Alexander HAMILTON *and the* Founding of the Nation

Alexander HAMILTON *and the* Founding of the Nation

Edited by

RICHARD B. MORRIS

THE DIAL PRESS 1957 NEW YORK

Library of Congress Catalog Number: 56-12132

DESIGNED BY WILLIAM R. MEINHARDT
PRINTED IN THE UNITED STATES OF AMERICA
BY THE HADDON CRAFTSMEN, SCRANTON, PA.

TO
ROBERT LIVINGSTON SCHUYLER

Acknowledgments

IN THE PREPARATION of this book I have benefited handsomely from the cooperation of the Alexander Hamilton Bicentennial Commission. Special thanks are due to the Commission's director, J. Harvie Williams, and to John Underhill and Richard C. Drum Hunt, Jr., of the Commission's staff. Dr. Frank Monaghan, historian of the Commission, made many valuable suggestions as to selections to be included and made available to me the detailed Hamilton chronology that has been prepared under his direction. His learning was frequently enlisted in an effort to resolve some of the unsettled issues of Hamilton scholarship. Acknowledgment must be made, too, to Professor Bower Aly of the University of Missouri for constructive leads to evaluating Hamilton's achievements as public speaker and rhetorician. My friend and colleague, Harold C. Syrett, executive director of the forthcoming multivolume edition of the papers of Alexander Hamilton, proved of invaluable assistance and placed at my disposal a set of the microfilm of the Hamilton Papers in the Library of Congress and his associate, Jacob E. Cooke, made a number of helpful suggestions. For the arduous work of transcribing and collating I had the good fortune to enlist the expert services of two indefatigable researchers, Miss Jean Gordon and Dr. Emil Oberholzer, Jr. The labors of typing were cheerfully assumed by Miss Sally Berkowitz. For permission to consult unpublished Hamilton materials and to use them in this volume I am indebted to the New York Historical Society, and particularly to Dr. Wayne Andrews of that institution, to the Manuscript Division of the New York Public Library, to Dr. Howard H. Peckham of the Clements Library, Ann Arbor, Mich., and to Roland Baughman, Curator of Special Collections, Columbia University. I am indebted, too, to Henry Bradley Martin of New York City for permission to examine the Washington copy of *The Federalist*.

R. B. M.

Alexander Hamilton After Two Centuries

As HE WAS about to assume the office of the Presidency George Washington remarked to a friend: "My movements to the chair of government will be accompanied by feelings not unlike those of a culprit who is going to the place of his execution." Washington's observation was indeed prophetic. Since the days of the Founding Fathers America's great public figures have been the recipients of much uncritical adulation and the targets of fierce vilification. They have been placed on a pedestal or kicked in the gutter. They have become transfigured into mythological heroes with saint-like attributes or into rascals whose motives have been impugned, whose personal lives have been invaded, and whose achievements belittled and distorted.

The career of Alexander Hamilton is an outstanding illustration of this ironic phenomenon of American politics. Endowed with exceptional precocity, consuming energy, and high ambition, Hamilton stood in the center of events from the earliest days of the Revolution until the late years of President Adams' administration. In the course of his public career he accumulated a wide variety of enemies. John Adams called him "the bastard brat of a Scots peddler." Jefferson charged him with being "not only a monarchist, but for a monarchy bottomed on corruption." The hired scribbler, Callender, defamed him as a Caligula, and Senator Maclay called him a crook. Since his own day he has been assailed as an enemy of democracy, a friend of reaction, an ally of the special interests, a High Tory who sought to erect a leviathan state, and an arch-plotter against the life of the republic.

That such charges were groundless was the sober judgment of many of Hamilton's contemporaries. Washington, perhaps Hamilton's greatest admirer and certainly his chief disciple, paid tribute to his enterprise, his quick perception, and "his judgment intuitively great." Granted that Hamilton was ambitious, Washington considered that his ambition was "of that laudable kind, which prompts a man to excel in whatever he takes in hand." The worldly Talleyrand, who knew him well, bracketed Hamilton with Napoleon and Fox. These three he considered the outstanding figures of that epoch. One political opponent conceded that Hamilton, "more than any other man, did the thinking of the time."

That Hamilton should have become a symbol of party, class, and faction is one of the ironies of American history. No man of his generation accomplished more to break down local barriers and sectional prejudices which had hampered the formation of a strong union. Save Washington, no man was more opposed to the spirit of party and faction. Yet, the Hamiltonian program fomented both the party spirit and partisanship. Hamilton did not foresee that the two-party system would prove a stabilizing force in American government. To him party was synonymous with disorder and instability.

Hamilton was one of our first great nationalists. "Think continentally," he counseled the young nation. He believed in the destiny of America and wished to confer upon the national government powers appropriate to its needs and opportunities. In *The Federalist* he shows how such national unity could be achieved without sacrificing states' rights and without jeopardizing individual liberties. His interpretation of the Constitution was both audacious and masterly. His enunciation of the doctrine of implied powers gave the nationalist Supreme Court the arguments for that broad construction which they put upon the Constitution. His interpretation of the taxing power opened up to the federal government sources of revenue essential to its needs prior to the adoption of the income tax amendment. A stanch advocate of separation of powers and checks and balances, Hamilton asserted the independence of the judiciary, and, of all the Founding Fathers, was most forceful in arguing for the right of the Supreme Court to declare laws of Congress unconstitutional. He believed that the courts were the safeguard of minority rights, and was confident that curbs upon judicial usurpation existed in the Constitution.

Hamilton was an administrative genius, perhaps the greatest America has yet produced. He believed in a strong executive, guarded the Presidency from encroachments upon its power by the legislative branch of the government, and assumed an influence in Washington's cabinet which is unmatched in the annals of the American cabinet system. Concerning himself with every phase of public policy, he was more than merely Secretary of the Treasury. He was in fact Washington's prime minister.

Hamilton's inventive mind grasped an extraordinary range of governmental problems—constitutional, economic, diplomatic, and military. His fiscal program was bold, original, and constructive, and firmly established American credit at home and abroad. To do so, he created a national debt and made effective use of the government's taxing power. With pardonable rhetoric Daniel Webster spoke of Hamilton's achievements: "He smote the rock of national resources and abundant streams of revenue gushed forth; he touched the dead corpse of public credit and it sprang upon its feet." The program injected confidence and buoyancy into the business community, but was received with less enthusiasm in other quarters. Farmers, small shopkeepers, and craftsmen saw little immediate advantage to them in the funding operations and rallied to Jefferson's opposition standard.

Hamilton was the friend of business enterprise, but he believed that business should be regulated in the interest of the general welfare, that competition should be fostered and monopoly discouraged. He did not subscribe to the view that business was not the business of government. Believing as he did in a government possessed with energy and initiative, he could scarcely be expected to allow the government to stand inert while the economy stagnated or was stifled by foreign competition. Hamilton advocated a nationally directed and controlled economy in the interest of private enterprise. He believed that the economy should be invigorated and protected by bounties and tariffs, by canals, roads, and other public improvements built by the federal government, and "by opening an asylum" to the poor and oppressed of other lands. He believed in maintaining a sound credit, in keeping the national debt within bounds, but he could scarcely be called a hard money man, and would today be considered an advocate of a managed currency. He recognized that private enterprise was subject to abuse. He castigated bank abuses as "pernicious," and insisted that "public utility" was "more truly the object of public banks than private profit."

Hamilton's remarkable grasp of national interest was evident in the direction he gave to the foreign policy of the Washington administration. He was a realist. He saw nothing "absurd" or "impracticable" in a league or alliance of nations, but cautioned Americans against becoming "the instruments of European greatness." He believed that a power friendly today could become an enemy tomorrow, "that peace or war will not always be left to our option." At the time of Jay's Treaty he opposed war with Great Britain because in his judgment a cessation of trade would "cut up credit by the roots," and above all because America needed time. It was too young and weak to involve itself in European wars. These ideas were given expression in Washington's Farewell Address, which in final form drew substantially upon Hamilton's "original draft." Hamilton's guiding principles were prudence, realism, discretion in speech, moderation in action, concern for the national interest. "Real firmness is good for every thing," he once counseled. "Strut is good for nothing."

Hamilton was an extraordinary advocate. As a speaker he was less effective with crowds than with assemblies and in the courtroom. He was an orator in the tradition of Pitt, Fox, and Burke. It was the kind of oratory that changed votes and persuaded judges. But it was as an essayist rather than an orator that Hamilton was most persuasive. *The Federalist* has justly become the classic of constitutional analysis and reasoning. Hamilton's *Phocion*, *Camillus*, and *Pacificus* letters are other powerful examples of a form of polemical writing that has unfortunately vanished from the literary scene. Flattering his readers by his appeal to logic and reason, Hamilton moved them to action by powerful emotional arguments. It need hardly be added that Hamilton wrote his own speeches and state papers. He did not need other men to fabricate ideas for him or ghost writers to dress them in literary garb.

It has been the fashion to pin the label of conservatism upon Hamilton, and in many respects he was profoundly conservative. But the program he, along with Madison, advocated in the Confederation period —the establishment of a strong national government, the creation of a new kind of republican federalism—was profoundly radical. It constituted a sharp break with the political ways of the past to which his opponents, the die-hard states'-rights particularists, wished to adhere.

Hamilton's brand of conservatism meant holding on to the tried and proven values of the past, but not standing still. He was not afraid of the new and the experimental. "There are epochs in human affairs when *novelty* even is useful," when "a change is necessary, if it be but for the sake of change," he wrote in advocating his program of Continental reforms as early as 1780. Hamilton believed in change and progress, but he hoped change would come by evolution rather than by volcanic eruption. There was, then, nothing paradoxical about the fact that Hamilton was an ardent defender of the American Revolution and an equally ardent foe of the French Revolution. The former, in Hamilton's eyes, was a political revolution actuated by principles of law, justice, and moderation, whereas the French Revolution, as he saw it, became a class struggle, employing violence and terror, and seeking imperialist ends through military aggrandisement.

Hamilton's enlightened conservatism, his devotion to "the mild reign of rational liberty," is perhaps best exemplified by his desire to conserve civil liberties, by his attachment to due process, to trial by jury, to the freedom of the press, and to the rights of minorities. He opposed loyalty oaths, indiscriminate confiscation of property, and religious tests for voting. "Let us not establish a tyranny," he warned at the time the Sedition Act was being considered by Congress.

In the last analysis it is the enduring quality of Hamilton's program which provides the true measure of his greatness as a statesman. Hamilton's successors in office found that his fiscal policies could not be rudely dethroned. "We can pay off his debts in fifteen years, but we can never get rid of his financial system," Jefferson grimly confessed on ascending to the Presidency. To justify the most significant accomplishment of his administration—the purchase of Louisiana—Jefferson had to adopt Hamilton's broad construction of the Constitution. Since that day the difference between the broad and the strict constructionists, between the Hamiltonians and the Jeffersonians, has been in large measure a difference bettween the party *in* power with responsibility and the party *out* of power and in opposition. Jefferson might have explained this philosophically by reminding us that "every difference of opinion is not a difference of principle."

Jefferson wanted "a wise and frugal government." Hamilton wanted a government that could act. Wars, unemployment, and the complexities and tensions of modern civilization have steadily foisted upon government new and awesome responsibilities. Woodrow Wilson once put the issue quite succinctly:

> We used to think in the old-fashioned days when life was very simple that all government had to do was to put on a policeman's uniform, and say, "Now don't anybody hurt anybody else." We used to say that the ideal of government was for every man to be left alone and not interfered with, except when he interfered with somebody else; and that the best government was the government that did as little governing as possible. That was the idea that obtained in Jefferson's time. But we are coming now to realize that life is so complicated that we are not dealing with the old conditions, and that the law has to step in and create new conditions under which we may live, the conditions which will make it tolerable for us to live.

The ends of government to which Wilson was pointing have in the course of time ranged beyond the vision of the Founding Fathers, but the means of achieving them are orthodox Hamiltonian means. Today neither of the two great parties would venture to challenge the effective exercise of political power for the general welfare. Were Alexander Hamilton alive in the mid-twentieth century he would find that both parties accept as axiomatic the Hamiltonian proposition that the central government must have effective powers.

In his Army Pay Book Hamilton, as a young Revolutionary officer, made various notes and jotted down a variety of quotations. One of them is surprisingly self-revealing. It is from an oration of Demosthenes, and, as entered by Hamilton, reads: "As a general marches at the head of his troops, so ought wise politicians, if I dare use the expression, to march at the head of affairs; insomuch that they ought not to wait the *event*, to know what measures to take; but the measures which they have taken ought to produce the *event*."

Truly it may be said that Hamilton constantly seized the initiative and kept ahead of events. Talleyrand said of Hamilton, "he has anticipated Europe." It may with as much accuracy be asserted that he anticipated America. The prophetic nature of much of Hamilton's thinking seems positively uncanny. It was Richard Rush, a Secretary of the Treasury from the opposition party, who paid tribute to Hamilton's direction of operations of the Treasury "with a forecast so luminous as still to throw a guiding light over the path of his successors." Hamilton envisioned America as a great industrial giant, whose manufacturing output would raise the general standard of living and stimulate both commerce and agriculture. Hamilton believed that the nation must be put into a strong posture of defense, that we could not rely upon the long-range peaceful intentions of foreign powers or count upon permanent alliances. He even warned of wars starting by surprise attacks without the formality of a declaration. Hamilton's alertness to the dangers of nullification, interposition, and secession take on sombre overtones in the light of later history. An advocate of the supremacy of the union, his views were to be upheld by Jackson and vindicated by Lincoln. Hamilton anticipated the later assumption by the Supreme Court of powers for the federal government on the basis of three clauses in the Constitution—the necessary and proper clause, the general welfare clause, and the commerce clause. These three clauses, as Hamilton interpreted them, have provided the constitutional foundation for much of the activity of our modern federal government in the fields of taxation, finance, business regulation, and social welfare, activities undreamed of when the nation was in its infancy. To Hamilton the enormous expansion of the power of the Presidency by the mid-twentieth century would have been less a surprise than a vindication of his notions of the need for administrative power, energy, and efficiency.

Hamilton's failures as a statesman are attributable more to personality and tactics than to basic principles. Hamilton carried courage in politics to the point of self-immolation. If there was any attacking to be done, he did not assign the task to someone else, but took it on himself. As Jefferson put it, he was truly the "Colossus of the Federalists," and the standing No. 1 target for the shafts of the opposition. Opinionated and self-assured, he lacked that understanding of the art of compromise, the mastery of which is so essential to the aspiring politician. Thus, he was inflexible when a little yielding would have made all the difference. The best example of this was his break with Madison over the question of discriminating between original and subsequent holders of public securities. Though probably impractical in operation, some sort of discrimination would have seemed fair and equitable and would certainly have been good politics. Hamilton lacked terminal facilities. He was candid, but he was also indiscreet. He wrote brilliantly, but he wrote too much and too often. His astonishing attack on President John Adams left Hamilton a party leader without a following.

With some justice it has been said that Hamilton loved his country more than he did his countrymen. He would not bow to what he called "the majesty of the multitude." Direct democracy, he felt, was unsuitable to a large nation like America. It would, he feared, prove tumultuous and fickle. But he was reconciled to the system of representative democracy set up in the Constitution. Although an admirer of the British constitution, he realized that only a republic was suited to the American temper. While Hamilton was often portrayed by his opponents as an enemy of the people, the fact is that he was less afraid of the people than he was of state political machines and state legislatures. In Hamilton's thinking the loyalty of the people to the national government was an essential weapon to counteract the separatist and divisive tactics of the antifederalists. It must be confessed that there were times when Hamilton had his doubts about the way democracy was working out, and that he was understandably less enthusiastic about democracy when his party was voted out of office than when it was in power. But he believed in the power of reason founded upon full disclosure of the facts, and he had faith in the force of an enlightened public opinion. "I desire above all things," he wrote, "to see the equality of political rights, exclusive of hereditary distinction, firmly established by a positive demonstration of its being consistent with the order and happiness of society."

In this book Hamliton is permitted to speak for himself, to present his basic ideas in his own words. A man of eloquence, a facile writer, a powerful polemicist, and an unrivalled master at drafting state papers that have endured, Hamilton, through his correspondence, pamphlets, and reports has left us a fascinating self-portrait. Herein is found Hamilton the man, the lover, the husband and father, the patriot and the statesman, the man who jealously guarded his integrity but stood loyally by his friends.

For reasons of space it has been necessary to excerpt much of Hamilton's writings, but every effort has been made to present an authoritative text. Wherever possible the selection is based upon the Hamilton Papers in the Library of Congress, the original newspaper articles or pamphlets, or Hamilton letters in other collections, in some cases newly uncovered. In addition, the text has drawn upon the two printed editions of Hamilton's writings, that of John C. Hamilton, published in 1850 (and hereinafter cited *Hamilton*) and the Centennial Edition of his writings, edited by Henry Cabot Lodge, and published in 1904 (hereinafter *Works*). Both editions, it should be added, are marred by errors of transcription as well as curious deletions, and must be used with caution.

Some of these writings go back almost two centuries, but they pose problems and suggest solutions which have as much significance today as when the nation was founded. These are times of challenge for America, a time anticipated by Hamilton, when this country at long last has assumed "an attitude correspondent with its great destinies." We can ill afford to ignore Hamiltonian means any more than we can neglect Jeffersonian ends if we wish to attain that delicate balance between liberty and security which will keep us free and secure peace in our time.

RICHARD B. MORRIS

An Alexander Hamilton Chronology

c.1755–57	[Jan. 11]	Alexander Hamilton born in Nevis, British West Indies, son of Rachel Faucitt Lavien and James Hamilton
1766		Hamilton becomes an apprentice clerk in the mercantile firm of Nicholas Cruger
1768	Feb. 19	Death of Rachel Faucitt Lavien at St. Croix, Virgin Islands
1772	Oct. 3	Publication of Hamilton's "Hurricane Letter" (dated Sept. 6) in *Royal Danish-American Gazette* of St. Croix.
1773	Summer	Sailed on *Thunderbolt* for Boston en route to New York
	Autumn	Entered King's College, now Columbia University, as a student with special status
1774	Dec. 15	*A Full Vindication*, Hamilton's first pamphlet
1775	Feb. 5	*The Farmer Refuted*
	June 15	First of two letters in Holt's *Journal* on Quebec Act
	Aug. 23	As a member of the militia company, "Corsicans" (later called "Hearts of Oak"), Hamilton first saw action in the rescue of cannon at the Battery; under direct bombardment from the British warship *Asia*
1776	March 14	Appointed captain in command of the Provincial Company of Artillery
	Aug. 27	Fought in Battle of Long Island
	Sept. 16	Harlem Heights, New York; first reputed personal meeting with Washington
	Oct. 28	Repulsed Hessian battalion at White Plains with his artillery
	Dec. 25	Fought at Trenton
1777	Jan. 3	At Princeton the first round of Hamilton's battery of two 4-pounders crashed into Nassau Hall

	March 1	Morristown, N.J.; appointed aide-de-camp to Washington with rank of lieutenant-colonel
	Oct. 30	Sent by Washington on mission to Gates
1778	Jan. 28	Drafted Washington's report to Congress on reorganization of the army
	June 28	With Major General Charles Lee at Monmouth Court House—"Let us all die here, rather than retreat!"
	Oct. 19	Publication of his first *Publius* letters deploring the weakness of Congress
1779	March 14	Morristown, N.J. Recommended raising of Negro troops
	Oct.	Unable to spare his aide, Washington refused Hamilton's request for a battalion command
[1779–80]		Submitted to "a member of Congress" his first plan to stabilize the public finances
1780	Sept. 3	Liberty Pole, Bergen County, N.J. Letter to James Duane expounding his views on government
	Sept. 25	Verplanck's Point, N.Y. Unsuccessful pursuit of the traitor Arnold
	Dec. 14	Married Elizabeth, daughter of General Philip Schuyler. [There were eight children of the marriage, the first Philip being born Jan. 22, 1782, and a second Philip on June 2, 1802, and was named after his elder brother killed in a duel the previous year. Between these two were: Angelica, b. Sept. 25, 1784; Alexander, May 16, 1786; James Alexander, April 14, 1788; John Church, Aug. 22, 1792; William Stephen, Aug. 4, 1797; and Eliza, Nov. 20, 1799]
1781	April 30	Morristown, N.J. Resigned as aide-de-camp to Washington
	July 12–July 4, 1782	Publication of the six *Continentalist* essays
	July 31	Dobb's Ferry, N.Y. Given command of battalion of light infantry.
	Oct. 14	Yorktown, Va. Commanded and personally led the assault and capture of Redoubt No. 10
1782	May 2	Appointed Receiver of Taxes for New York
	July	Albany, N.Y. Admitted to practice after three months' intensive study of the law.
	July 21	Urged New York legislature to pass a resolution for a general convention of the states to amend the Articles of Confederation
	July 22	Delegate to the Continental Congress from New York

1783	Nov. 25	Opened law office at 57 Wall Street, New York City
	Dec. 4	Attended Washington's farewell to his officers in Fraunces Tavern
1784		*Phocion Letters*
	Feb. 24	Founded and became a director of the Bank of New York
1785	Feb. 10	Associated in founding of The New York Society for Promoting the Manumission of Slaves
1786	Sept. 14	As a New York delegate to the Annapolis Convention, Hamilton drafted the resolution calling for a new convention to enlarge the powers of the federal government
1787	Jan. 12	Took seat in New York state Assembly
	May 25–Sept. 17	Federal Convention at Philadelphia
	Oct. 27	Publication of the first *Federalist* letter
1788	Jan. 22	Reappointed a delegate to the Continental Congress from New York
	June 17–July 26	Led fight for the ratification of the Constitution in the New York Convention, Poughkeepsie, N.Y.
1789	Sept. 11	Appointed Secretary of the Treasury
1790	Jan. 14	First Report on the Public Credit
	July 21	Agreed to location of national capital on Potomac in return for Jefferson's support of the assumption bill
	Dec. 13	Report on a National Bank
1791	Jan. 28	Report on the U. S. Mint
	Nov. 22	Charter for The Society for Establishing Useful Manufactures
	Dec. 5	Report on Manufactures
1793	Jan. 23	Giles' resolution criticizing Hamilton; Hamilton's rejoinder (Feb. 4–20)
	April 22	Washington's Proclamation of Neutrality
	Aug. 16	*No Jacobin* papers
1794	Feb. 1–8	*Americanus* papers
	Aug. 23–Sept. 2	*Tully* letters
	Sept. 30	Hamilton takes the field to suppress the Whisky Rebellion
1795	Jan. 16	Final (sometimes called Second) Report on the Public Credit
	Jan. 31	Resignation as Secretary of the Treasury
	Feb. 24	Argues in support of the carriage tax
	May	*Horatius* letter
	July 22	First of *Camillus* series
1796	May 15–Aug. 25	Prepared drafts of Washington's Farewell Address; delivered Sept. 19
	Dec. 6	*The Answer*

1797	Jan. 27	*The Warning*
	July 5	Disclosure by Hamilton of his liaison with Mrs. Reynolds
1798	Mar. 30–April 21	*The Stand*, a series of seven articles
	July 25	Appointed Inspector-General of the army with the rank of Major General
	Summer	Wrote letters to friends critical of the Alien and Sedition bills
1799	June 3	Death of his father, James Hamilton, at St. Vincent, B.W.I.
1800	June 2	Retires from the army
	Oct.	Criticism of the character and public conduct of President John Adams
1801	Feb. 17	Responsible for Jefferson's election as President over Burr by a majority of the states in the House of Representatives on the 26th roll call
	Nov. 16	Founded the New York *Evening Post*
	Nov. 23	Eldest son, Philip, mortally wounded in duel with George Eacker, a supporter of Aaron Burr
	Dec. 17	First of series of 18 articles analyzing and criticising Jefferson's policies
1804	Feb. 13	As counsel in *People v. Croswell*, argued in defense of the freedom of the press
	July 11	Mortally wounded by Burr in duel at Weehawken, N.J.
	July 12	Died in the home of William Bayard, New York City
	July 14	Buried with military honors in Trinity Churchyard, New York City

Contents

I. Alexander Hamilton After Two Centuries vii

II. A Hamilton Chronology xv

1. The Right of Revolution 1
   The Spirit of '76: Two different versions 22
   Revolution and Moderation 22
   Revolution as a Last Resort 25

2. Winning the Revolution 27
   The Burgoyne Campaign 31
   The Defense of Philadelphia 33
   Mission to Gates 34
   Plan for Reorganizing the Army 39
   With Lee at Monmouth 42
   Hamilton's Private War against Profiteers 47
   Recommended: A Fighting Parson 50
   The Treason of Arnold 50
   Hamilton and the Glory Road 61
   Mutiny 66

3. Building a New Nation 72
   Molding National Character 72
   Wanted: A Continental Government that Can Act 76
   Union Now: The Critical Weakness of the Confederation 90
   An Expanding Nation: New States and the West 112

4. On Government: Some Guiding Principles 122
   A Monarchy versus a Republic 122
   Democracy and the Role of the People 130
   On Classes, Parties, and Factions 139
   Some Political Tenets 143
   Competent Public Servants 144

5. Hamilton at the Federal Convention 145
A Chronology 145
Excerpts from His Speeches 149

6. The Fight for Ratification 160
The Federalist 160
The Great Debate 175

7. The Principles of Constitutional Government 181
The Powers of the President 181
The Treaty-making Power of the President 193
Treaties as the Supreme Law of the Land 207
The President's Power to Declare War 208
A Code of Presidential Etiquette 209
The Structure and Powers of Congress 211
The Senate 213
The Courts and Judicial Review 215
Separation of Powers—Checks and Balances 237
The Power to Tax 239
The Government and National Security 255
The Doctrine of Implied Powers 263
The Welfare Clause 269
The Bill of Rights 271
Nationalism, Federalism, and States' Rights 275
Nullification, Interposition, and Secession 280

8. Economic Program 285
Restoration of Public Credit 286
Hamilton's Report on the Public Credit 289
Arguments Against Discrimination 303
In Defense of Funding and Assumption 308
Reassurance to Washington 317
Avoiding an Excessive Public Debt 319
A Sound Tax Program 326
Principles and Objectives of Taxation 326
Hamilton's Tax Program 329
A National Bank 335
Report on a National Bank 343
A Sound but Flexible Currency 354
Encouragement of Trade 358
Encouragement of Manufactures 360
Encouragement of Labor 375
Encouragement of Agriculture 376

9. War and Peace 377
Some Maxims for the Conduct of Foreign Relations 377

British-American Relations 379
Jay's Treaty 381
The Camillus Letters 385
Deteriorating Relations 396
Franco-American Relations 400
Policy toward Spain and Latin-America 434
Administration of the Army 437
Treatment of the Indians 447

10. Liberty and Security 448
Human Rights and Due Process 448
Freedom and Bondage 454
Minority Rights and the Tories 456
Loyalty and Other Oaths 472
Freedom of the Press 475
Sedition and Insurrection 485

11. On Leaders and Leadership 495
The Washington-Hamilton Relationship 495
Hamilton's "Original Draft" of the Farewell Address 506
The Death of Washington 520
On Thomas Jefferson 521
On John Adams 527
On Aaron Burr 534
On George Clinton 543
On General Nathanael Greene 553
On von Steuben 557
On "Light Horse Harry" Lee 558
On Lafayette 559
On Robert Morris 560
On John Jay 561
On James Madison 561
On Edmund Randolph 562
On General James Wilkinson 563
On Gouverneur Morris 564
On Rufus King 565

12. On Life and Death 566
Birth, Youth, and Family Ties 566
Friendship 573
Husband and Father 574
Women: The Reynolds Affair 579
Integrity and Ambition 587
Education and Politics 600
Tragedy and Frustration 601
The Duel 602

1

The Right of Revolution

The sacred rights of mankind are not to be rummaged for among old parchments or musty records. They are written as with a sunbeam in the whole volume of human nature by the hand of the Divinity itself, and can never be erased or obscured by mortal power.

The pulse of Americans beats high in their country's cause.

Hamilton had been in New York a matter of months when the "Mohawk braves" dumped the tea in Boston harbor. Whatever loyalty the young West Indian may have still harbored toward George III did not prevent his ardent adherence to the cause of the colonists. In a series of letters to Holt's Journal *and in various broadsides the King's College student helped keep the agitation at fever pitch. By the time the first Continental Congress met in Philadelphia in the fall of '74 he had gone as far to the left as had Jefferson. That summer the Virginian had enunciated the doctrine that Parliament had no authority over the colonies. James Wilson of Philadelphia took a similar stand. In his* Novanglus *letters John Adams in December of '74 expounded the dominion theory of empire, the view that the colonies were tied to Great Britain by allegiance to the Crown alone. Writing at the same time as Adams, Hamilton came to identical conclusions about the constitutional relations of the various parts of the empire. He was goaded into action by a series of four* Westchester Farmer *pamphlets, in which an Anglican clergyman, Samuel Seabury, attacked the Congress. Hamilton's first salvo was* A Full Vindication. *Therein his appeal to natural rights revealed the new radical line, and his analysis of the cost of the Navigation Acts to the American colonies demonstrated that brilliant grasp of economic problems which both astonished and confounded his contemporaries.*

[December 15, 1774]

AND FIRST, LET me ask these restless spirits, Whence arises that violent antipathy they seem to entertain, not only to the natural rights of mankind, but to common sense and common modesty? That they are enemies to the natural rights of mankind is manifest, because they wish to see one part of their species enslaved by another. That they have an invincible aversion to common sense is apparent in many respects: they endeavor to persuade us that the absolute sovereignty of Parliament does not imply our absolute slavery; that it is a Christian duty to submit to be plundered of all we have, merely because some of our fellow-subjects are wicked enough to require it of us; that slavery, so far from being a great evil, is a great blessing; and even that our contest with Britain is founded entirely upon the petty duty of three pence per pound on East India tea, whereas the whole world knows it is built upon this interesting question, whether the inhabitants of Great Britain have a right to dispose of the lives and properties of the inhabitants of America, or not. And lastly, that these men have discarded all pretension to common modesty, is clear from hence: first, because they, in the plainest terms, call an august body of men, famed for their patriotism and abilities, fools or knaves; and of course the people whom they represented cannot be exempt from the same opprobrious appellations; and secondly, because they set themselves up as standards of wisdom and probity, by contradicting and censuring the public voice in favor of those men.

A little consideration will convince us that the Congress, instead of having "ignorantly misunderstood, carelessly neglected, or basely betrayed the interests of the colonies," have, on the contrary, devised and recommended the only effectual means to secure the freedom, and establish the future prosperity of America upon a solid basis. If we are not free and happy hereafter, it must proceed from the want of integrity and resolution in executing what they have concerted, not from the temerity or impolicy of their determinations. . . .

The only distinction between freedom and slavery consists in this: In the former state a man is governed by the laws to which he has given his consent, either in person or by his representative; in the latter, he is governed by the will of another. In the one case, his life and property are his own; in the other, they depend upon the pleasure of his master. It is easy to discern which of these two states is preferable. No man in his senses can hesitate in choosing to be free, rather than a slave.

That Americans are entitled to freedom is incontestable on every rational principle. All men have one common original: they participate in one common nature, and consequently have one common right. No reason can be assigned why one man should exercise any power or pre-eminence over his fellow creatures more than another; unless they have voluntarily vested him with it. Since, then, Americans have not, by any act of theirs, empowered the British Parliament to make laws for them, it follows they can have no just authority to do it.

Besides the clear voice of natural justice in this respect, the fundamental principles of the English constitution are in our favor. It has been repeatedly demonstrated that the idea of legislation or taxation, when the subject is not represented, is inconsistent with *that*. Nor is this all; our charters, the express conditions on which our progenitors relinquished their native countries, and came to settle in this, preclude every claim of ruling and taxing us without our assent.

Every subterfuge that sophistry has been able to invent, to evade or obscure this truth, has been refuted by the most conclusive reasonings; so that we may pronounce it a matter of undeniable certainty, that the pretensions of Parliament are contradictory to the law of nature, subversive of the British constitution, and destructive of the faith of the most solemn compacts.

What, then, is the subject of our controversy with the mother country? It is this: Whether we shall preserve that security to our lives and properties, which the law of nature, the genius of the British constitution, and our charters, afford us; or whether we shall resign them into the hands of the British House of Commons, which is no more privileged to dispose of them than the Great Mogul. What can actuate those men who labor to delude any of us into an opinion that the object of contention between the parent state and the colonies is only three pence duty upon tea; or that the commotions in America originate in a plan, formed by some turbulent men, to erect it into a republican government? The Parliament claims a right to tax us in all cases whatsoever; its late acts are in virtue of that claim. How ridiculous, then, is it to affirm that we are quarrelling for the trifling sum of three pence a pound on tea, when it is evidently the principle against which we contend.

. . . Though the manufacturers of Great Britain and Ireland and the inhabitants of the West Indies are not chargeable with any actual crime toward America, they may, in a political view, be esteemed criminal. In a civil society it is the duty of each particular branch to promote not only the good of the whole community, but the good of every other particular branch. If one part endeavors to violate the rights of another, the rest ought to assist in preventing the injury. When they do not, but remain neutral, they are deficient in their duty, and may be regarded, in some measure, as accomplices.

The reason of this is obvious from the design of civil society; which is, that the united strength of the several members might give stability and security to the whole body, and each respective member; so that one part cannot encroach upon another without becoming a common enemy, and eventually endangering the safety and happiness of all the other parts.

Since, then, the persons who will be distressed by the methods we are using for our own protection, have, by their neutrality, first committed a breach of an obligation similar to that which bound us to consult their emolument, it is plain the obligation upon us is annulled, and we are blameless in what we are about to do. . . .

No person that has enjoyed the sweets of liberty can be insensible of its infinite value, or can reflect on its reverse without horror and detestation. No person that is not lost to every generous feeling of humanity, or that is not stupidly blind to his own interest, could bear to offer himself and posterity as victims at the shrine of despotism, in preference to enduring the shortlived inconveniences that may result from an abridgment, or even entire suspension, of commerce.

Were not the disadvantages of slavery too obvious to stand in need of it, I might enumerate and describe the tedious train of calamities inseparable from it. I might show that it is fatal to religion and morality; that it tends to debase the mind, and corrupt its noblest springs of action. I might show that it relaxes the sinews of industry, clips the wings of commerce, and introduces misery and indigence in every shape.

Under the auspices of tyranny the life of the subject is often sported with, and the fruits of his daily toil are consumed in oppressive taxes, that serve to gratify the ambition, avarice, and lusts of his superiors. Every court minion riots in the spoils of the honest laborer, and despises the hand by which he is fed. The page of history is replete with instances that loudly warn us to beware of slavery.

Rome was the nurse of freedom. She was celebrated for her justice and lenity; but in what manner did she govern her dependent provinces? They were made the continual scene of rapine and cruelty. From thence let us learn how little confidence is due to the wisdom and equity of the most exemplary nations.

Should Americans submit to become the vassals of their fellow-subjects in Great Britain, their yoke will be peculiarly grievous and intolerable. A vast majority of mankind is entirely biassed by motives of self-interest. Most men are glad to remove any burthens off themselves, and place them upon the necks of their neighbors. We cannot, therefore, doubt but that the British Parliament, with a view to the ease and advantage of itself and its constituents, would oppress and grind the Americans as much as possible. Jealousy would concur with selfishness; and for fear of the future independence of America, if it should be permitted to rise to too great a height of splendor and opulence, every method would be taken to drain it of its wealth and restrain its prosperity. We are already suspected of aiming at independence, and that is one principal cause of the severity we experience. The same cause will always operate against us, and produce a uniform severity of treatment.

... We can live without trade of any kind. Food and clothing we have within ourselves. Our climate produces cotton, wool, flax, and hemp; which, with proper cultivation, would furnish us with summer apparel in abundance. The article of cotton, indeed, would do more; it would contribute to defend us from the inclemency of winter. We have sheep, which, with due care in improving and increasing them, would soon yield a sufficiency of wool. The large quantity of skins we have among us would never let us want a warm and comfortable suit. It would be no unbecoming employment for our daughters to provide silks of their own country. The silk-worm answers as well here as in any part of the world. Those hands which may be deprived of business by the cessation of commerce, may be occupied in various kinds of manufactures and other internal improvements. If, by the necessity of the thing, manufacturers should once be established, and take root among us, they will pave the way still more to the future grandeur and glory of America; and, by lessening its need of external commerce, will render it still securer against the encroachments of tyranny. . . .

The FARMER, I am inclined to hope, builds too much upon the present disunion of Canada, Georgia, the Floridas, the Mississippi, and Nova Scotia from other colonies. A little time, I trust, will awaken them from their slumbers, and bring them to a proper sense of their indiscretion. I please myself with the flattering prospect, that they will, erelong, unite in one indissoluble chain with the rest of the colonies. I cannot believe they will persist in such a conduct as must exclude them from the secure enjoyment of those heaven-descended immunities we are contending for.

... I am persuaded you love yourselves and children better than to let any designing men cheat you out of your liberty and property, to serve their own purposes. You would be a disgrace to your ancestors, and the bitterest enemies to yourselves, and to your posterity, if you did not act like men, in protecting and defending those rights you have hitherto enjoyed.

I say, my friends, I do not address you in particular, because I have any greater connection with you than with other people. I despise all false pretensions and mean arts. Let those have recourse to dissimulation and falsehood, who can't defend their cause without it. 'Tis my maxim to let the plain, naked truth speak for itself: and if men won't listen to it, 'tis their own fault: they must be contented to suffer for it. I am neither merchant nor farmer. I address you, because I wish well to my country, and of course to you, who are one chief support of it; and because an attempt has been made to lead you astray in particular. You are the men, too who would lose most, should you be foolish enough to counteract the prudent measures our worthy Congress has taken for the preservation of our liberties. Those who advise you to do it are not your friends, but your greatest foes. They would have you made slaves, that they may pamper themselves with the fruits of your honest labor. 'Tis the Farmer who is most oppressed in all countries where slavery prevails. . . .

Pray, who can tell me why a farmer in America is not as honest and good a man as a farmer in England? or why has not the one as good a right to what he has earned by his labor as the other? I can't, for my life, see any distinction between them. And yet, it seems, the English farmers are to be governed and taxed by their own Assembly, or Parliament; and the American farmers are not. The former are to choose their own representatives from among themselves, whose interest is connected with theirs, and over whom they have proper control. The latter are to be loaded with taxes by men three thousand miles off; by men who have no interest or connections among them, but whose interest it will be to burden them as much as possible, and over whom they cannot have the least restraint. How do you like this doctrine, my friends? Are you ready to own the English farmers for your masters? Are you willing to acknowledge their right to take your property from you, and when they please? I know you scorn the thougnt. You had rather die than submit to it. . . .

But being ruined by taxes is not the worst you have to fear. What security would you have for your lives? How can any of you be sure you would have the free enjoyment of your religion long? Would you put your religion in the power of any set of men living? Remember civil and religious liberty always go together: if the foundation of the one be sapped, the other will fall of course.

Call to mind one of our sister colonies, Boston. Reflect upon the situation of Canada; and then tell whether you are inclined to place any confidence in the justice and humanity of the Parliament. The port of Boston is blocked up, and an army planted in the town. . . .

The affair of Canada, if possible, is still worse. The English laws have been superceded by the French laws. The Romish faith is made the established religion of the land, and his Majesty is placed at the head of it. The free exercise of the Protestant faith depends upon the pleasure of the Governor and Council. The subject is divested of the right of trial by jury, and an innocent man may be imprisoned his whole life, without being able to obtain any trial at all. The Parliament was not contented with introducing arbitrary power and Popery in Canada, with its former limits; but they have annexed to it the vast tracts of land that surround all the colonies.

Does not your blood run cold, to think that an English Parliament should pass an act for the establishment of arbitrary power and Popery in such an extensive country? If they had any regard to the freedom and happiness of mankind, they would never have done it. If they had been friends to the Protestant cause, they would never have provided such a nursery for its great enemy; they would not have given such encouragement to Popery. The thought of their conduct, in this particular, shocks me. It must shock you, too, my friends. Beware of trusting yourselves to men who are capable of such an action! They may as well establish Popery in New York, and the other colonies, as they did in Canada. They had no more right to do it there than here. . . .

The high prices of goods are held up, to make you dissatisfied with the non-importation. If the argument on this head were true, it would be much better to subject yourselves to that disadvantage for a time, than to bring upon yourselves all the mischiefs I have pointed out to you. . . .

But I trust there is no danger that the prices of goods will rise much, if at all. The same Congress that put a stop to the importation of them, has also forbid raising the prices of them. The same committee that is to regulate the one, is also to regulate the other. All care will be taken to give no cause of dissatisfaction. Confide in the men whom you, and the rest of the continent, have chosen the guardians of our common liberties. They are men of sense and virtue. They will do nothing but what is really necessary for the security of your lives and properties. . . .

As to the courts of justice, no violence can, nor will, be used, to shut them up; but, if it should be found necessary, we may enter into solemn agreement to cease from all litigations at law, except in particular cases. We may regulate lawsuits in such a manner as to prevent any mischief that might arise from them. Restrictions may be laid on, to hinder merciless creditors from taking advantage of the times to oppress and ruin their debtors; but, at the same time, not to put it in the power of the debtors *wantonly* to withhold their just dues from their creditors when they are able to pay them. The law ruins many a good honest family. Disputes may be settled in a more friendly way. One or two virtuous neighbors may be chosen by each party to decide them. If the next Congress should think any regulations concerning the courts of justice requisite, they will make them; and proper persons will be appointed to carry them into execution, and to see that no individuals deviate from them. It will be your duty to elect persons whose fidelity and zeal for your interest you can depend upon, to represent you in *that* Congress, which is to meet in Philadelphia in May ensuing. . . .

I caution you, again and again, to beware of the men who advise you to forsake the plain path marked out for you by the Congress. They only mean to deceive and betray you. Our representatives in General Assembly cannot take any wiser or better course to settle our differences than our representatives in the Continental Congress have taken. If you join with the rest of America in the same common measure, you will be sure to preserve your liberties inviolate, but if you separate from them and seek for redress alone, and unseconded, you will certainly fall a prey to your enemies, and repent your folly as long as you live.

—*A Full Vindication of the Measures of the Congress from the Calumnies of their Enemies...* (New York: James Rivington, 1774), pp. 3, 5, 9-13, 20, 23-24, 35.

Hamilton's Full Vindication *provoked a reply from the* Westchester Farmer, *to whom Hamilton rejoined in* The Farmer Refuted. *This pamphlet is notable not only for its full-scale enunciation of the natural rights philisophy, but also for its farsighted critique of the military strategy which the colonists ought to follow in a war with Britain, a forecast of Washington's Fabian tactics. To the Tory argument that New York had no charter and therefore no charter rights, Hamilton replied by appealing to "the sacred rights of mankind."*

[February 5, 1775]

The first thing that presents itself is a wish, that "I had, explicitly, declared to the public my ideas of the *natural rights* of mankind. Man, in a state of nature (you say), may be considered as perfectly free from all restraint of *law* and *government*; and then, the weak must submit to the strong."

I shall, henceforth, begin to make some allowance for that enmity you have discovered to the *natural rights* of mankind. For, though ignorance of them, in this enlightened age, cannot be admitted as a sufficient excuse for you, yet it ought, in some measure, to extenuate your guilt. If you will follow my advice, there still may be hopes of your reformation. Apply yourself, without delay, to the study of the law of nature. I would recommend to your perusal, Grotius, Puffendorf, Locke, Montesquieu, and Burlemaqui. I might mention other excellent writers on this subject; but if you attend diligently to these, you will not require any others.

There is so strong a similitude between your political principles and those maintained by Mr. Hobbes, that, in judging from them, a person might very easily *mistake* you for a disciple of his. His opinion was exactly coincident with yours, relative to man in a state of nature. He held, as you do, that he was then perfectly free from all restraint of *law* and *government*. Moral obligation, according to him, is derived from the introduction of civil society; and there is no virtue but what is purely artificial, the mere contrivance of politicians for the maintenance of social intercourse. But the reason he ran into this absurd and impious doctrine was, that he disbelieved the existence of an intelligent, superintending principle, who is the governor, and will be the final judge, of the universe.

As you sometimes swear *by Him that made you,* I conclude your sentiments do not correspond with his in that which is the basis of the doctrine you both agree in; and this makes it impossible to imagine whence this congruity between you arises. To grant that there is a Supreme Intelligence who rules the world and has established laws to regulate the actions of His creatures, and still to assert that man, in a state of nature, may be considered as perfectly free from all restraints of *law* and *government,* appears, to a common understanding, altogether irreconcilable.

Good and wise men, in all ages, have embraced a very dissimilar theory. They have supposed that the Deity, from the relations we stand in to Himself and to each other, has constituted an eternal and immutable law, which is indispensably obligatory upon all mankind, prior to any human institution whatever.

This is what is called the law of nature, "which, being coeval with mankind, and dictated by God Himself, is, of course, superior in obligations to any other. It is binding over all the globe, in all countries, and at all times. No human laws are of any validity, if contrary to this; and such of them as are valid derive all their authority, mediately or immediately, from this original."—BLACKSTONE.

Upon this law depend the natural rights of mankind: the Supreme Being gave existence to man, together with the means of preserving and beautifying that existence. He endowed him with rational faculties, by the help of which to discern and pursue such things as were consistent with his duty and interest; and invested him with an inviolable right to personal liberty and personal safety.

Hence, in a state of nature, no man had any *moral* power to deprive another of his life, limbs, property, or liberty; nor the least authority to command or exact obedience from him, except that which arose from the ties of consanguinity.

Hence, also, the origin of all civil government, justly established, must be a voluntary compact between the rulers and the ruled, and must be liable to such limitations as are necessary for the security of the *absolute rights* of the latter; for what original title can any man, or set of men, have to govern others, except their own consent? To usurp dominion over a people in their own despite, or to grasp at a more extensive power than they are willing to intrust, is to violate that law of nature which gives every man a right to his personal liberty, and can therefore confer no obligation to obedience.

"The principal aim of society is to protect individuals in the enjoyment of those absolute rights which were vested in them by the immutable laws of nature, but which could not be preserved in peace without that mutual assistance and intercourse which is gained by the institution of friendly and social communities. Hence it follows, that the first and primary end of human laws is to maintain and regulate these absolute rights of individuals."—BLACKSTONE.

If we examine the pretensions of Parliament by this criterion, which is evidently a good one, we shall presently detect their injustice. First, they are subversive of our natural liberty, because an authority is assumed over us which we by no means assent to. And, secondly, they divest us of that moral security for our lives and properties, which we are entitled to, and which it is the primary end of society to bestow. For such security can never exist while we have no part in making the laws that are to bind us, and while it may be the interest of our uncontrolled legislators to oppress us as much as possible. . . .

The idea of colony does not involve the idea of slavery. There is a wide difference between the dependence of a free people and the submission of slaves. The former I allow, the latter I reject with disdain. Nor does the notion of a colony imply any subordination to our fellow subjects in the parent state while there is one common sovereign established. . . .

Admitting that the King of Great Britain was enthroned by virtue of an act of Parliament, and that he is King of America because he is King of Great Britain, yet the act of Parliament is not the *efficient cause* of his being the King of America. It is only the *occasion* of it. He is King of America by virtue of a compact between us and the Kings of Great Britain. These colonies were planted and settled by the grants, and under the protection, of English Kings, who entered into covenants with us, for themselves, their heirs, and successors; and it is from these covenants that the duty of protection on their part, and the duty of allegiance on ours, arise.

So that to disclaim the authority of a British Parliament over us does by no means imply the dereliction of our allegiance to British monarchs. Our compact takes no cognizance of the manner of their accession to the throne. It is sufficient for us that they are Kings of England. . . .

The right of Parliament to legislate for us cannot be accounted for upon any reasonable grounds. The constitution of Great Britain is very properly called a limited monarchy; the people having reserved to themselves a share in the legislature, as a check upon the regal authority, to prevent its degenerating into despotism and tyranny. The very aim and intention of the democratical part, or the House of Commons, is to secure the rights of the people. Its very being depends upon those rights. Its whole power is derived from them, and must be terminated by them.

It is the unalienable birthright of every Englishman, who can be considered as a *free agent,* to participate in framing the laws which are to bind him, either as to his life or property. But as many inconveniences would result from the exercise of this right in person, it is appointed by the constitution that he shall delegate it to another. Hence he is to give his vote in the election of some person he chooses to confide in as his representative. This right no power on earth can divest him of. It was enjoyed by his ancestors time immemorial, recognized and established by Magna Charta, and is essential to the existence of the constitution. Abolish this privilege, and the House of Commons is annihilated.

But what was the use and design of this privilege? To secure his life and property from the attacks of exorbitant power. And in what manner is this done? By giving him the election of those who are to have the disposal and regulation of them, and whose interest is in every respect connected with his.

The representative, in this case, is bound, by every possible tie, to consult the advantage of his constituents. Gratitude for the high and honorable trust reposed in him demands a return of attention and regard to the advancement of their happiness. Self interest, that most powerful incentive of human actions, points and attracts toward the same object. . . .

When we ascribe to the British House of Commons a jurisdiction over the colonies, the scene is entirely reversed. All these kinds of security immediately disappear; no ties of gratitude or interest remain. Interest, indeed, may operate to our prejudice. To oppress us may serve as a recommendation to their constituents, as well as an alleviation of their own incumbrances. The British patriots may, in time, be heard to court the gale of popular favor by boasting their exploits in laying some new impositions on their American vassals, and by that means lessening the burthens of their friends and fellow subjects.

But what merits still more serious attention is this: there seems to be already a jealously of our dawning splendor. It is looked upon as portentous of approaching independence. This, we have reason to believe, is one of the principal incitements to the present rigorous and unconstitutional proceedings against us. And though it may have chiefly originated in the calumnies of designing men, yet it does not entirely depend upon adventitious or partial causes, but is also founded in the circumstances of our country and situation. The boundless extent of territory we possess, the wholesome temperament of our climate, the luxuriance and fertility of our soil, the variety of our products, the rapidity of the growth of our population, the industry of our countrymen, and the commodiousness of our ports, naturally lead to a suspicion of independence, and would always have an influence pernicious to us. Jealousy is a predominant passion of human nature, and is a source of the greatest evils. Whenever it takes place between rulers and their subjects, it proves the bane of civil society. . . . The House of Commons receives all its authority from its electors, in consequence of the right they have to a share in the legislature. Its electors are freeholders, citizens, and others, in Great Britian. It follows, therefore, that all its authority is confined to Great Britain. This is demonstrative. Sophistry, by an artful play of ambigous terms, may perplex and obscure it, but reason can never confute it. The power which one society bestows upon any man, or body of men, can never extend beyond its own limits. The people of Great Britain may confer an authority over themselves, but they can never confer any over the people of America, because it is impossible for them to give *that* to another which they never possessed themselves. Now I should be glad to see an attempt to prove that a freeholder, citizen, or any other man in Great Britain, has any inherent right to the life, property, or liberty, of a freeholder, citizen, or any other man in America. He can have no original and intrinsic right, because nature has distributed an equality of rights to every man. He can have no secondary or derivative right, because the only thing which could give him that is wanting—the consent of the natural proprietor. . . .

When I say that the authority of Parliament is confined to Great Britain, I speak of it in its primitive and original state. Parliament may acquire an incidental influence over others, but this must be by their own free consent; for, without this, any power it might exercise would be mere usurpation, and by no means a just authority. . . .

It is said that "in every government there must be a supreme absolute authority lodged somewhere." . . .

This position, when properly explained, is evidently just. In every civil society there must be a supreme power to which all the members of that society are subject, for otherwise there could be no supremacy or subordination—that is, no government at all. But no use can be made of this principle beyond matter of fact. To infer from thence, that unless a supreme, absolute authority be vested in one part of an empire over all the other parts there can be no government in the whole, is false and absurd. Each branch may enjoy a distinct, complete legislature, and still good government may be preserved everywhere. It is in vain to assert that two or more distinct legislatures cannot exist in the same state. If by the same state, be meant the same individual community, it is true. Thus, for instance, there cannot be two supreme legislatures in Great Britain, or two in New York. But if by the same state be understood a number of individual societies or bodies politic united under one common head, then I maintain that there may be one distinct, complete legislature in each. Thus there may be one in Great Britain, another in Ireland, and another in New York; and still these several parts may form but one state. In order to do this there must indeed be some connecting, pervading principle; but this is found in the person and prerogative of the King. He it is that conjoins all these individual societies into one great body politic. He it is that is to preserve their mutual connexion and dependence, and make them all cooperate to one common end—the general good. His power is equal to the purpose, and his interest binds him to the due prosecution of it. . . .

The fundamental source of all your errors, sophisms, and false reasonings, is a total ignorance of the natural rights of mankind. Were you once to become acquainted with these, you could never entertain a thought, that all men are not, by nature, entitled to a parity of privileges. You would be convinced that natural liberty is a gift of the beneficent Creator to the whole human race, and that civil liberty is founded in that, and cannot be wrested from any people without the most manifest violation of justice. *Civil liberty is only natural liberty, modified and secured by the sanctions of civil society.* It is not a thing, in its own nature, precarious and dependent on human will and caprice, but it is conformable to the constitution of man, as well as necessary to the *well-being* of society.

Upon this principle colonists, as well as other men, have a right to civil liberty. For if it be conducive to the happiness of society (and reason and experience testify that it is), it is evident that every society, of whatsoever kind, has an absolute and perfect right to it, which can never be withheld without cruelty and injustice. The practice of Rome toward her colonies cannot afford the shadow of an argument against this. That mistress of the world was often unjust. And the treatment of her dependent provinces is one of the greatest blemishes in her history. Through the want of that civil liberty for which we are so warmly contending, they groaned under every species of wanton oppression. If we are wise we shall take warning from thence, and consider a like state of dependence as more to be dreaded than pestilence and famine.

The right of colonists, therefore, to exercise a legislative power, is an inherent right. It is founded upon the rights of all men to freedom and happiness. For civil liberty cannot possibly have any existence where the society for whom laws are made have no share in making them, and where the interest of their legislators is not inseparably interwoven with theirs. . . .

The foundation of the English constitution rests upon this principle: that no laws have any validity or binding force without the consent and approbation of the *people*, given in the persons of *their* representatives, periodically elected by *themselves*. This constitutes the democratical part of the government.

It is also undeniably certain, that no Englishman who can be deemed a *free agent* in a *political* view can be bound by laws to which he has not consented, either in person or by *his* representative. Or, in other words, every Englishman (exclusive of the mercantile and trading part of the nation) who possesses a freehold to the value of forty shillings per annum has a right to share in the legislature, which he exercises by giving his vote in the election of some person he approves of as his representative.

"The true reason," says Blackstone, "of requiring any qualification with regard to property in voters, is to exclude such persons as are *in so mean a situation* that they are esteemed to have *no will* of their own. If these persons had votes, they would be tempted to dispose of them under some undue influence or other. This would give a great, an artful, or a wealthy man a larger share in elections than is consistent with general liberty. If it were probable that every man would give his vote freely and without influence of any kind, then, upon the true theory and genuine principles of liberty, every member of the community, however poor, should have a vote in electing these delegates, to whose charge is committed the disposal of his property, his liberty, and his life. But since that can hardly be expected in persons of indigent fortunes, or such as are under the immediate dominion of others, all popular states have been obliged to establish certain qualifications, whereby some who are suspected to have no will of their own are excluded from voting, in order to set other individuals, whose wills may be supposed independent, more thoroughly upon a level with each other."

Hence, it appears that such "of the people as have no vote in the choice of representatives, and therefore are governed by laws to which they have not consented, either by themselves or by their representatives," are only those "persons who are *in so mean a situation* that they are esteemed to have *no will* of their own." Every *free agent*, every free man, possessing a freehold of forty shillings per annum, is, by the British constitution, entitled to a vote in the election of those who are invested with the disposal of his life, his liberty, and property.

It is therefore evident, to a demonstration, that unless a *free agent* in America be permitted to enjoy the same privilege, we are entirely stripped of the benefits of the constitution, and precipitated into an abyss of slavery. For we are deprived of that immunity which is the grand pillar and support of freedom. And this cannot be done without a direct violation of the constitution, which decrees to every *free agent* a share in the legislature. . . .

These considerations plainly show that the people in America, of all ranks and conditions, opulent as well as indigent (if subjected to the British Parliament), would be upon a less favorable footing than that part of the people of Great Britain who are *in so mean a situation* that they are supposed to have no will of their own. The injustice of this must be evident to every man of common sense.

Thus, sir, I have taken a pretty general survey of the American charters, and proved, to the satisfaction of every unbiased person, that they are entirely discordant with that sovereignty of Parliament for which you are an advocate. . . .

It is true that New York has no charter. But if it could support its claim to liberty in no other way, it might, with justice, plead the common principles of colonization: for it would be unreasonable to exclude one colony from the enjoyment of the most important privileges of the rest. There is no need, however, of this plea. The sacred rights of mankind are not to be rummaged for among old parchments or musty records. They are written, as with a sunbeam, in the whole *volume* of human nature, by the hand of the Divinity itself, and can never be erased or obscured by mortal power. . . .

But it is granted that Great Britain has a right to regulate the trade of the empire. The Congress have acknowledged it so far as concerned their constituents. You infer from thence that all parts of the empire must be subject to her. They need only be so far subject as is necessary for the end proposed, that is, the regulation of their trade. If you require any further subjection, you require *means* that are disproportionate to the *end*, which is unreasonable and not at all allowable.

With respect to the justice of submitting to impositions on our trade for the purpose of raising a revenue to support the navy by which it is protected, I answer that the exclusive regulation of our commerce for her own advantage is a sufficient tribute to Great Britain for protecting it. By this means a vast accession of wealth is annually thrown into her coffers. It is a matter of notoriety that the balance of trade is very much against us. After ransacking Spain, Portugal, Holland, the English, French, Spanish, Dutch, and Danish plantations, for money and bills of exchange, as remittances for the commodities we take from Great Britain, we are still always greatly in arrears to her. At a moderate computation, I am well informed that the profits she derives from us every year exceed two millions and a half sterling; and when we reflect that this sum will be continually increasing as we grow more and more populous, it must be evident that there is not the least justice in raising a revenue upon us by the imposition of special duties.

The right of Great Britain to regulate our trade upon this plan, it is now acknowledged, is not an inconsiderable matter. It is as much as any free people can concede, and as much as any just people would require. We are not permitted to procure manufactures anywhere else than from Great Britain, or Ireland. Our trade is limited and prescribed, in every respect, as is most for her interest. This is a plentiful source of wealth to her, as I have heretofore shown, and shall hereafter confirm by the testimony of some British writers.

But I have found out an argument, which I imagine will go very near convincing yourself of the absurdity of what you have offered on this head. It is short, but conclusive. "*The principal profits of our trade centre in Great Britain.*" How can you, my dear sir, after making this confession, entertain a single thought that it is incumbent upon us to suffer her to raise a revenue upon our trade? Are not the *principal profits* a sufficient recompense for protecting it? Surely you would not allow her the whole. . . .

A fondness for power is implanted in most men, and it is natural to abuse it when acquired. This maxim, drawn from the experience of all ages, makes it the height of folly to intrust any set of men with power which is not under every possible control; perpetual strides are made after more as long as there is any part withheld. We ought not, therefore, to concede any greater authority to the British Parliament than is absolutely necessary. There seems to be a necessity for vesting the regulation of our trade *there*, because in time our commercial interests might otherwise interfere with hers. But with respect to making laws for us, there is not the least necessity, or even propriety, in it. . . .

Had the rest of America passively looked on while a sister colony was subjugated, the same fate would gradually have overtaken all. The safety of the whole depends upon the mutual protection of every part. If the sword of oppression be permitted to lop off one limb without opposition, reiterated strokes will soon dismember the whole body. Hence, it was the duty and interest of all the colonies to succor and support the one which was suffering. It is sometimes sagaciously urged, that we ought to commiserate the distresses of the people of Massachusetts, but not intermeddle in their affairs, so far as perhaps to bring ourselves into like circumstances with them. This might be good reasoning, if our neutrality would not be more dangerous than our participation; but I am unable to conceive how the colonies in general would have any security against oppression, if they were once to content themselves with barely *pitying* each other, while Parliament was prosecuting and enforcing its demands. Unless they continually protect and assist each other, they must all inevitably fall a prey to their enemies.

Extraordinary emergencies require extraordinary expedients. The best mode of opposition was that in which there might be a union of councils. This was necessary to ascertain the boundaries of our rights, and to give weight and dignity to our measures, both in Great Britain and America. A Congress was accordingly proposed, and universally agreed to.

You, sir, triumph in the supposed *illegality* of this body: but granting your supposition were true, it would be a matter of no real importance. When the first principles of civil society are violated, and the rights of a whole people are invaded, the common forms of municipal law are not to be regarded. Men may then betake themselves to the law of nature; and, if they but conform their actions to that standard, all cavils against them betray either ignorance or dishonesty. There are some events in society, to which human laws cannot extend, but when applied to them, lose all their force and efficacy. In short, when human laws contradict or discountenance the means which are necessary to preserve the essential rights of any society, they defeat the proper end of all laws, and so become null and void. . . .

Whatever may may be said of the disciplined troops of Great Britain, the event of the contest must be extremely doubtful. There is a certain enthusiasm in liberty, that makes human nature rise above itself in acts of bravery and heroism. It cannot be expected that America would yield, without a magnanimous, persevering, and bloody struggle. The testimony of past ages, and the least knowledge of mankind, must suffice to convince us of the contrary. We have a recent instance, in *Corsica*, to what lengths a people will go in defense of its liberties; and if we take a view of the colonies in general, we must perceive that the pulse of Americans beats high in their country's cause.

. . . what reason have we to believe the arms of Great Britain would prevail? It will be replied: Because she can send against us some of the best troops in the world, either with respect to valor or discipline; and because we have only a raw, unexperienced militia to oppose them. Discipline and military skill are certainly matters of great importance, and give those to whom they belong a vast superiority; but they do not render them invincible. Superior numbers, joined to natural intrepidity and that animation which is inspired by a desire of freedom and a love of one's country, may very well overbalance those advantages. . . .

Let it be remembered that there are no large plains for the two armies to meet in and decide the contest by some decisive stroke; where any advantage gained by either side might be prosecuted till a complete victory was obtained. The circumstances of our country put it in our power to evade a pitched battle. It will be better policy to harass and exhaust the soldiery by frequent skirmishes and incursions than to take the open field with them, by which means they would have the full benefit of their superior regularity and skill. Americans are better qualified for that kind of fighting, which is most adapted to this country, than regular troops. Should the soldiery advance into the country, as they would be obliged to do if they had any inclination to subdue us, their discipline would be of little use to them. We should, in that case, be at least upon an equality with them, in any respect; and as we should have the advantage on many accounts, they would be likely to gain nothing by their attempts. . . .

You ask me: What resources have the colonies to pay, clothe, arm, and feed their troops? I refer you to the accounts of Virginia and Marblehead for an answer to this question. Our troops, on the spot with us, will be much more easily maintained than those of Britain at such a distance. We are not so poor and incumbered as to be unable to support those who are immediately employed in defending our liberties. Our country abounds in provisions. We have already materials enough among us, to keep us in clothes longer than Britain would have any appetite to continue her hostilities. Several of the colonies are pretty well stored with ammunition. France, Spain, and Holland would find means to supply us with whatever we wanted.

Let it not be said that this last is a bare *possibility;* that France and Spain have promised not to interfere in the dispute; and that Holland has long been a faithful ally to the British nation. There is the highest degree of probability in the case. A more desirable object to France and Spain than the disunion of these colonies from Great Britain cannot be imagined. Every dictate of policy and interest would prompt them to forward it by every possible means. They could not take any so effectual method to destroy the growing power of their great rival. The promises of princes and statesmen are of little weight. They never bind longer than till a strong temptation offers to break them; and they are frequently made with a sinister design. If we consult the known character of the French, we shall be disposed to conclude that their present seemingly pacific and friendly disposition is merely a piece of *finesse*, intended to dupe the administration into some violent measures with the colonies, that they may improve them to their own advantage. The most that can be expected is, that they would refrain from any open rupture with Britain. They would undoubtedly take every clandestine method to introduce among us, supplies of those things which we stood in need of to carry on the dispute. They would not neglect any thing in their power to make the opposition on our part as vigorous and obstinate as our affairs would admit of. . . .

But it seems to me a mark of great credulity to believe, upon the strength of their assurance, that France and Spain would not take a still more interesting part in the affair. The disjunction of these colonies from Britain, and the acquisition of a free trade with them, are objects of too inviting a complexion to suffer those kingdoms to remain idle spectators of the contention. If they found us inclined to throw ourselves upon their protection, they would eagerly embrace the opportunity to weaken their antagonists and strengthen themselves. Superadded to these general and prevailing inducements, there are others of a more particular nature. They would feel no small inconvenience in the loss of those supplies they annually get from us; and their islands in the West Indies would be in the greatest distress for want of our trade. . . .

Whatever opinion may be entertained of my sentiments and intentions, I attest that Being, whose all-seeing eye penetrates the inmost recesses of the heart, that I am not influenced (in the part I take) by any unworthy motive; that, if I am in an error, it is my judgment, not my heart, that errs; that I earnestly lament the unnatural quarrel between the parent state and the colonies, and most ardently wish for a speedy reconciliation—a perpetual and *mutually* beneficial union; that I am a warm advocate for limited monarchy, and an unfeigned well-wisher to the present Royal Family.

But, on the other hand, I am inviolably attached to the essential rights of mankind and the true interests of society. I consider civil liberty, in a genuine, unadulterated sense, as the greatest of terrestrial blessings. I am convinced that the whole human race is entitled to it, and that it can be wrested from no part of them without the blackest and most aggravated guilt.

I verily believe, also, that the best way to secure a permanent and happy union between Great Britain and the colonies, is to permit the latter to be as free as they desire. To abridge their liberties, or to exercise any power over them which they are unwilling to submit to, would be a perpetual source of discontent and animosity. A continual jealously would exist on both sides. This would lead to tyranny on the one hand, and to sedition and rebellion on the other. Impositions, not really grievous in themselves, would be thought so, and the murmurs arising from thence would be considered as the effect of a turbulent, ungovernable spirit. These jarring principles would at length throw all things into disorder, and be productive of an irreparable breach and a total disunion.

That harmony and mutual confidence may speedily be restored between all the parts of the British empire, is the favorite wish of one who feels the warmest sentiments of goodwill to mankind, who bears no enmity to you, and who is

A Sincere Friend to America

—*The Farmer Refuted: Or, A More Impartial and Comprehensive View of the Dispute between Great Britain and the Colonies, Intended as a Further Vindication of the Congress* (New York: James Rivington, 1775), pp. 5-16, 21-25, 38-43, 52, 70-78.

The passage of the Quebec Act in May, 1774, was regarded by the American colonists as a part of the "Intolerable" measures, on a par with the closing of the port of Boston and annulling the self-govern-

ment of Massachusetts. Fearing the loss of America, Britain hastened to win Canada by allowing it to remain French and Catholic. Save for the criminal law, the old French law was revived in Canada and the Catholic church given a privileged position. Following the lead of the Continental Congress, young Hamilton helped revive the anti-Catholic frenzy of the French and Indian Wars. How much damage this kind of prejudicial attack did to the American cause in Canada is difficult to ascertain. Despite religious differences many French Canadians were friendly to the American cause, and so were some of the clergy. The failure of America to win Canada must be attributed not so much to religious bigotry as to military inadequacy.

[June 15, 1775]

Here a power of a most extraordinary and dangerous nature is conferred. There must be an end of all liberty where the prince is possessed of such an exorbitant prerogative as enables him, at pleasure, to establish the most iniquitous, cruel, and oppressive courts of criminal, civil, and ecclesiastical jurisdiction; and to appoint temporary judges and officers, whom he can displace and change as often as he pleases. For what can more nearly concern the safety and happiness of subjects, than the wise economy, and equitable constitution of those courts in which trials for life, liberty, property, and religion are to be conducted? Should it ever comport with the designs of an ambitious and wicked minister, we may see an Inquisition erected in Canada, and priestly tyranny hereafter find as propitious a soil in America as it ever has in Spain or Portugal. . . .

The characteristic difference between a tolerated and established religion consists in this: With respect to the support of the former, the law is passive and improvident, leaving it to those who profess it to make as much, or as little, provision as they shall judge expedient; and to vary and alter that provision, as their circumstances may require. In this manner the Presbyterians and other sects are tolerated in England. They are allowed to exercise their religion without molestation, and to maintain their clergy as they think proper. These are wholly dependent upon their congregations, and can exact no more than they stipulate and are satisfied to contribute. But with respect to the support of the latter, the law is active and provident. Certain precise dues (tithes, etc.) are legally annexed to the clerical office, independent on the liberal contributions of the people; which is exactly the case with the Canadian priests; and, therefore, no reasonable, impartial man will doubt that the religion of the Church of Rome is established in Canada. While tithes were the free, though customary, gift of the people, as was the case before the passing of the act in question, the Roman Church was only in a state of toleration; but when the law came to take cognizance of them, and, by determining their permanent existence, destroyed the free agency of the people, it then resumed the nature of an establishment, which it had been divested of at the time of the capitulation. . . .

. . . Had there been really provision made, to be applied at the discretion of his Majesty, I should still consider this act as an atrocious infraction on the rights of Englishmen, in a point of the most delicate and momentous concern. No Protestant Englishman would consent to let the free exercise of his religion depend upon the mere pleasure of any man, however great or exalted. The privilege of worshipping the Deity in the manner his conscience dictates, which is one of the dearest he enjoys, must in that case be rendered insecure and precarious. Yet this is the unhappy situation to which the Protestant inhabitants of Canada are now reduced.

The will of the king must give law to their consciences. It is in his power to keep them for ever dispossessed of all religious immunities, and there is too much reason to apprehend that the same motives which instigated the act would induce him to give them as little future encouragement as possible.

—*Remarks on the Quebec Bill,* in *Works,* I, 184-185, 190-191, 193.

By the close of 1775 Hamilton was prominently associated with the radical leadership in New York, and alert to prevent the conservatives from controlling the new legislature.

NEW YORK, December 31, 1775

I have much reason to suspect that the Tories have it in contemplation to steal a march upon us if they can, in respect of a new Assembly. I believe the governor will shortly dissolve the old and issue writs for a new one. The motives for it, at this time, are probably these: It is hoped the attention of the people being engaged with their new institutions, Congresses, committees and the like; they will think the assembly of little importance and will not exert themselves as they ought to do, whereby the Tories may have the opportunity to elect their own creatures. Or at least it is expected the people may be thrown into divisions and ferments, injurious to present measures.

The Tories will be no doubt very artful and intriguing, and it behooves us to be very vigilant and cautious. I have thrown out a hand bill or two to give the necessary alarm, and shall second them by others.

It appears to me that as the best way to keep the attention of the people united and fixed to the same point it would be expedient that four of our Continental delegates should be candidates for this city and county: Mr. Livingston, Mr. Alsop, Mr. Lewis, Mr. Jay. The minds of all our friends will naturally tend to these, and the opposition will of course be weak and contemptible, for the Whigs, I doubt not, constitute a large majority of the people. If you approve the hint, I should wish for your presence here. Absence, you know, is not very favorable to the influence of any person, however great. I shall give you farther notice as I see the scheme advanced to be executed.

—To John Jay. Jay Papers (microfilm), Columbia Univ. Lib.

The Spirit of '76: Two different versions

ALBANY, August 13, 1782

As to the people, in the early periods of the war, near one-half of them were avowedly more attached to Great Britain than to their liberty, but the energy of the government has subdued all opposition. The State by different means has been purged of a large part of its malcontents; but there still remains, I dare say, a third, whose secret wishes are on the side of the enemy; the remainder sigh for peace, murmur at taxes, clamor at their rulers, change one incapable man for another more incapable, and, I fear, if left to themselves, would, too many of them, be willing to purchase peace at any price—not from inclination to Great Britain or disaffection to independence, but from mere supiness and avarice.

—To Robert Morris. *Hamilton Papers*, 1st ser.

March 30, 1798

When Great Britain attempted to wrest from us those rights, without which we must have descended from the rank of freemen, a keen and strong sense of injury and danger ran with electric swiftness through the breasts of our citizens. The mass and weight of talents, property, and character hastened to confederate in the public cause. The great body of our community everywhere burned with a holy zeal to defend it, and were eager to make sacrifices on the altar of their country.

—"The Stand," Part I. *Hamilton*, VII, 639.

Revolution and Moderation

Hamilton was ever the valiant defender of civil liberties. When the war ended he advocated fair treatment for the former Tories and scrupulous adherence to the terms of the treaty of peace with Great Britain. He never doubted the rightness of the Revolution, but insistently preached the virtue of moderation.

[1784]

Viewing the subject in every possible light, there is not a single interest of the community but dictates moderation rather than violence. That honesty is still the best policy; that justice and moderation are the surest supports of every government, are maxims which, however they may be called trite, are at all times true; though too seldom regarded, but rarely neglected with impunity.

*Were the people of America with one voice to ask: "What shall we do to perpetuate our liberties and secure our happiness?" the answer would be: "*GOVERN WELL,*" and you have nothing to fear either from internal disaffection or external hostility. Abuse not the power you possess, and you need never apprehend its diminution or loss. But if you make a wanton use of it, if you furnish another example that despotism may debase the government of the many as well as the few, you, like all others that have acted the same part, will experience that licentiousness is the forerunner to slavery.*

How wise was that policy of Augustus, who, after conquering his enemies, when the papers of Brutus were brought to him, which would have disclosed all his secret associates, immediately ordered them to be burnt. He would not even know his enemies, that they might cease to hate where they had nothing to fear.

How laudable was the example of Elizabeth, who, when she was transferred from the prison to the throne, fell upon her knees, and thanking Heaven for the deliverance it had granted her from her bloody persecutors, dismissed her resentment. "This act of pious gratitude," says her historian, "seems to have been the last circumstance in which she remembered any past injuries and hardships. With a prudence and magnanimity truly laudable, she buried all offences in oblivion, and received with affability even those who acted with the greatest virulence against her." She did more, she retained many of the opposite party in her councils.

The reigns of these two sovereigns are among the most illustrious in history. Their moderation gave a stability to their government which nothing else could have effected. This was the secret of uniting all parties.

—*A Letter from Phocion to the Considerate Citizens of New York p. 18.*

[1784]

If we set out with justice, moderation, liberality, and a scrupulous regard to the Constitution, the government will acquire a spirit and tone productive of permanent blessings to the community. If, on the contrary, the public councils are guided by humor, passion, and prejudice; if from resentment to individuals, or a dread of partial inconveniences, the Constitution is slighted, or explained away, upon every frivolous pretext, the future spirit of government will be feeble, distracted, and arbitrary. The rights of the subjects will be the sport of every party vicissitude. There will be no settled rule of conduct, but everything will fluctuate with the alternate prevalency of contending factions.

The world has its eye upon America. The noble struggle we have made in the cause of liberty has occasioned a kind of revolution in human sentiment. The influence of our example has penetrated the gloomy regions of despotism, and has pointed the way to enquiries which may shake it to its deepest foundations. Men begin to ask, every where: Who is this tyrant that dares to build his greatness on our misery and degradation? What commission has he to sacrifice millions to the wanton appetites of himself and a few minions that surround his throne?

To ripen enquiry into action, it remains for us to justify the revolution by its fruits.

If the consequences prove that we really have asserted the cause of human happiness, what may not be expected from so illustrious an example? In a greater or less degree the world will bless and imitate.

But if experience, in this instance, verifies the lesson long taught by the enemies of liberty, that the bulk of mankind are not fit to govern themselves; that they must have a master, and were only made for the rein and the spur; we shall then see the final triumph of despotism over liberty; the advocates of the latter must acknowledge it to be an *ignis fatuus*, and abandon the pursuit. With the greatest advantages for promoting it that ever a people had, we shall have betrayed the cause of human nature.

—*A Second Letter from Phocion*, pp. 42-43.

February 24, 1789

In all struggles for liberty, the leaders of the people have fallen under two principal discriminations; those who, to a conviction of the real usefulness of civil liberty, join a sincere attachment to the public good, and those who are of restless and turbulent spirit, impatient of control, and averse to all power or superiority which they do not themselves enjoy. With men of the latter description, this transition from demagogues to despots is neither difficult nor uncommon.

—*Letters of H. G., IV*, N. Y. *Daily Advertiser*, March 14, 1789.

February 8, 1794

There are two great errors in our reasoning upon this subject: one, that the combined powers will certainly attribute to us the same principles which they deem so exceptionable in France; the other, that our principles are in fact the same.

If left to themselves they will all, except one, naturally see in us a people who originally resorted to a revolution in government, as a refuge from encroachments on rights and privileges *antecedently* enjoyed, not as a people who from choice have sought a radical and entire change in the established government, in pursuit of new privileges and rights carried to an extreme, irreconcilable perhaps with any form of regular government. They will see in us a people who have a due respect for property and personal security; who, in the midst of our revolution, abstained with exemplary moderation from every thing violent or sanguinary, instituting governments adequate to the protection of persons and property; who, since the completion of our revolution, have in a very short period, from mere reasoning and reflection, without tumult or bloodshed, adopted a form of general government calculated, as well as the nature of things would permit, to remedy antecedent defects, to give strength and security to the nation, to rest the foundations of liberty on the basis of justice, order, and law; who at all times have been content to govern themselves, unmeddling with the affairs or governments of other nations; in fine, they will see in us sincere republicans, but decided enemies to licentiousness and anarchy; sincere republicans, but decided friends to the freedom of opinion, to the order and tranquility of all mankind. They will not see in us a people whose best passions have been misled, and whose best qualities have been perverted from their true aim by headlong, fanatical, or designing leaders, to the perpetration of acts from which humanity shrinks, to the commission of outrages over which the eye of reason weeps, to the profession and practice of principles which tend to shake the foundations of morality, to dissolve the social bands, to disturb the peace of mankind, to substitute confusion to order, anarchy to government.

—"Americanus," II. Draft in Hamilton's hand. Hamilton Papers, 1st ser.

Revolution as a Last Resort

[December, 1787]

If the representatives of the people betray their constituents, there is then no recourse left but in the exertion of that original right of self-defense which is paramount to all positive forms of government, and which against the usurpations of the national rulers may be exerted with infinitely better prospect of success than against those of the rulers of an individual state. In a single state, if the persons intrusted with supreme power become usurpers, the different parcels, subdivisions, or districts of which it consists, having no distinct government in each, can take no regular measures for defense. The citizens must rush tumultuously to arms, without concert, without system, without resource, except in their courage and despair. The usurpers, clothed with the forms of legal authority, can too often crush the opposition in embryo. The smaller the extent of the territory, the more difficult will it be for the people to form a regular or systematic plan of opposition, and the more easy will it be to defeat their early efforts. Intelligence can be more speedily obtained of their preparations and movements, and the military force in the possession of the usurpers can be more rapidly directed against the part where the opposition has begun. In this situation there must be a peculiar coincidence of circumstances to insure success to the popular resistance.

The obstacles to usurpation and the facilities of resistance increase with the increased extent of the state, provided the citizens understand their rights and are disposed to defend them. The natural strength of the people in a large community, in proportion to the artificial strength of the government, is greater than in a small, and of course more competent to a struggle with the attempts of the government to establish a tyranny. But in a confederacy the people, without exaggeration, may be said to be entirely the masters of their own fate. Power being almost always the rival of power, the general government will at all times stand ready to check the usurpations of the state governments, and these will have the same disposition towards the general government. The people, by throwing themselves into either scale, will infallibly make it preponderate. If their rights are invaded by either, they can make use of the other as the instrument of redress. How wise will it be in them by cherishing the union to preserve to themselves an advantage which can never be too highly prized!

—*The Federalist*, No. 28

2

Winning the Revolution

> The liberties of America are an infinite stake. We should not play a desperate game for it, or put it upon the issue of a single cast of the die.

"I wish there was a war." So wrote young Hamilton in 1769 in a letter to his friend Edward Stevens in which he expressed his dissatisfaction with "the grovelling condition of a clerk." The St. Croix clerk was to have his war perhaps sooner than he anticipated. At King's College he joined a Patriot volunteer band known as the "Corsicans" and drilled every morning before classes. In August of '75 his troop joined in a raid staged by Captain John Lamb to seize the cannon from the battery. When, on January 6, 1776, the New York Provincial Congress set up a company of artillery for the defense of the colony, Hamilton applied for command of the company, satisfied his seniors that he had adequate grasp of artillery and ballistics, and was commissioned on March 14th. He rounded up thirty men, equipped them out of his personal funds, and was a constant advocate of their interests, alert to support their claims to the same pay as the Continental troops.

May 26, 1776

I AM NOT personally interested in having an augmentation agreeably to the above rates, because my own pay will remain the same as that it now is: but I make this application on behalf of the company; as I am fully convinced such a disadvantageous distinction will have a very pernicious effect on the minds and behavior of the men. They do the same duty with the other companies, and think themselves entitled to the same pay. They have been already comparing accounts; and many marks of discontent have lately appeared on this score. As to the circumstance of our being confined to the defence of the colony, it will have little or no weight; for there are but few in the company, who would not as willingly leave the colony on any necessary expedition, as stay in it: and they will not, therefore, think it reasonable to have their pay curtailed on such a consideration.

—To the Provincial Congress of New York. *Hamilton*, I, 7-9.

July 26, 1776

My men, you are sensible, are, by their articles, entitled to the same subsistence with the Continental troops and it would be to them an insupportable discrimination, as well as a breach of the terms of their enlistment, to give them almost a third less provisions than the whole army besides receives. I doubt not you will readily put this matter upon a proper footing.

—To the Provincial Congress. *Hamilton*, I, 9.

Hamilton received his baptism under fire at the Battle of Long Island. When Washington sent part of his forces across the East River to prevent Howe from seizing Brooklyn Heights young Hamilton dispatched an anonymous note to the general pointing out the untenable position, as Howe was certain to land farther down in a flanking movement. He advised retreating to Manhattan, an action Washington did not order until the American left had been crumpled at Jamaica and forced back upon the main body at Brooklyn Heights. At White Plains, Hamilton's battery guarded Chatterton's Hill, protecting the withdrawal of Smallwood's militia. But it was at the Battle of Princeton that Hamilton first came to the attention of his chief. His cannon were brought to bear on Nassau Hall and he gave the order to fire when the British troops who had sought refuge there refused to surrender. By the time of the winter encampment at Morristown Hamilton's corps had been reduced to little more than a third of its full strength. On March 1, 1777, Hamilton was made a lieutenant-colonel and aide of Washington. From this time he was in close touch with the Committee of Correspondence of the New York Convention, comprising Gouverneur Morris, Robert R. Livingston, and William Allison, and sent them his astute observations on military and political affairs.

Years later the Chevalier de Pontigibaud, a French officer, reported in his Mémoires that Hamilton had considered the sending by the British of an invasion army to America as a serious blunder. A second mistake, Hamilton added, "was to give the two brothers Howe each a command. The general undertook scarcely anything by land in order to allow his brother, the admiral, the chance to distinguish himself at sea. All that the English need have done was to blockade our ports with twenty-five frigates and ten ships of the line. But, thank God, they did nothing of the sort!"

HEADQUARTERS, MORRISTOWN, March 22, 1777

The present time is so unfruitful of events that it affords no intelligence worthy of your notice. As to transactions of a military nature, I can only say that the British army continues to decrease by the daily loss of prisoners and deserters taken at and coming into the different posts, which is a striking symptom that the situation of affairs with the enemy is not so favorable as it might be; for when an army is in good humor and its affairs prosperous, desertion is a disease that seldom prevails in it.

—To Gouverneur Morris, *et al. Works*, IX, 47.

HEADQUARTERS, MORRISTOWN, April 5, 1777

As to your apprehensions of an attempt up the North River, I imagine you may discard any uneasiness on that score, although it will be at all times advisable to be on the watch against such a contingency. It is almost reduced to a certainty, that the principal views of the enemy, in the ensuing campaign, will be directed towards the southward, and to Philidelphia more immediately; of which idea, the discovery before mentioned, with respect to pilots, is no inconsiderable confirmation. Philadelphia is an object calculated to strike and attract attention. It has all along been the main source of supplies towards the war; and the getting it into their possession would deprive us of a wheel we could very badly spare, in the great political and military machine. They are sensible of this, and are equally sensible, that it contains, in itself, and is surrounded by, a prodigious number of persons attached to them, and inimicable to us, who would lend them all the assistance they could, in the further prosecution of their designs. It is also a common and well-grounded rule in war, to strike first and principally, at the capital towns and cities, in order to the conquest of a country.

I must confess I do not see any object equally interesting to draw their efforts to the northward. Operations merely for plundering and devastation can never answer their end; and if they could, one part of the continent would do nearly as well as another. And as to the notion of forming a junction with the northern army, and cutting off the communication between the Northern and Southern States, I apprehend it will do better in speculation than in practice. Unless the geography of the country is far different from any thing I can conceive, to effect this would require a chain of posts, and such a number of men at each as would never be practicable or maintainable, but to an immense army. In their progress, by hanging upon their rear, and seizing every opportunity of skirmishing, their situation might be rendered insupportably uneasy.

—To the Committee of the New York Convention. *Hamilton*, I, 17-19.

HEADQUARTERS, MORRIS TOWN, April 12, 1777.

I should be obliged to you to inform the convention that it is my opinion the General will not permit Mr. Le Roy to go into New York. It is a determined point with him to grant no such indulgence when any matter of the kind is referred to him, unless the person applying can assign the most substantial reasons for his request, and can also produce explicit credentials of his political principles and conduct being favourable to the American cause. I conclude from my being instructed to require his parole that he cannot give satisfaction on these points. If however he should obtain permission, I will execute the resolve transmitted to me. For the future, if the convention have cogent reasons for allowing any subject of the state to go into the enemy, as they are the best judges of all the circumstances concerning him, they had better send him in, without referring the matter particularly to the General.

—To Robert R. Livingston. Robert R. Livingston Coll., N. Y. Hist. Soc.

MIDDLE BROOK CAMP, June 2, 1777

. . . The enemy yesterday perpetrated a most barbarous butchery upon a Lieutenant Martin of ours. He was out with a scouting party, and met some of the British light horses. His men, 'tis said, quitted him. But however other matters may be, 'tis certain his dead body was found most horribly mangled. He had not a single bullet wound, but was hacked to pieces with a sword. He had several cuts in his head, each of which was sufficient to dispatch him; besides a number of more inconsiderable scars about his body and hands. It is evident that the most wanton and unnecessary cruelty might have been used towards him; for the greater part of his wounds must have been given him when utterly out of condition to resist. This may be relied on as a fact, for I saw his corps[e] as did also every officer and soldier in camp that chose it. The General sent him down to their lines with a letter to Lord Cornwallis, as an undeniable evidence of their brutality; but the letter was taken from the flag and sent in; the flag and the body not permitted to pass their outposts.

—To Robert R. Livingston, Robert R. Livingston Coll., N. Y. Hist. Soc.

HEADQUARTERS, CAMP AT MIDDLE BROOK, June 28, 1777

I know the comments that some people will make on our Fabian conduct. It will be imputed either to cowardice, or to weakness. But the more discerning, I trust, will not find it difficult to conceive, that it proceeds from the truest policy, and is an argument neither of the one nor the other.

The liberties of America are an infinite stake. We should not play a desperate game for it, or put it upon the issue of a single cast of the die. The loss of one general engagement may effectually ruin us, and it would certainly be folly to hazard it, unless our resources for keeping up an army were at an end, and some decisive blow was absolutely necessary; or unless our strength was so great as to give certainty of success. Neither is the case. America can in all probability maintain its army for years, and our numbers, though such as would give a reasonable hope of success, are not such as should make us entirely sanguine. . . .

On our part we are continually strengthening our political springs in Europe, and may every day look for more effectual aids than we have yet received. Our own army is continually growing stronger in men, arms, and discipline: we shall soon have an important addition of artillery, now on its way to join us. We can maintain our present numbers good, at least, by enlistments, while the enemy must dwindle away; and at the end of the summer the disparity between us will be infinitely great, and facilitate any exertions that may be made to settle the business with them. Their affairs will be growing worse, ours better; so that delay will ruin them. It will serve to perplex and fret them, and precipitate them into measures that we can turn to good account. Our business then is to avoid a general engagement, and to waste the enemy away by constantly goading their sides in a desultory, teasing way.

—To Robert R. Livingston. Robert R. Livingston Coll., N.Y. Hist. Soc.

The Burgoyne Campaign

[July, 1777]

The consequences of this northern affair will depend much upon the part that Howe acts. If he were to co-operate with Burgoyne it would demand our utmost efforts to counteract them. But if he should go towards the southward, all or most of the advantages of Burgoyne's success will be lost. He will either be obliged to content himself with the possession of Ticonderoga and the dependent fortresses, and with carrying on a partisan war the rest of the campaign, or he must precipitate himself into certain ruin by attempting to advance into the country with a very incompetent force. . . .

It may be asked, If, to avoid a general engagement, we give up objects of the first importance, what is to hinder the enemy from carrying every important point, and ruining us? My answer is, that our hopes are not placed in any particular city or spot of ground, but in the preserving a good army, furnished with proper necessaries, to take advantage of favorable opportunities, and waste and defeat the enemy by piecemeal. Every new post they take, requires a new division of their forces, and enables us to strike with our united force against a part of theirs: and such is their present situation, that another Trenton affair will amount to a complete victory on our part; for they are at too low an ebb to bear another stroke of the kind.

—To Dr. Hugh Knox. *Hamilton*, I, 31-34.

MORRIS TOWN, July 6, 1777

I am loth to risk a conjecture about Mr. Howe. He is such an un[in]telligible gentleman that no rule of interpretation can possibly be found out by which to unravel his designs. If he acted like a man of sense, he would wait quietly on Staten Island, and there concenter all his forces. He would draw around all the men that could be spared from Canada and all that are now at Rhode Island. With these and all the reinforcements he may receive from Europe, he would make a point of forcing us by some means or other to an action. In this his only hope lies, if he could defeat our army, and improve the moment of success he would go near effecting his purpose. But let him go to the Northward or to the Southward, every new post he takes weakens his main body, and makes it the more liable to be ruined by our collective strength.

—To Robert R. Livingston, Robert R. Livingston Coll., N. Y. Hist. Soc.

HEADQUARTERS, SMITH'S CLOVE,[1] July 22, 1777

I am doubtful whether Burgoyne will attempt to penetrate far, and whether he will not content himself with harassing our back settlements by parties assisted by the savages, who, it is to be feared, will pretty generally be tempted by the enemy's late successes to confederate in hostilities against us.

This doubt arises from some appearances that indicate a southern movement of General Howe's army, which, if it should really happen, will certainly be a barrier against any further impressions of Burgoyne; for it cannot be supposed he would be rash enough to plunge into the bosom of the country without an expectation of being met by General Howe. Things must prove very averse to us indeed, should he make such an attempt, and not be ruined by it. I confess, however, that the appearances I allude to do not carry a full evidence in my mind, because they are opposed by others of a contradictory kind, and because I cannot conceive upon what principle of common-sense or military propriety Howe can be running away from Burgoyne to the southward.

It is much to be wished he may, even though it should give him the possession of Philadelphia, which by our remoteness from it, may very well happen. In this case we may not only, if we think proper, retaliate,

[1] Between Stony Point and West Point.

by aiming a stroke at New York; but we may come upon him with the greatest part of our collective force, to act against that part which is under him. We shall then be certain that Burgoyne cannot proceed, and that a small force of Continental troops will be sufficient for that partisan war which he must carry on the rest of the campaign.

—To Gouverneur Morris. In Hamilton's hand. Hamilton Papers, 1st ser.

HEADQUARTERS, CORYELL'S FERRY, July 29, 1777

. . . When this last deduction is made, Burgoyne cannot advance with more than between five and six thousand men, to suppose him to act with his whole collective force; except Canadians and Indians, who are not, by any accounts, numerous.

Let us now take a view of our own force. When Glover's brigade gets up, and the recruits for the regiments there, now on their march, arrive, General Schuyler will have about five thousand Continental troops. Surely the Eastern States cannot sleep so soundly, when the danger is so imminent, but that they will reinforce him with eight or ten thousand militia. If this happens, and he cannot stop General Burgoyne's progress, it must proceed from other causes than the want of men. With about the same army last year, General Washington kept Howe with sixteen or seventeen thousand men at bay.

—To Gouverneur Morris. *Hamilton*, VI, 589-592.

The Defense of Philadelphia

Whether Hamilton's proposal to attack Howe's forces would have been more successful than the more cautious strategy of Washington can never be settled. At Brandywine Creek Washington narrowly escaped the destruction of his entire Army. In the course of withdrawal the General dispatched Hamilton and Captain Henry Lee with a small party to destroy military stores before they were seized by the enemy. Hamilton set torch to the stores, and narrowly escaped with his life when a large body of British horse road down upon him.

HEADQUARTERS, WILMINGTON September 1, 1777

. . . The enemy will have Philadelphia if they dare make a bold push for it, unless we fight them a pretty general action. I opine we ought to do it, and that we shall beat them soundly if we do. The militia seem pretty generally stirring. Our army is in high health and spirits. We shall, I hope, have twice the enemy's numbers. I would not only fight them, but I would attack them; for I hold it an established maxim, that there is three to one in favor of the party attacking.

—To Gouverneur Morris, Robert R. Livingston Coll., N. Y. Hist. Soc.

September 18, 1777

If Congress have not left Philadelphia they ought to do it immediately without fail; for the enemy have the means of throwing a party this night into the city. I just now passed the Valley Ford—in doing which a party of the enemy came down and fired upon us in the boat, by which means I lost my horse—one man was killed, and another wounded. The boats were abandoned, and will fall into their hands. I did all I could to prevent this, but to no purpose.

—To John Hancock, President of Congress. *Hamilton*, I, 34-35.

Mission to Gates

After the victory at Saratoga Gates could well have spared troops which Washington desperately needed to recapture Philadelphia. But Gates, puffed up with his newly-won importance, had not even deigned to notify his commander-in-chief of Burgoyne's surrender. To procure troops from both Gates and Israel Putnam Washington dispatched his aide Hamilton. Gates was adamant, but finally backed down under pressure and Putnam at length yielded grudgingly, when Hamilton presented him with "a positive order." Putnam's men had refused to march South until they received pay and clothing. The spectacle of a youthful lieutenant colonel issuing commands to a couple of major-generals has few precedents in military annals. Washington knew his man. "I approve entirely of all the steps you have taken," he later wrote Hamilton.

ALBANY November, 1777

I arrived here yesterday at noon, and waited upon General Gates immediately, on the business of my mission, but was sorry to find his ideas did not correspond with yours for drawing off the number of troops you directed. I used every argument in my power to convince him of the propriety of the measure, but he was inflexible in the opinion that two brigades at least of Continental troops should remain in and near this place. His reasons were that the intelligence of Sir Harry Clinton's having gone to join Burgoyne was not sufficiently authenticated to put it out of doubt; that there was therefore a possibility of his returning up the river, which might expose the finest arsenal in America (as he calls the one here) to destruction, should this place be left so bare of troops as I proposed, and that the want of conveniences and the difficulty of the roads would make it impossible to remove artillery and stores here for a considerable time; that the New England States would be left open to the depredations and ravages of the enemy; that it would put it out of his power to enterprise any thing against Ticonderoga, which he thinks might be done in the winter and which he considers it of importance to undertake.

The force of these reasons did by no means strike me, and I did every thing [in] my power to show they were unsubstantial, but all I could effect was to have one brigade dispatched in addition to those already marched. I found myself infinitely embarrassed, and was at a loss how to act. I felt the importance of strengthening you as much as possible, [but,] on the other hand, I found insuperable inconveniences in acting diametrically opposite [to] the opinion of a gentleman whose successes have raised him to the highest importance. General Gates has won the entire confidence of the Eastern States; if disposed to do it, by addressing himself to the prejudices of the people he would find no difficulty to render a measure odious which it might be said, with plausibility enough to be believed, was calculated to expose them to unnecessary danger, notwithstanding their exertions during the campaign had given them the fullest title to repose and security. General Gates has influence and interest elsewhere; he might use it if he please to discredit the measure there also. On the whole, it appeared to me dangerous to insist on sending more troops from hence while General Gates appeared so warmly opposed to it. Should any accident or inconvenience happen in consequence of it, there would be too fair a pretext for censure, and many people are too well disposed to lay hold of it. At any rate it might be considered as using him ill to take a step so contrary to his judgment in a case of this nature. These considerations, and others which I shall be more explicit in when I have the pleasure of seeing you, determined me not to insist upon sending either of the other brigades remaining here. I am afraid what I have done may not meet with your approbation, as not being perhaps fully warranted by your instructions, but I ventured to do what I though right, hoping that at least the goodness of my intention will excuse the error of my judgment.

I was induced to this relaxation the more readily, as I had directed to be sent on two thousand militia, which were not expected by you, and a thousand Continental troops out of those proposed to be left with General Putnam, which I have written to him, since I found how matters were circumstanced here, to forward to you with all dispatch.

—To Washington. *Hamilton Papers*, 1st ser.

ALBANY November 5, 1777

By inquiry I have learned that General Patterson's brigade, which is the one you propose to send, is by far the weakest of the three now here, and does not consist of more than about six hundred rank and file fit for duty. It is true that there is a militia regiment with it of about two hundred, but the term of service for which this regiment is engaged is so near expiring, that it would be past by the time the men could arrive at the place of their destination.

Under these circumstances, I cannot consider it either as compatible with the good of the service or my instructions from his Excellency, General Washington, to consent that that brigade be selected from the three to go to him; but I am under the necessity of desiring, by virtue of my orders from him, that one of the others be substituted instead of this,—either General Nixon's or General Glover's,—and that you will be pleased to give immediate orders for its embarkation.

Knowing that General Washington wished me to pay the greatest deference to your judgment, I ventured so far to deviate from the instructions he gave me, as to consent, in compliance with your opinion, that two brigades should remain here instead of one. At the same time, permit me to observe, that I am not myself sensible of the expediency of keeping more than one with the detached regiments in the neighborhood of this place, and that my ideas coincide with those of gentlemen whom I have consulted on the occasion, whose judgment I have much more reliance upon than on my own, and who must be supposed to have a thorough knowledge of all the circumstances. Their opinion is that one brigade and the regiments before mentioned would amply answer the purposes of this post. When I preferred your opinion to other considerations, I did not imagine you would pitch upon a brigade little more than half as large as the others; and, finding this to be the case, I indispensably owe it to my duty to desire, in his Excellency's name, that another may go instead of the one intended, and without loss of time. As it may be conducive to dispatch to send Glover's brigade, if agreeable to you, you will give orders accordingly.

—To General Gates. *Hamilton Papers*, 1st ser.

New Windsor November 10, 1777

I arrived here last night from Albany. Having given General Gates a little time to recollect himself, I renewed my remonstrances on the necessity and propriety of sending you more than one brigade of the three he had detained with him, and finally prevailed upon him to give orders for Glover's, in addition to Patterson's brigade, to march this way.

As it was thought conducive to expedition to send the troops by water as far as it could be done, I procured all the vessels that could be had at Albany fit for the purpose, but could not get more than sufficient to take Patterson's brigade. It was embarked the 7th instant, and I expected would have been [here] before this, but the wind has been contrary; though they must in all probability be here to-day.

General Glover's brigade marched at the same time on the east side of the river, the roads being much better than on this side. . . .

I am pained beyond expression to inform your Excellency that on my arrival I find every thing has been neglected and deranged by General Putnam, and that the two brigades—Poor's and Learned's—still remain here and on the other side of the river at Fishkill. Colonel Warner's militia, I am told, have been drawn to Peekskill to aid in an expedition against New York, which, it seems, is at this time the hobby-horse with General Putnam. Not the least attention has been paid to my order in your name for a detachment of one thousand men from the troops hitherto stationed at this post. Every thing is sacrificed to the whim of taking New York.

The two brigades of Poor and Learned it appears would not march for want of money and necessaries; several of the regiments having received no pay for six or eight months past. There has been a high mutiny among the former on this account, in which a captain killed a man, and was shot himself by his comrade. These difficulties, for want of proper management, have stopped the troops from proceeding. . . .

By Governor Clinton's advice, I have sent an [order] in the most emphatic terms to General Putnam immediately to dispatch all the Continental troops under him to your assistance and to detain the militia instead of them.

My opinion is that the only present use for troops in this quarter is to protect the country from the depredations of little plundering parties, and for carrying on the works necessary for the defence of the river. Nothing more ought to be thought of. 'Tis only wasting time and misapplying men to employ them in a farcical parade against New York, for in this it will undoubtedly terminate. New York is no object if it could be taken, and to take it would require more men than could be spared from more substantial purposes. Governor Clinton's ideas coincide with mine. . . .

If your Excellency agrees with me in opinion, it will be well to send instant directions to General Putnam, to pursue the object I have mentioned; for I doubt whether he will attend to any thing I shall say, notwithstanding it comes in the shape of a positive order.

—To Washington. Draft in Hamilton's hand. *Hamilton Papers,* 1st ser.

December 9, 1777

I cannot forbear confessing that I am astonished and alarmed beyond measure to find that all his Excellency's views have been hitherto frustrated, and that no single step of those I mentioned to you has been taken to afford him the aid he absolutely stands in need of, and by delaying which the cause of America is put to the utmost conceivable hazard. I so fully explained to you the general's situation that I could not entertain a doubt that you would make it the first object of your attention to reinforce him with that speed the exigency of affairs demanded, but I am sorry to say he will have too much reason to think other objects—in comparison with that, insignificant—have been uppermost. I speak freely and emphatically, because I tremble at the consequence of the delay that has happened. General Clinton's reinforcement is probably by this time with Mr. Howe. This will give him a decisive superiority over our army. What may be the issue of such a state of things I leave to the feelings of every friend to his country capable of foreseeing consequences. My expressions may perhaps have more warmth than is altogether proper, but they proceed from the overflowing of my heart, in a matter where I conceive this continent essentially interested. I wrote to you from Albany and desired you would send a thousand Continental troops of those first proposed to be left with you. This I understand has not been done. How the noncompliance can be answered to General Washington you can best determine. I now, sir, in the most explicit terms, by his Excellency's authority, give it as a positive order from him, that all the Continental troops under your command may be immediately marched to King's Ferry, there to cross the river and hasten to reinforce the army under him. The Massachusetts militia are to be detained instead of them until the troops coming from the northward arrive. When they do they will replace, as far as I am instructed, the troops you shall send away in consequence of this requisition.

—To General Putnam. *Works*, IX, 120-121.

For Gates Hamilton had nothing but contempt. After the humiliating defeat suffered by that general at the hands of Cornwallis at Camden, South Carolina, in mid-August, 1780, Hamilton dispatched these barbed comments to New York Congressman James Duane.

September 6, 1780

. . . What think you of the conduct of this great man? I am his enemy personally, for unjust and unprovoked attacks upon my character; therefore what I say of him ought to be received as from an enemy, and have no more weight than as it is consistent with fact and common sense. But did ever any one hear of such a disposition or such a flight? His best troops placed on the side strongest by nature, his worst on that weakest by nature, and his attack made with these. 'Tis impossible to give a more complete picture of military absurdity. It is equally against the maxims of war and common sense. We see the consequences. His left ran away, and left his right uncovered. His right wing turned on the left has in all probability been cut off. Though, in truth, the General seems to have known very little what became of his army. Had he placed his militia on his right, supported by the morass, and his Continental troops on his left, where it seems he was most vulnerable, his right would have been more secure, and his left would have opposed the enemy; and instead of going backward when he ordered to attack, would have gone forward. The reverse of what has happened might have happened.

But was there ever an instance of a general running away, as Gates has done, from his whole army? And was there ever so precipitate a flight? One hundred and eighty miles in three days and a half. It does admirable credit to the activity of a man at his time of life. But it disgraces the general and the soldier. I have always believed him to be very far short of a Hector, or a Ulysses. All the world, I think, will begin to agree with me.

But what will be done by Congress? Will he be changed or not? If he is changed, for God's sake overcome prejudice, and send Greene. You know my opinion of him. I stake my reputation on the events, give him but fair play.

But, above all things, let us have, without delay, a vigorous government, and a well constituted army for the war.

—To James Duane. *Hamilton*, I, 170.

Plan for Reorganizing the Army

A Committee of Conference was chosen by Congress on January 10, 1778, and directed, along with three members of the Board of War, to go to Valley Forge, and, in consultation with Washington, draft a plan for reorganization and reform of the army. Drafts were prepared by Hamilton, as Washington's aide-de-camp, which reflect Washington's views as well as those of his leading officers, but also bear the indubitable Hamilton stamp.

January 28, 1778

The numerous defects in our present military establishment, rendering many reformations and many new arrangements absolutely necessary, and Congress having been pleased to appoint you a committee, in concert with me, to make and recommend such as shall appear eligible, in pursuance of the various objects expressed in the resolution, for that purpose; I have, in the following sheets briefly delivered my sentiments upon such of them as appeared to me most essential, so far as observation has suggested and leisure permitted. These are submitted to consideration, and I shall be happy, if they are found conducive to remedying the evils and inconveniences we are now subject to, and putting the army upon a more respectable footing. Something must be done; important alterations must be made; necessity requires that our resources should be enlarged and our system improved, for without it, if the dissolution of the army should not be the consequence, at least its operations must be feeble, languid, and ineffectual.

As I consider a proper and satisfactory provision for officers as the basis of every other arrangement and regulation necessary to be made, since without officers no army can exist; and unless some measures be devised to place those officers in a more desirable condition, few of them would be able, if willing, to continue in it, I shall begin with a few reflections tending to prove the necessity of

A Half-pay and Pensionary Establishment.

A small knowledge of human nature will convince us, that with far the greatest part of mankind, interest is the governing principle, and that almost every man is more or less under its influence. Motives of public virtue may, for a time, or in particular instances, actuate men to the observance of a conduct purely disinterested, but they are not sufficient of themselves to produce a persevering conformity to the refined dictates of social duty. Few men are capable of making a continual sacrifice of all views of private interest or advantage, to the common good. It is in vain to exclaim against the depravity of human nature on this account, the fact is so, the experience of every age and nation has proved it, and we must in a great measure change the constitution of man, before we can make it otherwise. No institution not built on the presumptive truth of these maxims can succeed.

We find them exemplified in the American officers as well as in all other men. At the commencement of the dispute, in the first effusions of their zeal, and looking upon the service to be only temporary, they entered into it, without paying any regard to pecuniary or selfish considerations. But, finding its duration to be much longer than they at first expected, and that instead of deriving any advantage from the hardships and dangers to which they were exposed, they, on the contrary, were losers by their patriotism, and fell far short even of a competency to supply their wants; they have gradually abated in their ardor, and, with many, an entire disinclination to the service, under its present circumstances, has taken place. To this, in an eminent degree, must be ascribed the frequent resignations daily happening, and the more frequent importunities for permission to resign, and from some officers of the greatest merit. To this also, may we ascribe the apathy, inattention and neglect of duty, which pervade all ranks, and which will necessarily continue to increase, while an officer, instead of gaining, is impoverished by his commission, and conceives he is conferring, not receiving, a favor in holding it. There can be no tie upon men possessing such sentiments, nor can we adopt any method to oblige those to a punctual discharge of their duty, who are indifferent about their continuance in the service, and are often seeking a pretext to disengage themselves from it. Punishment, in this case, will be unavailing; but when an officer's commission is made valuable to him, and he fears to lose it, then may you exact obedience from him.

It is not indeed inconsistent with reason or justice, to expect, that one set of men should make sacrifice of property, domestic ease and happiness, encounter the rigors of the field, the perils and vicissitudes of war, to obtain those blessings which every citizen will enjoy in common with them, without some adequate compensation.

It must also be a comfortless reflection to any man, that, after he may have contributed to the securing of the rights of his country at the risk of his life and the ruin of his fortune, there would be no provision, to prevent himself and family, from sinking into indigence and wretchedness. I urge these sentiments with the greater freedom, because I cannot, and shall not receive the smallest benefit from the establishment, and have no other inducement for proposing it, than a full conviction of its utility and propriety.

Of completing the Regiments and altering their establishment.

The necessity of the first, in the most expeditious manner possible, is too self-evident to need illustrations or proof; and I shall, therefore, only beg leave to offer some reflections on the mode. Voluntary enlistments seem to be totally out of the question; all the allurements of the most exorbitant bounties, and every other inducement that could be thought of, have been tried in vain, and seem to have had little other effect than to increase the rapacity and raise the demands of those to whom they were held out. We may fairly infer that the country has been already pretty well drained of that class of men whose tempers, attachments, and circumstances disposed them to enter permanently, or for a length of time, into the army; and that the residue of such men, who, from different motives, have kept out of the army, if collected, would not augment our general strength in any proportion to what they require. If experience has demonstrated that little more can be done by voluntary enlistments, some other mode must be concerted, and no other presents itself than that of filling the regiments by drafts from the militia. This is a disagreeable alternative, but it is an unavoidable one.

As drafting for the war, or for a term of years, would probably be disgusting and dangerous, perhaps impracticable, I would propose an annual draft of men, without officers, to serve till the first day of January in each year. That on or before the first day of October preceding, these drafted men should be called upon to re-enlist for the succeeding year; and as an incitement to doing it, those being much letter and less expensive than raw recruits, a bounty of twenty-five dollars should be offered. That upon ascertaining at this period the number willing to re-engage, exact returns should be made to

Congress of the deficiency in each regiment and transmitted by them to the respective States, in order that they may have their several quotas immediately furnished and sent on to camp, for the service of the ensuing year, so as to arrive by or before the first day of January.

This method, though not so good as that of obtaining men for the war, is, perhaps, the best our circumstances will allow; and as we shall always have an established corps of experienced officers, may answer tolerably well. It is the only mode I can think of for completing our battalions in time, that promises the least prospect of success; the accomplishment of which is an object of the last importance; and it has this advantage, that the minds of the people being once reconciled to the experiment, it would prove a source of continual supplies hereafter.

Men drafted in this manner, should not, in the first instance, receive any bounty from the public; which being solemnly enjoined upon each State, and a stop put to the militia substitution laws, would probably be attended with very happy consequences.

A number of idle mercenary fellows would be thrown out of employment, precluded from their excessive wages as substitutes for a few weeks or months, and constrained to enlist in the Continental army. In speaking of abolishing the militia substitution laws, it is not meant to hinder a person, who might be drafted in the annual allotments from procuring a substitute in his stead, himself in consequence being excused. This indulgence would be admissible, and, considering all things, necessary, as there are many individuals whose dispositions and private affairs would make them irreconcilably adverse from giving their personal services for so long a duration, and with whom it would be impolitic to use compulsion. The allowance of substitution upon a smaller scale, in the occasional coming out of the militia for a few weeks, a month or two, is the thing meant to be reprobated. It is highly productive of the double disadvantage of preventing the growth of the army and depreciating our currency. . . .

—Plan of Reorganization of the Army addressed to Washington at Valley Forge, from two incomplete drafts in Hamilton's hand. *Hamilton*, II, 139-143, 150.

With Lee at Monmouth

In the late spring of '78 Clinton quit Philadelphia and moved his army toward New York across Jersey. Before leaving Valley Forge in pursuit, Washington called a council of war at which Major-General Charles Lee opposed bringing on a general action as "criminal," and won a majority of the general officers over to his view. Hamilton, who kept the minutes of the council, remarked: "I forbear to lift the veil from off these impotent councils," and spoke of "the characteristic imbecility of a council of war." The results of a second council of war, in Hamilton's opinion, "would have done honor to the most honorable society of widwives, and to them only."

Despite the cautious attitude of some of his officers, Washington dispatched an advance guard to establish contact with the enemy. Lee first declined the command in favor of Lafayette, then reasserted his command, then wavered again, and at the moment of contact with the enemy took over the reins once more. Hamilton, dispatched by Washington to obtain intelligence of the enemy's position, warned Lee that a British troop of cavalry deploying to the left of the American forces would soon be in a position to attack Lee's exposed flank. He advised Lee to counter-attack and Lee authorized Hamilton to give the order. Hamilton then reported back to Washington, who rode up at breakneck pace. When Washington reached the field Lee's troops were in wild disorder. Whether or not he called Lee "a damned poltroon" as tradition would have it, he was in a towering rage and reputedly swore "till the leaves shook on the trees." (In later life Hamilton denied that Washington used profanity on this occasion.) Meantime Hamilton rallied the fleeing men who turned upon the British and swept them with a withering fire.

If Hamilton was one of the heroes of the day (he had his horse shot from under him), Lee was the villain. Washington placed Lee under arrest and convened a court-martial. There Hamilton testified against Lee, asserting that he "seemed to be under a hurry of mind," and that, while his men retreated, he sat on his horse, "doing nothing that I saw." In his own defense, Lee stated that after Washington had galloped on to hearten Lafayette, Hamilton had flourished his sword and exclaimed, "That's right, my dear General, and I will stay, and we will all die here on this spot." This testimony was confirmed in part. Lee, found guilty and suspended from his command for one year, was dropped from the army. A repercussion of the affair was a duel between Hamilton's bosom friend, John Laurens, an aide of Washington, and Lee, who had made disparaging remarks about the general.

July 5, 1778

We have made another detachment of a thousand men under General Wayne, and formed all the detached troops into an advanced corps, under the command of the Marquis de Lafayette. The project was that this advanced corps should take the first opportunity to attack the enemy's rear on a march, to be supported or covered, as circumstances should require, by the whole army. General Lee's conduct with respect to the command of this corps was truly childish.

According to the incorrect notions of our army, his seniority would have entitled him to the command of the advanced corps; but he in the first instance declined it in favor of the Marquis. Some of his friends having blamed him for doing it, and Lord Stirling having shown a disposition to interpose his claim, General Lee very inconsistently reasserted his pretensions. The matter was a second time accommodated. General Lee and Lord Stirling agreed to let the Marquis command. General Lee, a little time after, recanted again, and became very importunate. The General [Washington], who had all along observed the greatest candor in the matter, grew tired of such fickle behavior, and ordered the Marquis to proceed.

I never saw the General to so much advantage. His coolness and firmness were admirable. He instantly took measures for checking the enemy's advance, and giving time to the army, which was very near, to form and make a proper disposition. He then rode back, and had the troops formed on a very advantageous piece of ground, in which, and in other transactions of the day, General Lee and Lord Stirling rendered very essential service, and did themselves great honor. America owes a great deal to General Washington for this day's work. A general rout, dismay, and disgrace would have attended the whole army in any other hands but his. By his own good sense and fortitude, he turned the fate of the day. Other officers have great merit in performing their parts well, but he directed the whole with the skill of a master workman. He did not hug himself at a distance and leave an Arnold to win laurels for him, but by his own presence he brought order out of confusion, animated his troops, and led them to success. After a tribute to Wayne, Steward, Ramsey, Olney, Livingston, Barber, Cilley, Parker, Craig, and Oswald, the behavior of the officers and men was such as could not easily be surpassed. Our troops, after the first impulse from mismanagement, behaved with more spirit and moved with greater order than the British troops. You know my way of thinking of our army, and that I am not apt to flatter it. I assure you I never was pleased with them before this day. What think you now of General Lee? Whatever a court martial may decide, I shall continue to believe and say—his conduct was monstrous and unpardonable.

—To Elias Boudinot. *Works*, IX, 140-142.

July 14, 1778 (?)

Since the giving my evidence at the Court Martial, I have been endeavoring to recollect more particularly the import of the conversation between General Lee and myself, that happened in the field the day of the action, and which was the subject of discussion yesterday before the court. My memory will not serve me on the occasion, in so clear a manner as I could wish; but I have been able to form some more distinct ideas, than those expressed when I was interrogated by General Lee, which I communicate to you to make what use of them you think proper. On my making some remarks to General Lee which I now forget, he asked me the following questions, or others to the same effect, and I think partly in the same words—"Do I appear to you to have lost my senses, or do I not possess myself?"

My answer to these questions I do not perfectly recollect, but I remember that it was a favorable one, though I am unable to determine to what extent. It will be readily conceived that so singular and unexpected a question was not a little embarrassing, and it is possible I may have replied in terms of less reserve and caution than I should have done at a moment of greater tranquillity and cooler reflection. I perfectly remember what passed in my mind upon the occasion with respect to General Lee's conduct, and, from the most deliberate and unbiassed retrospect of it, my judgment entirely coincides with what I then thought. His answers to what was said to him were pertinent, and his behavior had not the least appearance of concern on the score of personal security. So far he possessed himself and could not be said to have lost his senses according to his own expressions. But he certainly did not appear to me to be in that collected state of mind or to have that kind of self-possession which is an essential requisite of *the General*, and which alone can enable him in critical emergencies to take his measures with the promptitude and decision they require. A certain indecision, improvidence, and hurry of spirits to the best of my recollection were apparent. These were my thoughts at the time, and it is natural for me to believe that what I replied to General Lee could not be inconsistent with them.

This letter I mean as explanatory to my testimony of yesterday, founded upon my reflections since, and if it can be done with propriety, I shall be glad it may be admitted by the court as such.

—To Lord Stirling. *Ibid.*, 142-144.

[December 24, 1778]

General Lee, attended by Major Edwards, and Col. Laurens, attended by Col. Hamilton, met agreeable to appointment on Wednesday afternoon at half-past three in a wood situate near the four-mile stone on the Point-no-point road. Pistols having been the weapons previously fixed upon, and the combatants being provided with a brace each, it was asked in what manner they were to proceed. General Lee proposed to advance upon one another and each fire at what time and distance he thought proper. Col. Laurens expressed his preference of this mode, and agreed to the proposal accordingly.

They approached each other within about five or six paces and exchanged a shot almost at the same moment. As Col Laurens was preparing for a second discharge, General Lee declared himself wounded. Col. Laurens, as if apprehending the wound to be more serious than it proved, advanced towards the General to offer his support. The same was done by Col. Hamilton and Major Edwards under a similar apprehension. General Lee then said the wound was inconsiderable—less than he had imagined at the first stroke of the ball, and proposed to fire a second time. This was warmly opposed both by Col. Hamilton and Major Edwards, who declared it to be their opinion, that the affair should terminate as it then stood. But General Lee repeated his desire that there should be a second discharge, and Col. Laurens agreed to the proposal. Col. Hamilton observed that unless the General was influenced by motives of personal enmity, he did not think the affair ought to be pursued any further; but as General Lee seemed to persist in desiring it, he was too tender of his friend's honor to persist in opposing it. The combat was then going to be renewed; but Major Edwards again declaring his opinion, that the affair ought to end where it was, General Lee then expressed his confidence in the honor of the gentlemen concerned as seconds, and said he should be willing to comply with whatever they should coolly and deliberately determine. Col. Laurens consented to the same. . . .

During the interview a conversation to the following purport passed between General Lee and Col. Laurens. On Col. Hamilton's intimating the idea of personal enmity, as before mentioned, General Lee declared he had none, and had only met Col. Laurens to defend his own honor; that Mr. Laurens best knew whether there was any on his part. Col. Laurens replied, that General Lee was acquainted with the motives that had brought him there, which were that he had been informed, from what he thought good authority, that General Lee had spoken of General Washington in the grossest and most opprobrious terms of personal abuse, which he, Col. Laurens, thought himself bound to resent, as well on account of the relation he bore to General Washington, as from motives of personal friendship and respect for his character. General Lee acknowledged that he had given his opinion against General Washington's military character to his particular friends, and might perhaps do it again. He said every man had a right to give his sentiments freely of military characters, and that he did not think himself personally accountable to Col. Laurens for what he had done in that respect. But he said he never had spoken of General Washington in the terms mentioned, which he could not have done, as well because he had always esteemed General Washington as a man, as because such abuse would be incompatible with the character he would ever wish to sustain as a gentleman.

Upon the whole we think it a piece of justice to the two gentlemen to declare, that after they met their conduct was strongly marked with all the politeness, generosity, coolness, and firmness that ought to characterize a transaction of this nature.

—Alexander Hamilton and E. Edwards, "Narrative of an Affair of Honor between General Lee and Colonel Laurens." Draft in Hamilton Papers, 1st ser.

Hamilton's Private War against Profiteers

In his later career Hamilton was criticized for a seeming tenderness toward speculators and stock-jobbers. No such criticism could be levelled against him during the years of the Revolution. As a soldier, he shared Washington's shock and disgust at civilian profiteers and monopolists. "Speculators are as thick and as industrious as bees, and as active and wicked as the devil himself," Caesar Rodney of Delaware observed. No speculator was more venal than Congressman Samuel Chase of Maryland. Taking advantage of inside information of the intentions of the government to make a secret purchase of grain for the use of the French fleet, Chase sent agents to corner the market. When Hamilton learned the facts he tossed off a number of fiery letters to Holt's Journal under the pseudonym Publius. Chase was investigated by his own state legislature, but was cleared by a strictly partisan vote.

October 19, 1778

SIR:—While every method is taken to bring to justice those men whose principles and practices have been hostile to the present revolution, it is to be lamented that the conduct of another class, equally criminal, and, if possible, more mischievous, has hitherto passed with impunity, and almost without notice. I mean that tribe who, taking advantage of the times, have carried the spirit of monopoly and extortion to an excess which scarcely admits of a parallel. Emboldened by the success of progressive impositions, it has extended to all the necessaries of life. The exorbitant price of every article, and the depreciation upon our currency, are evils derived essentially from this source. When avarice takes the lead in a state, it is commonly the forerunner of its fall. How shocking is it to discover among ourselves, even at this early period, the strongest symptoms of this fatal disease.

There are men in all countries, the business of whose lives it is to raise themselves above indigence by every little art in their power. When these men are observed to be influenced by the spirit I have mentioned, it is nothing more than might be expected, and can only exicite contempt. When others, who have characters to support, and credit enough in the world to satisfy a moderate appetite for wealth, in an honorable way, are found to be actuated by the same spirit, our contempt is mixed with indignation. But when a man, appointed to be the guardian of the state and the depositary of the happiness and morals of the people, forgetful of the solemn relation in which he stands, descends to the dishonest artifices of a mercantile projector, and sacrifices his conscience and his trust to pecuniary motives, there is no strain of abhorrence of which the human mind is capable, no punishment the vengeance of the people can inflict, which may not be applied to him with justice. If it should have happened that a member of C—ss had been this degenerate character, and has been known to turn the knowledge of secrets to which his office gave him access to the purposes of private profit, by employing emissaries to engross an article of immediate necessity to the public service, he ought to feel the utmost rigor of public resentment, and be detested as a traitor of the worst and most dangerous kind.

—*Publius,* in *N.Y. Journal, and the General Advertiser* (Poughkeepsie, John Holt), Oct. 19, 1778.

October 26, 1778

SIR:—The honor of being a hero of a public panegyric is what you could hardly have aspired to, either from your talents, or from your good qualities. The partiality of your friends has never given you credit for more than mediocrity in the former; and experience has proved that you are indebted for all your consequence to the reverse of the latter. Had you not struck out a new line of prostitution for yourself, you might still have remained unnoticed and contemptible—your name scarcely known beyond the little circle of your electors and clients, and recorded only in the journals of C——ss. But you have now forced yourself into view, in a light too singular and conspicuous to be overlooked, and have acquired an undisputed title to be immortalized in infamy. . . .

It is unfortunate for the reputation of Governor Johnstone,[1] and for the benevolent purposes of his royal master, that he was not acquainted with the frailties of your character before he made his experiment on men whose integrity was above temptation. If he had known you, and had thought your services worth purchasing, he might have played a sure game, and avoided the risk of exposing himself to contempt and ridicule. And you, sir, might have made your fortune at one decisive stroke.

It is a matter of curious inquiry, what could have raised you in the first instance, and supported you since in your present elevation. I

[1] One of the commissioners sent over from England in 1778 to effect a reconciliation with America, Johnstone was accused of attempting to bribe American patriot leaders.

never knew a single man but was ready to do ample justice to your demerit. The most indulgent opinion of the qualifications of your head and heart could not offend the modest delicacy of your ear, or give the smallest cause of exultation to your vanity. It is your lot to have the peculiar privilege of being universally despised. Excluded from all resource to your abilities or virtues, there is only one way in which I can account for the rank you hold in the political scale. There are seasons in every country when noise and impudence pass current for worth; and in popular commotions especially, the clamors of interested and factious men are often mistaken for patriotism. You prudently took advantage of the commencement of the contest, to ingratiate yourself in the favor of the people, and gain an ascendant in their confidence by appearing a zealous assertor of their rights. No man will suspect you of the folly of public spirit—a heart notoriously selfish exempts you from any charge of this nature, and obliges us to resolve the part you took into opposite principles. A desire of popularity and a rivalship with the ministry will best explain them. Their attempt to *confine* the sale of a lucrative article of commerce to the East India Company, must have been more unpardonable in the sight of a *monopolist* than the most daring attack upon the public liberty. There is a vulgar maxim which has pointed emphasis in your case, and has made many notable patriots in this dispute.

It sometimes happens that a temporary caprice of the people leads them to make choice of men whom they neither love nor respect; and that they afterward, from an indolent and mechanical habit natural to the human mind, continue their confidence and support merely because they had once conferred them. I cannot persuade myself that your influence rests upon a better foundation, and I think the finishing touch you have given to the profligacy of your character must rouse the recollection of the people, and force them to strip you of a dignity which sets so awkwardly upon you, and consign you to that disgrace which is due to a scandalous perversion of your trust.

When you resolved to avail yourself of the extraordinary demand for the article of flour which the wants of the French fleet must produce, and which your official situation early impressed on your attention, to form connections, for monopolizing that article, and raising the price upon the public more than an hundred per cent; when by your intrigues and studied delays you protracted the determination of the C—tt—e of C—ss on the proposals made by Mr. W—sw—th, C—ss—y G—n—l,[1] for procuring the necessary supplies for the public use, to give your agents time to complete their purchases;—I say when you were doing all this, and engaging in a traffic infamous in itself, repugnant to your station, and ruinous to your country, did you pause and allow yourself a moment's reflection on the consequences? Were

[1] Jeremiah Wadsworth, Commissary General.

you infatuated enough to imagine you would be able to conceal the part you were acting? Or had you conceived a thorough contempt of reputation, and a total indifference to the opinion of the world? Enveloped in the promised gratifications of your avarice, you probably forgot to consult your understanding, and lost sight of every consideration that ought to have regulated the man, the citizen, the statesman.

I am aware that you could never have done what you have without first obtaining a noble victory over every sentiment of honor and generosity. You have therefore nothing to fear from the reproaches of your own mind. Your insensibility secures you from remorse. But there are arguments powerful enough to extort repentance, even from a temper as callous as yours. You are a man of the world, sir; your self-love forces you to respect its decisions, and your utmost credit with it will not bear the test of your recent enormities, or screen you from the fate you deserve.

—"Publius," in *N. Y. Journal*, Oct. 26, 1778.

Recommended: A Fighting Parson

July 6, 1780

Doctor W. Mendy is one of those characters that for its honesty, simplicity, and helplessness interests my humanity.

He is exceedingly anxious to be in the Service, and, I believe, has been forced out of it not altogether by fair play. He is just what I should like for a military parson, except that he does not whore or drink. He will fight, and he will not insist upon your going to heaven whether you will or not. He tells me there is a vacancy in your Brigade. I should be really happy if, through your influence, he can fill it. Pray take care of this good old man.

—To General Anthony Wayne. (Copy).
Hamilton Papers, N. Y. Pub. Lib.

The Treason of Arnold

Hamilton was at West Point on the blackest day of the Revolution. He has left us a full and dramatic account of Arnold's treason and Andrés plight. The letter of September 30th, signed A B (or A H), and addressed to General Clinton in New York is believed to be Hamilton's as it employs much the same language as he used in his long letter to Laurens. Lieutenant Colonel Simcoe of the British army insisted that this letter came from Hamilton. While Washington could not with propriety formally request the exchange, there is no question that he would have wanted to get his hands on Benedict Arnold. As for Peggy Shippen Arnold, she was probably a good deal less innocent than she seemed at the time to the young and impressionable Hamilton.

VERPLANCK'S POINT September 25, 1780

You will see by the enclosed that we are too late. Arnold went by water to the *Vulture*. I shall write to General Greene, advising him, without making a bustle, to be in readiness to march, and even to detach a brigade this way; for, though I do not believe the project will go on, yet it is possible Arnold has made such dispositions with the garrison as may tempt the enemy, in its present weakness, to make the stroke this night, and it seems prudent to be providing against it. I shall endeavor to find Meigs, and request him to march to the garrison, and shall make some arrangements here. I hope your Excellency will approve these steps, as there may be no time to be lost. The *Vulture* is gone down to New York.

—To Washington. *Works*, IX, 205-206.

VERPLANKS POINT 25th September, 1780

There has just been unfolded at this place a scene of the blackest treason. Arnold has fled to the enemy—André, the British Adjutant-General, is in our possession as a spy. His capture unravelled the mystery.

West Point was to have been the sacrifice. All the dispositions have been made for the purpose, and 't is possible, though not probable, we may still see the execution. The wind is fair. I came here in pursuit of Arnold, but was too late. I advise your putting the army under marching orders and detaching a brigade immediately this way.

—To General Nathanael Greene. *Hamilton*, I, 185.

September 25, 1780

Arnold, hearing of the plot being detected, immediately fled to the enemy. I went in pursuit of him, but was much too late; and could hardly regret the disappointment, when, on my return, I saw an amiable woman, frantic with distress for the loss of a husband she tenderly loved; a traitor to his country and to his fame; a disgrace to his connections: it was the most affecting scene I ever was witness to. She, for a considerable time, entirely lost herself. The General went up to see her, and she upbraided him with being in a plot to murder her child. One moment she raved, another she melted into tears. Sometimes she pressed her infant to her bosom, and lamented its fate, occasioned by the imprudence of its father, in a manner that would have pierced insensibility itself. All the sweetness of beauty, all the loveliness of innocence, all the tenderness of a wife, and all the fondness of a mother showed themselves in her appearance and conduct. We have every reason to believe that she was entirely unacquainted with the plan, and that the first knowledge of it was when Arnold went to tell her he must banish himself from his country and from her forever. She instantly fell into a convulsion, and he left her in that situation.

This morning she is more composed. I paid her a visit, and endeavored to sooth her by every method in my power, though you may imagine she is not easily to be consoled. Added to her other distresses, she is very apprehensive the resentment of her country will fall upon her (who is only unfortunate) for the guilt of her husband.

I have tried to persuade her that her fears are ill-founded, but she will not be convinced. She received us in bed, with every circumstance that would interest our sympathy; and her sufferings were so eloquent, that I wished myself her brother, to have a right to become her defender. As it is, I have entreated her to enable me to give her proofs of my friendship. Could I forgive Arnold for sacrificing his honor, reputation, and duty, I could not forgive him for acting a part that must have forfeited the esteem of so fine a woman. At present she almost forgets his crime in his misfortunes; and her horror at the guilt of the traitor is lost in her love of the man. But a virtuous mind cannot long esteem a base one; and time will make her despise if it cannot make her hate.

—To Elizabeth Schuyler. *Hamilton,* I, 186-187.

Sept. 30, [17]80

Sir,

It has so happened in the course of events, that Major André Adjutant General of your army has fallen into our hands. He was captured in such a way as will according to the laws of war justly affect his life. Though an enemy his virtues and his accomplishments are admired. Perhaps he might be released for General Arnold, delivered up without restriction or condition, which is the prevailing wish. Major André's character and situation seem to demand this of your justice and friendship. Arnold appears to have been the guilty author of the michief; and ought more properly to be the victim, as there is great reason to believe he meditated a double treachery, and had arranged the interview in such a manner, that if discovered in the first instance, he might have it in his power to sacrifice Major André to his own safety.

I have the honor to be etc. A B [or A H][1]

No time is to be lost.

Endorsed by General Clinton: "Hamilton W aid de camp received after A death."

—To Sir Henry Clinton, New York. Clinton Papers, William L. Clements Lib.

[1] Hamilton used the pseudonym "A. B." for his "Continentalist" letters, the first of which was dated July 12, 1781.

TAPPAN October 2, 1780

Poor André suffers to-day. Every thing that is amiable in virue, in fortitude, in delicate sentiment, and accomplished manners, pleads for him; but hard-hearted policy calls for a sacrifice. He must die. I send you my accounts of Arnold's affair; and to justify myself to your sentiments, I must inform you that I urged a compliance with André's request to be shot; and I do not think it would have had an ill effect; but some people are only sensible to motives of policy, and sometimes, from a narrow disposition, mistake it.

When André's tale comes to be told, and present resentment is over, the refusing him the privilege of choosing the manner of his death will be branded with too much obstinacy.

It was proposed to me to suggest to him the idea of an exchange for Arnold; but I knew I should have forfeited his esteem by doing it, and therefore declined it. As a man of honor, he could but reject it, and I would not for the world have proposed to him a thing which must have placed me in the unamiable light of supposing him capable of meanness, or of not feeling myself the impropriety of the measure. I confess to you I had the weakness to value the esteem of a dying man, because I reverenced his merit.

—To Elizabeth Schuyler. *Hamilton, I,* 187.

[October, 1780]

Since my return from Hartford, my dear Laurens, my mind has been too little at ease to permit me to write to you sooner. It has been wholly occupied by the affecting and tragic consequences of Arnold's treason. My feelings were never put to so severe a trial. You will no doubt have heard the principal facts before this reaches you. But there are particulars, to which my situation gave me access, that cannot have come to your knowledge from public report, which I am persuaded you will find interesting.

From several circumstances, the project seems to have originated with Arnold himself, and to have been long premeditated. The first overture is traced back to some time in June last. It was conveyed in a letter to Colonel Robinson, the substance of which was that the ingratitude he had experienced from his country, concurring with other causes, had entirely changed his principles; that he now only sought to restore himself to the favor of his king by some signal proof of his repentance, and would be happy to open a correspondence with Sir Henry Clinton for that purpose. About this period he made a journey to Connecticut, on his return from which to Philadelphia, he solicited the command of West Point, alleging that the effects of his wounds had disqualified him for the active duties of the field. The sacrifice of this important post was the atonement he intended to make. General Washington hesitated the less to gratify an officer who had rendered such eminent services, as he was convinced the post might be safely intrusted to one who had given so many distinguished specimens of his bravery. In the beginning of August he joined the army, and renewed his application. The enemy, at this juncture, had embarked the greatest part of their forces on an expedition to Rhode Island, and our army was in motion to compel them to relinquish the enterprise, or to attack New York in its weakened state. The General offered Arnold the left wing of the army, which he declined, on the pretext already mentioned, but not without visible embarrassment. He certainly might have executed the duties of such a temporary command, and it was expected, from his enterprising temper, that he would gladly have embraced so splendid an opportunity. But he did not choose to be diverted a moment from his favorite object, probably from an apprehension that some different disposition might have taken place, which would have excluded him. The extreme solicitude he discovered to get possession of the post would have led to a suspicion of treachery, had it been possible from his past conduct to have supposed him capable of it.

The correspondence thus begun was carried on between Arnold and Major André, Adjutant-General to the British army, in behalf of Sir Henry Clinton, under feigned signatures, and in a mercantile disguise. In an intercepted letter of Arnold's, which lately fell into our hands, he proposes an interview, "to settle the risks and profits of the copartnership," and, in the same style of metaphor, intimates an expected augmentation of the garrison, and speaks of it as the means of extending their traffic. It appears, by another letter, that André was to have met him on the lines, under the sanction of a flag, in the character of Mr. John Anderson. But some cause or other not known prevented this interview.

The twentieth of last month, Robinson and André went up the river in the *Vulture*, sloop-o-war. Robinson sent a flag to Arnold with two letters: one to General Putnam, inclosed in another to himself, proposing an interview with Putnam, or, in his absence, with Arnold, to adjust some private concerns. The one to General Putnam was evidently meant as a cover to the other, in case, by accident, the letters should have fallen under the inspection of a third person.

General Washington crossed the river on his way to Hartford the day these despatches arrived. Arnold, conceiving he must have heard of the flag, thought it necessary, for the sake of appearances, to submit the letters to him, and ask his opinion of the propriety of complying with the request. The General, with his usual caution, though without the least surmise of the design, dissuaded him from it, and advised him to reply to Robinson that whatever related to his private affairs must be of a civil nature, and could only be properly addressed to the civil authority. This reference fortunately deranged the plan, and was the first link in the chain of events that led to the detection. The interview could no longer take place in the form of a flag, but was obliged to be managed in a secret manner.

Arnold employed one Smith to go on board the *Vulture* on the night of the twenty-second, to bring André on shore, with a pass for Mr. John Anderson. André came ashore accordingly, and was conducted within a picket of ours to the house of Smith, where Arnold and he remained together in close conference all that night and the day following. At daylight, in the morning, the commanding officer at King's Ferry, without the privity of Arnold, moved a couple of pieces of cannon to a point opposite to where the *Vulture* lay, and obliged her to take a more remote station. This event, or some lurking distrust, made the boatmen refuse to convey the two passengers back, and disconcerted Arnold so much that, by one of those strokes of infatuation which often confound the schemes of men conscious of guilt, he insisted on André's exchanging his uniform for a disguise, and returning in a mode different from that in which he came. André, who had been undesignedly brought within our posts in the first instance, remonstrated warmly against this new and dangerous expedient. But Arnold persisting in declaring it impossible for him to return as he came, he at length reluctantly yielded to his directions, [and consented to change his dress and take the route he recommended].[1] Smith furnished the disguise, and in the evening passed King's Ferry with him and proceeded to Crompond, where they stopped the remainder of the night, at the instance of a militia officer, to avoid being suspected by him. The next morning they resumed their journey, Smith accompanying André a little beyond Pine's Bridge, where he left him. He had reached Tarrytown, when he was taken up by three militiamen, who rushed out of the woods and seized his horse.

At this critical moment his presence of mind forsook him. Instead of producing his pass, which would have extricated him from our parties, and could have done him no harm with his own, he asked the militiamen if they were of the *upper* or *lower* party; descriptive appellations known among the enemy's refugee corps. The militiamen replied they were of the lower party, upon which he told them he was a British officer, and pressed them not to detain him, as he was upon urgent business. This confession removed all doubts, and it was in vain he afterwards produced his pass. He was instantly forced off to a place of greater security, where, after a careful search, there were found concealed in the feet of his stockings several papers of importance, delivered to him by Arnold! Among these were a plan of the fortifications of West Point; a memorial from the engineer on the attack and defence of the place; returns of the garrison, cannon, and stores; copy of the minutes of a council of war held by General

[1] Not in MS. copy. See *Works*, IX, 209-223.

Washington a few weeks before. The prisoner at first was inadvertently ordered to Arnold, but on recollection, while still on the way, he was countermanded and sent to Old Salem. The papers were enclosed in a letter to General Washington, which, having taken a route different from that by which he returned, made a circuit that afforded leisure for another letter, through an ill-judged delicacy, written to Arnold with information of Anderson's capture, to get to him an hour before General Washington arrived at his quarters; time enough to elude the fate that awaited him. He went down the river on his barge to the *Vulture* with such precipitate confusion that he did not take with him a single paper useful to the enemy. On the first notice of the affair he was pursued, but much too late to be overtaken.

There was some color for imagining that it was a part of the plan to betray the General into the hands of the enemy. Arnold was very anxious to ascertain from him the precise day of his return, and the enemy's movements seem to have corresponded to this point. But if it was really the case it was very injudicious. The success must have depended on surprise, and as the officers at the advanced posts were not in the secret their measures might have given the alarm, and General Washington, taking the command of the post, might have rendered the whole scheme abortive. Arnold, it is true, had so dispersed the garrison as to have made a defence difficult but not impracticable; and the acquisition of West Point was of such magnitude to the enemy that it would have been unwise to connect it with any other object, however great, which might make the obtaining of it precarious.

Arnold, a moment before the setting out, went into Mrs. Arnold's apartment, and informed her that some transactions had just come to light which must forever banish him from his country. She fell into a swoon at this declaration: and he left her in it to consult his own safety, till the servants, alarmed by her cries, came to her relief. She remained frantic all day, accusing every one who approached her with an intention to murder her child (an infant in her arms), and exhibiting every other mark of the most genuine and agonizing distress. Exhausted by the fatigue and tumult of her spirits, her phrensy subsided towards evening, and she sank into all the sadness of affliction. It was impossible not to have been touched with her situation. Every thing affecting in female tears, or in the misfortunes of beauty; every thing pathetic in the wounded tenderness of a wife, or in the apprehensive fondness of a mother; and, till I have reason to change the opinion, I will add, every thing amiable in suffering innocence conspired to make her an object of sympathy to all who were present. She experienced the most delicate attentions and every friendly office, till her departure for Philadelphia.

André was, without loss of time, conducted to the headquarters of the army, where he was immediately brought before a Board of General Officers, to prevent all possibility of misrepresentation, or cavil on the part of the enemy. The Board reported that he ought to be considered as a spy, and, according to the laws of nations, to suffer death, which was executed two days after.

Never, perhaps, did a man suffer death with more justice, or deserve it less. The first step he took after his capture was to write a letter to General Washington, conceived in terms of dignity without insolence, and apology without meanness. The scope of it was to vindicate himself from the imputation of having assumed a mean character for treacherous or interested purposes; asserting that he had been involuntarily an impostor; that contrary to his intention, which was to meet a person for intelligence on neutral ground, he had been betrayed within our posts, and forced into the vile condition of an enemy in disguise; soliciting only that, to whatever rigor policy might devote him, a decency of treatment might be observed, due to a person who, though unfortunate, had been guilty of nothing dishonorable. His request was granted in its full extent; for, in the whole progress of the affair, he was treated with the most scrupulous delicacy. When brought before the Board of Officers he met with every mark of indulgence, and was required to answer no interrogatory which could even embarrass his feelings. On his part, while he carefully concealed every thing that might involve others, he frankly confessed all the facts relating to himself; and, upon his confession, without the trouble of examining a witness, the Board made their report. The members of it were not more impressed with the candor and firmness, mixed with a becoming sensibility, which he displayed, than he was penetrated with their liberality and politeness. He acknowledged the generosity of the behavior towards him in every respect, but particularly in this, in the strongest terms of manly gratitude. In a conversation with a gentleman who visited him after his trial, he said he flattered himself he had never been illiberal; but if there were any remains of prejudice in his mind, his present experience must obliterate them.

In one of the visits I made to him (and I saw him several times during his confinement), he begged me to be the bearer of a request to the General, for permission to send an open letter to Sir Henry Clinton. "I forsee my fate," said he, "and though I pretend not to play the hero, or to be indifferent about life, yet I am reconciled to whatever may happen, conscious that misfortune, not guilt, has brought it upon me. There is only one thing that disturbs my tranquillity. Sir Henry Clinton has been too good to me; he has been lavish of his kindness. I am bound to him by too many obligations, and love him too well, to bear the thought that he should reproach himself, or that others should reproach him, on the supposition of my having conceived myself obliged, by his instructions, to run the risk I did. I would not for the world leave a sting in his mind that should imbitter his future days." He could scarce finish the sentence, bursting into tears in spite of his efforts to suppress them, and with difficulty collected himself enough afterwards to add, "I wish to be permitted to assure him I did not act under this impression, but submitted to a necessity imposed upon me, as contrary to my own inclination as to his orders." His request was readily complied with, and he wrote the letter annexed, with which I dare say you will be as much pleased as I am, both for the diction and sentiment.

When his sentence was announced to him he remarked that since it was his lot to die, there was still a choice in the mode, which would make a material difference in his feelings, and he would be happy, if possible, to be indulged with a professional death. He made a second application, by letter, in concise but persuasive terms. It was thought this indulgence, being incompatible with the customs of war, could not be granted, and it was therefore determined, in both cases, to evade an answer, to spare him the sensations which a certain knowledge of the intended mode would inflict.

In going to the place of execution, he bowed familiarly as he went along, to all those with whom he had been acquainted in his confinement. A smile of complacency expressed the serene fortitude of his mind. Arrived at the fatal spot, he asked, with some emotion, "Must I die in this manner?" He was told that it had been unavoidable. "I am reconciled to my fate," said he, "but not to the mode." Soon, however, recollecting himself, he added: "It will be but a momentary pang," and, springing upon the cart, performed the last offices to himself, with a composure that excited the admiration and melted the hearts of the beholders. Upon being told that the final moment was at hand, and asked if he had anything to say, he answered: "Nothing but to request you will witness to the world that I die like a brave man." Among the extraordinary circumstances that attended him, in the midst of his enemies, he died universally esteemed and universally regretted.

There was something singularly interesting in the character and fortunes of André. To an excellent understanding, well improved by education and travel, he united a peculiar elegance of mind and manners, and the advantage of a pleasing person. 'Tis said he possessed a pretty taste for the fine arts, and had himself attained some proficiency in poetry, music, and painting. His knowledge appeared without ostentation, and embellished by a diffidence that rarely accompanies so many talents and accomplishments: which left you to suppose more than appeared. His sentiments were elevated, and inspired esteem: they had a softness that conciliated affection. His elocution was handsome; his address easy, polite, and insinuating. By his merit he had acquired the unlimited confidence of his general, and was making a rapid progress in military rank and reputation. But in the height of his career, flushed with new hopes from the execution of a project, the most beneficial to his party that could be devised, he was at once precipitated from the summit of prosperity, and saw all the expectations of his ambition blasted, and himself ruined.

The character I have given of him, is drawn partly from what I saw of him myself, and partly from information. I am aware that a man of real merit is never seen in so favorable a light as through the medium of adversity: the clouds that surround him are shades that set off his good qualities. Misfortune cuts down the little vanities that, in prosperous times serve as so many spots in his virtues; and gives a tone of humility that makes his worth more amiable. His spectators, who enjoy a happier lot, are less prone to detract from it, through envy, and are more disposed, by compassion, to give him the credit he deserves, and perhaps even to magnify it.

I speak not of André's conduct in this affair as a philosopher, but as a man of the world. The authorized maxims and practices of war are the satires of human nature. They countenance almost every species of seduction as well as violence; and the general that can make most traitors in the army of his adversary is frequently most applauded.

On this scale we acquit André; while we could not but condemn him, if we were to examine his conduct by the sober rules of philosophy and moral rectitude. It is, however, a blemish on his fame, that he once intended to prostitute a flag: about this, a man of nice honor ought to have had a scruple; but the temptation was great: let his misfortunes cast a veil over his error.

Several letters from Sir Henry Clinton, and others, were received in the course of the affair, feebly attempting to prove that André came out under the protection of a flag, with a passport from a general officer in active service; and consequently could not be justly detained. Clinton sent a deputation, composed of Lieutenant-General Robinson, Mr. Elliot, and Mr. William Smith, to represent, as he said, the true state of Major André's case. General Greene met Robinson, and had a conversation with him, in which he reiterated the pretence of a flag, urged André's release as a personal favor to Sir Henry Clinton, and offered any friend of ours in their power in exchange. Nothing could have been more frivolous than the plea which was used. The fact was, that besides the time, manner, object of the interview, change of dress, and other circumstances, there was not a single formality customary with flags; and the passport was not to Major André, but to Mr. Anderson. But had there been, on the contrary, all the formalities, it would be an abuse of language to say that the sanction of a flag for corrupting an officer to betray his trust, ought to be respected. So unjustifiable a purpose would not only destroy its validity, but make it an aggravation.

André, himself, has answered the argument, by ridiculing and exploding the idea, in his examination before the Board of Officers. It was a weakness to urge it.

There was, in truth, no way of saving him. Arnold or he must have been the victim; the former was out of our power.

It was by some suspected Arnold had taken his measures in such a manner, that if the interview had been discovered in the act, it might have been in his power to sacrifice André to his own security. This surmise of double treachery made them imagine Clinton might be induced to give up Arnold for André; and a gentleman took occasion to suggest this expedient to the latter as a thing that might be proposed by him. He declined it. The moment he had been capable of so much fraility, I should have ceased to esteem him.

The infamy of Arnold's conduct previous to his desertion is only equalled by his baseness since. Beside the folly of writing to Sir Henry Clinton, assuring him that André had acted under a passport from him, and according to his directions while commanding officer at a post, and that, therefore, he did not doubt he would be immediately sent in, he had the effrontery to write to General Washington in the same spirit, with the addition of a menace of retaliation, if the sentence should be carried into execution. He has since acted the farce of sending in his resignation. This man is, in every sense, despicable. Added to the scene of knavery and prostitution during his command in Philadelphia, which the late seizure of his papers has unfolded, the history of his command at West Point is a history of little, as well as great villanies. He practised every dirty act of peculation, and even stooped to connections with the sutlers of the garrison to defraud the public.

To his conduct, that of the captors of André forms a striking contrast. He tempted them with the offer of his watch, his horse, and any sum of money they should name. They rejected his offers with indignation, and the gold that could seduce a man high in the esteem and confidence of his country, who had the remembrance of past exploits, the motives of present reputation and future glory, to prop his integrity, had no charms for three simple peasants, leaning only on their virtue and an honest sense of their duty. While Arnold is handed down with execration to future times, posterity will repeat with reverence the names of Van Wart, Paulding, and Williams.

I congratulate you, my friend, on our happy escape from the mischiefs with which this treason was big. It is a new comment on the value of an honest man, and, [if it were possible, would endear you] to me [more than ever.][1]

—To John Laurens. Date in later hand. Hamilton Papers, 1st ser.

[1] Bracketed material now illegible.

Washington's postscript to this episode is worth remembering. "Traitors are the growth of every country," he reminded us, "and in a revolution of the present nature, it is more to be wondered at, that the catalogue is so small than that there have been found a few."

Hamilton and the Glory Road

As Washington's secretary and chief dispatch writer Hamilton felt his road to military glory blocked. He finally quit Washington's military family, but constantly sought an assignment in the field. At length Washington yielded to his importunities and, ignoring seniority, gave him a command for the Yorktown campaign. There Hamilton acquitted himself brilliantly, leading the attack on the redoubt on the right. At Yorktown Hamilton had his brief moment of military glory.

November 22, 1780

Some time last fall, when I spoke to your Excellency about going to the southward, I explained to you candidly my feelings with respect to military reputation, and how much it was my object to act a conspicuous part in some enterprise that might perhaps raise my character as a soldier above mediocrity. You were so good as to say you would be glad to furnish me with an occasion. When the expedition to Staten Island was afoot, a favorable one seemed to offer. There was a battalion without a field officer, the command of which, I thought, as it was accidental, might be given to me without inconvenience. I made an application for it through the Marquis, who informed me of your refusal on two principles—one, that the giving me a whole battalion might be a subject of dissatisfaction; the other, that if any accident should happen to me, in the present state of your family, you would be embarrassed for the necessary assistance.

The project you now have in contemplation affords another opportunity. I have a variety of reasons that press me to desire ardently to have it in my power to improve it. I take the liberty to observe that the command may now be proportioned to my rank, and that the second objection ceases to operate, as, during the period of establishing our winter-quarters, there will be a suspension of material business . . .

—To Washington. Hamilton Papers, 1st ser.

[De Peyster's Point April 27, 1781]

I imagine your Excellency has been informed that in consequence of the resolution of Congress for granting commissions to aids-de-camp appointed under the former establishment, I have obtained one of lieutenant-colonel in the army of the United States, bearing rank since the first of March, 1777.

It is become necessary to me to apply to your Excellency to know in what manner you foresee you will be able to employ me in the ensuing campaign. I am ready to enter into activity whenever you think proper, though I am not anxious to do it till the army takes the field, as before that period I perceive no object.

Unconnected as I am with any regiment, I can have no other command than in a light corps, and I flatter myself my pretensions to this are good.

Your Excellency knows I have been in actual service since the beginning of '76. I began in the line, and had I continued there I ought in justice to have been more advanced in rank than I now am. I believe my conduct in the different capacities in which I have acted has appeared to the officers of the army in general such as to merit their confidence and esteem; and I cannot suppose them to be so ungenerous as not to see me with pleasure put into a situation still to exercise the disposition I have always had of being useful to the United States. I mention these things only to show that I do not apprehend the same difficulties can exist in my case (which is peculiar) that have opposed the appointments to commands of some other officers not belonging to what is called the line. Though the light infantry is chiefly formed, yet being detached to the southward, I take it for granted there will be a vanguard by detachment formed for this army.

—To Washington. Copy; date in later hand. Hamilton Papers, 1st ser.

De Peyster's Point May 2, 1781

I am extremely sorry to have embarrassed you by my late application, and that you should think there are insuperable obstacles to a compliance with it. Having renounced my expectations, I have no other inducement for troubling your Excellency with a second letter, than to obviate the appearance of having desired a thing inconsistent with the good of the service, while I was acquainted with the circumstances that made it so. . . .

I cannot forbear repeating that my case is peculiar and dissimilar to all the former. It is distinguished by the circumstances I have before intimated: my early entrance into the service; my having made the campaign of '76, the most disagreeable of the war, at the head of a company of artillery, and having been entitled in that corps to a rank equal in degree, and more ancient in date, than I now possess; my having made all the subsequent campaigns in the family of the Commander-in-Chief, in a constant course of important and laborious service. These are my pretensions, at this advanced period of the war, to being employed in the only way which my situation admits; and I imagine they would have their weight in the minds of the officers in general. I only urge them a second time as reasons which will not suffer me to view the matter in the same light with your Excellency, or to regard as impracticable my appointment in a light corps, should there be one formed. I entreat that they may be understood in this sense only. I am incapable of wishing to obtain any object by importunity. I assure your Excellency that I am too well persuaded of your candor to attribute your refusal to any other cause than an apprehension of inconveniences that may attend the appointment.

P. S.—I have used the term brevet in the sense your Excellency appears to have understood it in, as signifying, in general, all officers not attached to any established corps. Congress seem, however, to have made a distinction: they only give a kind of warrant to those whom they designate as brevet officers. Mine is a regular commission.

—To Washington. Hamilton Papers, 1st ser.

CAMP NEAR DOBBS FERRY July 10, 1781

The day before yesterday I arrived here, but for want of an opportunity could not write any sooner; indeed, I know of none now. Finding, when I came here, that nothing was said on the subject of a command, I wrote the General a letter, and inclosed him my commission. This morning Tilghman came to me in his name, pressed me to retain my commission, with an assurance that he would endeavor, by all means, to give me a commond, nearly such as I could have desired in the present circumstances of the army. Though I know you would be happy to hear I had rejected this proposal, it is a pleasure my reputation would not permit me to afford you. I consented to retain my commission, and accept the command. I quarter, at present, by a very polite and warm invitation, with General Lincoln, and experience from the officers of both armies every mark of esteem. * * *

—To Elizabeth Hamilton. *Hamilton, I*, 266-267.

CAMP BEFORE YORKTOWN October 15, 1781

I have the honor to render you an account of the corps under my command in your attack of last night upon the redoubt on the left of the enemy's lines.

Agreeably to your orders, we advanced in two columns with unloaded arms: the right, composed of Lieutenant-Colonel Gimat's battalion and my own, commanded by Major Fish; the left, of a detachment commanded by Lieutenant-Colonel Laurens, destined to take the enemy in reverse, and intercept their retreat. The column on the right was preceded by a vanguard of twenty men, led by Lieutenant Mansfield, and a detachment of sappers and miners, commanded by Captain Gilliland, for the purpose of removing obstructions.

The redoubt was commanded by Major Campbell, with a detachment of British and German troops, and was completely in a state of defence.

The rapidity and immediate success of the assault are the best comment on the behavior of the troops. Lieutenant-Colonel Laurens distinguished himself by an exact and vigorous execution of his part of the plan, by entering the enemy's works with his corps among the foremost, and making prisoner the commanding officer of the redoubt. Lieutenant-Colonel Gimat's battalion, which formed the van of the right attack, and which fell under my immediate observation, encouraged by the decisive and animated example of their leader, advanced with an ardor and resolution superior to every obstacle. They were well seconded by Major Fish, with the battalion under his command, who, when the front of the column reached the abatis, unlocking his corp to the left, as he had been directed, advanced with such celerity as to arrive in time to participate in the assault.

Lieutenant Mansfield deserves particular commendation for the coolness, firmness, and punctuality with which he conducted the vanguard. Captain Olney, who commanded the first platoon of Gimat's battalion, is entitled to peculiar applause. He led his platoon into the work with exemplary intrepidity, and received two bayonet wounds. Captain Gilliland, with the detachment of sappers and miners, acquitted themselves in a manner that did them great honor.

I do but justice to the several corps when I have the pleasure to assure you there was not an officer nor soldier whose behavior, if it could be particularized, would not have a claim to the warmest approbation. As it would have been attended with delay and loss to wait for the removal of the abatis and palisades, the ardor of the troops was indulged in passing over them.

There was a happy coincidence of movements. The redoubt was in the same moment enveloped and carried in every part. The enemy are entitled to the acknowledgment of an honorable defence.

Permit me to have the satisfaction of expressing our obligations to Col. Armand, Capt. Legongne, the Chevalier De Fontevieux, and Capt. Bedkin, officers of his corps, who, acting upon this occasion as volunteers, proceeded at the head of the right column, and, entering the redoubt among the first, by their gallant example contributed to the success of the enterprise.

Our killed and wounded you will perceive by the enclosed return. I sensibly felt, at a critical period, the loss of the assistance of Lieutenant-Colonel Gimat, who received a musket ball in his foot, which obliged him to retire from the field. Captain Bets, of Laurens's corps, Captain Hunt and Lieutenant Mansfield, of Gimat's were wounded with the bayonet in gallantly entering the work. Captain Kirkpatrick, of the corps of sappers and miners, received a wound in the ditch.

Inclosed is a return of the prisoners. The killed and wounded of the enemy did not exceed eight. Incapable of imitating examples of barbarity, and, forgetting recent provocations, the soldiery spared every man who ceased to fight.

—To Lafayette. *Hamilton*, I, 270-272.

March, 1782

You cannot imagine how entirely domestic I am growing. I lose all taste for the pursuits of ambition. I sigh for nothing but the company of my wife and my baby. The ties of duty alone, or imagined duty, keep me from renouncing public life altogether. It is, however, probable I may not any longer be engaged in it. I have explained to you the difficulties which I met with in obtaining a command last campaign. I thought it incompatible with the delicacy due to myself to make any application this campaign. I have expressed this sentiment in a letter to the General, and, retaining my rank only, have relinquished the emoluments of my commission, declaring myself, notwithstanding, ready at all times to obey the calls of the public. I don't expect to hear any of these, unless the state of our affairs should change for the worse, and, lest by any unforeseen accident that would happen, I choose to keep myself in a situation again to contribute my aid. This prevents a total resignation.

—To Richard K. Meade. *Hamilton*, I, 275-276.

August 10, 1802

Finding that a story, long since propagated, under circumstances which it was expected would soon consign it to oblivion (and by which I have been complimented at the expense of Generals Washington and Lafayette), has of late been revived, and has acquired a degree of importance by being repeated in different publications, as well in Europe as America, it becomes a duty to counteract its currency and influence by an explicit disavowal. The story imports in substance, that General Lafayette, with the approbation or connivance of General Washington, ordered me, as the officer who was to command the attack on a British redoubt, in the course of the siege of York Town, to put to death all those of the enemy who should happen to be taken in the redoubt, and that, through motives of humanity, I forebore to execute the order. Positively and unequivocally I declare, that no such nor similar order, nor any intimation nor hint resembling it, was ever by me received, or understood to have been given. It is needless to enter into an explanation of some occurrences on the occasion alluded to, which may be conjectured to have given rise to the calumny. It is enough to say that they were entirely disconnected with any act of either of the generals who have been accused.

—To the Editor of the "Evening Post". *Works*, X, 441-442.

Mutiny

In the winter and spring of '83 the army verged on mutiny. Its demands for back pay and half pay had not been met and some officers urged desperate measures. Hamilton's letter to Washington, written from Congress, voiced this discontent and takes on special significance, first because it alerted Washington to the necessity of directing or controlling the protest movement in the army, and second because it placed the claims of the army ahead of the claims of all other public creditors, whose interests were ever dear to Hamilton. In one important respect Washington did not take Hamilton's advice. He did not assume the leadership of the movement to obtain justice for the veterans, but he did assert himself at the strategic moment to prevent the use of force. A few officers at Washington's main camp near Newburgh, N. Y., had concocted a plan to use force. The plotters had called a meeting for March 15th. To their consternation Washington appeared and denounced the proposals. Hamilton also repudiated the resort to force to redress grievances. When, in June of that year, a detachment of mutineers headed East toward Philadelphia while Congress was in session, Hamilton made strenuous efforts to head them off. When that proved impossible and the state and local authorities uncooperative, Congress fled to Princeton to avoid further humiliation. For this action, Hamilton and Congress were criticized, but his defense is most persuasive. He opposed running away, but defended that course when it was adopted. Hamilton denounced the conduct of John Dickinson, president of the state of Pennsylvania, and the state Executive Council, as "to the last degree weak and disgusting," and charged that they refused to act "till some outrage should have been committed by the troops."

PHILADELPHIA, February 7, 1783

Flattering myself that your knowledge of me will induce you to receive the observations I make, as dictated by a regard to the public good, I take the liberty to suggest to you my ideas on some matters of delicacy and importance. I view the present juncture as a very interesting one. I need not observe how far the temper and situation of the army may make it so. The state of our finances was perhaps never more critical. I am under injunctions which will not permit me to disclose some facts that would at once demonstrate this position. . . . It is however certain that there has scarcely been a period of the Revolution which called more for wisdom and decision in Congress. Unfortunately for us, we are a body not governed by reason or foresight, but by circumstances. It is probable we shall [not] take the proper measures; and if we do not a few m[onths] may open an embarrassing scene. This will be the ca[se,] whether we have peace or a continuance of the war.

If the war continues, it would seem th[at] the army must in June subsist itself *to defend the* [*country?*][1] If peace should take place it *will* subsist itself to pro[cure] justice to itself. It appears to be a prevailing opinion in the army that the disposition to recompense their s[ervices] will cease with the necessity for them; and that if they [once] lay down their arms, they part with the means of ob[taining] justice. It is to be lamented that appearances aff[ord] too much ground for their distrust.

It becomes a serious inquiry what is the true line of policy? The claims of the army urged with moderation, but with firmness, may operate on those weak minds which are influenced by their apprehensions more than by their judgments, so as to produce a concurrence in the measures which the exigencies of affairs demand. They may add weight to the applications of Congress to the several states. So far an useful turn may be given to them. But the difficulty will be to keep a *complaining* and *suffering* army within the bounds of moderation.

This Your Excellency's influence must effect. In order to [do] it, it will be advisable not to discountenance their endeavours to procure redress, but rather by the intervention of confidential and prudent persons *to take the direction of them*. This however must not appear: it is of moment to the public tranquillity, that your Excellency should preserve the confidence of the army without losing that of the people. This will enable you in case of extremity to guide the torrent, and to bring order, perhaps even good, out of confusion. 'Tis a part that requires address; but 'tis one which your own situation as well as the welfare of the community points out.

I will not conceal from your Excellency a truth which it is necessary you should know. An idea is propagated in the army that delicacy carried to an extreme prevents your espousing its interests with sufficient warmth. The falsehood of this opinion no one can be better acquainted with than myself; but it is not the less mischievous for being false. Its tendency is to impair that influence which you may exert with advantage, should any commotions unhappily ensue, to moderate the pretensions of the army and make their conduct correspond with their duty.

The great *desideratum* at present is the establishment of general funds, which alone can do justice to the creditors of the United States (of whom the army forms the most meritorious class), restore public

[1] Manuscript mutilated. The word "country" found in the printed texts may have been in the manuscript but the space seems insufficient for a word of that length.

credit, and supply the future wants of Government. This is the object of all men of sense; in this the influence of the army, properly directed, may cooperate.

The intimations I have thrown out will suffice to give your Excellency a proper conception of my sentiments. You will judge of their reasonableness or fallacy; but I persuade myself you will do justice to my motives. . . .

(P. S.) General Knox has the confidence of the army and is a man of sense. I think he may be safely made use of. Situated as I am your Excellency will feel the confidential nature of these observations.

—To Washington. Hamilton Papers, 1st ser.[2]

PHILADELPHIA March 17, 1783

. . . I cannot forbear adding that if no excesses take place I shall not be sorry that ill-humors have appeared. I shall not regret importunity, if temperate, from the army. . . .

P.S.—Your Excellency mentions that it has been surmised the plan in agitation was formed in Philadelphia, that combinations have been talked of between the public creditors and the army, and that members of Congress had encouraged the idea. This is partly true. I have myself urged in Congress the propriety of uniting the influence of the public creditors, and the army as part of them, to prevail upon the States to enter into their views. I have expressed the same sentiments out-of-doors. Several other members of Congress have done the same. The meaning, however, of all this was simply that Congress should adopt such a plan as would embrace the relief of all the public creditors, including the army, in order that the personal influence of some, the connections of others, and a sense of justice to the army, as well as the apprehension of ill consequences, might form a mass of influence in each State in favor of the measures of Congress. In this view, as I mentioned to your Excellency in a former letter, I thought the discontents of the army might be turned to a good account. I am still of opinion that their earnest but respectful applications for redress will have a good effect. As to any combination of *force*, it would only be productive of the horrors of a civil war, might end in the ruin of the country, and would certainly end in the ruin of the army.

—To Washington. Draft in Hamilton's hand. Hamilton Papers, 1st ser.

PHILADELPHIA March 25, 1783

I sincerely wish *ingratitude* was not so natural to the human heart as it is. I sincerely wish there were no seeds of it in those who direct

[2] Hamilton at the foot of the letter appears to have written a "7" over a "13." The earlier date would appear correct, as the letter bears an endorsement in Washington's hand of Feb. 7. N. Y. Pub. Lib. copy is endorsed Feb. 13 in later hand.

the councils of the United States. But while I urge the army to moderation, and advise your Excellency to take the direction of their discontents, and endeavor to confine them within the bounds of duty, I cannot, as an honest man, conceal from you that I am afraid their distrusts have too much foundation. Republican jealousy has in it a principle of hostility to an army, whatever be their merits, whatever be their claims to the gratitude of the community. It acknowledges their services with unwillingness, and rewards them with reluctance. I see this temper, though smothered with great care, involuntarily breaking out upon too many occasions. I often feel a mortification, which it would be impolitic to express, that sets my passions at variance with my reason. Too many, I perceive, if they could do it with safety or color, would be glad to elude the just pretensions of the army. I hope this is not the prevailing disposition.

But supposing the country ungrateful, what can the army do? It must submit to its hard fate. To seek redress by its arms would end in its ruin. The army would moulder by its own weight, and for want of the means of keeping together the soldiers would abandon their officers; there would be no chance of success without having recourse to means that would reverse our revolution. I make these observations, not that I imagine your Excellency can want motives to continue your influence in the path of moderation, but merely to show why I canot myself enter into the views of coercion which some gentlemen entertain, for I confess, could force avail, I should almost wish to see it employed. I have an indifferent opinion of the honesty of this country, and ill forebodings as to its future system.

Your Excellency will perceive I have written with sensations of chagrin, and will make allowance for coloring, but the general picture is too true. God send us all more wisdom.

—To Washington. Hamilton's hand. Hamilton Papers, 1st ser.

[April, 1783]

The matter with respect to the army which has occasioned most altercation in Congress and most dissatisfaction in the army, has been the half-pay. The opinions on this head have been two: one party was for referring the several lines to their States, to make such commutation as they should think proper; the other, for making the commutation by Congress, and funding it on Continental security. I was of this last opinion, and so were all those who will be represented as having made use of the army as puppets.

—To Washington. Hamilton's hand. Dated in endorsement by Washington; probably written April 9. Hamilton Papers, 1st ser.

[PHILADELPHIA June 19, 1783]

The Instructions to Major Jackson [Assistant Secretary of War]

Sir:

Information having been received that a detachment of about eighty mutineers are on their way from Lancaster to this place, you will please proceed to meet them, and to endeavor by every prudent method to engage them to return to the post they have left. You will inform them of the orders that have been given, permitting them to remain in service till their accounts shall have been settled, if they prefer it to being furloughed, and of the allowance of pay which has been made to the army at large, and in which they are to be included. You will represent to them that their accounts cannot be settled without their officers, whom they have left behind them at Lancaster. You will represent to them with coolness but energy the impropriety of such irregular proceedings, and the danger they will run by persisting in an improper conduct. You will assure them of the best intentions in Congress to do them justice, and of the absurdity of their expecting to procure it more effectually by intemperate proceedings. You will point out to them the tendency which such proceedings may have to raise the resentments of their country, and to indispose it to take effectual measures for their relief. In short, you will urge every consideration in your power to induce them to return, at the same time avoiding whatever may tend to irritate. If they persist in coming to town, you will give the earliest notice to us of their progress and disposition. Should they want provisions, you will assure them of a supply, if they will remain where they are, which you are to endeavor to persuade them to do, in preference to coming to town.

I am, sir,

Your most obedient servant,

A. HAMILTON,

In behalf of the Committee.

—*Journal of the Cont. Cong.*, XXIV, 415-416.

PRINCETOWN June 29, 1783

I am informed that among other disagreeable things said about the removal of Congress from Philadelphia, it is insinuated that it was a contrivance of some members to get them out of the State of Pennsylvania into one of those to which they belonged; and I am told that this insinuation has been pointed at me in particular.

Though I am persuaded that all disinterested persons will justify Congress in quitting a place where they were told they were not to expect support (for the conduct of the Council amounted to that), yet I am unwilling to be held up as having had an extraordinary agency in the measure for interested purposes when the fact is directly the reverse. As you were a witness to my conduct and opinions through the whole of the transaction, I am induced to trouble you for your testimony upon this occasion. I do not mean to make a public use of it, but, through my friends, to vindicate myself from the imputations I have mentioned.

—To James Madison, Jr. Hamilton's hand. Hamilton Papers, 1st ser.

On October 16, 1783, Madison wrote Hamilton from Princeton supporting the latter's version of the removal of Congress, to which Hamilton had yielded "more in compliance with the peremptory expostulations of others than with any disposition of your own mind."

[1783]

This was not to be considered as the disorderly riot of an unarmed mob, but as the deliberate mutiny of an incensed soldiery, carried to the utmost point of outrage short of assassination. The licentiousness of an army is to be dreaded in every government, but in a republic it is more particularly to be restrained; and when directed against the civil authority, to be checked with energy and punished with severity. The merits and sufferings of the troops might be a proper motive for mitigating punishment, when it was in the power of the government to inflict it; but it was no reason for relaxing in the measures necessary to put itself in that situation. Its authority was first to be vindicated, and then its clemency to be displayed.

The rights of government are as essential to be defended as the rights of individuals. The security of the one is inseparable from that of the other. And, indeed, in every new government, especially of the popular kind, the great danger is that public authority will not be sufficiently respected. . . .

Congress were not only right in adopting measures of coercion, but they were also right in resolving to change their situation if proper exertions were not made by the particular government and citizens of the place where they resided. The want of such exertions would evince some defect, no matter where, that would prove they ought to have no confidence in their situation. They were, to all intents and purposes, in the power of a lawless, armed banditti, enraged, whether justly or not, against them. However they might have had a right to expose their own persons to insult and outrage, they had no right to expose the character of representatives, or dignity of the States they represented, or of the Union.

—To John Dickinson. Works, IX, 367-368, 373.

3

Building a New Nation

We are laboring hard to establish in this country principles more and more *national* . . .

Perhaps because he knew no native allegiance to any of the original states Hamilton was among the foremost figures of the Revolution to think in continental terms. Hamilton aimed to impart vigor into the Federal government, to tighten the bonds of union, to build a strong nation. The idea that loyalty to the new nation should transcend state attachments was truly a revolutionary concept. It constituted a more thoroughgoing break with the political system of the past than that of the particularists who were content with severing the ties of empire and returning to the state autonomy that had in large measure existed before the year 1763. Along with his ideas on the need for a stronger union, for a system of Federal taxation and a national bank, Hamilton gave a good deal of thought to the subject of national character while the war with Britain was still being waged. He constantly sought to reconcile national patriotism with existing state loyalties.

Molding National Character

HEADQUARTERS March 12, 1778

. . . Whatever refined politicians may think, it is of great consequence to preserve a national character; and, if it should once seem to be a system in any State to violate its faith whenever it is the least inconvenient to keep it, it will unquestionably have an ill effect upon foreign negotiations, and tend to bring Government at home in contempt, and, of course, to destroy its influence. . . .

For my own part, I have so much of the milk of humanity in me, that I abhor such *Neronian* maxims; and I look upon the old proverb that *honesty is the best policy* to be so generally true, that I can never expect any good from a system at real deviation from it; and I never can adopt the reasonings of some *American* politicians, deducible from their practice, that no regard is to be paid to national character or the rules of good faith.

I dwell upon the faults of Congress, because I think they strike at the vitals of our opposition and of our future prosperity; and with this idea, I cannot but wish that every gentleman of influence in the country should think with me.

—To Governor George Clinton. *Works,* IX, 129-131.

July 19, 1781

The security, therefore, of the public liberty must consist in such a distribution of the sovereign power, as will make it morally impossible for one part to gain ascendancy over the others, or for the whole to unite in a scheme of usurpation.

In federal governments, each member has a distinct sovereignty, makes and executes laws, imposes taxes, distributes justice, and exercises every other function of government. It has always within itself the means of revenue; and on an emergency, can levy forces. . . .

The particular governments will have more empire over the minds of their subjects than the general one, because their agency will be more direct, more uniform, and more apparent. The people will be habituated to look up to them as the arbiters and guardians of their personal concerns, by which the passions of the vulgar, if not of all men, are most strongly affected; and in every difference with the confederated body, will side with them against the common sovereign.

—"The Continentalist," No. II. *N. Y. Packet,* July 19, 1781.

July 4, 1782

. . . There is something noble and magnificent in the perspective of a great Federal Republic, closely linked in the pursuit of a common interest, tranquil and prosperous at home, respectable abroad; but there is something proportionably diminutive and contemptible in the prospect of a number of petty states, with the appearance only of union, jarring, jealous and perverse, without any determined direction, fluctuating and unhappy at home, weak and insignificant by their dissensions in the eyes of other nations. Happy America, if those to whom thou hast intrusted the guardianship of thy infancy know how to provide for thy future repose, but miserable and undone, if their negligence or ignorance permits the spirit of discord to erect her banner on the ruins of thy tranquillity!

—"The Continentalist," No. VI. *N.Y. Packet,* July 4, 1782.

[1787]

Can our national character be preserved without paying our debts? Can the Union subsist without revenue? Have we realized the consequences which would attend its dissolution?

If these States are not united under a Federal Government they will infallibly have wars with each other; and their divisions will subject them to all the mischiefs of foreign influence and intrigue. The human passions will never want objects of hostility. The Western territory is an obvious and fruitful source of contest. Let us also cast our eye upon the map of this State, intersected from one extremity to the other by a large navigable river. In the event of a rupture with them, what is to hinder our metropolis from becoming a prey to our neighbors? Is it even supposable that they would suffer it to remain the nursery of wealth to a distinct community?

These subjects are delicate, but it is necessary to contemplate them, to teach us to form a true estimate of our situation.

Wars with each other would beget standing armies—a source of more real danger to our liberties than all the powers that could be conferred upon the representatives of the Union. And wars with each other would lead to opposite alliances with foreign powers, and plunge us into all the labyrinths of European politics.

The Romans, in their progress to universal dominion, when they conceived the project of subduing the refractory spirit of the Grecian republics which composed the famous Achaian League, began by sowing dissensions among them, and instilling jealousies of each other, and of the common head, and finished by making them a province of the Roman empire.

The application is easy: if there are any foreign enemies, if there are any domestic foes to this country, all their arts and artifices will be employed to effect a dissolution of the Union. This cannot be better done than by sowing jealousies of the Federal head, and cultivating in each State an undue attachment to its own power.

—Speech on the Revenue System before the New York legislature. *Works*, II, 222-223.

[December, 1787]

An objection, of a nature different from that which has often been stated and answered, in my last address, may perhaps be likewise urged against the principle of legislation for the individual citizens of America. It may be said that it would tend to render the government of the Union too powerful, and to enable it to absorb those residuary authorities, which it might be judged proper to leave with the states for local purposes. . . .

It is a known fact in human nature, that its affections are commonly weak in proportion to the distance or diffusiveness of the object.

Upon the same principle that a man is more attached to his family than to his neighborhood, to his neighborhood than to the community at large, the people of each state would be apt to feel a stronger bias towards their local governments than towards the government of the Union; unless the force of that principle should be destroyed by a much better administration of the latter. . . .

There is one transcendent advantage belonging to the province of the state governments, which alone suffices to place the matter in a clear and satisfactory light. I mean the ordinary administration of criminal and civil justice. This, of all others, is the most powerful, most universal, and most attractive source of popular obedience and attachment. . . .

The operations of the national government, on the other hand, falling less immediately under the observation of the mass of the citizens, the benefits derived from it will chiefly be perceived and attended to by speculative men. Relating to more general interests, they will be less apt to come home to the feelings of the people; and, in proportion, less likely to inspire an habitual sense of obligation, and an active sentiment of attachment.

—*The Federalist* No. 17.

June 21, 1788

. . . It has been asserted that the interests, habits, and manners of the Thirteen States are different; and hence it is inferred that no general free government can suit them. This diversity of habits, etc., has been a favorite theme with those who are disposed for a division of our empire, and, like many other popular objections, seems to be founded on fallacy. I acknowledge that the local interests of the states are in some degree various, and that there is some difference in the manners and habits. But this I will presume to affirm, that from New Hampshire to Georgia the people of America are as uniform in their interests and manners as those of any established in Europe.

—Speech on the Constitution, *Debates of the N.Y. Convention*, pp. 46-47.

December 16, 1796

We are laboring hard to establish in this country principles more and more *national* and free from all foreign ingredients, so that we may be neither "Greeks nor Trojans," but truly Americans.

—To Rufus King. *Hamilton*, VI, 187-188.

February 21, 1797

. . . Mental debasement is the greatest misfortune that can befall a people. The most pernicious of conquests which a state can experience is a conquest over that elevated sense of its own rights which inspires a due sensibility to insult and injury; over that virtuous and generous pride of character, which prefers any peril or sacrifice to a final submission to oppression, and which regards national ignominy as the greatest of national calamities.

—"Americus", in *The Warning*, Part III. Draft in Hamilton's hand. Hamilton Papers, 1st ser.

October 2, 1798

. . . I anticipate with you that this country will, erelong, assume an attitude correspondent with its great destinies—majestic, efficient, and operative of great things. A noble career lies before it.

—To Rufus King. *Works*, X, 321.

February 27, 1800

I observe more and more that by the jealousy and envy of some, the miserliness of others, and the concurring influence of *all foreign powers*, America, if she attains to greatness, must *creep* to it. Will it be so? Slow and sure is no bad maxim. *Snails* are a wise generation.

—To Theodore Sedgwick. Hamilton's hand. Hamilton Papers, 1st ser.

Wanted: A Continental Government that Can Act

The course of the Revolution disclosed the difficulties of carrying on an effective war program without a strong executive and of securing cooperative action from the thirteen independent states even when they were fighting for survival. Hamilton was a Continentalist. He believed in a strong federal government with power to act. In a number of amazing letters, some of them written as early as 1778, he stressed the importance of having a Continental Congress with both prestige and power. Perhaps most notable among this series of letter was the one written in 1780 to James Duane, in which he urged that Congress be given "complete sovereignty" with certain limitations. He spelled out his ideas at greater length in a series of "Continentalist" newspaper letters the following year.

HEADQUARTERS February 13, 1778

There is a matter which often obtrudes itself upon my mind, and which requires the attention of every person of sense and prudence among us—I mean a degeneracy of representation in the great council of America. It is a melancholy truth, sir, the effects of which we daily see and feel, that there is not so much wisdom in a certain body as there ought to be, and as the success of our affairs absolutely demands. Many members of it are, no doubt, men in every respect fit for the trust, but this cannot be said of it as a body. Folly, caprice, a want of foresight, comprehension, and dignity characterize the general tenor of their action. Of this, I dare say, you are sensible, though you have not, perhaps, so many opportunities of knowing it as I have. Their conduct, with respect to the army especially, is feeble, indecisive, and improvident—insomuch that we are reduced to a more terrible situation than you can conceive. False and contracted views of economy have prevented them, though repeatedly urged to it, from making that provision for officers which was requisite to interest them in the service, which has produced such carelessness and indifference to the service as is subversive to every officer-like quality. They have disgusted the army by repeated instances of the most whimsical favoritism in their promotions, and by an absurb prodigality of rank to foreigners and to the meanest staff of the army. They have not been able to summon resolution enough to withstand the impudent importunity and vain boasting of foreign pretenders, but have manifested such a ductility and inconsistency in their proceedings as will warrant the charge of suffering themselves to be bullied by every petty rascal who comes armed with ostentatious pretensions of military merit and experience. Would you believe it, sir, it is become almost proverbial in the mouths of the French officers and other foreigners, that they have nothing more to do to obtain whatever they please than to assume a high tone and assert their own merit with confidence and perseverance? These things wound my feelings as a Republican more than I can express, and in some degree make me comtemptible in my own eyes. . . .

America once had a representation that would do honor to any age or nation. The present falling off is very alarming and dangerous. What is the cause? or how is it to be remedied?—are questions that the welfare of these States requires should be well attended to. The great men who composed our first council; are they dead, have they deserted the cause, or what has become of them? Very few are dead and still fewer have deserted the cause; they are all, except the few who still remain in Congress, either in the field or in the civil offices of their respective States; for the greater part are engaged in the later. The only remedy then is to take them out of these employments and return them to the place where their presence is infinitely more important.

Each State, in order to promote its own external government and prosperity, has selected its best members to fill the offices within itself, and conduct its own affairs. Men have been fonder of the emoluments and conveniences of being employed at home; and local attachment falsely operating has made them more provident for the particular interests of the State to which they belonged, than for the common interests of the Confederacy. This is a most pernicious mistake and must be corrected. . . . You should not beggar the councils of the United States to enrich the administration of the several members. Realize to yourself the consequence of having a Congress despised at home and abroad. How can the common force be exerted if the power of collecting it be put in weak, foolish, and unsteady hands? How can we hope for success in our European negotiations, if the nations of Europe have no confidence in the wisdom and vigor of the great Continental Government? This is the object on which their eyes are fixed; hence it is, America will derive its importance or insignificance in their estimation. . . .

—To Governor George Clinton. *Works*, IX, 122-127.

May 14, 1780

This will be handed you by the Marquis [de Lafayette], who brings us very important intelligence.[1] The General communicates the substance of it in a private letter to you, and proposes a measure which all deem essential. For God's sake, my dear sir, engage Congress to adopt it, and come to a speedy decision. We have not a moment to lose. Were we to improve every instant of the interval, we should have too little time for what we have to do. The expected succor may arrive in the beginning of June; in all probability it will not be later than the middle. In the last case we have not a month to make our preparations in, and in this short period we must collect men, form magazines, and do a thousand things of as much difficulty as importance. The propriety of the measure proposed is so obvious that an hour ought to decide it, and if any new members are to come, they ought to set out instantly with all expedition for headquarters. . . .

Again, my dear sir, I must entreat you to use the spur on the present occasion. The fate of America is perhaps suspended on the issue; if we are found unprepared, it must disgrace us in the eyes of all Europe, besides defeating the good intentions of our allies, and losing the happiest opportunity we ever have had to save ourselves.

—To James Duane. *Hamilton*, I, 137-138.

LIBERTY POLE September 3, 1780

I shall now propose the remedies which appear to me applicable to our circumstances, and necessary to extricate our affairs from their present deplorable situation.

The first step must be to give Congress powers competent to the public exigencies. This may happen in two ways: one by resuming and exercising the discretionary powers I suppose to have originally

[1] News of the dispatching of the French fleet with the army under Rochambeau. Washington urged that Congress cooperate with the French. Congress appointed a committee to facilitate combined Franco-American operations.

vested in them for the safety of the States, and resting their conduct on the candor of their countrymen and the necessity of the conjecture; the other, by calling immediately a Convention of all the States, with full authority to conclude finally upon a General Confederation, stating to them beforehand, explicitly, the evils arising from a want of power in Congress, and the impossibility of supporting the contest on its present footing, that the delegates may come possessed of proper sentiments as well as proper authority to give efficacy to the meeting. Their commission should include a right of vesting Congress with the whole, or a proportion, of the unoccupied lands, to be employed for the purpose of raising a revenue; reserving the jurisdiction to the States by whom they are granted. . . .

The Confederation, in my opinion, should give Congress complete sovereignty, except as to that part of internal police which relates to the rights of property and life among individuals, and to raising money by internal taxes. It is necessary that every thing belonging to this should be regulated by the State Legislatures. Congress should have complete sovereignty in all that relates to war, peace, trade, finance; and to the management of foreign affairs; the right of declaring war; of raising armies, officering, paying them, directing their motions in every respect; of equipping fleets, and doing the same with them; of building fortifications, arsenals, magazines, etc., etc.; of making peace on such conditions as they think proper; of regulating trade, determining with what countries it shall be carried on; granting indulgences; laying prohibitions on all the articles of export or import; imposing duties; granting bounties and premiums for raising, exporting or importing, and applying to their own use, the product of these duties—only giving credit to the States on whom they are raised in the general account of revenues and expenses; instituting Admiralty Courts, etc.; of coining money; establishing banks on such terms, and with such privileges as they think proper; appropriating funds, and doing whatever else relates to the operations of finance; transacting every thing with foreign nations; making alliances, offensive and defensive, treaties of commerce, etc., etc.

The Confederation should provide certain perpetual revenues, productive and easy of collection; a land tax, poll tax, or the like; which, together with the duties on trade, and the unlocated lands, would give Congress a substantial existence, and a stable foundation for their schemes of finance. What more supplies were necessary should be occasionally demanded of the States, in the present mode of quotas.

The second step I would recommend is, that Congress should instantly appoint the following great officers of State: A Secretary of Foreign Affairs, a President of War, a President of Marine, a Financier, a President of Trade. Instead of this last, a Board of Trade may be preferable, as the regulations of trade are slow and gradual, and require prudence and experience more than other qualities, for which Boards are very well adapted.

Congress should choose for these offices men of the first abilities, property, and character in the Continent, and such as have had the best opportunities of being acquainted with the several branches. General Schuyler, whom you mentioned, would make an excellent President of War; General M'Dougall a very good President of Marine. Mr. Robert Morris would have many things in his favor for the department of finance. He could, by his own personal influence, give great weight to the measures he should adopt. I dare say men, equally capable, may be found for the other departments. . . .

The placing the officers upon half-pay during life would be a great stroke of policy, and would give Congress a stronger tie upon them than any thing else they can do. No man that reflects a moment but will prefer a permanent provision of this kind to any temporary compensation. Nor is it opposed to economy; the difference between this and between what has been already done will be insignificant. The benefit of it to the widows should be confined to those whose husbands die during the war. As to the survivors, not more than one half, on the usual calculation of men's lives, will exceed the seven years for which the half-pay is already established. Besides this, whatever may be the visionary speculations of some men at this time, we shall find it indispensable, after the war, to keep on foot a considerable body of troops, and all the officers, retained for this purpose must be deducted out of the half-pay list. If any one will take the pains to calculate the expense of these principles, I am persuaded he will find the addition of expense, from the establishment proposed, by no means a national object.

The advantages of securing the attachment of the army to Congress, and binding them to the services by substantial ties, are immense. We should then have discipline,—an army in reality as well as in name. Congress would then have a solid basis of authority and consequence; for, to me, it is an axiom, that in our constitution an army is essential to the American Union.

The providing of supplies is the pivot of every thing else (though a well-constituted army would, not in a small degree, conduce to this by giving consistency and weight to government). There are four ways, all of which must be united: a foreign loan; heavy pecuniary taxes; a tax in kind; a bank founded on public and private credit. . . .

How far it may be practicable to erect a bank on the joint credit of the public and of individuals can only be certainly determined by the experiment. But it is of so much importance, that the experiment ought to be fully tried. When I saw the subscriptions going on to the bank established for supplying the army, I was in hopes it was only the embryo of a more permanent and extensive establishment. But I have reason to believe I shall be disappointed. It does not seem to be at all conducted on the true principles of a bank.

The directors of it are purchasing with their stock instead of bank-notes, as I expected, in consequence of which it must turn out to be a mere subscription of a particular sum of money for a particular purpose.

Paper credit never was long supported in any country, on a national scale, where it was not founded on a joint basis of public and private credit. An attempt to establish it on public credit alone in France, under the auspices of Mr. Law, had nearly ruined the kingdom. We have seen the effects of it in America, and every successive experiment proves the futility of the attempt. Our new money is depreciating almost as fast as the old, though it has, in some States, as real funds as paper-money ever had. The reason is that the moneyed men have not an immediate interest to uphold its credit. They may even, in many ways, find it their interest to undermine it. The only certain manner to obtain a permanent paper credit is to engage the moneyed interest immediately in it, by making them contribute the whole or part of the stock, and giving them the whole or part of the profits.

The invention of banks on the modern principle, originated in Venice. There the public and a company of moneyed men are mutually concerned. The Bank of England unites public authority and faith with private credit, and hence we see what a vast fabric of paper credit is raised on a visionary basis. Had it not been for this, England would never have found sufficient funds to carry on her wars; but with the help of this, she has done, and is doing, wonders. The Bank of Amsterdam is on a similar foundation.

And why can we not have an American Bank? Are our moneyed men less enlightened to their own interest, or less enterprising in the pursuit? I believe the fault is in government, which does not exert itself to engage them in such a scheme. It is true the individuals in America are not very rich, but this would not prevent their instituting a bank; it would only prevent its being done with such ample funds as in other countries. Have they not sufficient confidence in the government, and in the issue of the cause? Let the government endeavor to inspire that confidence, by adopting the measures I have recommended, or others equivalent to them. Let it exert itself to procure a solid confederation; to establish a good plan of executive administration; to form a permanent military force; to obtain, at all events, a foreign loan. If these things were in a train of vigorous execution, it would give a new spring to our affairs; government would recover its respectability, and individuals would renounce their diffidence. . . .

The first step to establishing the bank will be to engage a number of moneyed men of influence to relish the project and make it a business. The subscribers to that lately established are the fittest persons that can be found, and their plan may be interwoven.

The outlines of my plan would be to open subscriptions in all the states, for the stock, which we will suppose to be one million of pounds. Real property of every kind, as well as specie, should be deemed good stock, but at least a fourth part of the subscription should be in specie or plate. There should be one great company, in three divisions: in Virginia, Philadelphia, and at Boston; or two, at Philadelphia and Boston. The Bank should have a right to issue bank-notes, bearing two per cent interest, for the whole of their stock, but not to exceed it. These notes may be payable every three months or oftener, and the faith of government must be pledged for the support of the bank. It must therefore have a right, from time to time, to inspect its operations, and must appoint inspectors for the purpose.

The advantages of the bank may consist in this: in the profits of the contracts made with government, which should bear interest to be annually paid in specie; in the loan of money at interest, say six per cent; in purchasing lives by annuities, as practised in England, etc. The benefit resulting to the company is evident from the consideration, that they may employ in circulation a great deal more money than they have specie in stock, on the credit of the real property which they will have in other use. This money will be employed either in fulfilling their contracts with the public, by which also they will gain a profit, or in loans at an advantageous interest, or in annuities.

The bank may be allowed to purchase plate and bullion, and coin money, allowing government a part of the profit. I [should] make the bank-notes bear interest, to obtain a readie[r] currency, and to induce the holders to prefer them to specie, to prevent too great a run upon the bank, at any time, beyond its ability to pay. . . .

. . . There are epochs in human affairs when *novelty* even is useful. If a general opinion prevails that the old way is bad, whether true or false, and this obstructs or relaxes the operations of the public service, a change is necessary, if it be but for the sake of change. This is exactly the case now. 'Tis an universal sentiment that our present system is a bad one, and that things do not go right on this account. The measure of a Convention would revive the hopes of the people and give a new direction to their passions, which may be improved in carrying points of substantial utility. . . .

I wish, too, Congress would always consider that a kindness consists as much in the manner as in the thing. The best things done hesitatingly and with an ill grace lose their effect, and produce disgust rather than satisfaction or gratitude. In what Congress have at any time done for the army, they have commonly been too late. They have seemed to yield to importunity rather than to sentiments of justice or to a regard to the accommodation of their troops. An attention to this idea is of more importance than it may be thought. I, who have seen all the workings and progress of the present discontents, am convinced that a want of this has not been among the most inconsiderable causes.

—To James Duane. Hamilton Papers, 1st ser.

August 9, 1781

. . . Our whole system is in disorder; our currency depreciated, till in many places it will hardly obtain a circulation at all; public credit at its lowest ebb; our army deficient in numbers, and unprovided with every thing; the government, in its present condition, unable to command the means to pay, clothe, or feed their troops; the enemy making an alarming progress in the Southern states, lately in complete possession of two of them, though now in part rescued by the genius and exertions of a General without an army; a force under Cornwallis still formidable to Virginia.

We ought to blush to acknowledge that this is a true picture of our situation, when we reflect that the enemy's whole force in the United States, including their American levies and the late reinforcements, is little more than fourteen thousand effective men; that our population, by recent examination, has been found to be greater than at the commencement of war; that the quantity of our specie has also increased; that the country abounds with all the necessaries of life; and has a sufficiency of foreign commodities, with a considerable and progressive commerce; that we have, beyond comparison, a better stock of warlike materials than when we began the contest, and an ally as willing as able to supply our further wants; and that we have on the spot five thousand auxiliary troops, paid and subsisted by that ally, to assist in our defence.

Nothing but a GENERAL DISAFFECTION of the PEOPLE or MISMANAGEMENT in their RULERS can account for the figure we make, and for the distresses and perplexities we experience contending against so small a force. Our enemies themselves must now be persuaded that the first is not the cause, and we know it is not.

—"The Continentalist No. III," in *N.Y. Packet*, Aug. 9, 1781.

August 30, 1781

The preceding numbers are chiefly intended to confirm an opinion, already pretty generally received, that it is necessary to augment the powers of the Confederation. The principal difficulty yet remains to fix the public judgment definitely on the points which ought to compose that augmentation.

It may be pronounced with confidence that nothing short of the following articles can suffice.

1st.—The Power of Regulating Trade, comprehending a right of granting bounties and premiums by way of encouragement, of imposing duties of every kind as well for revenue as regulation, of appointing all officers of the customs, and of laying embargoes in extraordinary emergencies.

2d.—A moderate land tax, throughout the United States, of a specific rate per pound or per acre,[1] granted to the Federal Government in perpetuity, and, if Congress think proper, to be levied by their own collectors.

3d.—A moderate capitation tax on every male[2] inhabitant above fifteen years of age, exclusive of common soldiers, common seamen, day laborers, cottagers, and paupers, to be also vested in perpetuity, and with the same condition of collection.

4th.—The disposal of all unlocated land for the benefit of the United States (so far as respects the profits of the first sale and the quit-rents), the jurisdiction remaining to the respective States in whose limits they are contained.

5th.—A certain proportion of the product of all mines discovered, or to be discovered, for the same duration, and with the same right of collection as in the second and third articles.

6th.—The appointment of all land (as well as naval) officers of every rank.

The three first articles are of IMMEDIATE NECESSITY; the last three would be of great present, but of much greater future, utility; the whole combined would give solidity and permanency to the Union.

The great defect of the Confederation is, that it gives the United States no property; or, in other words, no revenue, nor the means of acquiring it, inherent in themselves and independent on the temporary pleasure of the different members. And power without revenue, in political society, is a name. While Congress continue altogether dependent on the occasional grants of the several States, for the means of defraying the expenses of the Federal Government, it can neither have dignity, vigor, nor *credit*. Credit supposes specific and permanent funds for the punctual payment of interest, with a moral certainty of the final redemption of the principal.

—"The Continentalist No. IV," in *N.Y. Packet*, Aug. 30, 1781.

July 4, 1782

. . . The great art is to distribute the public burthens well, and not suffer them, either first or last, to fall too heavily on parts of the

[1] Two pence an acre on cultivated, and a halfpenny on uncultivated, land would answer the purpose, and would be so moderate as not to be felt; a small tax on uncultivated land would have the good effect of obliging the proprietor either to cultivate it himself or to dispose of it to some persons that would do it.

[2] Suppose a dollar, or even half a dollar, per head.

community, else distress and disorder must ensue; a shock given to any part of the political machine vibrates through the whole. . . .

. . . The nature of our popular institutions requires a numerous magistracy, for whom competent provision must be made, or we may be certain our affairs will always be committed to improper hands, and experience will teach us that no government costs so much as a bad one.

We may preach, till we are tired of the theme, the necessity of disinterestedness in republics, without making a single proselyte. The virtuous declaimer will neither persuade himself nor any other person to be content with a double mess of porridge, instead of a reasonable stipend for his services. We might as soon reconcile ourselves to the Spartan community of goods and wives, to their iron coin, their long beards, or their black broth. There is a total dissimilarity in the circumstances as well as the manners of society among us, and it is as ridiculous to seek for models in the small ages of Greece and Rome, as it would be to go in quest of them among the Hottentots and Lapoons[1]. . . .

The Federal Government should neither be independent nor too much dependent. It should neither be raised above responsibility or control, nor should it want the means of maintaining its own weight, authority, dignity, and credit. To this end, permanent funds are indispensable, but they ought to be of such a nature and so moderate in their amount as never to be inconvenient. Extraordinary supplies can be the objects of extraordinary emergencies, and in that salutary medium will consist our true wisdom. . . .

The genius of liberty reprobates every thing arbitrary or discretionary in taxation. It exacts that every man, by a definite and general rule, should know what proportion of his property the state demands. Whatever liberty we may boast in theory, it cannot exist in fact while assessments continue. . . .

The establishment of permanent funds would not only answer the public purposes infinitely better than temporary supplies, but it would be the most effectual way of easing the people. With this basis for procuring credit, the amount of present taxes might be greatly diminished. Large sums of money might be borrowed abroad at a low interest, and introduced into the country, to defray the current expenses and pay the public debts; which would not only lessen the demand for immediate supplies, but would throw more money into circulation, and furnish the people with greater means of paying the taxes. . . .

The product of the three foregoing articles will be as little as can be required to enable Congress to pay their debts and restore order into their finances. In addition to them:

[1] Lapps.

The disposal of the unlocated lands will hereafter be a valuable source of revenue and an immediate one of credit. As it may be liable to the same condition with the duties on trade—that is, the product of the sales within each state to be credited to that state,—and as the rights of jurisdiction are not infringed, it seems to be susceptible of no reasonable objection.

Mines in every country constitute a branch of revenue. In this, where nature has so richly impregnated the bowels of the earth, they may in time become a valuable one; and as they require the care and attention of government to bring them to perfection, this care and a share in the profits of it will very properly devolve upon Congress. All the precious metals should absolutely be the property of the Federal Government, and with respect to the others it should have a discretionary power of reserving, in the nature of a tax, such part as it may judge not inconsistent with the encouragement due to so important an object. This is rather a future than a present resource. . . .

—"The Continentalist," No. VI. *N. Y. Packet*, July 4, 1782.

August 15, 1782

Peace made, my dear friend, a new scene opens. The object then will be to make our independence a blessing. To do this we must secure our Union on solid foundations—a herculean task,—and to effect which, mountains of prejudice must be levelled! It requires all the virtue and all the abilities of the country. Quit your sword, my friend; put on the toga. Come to Congress. We know each other's sentiments; our views are the same. We have fought side by side to make America free; let us hand in hand struggle to make her happy.

—To John Laurens. Works, IX, 280-281.

Congress could not raise revenue to meet its bills. Under the Articles of Confederation the only means allowed Congress was that of requisitions upon the states. That means had been found highly unsatisfactory. In 1781 Congress proposed an amendment to the Articles, whereby it would be empowered to levy a five per cent duty on imports to pay the Revolutionary debt. Rhode Island refused her assent. Hamilton was properly alarmed.

December 11, 1782

Congress are equally affected and alarmed by the information they have received that the Legislature of your State, at their last meeting, have refused their concurrence in establishing a duty on imports. They consider this measure as so indispensable to the prosecution of the war, that a sense of duty and regard to the common safety compel them to renew their efforts to engage a compliance with it. And in this view they have determined to send a deputation of three members to your State, as expressed in the inclosed resolution. The gentleman they have appointed will be able to lay before you a full and just representation of public affairs, from which, they flatter themselves, will result a conviction of the propriety of their solicitude upon the present occasion. Convinced by past experience of the zeal and patriotism of the State of Rhode Island, they cannot doubt that it will yield to those urgent considerations which flow from a knowledge of our true situation.

They will only briefly observe that the increasing discontents of the army, the loud clamors of the public creditors, and the extreme disproportion between the public supplies and the demands of the public service, are so many invincible arguments for the fund recommended by Congress. They feel themselves unable to devise any other that will be more efficacious, less exceptionable, or more generally agreeable; and if this is refused, they anticipate calamities of the most menacing nature—with this consolation, however, that they have faithfully discharged their trust, and that the mischiefs which follow cannot be attributed to them.

A principal object of the proposed fund is to *procure loans abroad.* If no security can be held out to lenders, the success of these must necessarily be very limited. The last accounts on the subject were not flattering; and when intelligence shall arrive in Europe that the State of Rhode Island has disagreed to the only fund which has yet been devised, there is every reason to apprehend it will have a fatal influence upon their future progress.

Deprived of this resource, our affairs must in all probability hasten to a dangerous crisis, and these States be involved in greater embarrassments than they have yet experienced, and from which it may be much more difficult to emerge. Congress will only add a request to your Excellency, that if the Legislature should not be sitting, it may be called together as speedily as possible, to enable the gentlemen whom they have deputed to perform the purpose of their mission.

—To the Governor of Rhode Island. *Hamilton,* I, 322-323.

In letters public and private Hamilton continued to hammer away at the theme of strong union. At the Annapolis Convention of September, 1786, at which New York, New Jersey, Delaware, Pennsylvania, and Virginia were represented, Hamilton drafted the notable address to the states, which the Convention adopted on September 14th. Cautiously endorsed by Congress, this report led to the calling of the Constitutional Convention in Philadelphia.

[1783]

Congress stand in a very delicate and embarrassing situation. On the one hand they are blamed for not doing what they have no means of doing; on the other their attempts are branded with the imputations of a spirit of encroachment and a lust of power.

In these circumstances, it is the duty of all those who have the welfare of the community at heart to unite their efforts to direct the attention of the people to the true source of the public disorders—the want of an efficient general government,—and to impress upon them this conviction, that these States, to be happy, must have a stronger bond of Union and a Confederation capable of drawing forth the resources of the country. This will be a more laudable occupation than that of cavilling against measures the imperfection of which is the necessary result of the Constitution.

—"Vindication of Congress," Hamilton Papers, 1st ser.

ANNAPOLIS September 14, 1786

. . . Deeply impressed, however, with the magnitude and importance of the object confided to them on this occasion, your Commissioners cannot forbear to indulge an expression of their earnest and unanimous wish that speedy measures may be taken to effect a general meeting of the States in a future convention for the same, and such other purposes as the situation of public affairs may be found to require.

If in expressing this wish, or intimating any other sentiment, your Commissioners should seem to exceed the strict bounds of their appointment, they entertain a full confidence that a conduct dictated by an anxiety for the welfare of the United States will not fail to receive an indulgent construction.

In this persuasion, your Commissioners submit an opinion that the idea of extending the powers of their deputies to other subjects than those of commerce, which had been adopted by the State of New Jersey, was an improvement on the original plan, and will deserve to be incorporated into that of a future convention. They are the more naturally led to this conclusion, as, in the course of their reflections on the subject, they have been induced to think that the power of regulating trade is of such comprehensive extent, and will enter so far into the general system of the Federal Government, that to give it efficacy, and to obviate questions and doubts concerning its precise nature and limits, may require a correspondent adjustment of other parts of the Federal system.

That there are important defects in the system of the Federal Government is acknowledged by the acts of all those States which have concurred in the present meeting; that the defects upon a closer examination may be found greater and more numerous than even these acts imply, is at least so far probable, from the embarrassments which characterize the present state of our national affairs, foreign and domestic, as may reasonably be supposed to merit a deliberate and candid discussion in some mode which will unite the sentiments and councils of all the States. In the choice of the mode, your Commissioners are of the opinion that a Convention of deputies from the different States for the special and sole purpose of entering into this investigation, and digesting a plan of supplying such defects as may be discovered to exist, will be entitled to a preference, from considerations which will occur without being particularized.

Your Commissioners decline an enumeration of those national circumstances on which their opinion respecting the propriety of a future convention, with more enlarged powers, is founded, as it would be an useless intrusion of facts and observations, most of which have been frequently the subject of public discussion, and none of which can have escaped the penetration of those to whom they would in this instance be addressed. They are, however, of a nature so serious as, in the view of your Commissioners, to render the situation of the United States delicate and critical, calling for an exertion of the united virtue and wisdom of all the members of the Confederacy.

Under this impression your Commissioners, with the most respectful deference, beg leave to suggest their unanimous conviction, that it may essentially tend to advance the interests of the Union, if the States, by whom they have been respectively delegated would themselves concur, and use their endeavors to procure the concurrence of the other States in the appointment of Commissioners to meet at Philadelphia on the second Monday in May next, to take into consideration the situation of the United States, to devise such further provisions as shall appear to them necessary to render the Constitution of the Federal Government adequate to the exigencies of the Union; and to report such an act for that purpose to the United States in Congress assembled, as when agreed to, by them, and afterwards confirmed by the Legislature of every State, will effectually provide for the same. . . .

—To the Legislatures of Virginia, Delaware, Pennsylvania, New Jersey, and New York, "Report of the Annapolis Convention," *Documents Illustrative of the Formation of the Union of of the American States* (Washington, D. C., 1927), pp. 41-43.

The problem of the federal revenue reached a crisis in 1787, when the New York legislature refused to grant Congress the power to levy a duty on imports, a power specifically restricted to a twenty-five year period. New York's action blocked that unanimous consent which was necessary in order to validate an amendment to the Articles. In his speech in support of the revenue amendment Hamilton once again enunciated the doctrine of a union with broad powers.

[1787]

In the commencement of the Revolution delegates were sent to meet in Congress with large discretionary powers. In short, generally speaking, with full power "to take care of the republic." In the whole of this transaction the idea of an Union of the colonies was carefully held up. It pervaded all our public acts.

In the Declaration of Independence we find it continued and confirmed. That declaration, after setting forth its motives and causes, proceeds thus: "We, therefore, the representatives of the United States of America in General Congress assembled, appealing to the Supreme Judge of the world for the rectitude of our intentions, do in the name and by the authority of the good people of these colonies, solemnly publish and declare that these United Colonies are, and of right ought to be, free and independent states; that they are absolved from all allegiance to the British Crown, and that all political connection between them and the state of Great Britain is, and ought to be, totally dissolved; and that, as free and independent states, they have full power to levy war, conclude peace, contract alliances, establish commerce, and do all other acts and things that independent states may of right do."

Hence we see that the Union and Independence of these States are blended and incorporated in one and the same act; which, taken together, clearly imports that the United States had in their origin full power to do all acts and things which independent states may of right do; or, in other words, full power of sovereignty.

Accordingly, we find that upon the authority of that act, only approved by the several States, they did levy war, contract alliances, and exercise other high powers of sovereignty, even to the appointment of a dictator, prior to the present Confederation.

—Speech on the Revenue System before the New York legislature. *Works*, II, 200-201.

Union Now: The Critical Weakness of the Confederation

We are ripening for a dissolution.

The more I see, the more I find reason for those who love this country to weep over its blindness.

Like a majority of the Founding Fathers Hamilton viewed the political drift with considerable alarm. As Hamilton saw it the nation was heading toward a crisis. Washington, Jay, Knox, Madison, and other sober men of affairs were of the same mind. But no one saw the perils earlier than Hamilton, and no one kept pounding away at the theme during the Confederation period more insistently. It was only proper that he should assume the task of explaining the weaknesses of the Confederation in the celebrated Federalist *papers, written to win ratification of the Constitution.*

Some antifederalist contemporaries were less perturbed about conditions than were Hamilton and Washington, and some recent historians have implied that all this talk of crisis was part of a Federalist plot to pressure the public into granting strong powers to the Federal government. But the antifederalists failed to convince the public of their day, and the dissenting historians have never successfully refuted the mountain of facts—constitutional, diplomatic, and economic—which Hamilton marshalled in support of his views.

LIBERTY POLE September 3, 1780

The fundamental defect is a want of power in Congress. It is hardly worth while to show in what this consists, as it seems to be universally acknowledged; or to point out how it has happened, as the only question is how to remedy it. It may, however, be said, that it has originated from three causes: an excess of the spirit of liberty, which has made the particular States show a jealousy of all power not in their own hands,—and this jealousy has led them to exercise a right of judging in the last resort of the measures recommended by Congress, and of acting according to their own opinions of their propriety, or necessity; a diffidence, in Congress, of their own powers, by which they have been timid and indecisive in their resolutions, constantly making concessions to the States, till they have scarcely left themselves the shadow of power; a want of sufficient means at their disposal to answer the public exigencies, and of vigor to draw forth those means, which have occasioned them to depend on the States individually to fulfill their engagements with the army,—the consequence of which has been to ruin their influence and credit with the army, to establish its dependence on each State separately, rather than on *them*—that is, rather than on the whole collectively.

It may be pleaded that Congress had never any definitive powers granted them, and of course could exercise none, could do nothing more than recommend. The manner in which Congress was appointed would warrant, and the public good required that they should have considered themselves as vested with full power *to preserve the republic from harm.* They have done many of the highest acts of sovereignty, which were always cheerfully submitted to: The declaration of independence, the declaration of war, the levying of an army, creating a navy, emitting money, making alliances with foreign powers, appointing a dictator, etc. All these implications of a complete sovereignty were never disputed, and ought to have been a standard for the whole conduct of administration. Undefined powers are discretionary powers, limited only by the object for which they were given; in the present case the independence and freedom of America. The Confederation made no difference, for as it has not been generally adopted, it had no operation. But from what I recollect of it, Congress have even descended from the authority which the spirit of that act gives them, while the particular States have no further attended to it than as it suited their pretensions and convenience. It would take too much time to enter into particular instances, each of which separately might appear inconsiderable, but united are of serious import. I only mean to remark, not to censure.

But the Confederation itself is defective, and requires to be altered. It is neither fit for war nor peace. The idea of an uncontrollable sovereignty in each State over its internal police will defeat the other powers given to Congress, and make our union feeble and precarious. . . .

The Confederation, too, gives the power of the purse too entirely to the State Legislatures. It should provide perpetual funds, in the disposal of Congress, by a land tax, poll tax, or the like. All imposts upon commerce ought to be laid by Congress, and appropriated to their use. For, without certain revenues, a government can have no power. That power which holds the purse-strings absolutely, must rule. This seems to be a medium which, without making Congress altogether independent, will tend to give reality to its authority.

Another defect in our system is want of method and energy in the administration. This has partly resulted from the other defect; but in a great degree from prejudice, and the want of a proper executive. Congress have kept the power too much in their own hands, and have meddled too much with details of every sort. Congress is, properly, a deliberative corps, and it forgets itself when it attempts to play the executive. It is impossible such a body, numerous as it is, and constantly fluctuating, can ever act with sufficient decision or with system. Two thirds of the members, one half the time, cannot know what has gone before them, or what connection the subject in hand has to what has been transacted on former occasions. The members who have been more permanent, will only give information that promotes the side they espouse in the present case, and will as often mislead as enlighten. The variety of business must distract, and the proneness of every assembly to debate must at all times delay.

Lately, Congress, convinced of these inconveniences, have gone into the measure of appointing Boards. But this is, in my opinion, a bad plan.

A single man in each department of the administration would be greatly preferable. It would give us a chance of more knowledge, more activity, more responsibility, and, of course, more zeal and attention. Boards partake of a part of the inconveniences of larger assemblies. Their decisions are slower, their energy less, their responsibility more diffused. They will not have the same abilities and knowledge as an administration by single men. Men of the first pretensions will not so readily engage in them, because they will be less conspicuous, of less importance, have less opportunity of distinguishing themselves. The members of Boards will take less pains to inform themselves and arrive to eminence, because they have fewer motives to do it. All these reasons conspire to give a preference to the plan of vesting the great executive departments of the State in the hands of individuals. As these men will be, of course, at all times under the direction of Congress, we shall blend the advantages of a monarchy and republic in our constitution. . . .

A third defect is the fluctuating constitution of our army. This has been a pregnant source of evil; all our military misfortunes, three fourths of our civil embarrassments, are to be ascribed to it. . . .

The imperfect and unequal provision made for the army is a fourth defect, which you will find delineated in the same letter. Without a speedy change the army must dissolve. It is now a mob, rather than an army; without clothing, without pay, without provision, without morals, without discipline. We begin to hate the country for its neglect of us. The country begin to hate us for our oppressions of them. Congress have long been jealous of us. We have now lost all confidence in them, and give the worst construction to all they do. Held together by the slenderest ties, we are ripening for a dissolution.

—To James Duane. Hamilton Papers, 1st ser.

July 12, 1781

In comparison of our governments with those of the ancient republics, we must, without hesitation, give the preference to our own; because every power with us is exercised by representation, not in tumultuary assemblies of the collective body of the people, where the art or impudence of the ORATOR OR TRIBUNE, rather than the utility or justice of the measure, could seldom fail to govern. Yet, whatever may be the advantage on our side in such a comparison, men who estimate the value of institutions, not from prejudices of the moment, but from experience and reason, must be persuaded that the same JEALOUSY OF POWER has prevented our reaping all the advantages from the examples of other nations which we ought to have done, and has rendered our constitutions in many respects feeble and imperfect.

Perhaps the evil is not very great in respect to our constitutions; for, notwithstanding their imperfections, they may for some time be made to operate in such a manner as to answer the purposes of the common defence and the maintenance of order; and they seem to have, in themselves, and in the progress of society among us, the seeds of improvement.

But this is not the case with respect to the FEDERAL GOVERNMENT; if it is too weak at first, it will continually grow weaker. The ambition and local interests of the respective members will be constantly undermining and usurping upon its prerogatives till it comes to a dissolution, if a partial combination of some of the more powerful ones does not bring it to a more SPEEDY and VIOLENT END.

—"The Continentalist No. I," in *N. Y. Packet and the American Advertiser* (Fishkill: Samuel Loudon), July 12, 1781.

ALBANY July 13, 1782

I shall to-morrow morning commence a journey to Poughkeepsie, where the Legislature are assembled, and I will endeavor by every step in my power to second your views, though, I am sorry to add, without very sanguine expectations. I think it probable the Legislature will do something, but whatever momentary effort they may make, till the entire change of their present system very little will be done. To effect this, mountains of prejudice and particular interest are to be levelled. For my own part, considering the late serious misfortune of our ally, the spirit of reformation, of wisdom, and of unanimity, which seems to have succeeded to that of blunder, perverseness, and dissension in the British Government, and the universal reluctance of these States to do what is right, I cannot help viewing our situation as critical, and I feel it the duty of every citizen to exert his faculties to the utmost to support the measures, especially those solid arrangements of finance on which our safety depends.

—To Robert Morris. Hamilton's hand. Hamilton Papers, 1st ser.

POUGHKEEPSIE July 22, 1782

Both Houses have unanimously passed a set of resolutions, to be transmitted to Congress and the several States, proposing a convention of the States, to enlarge the powers of Congress and vest them with funds. I think this a very eligible step, though I doubt of the concurrence of the other States; but I am certain without it they will never be brought to cooperate in any reasonable or effectual plan. Urge reforms or exertions, and the answer constantly is: What avails it for one State to make them without the concert of the others? It is in vain to expose the futility of this reasoning; it is founded in all those passions which have the strongest influence on the human mind.

—To Robert Morris. Hamilton's hand. Hamilton Papers, 1st ser.

[September 28, 1782]

. . . The more I see, the more I find reason for those who love this country to weep over it blindness.

—To Robert Morris. Draft possibly in Hamilton's hand. Dated in later hand. Hamilton Papers, 1st ser.

January 12, 1783

. . . Every day proves more and more the insufficiency of the Confederation. The proselytes to this opinion are increasing fast, and many of the most sensible men acknowledge the wisdom of the measure recommended by your Legislature at their last sitting.

—To Governor Clinton. *Works*, IX, 309.

[Spring of 1783][1]

Whereas, in the opinion of this Congress, the Confederation of the United States is defective in the following essential points, to wit:

Firstly, and generally: "In confining the power of the Federal Government within too narrow limits; withholding from it that efficacious authority and influence, in all matters of general concern, which are indispensable to the harmony and welfare of the whole; embarrassing general provisions by unnecessary details and inconvenient exceptions incompatible with their nature, tending only to create jealousies and disputes respecting the proper bounds of the authority of the United States, and of that of the particular States, and a mutual interference of the one with the other. . . .

Eleven other points are made by Hamilton to underscore the defects of the Confederation: There is no separation of powers. There is no Federal judiciary. Congress has the power to vote taxes but not to collect them. The attempt to fix the proportionate share which each state must bear of the common expenses is attended with expense, difficulty, and uncertainty. Congress is authorized to borrow money and issue paper, but not empowered to establish funds to secure repayment of money borrowed or redemption of bills emitted. Proper provisions for defense are lacking. The United States does not have general supervision of trade. The treaty-making power of the government is restrained. The United States has the sole power of regulating the alloy and value of its coin or that of the states, but does not have the power to regulate foreign coin in circulation. The assent of nine states is required for matters of importance. The United States does not have the power to pass laws in support of the laws of nations.

[1] Some time after March 20, 1783, when Hamilton unsuccessfully proposed that Congress be empowered to nominate its own officers to collect the revenue from individuals, these resolutions appear to have been prepared, but not presented to Congress.

And whereas, experience hath clearly manifested that the powers reserved to the Union in the Confederation are unequal to the purpose of effectually drawing forth the resources of the respective members, *for the common welfare and defence;* whereby the United States have, upon several occasions, been exposed to the most critical and alarming situations; have wanted an army adequate to their defence, and proportioned to the abilities of the country; have, on account of that deficiency, seen essential posts reduced, others eminently endangered, whole states, and large parts of others overrun and ravaged by small bodies of the enemy's forces; have been destitute of sufficient means of feeding, clothing, paying, and appointing that army; by which the troops, rendered less efficient for military operations, have been exposed to sufferings which nothing but unparalleled patience, perseverance, and patriotism could have endured; whereby, also, the United States have been too often compelled to make the administration of their affairs a succession of temporary expedients, inconsistent with order, economy, energy, or a scrupulous adherence to the public engagements; and now find themselves, at the close of a glorious struggle for independence, without any certain means of doing justice to those who have been its principal supporters,—to an army which has bravely fought and patiently suffered, to citizens who have cheerfully lent their money, and to others who have in different ways contributed their property and their personal service to the common cause; obliged to rely, for the only effectual mode of doing that justice, by funding the debt on solid securities, on the precarious concurrence of thirteen distinct deliberatives, the dissent of either of which may defeat the plan, and leave these states, at this early period of their existence, involved in all the disgrace and mischiefs of violated faith and national bankruptcy. . . .

And whereas, it is essential to the happiness and security of these states, that their union should be established on the most solid foundations; and it is manifest that this desirable object cannot be effected but by a government capable, both in peace and war, of making every member of the Union contribute, in just proportion, to the common necessities, and of combining and directing the forces and wills of the several parts to a general end; to which purposes, in the opinion of Congress, the present Confederation is altogether inadequate.

And whereas, on the spirit which may direct the councils and measures of these states at the present juncture may depend their future safety and welfare, Congress conceives it to be their duty freely to state to their constituents the defects which, by experience, have been discovered in the present plan of the Federal Union, and solemnly to call their attention to a revisal and amendment of the same.

Therefore, *Resolved,* That it be earnestly recommended to the several States to appoint a Convention to meet at , on the day of , with full powers to revise the Confederation, and to adopt and propose such alterations as to them shall appear necessary; to be finally approved or rejected by the States respectively; and that a Committee of be appointed to prepare an address upon the subject.

[Endorsement in Hamilton's hand.] Intended to be submitted to Congress in seventeen hundred and eighty-three, but abandoned for want of support!"

—Resolutions for a General Convention. J. C. Hamilton, *History of the Republic*, II, 571-578.

April [1787]

One more observation will conclude what I have to say. The present situation of our national affairs appears to me peculiarly critical. I know not what may be the result of the disordered state of our government. I am, therefore, the more solicitous to guard against danger from abroad.

—Speech on Acceding to the Independence of Vermont. *Hamilton*, II, 389-390.

[December, 1787]

. . . In pursuance of the plan which I have laid down for the discussion of the subject, the point next in order to be examined is the "insufficiency of the present Confederation to the preservation of the Union." . . .

We may indeed with propriety be said to have reached almost the last stage of national humiliation. There is scarcely anything that can wound the pride or degrade the character of an independent nation which we do not experience. Are there engagements to the performance of which we are held by every tie respectable among men? These are the subjects of constant and unblushing violation. Do we owe debts to foreigners and to our own citizens contracted in a time of imminent peril for the preservation of our political existence? These remain without any proper or satisfactory provision for their discharge. Have we valuable territories and important posts in the possession of a foreign power which, by express stipulation, ought long since to have been surrendered? These are still retained, to the prejudice of our interests, not less than of our rights. Are we in a condition to resent or to repel the aggression? We have neither troops, nor treasury, nor government.[1] Are we even in a condition to remonstrate with dignity? The just imputations on our own faith, in respect to the same treaty, ought first to be removed. Are we entitled by nature and compact to a free participation in the navigation of the Mississippi?

[1] "I mean for the Union."—Publius

Spain excludes us from it. Is public credit an indispensable resource in time of public danger? We seem to have abandoned its cause as desperate and irretrievable. Is commerce of importance to national wealth? Ours is at the lowest point of declension. Is respectability in the eyes of foreign powers a safeguard against foreign encroachments? The imbecility of our government even forbids them to treat with us. Our ambassadors abroad are the mere pageants of mimic sovereignty. Is a violent and unnatural decrease in the value of land a symptom of national distress? The price of improved land in most parts of the country is much lower than can be accounted for by the quantity of waste land at market, and can only be fully explained by that want of private and public confidence, which is so alarmingly prevalent among all ranks, and which has a direct tendency to depreciate property of every kind. Is private credit the friend and patron of industry? That most useful kind which relates to borrowing and lending is reduced within the narrowest limits, and this still more from an opinion of insecurity than from the scarcity of money. To shorten an enumeration of particulars which can afford neither pleasure nor instruction, it may in general be demanded, what indication is there of national disorder, poverty, and insignificance that could befall a community so peculiarly blessed with natural advantages as we are, which does not form a part of the dark catalogue of our public misfortunes?. . .

The great and radical vice in the construction of the existing Confederation is in the principle of LEGISLATION for STATES or GOVERNMENTS, in their CORPORATE or COLLECTIVE CAPACITIES, and as contradistinguished from the INDIVIDUALS of which they consist. Though this principle does not run through all the powers delegated to the Union, yet it pervades and governs those on which the efficacy of the rest depends. Except as to the rule of apportionment, the United States has an indefinite discretion to make requisitions for men and money; but they have no authority to raise either, by regulations extending to the individual citizens of America. The consequence of this is, that though in theory their resolutions concerning those objects are laws, constitutionally binding on the members of the Union, yet in practice they are mere recommendations which the States observe or disregard at their option.

It is a singular instance of the capriciousness of the human mind, that after all the admonitions we have had from experience on this head, there should still be found men who object to the new Constitution, for deviating from a principle which has been found the bane of the old, and which is in itself evidently incompatible with the idea of GOVERNMENT; a principle, in short, which, if it is to be executed at all, must substitute the violent and sanguinary agency of the sword to the mild influence of the magistracy. . . .

Government implies the power of making laws. It is essential to the idea of a law, that it be attended with a sanction; or, in other words, a penalty or punishment for disobedience. If there be no penalty annexed to disobedience, the resolutions or commands which pretend to be laws will, in fact, amount to nothing more than advice or recommendation. This penalty, whatever it may be, can only be inflicted in two ways: by the agency of the courts and ministers of justice, or by military force; by the COERCION of the magistracy, or by the COERCION of arms. The first kind can evidently apply only to men; the last kind must of necessity, be employed against bodies politic, or communities, or States. It is evident that there is no process of a court by which the observance of the laws can, in the last resort, be enforced. Sentences may be denounced against them for violations of their duty; but these sentences can only be carried into execution by the sword. In an association where the general authority is confined to the collective bodies of the communities that compose it, every breach of the laws must involve a state of war; and military execution must become the only instrument of civil obedience. Such a state of things can certainly not deserve the name of government, nor would any prudent man choose to commit his happiness to it.

There was a time when we were told that breaches, by the States, of the regulations of the federal authority were not to be expected; that a sense of common interest would preside over the conduct of the respective members, and would beget a full compliance with all the constitutional requisitions of the Union. This language, at the present day, would appear as wild as a great part of what we now hear from the same quarter will be thought, when we shall have received further lessons from the best oracle of wisdom, experience. It at all times betrayed an ignorance of the true springs by which human conduct is actuated, and belied the original inducements to the establishment of civil power. Why has government been instituted at all? Because the passions of men will not conform to the dictates of reason and justice, without constraint. Has it been found that bodies of men act with more rectitude or greater disinterestedness than individuals? The contrary of this has been inferred by all accurate observers of the conduct of mankind; and the inference is founded upon obvious reasons. Regard to reputation has a less active influence, when the infamy of a bad action is to be divided abong a number, than when it is to fall singly upon one. A spirit of faction, which is apt to mingle its poison in the deliberations of all bodies of men, will often hurry the persons of whom they are composed into improprieties and excesses, for which they would blush in a private capacity.

In addition to all this, there is, in the nature of sovereign power, an impatience of control, that disposes those who are invested with the exercise of it, to look with an evil eye upon all external attempts to restrain or direct its operations. From this spirit it happens, that in every political association which is formed upon the principle of uniting in a common interest a number of lesser sovereignties, there will be found a kind of eccentric tendency in the subordinate or inferior orbs, by the operation of which there will be a perpetual effort in each to fly off from the common centre. This tendency is not difficult to be accounted for. It has its origin in the love of power. Power controlled or abridged is almost always the rival and enemy of that power by which it is controlled or abridged. This simple proposition will teach us, how little reason there is to expect, that the persons intrusted with the administration of the affairs of the particular members of a confederacy will at all times be ready, with perfect good-humor, and an unbiased regard to the public weal, to execute the resolutions or decrees of the general authority. The reverse of this results from the constitution of human nature.

If, therefore, the measures of the Confederacy cannot be executed without the intervention of the particular administrations, there will be little prospect of their being executed at all. The rulers of the respective members, whether they have a constitutional right to do it or not, will undertake to judge of the propriety of the measures themselves. They will consider the conformity of the thing proposed or required to their immediate interests or aims; the momentary conveniences or inconveniences that would attend its adoption. All this will be done; and in a spirit of interested suspicious scrutiny, without that knowledge of national circumstances and reasons of state, which is essential to a right judgment, and with that strong predilection in favor of local objects, which can hardly fail to mislead the decision. The same process must be repeated in every member of which the body is constituted; and the execution of the plans, framed by the councils of the whole, will always fluctuate on the discretion of the ill-informed and prejudiced opinion of every part. Those who have been conversant in the proceedings of popular assemblies; who have seen how difficult it often is, where there is no exterior pressure of circumstances, to bring them to harmonious resolutions on important points, will readily conceive how impossible it must be to induce a number of such assemblies, deliberating at a distance from each other, at different times, and under different impressions, long to coöperate in the same views and pursuits.

In our case, the concurrence of thirteen distinct sovereign wills is requisite, under the Confederation, to the complete execution of every important measure that proceeds from the Union. It has happened as was to have been foreseen. The measures of the Union have not been executed; the delinquencies of the states have, step by step, matured themselves to an extreme, which has, at length, arrested all the wheels of the national government, and brought them to an awful stand. Congress at this time scarcely possesses the means of keeping up the forms of administration, till the states can have time to agree upon a more substantial substitute for the present shadow of a federal government. Things did not come to this desperate extremity at once. The causes which have been specified produced at first only unequal and disproportionate degrees of compliance with the requisitions of the Union. The greater deficiencies of some states furnished the pretext of example and temptation of interest to the complying, or to the least delinquent states. Why should we do more in proportion than those who are embarked with us in the same political voyage? Why should we consent to bear more than our proper share of the common burden? These were suggestions which human selfishness could not withstand, and which even speculative men, who looked forward to remote consequences, could not, without hesitation, combat. Each state, yielding to the persuasive voice of immediate interest or convenience, has successively withdrawn its support, till the frail and tottering edifice seems ready to fall upon our heads, and to crush us beneath its ruins.

—*The Federalist* No. 15.

December 4, 1787

. . . It has been seen that delinquencies in the members of the Union are its natural and necessary offspring; and that whenever they happen, the only constitutional remedy is force, and the immediate effect of the use of it, civil war. . . . When the sword is once drawn, the passions of men observe no bounds of moderation. The suggestions of wounded pride, the instigations of irritated resentment, would be apt to carry the states against which the arms of the Union were exerted, to any extremes necessary to avenge the affront or to avoid the disgrace of submission. The first war of this kind would probably terminate in a dissolution of the Union.

This may be considered as the violent death of the Confederacy. Its more natural death is what we now seem to be on the point of experiencing, if the federal system be not speedily renovated in a more substantial form. . . .

The result of these observations to an intelligent mind must be clearly this, that if it be possible at any rate to construct a federal government capable of regulating the common concerns and preserving the general tranquillity, it must be founded, as to the objects committed to its care, upon the reverse of the principle contended for by the opponents of the proposed Constitution. It must carry its agency to the persons of the citizens. It must stand in need of no intermediate legislation; but must itself be empowered to employ the arm of the ordinary magistrate to execute its own resolutions. . . .

To this reasoning it may perhaps be objected, that if any state should be disaffected to the authority of the Union, it could at any time obstruct the execution of its laws, and bring the matter to the same issue of force, with the necessity of which the opposite scheme is reproached.

The plausibility of this objection will vanish the moment we advert to the essential difference between a mere NON-COMPLIANCE and a DIRECT and ACTIVE RESISTANCE. If the interposition of the state legislatures be necessary to give effect to a measure of the Union, they have only NOT TO ACT, or to ACT EVASIVELY, and the measure is defeated. This neglect of duty may be disguised under affected but unsubstantial provisions, so as not to appear, and of course not to excite any alarm in the people for the safety of the Constitution. The state leaders may even make a merit of their surreptitious invasions of it on the ground of some temporary convenience, exemption, or advantage.

But if the execution of the laws of the national government should not require the intervention of the state legislatures, if they were to pass into immediate operation upon the citizens themselves, the particular governments could not interrupt their progress without an open and violent exertion of an unconstitutional power. No omissions nor evasions would answer the end. They would be obliged to act, and in such a manner as would leave no doubt that they had enroached on the national rights. An experiment of this nature would always be hazardous in the face of a constitution in any degree competent to its own defence, and of a people enlightened enough to distinguish between a legal exercise and an illegal usurpation of authority. The success of it would require not merely a factious majority in the legislature, but the concurrence of the courts of justice and of the body of the people. If the judges were not embarked in a conspiracy with the legislature, they would pronounce the resolutions of such a majority to be contrary to the supreme law of the land, unconstitutional, and void. If the people were not tainted with the spirit of their state representatives, they, as the natural guardians of the Constitution, would throw their weight into the national scale and give it a decided preponderance in the contest. Attempts of this kind would not often be made with levity or rashness, because they could seldom be made without danger to the authors, unless in cases of a tyrannical exercise of the federal authority.

—*The Federalist* No. 16.

[December, 1787]

The next most palpable defect of the subsisting Confederation is the total want of a SANCTION to its laws. The United States, as now composed, have no powers to exact obedience, or punish disobedience to their resolutions, either by pecuniary mulcts, by a suspension or divestiture of privileges, or by any other constitutional mode. There is no express delegation of authority to them to use force against delinquent members; and if such a right should be ascribed to the federal head, as resulting from the nature of the social compact between the States, it must be by inference and construction, in the face of that part of the second article, by which it is declared, "that each State shall retain every power, jurisdiction, and right, not *expressly* delegated to the United States in Congress assembled." There is, doubtless, a striking absurdity in supposing that a right of this kind does not exist, but we are reduced to the dilemma either of embracing that supposition, preposterous as it may seem, or of contravening or explaining away a provision, which has been of late a repeated theme of the eulogies of those who oppose the new Constitution; and the want of which, in that plan, has been the subject of much plausible animadversion, and severe criticism. If we are unwilling to impair the force of this applauded provision, we shall be obliged to conclude, that the United States afford the extraordinary spectacle of a government destitute even of the shadow of constitutional power to enforce the execution of its own laws. . . .

The want of a mutual guaranty of the State governments is another capital imperfection in the federal plan. There is nothing of this kind declared in the articles that compose it; and to imply a tacit guaranty from considerations of utility, would be a still more flagrant departure from the clause which has been mentioned, than to imply a tacit power of coercion from the like considerations. The want of a guaranty, though it might in its consequences endanger the Union, does not so immediately attack its existence as the want of a constitutional sanction to its laws.

Without a guaranty the assistance to be derived from the Union in repelling those domestic dangers which may sometimes threaten the existence of the State constitutions, must be renounced. Usurpation may rear its crest in each State, and trample upon the liberties of the people, while the national government could legally do nothing more than behold its encroachments with indignation and regret. A successful faction may erect a tyranny on the ruins of order and law, while no succor could constitutionally be afforded by the Union to the friends and supporters of the government. The tempestuous situation from which Massachusetts has scarcely emerged, evinces that dangers of this kind are not merely speculative. Who can determine what might have been the issue of her late convulsions, if the malcontents had been headed by a Cæsar or by a Cromwell? Who can predict what effect a despotism, established in Massachusetts, would have upon the liberties of New Hampshire or Rhode Island, of Connecticut or New York? . . .

It could be no impediment to reforms of the State constitutions by a majority of the people in a legal and peaceable mode. This right would remain undiminished. The guaranty could only operate against changes to be effected by violence. Towards the preventions of calamities of this kind, too many checks cannot be provided. The peace of society and the stability of government depend absolutely on the efficacy of the precautions adopted on this head. Where the whole power of the government is in the hands of the people, there is the less pretence for the use of violent remedies in partial or occasional distempers of the State. The natural cure for an ill-administration, in a popular or representative constitution, is a change of men. A guaranty by the national authority would be as much levelled against the usurpations of rulers as against the ferments and outrages of faction and sedition in the community.

The principle of regulating the contributions of the States to the common treasury by QUOTAS is another fundamental error in the Confederation. Its repugnancy to an adequate supply of the national exigencies has been already pointed out, and has sufficiently appeared from the trial which has been made of it. I speak of it now solely with a view to equality among the States. Those who have been accustomed to contemplate the circumstances which produce and constitute national wealth, must be satisfied that there is no common standard or barometer by which the degrees of it can be ascertained. Neither the value of lands, nor the numbers of the people, which have been successively proposed as the rule of State contributions, has any pretension to being a just representative. . . .

Let Virginia be contrasted with North Carolina, Pennsylvania with Connecticut, or Maryland with New Jersey, and we shall be convinced that the respective abilities of those States, in relation to revenue, bear little or no analogy to their comparative stock in lands or to their comparative population. The position may be equally illustrated by a similar process between the counties of the same State. No man who is acquainted with the State of New York will doubt that the active wealth of Kings County bears a much greater proportion to that of Montgomery than it would appear to be if we should take either the total value of the lands or the total number of the people as a criterion!

The wealth of nations depends upon an infinite variety of causes. Situation, soil, climate, the nature of the productions, the nature of the government, the genius of the citizens, the degree of information they possess, the state of commerce, of arts, of industry,—these circumstances and many more, too complex, minute, or adventitious to admit of a particular specification, occasion differences hardly conceivable in the relative opulence and riches of different countries. The consequence clearly is that there can be no common measure of national wealth, and, of course, no general or stationary rule by which the ability of a state to pay taxes can be determined. The attempt, therefore, to regulate the contributions of the members of a confederacy by any such rule, cannot fail to be productive of glaring inequality and extreme oppression.

This inequality would of itself be sufficient in America to work the eventual destruction of the Union, if any mode of enforcing a compliance with its requisitions could be devised. The suffering States would not long consent to remain associated upon a principle which distributes the public burdens with so unequal a hand, and which was calculated to impoverish and oppress the citizens of some States, while those of others would scarcely be conscious of the small proportion of the weight they were required to sustain. This, however, is an evil inseparable from the principle of quotas and requisitions.

There is no method of steering clear of this inconvenience, but by authorizing the national government to raise its own revenues in its own way. Imposts, excises, and, in general, all duties upon articles of consumption, may be compared to a fluid, which will, in time, find its level with the means of paying them. The amounts to be contributed by each citizen will in a degree be at his own option, and can be regulated by an attention to his resources. The rich may be extravagant, the poor can be frugal; and private oppression may always be avoided by a judicious selection of objects proper for such impositions. . . .

It is a signal advantage of taxes on articles of consumption, that they contain in their own nature a security against excess. They prescribe their own limit; which cannot be exceeded without defeating the end proposed,—that is, an extension of the revenue. When applied to this object, the saying is as just as it is witty, that, "in political arithmetic, two and two do not always make four." If duties are too high, they lessen the consumption; the collection is eluded; and the product to the treasury is not so great as when they are confined within proper and moderate bounds. This forms a complete barrier against any material oppression of the citizens by taxes of this class, and is itself a natural limitation of the power of imposing them.

Impositions of this kind usually fall under the denomination of indirect taxes, and must for a long time constitute the chief part of the revenue raised in this country. Those of the direct kind, which principally relate to land and buildings, may admit of a rule of apportionment. Either the value of land, or the number of the people, may serve as a standard. The state of agriculture and the populousness of a country have been considered as nearly connected with each other. And, as a rule, for the purpose intended, numbers, in the view of simplicity and certainty, are entitled to a preference.

—*The Federalist* No. 21.

December 14, 1787

IN ADDITION to the defects already enumerated in the existing federal system, there are others of not less importance, which concur in rendering it altogether unfit for the administration of the affairs of the Union.

The want of a power to regulate commerce is by all parties allowed to be of the number. . . . It is indeed evident, on the most superficial view, that there is no object, either as it respects the interest of trade or finance, that more strongly demands a federal superintendence. The want of it has already operated as a bar to the formation of beneficial treaties with foreign powers, and has given occasions of dissatisfaction between the States. No nation acquainted with the nature of our political association would be unwise enough to enter into stipulations with the United States, by which they conceded privileges of any importance to them, while they were apprised that the engagements on the part of the Union might at any moment be violated by its members, and while they found from experience that they might enjoy every advantage they desired in our markets, without granting us any return but such as their momentary convenience might suggest. . . .

Several states have endeavored, by separate prohibitions, restrictions, and exclusions, to influence the conduct of [Great Britain] in this particular, but the want of concert, arising from the want of a general authority and from clashing and dissimilar views in the State, has hitherto frustrated every experiment of the kind, and will continue to do so as long as the same obstacles to a uniformity of measures continue to exist.

The interfering and unneighborly regulations of some States, contrary to the true spirit of the Union, have, in different instances, given just cause of umbrage and complaint to others, and it is to be feared that examples of this nature, if not restrained by a national control, would be multiplied and extended till they became not less serious sources of animosity and discord than injurious impediments to the intercourse between the different parts of the Confederacy. "The commerce of the German empire* is in continual trammels from the multiplicity of the duties which the several princes and states exact upon the merchandises passing through their territories, by means of which the fine streams and navigable rivers with which Germany is so happily watered are rendered almost useless." Though the genius of the people of this country might never permit this description to be strictly applicable to us, yet we may reasonably expect, from the gradual conflicts of State regulations, that the citizens of each would at length come to be considered and treated by the others in no better light than that of foreigners and aliens.

The power of raising armies, by the most obvious construction of the articles of the Confederation, is merely a power of making requisitions upon the States for quotas of men. This practice, in the course of

* Encyclopedia, article "Empire."—PUBLIUS

the late war, was found replete with obstructions to a vigorous and to an economical system of defence. It gave birth to a competition between the States which created a kind of auction for men. In order to furnish the quotas required of them, they outbid each other till bounties grew to an enormous and insupportable size. The hope of a still further increase afforded an inducement to those who were disposed to serve to procrastinate their enlistment, and disinclined them from engaging for any considerable periods. Hence, slow and scanty levies of men, in the most critical emergencies of our affairs; short enlistments at an unparalleled expense; continual fluctuations in the troops, ruinous to their discipline and subjecting the public safety frequently to the perilous crisis of a disbanded army. Hence, also, those oppressive expedients for raising men which were upon several occasions practised, and which nothing but the enthusiasm of liberty would have induced the people to endure.

This method of raising troops is not more unfriendly to economy and vigor than it is to an equal distribution of the burden. The States near the seat of war, influenced by motives of self-preservation, made efforts to furnish their quotas, which even exceeded their abilities; while those at a distance from danger were, for the most part, as remiss as the others were diligent, in their exertions. The immediate pressure of this inequality was not in this case, as in that of the contributions of money, alleviated by the hope of a final liquidation. The States which did not pay their proportions of money might at least be charged with their deficiencies; but no account could be formed of the deficiences in the supplies of men. We shall not, however, see much reason to regret the want of this hope, when we consider how little prospect there is, that the most delinquent States will ever be able to make compensation for their pecuniary failures. The system of quotas and requisitions, whether it be applied to men or money, is, in every view, a system of imbecility in the Union, and of inequality and injustice among the members.

The right of equal suffrage among the States is another exceptionable part of the Confederation. Every idea of proportion and every rule of fair representation conspire to condemn a principle, which gives to Rhode Island an equal weight in the scale of power with Massachusetts, or Connecticut, or New York; and to Delaware an equal voice in the national deliberations with Pennsylvania, or Virginia, or North Carolina. Its operation contradicts the fundamental maxim of republican government, which requires that the sense of the majority should prevail. Sophistry may reply, that sovereigns are equal, and that a majority of the votes of the States will be a majority of confederated America. But this kind of logical legerdemain will never counteract the plain suggestions of justice and common-sense. It may happen that this majority of States is a small minority of the people of America*; and two thirds of the people of America could not long be persuaded, upon the credit of artificial distinction and syllogistic subtleties, to submit their interests to the management and disposal of one third. . . .

It may be objected to this, that not seven but nine States, or two thirds of the whole number, must consent to the most important resolutions; and it may be thence inferred, that nine States would always comprehend a majority of the Union. But this does not obviate the impropriety of an equal vote between States of the most unequal dimensions and populousness; nor is the inference accurate in point of fact; for we can enumerate nine States which contain less than a majority of the people†; and it is constitutionally possible that these nine may give the vote. . . .

But this is not all: what at first sight may seem a remedy, is, in reality, a poison. To give a minority a negative upon the majority (which is always the case where more than a majority is requisite to a decision), is, in its tendency, to subject the sense of the greater number to that of the lesser. Congress, from the non-attendance of a few States, have been frequently in the situation of a Polish diet, where a single VETO has been sufficient to put a stop to all their movements. A sixtieth part of the Union, which is about the proportion of Delaware and Rhode Island, has several times been able to oppose an entire bar to its operations. This is one of those refinements which, in practice, has an effect the reverse of what is expected from it in theory. The necessity of unanimity in public bodies, or of something approaching towards it, has been founded upon a supposition that it would contribute to security. But its real operation is to embarrass the administration, to destroy the energy of the government, and to substitute the pleasure, caprice, or artifices of an insignificant, turbulent, or corrupt junto, to the regular deliberations and decisions of a respectable majority. In those emergencies of a nation, in which the goodness or badness, the weakness or strength of its government, is of the greatest importance, there is commonly a necessity for action. The public business must, in some way or other, go forward. If a pertinacious minority can control the opinion of a majority, respecting the best mode of conducting it, the majority, in order that something may be done, must conform to the views of the minority; and thus the sense of the smaller number will overrule that of the greater, and give a tone to the national proceedings. . . .

It is not difficult to discover, that a principle of this kind gives greater scope to foreign corruption, as well as to domestic faction, than

* New Hampshire, Rhode Island, New Jersey, Delaware, Georgia, South Carolina, and Maryland are a majority of the whole number of the States, but they do not contain one third of the people.—PUBLIUS

† Add New York and Connecticut to the foregoing seven, and they will be less than a majority.—PUBLIUS

that which permits the sense of the majority to decide; though the contrary of this has been presumed. The mistake has proceeded from not attending with due care to the mischiefs that may be occasioned by obstructing the progress of government at certain critical seasons. When the concurrence of a large number is required by the Constitution to the doing of any national act, we are apt to rest satisfied that all is safe, because nothing improper will be likely *to be done;* but we forget how much good may be prevented, and how much ill may be produced, by the power of hindering the doing what may be necessary, and of keeping affairs in the same unfavorable posture in which they may happen to stand at particular periods.

Suppose, for instance, we were engaged in a war, in conjunction with one foreign nation, against another. Suppose the necessity of our situation demanded peace, and the interest or ambition of our ally led him to seek the prosecution of war, with views that might justify us in making separate terms. In such a state of things, this ally of ours would evidently find it much easier, by his bribes and intrigues, to tie up the hands of government from making peace, where two thirds of all the votes were requisite to that object, than where a simple majority would suffice. In the first case, he would have to corrupt a smaller number; in the last, a greater number. . . .

Evils of this description ought not to be regarded as imaginary. One of the weak sides of republics, among their numerous advantages, is that they afford too easy an inlet to foreign corruption. An hereditary monarch, though often disposed to sacrifice his subjects to his ambition, has so great a personal interest in the government and in the external glory of the nation, that it is not easy for a foreign power to give him the equivalent for what he would sacrifice by treachery to the state. The world has accordingly been witness to few examples of this species of royal prostitution, though there have been abundant specimens of every other kind.

In republics, persons elevated from the mass of the community, by the suffrages of their fellow-citizens, to stations of great preeminence and power, may find compensations for betraying their trust, which, to any but minds animated and guided by superior virtue, may appear to exceed the proportion of interest they have in the common stock, and to overbalance the obligations of duty. Hence it is that history furnishes us with so many mortifying examples of the prevalency of foreign corruption in republican governments. . . .

A circumstance which crowns the defects of the Confederation remains yet to be mentioned,—the want of a judiciary power. Laws are a dead letter without courts to expound and define their true meaning and operation. The treaties of the United States, to have force at all, must be considered as part of the law of the land. Their true import, as far as respects individuals, must, like all other laws, be ascertained by judicial determinations. To produce uniformity in these determinations, they ought to be submitted, in the last resort, to one SUPREME TRIBUNAL. . . .

The treaties of the United States, under the present Constitution, are liable to the infractions of thirteen different legislatures, and as many different courts of final jurisdiction, acting under the authority of those legislatures. The faith, the reputation, the peace of the whole Union, are thus continually at the mercy of the prejudices, the passions, and the interests of every member of which it is composed. Is it possible that foreign nations can either respect or confide in such a government? Is it possible that the people of America will longer consent to trust their honor, their happiness, their safety, on so precarious a foundation?

In this review of the Confederation, I have confined myself to the exhibition of its most material defects; passing over those imperfections in its details by which even a great part of the power intended to be conferred upon it has been in a great measure rendered abortive. It must be by this time evident to all men of reflection, who can divest themselves of the prepossessions of preconceived opinions, that it is a system so radically vicious and unsound, as to admit not of amendment but by an entire change in its leading features and characters.

The organization of Congress is itself utterly improper for the exercise of those powers which are necessary to be deposited in the Union. A single assembly may be a proper receptacle of those slender, or rather fettered, authorities, which have been heretofore delegated to the federal head; but it would be inconsistent with all the principles of good government, to intrust it with those additional powers which, even the moderate and more rational adversaries of the proposed Constitution admit, ought to reside in the United States. If that plan should not be adopted, and if the necessity of the Union should be able to withstand the ambitious aims of those men who may indulge magnificent schemes of personal aggrandizement from its dissolution, the probability would be, that we should run into the project of conferring supplemental powers upon Congress, as they are now constituted; and either the machine, from the intrinsic feebleness of its structure, will moulder into pieces, in spite of our ill-judged efforts to prop it; or, by successive augmentations of its force and energy, as necessity might prompt, we shall finally accumulate, in a single body, all the most important prerogatives of sovereignty, and thus entail upon our posterity one of the most execrable forms of government that human infatuation ever contrived. Thus we should create in reality that very tyranny which the adversaries of the new Constitution either are, or affect to be, solicitous to avert.

It has not a little contributed to the infirmities of the existing federal system, that it never had a ratification by the PEOPLE. Resting on no better foundation than the consent of the several legislatures, it has been exposed to frequent and intricate questions concerning the validity of its powers, and has, in some instances, given birth to the enormous doctrine of a right of legislative repeal. Owing its ratification to the law of a State, it has been contended that the same authority might repeal the law by which it was ratified. However gross a heresy it may be to maintain that a *party* to a *compact* has a right to revoke that *compact*, the doctrine itself has had respectable advocates. The possibility of a question of this nature proves the necessity of laying the foundations of our national government deeper than in the mere sanction of delegated authority. The fabric of American empire ought to rest on the solid basis of THE CONSENT OF THE PEOPLE. The streams of national power ought to flow immediately from that pure, original fountain of all legitimate authority.

—*The Federalist* No. 22.

[June 20, 1788]

. . . I will not agree with gentlemen who trifle with the weaknesses of our country; and suppose that they are enumerated to answer a party purpose, and to terrify with ideal dangers. No; I believe these weaknesses to be real, and pregnant with destruction. Yet, however weak our country may be, I hope we shall never sacrifice our liberties. If therefore, on a full and candid discussion, the proposed system shall appear to have that tendency, for God's sake, let us reject it! But, let us not mistake words for things, nor accept doubtful surmises as evidence of truth.

—Speech on the Compromises of the Constitution, in *Debates and Proceedings of the Con-Poughkeepsie on the 17th June 1788 to deliberate on the Form of Federal Government recom-vention of the State of New York, Assembled at mended by the General Convention of Philadelphia*. Taken in Short Hand. (New York: Francis Childs, 1788), p. 21.

June 21, 1788

Suggestions, Sir, of an extraordinary nature have been frequently thrown out in the course of the present political controversy. It gives me pain to dwell on topics of this kind; and I wish they might be dismissed. We have been told that the old Confederation has proved inefficacious, only because intriguing and powerful men, aiming at a revolution, have been for ever instigating the people and rendering them disaffected to it. This, Sir, is a false insinuation. I will venture to assert that no combination of designing men under Heaven will be capable of making a government unpopular which is in its principles a wise and good one, and vigorous in its operations.

The Confederation was framed amidst the agitation and tumult of society. It was composed of unsound materials, put together in haste. Men of intelligence discovered the feebleness of the structure in the first stages of its existence, but the great body of the people, too much engrossed with their distresses to contemplate any but the immediate cause of them, were ignorant of the defects of their Constitution. But, when the dangers of war were removed, they saw clearly what they had suffered, and what they had yet to suffer from a feeble form of government. There was no need of discerning men to convince the people of their unhappy situation. The complaint was co-extensive with the evil, and both were common to all classes of the community.

—Speech on the Constitution, *Debates of the N.Y. Convention*, p. 40.

An Expanding Nation: New States and the West

The first test of Hamilton's principle of government by consent of the governed came when the issue of Vermont's independence aroused the inhabitants of New York. The area of Vermont had long been claimed by New York, a claim which had been recognized by the British government. The settlers of the Green Mountain State declared their independence in 1777. Failing to obtain recognition from Congress, Ethan Allen and his brother Ira entered into negotiations with Governor Haldimand of Canada with a view to making Vermont a British province. Whether the Allens meant business will never be determined. Hamilton's fair-minded stand led to New York's agreement to recognize the territorial claims of Vermont, and in 1791 that state was admitted into the Union.

April [1787]

The first objection is drawn from that great principle of the social compact,—that the chief object of government is to protect the rights of individuals by the united strength of the community. The justness of this principle is not to be disputed, but its extent remains to be ascertained. It must be taken with this limitation: The united strength of the community ought to be exerted for the protection of individuals so far as there is a rational prospect of success; so far as is consistent with the safety and well-being of the whole. The duty of a nation is always limited by these considerations: It is bound to make efforts and encounter hazards for the protection of its members, proportioned to its abilities, warranted by a reasonable expectation of a favorable issue, and compatible with its eventual security. But it is not bound to enter into or prosecute enterprises of a manifest rashness and folly;

or which, in the event of success, would be productive of more mischief than good. . . .

The tendency of the principle contended for, on the application of it in argument, has been to prove that the State ought to employ the common strength of the society to protect the rights of its citizens, interested in the district of territory in question, by reducing the revolted inhabitants of that district to an obedience to its laws. The inquiry therefore is: Can this be done? Is the State in a situation to undertake it? Is there a probability that the object will be more attainable at a future day? Is there not rather a probability that it will be every day more out of our reach, and that leaving things in their present state will be attended with serious dangers and inconveniences? Is it even desirable, if practicable, to reduce the people in question under subjection to this State?

In pursuing this inquiry we ought to bear in mind that a nation is never to regulate its conduct by remote possibilities or mere contingencies, but by such probability as may reasonably be inferred from the existing state of things and the usual course of human affairs. . . .

The scheme of coercion would ill suit even the disposition of our own citizens. The habits of thinking to which the Revolution has given birth, are not adapted to the idea of a contest for dominion over a people disinclined to live under our government. And, in reality, it is not the interest of the State ever to regain dominion over them by force. We shall do well to advert to the nature of our government, and to the extent of this State, according to its acknowledged limits. Are we sure we shall be able to govern what we already possess? or would it be wise to wish to try the strength of our government over a numerous body of people disaffected to it, and compelled to submit to its authority by force? For my part I should regard the reunion of Vermont to this State as one of the greatest evils that could befall it; as a source of continual embarrassment and disquietude. . . .

. . . the policy of the measure results from two important considerations. The one, that by the union of Vermont to the Confederacy, it must of course bear a proportion of the public burdens; the other, that it would be detached from the completion of a connection, already in all appearance begun, with a foreign power. The incorporation of Vermont into the Confederacy is by the bill made an express condition of the acknowledgment of their independence. . . .

But laying aside every supposition of this nature, there are motives of interest which would dispose the British Government to cultivate Vermont. A connection with Vermont will hereafter conduce to the security of Canada, and to the preservation of the Western posts. That Great Britain means to retain these posts, may be inferred from the interest she has in doing it. The ostensible reason for not having delivered them up heretofore, is the infractions of the treaty on our part; but though these infractions in some instances cannot be denied, it may fairly be presumed that they are nothing more than the pretext for withholding the posts, while the true motive is the prodigious advantage which the monopoly of the fur trade affords to the commerce of the English nation. . . .

I shall say a little in answer to these observations drawn from the examples of Roman magnanimity. Neither the manners nor the genius of Rome are suited to the republic or to the age we live in. All her maxims and habits were military; her government was constituted for war. Ours is unfit for it; and our situation, still less than our Constitution, invites us to emulate the conduct of Rome, or to attempt a display of unprofitable heroism.

—Speech in the New York Assembly. *Hamilton,* II, 376, 377, 379, 383, 385, 389.

Tied in to the admission of Vermont was the application of Kentucky for statehood, one balancing the other in the sectional alignment. John Brown, the Virginia delegate who was spokesman for Kentucky, regarded Hamilton as the leader of the eastern opposition. The following resolution did not result in quick action, as the committee set up thereunder reported that Congress under the Articles lacked the power to act and the question was deferred for determination by the new government. At the Poughkeepsie Convention Hamilton took the early admission of Kentucky for granted. It came about in 1792.

June 2, 1788

Resolved, That in their opinion it is expedient that the District of Kentucke be erected into an independent State, and they therefore submit the following resolution—That the address and resolutions from the District of Kentucke, with the acts of the Legislature of Virginia therein specified, be referred to a committee of [a member from each State], to prepare and report a proper act for acceding to the independence of the said District of Kentucke, and for receiving the same into the Union as a member thereof, in a mode conformable to the Articles of Confederation.

—Resolution in Congress. *Hamilton,* II, 426.

Hamilton's "Report of a Uniform System for the Disposition of the Lands" reflected the views of Eastern business interests who were more interested in land speculation than in actual settlement, along with his own interest, as Secretary of the Treasury, in securing revenue. Hence, the plan gave priority to revenue from sales to big speculators over actual farmers. One surprisingly democratic feature of the plan was his proposal of a price of thirty cents per acre as against two dollars per acre fixed under the Land Act of 1796.

July 22, 1790

That on the formation of a plan for the disposition of the vacant lands of the United States, there appears [*sic*] to be two leading objects of consideration: one, the facility of advantageous sale according to the probable course of purchases; the other, the accommodation of individuals now inhabiting the western country, or who may hereafter emigrate thither.

The former, as an operation of finance, claims primary attention; the latter is important, as it relates to the satisfaction of the inhabitants of the western country. It is desirable, and it does not appear impracticable, to conciliate both. . . .

That no land shall be sold, except such in respect to which the titles of the Indian tribes shall have been previously extinguished.

That a sufficient tract or tracts shall be reserved and set apart for satisfying the subscribers to the proposed loan in the public debt; but that no location shall be for less than five hundred acres.

That convenient tracts shall from time to time be set apart for the purpose of locations by actual settlers, in quantities not exceeding to one person one hundred acres.

That other tracts shall from time to time be set apart for sales in townships of ten miles square, except where they shall adjoin upon a boundary of some prior grant, or of a tract so set apart, in which cases there shall be no greater departure from such form of location than may be absolutely necessary. . . .

That the price shall be thirty cents per acre, to be paid either in gold or silver, or in public securities, computing those which shall bear an immediate interest of six per cent. as at par with gold and silver; and those which shall bear a future or less interest, if any there shall be, at a proportional value.

—To the House of Representatives. *Hamilton*, III, 84-85, 86.

Hamilton was properly concerned about securing peace on the frontiers and fair dealings for the Indians. Citizen Edmond Genêt, the fiery French minister to the United States, had other ideas. He backed a military expedition against Spanish Louisiana. George Rogers Clark was made major general of the "Independent and Revolutionary Legion of the Mississippi" and the secret approval of Secretary of State Jefferson was obtained for the expedition. After Genêt's recall the movement collapsed, but Hamilton remained on the constant alert.

September 25, 1794

. . . The obligation upon the United States to afford adequate protection to the inhabitants of the frontiers is no doubt of the highest and most sacred kind. But there is a duty no less strong upon those inhabitants to avoid giving occasion to hostilities by an irregular and improper conduct, and upon the local governments sincerely and effectually to punish and repress instances of such conduct, and the spirit which produces them. If these inhabitants can with impunity thwart all the measures of the United States for restoring or preserving peace, if they can with impunity commit depredations and outrages upon the Indians, and that in violation of the faith of the United States, pledged not only in their general treaties, but even in the special (and among all nations peculiarly sacred) case of a safe conduct, as in the instance of the attack upon the Indians while encamped within our protection, on the 10th of May last, can it be surprising if such circumstances should abate the alacrity of the national councils to encounter those heavy expenses which the protection of the frontiers occasions, and the readiness of the citizens of the United States distant from the scenes of danger to acquiesce in the burdens they produce?

. . . The President learns with great pleasure the measures your Excellency had begun and was about to pursue for the removal of the settlers under General Clarke. It is impossible to conceive a settlement more unjustifiable in its pretexts, or more dangerous in its principle than that which he is attempting. It is not only a high-handed usurpation of the rights of the general and State governments, and a most unwarrantable encroachment upon those of the Indians, but proceeding upon the idea of a separate and independent government, to be erected on a *military basis,* it is essentially hostile to our republican systems of government, and is pregnant with incalculable mischiefs. It deeply concerns the great interests of the country that such an establishment should not be permitted to take root, and that the example should be checked by adequate punishment, in doing which no time is to be lost, for such is the nature of the establishment that it may be expected rapidly to attain to a formidable magnitude, involving great expense and trouble to subvert it.

—To George Matthews, Governor of Georgia.
Hamilton, V, 33-37.

Hamilton wanted a balanced national economy. He did not want a rapid expansion of the West to take place at the expense of Eastern development. At the same time, he recognized the deep sectional sentiment that prevailed in the West and was concerned about keeping the region loyal to the union.

[1795-98]

No one has been more uniformly nor more entirely than myself in favor of the system of giving a free course to the population and settlement of our interior country, and of securing to it by the best efforts of the government the enjoyment of those collateral advantages on which its prosperity must depend. This, in my opinion, is preferable as the most natural policy, and as that which will best secure and cement the unity of the empire. But with this policy adopted, in my most unqualified manner, I am far from regarding it as wise to give or occasion any extraordinary impulse to a transfer of people from the settled to the unsettled parts of the country. This is to retard the progress in general improvement, and to impair for a greater length of time the vigor of the nation, by scattering too widely and sparsely the elements of resource and strength. It is to weaken government by enlarging too rapidly the sphere of its action, and weakening by stretching out the links of connection between the different parts.

The true politician will content himself by seeing new settlements formed by the current of a redundant population; he will submit, because it is unnatural, and would be fruitless and unwise, to oppose even a greater transfer than the mere surplus, by the attractions to emigration which new countries hold out; he will seek to tie the emigrants to the friends and brethren they have, by a kind and liberal conduct of the government towards them, by efficacious protection, and by sincere, persevering, and energetic endeavors to obtain for them the free and full enjoyment of those rights and advantages which local situation requires. But he will not accelerate this transfer by accumulating artificial disadvantages on the already settled parts of the country; he will even endeavor to avoid this by removing such disadvantages if casual causes have produced them.

—"Defence of the Funding System," II. Hamilton Papers, 1st ser.

October 31, 1799

In regard to the citizens of the Western country, as far as your agency may be concerned, you will do every thing to foster goodwill and attachment toward the Government of the United States. A firm and cordial union is certainly the vital interest of every part of our country.

—To Wilkinson. Draft in Hamilton's hand. Hamilton Papers, 1st ser.

Hamilton's ideas on Louisiana constituted a curious blend of prophetic vision and obtuseness. Perhaps his judgment was colored by his lack of confidence in the administration responsible for the final negotiations. Thus, he was wrong when he said that there was no chance of buying the territory, but his brilliant analysis of the military and diplomatic reasons for Napoleon's sale to the American commissioners demonstrated his masterly grasp of international affairs. Again, his fear that constitutional government could not control such vast stretches of settled land led him to underestimate the importance of western settlement. Hamilton's interest in the West was commercial rather than agricultural. Over the years various plans had been concocted to seize or dismember the West. Hamilton's arch-foe, Aaron Burr, was to evolve some such plan within a few years, but he scattered his shots in so many directions that he fooled everybody about his exact intentions, including his closest confederates.

March 27, 1798

If *Spain* would cede Louisiana to the United States, I would accept it absolutely if obtainable absolutely, or with an engagement to *restore*, if it cannot be obtained absolutely.

—To Timothy Pickering. Hamilton's hand. Hamilton Papers, 1st ser.

GRANGE (NEW YORK) December 29, 1802

. . . You know my general theory as to our Western affairs. I have always held that the *unity of our empire* and the best interests of our nation require that we shall annex to the United States all the territory east of the Mississippi, New Orleans included. Of course I infer that, in an emergency like the present, energy is wisdom.

—To General Charles Cotesworth Pinckney. *Hamilton*, VI, 551-552.

February 8, 1803

Since the question of independence, none has occurred more deeply interesting to the United States than the cession of Louisiana to France. This event threatens the early dismemberment of a large portion of the country; more immediately, the safety of all the Southern States; and remotely, the independence of the whole Union. . . .

The strict right to resort at once to WAR, if it should be deemed expedient, cannot be doubted. . . .

The whole is then a question of expediency. Two courses only present: First, to negotiate, and endeavor to purchase; and if this fails, to go to war. Secondly, to seize at once on the Floridas and New Orleans, and then negotiate.

A strong objection offers itself to the first. There is not the most distant probability that the ambitious and aggrandizing views of Buonaparte will commute the territory for money. Its acquisition is of immense importance to France, and has long been an object of her extreme solicitude. The attempt, therefore, to purchase, in the first instance, will certainly fail; and in the end, war must be resorted to, under all the accumulation of difficulties caused by a previous and strongly fortified possession of the country by our adversary.

The second plan is, therefore, evidently the best. First, because effectual; the acquisition easy; the preservation afterwards easy. The evils of a war with France at this time are certainly not very formidable: her fleet crippled and powerless; her treasury empty; her resources almost dried up; in short, gasping for breath after a tremendous conflict, which, though it left her victorious, left her nearly exhausted under her extraordinary exertions. On the other hand, we might count with certainty on the aid of Great Britain with her powerful navy.

Secondly, this plan is preferable, because it affords us the only chance of avoiding a long-continued war. When we have once taken possession the business will present itself to France in a new aspect. She will then have to weigh the immense difficulties, if not the utter impracticability, of wresting it from us. In this posture of affairs she will naturally conclude it is her interest to bargain. Now it may become expedient to terminate hostilities by a purchase, and a cheaper one may reasonably be expected.

—"Pericles," *New York Evening Post*, February 8, 1803.

July 5, 1803

Purchase of Louisiana.—At length the business of New Orleans has terminated favorably to this country. Instead of being obliged to rely any longer on the force of treaties, for a place of deposit, the jurisdiction of the territory is now transferred to our hands and in future the navigation of the Mississippi will be ours unmolested. This, it will be allowed, is an important acquisition; not, indeed, as territory, but as being essential to the peace and prosperity of our Western country, and as opening a free and valuable market to our commercial states. This purchase has been made during the period of Mr. Jefferson's presidency, and will, doubtless, give eclat to his administration. Every man, however, possessed of the least candor and reflection will readily acknowledge that the acquisition has been soley owing to a fortuitous concurrence of unforeseen and unexpected circumstances, and not to any wise or vigorous measures on the part of the American government.

As soon as we experienced from Spain a direct infraction of an important article of our treaty, in withholding the deposit of New Orleans, it afforded us justifiable cause of war, and authorized immediate hostilities. Sound policy unquestionably demanded of us to begin with a prompt, bold and vigorous resistance against the injustice; to seize the object at once; and having this *vantage ground*, should we have thought it advisable to terminate hostilities by a purchase, we might then have done it on almost our own terms. This course, however, was not adopted, and we were about to experience the fruits of our folly, when another nation has found it her interest to place the French Government in a situation substantially as favorable to our views and interest as those recommended by the federal party here, excepting indeed that we should probably have obtained the same object on better terms.

On the part of France the short interval of peace has been wasted in repeated and fruitless efforts to subjugate St. Domingo; and those means which were originally destined to the colonization of Louisiana had been gradually exhausted by the unexpected difficulties of this ill-starred enterprise.

To the deadly climate of St. Domingo, and to the courage and obstinate resistance made by its black inhabitants are we indebted for the obstacles which delayed the colonization of Louisiana, till the auspicious moment, when a rupture between England and France gave a new turn to the projects of the latter, and destroyed at once all her schemes as to this favorite object of her ambition.

It was made known to Bonaparte that among the first objects of England would be the seizure of New Orleans, and that preparations were even then in a state of forwardness for that purpose. The First Consul could not doubt, that if an English fleet was sent thither, the place must fall without resistance; it was obvious, therefore, that it would be in every shape preferable that it should be placed in the possession of a neutral power; and when, besides, some millions of money, of which he was extremely in want, were offered him, to part with what he could no longer hold, it affords a moral certainty that it was to an accidental state of circumstances, and not to wise plans, that this cession, at this time, has been owing. . . . The real truth is, Bonaparte found himself absolutely compelled by situation to relinquish his darling plan of colonizing the banks of the Mississippi; and thus have the Government of the United States, by the unforeseen operation of events, gained what the feebleness and pusillanimity of its miserable system of measures could never have acquired.—Let us then, with all due humility, acknowledge this as another of those signal instances of the kind interpositions of an over-ruling Providence, which we more especially experienced during our Revolutionary War, and by which we have more than once been saved from the consequences of our errors and perverseness.

We are certainly not disposed to lessen the importance of this acquisition to the country, but it is proper that the public should be correctly informed of its real value and extent as well as of the terms on which it has been acquired. . . .

Those disposed to magnify its values will say, that this western region is important as keeping off a troublesome neighbor, and leaving us in the quiet possession of the Mississippi. Undoubtedly this has some force, but on the other hand it may be said, that the acquisition of New Orleans is perfectly adequate to every purpose; for whoever is in possession of that has the uncontrolled command of the river. Again, it may be said, and this probably is the most favorable point of view in which it can be placed, that although not valuable to the United States for settlement, it is so to Spain, and will become more so, and therefore at some distant period will form an object which we may barter with her for the Floridas, obviously of far greater value to us than all the immense, undefined region west of the river.

It has been usual for the American writers on this subject to include the Floridas in their ideas of Louisiana, as the French formerly did, and the acquisition has derived no inconsiderable portion of its value and importance with the public from this view of it. It may, however, be relied on, that no part of the Floridas, not a foot of land on the east of the Mississippi, excepting New Orleans, falls within the present cession. As to the unbounded region west of the Mississippi, it is, with the exception of a very few settlements of Spaniards and Frenchmen bordering on the banks of the river, a wilderness through which wander numerous tribes of Indians. And when we consider the present extent of the United States, and that not one sixteenth part of its territory is yet under occupation, the advantage of the acquisition, as it relates to actual settlement, appears too distant and remote to strike the mind of a sober politician with much force. This, therefore, can only rest in speculation for many years, if not centuries to come, and consequently will not perhaps be allowed very great weight in the account by the majority of readers. But it may be added, that should our own citizens, more enterprising than wise, become desirous of settling this country, and emigrate thither, it must not only be attended with all the injuries of a too widely dispersed population, but by adding to the great weight of the western part of our territory, must hasten the dismemberment of a large portion of our country, or a dissolution of the government. On the whole, we think it may with candor be said, that whether the possession at this time of any territory west of the river Mississippi will be advantageous, is at best extremely problematical. For ourselves, we are very much inclined to the opinion, that after all, it is the Island of New Orleans by which the command of a free navigation of the Mississippi is secured, that gives to this interesting cession its greatest value and will render it in every view of immense benefit to our country. By this cession we hereafter shall hold within our own grasp, what we have heretofore enjoyed only by the uncertain tenure of a treaty, which might be broken at the pleasure of another, and (governed as we now are) with perfect impunity. Provided therefore we have not purchased it too dear, there is all the reason for exultation which the friends of the administration display, and which all Americans may be allowed to feel.

—*N. Y. Evening Post*, July 5, 1803.

4

On Government: Some Guiding Principles

A Monarchy versus a Republic

I am affectionately attached to the republican theory.

Because Hamilton at the Constitutional Convention had expressed his admiration of the constitutional monarchy of Great Britain and favored a "high tone" for the new government, he was time after time charged with harboring monarchical sentiments and even of being privy to alleged plots to place a European prince at the head of the new national government. Hamilton frankly conceded that a monarchy was not in tune with American sentiment and stanchly supported the principles of republicanism. Even at the end of his career the ugly rumor of his attachment to monarchical schemes was spread by political opponents. Hamilton quickly scotched this smear campaign and convincingly disavowed harboring such "un-American" ideas. "However much we may differ on other political subjects," wrote his old foe, George Clinton, "we agree in sentiment in this." Such a charge against Hamilton was termed by Clinton as "odious and disreputable."

January 19, 1787

I CANNOT FORBEAR remarking that it is a common artifice to endeavor to insinuate a resemblance between the king under the former government and Congress, although no two things could be more unlike each other. Nothing can be more dissimilar than a monarch, permanent, hereditary, the source of honor and emolument; and a republican body, composed of individuals appointed annually, liable to be recalled within the year, and subject to a continual rotation, which, with few exceptions, is the fountain neither of honor nor emolument. If we exercise our judgments, we shall plainly see that no such resemblance exists, and that all inferences deducted from the comparison must be false.

Upon every occasion, however foreign such observations may be, we hear a loud cry raised about the danger of intrusting power to Congress; we are told it is dangerous to trust power anywhere; that power is liable to abuse,—with a variety of trite maxims of the same kind. General propositions of this nature are easily framed, the truth of which cannot be denied, but they rarely convey any precise idea. To these we might oppose other propositions, equally true and equally indefinite. It might be said that too little power is as dangerous as too much; that it leads to anarchy, and from anarchy to despotism. But the question still recurs: What is the too much or too little? Where is the measure or standard to ascertain the happy mean?

Power must be granted, or civil society cannot exist; the possibility of abuse is no argument against the thing. This possibility is incident to every species of power, however placed or modified.

—Speech to the New York Assembly. *Works,* VIII, 15-16.

June 21, 1788

. . . We have been told that the spirit of patriotism and love of liberty are almost extinguished among the people, and that it has become a prevailing doctrine, that republican principles ought to be hooted out of the world. Sir, I am confident that such remarks as these are rather occasioned by the heat of argument, than by a cool conviction of their truth and justice. As far as my experience has extended, I have heard no such doctrine, nor have I discovered any diminution of regard for those rights and liberties, in defence of which the people have fought and suffered. There have been, undoubtedly, some men who have had speculative doubts on the subject of government, but the principles of republicanism are founded on too firm a basis to be shaken by a few speculative and skeptical reasoners. Our error has been of a very different kind. We have erred through excess of caution, and a zeal false and impracticable. Our counsels have been destitute of consistency and stability. I am flattered with a hope, Sir, that we have now found a cure for the evils under which we have so long labored. I trust that the proposed Constitution affords a genuine specimen of representative and republican government; and that it will answer, in an eminent degree, all the beneficial purposes of society.

—Speech on the Constitution, *Debates of the N.Y. Convention,* pp. 40, 41.

June 24, 1788

. . . We all, with equal sincerity, profess to be anxious for the establishment of a republican government, on a safe and solid basis. It is the object of the wishes of every honest man in the United States;

and I presume I shall not be disbelieved when I declare, that it is an object, of all others, the nearest and most dear to my own heart. The means of accomplishing this great purpose become the most important study which can interest mankind.

—Speech on the United States Senate, *Debates of the N.Y. Convention*, p. 70.

May 26, 1792

A word on another point. I am told that serious apprehensions are disseminated in your State as to the existence of a monarchical party meditating the destruction of State and republican government. If it is possible that so absurd an idea can gain ground, it is necessary that it should be combated. I assure you, on my private faith and honor as a man, that there is not, in my judgment, a shadow of foundation for it. A very small number of men indeed may entertain theories less republican than Mr. Jefferson and Mr. Madison, but I am persuaded there is not a man among them who would not regard as both criminal and visionary any attempt to subvert the republican system of the country. . . .

As to my own political creed, I give it to you with the utmost sincerity. I am affectionately attached to the republican theory. I desire above all things to see the equality of political rights, exclusive of all hereditary distinction, firmly established by a practical demonstration of its being consistent with the order and happiness of society. As to State governments, the prevailing bias of my judgment is that if they can be circumscribed within bounds, consistent with the preservation of the national government, they will prove useful and salutary. . . . As to any combination to prostrate the State governments, I disavow and deny it. From an apprehension lest the judiciary should not work efficiently or harmoniously, I have been desirous of seeing some national scheme of connection adopted as an amendment to the Constitution, otherwise I am for maintaining things as they are; though I doubt much the possibility of it, from a tendency in the nature of things towards the preponderancy of the state governments.

I said that I was affectionately attached to the republican theory. This is the real language of my heart, which I open to you in the sincerity of friendship; and I add that I have strong hopes of the success of that theory; but, in candor, I ought also to add that I am far from being without doubts. I consider its success as yet a problem. It is yet to be determined by experience whether it be consistent with that stability and order in government which are essential to public strength and private security and happiness.

On the whole, the only enemy which Republicanism has to fear in this country is in the spirit of faction and anarchy. . . .

If I were disposed to promote monarchy and overthrow State

governments, I would mount the hobby-horse of popularity; I would cry out "usurpation," "danger to liberty," etc., etc.; I would endeavor to prostrate the national government, raise a ferment, and then "ride in the whirlwind, and direct the storm." That there are men acting with Jefferson and Madison who have this in view, I verily believe; I could lay my finger on some of them. That Madison does not mean it, I also verily believe; and I rather believe the same of Jefferson, but I read him upon the whole thus: "A man of profound ambition and violent passions."

—To Colonel Edward Carrington. *Works*, IX, 532-535.

August 18, 1792

OBJECTION 14.—The ultimate object of all [this is to prepare the way for a change from the present republican form of government to that of a monarchy, of which the British constitution is to be the model.]*

ANSWER.—To this there is no other answer than a flat denial, except this: that the project, from its absurdity, refutes itself.

The idea of introducing a monarchy or aristocracy into this country, by employing the influence and force of a government continually changing hands, toward it, is one of those visionary things that none but madmen could meditate, and that no wise man will believe.

If it could be done at all, which is utterly incredible, it would require a long series of time, certainly beyond the life of any individual, to effect it. Who, then, would enter into such a plot? for what purpose of interest or ambition?

To hope that the people may be cajoled into giving their sanctions to such institutions is still more chimerical. A people so enlightened and so diversified as the people of this country can surely never be brought to it, but from convulsions and disorders, in consequence of the arts of popular demagogues.

The truth unquestionably is, that the only path to a subversion of the republican system of the country is by flattering the prejudices of the people, and exciting their jealousies and apprehensions, to throw affairs into confusion, and bring on civil commotion. Tired at length of anarchy or want of government, they may take shelter in the arms of monarchy for repose and security.

Those, then, who resist a confirmation of public order are the true artificers of monarchy. Not that this is the intention of the generality of them. Yet it would not be difficult to lay the finger upon some of their party who may justly be suspected. When a man, unprincipled in private life, desperate in his fortune, bold in his temper, possessed of considerable talents, having the advantage of military habits, despotic in his ordinary demeanor, known to have

* Material in brackets not found in Hamilton's own draft, but supplied by Lodge.

scoffed in private at the principles of liberty; when such a man is seen to mount the hobby-horse of popularity, to join in the cry of danger to liberty, to take every opportunity of embarrassing the general government and bringing it under suspicion, to flatter and fall in with all the nonsense of the zealots of the day, it may justly be suspected that his object is to throw things into confusion, that he may "ride the storm and direct the whirlwind."[1]

It has aptly been observed, that *Cato* was the Tory, *Caesar* the Whig of his day. The former frequently resisted, the latter always flattered, the follies of the people. Yet the former perished with the republic—the latter destroyed it. . . .

No popular government was ever without its Catilines and its Caesars—these are its true enemies. . . .

It is curious to observe the anticipations of the different parties. One side appears to believe that there is a serious plot to overturn the State governments, and substitute a monarchy to the present republican system. The other side firmly believes that there is a serious plot to overturn the general government, and elevate the separate power of the States upon its ruins. Both sides may be equally wrong, and their mutual jealousies may be naturally causes of the appearances which mutually disturb them and sharpen them against each other.

OBJECTION 15.—This charge, [that this change (i. e., from a republic to a monarchy) was contemplated in the convention, they say is no secret, because its partisans have made none of it—to effect it then was impracticable; but they are still eager after their object, and are predisposing every thing for its ultimate attainment.]*

ANSWER.—This is a palpable misrepresentation. No man that I know of contemplated the introducing into this country a monarchy. A very small number (not more than three or four) manifested theoretical opinions favorable in the abstract to a constitution like that of Great Britain; but every one agreed that such a constitution, except as to the general distribution of departments and powers, was out of the question in reference to this country. The member who was most explicit on this point (a member from New York) declared in strong terms that the republican theory ought to be adhered to in this country as long as there was any chance of its success; that the idea of a perfect equality of political rights among the citizens, exclusive of all permanent or hereditary distinctions, was of a nature to engage the good wishes of every good man, whatever might be his theoretic doubts; that it merited his best efforts to give success to it in practice; that hitherto, from an incompetent structure of the government, it had not had a fair trial, and that the endeavor ought then to

[1] Hamilton is referring to Aaron Burr, at that time a candidate for the Vice-Presidency.—Ed.

* Not in draft.

be to secure to it a better chance of success by a government more capable of energy and order.

There is not a man at present in either branch of the Legislature who, that I recollect, had held language in the convention favorable to monarchy.

The basis, therefore, of this suggestion fails.

—To Washington, "Objections and Answers Respecting the Administration of the Government." Hamilton Papers, 1st ser.

September 11, 1792

A writer in the Gazette of Saturday last, after several observations with regard to certain charges which have been lately brought forward against the Secretary of State, proceeds to make or insinuate several charges against another political character. . . .

As to the charges which have been brought against the other public character alluded to, I shall assert, generally, from a long, intimate, and confidential acquaintance with him, added to some other means of information, that the matters charged, as far as they are intelligible, are either grossly misrepresented or palpably untrue. . . .

The charge of which I shall take more particular notice, is contained in the following passage:

"Let him explain the public character, who, if uncontradicted fame is to be regarded, *opposed* the Constitution in the Grand Convention, because it was too *republican,* and advocated the *British monarchy as the perfect standard* to be approached as nearly as the people could be *made to bear.*" This I affirm to be a gross misrepresentation. To prove it is so, it were sufficient to appeal to a single fact, namely, that the gentleman alluded to was the only member from the State to which he belonged who signed the Constitution, and it is notorious, against the prevailing weight of the official influence of the State, and against what would probably be the opinion of a large majority of his fellow-citizens, till better information should correct their first impressions.

How, then can he be believed to have opposed a thing which he actually agreed to, and that in so unsupported a situation, and under circumstances of such peculiar responsibility? To this I shall add two more facts. One, that the member in question never made a proposition to the Convention which was not conformable to the republican theory. The other, that the highest-toned of any of the propositions made by him was actually voted for by the representation of several States, including some of the principal ones; and including individuals who, in the estimation of those who deem themselves the only republicans, are pre-eminent for republican character. More than this I am not at liberty to say.

It is a matter generally understood, that the deliberations of the Convention, which were carried on in private, were to remain undisturbed. And every prudent man must be convinced of the propriety both of the one and the other. Had the deliberations been open while going on, the clamors of faction would have prevented any satisfactory result; had they been afterwards disclosed, much food would have been afforded to inflammatory declamation. Propositions made without due reflection, and perhaps abandoned by the proposers themselves, on more mature reflection, would have been handles for a profusion of ill-natured accusation.

Every infallible declaimer, taking his own ideas as the perfect standard, would have railed without measure or mercy at every member of the Convention who had gone a single line beyond his standard.

—"Amicus." *Hamilton,* VII, 31-33.

September 29, 1792

It is not unusual to defend one post by attacking another. Aristides has shown a disposition to imitate this policy. He by clear implication tells us, and doubtless means it as a justification of the person whom he defends, that attachment to *aristocracy, monarchy, hereditary succession,* a *titled order of nobility,* and all the *mock pageantry* of kingly government form the *appropriate* and *prominent* features in the character to which he boasts Mr. Jefferson's opposition, and which it seems to be a principal part of the business of his Gazette to depreciate. This is no more than what has been long matter for malevolent insinuation. I mistake, however, the man to whom it is applied, if he fears the strictest scrutiny into his political principles and conduct; if he does not wish there "were windows in the breast," and that assembled America might witness the inmost springs of his public actions. I mistake him—however a turn of mind less addicted to *dogmatizing* then *reasoning,* less fond of *hypotheses* than *experience,* may have led to speculative doubts concerning the probable success of the republican theory—if he has not uniformly and ardently, since the experiment of it began in the United States, *wished* it success; if he is not sincerely desirous that the sublime idea of a perfect equality of rights among citizens, exclusive of hereditary distinctions, may be practically justified and realized; and if among the sources of the regret which his language and conduct have testified, at the overdriven maxims and doctrines that too long withstood the establishment of firm government in the United States, and now embarrass the execution of the government which has been established, a *principal one* has not been their tendency to counteract a *fair trial* of the theory to which he is represented to be adverse. I mistake him, if his measures proceeding upon the ground of a liberal and efficient exercise of the powers of the national government, have had any other object than to give it stability and duration: *the only solid and rational expedient for preserving republican government in the United States.*

It has been pertinently remarked by a judicious writer, that *Caesar*, who *overturned* the republic, was the WHIG, *Cato*, who *died* for it, the TORY, of Rome; such, at least, was the common cant of political harangues, the insidious tale of hypocritical demagogues.

—"Catullus to Aristides". *Hamilton*, VII, 52-53.

[1801]

In regard to these sects, which compose the pith and essence of the anti-federal party, we believe it to be true that the contest between us is indeed a war of principles—a war between tyranny and liberty, but not between monarchy and republicanism. It is a contest between the tyranny of Jacobinism, which confounds and levels every thing, and the mild reign of rational liberty, which rests on the basis of an efficient and well-balanced government, and through the medium of stable laws shelters and protects the life, the reputation, the civil and religious rights of every member of the community.

—Address to the Electors of the State of New York. *Hamilton*, VII, 743-744.

February 27, 1804

It is now a long time since a very odious slander has been in circulation to the prejudice of my character.

It has come to my ears in more than one way, but always, till lately, without the disclosure of any source to which I could resort for explanation or detection. Within a few days, Mr. Kane, of this city, related to me a story as coming from Judge Purdy, in substance very similar to the calumny to which I have alluded. The amount of his information, and the result of an interview with Judge Purdy, are contained in the enclosed paper.[1] You will observe, sir, that your name is implicated in the transaction. With what warrant, it would be improper for me to prejudge. But the very mention of your name adds importance to the affair, and increases the motives to investigation. The charge, even in the mitigated form to which it is reduced by Judge Purdy's admission, is of a nature too derogatory to permit me to pass it lightly over. It is essential that its origin and progress should be traced as fully as may be practicable, in order to the thorough exposure of its falsehood and malignity.

The assertions of Judge Purdy authorize me to appeal to you for a frank and candid explanation of so much of the matter as relates to yourself. This explanation I request as speedily as may be.

—To Governor George Clinton. Draft in Hamilton's hand. Hamilton Papers, 1st ser.

[1] The paper, a statement by James Kane, reported Purdy's assertion that Hamilton and others, either in 1798 or prior to the Constitutional Convention, sought to establish a monarchy in the United States. Purdy's authority for the assertion was Governor Clinton, who disavowed all knowledge of it.

March 9, 1804

I shall not only rely on the assurance which you give as to the future communication of the copy of the letter in question, should it hereafter come to your hands, but I will take the liberty to add a request, that you will be pleased to make known to me any other circumstances, if any should reach you, which may serve to throw light upon the affair. I feel an anxiety that it should be thoroughly sifted, not merely on my own account, but from a conviction that the pretended existence of such a project, long travelling about in whispers, has had no inconsiderable influence in exciting false alarms, and unjust suspicions to the prejudice of a number of individuals, every way worthy of public confidence, men who have always faithfully supported the existing institutions of the country, and who would disdain to be concerned in an intrigue with any foreign power, or its agents, either for introducing monarchy, or for promoting or upholding any other scheme of government within the United States.

—To Governor George Clinton. Draft in Hamilton's hand. Hamilton Papers, 1st ser.

Democracy and the Role of the People

> It is a false calculation, that the people of this country can ever be ultimately deceived.

Antifederalist propaganda created an image of Hamilton as the arch-foe of democracy. Actually, Hamilton in the early portion of his career enthusiastically supported popular government and went so far as to criticize the New York state constitution of 1777 because it was not democratic enough to suit him. Sharing as he did the pessimistic view of human nature with other Founding Fathers, Hamilton would be expected to temper his initial enthusiasm for mass action, to support representative rather than direct democracy, and to seize upon the system of checks and balances as a curb on the "imprudence" of democracy. Hamilton's real enemy was not the people but the state machines. He saw the people as a check upon unlimited state sovereignty and he was ever zealous in tightening the bonds between the people and the federal government. At the Constitutional Convention he fought successfully for the election of members of the House of Representatives by the people instead of by state legislatures and subsequently he advocated selecting the Presidential electors by the people. Despite the increasing conservatism of his later years he never abandoned these principles.

HEADQUARTERS, MORRIS TOWN May 7, 1777

I thank you for the favor of the pamphlet containing your form of government, which, without flattery, I consider as far more judicious and digested than anything of the kind that as yet appeared among us; though I am not so unreserved in my approbation as to think it free from defects. While I view it, in the main, as a wise and excellent system, I truly confess it appears to me to have some faults, which I could wish did not exist. Were it not too late to discuss particulars for any useful end, or could my judgment have any weight in the matter, which is the work of so many far more able and discerning than I can pretend to be, I should willingly descend to an exhibition of those parts I dislike, and my reasons for disapproving. But, in the present situation of things, it would be both useless and presumptuous. . . .

—To Gouverneur Morris and Committee of the New York Convention. Robert R. Livingston Coll., N. Y. Hist. Soc.

HEADQUARTERS, MORRIS TOWN May 19, 1777

I partly agree and partly disagree with you respecting the deficiencies of your constitution. That there is a want of vigor in the executive I believe will be found true. To determine the qualifications proper for the chief executive Magistrate requires the deliberate wisdom of a select assembly, and cannot be safely lodged with the people at large. That instability is inherent in the nature of popular government, I think very disputable; unstable democracy is an epithet frequently in the mouths of politicians; but I believe that from a strict examination of the matter, from the records of history, it will be found that the fluctuations of governments in which the popular principle has borne a considerable sway has proceeded from its being compounded with other principles; and from its being made to operate in an improper channel. Compound governments, though they may be harmonious in the beginning, will introduce different interests; and these interests will clash, throw the state into convulsions, and produce a change or dissolution. When the deliberative or judicial powers are vested wholly or partly in the collective body of the people, you must expect error, confusion and instability. But a representative democracy, where the right of election is well secured and regulated, and the exercise of the legislative, executive and judiciary authorities is vested in select persons chosen really and not nominally by the people, will in my opinion be most likely to be happy, regular and durable.

That complexity of your legislature will occasion delay and dilatoriness is evident and I fear may be attended with a much greater evil; as expedition is not very material in making laws, especially when the government is well digested and matured by time. The evil I mean is, that in time your Senate, from the very name and from the mere circumstances of its being a separate member of the legislature, will be liable to degenerate into a body purely aristocratical. And I think the danger of an abuse of power from a simple legislature would not be very great in a government where the equality and fulness of popular representation is so wisely provided as in yours.

On the whole, though, I think these are the defects intimated. I think your Government far the best that we have yet seen, and capable of giving long and substantial happiness to the people. . . .
[P.S.] Relying on your punctuality in favoring me with any important intelligence your way, I am likely to lose a beaver hat, which was staked against the truth of the report of the stores at St. John's being destroyed. If you forget me in future, certainly I will excommunicate you.

—To Robert R. Livingston. Robert R. Livingston Coll., N. Y. Hist. Soc.

December 16, 1782

The truth is, the security intended to the general liberty in the Confederation consists in the frequent election, and in the rotation, of the members of Congress, by which there is a constant and an effectual check upon them. This is the security which the people in every State enjoy against the usurpations of their internal governments; and it is the true source of security in a representative republic. The government, so constituted, ought to have the means necessary to answer the end of its institution. By weakening its hands too much, it may be rendered incapable of providing for the interior harmony or the exterior defence of the State.

—Report on Impost Duty. *Works*, II, 187.

July 6, 1786

. . . some alterations in the original Constitution will be proper, as well in deference to the sense of many of our fellow citizens, as in conformity to the true spirit of the institution itself. The alterations they have in view respect principally the duration or succession of the society, and the distinction between honorary and regular members. As to the first, the provision intended to be made appears to them to be expressed in terms not sufficiently explicit; and, as far as it may intend, an *hereditary succession* by right of primogeniture, is liable to this objection—*that it refers to birth what ought to belong to merit only:* a principle inconsistent with the genius of the society founded on friendship and patriotism. As to the second, the distinction holds up an odious difference between men who have served their country in one way, and those who have served it in another, and improper in a society where the character of patriot ought to be an equal title to all its members.

—Report for the Society of the Cincinnati. *Hamilton*, II, 335-336.

Debate on a New York State election bill enabling the election inspector to take aside any illiterate person and examine him privately concerning his ballot.

January 23, 1787

Col. Hamilton thought it was very apparent, if the clause prevailed, that it would tend to increase rather than prevent an improper influence. For, though an inspector takes an oath that his conduct shall be impartial, yet he can easily interpret the oath so as to correspond with his own wishes. If he is an honest man, he will think the public good concerned in promoting a candidate to whom he is attached; and under this impression may see no harm in recommending him to a person offering his vote. His suggestion will be generally attended with success, and the consequence will be that the inspector will have the disposition of the votes of almost all unlettered persons in favor of the party to which he inclines. Here, then, is a more concentred influence over the illiterate and uninformed part of the community, than they would have been subject to if left to themselves. Here they will be liable to an influence more dangerous than the one we wish to avoid. The question then is, whether it is better to leave them to an accidental influence or imposition, or to subject them to a more regular and extensive influence. The appointment of inspectors will then become more than it is, an object of party, and it will always be in their power to turn the scale of a contested election. On the contrary, if the voters are left to themselves, the activity of the different parties will make the chance equal; and the influence on one hand will be balanced by an equal degree on the other.

—Speech in the New York Assembly. *Works,* VIII, 17-18.

January 27, 1787

. . . Let us take care that the persons to elect are properly qualified, that they are in such a situation in point of property as not to be absolutely indigent and dependent, and let us trust to them the care of choosing proper persons to represent them. The Constitution will not presume that whole districts and counties of electors duly qualified will choose men improper for the trust. Let us, on our part, be cautious how we abridge the freedom of choice allowed them by the Constitution, or the right of being elected, which every citizen may claim under it. I hold it to be a maxim which ought to be sacred in our form of government, that no man ought to be deprived of any right or privilege which he enjoys under the Constitution, but for some offence proved in due course of law. To declare qualifications or disqualifications by general descriptions in legislative acts, would be to invade this important principle. It would be to deprive in the gross all those who had not the requisite qualifications, or who were objects of those disqualifications, to that right to a share in the administration of the republic which the Constitution gives them, and that without any offence to incur a forfeiture. . . .

But let us pursue the subject a little further: commerce, it will be admitted, leads to an increase of individual property; property begets influence. Though a Legislature composed as we are will always take care of the rights of the middling and lower classes, suppose the majority of the Legislature to consist at a future day of wealthy men, what would hinder them, if the right of innovating on the Constitution be admitted, from declaring that no man not worth ten thousand pounds should be eligible to a seat in either House? Would not this introduce a principle fatal to the genius of our present Constitution?

In making this observation, I cannot be suspected of wishing to increase the jealousy—already sufficiently high—of men of property. My situation, prospects, and connections forbid the supposition. But I mean to lay honestly before you the dangers to which we expose ourselves by letting in the principle which the clause under consideration rests upon. I give no opinion on the expediency of the exclusion proposed. I only say, in my opinion the Constitution does not permit it, and I shall be against any qualification or disqualification—either of electors or elected—not prescribed by the Constitution. To me it appears that the qualifications of both ought to be fundamental in a republican government, not liable to be varied or added to by the Legislature, and that they should for ever remain where the Constitution has left them. I see no other safe ground. It is to be lamented that men, to carry some favorite point in which their party or prejudices are interested, will inconsiderately introduce principles and precedents which lead to successive innovations destructive of the liberty of the subject and the safety of the government. For my part, I shall uniformly oppose every innovation not known in the provisions of the Constitution.

—Speech in the New York Assembly. *Works*, VIII, 25-28.

October 17, 1787

. . . I am not one of those who gain an influence by cajoling the unthinking mass (tho' I pity their delusions), and ringing in their ears the gracious sound of their *absolute Sovereignty*. I despise the trick of such dirty policy. I know there are Citizens, who, to gain their own private ends, enflame the minds of the well-meaning, tho' less intelligent parts of the community, by sating their vanity with that cordial and unfailing specific, that *all power is seated in the people*. For my part, I am not much attached to the *majesty of the multitude*, and therefore waive all pretensions (founded on such conduct), to their countenance. I consider them in general as very ill qualified to judge for themselves what government will best suit their peculiar situations; nor is this to be wondered at. The science of government is not easily understood. . . . If truth, then, is permitted to speak, the mass of the people of America (any more than the mass of other countries) cannot judge with any degree of precision concerning the fitness of this New Constitution to the peculiar situation of America; they have, however, done wisely in delegating the power of framing a government to those every way worthy and well-qualified; and, if this Government is snatched, untasted, from them, it may not be amiss to inquire into the causes which will probably occasion their disappointment.

Out of several, which present to my mind, I shall venture to select *one*, baneful enough, in my opinion, to work this dreadful evil. There are always men in society of some talents, but more ambition, in quest of *that* which it would be impossible for them to obtain in any other way than by working on the passions and prejudices of the less discerning classes of citizens and yeomanry. It is the plan of men of this stamp to frighten the people with ideal bugbears, in order to mould them to their own purposes. The unceasing cry of these designing croakers is, My friends, your liberty is invaded! Have you thrown off the yoke of one tyrant to invest yourselves with that of another? Have you fought, bled and conquered for *such a change?* If you have—go—retire into silent obscurity, and kiss the rod that scourges you.

To be serious: These state empirics leave no species of deceit untried to convince the unthinking people that they have power to do—what? Why truly to do much mischief, and to occasion anarchy and wild uproar. And for what reason do these political jugglers incite the peaceably disposed to such extravagant commotions? Because until the people really discover that they have *power*, by some outrageous act, they never can become of any importance. The misguided people never reflect during this frenzy, that the moment they become riotous, they renounce from that moment, their independence, and commence vassals to their ambitious leaders, who instantly, and with a high hand, rob them of their consequence, and apply it to their own present and future aggrandizement; nor will these tyrants over the people stick at sacrificing *their* good, if an advantageous compromise be effected for *themselves*.

—"Caesar," II. N. Y. *Daily Advertiser*, Oct. 17, 1787.[1]

[1] Two "Caesar" letters were written in reply to George Clinton who attacked the proposed Constitution in a series of seven letters to the press under the pseudonym of "Cato." The "Caesar" letters were contemporaneously ascribed to Hamilton. Among the Clinton Papers in the New York State Library is a copy of the letter from Hamilton which reputedly accompanied the initial "Caesar" essay. Actually it is in the handwriting of John Lamb, a political opponent of Hamilton. If Hamilton did write these letters, he demonstrated an astounding reversal in tactics, for within ten days, with the publication of the first *Federalist* paper, he appealed to enlightened public opinion and took an entirely different tone toward the voters.

June 21, 1788

. . . Sir, the general sense of the people will regulate the conduct of their representatives. I admit that there are exceptions to this rule. There are certain conjunctures when it may be necessary and proper to disregard the opinions which the majority of the people have formed; but, in the general course of things, the popular views, and even prejudices, will direct the actions of the rulers.

All governments, even the most despotic, depend, in a great degree, on opinion. In free republics it is most peculiarly the case. In these the will of the people makes the essential principle of the government, and the laws which control the community receive their tone and spirit from the public wishes. It is the fortunate situation of our country, that the minds of the people are exceedingly enlightened and refined. Here, then, we may expect the laws to be proportionately agreeable to the standard of a perfect policy, and the wisdom of public measures to consist with the most intimate conformity between the views of the representative and his constituent.

—Speech on the Constitution, *Debates of the N. Y. Convention*, p. 36.

June 21, 1788

It has been observed that a pure democracy, if it were practicable, would be the most perfect government. Experience has proved, that no position in politics is more false than this. The ancient democracies, in which the people themselves deliberated, never possessed one feature of good government. Their very character was tyranny; their figure deformity. When they assembled, the field of debate presented an ungovernable mob, not only incapable of deliberation, but prepared for every enormity. In these assemblies the enemies of the people brought forward their plans of ambition systematically. They were opposed by their enemies of another party; and it became a matter of contingency, whether the people subjected themselves to be led blindly by one tyrant or by another.

—Speech on the Constitution, *Debates of the N. Y. Convention*, p. 37.

June 21, 1788

We hear constantly a great deal which is more calculated to awake our passions and create prejudices than to conduct us to truth and teach us our real interests. I do not suppose this to be the design of gentlemen. Why, then, are we told so often of an aristocracy? For my part, I hardly know the meaning of this word as it is applied. If all we hear be true, this government is really a very bad one. But who are the aristocracy among us? Where do we find men elevated to a perpetual rank among our fellow citizens, and possessing powers entirely independent of them? The arguments of the gentlemen only go to prove that there are men who are rich, men who are poor; some who are wise, and others who are not; that, indeed, every distinguished man is an aristocrat. . . . Does the new government render a rich man more eligible than a poor one? No! It requires no such qualification. It is bottomed on the broad and equal principle of your state constitution. . . .

It is a harsh doctrine, that men grow wicked in proportion as they improve and enlighten their minds. Experience has by no means justified us in the supposition that there is more virtue in one class of men than in another. Look through the rich and the poor of the community; the learned and the ignorant. Where does virtue predominate? The difference indeed consists, not in the quantity, but kind of vices, which are incident to the various classes; and here the advantage of character belongs to the wealthy. Their vices are probably more favorable to the prosperity of the state than those of the indigent, and partake less of moral depravity.

—Speech on the Constitution, *Debates of the N. Y. Convention*, pp. 39-40.

June 21, 1788

After all, Sir, we must submit to this idea, that the true principle of a republic is that the people should choose whom they please to govern them. Representation is imperfect in proportion as the current of popular favor is checked. This great source of free government, popular election, should be perfectly pure, and the most unbounded liberty allowed. Where this principle is adhered to; where, in the organization of the government, the legislative, executive, and judicial branches are rendered distinct; where, again, the legislative is divided into separate houses, and the operations of each are controlled by various checks and balances, and above all by the vigilance and weight of the state governments, to talk of tyranny and the subversion of our liberties, is to speak the language of enthusiasm. This balance between the National and State governments ought to be dwelt on with peculiar attention, as it is of the utmost importance. It forms a double security to the people. If one encroaches on their rights they will find a powerful protection in the other. Indeed, they will both be prevented from overpassing their constitutional limits by a certain rivalship, which will ever subsist between them. I am persuaded that a firm union is as necessary to perpetuate our liberties as it is to make us respectable; and experience will probably prove that the national government will be as natural a guardian of our freedom as the state legislatures themselves.

—Speech on the Constitution, *Debates of the N. Y. Convention*, p. 40.

June 21, 1788

Sir, there is something in an argument that has been urged, which, if it proves any thing, concludes against all union and all governments; it goes to prove that no powers should be intrusted to any body of men, because they may be abused. This is an argument of possibility and chance—one that would render useless all reasonings upon the probable operation of things, and defeat the established principles of natural and moral causes. It is a species of reasoning sometimes used to excite popular jealousies, but is generally discarded by wise and discerning men.

—Speech on the Constitution, *Debates of the N. Y. Convention*, p. 46.

December 14, 1790

. . . Public opinion being the ultimate arbiter of every measure of government, it can scarcely appear improper, in deference to that, to accompany the origination of any new proposition with explanations, which the superior information of those to whom it is immediately addressed would render superfluous.

—Report of the Secretary of the Treasury to the House of Representatives on a National Bank. Hamilton Papers, 2nd ser.

[1795]

. . . It is a false calculation, that the people of this country can ever be ultimately deceived.

—"Camillus," No. 9. Draft in Hamilton's hand. Hamilton Papers, 1st ser.

March 4, 1802

You have seen certain resolutions unanimously pass our Legislature for amending the Constitution; 1st, by designating separately the candidates for President and Vice-President; 2d, by having electors chosen by the people in districts under the direction of the national Legislature.

After mature reflection, I was thoroughly confirmed in my full impression, that it is true federal policy to promote the adoption of these amendments.

Of the first, not only because it is in itself right, that the people should know whom they are choosing, and because the present mode gives all possible scope to intrigue, and is dangerous (as we have seen) to the public tranquillity; but because in every thing which gives opportunity for juggling arts, our adversaries will nine times out of ten excel us.

Of the second, because it removes thus far the intervention of the State governments, and strengthens the connection between the Federal head and the people, and because it diminishes the means of party combination, in which also, the burning zeal of our opponents will be generally an overmatch for our temperate flame.

—To Gouverneur Morris. Draft in Hamilton's hand. Hamilton Papers, 1st ser.

On Classes, Parties, and Factions

We are attempting by this Constitution to abolish factions and to unite all parties for the general welfare.

Hamilton, along with Washington and Madison, deplored "the violence of faction," which, they felt, a strong union could control. In the tenth Federalist *Madison regarded the protection of "the faculties of men" as the "first object of government." From these faculties, he held, the right of property originated, and he argued that it was the task of the government to protect the acquisition of property as well as its possession. Madison recognized a number of sources of faction, among them religion and politics, but felt that "the most common and durable source" was "the various and unequal distribution of property." The regulation of the differing economic interests of society was, in his opinion "the principal task of modern legislation."*

With all this Hamilton would have agreed. He recognized the multiplicity of interests in the commonwealth. There were the rich and the poor, the commercial and the noncommercial interests, the North and the South, the large states and the small states. In his opinion the Constitution was a compromise of these clashing interests, but he frankly confessed that an important source of its support was the group of public creditors.

Hamilton and Washington were uniformly opposed to the party system. It was Hamilton's failure to recognize the inevitability of such a development which constituted, perhaps, his major weakness as a politician. With greater realism and less consistency, Madison plunged headlong into the leadership of a party of the opposition. The tragic drift in America after 1820 proved the prescience of Hamilton's views about the dangers of sectionalism; Revolutionary events in Europe since 1789 underscored for Americans the perils of political organization along class lines.

June 20, 1788

Sir, the natural situation of this country seems to divide its interests into different classes. There are navigating and non-navigating States. The Northern are properly the navigating States; the Southern appear to possess neither the means nor the spirit of navigation. This difference in situation naturally produces a dissimilarity of interests and views respecting foreign commerce.

—Speech on the Compromises of the Constitution, *Debates of the N.Y. Convention*, p. 25.

June 25, 1788

Much has been said about factions. As far as my observation has extended, factions in Congress have arisen from attachment to state prejudices. We are attempting by this Constitution to abolish factions and to unite all parties for the general welfare.

—Speech on the United States Senate, *Debates of the N. Y. Convention*, p. 83.

January 8, 1788

. . . There are strong minds in every walk of life that will rise superior to the disadvantages of situation, and will command the tribute due to their merit, not only from the classes to which they particularly belong, but from the society in general. The door ought to be equally open to all; and I trust, for the credit of human nature, that we shall see examples of such vigorous plants flourishing in the soil of federal as well as of state legislation; but occasional instances of this sort will not render the reasoning founded upon the general course of things, less conclusive.

The subject might be placed in several other lights that would lead to the same result; and in particular it might be asked, What greater affinity or relation of interest can be conceived between the carpenter and blacksmith, and the linen manufacturer or stocking-weaver, than between the merchant and either of them? It is notorious that there are often as great rivalships between different branches of the mechanic or manufacturing arts as there are between any of the departments of labor and industry; so that, unless the representative body were to be far more numerous than would be consistent with any idea of regularity or wisdom in its deliberations, it is impossible that what seems to be the spirit of the objection we have been considering should ever be realized in practice. . . .

—*The Federalist* No. 36.

February 26, 1788

We have seen that an uncontrollable power over the elections to the federal government could not, without hazard, be committed to the state legislatures. Let us now see, what would be the danger on the other side; that is, from confiding the ultimate right of regulating its own elections to the Union itself. It is not pretended that this right would ever be used for the exclusion of any state from its share in the representation. The interest of all would, in this respect at least, be the security of all. But it is alleged that it might be employed in such a manner as to promote the election of some favorite class of men in exclusion of others, by confining the places of election to particular districts, and rendering it impracticable to the citizens at large to partake in the choice. Of all chimerical suppositions, this seems to be the most chimerical. . . .

But what is to be the object of this capricious partiality in the national councils? Is it to be exercised in a discrimination between the different kinds of property, or between the different degrees of property? Will it lean in favor of the landed interest, or the moneyed interest, or the mercantile interest, or the manufacturing interest? Or, to speak in the fashionable language of the adversaries to the Constitution, will it court the elevation of "the wealthy and well-born," to the exclusion and debasement of the rest of the society?

If this partiality is to be exerted in favor of those who are concerned in any particular description of industry or property, I presume it will readily be admitted, that the competition for it will lie between landed men and merchants. And I scruple not to affirm, that it is infinitely less likely in the national councils than that the one or the other of them should predominate in all the local councils. The inference will be that a conduct tending to give an undue preference to either is much less to be dreaded from the former than from the latter. . . .

In a country consisting chiefly of the cultivators of land, where the rules of an equal representation obtain, the landed interest must, upon the whole, preponderate in the government. As long as this interest prevails in most of the state legislatures so long it must maintain a correspondent superiority in the national Senate, which will generally be a faithful copy of the majorities of those assemblies. . . .

I the rather consult brevity in discussing the probability of a preference founded upon discrimination between the different kinds of industry and property, because, as far as I understand the meaning of the objectors, they contemplate a discrimination of another kind. They appear to have in view, as the objects of the preference with which they endeavor to alarm us, those whom they designate by the description of "the wealthy and the well-born." These, it seems, are to be exalted to an odious preeminence over the rest of their fellow citizens. At one time, however, their elevation is to be a necessary consequence of the smallness of the representative body; at another time it is to be effected by depriving the people at large of the opportunity of exercising their right of suffrage in the choice of that body.

But upon what principle is the discrimination of the places of election to be made in order to answer the purpose of the meditated preference? Are "the wealthy and the well-born," as they are called, confined to particular spots in the several states? Have they, by some miraculous instinct of foresight, set apart in each of them a common place of residence? Are they only to be met with in the towns or cities? Or are they, on the contrary, scattered over the face of the country as avarice or chance may have happened to cast their own lot or that of their predecessors? . . .

With a disposition to invade the essential rights of the community, and with the means of gratifying that disposition, is it presumable that the persons who were actuated by it would amuse themselves in the ridiculous task of fabricating election laws for securing a preference to a favorite class of men? Would they not be likely to prefer a conduct better adapted to their own immediate aggrandizement? Would they not rather boldly resolve to perpetuate themselves in office by one decisive act of usurpation, than to trust to the precarious expedients which, in spite of all the precautions that might accompany them, might terminate in the dismission, disgrace, and ruin of their authors? Would they not fear that citizens, not less tenacious than conscious of their rights, would flock from the remote extremes of their respective states to the places of election, to overthrow their tyrants, and to substitute men who would be disposed to avenge the violated majesty of the people?

—*The Federalist* No. 60.

August 18, 1792

It is certainly much to be regretted that party discriminations are so far geographical as they have been, and that ideas of a severance of the Union are creeping in both North and South. . . .

—To Washington, "Objections and Answers Respecting the Administration of the Government." Hamilton Papers, 1st ser.

[1795-98]

In hinting at the possible subversion of the government, it may be proper to explain the foundation of this idea. The public creditors, who consisted of various descriptions of men, a large proportion of them very meritorious and very influential, had had a considerable agency in promoting the adoption of the new Constitution, for this peculiar reason, among the many weighty reasons which were common to them as citizens and proprietors, that it exhibited the prospect of a government able to do justice to their claims. Their disappointment and disgust, quickened by the sensibility of private interest, could not but have been extreme.

There was another class of men, and a very weighty one, who had had great share in the establishment of the Constitution, who, though not personally interested in the debt, considered the maxims of public credit as of the essence of good government, as intimately connected by the analogy and sympathy of principles with the security of property in general, and as forming an inseparable portion of the great system of political order. These men, from sentiment, would have regarded their labors in supporting the Constitution as in a great measure lost; they would have seen the disappointments of their hopes in the unwillingness of the government to do what they esteemed justice, and to pursue what they called an honorable policy; and they would have regarded this failure as an augury of the continuance of the fatal system which had for some time prostrated the national honor, interest, and happiness. The disaffection of a part of these classes of men might have carried a considerable reinforcement to the enemies of the government.

—"Defence of the Funding System," II. Draft in Hamilton's hand; dated in later hand. Hamilton Papers, 1st ser.

Some Political Tenets

June 25, 1788

There are two objects in forming systems of government—safety for the people, and energy in the administration. When these objects are united, the certain tendency of the system will be to the public welfare. If the latter object be neglected, the people's security will be as certainly sacrificed as by disregarding the former. Good constitutions are formed upon a comparison of the liberty of the individual with the strength of government. If the tone of either be too high, the other will be weakened too much. It is the happiest possible mode of conciliating these objects, to institute one branch peculiarly endowed with sensibility, another with knowledge and firmness.

—Speech on the United States Senate, *Debates of the N.Y. Convention*, p. 81.

June 28, 1788

. . . Constitutions should consist only of general provisions; the reason is that they must necessarily be permanent, and that they cannot calculate for the possible change of things.

—Speech on the United States Senate, *Debates of the N.Y. Convention*, p. 115.

[1790]

A weak and embarrassed government never fails to be unpopular. It attaches to itself the disrespect incident to weakness, and, unable to promote the public happiness, its impotencies are its crimes. Without the assumption, the government would have been for a long time at least under all the entanglements and imbecilities of a complicated clashing and disordered system of finance.

—"Defence of the Funding System," II. Hamilton Papers, 1st ser.

January 6, 1799

. . . 'T is needless to detail to you my political tenets. I shall only say that I hold with *Montesquieu*, that a government must be fitted to a nation, as much as a coat to the individual; and, consequently, that what may be good at Philadelphia may be bad at Paris, and ridiculous at Petersburgh.

—To Lafayette. Copy. Hamilton Papers, 1st ser.

Competent Public Servants

[September 1, 1790]

I shall only remark, that changes of public servants ought never to be made but for cogent reasons. If lightly made, they are not only chargeable with injustice and are a symptom of fickleness in the public counsels, but they destroy the motives to good conduct, and, in money concerns especially, are apt to beget a disposition to make the most of possession while it lasts.

—To William Short (Cabinet Paper). *Hamilton,* IV, 40.

December 7, 1796

There is a subject which has dwelt long and much upon my mind, which I cannot omit this opportunity of suggesting. It is the compensation to our public officers, especially those in the most important stations. Every man acquainted with the expense, even of the most frugal plan of living in our great cities, must be sensible of their inadequateness. The impolicy of such defective provisions seems not to have been sufficiently weighed.

No plan of governing is well founded, which does not regard man as a compound of selfish and virtuous passions. To expect him to be wholly guided by the latter, would be as great an error as to suppose him wholly destitute of them. Hence the necessity of adequate rewards for those services of which the public stand in need. Without them, the affairs of a nation are likely to get sooner or later into incompetent or unfaithful hands.

. . . If the rewards of the government are scanty, those who have talents without wealth, and are too virtuous to abuse their stations, cannot accept public offices without a sacrifice of interest; which, in ordinary times, may hardly be justified by their duty to themselves and their families. If they have talents without virtue, they may, indeed, accept offices to make a dishonest and improper use of them. The tendency then is to transfer the management of public affairs to wealthy but incapable hands, or to hands which, if capable, are as destitute of integrity as of wealth.

—Part of Washington's Speech to Congress. Draft in Hamilton's hand. Hamilton Papers, 1st ser.

5

Hamilton at the Federal Convention

A Chronology

May 25—Attends opening session as delegate from New York. Nominates William Jackson as Secretary of the Convention.

**May 29*.—Raises the basic issue whether the United States "were susceptible of one government." (McHenry, *Documents Illustrative of the Formation of the Union of the American States* [Washington, D. C., 1927—hereinafter called *Documents*], p. 926). Randolph plan presented.

May 30—Moves to alter the resolution so as to read "that the rights of suffrage in the National Leguslature ought to be proportioned to the number of free inhabitants." Seconded by Spaight. This was a modification of the Randolph Plan, which had proposed that "the rights of suffrage in the National Legislature ought to be proportioned to the quotas of contribution, or to the number of free inhabitants, as the one or the other rule may seem best in different cases." (Madison, *Documents*, p. 123)

June 4—Wilson and Hamilton move that Gerry's proposals be amended "so as to give the Executive an absolute negative on the laws." "There was no danger, they thought, of such a power being too much exercised. It was mentioned by Col. Hamilton that the King of Great Britain had not exerted his negative since the Revolution." (Madison, *Documents*, pp. 147, 148)

June 5—Proposes that the executive nominate the judges, and that the Senate have the right of approving or rejecting. (Pierce, *Documents*, p. 94)

June 11—Wilson and Hamilton move that "the right of suffrage in the second branch [Senate] ought to be according to the same rule as in the first branch." Carried (Madison, *Documents*, p. 190)

* Speeches excerpted below.

**June 18*—Speech on the Randolph and Paterson Plans, particularly opposing the latter on the ground that "no amendment of the Confederation, leaving the states in possession of their sovereignty could possibly answer the purpose." Proposes own plan. (Madison, *Documents*, p. 215; Yates, *Secret Debates;* Lansing in Strayer, *The Delegate from New York*, pp. 64-70)

June 21—On motion of Pinckney that the House of Representatives should be elected in such manner as the legislature of each state should direct instead of by the people, Hamilton speaks in opposition, arguing that the transfer of the election from the people to the state legislatures "would essentially vitiate the plan. It would increase the state influence which could not be too watchfully guarded against. All, too, must admit the possibility in case the general government should maintain itself, that the state governments might gradually dwindle into nothing. The system therefore should not be engrafted on what might possibly fail." (Madison, *Documents*, pp. 252, 253) In Yates's account, Hamilton asserts that election "directly by the people" is "essential to the democratic rights of the community." (*Secret Debates*). According to Lansing's account, Hamilton declares: "If you permit legislatures to elect you will have *state interests* represented." (Strayer, p. 76)

—— Hamilton opposes proposal that representatives to the lower house be chosen for three years on the ground that "the British House of Commons were elected septennially, yet the democratic spirit of that Constitution had not ceased. Frequency of elections tended to make the people listless to them; and to facilitate the success of little cabals." (Madison, *Documents*, p. 256)

June 22—Supports resolution that members of the National Legislature receive "fixed stipends to be paid out of the National Treasury," expressing "strenuous" opposition to making Congress "dependent on the legislative rewards of the states. Those who pay are the masters of those who are paid." Stresses the "difference between the feelings and views of the people and the governments of the states." Holds that the latter, "from the personal interest and official inducements" would be "unfriendly to the General Government." (Madison, *Documents*, p. 258)

—— Favors Gorham's motion to strike out the provision making members of the House ineligible to other offices during their term and for one year thereafter. Admits "inconveniences on both sides." "We must take man as we find him, and if we expect him to serve the public must interest his passions in doing so. A reliance on pure patriotism had been the source of many of our errors." Regarding the possible effects of such a reform in Great Britain, he cites a remark attributed to "one of the ablest politicians" (Hume) to the effect that "all that influence on the side of the Crown, which went under the name of *corruption*" was "an essential part of the weight which maintained the equilibrium of the Constitution." (Madison, *Documents*, p. 261; cf. Yates, *Secret Debates*)

**June 26*—Gorham moves that Senators serve for a six-year term, one third to be elected every second year. Read amends the motion, to make the term nine years, one third going out triennially. Madison, supporting the idea of a long term for Senators, points to the rise of a "leveling spirit" and urges that this was one way of guarding against that spirit "on republican principles." Hamilton supports Madison. (Madison, *Documents*, pp. 281, 282)

June 28—As a result of intensified debates over the suffrage in the lower house, Franklin urges that a clergyman be invited to offer prayers at the beginning of each session. "Mr. Hamilton and several others expressed their apprehensions that however proper such a resolution might have been at the beginning of the convention, it might at this late day, in the first place, bring on it some disagreeable animadversions, and, in the second place, lead the public to believe that the embarrassments and dissensions within the Convention had suggested this measure." The session adjourns without vote on the motion. (Madison, *Documents*, p. 296)[1]

**June 29*—Hamilton's last speech before leaving the Convention for an absence of some six weeks deals with the crucial issue of representation in the lower house. He opposes equality of the states in the House of Representatives. (Reports of Madison, King and Brearley, *Documents*, pp. 301, 302, 867, 868, 906, 907)

June 30—"Mr. Hamilton left this morning." (Lansing in Strayer, p. 96)

August 13—Speaks in opposition to proposal of Gerry that representatives in the lower house in future be confined to native-born Americans; opposes "embarrassing the government with minute restrictions." While conceding some dangers, he asserts that "the advantages of encouraging foreigners was obvious and admitted." "Persons in Europe of moderate fortunes will be fond of coming here where they will be on a level with the first citizens." Moves that eligibility be based merely on "citizenship and inhabitancy." (Madison, *Documents*, p. 524)

**Sept. 6*—Proposes electing the President by a plurality of electoral votes. (Madison and McHenry notes, *Documents*, pp. 675, 948)

Sept. 8—Vigorously supports motion of Williamson to increase the number of members of the House of Representatives. "He avowed himself a friend to a vigorous Government, but would declare at the same time that he held it essential that the popular branch of it

[1] According to a later version, Hamilton added that he was confident the convention could transact the business entrusted to its care without "the necessity of calling in foreign aid!" Jonathan Dayton to William Steele (Sept., 1825), *National Intelligencer*, Aug. 25, 1826.

should be on a broad foundation. He was seriously of opinion that the House of Representatives was on so narrow a scale as to be really dangerous, and to warrant a jealousy in the people for their liberties. He remarked that the connection between the President and Senate would tend to perpetuate him by corrupt influence. It was the more necessary on this account that a numerous representation in the other branch of the legislature should be established." (Madison, *Documents*, p. 694)

— Appointed a member of a Committee on Style to revise the draft Constitution along with Gouverneur Morris, James Madison, William Samuel Johnson, and Rufus King.

Sept. 10—Favors the proposition that on application of the legislatures of two thirds of the states Congress should call a Convention to amend the Constitution. "There was no greater evil in subjecting the people of the United States to the major voice than the people of a particular state. The lack of an easy mode of amending was a serious flaw in the Articles of Confederation." Instead of giving the power to the state legislatures, Hamilton proposes that Congress be empowered to call a Convention whenever two thirds of each branch should concur. Then seconds Madison's motion providing that by a two-thirds vote of both Houses or on the application of two-thirds of the legislatures of the several states Congress shall propose amendments to the Constitution, which shall be valid when ratified by three fourths of the state legislatures or by conventions in three fourths of the states (Article V). (Madison, *Documents*, p. 695)

— Concurs with Gerry "as to the indecorum of not requiring the approbation" of the Continental Congress to the change in government. Considers this "a necessary ingredient in the transaction." Proposes that if Congress should approve, the Constitution be sent to the state legislatures and referred to the state conventions, "each legislature declaring that if the convention of the state should think the plan ought to take effect among nine ratifying states, the same should take effect accordingly." Formally moves that the ratifying conventions "be chosen by the people" in each state; seconded by Gerry. Motion defeated. Wilson, Clymer, King, and Rutledge speak against it. (Madison, *Documents*, p. 697)

**Sept. 17*—The engrossed Constitution is read. Hamilton urges every member to sign. He is the only signer from New York. (Madison, *Documents*, p. 742)

July 3, 1787

In my passage through the Jerseys, and since my arrival here, I have taken particular pains to discover the public sentiment, and I am more and more convinced that this is the critical opportunity for establishing the prosperity of this country on a solid foundation. I have conversed with men of information, not only in this city, but from different parts of the State, and they agree that there has been an astonishing revolution for the better in the minds of the people. The prevailing apprehension among thinking men is, that the Convention, from the fear of shocking the popular opinion, will not go far enough. They seem to be convinced that a strong, well-mounted government will better suit the popular palate than one of a different complexion. Men in office are indeed taking all possible pains to give an unfavorable impression of the Convention, but the current seems to be moving strongly the other way.

A plain but sensible man, in a conversation I had with him yesterday, expressed himself nearly in this manner: The people begin to be convinced that "their excellent form of government," as they have been used to call it, will not answer their purpose, and that they must substitute something not very remote from that which they have lately quitted.

These appearances, though they will not warrant a conclusion that the people are yet ripe for such a plan as I advocate, yet serve to prove that there is no reason to despair of their adopting one equally energetic, if the Convention should think proper to propose it. They serve to prove that we ought not to allow too much weight to objections drawn from the supposed repugnance of the people to an efficient constitution. I confess I am more and more inclined to believe that former habits of thinking are regaining their influence with more rapidity than is generally imagined. . . .

I own it to you, sir, that I am seriously and deeply distressed at the aspect of the counsels which prevailed when I left Philadelphia. I fear that we shall let slip the golden opportunity of rescuing the American empire from disunion, anarchy, and misery.

—To Washington. Hamilton's hand. Hamilton Papers, 1st ser.

On July 10th Washington wrote Hamilton: "I am sorry you went away. I wish you were back."

Excerpts from his Speeches

May 29, 1787

It was observed by Mr. Hamilton before adjourning that it struck him as a necessary and preliminary inquiry to the propositions from Virginia whether the United States were susceptible of one government, or required a separate existence connected only by leagues offensive and defensive and treaties of commerce.

—Notes of James McHenry, *Documents Illustrative of the Formation of the Union of the American States*, 69th Congress, 1st Sess., House Doc. No. 398 (Washington, 1927) (hereinafter *Documents*), p. 926.

June 18, 1787

Mr. Hamilton said that he had been hitherto silent on the business before the convention, partly from respect to others whose superior abilities, age, and experience rendered him unwilling to bring forward ideas dissimilar to theirs, and partly from his delicate situation with respect to his own state, to whose sentiments, as expressed by his colleagues, he could by no means accede. The crisis, however, which now marked our affairs was too serious to permit any scruples whatever to prevail over the duty imposed on every man to contribute his efforts for the public safety and happiness. . . .

The states sent us here to provide for the exigencies of the Union. To rely on and propose any plan not adequate to these exigencies, merely because it was not clearly within our powers, would be to sacrifice the means to the end. It may be said that the *states* cannot *ratify* a plan not within the purview of the Articles of Confederation providing for alterations and amendments. But may not the states themselves, in which no constitutional authority equal to this purpose exists in the legislatures, have had in view a reference to the people at large? In the Senate of New York a proviso was moved that no act of the convention should be binding until it should be referred to the people and ratified; and the motion was lost by a single voice only, the reason assigned against it being that it might possibly be found an inconvenient shackle.

The great question is: What provision shall we make for the happiness of our country?

Hamilton enumerates the "great and essential" principles necessary for the support of government as an active and constant interest in supporting it, the love of power, which has caused demagogues "to hate the control of the General Government," the habitual attachment of the people to the states, a coercion of law or of arms, and "influence," which he defines as "a dispensation of those regular honors and emoluments which produce an attachment to the government." He then points out that in previous federations, ancient and modern, state or local power crippled effective union.

. . . How then are all these evils to be avoided? Only by such a complete sovereignty in the General Government as will turn all the strong principles and passions above-mentioned on its side. Does the scheme of New Jersey produce this effect? Does it afford any substantial remedy whatever? On the contrary it labors under great defects, and the defect of some of its provisions will destroy the efficacy of others. It gives a direct revenue to Congress, but this will not be sufficient. The balance can only be supplied by requisitions; which experience proves cannot be relied on. If states are to deliberate on the mode, they will also deliberate on the object, of the supplies; and will grant or not grant as they approve or disapprove of it. The delinquency of one will invite and countenance it in others. Quotas, too, must, in the nature of things, be so unequal, as to produce the same evil. . . .

Mr. Paterson's plan provides no remedy. If the powers proposed were adequate, the organization of Congress is such that they could never be properly and effectually exercised. The members of Congress being chosen by the states and subject to recall, represent all the local prejudices. Should the powers be found effectual, they will from time to time be heaped on them, till a tyrannic sway shall be established. The general power, whatever be its form, if it preserves itself, must swallow up the state powers. Otherwise, it will be swallowed up by them. It is against all the principles of good government to vest the requisite powers in such a body as Congress. Two sovereignties cannot co-exist within the same limits. Giving powers to Congress must eventuate in a bad government or in no government. The plan of New Jersey, therefore, will not do. What, then, is to be done? Here he was embarrassed. The extent of the country to be governed discouraged him. The expense of a General Government was also formidable; unless there was such a diminution of expense on the side of the state governments as the case would admit. If they were extinguished, he was persuaded that great economy might be obtained by substituting a General Government.

He did not mean, however, to shock the public opinion by proposing such a measure. On the other hand, he saw no *other* necessity for declining it. They are not necessary for any of the great purposes of commerce, revenue, or agriculture. Subordinate authorities, he was aware, would be necessary. There must be district tribunals, corporations for local purposes. But *cui bono* the vast and expensive apparatus now appertaining to the states? The only difficulty of a serious nature which occurred to him was that of drawing representatives from the extremes to the center of the community. What inducements can be offered that will suffice? The moderate wages for the first branch would only be a bait to little demagogues. Three dollars or thereabouts, he supposed, would be the utmost. The Senate, he feared, from a similar cause, would be filled by certain undertakers who wish for particular offices under the government. This view of the subject almost led him to despair that a republican government could be established over so great an extent. He was sensible, at the same time, that it would be unwise to propose one of any other form. In his private opinion, he had no scruple in declaring, supported as he was by the opinions of so many of the wise and good, that the British government was the best in the world; and that he doubted much whether anything short of it would do in America. He hoped gentlemen of different opinions would bear with him in this, and begged them to recollect the change of opinion on this subject which had taken place, and was still going on. It was once thought that the power of Congress was amply sufficient to secure the end of their institution. The error was now seen by every one. The members most tenacious of republicanism . . . were as loud as any in declaiming against the vices of democracy. This progress of the public mind led him to anticipate the time when others as well as himself would join in the praise bestowed by Mr. Neckar on the British constitution, namely, that it is the only government in the world "which unites public strength with individual security."

In every community where industry is encouraged there will be a division of it into the few and the many. Hence, separate interests will arise. There will be debtors and creditors, etc. Give all power to the many, they will oppress the few. Give all power to the few, they will oppress the many. Both, therefore, ought to have the power that each may defend itself against the other. To the want of this check we owe our paper money, instalment laws, etc. To the proper adjustment of it the British owe the excellence of their constitution. Their House of Lords is a most noble institution. Having nothing to hope for by a change, and a sufficient interest by means of their property in being faithful to the national interest, they form a permanent barrier against every pernicious innovation whether attempted on the part of the Crown or of the Commons. . . .

Gentlemen differ in their opinions concerning the necessary checks, from the different estimates they form of the human passions. They suppose seven years a sufficient period to give the Senate an adequate firmness, from not duly considering the amazing violence and turbulence of the democratic spirit. When a great object of government is pursued which seizes the popular passions, they spread like wildfire and become irresistible. He appealed to the gentlemen from the New England states whether experience had not there verified the remark. As to the Executive, it seemed to be admitted that no good one could be established on republican principles. Was not this giving up the merits of the question; for can there be a good government without a good Executive? The English model was the only good one on this subject. The hereditary interest of the king was so interwoven with that of the nation, and his personal emolument so great, that he was placed above the danger of being corrupted from abroad, and, at the same time, was both sufficiently independent and sufficiently controlled to answer the purpose of the institution at home. One of the weak sides of republics was their being liable to foreign influence and corruption. Men of little character, acquiring great power, become easily the tools of intermeddling neighbors. . . .

What is the inference from all these observations? That we ought to go as far, in order to attain stability and permanency, as republican principles will admit. Let one branch of Legislature hold their places for life, or, at least, during good behavior. Let the Executive, also, be for life. He appealed to the feelings of the members present whether a term of seven years would induce the sacrifice of private affairs, which an acceptance of public trust would require, so as to ensure the services of the best citizens. On this plan we should have in the Senate a permanent will, a weighty interest, which would answer essential purposes. But is this a republican government? it will be asked. Yes, if all the magistrates are appointed and vacancies are filled by the people, or a process of election originating with the people. He was sensible that an Executive, constituted as he proposed, would have, in fact, but little of the power and independence that might be necessary. On the other plan of appointing him for seven years, he though the Executive ought to have but little power. He would be ambitious, with the means of making creatures; and as the object of his ambition would be to *prolong* his power, it is probable that in case of a war he would avail himself of the emergency to evade or refuse a degradation from his place. An Executive for life has not this motive for forgetting his fidelity, and will therefore be a safer depository of power. . . .

Having made these observations, he would read to the committee a sketch of a plan which he should prefer to either of those under consideration. He was aware that it went beyond the ideas of most members. But will such a plan be adopted out of doors? In return he would ask, Will the people adopt the other plan? At present they will adopt neither. But he sees the Union dissolving, or already dissolved. He sees evils operating in the states which must soon cure the people of their fondness for democracies. . . . He did not mean to offer the paper he had sketched as a proposition to the committee. It was meant only to give a more correct view of his ideas, and to suggest the amendments which he should probably propose to the plan of Mr. Randolph, in the proper stages of its future discussion.

—Debates of the Federal Convention as reported by James Madison. *Documents*, pp. 215-223.

Hamilton then presented his own plan, of which at least six reports are extant. His proposals went considerably beyond the Randolph Plan in the extent to which they would have centralized power in the national government. His plan vested "the supreme legislative power of the United States of America" in two houses. The lower house was to be elected by the people for a three-year term, the Senate elected by electors chosen by the people to serve during good behavior. The chief executive was to be elected by electors chosen by still other electors, who were in turn chosen by the people. He was to serve during good behavior and have an absolute veto. The supreme judicial authority was to vest in twelve federal judges to hold office during good behavior. All government officials were liable to impeachment before a special court comprising the chief judges of the highest court of each state. "All laws of the particular states contrary to the Constitution or laws of the United States to be utterly void," and to prevent such laws from being enacted, the governor of each state, under Hamilton's plan, was to be appointed by the federal government and to be given a veto over the laws passed by his respective state legislature. Exclusive authority over the military and naval forces was to vest in the federal government.[1]

Madison noted that Hamilton's speech introducing the plan, as written down by him, "was seen by Mr. Hamilton who approved its correctness, with one or two verbal changes, which were made as he suggested." Judge Yates, a colleague of Hamilton's from New York, who differed with him politically, incorporated some explanatory matter in his own report of the speech and attributed to Hamilton a few pungent remarks not recorded by Madison.

All communities divide themselves into the few and the many. The first are the rich and well-born, the other the mass of the people. The voice of the people has been said to be the voice of God; and, however generally this maxim has been quoted and believed, it is not true in fact. The people are turbulent and changing; they seldom judge or determine right. Give, therefore, to the first class a distinct, permanent share in the government. They will check the unsteadiness of the second, and, as they cannot receive any advantage by a change, they therefore will ever maintain good government. Can a democratic assembly, who annually revolve in the mass of the people, be supposed steadily to pursue the public good? Nothing but a permanent body can check the imprudence of democracy. Their turbulent and uncontrolling disposition requires checks. . . .

I confess that this plan and that from Virginia are very remote from the idea of the people. Perhaps the Jersey plan is nearest their expectation. But the people are gradually ripening in their opinions of government; they begin to be tired of an excess of democracy; and

[1] Hamilton's version (probably a later insertion) provided for the Supreme Court judges to sit on the court of impeachment along with the chief judges of the state courts and also specified twelve Supreme Court judges. Madison omitted the second stage of electors for choosing the President, but all the other accounts, including Hamilton's own copy, specify a two-stage electoral college. Madison's account is in *Documents*, pp. 224, 225. Four other versions are found in *ibid.*, pp. 981-988. John Lansing, Jr.'s version is in Joseph R. Strayer, ed., *The Delegate from New York* (Princeton, 1939), pp. 119-122.

what even is the Virginia plan, but *pork still, with a little change of the source.*

—*Notes of the Secret Debates of the Federal Convention of 1787, Taken by the Late Hon. Robert Yates, Chief Justice of the State of New York* (G. Templeman: Washington, 1836).

Lansing's version of Hamilton's remarks about the prospects for democracy differ somewhat from Yates's. Instead of the people tiring of an excess of democracy, Lansing has Hamilton say that "the principal citizens of every state are tired of democracy." Hamilton's brief of his speech, found in the Hamilton Papers, is an additional lead to what he said that day:

Society naturally divides itself into two political divisions—the very *few* and the *many*, who have distinct interests.

If government in the hands of the *few*, they will tyrannize over the many.

If [in] the hands of the many, they will tyrannize over the few. It ought to be in the hands of both; and they should be separated.

This separation must be permanent.

Representation alone will not do.

Demagogues will generally prevail.

And if separated, they will need a mutual check.

This check is a monarch.

June 19, 1787

I agree to the proposition. I did not intend yesterday a total extinguishment of state governments; but my meaning was, that a national government ought to be able to support itself without the aid or interference of the state governments, and that therefore it was necessary to have full sovereignty. Even with corporate rights the states will be dangerous to the national government, and ought to be extinguished, new modified, or reduced to a smaller scale. . . .

Mr. Wilson. The declaration of independence preceded the state constitutions. What does this declare? In the name of the people of these states, we are declared to be free and independent. The power of war, peace, alliances and trade are declared to be vested in Congress.

Mr. Hamilton. I agree to Mr. Wilson's remark. Establish a weak government and you must at times overleap the bounds. Rome was obliged to create dictators. Cannot you make propositions to the people because we before confederated on other principles? The people can yield to them, if they will. The three great objects of government, *agriculture*, *commerce*, and *revenue*, can only be secured by a general government.

—Yates, *Secret Debates.*

The more close the union of the states, and the more complete the authority of the whole, the less opportunity will be allowed [to] the stronger states to injure the weaker.

—Madison's Debates, *Documents*, p. 240.

June 26, 1787

[Hamilton on the tenure of Senators] He did not mean to enter particularly into the subject. He concurred with Mr. Madison in thinking we were now to decide for ever the fate of republican government;[1] and that if we did not give to that form due stability and wisdom, it would be disgraced and lost among ourselves, disgraced and lost to mankind forever. He acknowledged himself not to think favorably of republican government; but addressed his remarks to those who did think favorably of it, in order to prevail on them to tone their government as high as possible. He professed himself to be as zealous an advocate for liberty as any man whatever; and trusted he should be as willing a martyr to it, though he differed as to the form in which it was most eligible. He concurred, also, in the general observations of Mr. Madison on the subject, which might be supported by others if it were necessary. It was certainly true that nothing like an equality of property existed; that an inequality would exist as long as liberty existed, and that it would unavoidably result from that very liberty itself. This inequality of property constituted the great and fundamental distinction in society. When the tribunitial power had levelled the boundary between the *patricians* and *plebians*, what followed? The distinction between rich and poor was substituted. . . .

—Madison's Debates, *Documents*, pp. 281, 282.

June 29, 1787

[Opposing equality of the states in the House of Representatives.] This position cannot be correct. Facts plainly contradict it. The parliament of Great Britain asserted a supremacy over the whole empire, and the celebrated Judge Blackstone labors for the legality of it, although many parts were not represented. This parliamentary power we opposed as contrary to our colonial rights. With that exception, throughout that whole empire it is submitted to. May not the smaller and greater states so modify their respective rights as to establish the general interest of the whole, without adhering to the right of equality? Strict representation is not observed in any of the state governments. The senate of New York are chosen by persons of certain qualifications

[1] Both the Madison and Yates versions speak of republican government. Lansing's account has Hamilton consider "the cause of democracy" and declare his attachment to a free government, for which he would "chearfully become a martyr." He is for "tuning the government high" to prevent "the occasional violence of democracy" and the "tyranny of the despot." Strayer, *The Delegate from New York*, pp. 84, 85.

to the exclusion of others. The question, after all, is, is it our interest in modifying this general government to sacrifice individual rights to the preservation of the rights of an *artificial* being, called states? There can be no truer principle than this—that every individual of the community at large has an equal right to the protection of government.

—Yates, *Secret Debates.*

Men are naturally equal, and societies or states, when fully independent, are also equal. It is as reasonable, and may be as expedient, that states should form leagues or compacts and lessen or part with their national equality as that men should form the social compact and, in doing so, lessen or surrender the natural equality of men. This is done in every society; and the grant to the society affects persons and property. Age, minority and estates are all affected.

A man may not become an elector or elected unless of a given age and having a certain estate. Let the people be represented according to numbers, the people will be free. Every office will be equally open to all and the majority of the people are to make the laws. Yet, it is said that the states will be destroyed and the people will be slaves. This is not so. The people are free at the expense of an artificial and ideal equaltiy of the states.

—Notes of Rufus King in the Federal Convention, *Documents*, pp. 867, 868.

In the notes of David Brearley Hamilton is reported to have urged during the debate of June 29th "that the general government will act not only upon the states but upon individuals."[1] *His colleague Lansing attributed this peroration to Hamilton: "This is a critical moment of American liberty. It is a miracle that we have met." Hamilton urged: "We must devise a system on the spot," one that is "strong and nervous, hoping that the good sense and principal necessity of our affairs will reconcile the people to it."*[2]

September 6, 1787

Mr. Hamilton said that he had been restrained from entering into the discussions by his dislike of the scheme of government in general; but as he meant to support the plan to be recommended as better than nothing, he wished in this place to offer a few remarks. He liked the new modification, on the whole, better than in the printed report. In this the President was a Monster elected for seven years, and ineligible afterwards; having great powers in appointments to office and continually tempted by this constitutional disqualification

[1] *Documents*, pp. 906, 907.
[2] Strayer, pp. 93, 94.

to abuse them in order to subvert the Government. Although he should be made re-eligible, still if appointed by the Legislature, he would be tempted to make use of corrupt influence to be continued in office. It seemed particularly desirable, therefore, that some other mode of election should be devised. Considering the different views of different states, and the different districts, Northern, Middle, and Southern, he concurred with those who thought that the votes would not be concentered, and that the appointment would consequently in the present mode devolve on the Senate. The nomination to offices will give great weight to the President. Here then is a mutual connection and influence that will perpetuate the President and aggrandize both him and the Senate. What is to be the remedy? He saw none better than to let the highest number of ballots, whether a majority or not, appoint the President. What was the objection to this? Merely that too small a number might appoint. But as the plan stands, the Senate may take the candidate having the smallest number of votes and make him President.

—Madison's Debates. *Documents*, pp. 675, 676.

James McHenry's account of Hamilton's speech accords substantially with Madison's, but he attributes to him these additional remarks: "He does not agree with those persons who say they will vote against the report because they cannot get all parts of it to please them. He will take any system which promises to save America from the dangers with which she is threatened."[1]

September 17, 1787

Mr. Hamilton expressed his anxiety that every member should sign. A few characters of consequence, by opposing or even refusing to sign the Constitution, might do infinite mischief by kindling the latent sparks which lurk under an enthusiasm in favor of the Convention which may soon subside. No man's ideas were more remote from the plan than his were known to be; but is it possible to deliberate between anarchy and convulsion on one side, and the chance of good to be expected from the plan on the other?

—Madison's Debates. *Documents*, p. 742.

September 15, 1803[2]

. . . The highest-toned propositions which I made in the convention were for a President, Senate, and Judges during good behavior—a House of Representatives for three years. Though I would have enlarged the legislative power of the general government, yet I never

[1] Papers of James McHenry. *Documents*, p. 948.

[2] Dated Sept. 15-16; endorsed Sept. 15.

contemplated the abolition of the State governments, but on the contrary, they were, in some particulars, constituent parts of my plan. This plan was, in my conception, conformable with the strict theory of a government purely republican, the essential criteria of which are that the principal organs of the executive and legislative departments be elected by the people, and hold their offices by a *responsible* and temporary or *defeasible* tenure. A vote was taken on the proposition respecting the executive. Five States were in favor of it, among these Virginia, and though, from the manner of voting—by delegations,—individuals were not distinguished, it was morally certain, from the known situation of the Virginia members (six in number, two of them, *Mason* and *Randolph,* professing popular doctrines), that *Madison* must have concurred in the vote of Virginia; thus, if I sinned against *republicanism,* Mr. Madison was not less guilty. I may truly then say that I never proposed either a President or Senate for life, and that I neither recommended nor mediated the annihilation of the State governments. And I may add that, in the course of the discussions in the convention, neither the propositions thrown out for debate, nor even those voted in the earlier stages of the deliberation, were considered as evidences of a definitive opinion in the proposer or voter. It appeared to me to be in some sort understood that, with a view to free investigation, experimental propositions might be made, which were to be received merely as suggestions for consideration. Accordingly, it is a fact that my final opinion was against an Executive during good behavior, on account of the increased danger to the public tranquillity incident to the election of a magistrate of this degree of permanency. In the plan of a constitution which I drew up while the convention was sitting, and which I communicated to Mr. Madison about the close of it, perhaps a day or two after, the office of President has no greater duration than for three years. This plan was predicated upon these bases: 1. That the political principles of the people of this country would endure nothing but republican government. 2. That in the actual situation of the country, it was in itself right and proper that the republican theory should have a fair and full trial. 3. That to such a trial it was essential that the government should be so constructed as to give all the energy and stability reconcilable with the principles of that theory.

These were the genuine sentiments of my heart, and upon them I acted. I sincerely hope that it may not hereafter be discovered that, through want of sufficient attention to the last idea, the experiment of republican government, even in this country, has not been as complete, as satisfactory, and as decisive as could be wished.

—To Timothy Pickering. Hamilton Papers, 1st ser.

6

The Fight for Ratification

The Federalist

> The establishment of a Constitution in time of profound peace by the voluntary consent of a whole people is a PRODIGY, to the completion of which I look forward with trembling anxiety.

When Hamilton affixed his name to the Constitution he put aside his doubts and plunged into the fight for its ratification. Aside from his shrewd political maneuvers, he made two epochal contributions. Collaborating with James Madison and John Jay, he wrote a series of letters to the New York press, published in book form in May, 1788, as The Federalist. In addition, he made a series of great speeches before the New York Convention.

All the Federalist papers were signed with the pseudonym "Publius," and the three authors evidently agreed to keep the identity of the authorship of the individual letters a secret. Writing to Madison from Paris in November, 1788, Jefferson praised The Federalist as "the best commentary on the principles of government which ever was written." He correctly assumed that most of it was written by one person, and that "in some parts it is discoverable that the author means only to say what may be best said in defense of opinions in which he did not concur." If Jefferson was referring to Madison—and the circumstantial evidence of his intent points in that direction—his description more accurately fitted Hamilton, who wrote at the very least two-thirds of The Federalist papers.

For a time the mystery of authorship seemed to be resolved. On the day before the fatal duel at Weehawken, Hamilton visited the New York law offices of his friend Egbert Benson. Learning that Benson was out of town, Hamilton walked around the room, stopped in front of one of the bookcases, took from it a volume of Pliny's Letters, and rather ostentatiously slipped into the book a small piece of paper. Then he returned the book to the shelf and left the office. After Hamilton's death the scrap of paper was located. It bore the following notation:

No. 2, 3, 4, 5, 64—J[ay]
No. 10, 14, 37 to 48 inclusive—M[adison]
No. 18, 19, 20—M[adison] and H[amilton] jointly
All the others by H[amilton]

Some years later, when this list was made public, Madison felt called upon to make certain revisions. He claimed authorship, in addition, of Nos. 18, 19, and 20, and of 49 to 58 and of 62 to 64. This revised list was wrong in at least one respect. It failed to credit Jay with No. 64, a copy of which in Jay's hand is found in his personal papers. The mystery was heightened by the conflicting evidence offered by notations in various copies of The Federalist in the hands of the friends of the collaborators. Thus, Jefferson's copy contains on the fly-leaf notations by Jefferson which substantially agree with Madison's later list, although he also credited Madison with No. 17 (clearly Hamilton's). On the other hand, Washington's copy (which erroneously credits Jay with Nos. 1 and 54) agrees substantially with Hamilton's list.

Internal evidence from the plan, structure, and literary phrasing of the letters, while by no means conclusive, tends to support Madison's claims. It is likely that Hamilton and Madison, who were in complete harmony on this project, exchanged ideas, that Hamilton made insertions or corrections on some of Madison's letters, and on this basis claimed joint authorship of letters largely from the pen of the Virginian. Chancellor Kent, a knowledgeable New York Federalist who was a close friend of Hamilton's, was led, on the basis of his study of the internal evidence, to support the claims of Madison's friends. Some divergence in emphasis and point of view between Hamilton and Madison may be found in The Federalist, but, taken as a whole, it is an outstanding example of intellectual teamwork. The mystery of authorship is still not completely resolved, but the excerpts included in this volume are confined to portions of The Federalist which are indisputably Hamilton's.

The initial letters stressed the basis, need, and advantages of a strong federal union.

October 27, 1787

To the People of the State of New York:

AFTER an unequivocal experience of the inefficiency of the subsisting federal government, you are called upon to deliberate on a new Constitution for the United States of America. The subject speaks its own importance; comprehending in its consequences nothing less than the existence of the UNION, the safety and welfare of the parts of which it is composed, the fate of an empire in many respects the most interesting in the world. It has been frequently remarked that it seems to have been reserved to the people of this country, by their conduct and example, to decide the important question, whether societies of men are really capable or not of establishing good government from reflection and choice, or whether they are forever destined to depend for their political constitutions on accident and force. If there be any truth in the remark, the crisis at which we are arrived may with propriety be regarded as the era in which that decision is to be made; and a wrong election of the part we shall act may, in this view, deserve to be considered as the general misfortune of mankind.

This idea will add the inducements of philanthropy to those of patriotism, to heighten the solicitude which all considerate and good men must feel for the event. Happy will it be if our choice should be directed by a judicious estimate of our true interests, unperplexed and unbiased by considerations not connected with the public good. But this is a thing more ardently to be wished than seriously to be expected. The plan offered to our deliberations affects too many particular interests, innovates upon too many local institutions, not to involve in its discussion a variety of objects foreign to its merits, and of views, passions and prejudices little favorable to the discovery of truth.

Among the most formidable of the obstacles which the new Constitution will have to encounter may readily be distinguished the obvious interest of a certain class of men in every State to resist all changes which may hazard a diminution of the power, emolument, and consequence of the offices they hold under the State establishments; and the perverted ambition of another class of men, who will either hope to aggrandize themselves by the confusions of their country, or will flatter themselves with fairer prospects of elevation from the subdivision of the empire into several partial confederacies than from its union under one government.

It is not, however, my design to dwell upon observations of this nature. I am well aware that it would be disingenous to resolve indiscriminately the opposition of any set of men (merely because their situations might subject them to suspicion) into interested or ambitious views. Candor will oblige us to admit that even such men may be actuated by upright intentions; and it cannot be doubted that much of the opposition which has made it appearance, or may hereafter make its appearance, will spring from sources, blameless at least, if not respectable—the honest errors of minds led astray by preconceived jealousies and fears. So numerous indeed and so powerful are the causes which serve to give a false bias to the judgment, that we, upon many occasions, see wise and good men on the wrong as well as on the right side of questions of the first magnitude to society. This circumstance, if duly attended to, would furnish a lesson of moderation to those who are ever so much persuaded of their being in the right in any controversy. And a further reason for caution, in this respect, might be drawn from the reflection that we are not always sure that those who advocate the truth are influenced by purer principles than their antagonists. Ambition, avarice, personal animosity, party opposition, and many other motives not more laudable than these, are apt to operate as well upon those who support as those who oppose the right side of a question. Were there not even inducements to moderation, nothing could be more ill-judged than that intolerant spirit which has, at all times, characterized political parties. For in politics, as in religion, it is equally absurd to aim at making proselytes by fire and sword. Heresies in either can rarely be cured by persecution. . . .

An enlightened zeal for the energy and efficiency of government will be stigmatized as the offspring of a temper fond of despotic power and hostile to the principles of liberty. An over-scrupulous jealousy of danger to the rights of the people, which is more commonly the fault of the head than of the heart, will be represented as mere pretence and artifice, the stale bait for popularity at the expense of the public good. It will be forgotten, on the one hand, that jealousy is the usual concomitant of love, and that the noble enthusiasm of liberty is apt to be infected with a spirit of narrow and illiberal distrust. On the other hand, it will be equally forgotten that the vigor of government is essential to the security of liberty; that, in the contemplation of a sound and well-informed judgment, their interest can never be separated; and that a dangerous ambition more often lurks behind the specious mask of zeal for the rights of the people than under the forbidding appearance of zeal for the firmness and efficiency of government. History will teach us that the former has been found a much more certain road to the introduction of despotism than the latter, and that of those men who have overturned the liberties of republics, the greatest number have begun their career by paying an obsequious court to the people; commencing demagogues, and ending tyrants.

In the course of the preceding observations, I have had an eye, my fellow-citizens, to putting you upon your guard against all attempts, from whatever quarter, to influence your decison in a matter of the utmost moment to your welfare, by any impressions other than those which may result from the evidence of truth. You will, no doubt, at the same time, have collected from the general scope of them, that they proceed from a source not unfriendly to the new Constitution. Yes, my countrymen, I own to you that, after having given it an attentive consideration, I am clearly of opinion it is your interest to adopt it. I am convinced that this is the safest course for your liberty, your dignity, and your happiness. I affect not reserves which I do not feel. I will not amuse you with an appearance of deliberation when I have decided. I frankly acknowledge to you my convictions, and I will freely lay before you the reasons on which they are founded. The consciousness of good intentions disdains ambiguity. I shall not, however, multiply professions on this head. My motives must remain in the depository of my own breast. My arguments will be open to all, and may be judged of by all. They shall at least be offered in a spirit which will not disgrace the cause of truth.

I propose, in a series of papers, to discuss the following interesting particulars:—*The utility of the* UNION *to your political prosperity—The insufficiency of the present Confederation to preserve that Union—The necessity of a government at least equally energetic with the one proposed, to the attainment of this object—The conformity of the proposed Constitution to the true principles of republican government—Its analogy to your own State constitution*—and lastly, *The additional security which its adoption will afford to the preservation of that species of government, to liberty, and to property.*

In the progress of this discussion I shall endeavor to give a satisfactory answer to all the objections which shall have made their appearance, that may seem to have any claim to your attention.

It may perhaps be thought superfluous to offer arguments to prove the utility of the UNION, a point, no doubt, deeply engraved on the hearts of the great body of the people in every State, and one, which it may be imagined, has no adversaries. But the fact is, that we already hear it whispered in the private circles of those who oppose the new Constitution, that the thirteen States are of too great extent for any general system, and that we must of necessity resort to separate confederacies of distinct portions of the whole. This doctrine will, in all probability, be gradually propagated, till it has votaries enough to countenance an open avowal of it. For nothing can be more evident, to those who are able to take an enlarged view of the subject, than the alternative of an adoption of the new Constitution or a dismemberment of the Union. It will therefore be of use to begin by examining the advantages of that Union, the certain evils, and the probable dangers, to which every State will be exposed from its dissolution. . . .

PUBLIUS

—*The Federalist* No. 1 (Original, McLean ed., 1788).

[November, 1787]

. . . The causes of hostility among nations are innumerable. There are some which have a general and almost constant operation upon the collective bodies of society. Of this description are the love of power or the desire of pre-eminence and dominion—the jealousy of power, or the desire of equality and safety. There are others which have a more circumscribed though an equally operative influence within their spheres. Such are the rivalships and competitions of commerce between commercial nations. And there are others, not less numerous than either of the former, which take their origin entirely in private passions; in the attachments, enmities, interests, hopes, and fears of leading individuals in the communities of which they are members. . . .

The celebrated Pericles, in compliance with the resentment of a prostitute,[1] at the expense of much of the blood and treasure of his countrymen, attacked, vanquished, and destroyed the city of the *Samnians*. The same man, stimulated by private pique against the Megarensians,[2] another nation of Greece, or to avoid a prosecution with which he was threatened as an accomplice in a supposed theft of the statutary Phidias,[3] or to get rid of the accusations prepared to be brought against him for dissipating the funds of the state in the purchase of popularity,[4] or from a combination of all these causes, was the primitive author of that famous and fatal war, distinguished in the Grecian annals by the name of the *Peloponnesian* war; which, after various vicissitudes, intermissions, and renewals, terminated in the ruin of the Athenian commonwealth. . . .

The influence which the bigotry of one female,[5] the petulance of another,[6] and the cabals of a third,[7] had in the contemporary policy, ferments, and pacifications, of a considerable part of Europe, are topics that have been too often descanted upon not to be generally known.

To multiply examples of the agency of personal considerations in the production of great national events, either foreign or domestic, according to their direction, would be an unnecessary waste of time. . . . Perhaps, however, a reference, tending to illustrate the general principle, may with propriety be made to a case which has lately happened among ourselves. If Shays had not been a *desperate debtor*, it is much to be doubted whether Massachusetts would have been plunged into a civil war.

But notwithstanding the concurring testimony of experience, in this particular, there are still to be found visionary or designing men, who stand ready to advocate the paradox of perpetual peace between the States, though dismembered and alienated from each other. . . .

From this summary of what has taken place in other countries,

[1] Aspasia, vide *Plutarch's Life of Pericles*.—Publius

[2] *Ibid.*—Publius

[3] *Ibid.*—Publius

[4] *Ibid.* Phidias was supposed to have stolen some public gold, with the connivance of Pericles, for the embellishment of the statue of Minerva.—Publius

[5] Madame de Maintenon.—Publius

[6] Duchess of Marlborough.—Publius

[7] Madame de Pompadour.—Publius

whose situations have borne the nearest resemblance to our own, what reason can we have to confide in those reveries which would seduce us into an expectation of peace and cordiality between the members of the present confederacy, in a state of separation? . . . Is it not time to awake from the deceitful dream of a golden age, and to adopt as a practical maxim for the direction of our political conduct that we, as well as the other inhabitants of the globe, are yet remote from the happy empire of perfect wisdom and perfect virtue?

Let the point of extreme depression to which our national dignity and credit have sunk, let the inconveniences felt everywhere from a lax and ill administration of government, let the revolt of a part of the State of North Carolina, the late menacing disturbance in Pennsylvania, and the actual insurrections and rebellions in Massachusetts, declare—!

—*The Federalist* No. 6.

[November, 1787]

It is sometimes asked, with an air of seeming triumph, what inducements could the States have, if disunited, to make war upon each other? It would be a full answer to this question to say—precisely the same inducements which have, at different times, deluged in blood all the nations in the world. But, unfortunately for us, the question admits of a more particular answer. There are causes of differences within our immediate contemplation, of the tendency of which, even under the restraints of a federal constitution, we have had sufficient experience to enable us to form a judgment of what might be expected if those restraints were removed.

Territorial disputes have at all times been found one of the most fertile sources of hostility among nations. Perhaps the greatest proportion of wars that have desolated the earth have sprung from this origin. This cause would exist among us in full force. We have a vast tract of unsettled territory within the boundaries of the United States. There still are discordant and undecided claims between several of them, and the dissolution of the Union would lay a foundation for similar claims between them all. . . .

In the wide field of Western territory, therefore, we perceive an ample theatre for hostile pretensions, without any umpire or common judge to interpose between the contending parties. To reason from the past to the future, we shall have good ground to apprehend, that the sword would sometimes be appealed to as the arbiter of their differences. The circumstances of the dispute between Connecticut and Pennsylvania, respecting the land at Wyoming, admonish us not to be sanguine in expecting an easy accommodation of such differences. . . .

The competitions of commerce would be another fruitful source of contention. The states less favorably circumstanced would be desirous of escaping from the disadvantage of local situation, and of sharing in the advantage of their more fortunate neighbors. Each state, or separate confederacy, would pursue a system of commercial policy peculiar to itself. This would occasion distinctions, preferences, and exclusions, which would beget discontent. . . .

The public debt of the Union would be a further cause of collision between the separate states or confederacies. The apportionment, in the first instance, and the progressive extinguishment afterward, would be alike productive of ill-humor and animosity. . . .

Laws in violation of private contracts, as they amount to aggressions on the rights of those states whose citizens are injured by them, may be considered as another probable source of hostility. We are not authorized to expect that a more liberal or more equitable spirit would preside over the legislations of the individual states hereafter, if unrestrained by any additional checks, than we have heretofore seen in too many instances disgracing their several codes. . . .

—*The Federalist* No. 7.

November 20, 1787

. . . War between the states, in the first period of their separate existence, would be accompanied with much greater distresses than it commonly is in those countries where regular military establishments have long obtained. The disciplined armies always kept on foot on the continent of Europe, though they bear a malignant aspect to liberty and economy, have, notwithstanding, been productive of the signal advantage of rendering sudden conquests impracticable, and of preventing that rapid desolation which used to mark the progress of war prior to their introduction. . . .

In this country the scene would be altogether reversed. The jealousy of military establishments would postpone them as long as possible. The want of fortifications, leaving the frontiers of one state open to another, would facilitate inroads. The populous states would, with little difficulty, overrun their less populous neighbors. . . . The violent destruction of life and property incident to war, the continual effort and alarm attendant on a state of continual danger, will compel nations the most attached to liberty to resort for repose and security to institutions which have a tendency to destroy their civil and political rights. To be more safe, they at length become willing to run the risk of being less free.

The institutions chiefly alluded to are STANDING ARMIES and the correspondent appendages of military establishments. . . . The weaker states or confederacies would first have recourse to them to put themselves upon an equality with their more potent neighbors. They would endeavor to supply the inferiority of population and resources by a more regular and effective system of defense, by disciplined troops, and by fortifications. They would, at the same time, be necessitated to strengthen the executive arm of government, in doing which their constitutions would acquire a progressive direction towards monarchy. It is of the nature of war to increase the executive at the expense of the legislative authority. . . .

If we are wise enough to preserve the Union, we may for ages enjoy an advantage similar to that of an insulated situation. Europe is at a great distance from us. Her colonies in our vicinity will be likely to continue too much disproportioned in strength to be able to give us any dangerous annoyance. Extensive military establishments cannot, in this position, be necessary to our security. But if we should be disunited, and the integral parts should either remain separated, or, which is most probable, should be thrown together into two or three confederacies, we should be, in a short course of time, in the predicament of the continental powers of Europe—our liberties would be a prey to the means of defending ourselves against the ambition and jealousy of each other. . . .

—*The Federalist* No. 8.

[November, 1787]

A FIRM Union will be of the utmost moment to the peace and liberty of the States, as a barrier against domestic faction and insurrection. It is impossible to read the history of the petty republics of Greece and Italy without feeling sensations of horror and disgust at the distractions with which they were continually agitated, and at the rapid succession of revolutions by which they were kept in a state of perpetual vibration between the extremes of tyranny and anarchy. If they exhibit occasional calms, these only serve as short-lived contrasts to the furious storms that are to succeed. . . .

From the disorders that disfigure the annals of those republics the advocates of despotism have drawn arguments, not only against the forms of republican government, but against the very principles of civil liberty. They have decried all free government as inconsistent with the order of society, and have indulged themselves in malicious exultation over its friends and partisans. Happily for mankind, stupendous fabrics reared on the basis of liberty, which have flourished for ages, have, in a few glorious instances, refuted their gloomy sophisms. And I trust, America will be the broad and solid foundation of other edifices, not less magnificent, which will be equally permanent monuments of their errors.

But it is not to be denied that the portraits they have sketched of republican government were too just copies of the originals from which they were taken. If it had been found impracticable to have devised models of a more perfect structure, the enlightened friends to liberty would have been obliged to abandon the cause of that species of government as indefensible. The science of politics, however, like most other sciences, has received great improvement. The efficacy of various principles is now well understood, which were either not known at all, or imperfectly known to the ancients. The regular distribution of power into distinct departments; the introduction of legislative balances and checks; the institution of courts composed of judges holding their offices during good behavior; the representation of the people in the legislature by deputies of their own election: these are wholly new discoveries, or have made their principal progress towards perfection in modern times. They are means, and powerful means, by which the excellences of republican government may be retained and its imperfections lessened or avoided. . . .

The definition of a *confederate republic* seems simply to be "an assemblage of societies," or an association of two or more states into one state. The extent, modifications, and objects of the federal authority are mere matters of discretion. So long as the separate organization of the members be not abolished; so long as it exists, by a constitutional necessity, for local purposes; though it should be in perfect subordination to the general authority of the union, it would still be, in fact and in theory, an association of states, or a confederacy. The proposed Constitution, so far from implying an abolition of the State governments, makes them constituent parts of the national sovereignty, by allowing them a direct representation in the Senate, and leaves in their possession certain exclusive and very important portions of sovereign power. This fully corresponds, in every rational import of the terms, with the idea of a federal government. . . .

—*The Federalist* No. 9

[November, 1787]

The importance of the Union, in a commercial light, is one of those points about which there is at least room to entertain a difference of opinion, and which has, in fact, commanded the most general assent of men who have any acquaintance with the subject. This applies as well to our intercourse with foreign countries as with each other. . . .

A further resource for influencing the conduct of European nations toward us, in this respect, would arise from the establishment of a federal navy. . . . A price would be set not only upon our friendship, but upon our neutrality. By a steady adherence to the Union, we may hope, erelong, to become the arbiter of Europe in America, and to be able to incline the balance of European competitions in this part of the world as our interest may dictate. . . .

Under a vigorous national government, the natural strength and resources of the country, directed to a common interest, would baffle all the combinations of European jealousy to restrain our growth. This situation would even take away the motive to such combinations, by inducing an impracticability of success. An active commerce, an extensive navigation, and a flourishing marine would then be the offspring of moral and physical necessity. We might defy the little arts of the little politicians to control or vary the irresistible and unchangeable course of nature.

But in a state of disunion, these combinations might exist and might operate with success. It would be in the power of the maritime nations, availing themselves of our universal impotence, to prescribe the conditions of our political existence; and as they have a common interest in being our carriers, and still more in preventing our becoming theirs, they would in all probability combine to embarrass our navigation in such a manner as would in effect destroy it, and confine us to a PASSIVE COMMERCE. We should then be compelled to content ourselves with the first price of our commodities, and to see the profits of our trade snatched from us to enrich our enemies and persecutors. That unequalled spirit of enterprise, which signalizes the genius of the American merchants and navigators, and which is in itself an inexhaustible mine of national wealth, would be stifled and lost, and poverty and disgrace would overspread a country which, with wisdom, might make herself the admiration and envy of the world.

There are rights of great moment to the trade of America which are rights of the Union. I allude to the fisheries, to the navigation of the Western lakes, and to that of the Mississippi. The dissolution of the Confederacy would give room for delicate questions concerning the future existence of these rights; which the interest of more powerful partners would hardly fail to solve to our disadvantage. The disposition of Spain with regard to the Mississippi needs no comment. France and Britain are concerned with us in the fisheries, and view them as of the utmost moment to their navigation. . . . This branch of trade ought not to be considered as a partial benefit. . . . As a nursery of seamen, it now is, or, when time shall have more nearly assimilated the principles of navigation in the several states, will become a universal resource. To the establishment of a navy it must be indispensable.

To this great national object, a NAVY, union will contribute in various ways. . . . A navy of the United States, as it would embrace the resources of all, is an object far less remote than a navy of any single state or partial confederacy, which would only embrace the resources of a single part. . . .

I shall briefly observe, that our situation invites and our interests prompt us to aim at an ascendant in the system of American affairs. The world may politically, as well as geographically, be divided into four parts, each having a distinct set of interests. Unhappily for the other three, Europe, by her arms and by her negotiations, by force and by fraud, has, in different degrees, extended her dominion over them all. Africa, Asia, and America, have successively felt her domination. The superiority she has long maintained has tempted her to plume herself as the Mistress of the World, and to consider the rest of mankind as created for her benefit. Men admired as profound philosophers have, in direct terms, attributed to her inhabitants a physical superiority and have gravely asserted that all animals, and with them the human species, degenerate in America—that even dogs cease to bark after having breathed awhile in our atmosphere. Facts have too long supported these arrogant pretensions of the Europeans. It belongs to us to vindicate the honor of the human race, and to teach that assuming brother, moderation. Union will enable us to do it. Disunion will add another victim to his triumphs. Let Americans disdain to be the instruments of European greatness! Let the thirteen States, bound together in a strict and indissoluble Union, concur in erecting one great American system, superior to the control of all transatlantic force or influence, and able to dictate the terms of the connection between the old and the new world!

—*The Federalist* No. 11.

November 27, 1787

. . . The prosperity of commerce is now perceived and acknowledged by all enlightened statesmen to be the most useful as well as the most productive source of national wealth, and has accordingly become a primary object of their political cares. . . .

The ability of a country to pay taxes must always be proportioned, in a great degree, to the quantity of money in circulation, and to the celerity with which it circulates. Commerce, contributing to both of these objects, must of necessity render the payment of taxes easier, and facilitates the requisite supplies to the treasury. . . .

If . . . there be but one government pervading all the states, there will be, as to the principal part of our commerce, but ONE SIDE to guard—the ATLANTIC COAST. Vessels arriving directly from foreign countries, laden with valuable cargoes, would rarely choose to hazard themselves to the complicated and critical perils which would attend attempts to unlade prior to their coming into port. They would have to dread both the dangers of the coast, and of detection, as well after as before their arrival at the places of their final destination. An ordinary degree of vigilance would be competent to the prevention of any material infractions upon the rights of the revenue. A few armed vessels, judiciously stationed at the entrance of our ports, might at a small expense be made useful sentinels of the laws. . . .

What will be the consequence, if we are not able to avail ourselves of the resource in question in its full extent? A nation cannot long exist without revenues. Destitute of this essential support, it must resign its independence, and sink into the degraded condition of a province. This is an extremity to which no government will of choice accede.

Revenue, therefore, must be had at all events. In this country, if the principal part be not drawn from commerce, it must fall with oppressive weight upon land. It has been already intimated that excises, in their true signification, are too little in unison with the feelings of the people, to admit of great use being made of that mode of taxation; nor, indeed, in the states where almost the sole employment is agriculture, are the objects proper for excise sufficiently numerous to permit very ample collections in that way. Personal estate . . . from the difficulty in tracing it, cannot be subjected to large contributions by any other means than by taxes on consumption. In populous cities it may be enough the subject of conjecture to occasion the oppression of individuals without much aggregate benefit to the state; but beyond these circles, it must, in a great measure, escape the eye and the hand of the tax-gatherer. As the necessities of the state, nevertheless, must be satisfied in some mode or other, the defect of other resources must throw the principal weight of public burdens on the possessors of land. And as, on the other hand, the wants of the government can never obtain an adequate supply, unless all the sources of revenue are open to its demands, the finances of the community, under such embarrassments, cannot be put into a situation consistent with its respectability or its security. Thus we shall not even have the consolations of a full treasury to atone for the oppression of that valuable class of the citizens who are employed in the cultivation of the soil. But public and private distress will keep pace with each other in gloomy concert; and unite in deploring the infatuation of those counsels which led to disunion.

—*The Federalist* No. 12.

[November, 1787]

As connected with the subject of revenue, we may with propriety consider that of economy. The money saved from one object may be usefully applied to another, and there will be so much the less to be drawn from the pockets of the people. If the states are united under one government; there will be but one national civil list to support; if they are divided into several confederacies, there will be as many different national civil lists to be provided for—and each of them, as to the principal departments coextensive with that which would be necessary for a government of the whole. The entire separation of the states into thirteen unconnected sovereignties is a project too extravagant and too replete with danger to have many advocates. . . .

Nothing can be more evident than that the thirteen states will be able to support a national government better than one half, or one third, or any number less than the whole.

—*The Federalist* No. 13.

Hamilton concluded The Federalist *with a summary and final plea for ratification.*

[May, 1788]

To the People of the State of New York:

. . . Thus have I, fellow-citizens, executed the task I had assigned to myself; with what success, your conduct must determine. I trust at least you will admit that I have not failed in the assurance I gave you respecting the spirit with which my endeavors should be conducted. I have addressed myself purely to your judgments, and have studiously avoided those asperities which are too apt to disgrace political disputants of all parties, and which have been not a little provoked by the language and conduct of the opponents of the Constitution. The charge of a conspiracy against the liberties of the people, which has been indiscriminately brought against the advocates of the plan, has something in it too wanton and too malignant, not to excite the indignation of every man who feels in his own bosom a refutation of the calumny. The perpetual changes which have been rung upon the wealthy, the well-born, and the great, have been such as to inspire the disgust of all sensible men. . . .

I shall not dissemble that I feel an entire confidence in the arguments which recommend the proposed system to your adoption, and that I am unable to discern any real force in those by which it has been opposed. I am persuaded that it is the best which our political situation, habits, and opinions will admit, and superior to any the revolution has produced. . . .

No advocate of the measure can be found, who will not declare as his sentiment, that the system, though it may not be perfect in every part, is, upon the whole, a good one; is the best that the present views and circumstances of the country will permit; and is such an one as promises every species of security which a reasonable people can desire.

I answer in the next place, that I should esteem it the extreme of imprudence to prolong the precarious state of our national affairs, and to expose the Union to the jeopardy of successive experiments, in the chimerical pursuit of a perfect plan. I never expect to see a perfect work from imperfect man. The result of the deliberation of all collective bodies must necessarily be a compound, as well of the errors and prejudices, as of the good sense and wisdom, of the individuals of whom they are composed. . . .

The reasons assigned in an excellent little pamphlet lately published in this city, are unanswerable to show the utter improbability of assembling a new convention, under circumstances in any degree so favorable to a happy issue, as those in which the late convention met, deliberated, and concluded. I will not repeat the arguments there used, as I presume the production itself has had an extensive circulation. It is certainly well worthy the perusal of every friend to his country. There is, however, one point of light in which the subject of amendments still remains to be considered, and in which it has not yet been exhibited to public view. I cannot resolve to conclude without first taking a survey of it in this aspect.

It appears to me susceptible of absolute demonstration, that it will be far more easy to obtain subsequent than previous amendments to the Constitution. The moment an alteration is made in the present plan, it becomes, to the purpose of adoption, a new one, and must undergo a new decision of each State. To its complete establishment throughout the Union, it will therefore require the concurrence of thirteen States. If, on the contrary, the Constitution proposed should once be ratified by all the States as it stands, alterations in it may at any time be effected by nine States. Here, then, the chances are as thirteen to nine in favor of subsequent amendment, rather than of the original adoption of an entire system. . . .

The zeal for attempts to amend, prior to the establishment of the Constitution, must abate in every man who is ready to accede to the truth of the following observations of a writer equally solid and ingenious: "To balance a large state or society [says he], whether monarchical or republican, on general laws, is a work of so great difficulty, that no human genius, however comprehensive, is able, by the mere dint of reason and reflection, to effect it. The judgments of many must unite in the work; EXPERIENCE must guide their labor; TIME must bring it to perfection, and the FEELING of inconveniences must correct the mistakes which they *inevitably* fall into in their first trials and experiments."[1] These judicious reflections contain a lesson of moderation to all the sincere lovers of the Union, and ought to put them upon their guard against hazarding anarchy, civil war, a perpetual alienation of the States from each other, and perhaps the military despotism of a victorious demagogue, in the pursuit of what they are not likely to obtain, but from TIME and EXPERIENCE. It may be in me a defect of political fortitude, but I acknowledge that I cannot entertain an equal tranquillity with those who affect to treat the dangers of a longer continuance in our present situation as imaginary. A NATION, without a NATIONAL GOVERNMENT, is, in my view, an awful spectacle. The establishment of a Constitution, in time of profound peace, by the voluntary consent of a whole people, is a PRODIGY, to the completion of which I look forward with trembling anxiety. I can reconcile it to no rules of prudence to let go the hold we now have, in so arduous an enterprise, upon seven out of the thirteen States, and after having passed over so considerable a part of the ground, to recommence the course. I dread the more the consequences of new attempts, because I KNOW that POWERFUL INDIVIDUALS, in this and in other States, are enemies to a general national government in every possible shape. PUBLIUS

—*The Federalist* No. 85.

[1] Hume's *Essays*, vol. i., p. 128—The rise of arts and sciences.

In the spring of 1788 Hamilton and Madison kept in close touch with each other, relaying information on the progress of ratification in their respective states where the issues were contested most bitterly. By 1800 they were political adversaries and it might have been embarrassing to both of them had the authorship of the individual Federalist *papers been publicly disclosed.*

April 3, 1788

. . . I send you the *Federalist* from the beginning to the conclusion of the commentary on the Executive Branch. If our suspicions of the author be right, he must be too much engaged to make a rapid progress in what remains. The Court of Chancery and a Circuit Court are now sitting.

—To James Madison. *Hamilton,* I, 450-451.

April 7, 1800

I would readily comply with the wish of Mr. Evans, was I sure that it would not be a breach of propriety towards Mr. Madison. But if my memory does not deceive me, there was a sort of understanding between us that there should be no disclosure but by mutual consent. You will be sensible that I ought to be peculiarly circumspect with regard to this gentleman.

—To Oliver Wolcott. *Works,* X, 368.

The Great Debate

Hamilton anxiously awaited word of the fate of the Constitution in Virginia and New Hampshire. The latter state, the ninth, ratified on June 21st, Virginia four days later.

May 19, 1788

. . . We think here that the situation of your State is critical. Let me know what you now think of it. I believe you meet nearly at the time we do. It will be of vast importance that an exact communication should be kept up between us at that period; and the moment *any decisive* question is taken, if favorable, I request you to dispatch an express to me, with pointed orders to make all possible diligence, by changing horses, etc.

—To James Madison. *Hamilton,* I, 453-454.

June 6, 1788

. . . permit me to request that the instant you have taken a decisive vote in favor of the Constitution, you send an express to me at Poughkeepsie. Let him take the *shortest route* to that place, change horses on the road, and use all possible diligence. I shall with pleasure defray all expenses, and give a liberal reward to the person. As I suspect an effort will be made to precipitate us, all possible *safe* dispatch on your part, as well to obtain a decision as to communicate the intelligence of it, will be desirable.

—To John Sullivan, President of the State of New Hampshire. *Works*, IX, 432.

Hamilton's speeches at the Poughkeepsie Convention rank among the most persuasive oratorical efforts in American history. These speeches actually changed votes. Since the antifederalists constituted a majority of the delegates, Hamilton felt that a full and thorough discussion of the Constitution was essential if the opposition was to be persuaded against their initial prejudices. Time was on his side, provided the Convention could be held in session. James Kent, later Chancellor of New York, heard Hamilton's speeches and observed that he "maintained the ascendancy on every question" and carried the burden of the debate for his side. Hamilton felt it necessary to reassure the delegates that the new Constitution would not impair state sovereignty.

June 20, 1788

The state governments possess inherent advantages, which will ever give them an influence and ascendancy over the national government, and will for ever preclude the possibility of federal encroachments. That their liberties, indeed, can be subverted by the federal head, is repugnant to every rule of political calculation.

—Speech on the Compromises of the Constitution, *Debates of the N. Y. Convention*, p. 27.

June 21, 1788

. . . let us consider the powers of the national government, and compare them with the objects of state legislation. The powers of the new government are general, and calculated to embrace the aggregate interests of the Union, and the general interest of each state, so far as it stands in relation to the whole. The object of the state governments is to provide for their internal interests, as unconnected with the United States, and as composed of minute parts or districts. A particular knowledge, therefore, of the local circumstances of any state, as they may vary in different districts, is unnecessary for the federal representative. As he is not to represent the interests or local wants of the county of Dutchess or Montgomery, neither is it necessary that he should be acquainted with their particular resources. But in the state governments, as the laws regard the interest of the people, in all their various minute divisions, it is necessary that the smallest interests should be represented. . . .

Sir, in my experience of public affairs, I have constantly remarked, in the conduct of the members of Congress, a strong and uniform attachment to the interests of their own State. These interests have on many occasions been adhered to with an undue and illiberal pertinacity, and have too often been preferred to the welfare of the Union. This attachment has given birth to an unaccommodating spirit of party, which has frequently embarrassed the best measures....

Sir, the most powerful obstacle to the members of Congress betraying the interests of their constituents, is the state legislatures themselves, who will be standing bodies of observation, possessing the confidence of the people, jealous of federal encroachments, and armed with every power to check the first essays of treachery. They will institute regular modes of enquiry. The complicated domestic attachments which subsist between state legislators and their electors, will ever make them vigilant guardians of the people's rights. Possessed of the means and the disposition of resistance, the spirit of opposition will be easily communicated to the people, and, under the conduct of an authorized body of leaders, will act with weight and system. Thus it appears that the very structure of the Confederacy affords the surest preventives from error, and the most powerful checks to misconduct.

—Speech on the Constitution, *Debates of the N. Y. Convention*, pp. 45-46.

June 24, 1788

. . . Whenever, therefore, Congress shall meditate any infringement of the state constitutions, the great body of the people will naturally take part with their domestic representatives. Can the general government withstand such a united opposition? Will the people suffer themselves to be stripped of their privileges? Will they suffer their legislatures to be reduced to a shadow and a name? The idea is shocking to common sense. . . . Thus, whatever constitutional provisions are made to the contrary, every government will be at last driven to the necessity of subjecting the partial to the universal interest. The gentlemen ought always, in their reasoning, to distinguish between the real, genuine good of a state, and the opinions and prejudices which may prevail respecting it. The latter may be opposed to the general good, and consequently ought to be sacrificed; the former is so involved in it that it never can be sacrificed.

—Speech on the United States Senate, *Debates of the N.Y. Convention*, p. 73.

June 27, 1788

It has been advanced as a principle, that no government but a despotism can exist in a very extensive country. This is a melancholy consideration indeed. If it were founded on truth, we ought to dismiss the idea of a republican government, even for the state of New York. This idea has been taken from a celebrated writer, who, by being misunderstood, has been the occasion of frequent fallacies in our reasoning on political subjects. But the position has been misapprehended; and its application is entirely false and unwarrantable. It relates only to democracies, where the whole body of the people meet to transact business, and where representation is unknown. Such were a number of ancient and some modern independent cities. Men who read without attention have taken these maxims respecting the extent of country, and, contrary to their proper meaning, have applied them to republics in general. This application is wrong in respect to all representative governments, but especially in relation to a confederacy of states, in which the supreme legislature has only general powers and the civil and domestic concerns of the people are regulated by the laws of the several states. This distinction being kept in view, all the difficulty will vanish, and we may easily conceive that the people of a large country may be represented as truly as those of a small one. An assembly constituted for general purposes may be fully competent to every federal regulation, without being too numerous for deliberate conduct. If the state governments were to be abolished, the question would wear a different face; but this idea is inadmissible. They are absolutely necessary to the system. Their existence must form a leading principle in the most perfect constitution we could form. I insist that it never can be the interest or desire of the national legislature to destroy the state governments. It can derive no advantage from such an event; but, on the contrary, would lose an indispensable support, a necessary aid in executing the laws and conveying the influence of government to the doors of the people. . . .

There are certain social principles in human nature, from which we may draw the most solid conclusions with respect to the conduct of individuals and of communities. We love our families more than our neighbors; we love our neighbors more than our countrymen in general. The human affections, like the solar heat, lose their intensity as they depart from the center; and become languid in proportion to the expansion of the circle on which they act. On these principles, the attachment of the individual will be first and for ever secured by the state governments. . . . The state officers will ever be important, because they are necessary and useful. Their powers are such as are extremely interesting to the people, such as affect their property, their liberty, and life. What is more important than the administration of justice, and the execution of the civil and criminal laws? Can the state governments become insignificant, while they have the power of raising money independently and without control? If they are really useful,—

if they are calculated to promote the essential interests of the people, they must have their confidence and support. The states can never lose their powers till the whole people of America are robbed of their liberties.

—Speech on the United States Senate, *Debates of the N.Y. Convention*, pp. 106-108.

June 28, 1788

. . . Congress will have every means of knowledge that any legislature can have. From general observations, and from the revenue systems of the several states, they will derive information as to the most eligible modes of taxation. If a land tax is the object, cannot Congress procure as perfect a valuation as any other assembly? Can they not have all the necessary officers for assessment and collections? Where is the difficulty? Where is the evil? They never can oppress a particular State by an unequal imposition, because the Constitution has provided a fixed ratio, a uniform rule, by which this must be regulated. The system will be founded upon the most easy and equal principles—to draw as much as possible from direct taxation, to lay the principal burdens on the wealthy, etc.

—Speech on the United States Senate, *Debates of the N.Y. Convention*, pp. 116-118.

Once New Hampshire had ratified, the issue now became, should New York refuse to join a government already established? The antifederalists insisted on contingent ratification, qualifying acceptance of the Constitution by insisting that certain amendments be adopted. Hamilton then produced an opinion by Madison that a conditional ratification would be inadmissible. The antifederalists then capitulated, with the final vote for ratification, 30-27. To satisfy the legitimate criticism that no bill of rights had been incorporated in the Constitution Hamilton drafted a special form of ratification expressly asserting that certain rights could not be abridged by the federal government. The formal ratification on July 26, 1788, drew in part on Hamilton's draft, but spelled out the bill of rights in considerable detail and avoided incorporating the favorable comments about the Constitution which Hamilton had proposed.

July, 1788

. . . Congress will, I presume, recommend certain amendments to render the *structure* of the government more secure. This will satisfy the more considerate and honest opposers of the Constitution, and with the aid of them will break up the party.

—To James Madison. *Hamilton*, I, 464-465.

[July, 1788]

DRAFT OF PROPOSED RATIFICATION OF THE CONSTITUTION OF THE UNITED STATES, WITH SPECIFIED AMENDMENTS

We, the delegates of the people of the State of New York in Convention assembled, having maturely considered the Constitution for the United States, agreed to on the 17th day of September, in the year 1787, at Philadelphia, in the commonwealth of Pennsylvania, by the Convention then and there convened, and having also seriously and deliberately considered the present situation of the United States, and being convinced that it is advisable to adopt the said Constitution, do declare and make known, in the name and behalf of the people aforesaid, that the powers granted in and by the said Constitution, being derived from the people of the United States, may be resumed by them whenever they shall judge it necessary to their happiness; that every power not granted thereby remains either to them or their respective State governments, to whom they may have delegated the same; that therefore no right of any kind, either of the people of the respective States or of the said governments, can be cancelled, abridged, restrained, or modified by Congress, or by any officer or department of the United States, except in conformity to the powers given by the said Constitution, that among other essential rights, the liberty of conscience and of the press cannot be cancelled or abridged by any authority of the United States.

With these impressions, with a firm reliance on the blessing of Providence upon a government framed under circumstances which afford a new and instructive example of wisdom and moderation to mankind; with an entire conviction that it will be more prudent to rely, for whatever amendments may be desirable in the said Constitution, on the mode therein prescribed, than either to embarrass the Union or hazard dissensions in any part of the community by pursuing a different course, and with a full confidence that the amendments which shall have been proposed will receive an early and mature consideration, and that such of them as may in any degree tend to the real security and permanent advantage of the people, will be adopted: We, the said delegates, in the name and behalf of the PEOPLE of this State, Do, by these presents, assent to and RATIFY the Constitution aforesaid, hereby announcing to all those whom it may concern, that the said Constitution is binding upon the said people according to an authentic copy hereunto annexed.

—*Works*, II, 95-97.

7

The Principles of Constitutional Government

The Powers of the President

Energy in the Executive is a leading character in the definition of good government.

Hamilton, who firmly believed that a government should have energy for the tasks at hand, felt that a vigorous executive was not inconsistent with republican government. In The Federalist *he gives us a masterly analysis of the kind of strong executive he envisioned under the Constitution, being careful at the same time to reassure his readers that such a President would not be a monarch.*

March 11, 1788

. . . It is impossible not to bestow the imputation of deliberate imposture and deception upon the gross pretence of a similitude between a king of Great Britain and a magistrate of the character marked out for that of the President of the United States. It is still more impossible to withhold that imputation from the rash and barefaced expedients which have been employed to give success to the attempted imposition. . . .

—*The Federalist* No. 67.

March 14, 1788

. . . Nothing was more to be desired than that every practicable obstacle should be opposed to cabal, intrigue, and corruption. These mighty adversaries of republican government might naturally have been expected to make their approaches from more than one quarter, but chiefly from the desire in foreign powers to gain an improper ascendant in our councils. How could they better gratify this, than by raising a creature of their own to the chief magistracy of the Union? But the convention have guarded against all danger of this sort, with the most provident and judicious attention. They have not made the appointment of the President to depend on any preexisting bodies of men who might be tampered with beforehand to prostitute their votes; but they have referred it in the first instance to an immediate act of the people of America, to be exerted in the choice of persons for the temporary and sole purpose of making the appointment. And they have excluded from eligibility to this trust all those who from situation might be suspected of too great devotion to the President in office. No senator, representative, or other person holding a place of trust or profit under the United States can be of the numbers of the electors. Thus without corrupting the body of the people, the immediate agents in the election will at least enter upon the task free from any sinister bias. Their transient existence, and their detached situation . . . afford a satisfactory prospect of their continuing so to the conclusion of it. . . .

Another and no less important desideratum was that the Executive should be independent for his continuance in office on all but the people themselves. He might otherwise be tempted to sacrifice his duty to his complaisance for those whose favor was necessary to the duration of his official consequence. This advantage will also be secured by making his reelection to depend on a special body of representatives, deputed by the society for the single purpose of making the important choice. . . .

The process of election affords a moral certainty, that the office of President will never fall to the lot of any man who is not in an eminent degree endowed with the requisite qualifications. Talents for low intrigue, and the little arts of popularity, may alone suffice to elevate a man to the first honors in a single State; but it will require other talents, and a different kind of merit, to establish him in the esteem and confidence of the whole Union, or of so considerable a portion of it as would be necessary to make him a successful candidate for the distinguished office of President of the United States. It will not be too strong to say, that there will be a constant probability of seeing the station filled by characters preeminent for ability and virtue. . . .

—*The Federalist* No. 68.

March 14, 1788

I PROCEED now to trace the real characters of the proposed Executive, as they are marked out in the plan of the convention. This will serve to place in a strong light the unfairness of the representations which have been made in regard to it.

The first thing which strikes our attention is, that the executive authority, with few exceptions, is to be vested in a single magistrate.

This will scarcely, however, be considered as a point upon which any comparison can be grounded; for if, in this particular, there be a resemblance to the king of Great Britain, there is not less a resemblance to the Grand Seignior, to the khan of Tartary, to the Man of the Seven Mountains, or to the governor of New York.

That magistrate is to be elected for *four* years; and is to be reëligible as often as the people of the United States shall think him worthy of their confidence. In these circumstances there is a total dissimilitude between *him* and a king of Great Britain, who is an *hereditary* monarch, possessing the crown as a patrimony descendible to his heirs forever; but there is a close analogy between *him* and a governor of New York, who is elected for *three* years, and is reëligible without limitation or intermission. If we consider how much less time would be requisite for establishing a dangerous influence in a single State, than for establishing a like influence throughout the United States, we must conclude that a duration of *four* years for the Chief Magistrate of the Union is a degree of permanency far less to be dreaded in that office, than a duration of *three* years for a corresponding office in a single State.

The President of the United States would be liable to be impeached, tried, and, upon conviction of treason, bribery, or other high crimes or misdemeanors, removed from office; and would afterwards be liable to prosecution and punishment in the ordinary course of law. The person of the king of Great Britain is sacred and inviolable; there is no constitutional tribunal to which he is amenable; no punishment to which he can be subjected without involving the crisis of a national revolution. . . .

The President of the United States is to have power to return a bill, which shall have passed the two branches of the legislature, for reconsideration; and the bill so returned is to become a law, if, upon that reconsideration, it be approved by two thirds of both houses. The king of Great Britain, on his part, has an absolute negative upon the acts of the two houses of Parliament. The disuse of that power for a considerable time past does not affect the reality of its existence; and is to be ascribed wholly to the crown's having found the means of substituting influence to authority, or the art of gaining a majority in one or the other of the two houses, to the necessity of exerting a prerogative which could seldom be exerted without hazarding some degree of national agitation. The qualified negative of the President differs widely from this absolute negative of the British sovereign. . . .

The President is to be the "commander-in-chief of the army and navy of the United States, and of the militia of the several States, when called into the actual service of the United States. He is to have power to grant reprieves and pardons for offences against the United

States, *except in cases of impeachment;* to recommend to the consideration of Congress such measures as he shall judge necessary and expedient; to convene, on extraordinary occasions, both houses of the legislature, or either of them, and, in case of disagreement between them *with respect to the time of adjournment*, to adjourn them to such time as he shall think proper; to take care that the laws be faithfully executed; and to commission all officers of the United States." In most of these particulars, the power of the President will resemble equally that of the king of Great Britain and of the governor of New York. The most material points of difference are these:—*First*. The President will have only the occasional command of such part of the militia of the nation as by legislative provision may be called into the actual service of the Union. The king of Great Britain and the governor of New York have at all times the entire command of all the militia within their several jurisdictions. In this article, therefore, the power of the President would be inferior to that of either the monarch or the governor. *Secondly*. The President is to be commander-in-chief of the army and navy of the United States. In this respect his authority would be nominally the same with that of the king of Great Britain, but in substance much inferior to it. . . . *Thirdly*. The power of the President, in respect to pardons, would extend to all cases, *except those of impeachment*. . . . *Fourthly*. The President can only adjourn the national legislature in the single case of disagreement about the time of adjournment. The British monarch may prorogue or even dissolve the Parliament. The governor of New York may also prorogue the legislature of this State for a limited time; a power which, in certain situations, may be employed to very important purposes.

The President is to have power, with the advice and consent of the Senate, to make treaties, provided two thirds of the senators present concur. The king of Great Britain is the sole and absolute representative of the nation in all foreign transactions. He can of his own accord make treaties of peace, commerce, alliance, and of every other description. It has been insinuated, that his authority in this respect is not conclusive, and that his conventions with foreign powers are subject to the revision, and stand in need of the ratification, of Parliament. But I believe this doctrine was never heard of, until it was broached upon the present occasion. Every jurist* of that kingdom, and every other man acquainted with its Constitution, knows, as an established fact, that the prerogative of making treaties exists in the crown in its utmost plentitude; and that the compacts entered into by the royal authority have the most legal validity and perfection, independent of any other sanction. . . .

Hence it appears that, except as to the concurrent authority of the President in the article of treaties, it would be difficult to determine

* *Vide* Blackstone's "Commentaries," vol. i., p. 257.—Publius

whether that magistrate would in the aggregate, possess more or less power than the Governor of New York. And it appears yet more unequivocally, that there is no pretence for the parallel which has been attempted between him and the king of Great Britain. . . .

—*The Federalist* No. 69.

March 18, 1788

There is an idea, which is not without its advocates, that a vigorous Executive is inconsistent with the genius of republican government. The enlightened well-wishers to this species of government must at least hope that the supposition is destitute of foundation; since they can never admit its truth, without at the same time admitting the condemnation of their own principles. Energy in the Executive is a leading character in the definition of good government. It is essential to the protection of the community against foreign attacks; it is not less essential to the steady administration of the laws; to the protection of property against those irregular and high-handed combinations which sometimes interrupt the ordinary course of justice; to the security of liberty against the enterprises and assaults of ambition, of faction, and of anarchy. . . .

The ingredients which constitute energy in the Executive are, first, unity; secondly, duration; thirdly, an adequate provision for its support; fourthly, competent powers.

The ingredients which constitute safety in the republican sense are, first, a due dependence on the people; secondly, a due responsibility . . . .

The idea of a council to the Executive, which has so generally obtained in the State constitutions, has been derived from that maxim of republican jealousy which considers power as safer in the hands of a number of men than of a single man. If the maxim should be admitted to be applicable to the case, I should contend that the advantage on that side would not counterbalance the numerous disadvantages on the opposite side. But I do not think the rule at all applicable to the executive power. I clearly concur in opinion, in this particular, with a writer whom the celebrated Junius pronounces to be "deep, solid, and ingenious," that "the executive power is more easily confined when it is ONE";[1] that it is far more safe there should be a single object for the jealousy and watchfulness of the people; and, in a word, that all multiplication of the Executive is rather dangerous than friendly to liberty. . . .

—*The Federalist* No. 70.

March 18, 1788

DURATION in office has been mentioned as the second requisite to the energy of the Executive authority. This has relation to two objects:

[1] De Lolme.—PUBLIUS

to the personal firmness of the executive magistrate, in the employment of his constitutional powers; and to the stability of the system of administration which may have been adopted under his auspices. With regard to the first, it must be evident, that the longer the duration in office, the greater will be the probability of obtaining so important an advantage. It is a general principle of human nature, that a man will be interested in whatever he possesses, in proportion to the firmness or precariousness of the tenure by which he holds it; will be less attached to what he holds by a momentary or uncertain title, than to what he enjoys by a durable or certain title; and, of course, will be willing to risk more for the sake of the one, than for the sake of the other. . . .

There are some who would be inclined to regard the servile pliancy of the Executive to a prevailing current, either in the community or in the legislature, as its best recommendation. But such men entertain very crude notions, as well of the purposes for which government was instituted, as of the true means by which the public happiness may be promoted. The republican principle demands that the deliberate sense of the community should govern the conduct of those to whom they intrust the management of their affairs; but it does not require an unqualified complaisance to every sudden breeze of passion, or to every transient impulse which the people may receive from the arts of men, who flatter their prejudices to betray their interests. It is a just observation, that the people commonly *intend* the PUBLIC GOOD. This often applies to their very errors. But their good sense would despise the adulator who should pretend that they always *reason right* about the *means* of promoting it. They know from experience that they sometimes err; and the wonder is that they so seldom err as they do, beset, as they continually are, by the wiles of parasites and sycophants, by the snares of the ambitious, the avaricious, the desperate, by the artifices of men who possess their confidence more than they deserve it, and of those who seek to possess rather than to deserve it. When occasions present themselves, in which the interests of the people are at variance with their inclinations, it is the duty of the persons whom they have appointed to be the guardians of those interests, to withstand the temporary delusion, in order to give them time and opportunity for more cool and sedate reflection. . . .

But however inclined we might be to insist upon an unbounded complaisance in the Executive to the inclinations of the people, we can with no propriety contend for a like complaisance to the humors of the legislature. The latter may sometimes stand in opposition to the former, and at other times the people may be entirely neutral. In either supposition, it is certainly desirable that the Executive should be in a situation to dare to act his own opinion with vigor and decision. . . .

It may perhaps be asked, how the shortness of the duration in office can affect the independence of the Executive on the legislature, unless the one were possessed of the power of appointing or displacing the other. One answer to this inquiry may be drawn from the principle already remarked—that is from the slender interest a man is apt to take in a short-lived advantage, and the little inducement it affords him to expose himself, on account of it, to any considerable inconvenience or hazard. Another answer, perhaps more obvious, though not more conclusive, will result from the consideration of the influence of the legislative body over the people; which might be employed to prevent the reëlection of a man who, by an upright resistance to any sinister project of that body, should have made himself obnoxious to its resentment.

It may be asked also, whether a duration of four years would answer the end proposed; and if it would not, whether a less period, which would at least be recommended by greater security against ambitious designs, would not, for that reason, be preferable to a longer period, which was, at the same time, too short for the purpose of inspiring the desired firmness and independence of the magistrate.

It cannot be affirmed, that a duration of four years, or any other limited duration, would completely answer the end proposed; but it would contribute towards it in a degree which would have a material influence upon the spirit and character of the government. Between the commencement and termination of such a period, there would always be a considerable interval, in which the prospect of annihilation would be sufficiently remote, not to have an improper effect upon the conduct of a man imbued with a tolerable portion of fortitude; and in which he might reasonably promise himself, that there would be time enough before it arrived, to make the community sensible of the propriety of the measures he might incline to pursue. Though it be probable that, as he approached the moment when the public were, by a new election, to signify their sense of his conduct, his confidence, and with it his firmness, would decline; yet both the one and the other would derive support from the opportunities which his previous continuance in the station had afforded him, of establishing himself in the esteem and good-will of his constituents. He might, then, hazard with safety, in proportion to the proofs he had given of his wisdom and integrity, and to the title he had acquired to the respect and attachment of his fellow-citizens. As, on the one hand, a duration of four years will contribute to the firmness of the Executive in a sufficient degree to render it a very valuable ingredient in the composition; so, on the other, it is not enough to justify any alarm for the public liberty. . . .

—*The Federalist* No. 71.

March 21, 1788

With a positive duration of considerable extent, I connect the circumstances of reëligibility. The first is necessary to give to the officer himself the inclination and the resolution to act his part well, and to the community time and leisure to observe the tendency of his measures, and thence to form an experimental estimate of their merits. The last is necessary to enable the people, when they see reason to approve of his conduct, to continue him in his station, in order to prolong the utility of his talents and virtues, and to secure to the government the advantage of permanency in a wise system of administration.

Nothing appears more plausible at first sight, nor more ill-founded upon close inspection than a scheme which in relation to the present point has had some respectable advocates,—I mean that of continuing the chief magistrate in office for a certain time, and then excluding him from it, either for a limited period or forever after. This exclusion, whether temporary or perpetual, would have nearly the same effects, and these effects would be for the most part rather pernicious than salutary.

One ill effect of the exclusion would be a diminution of the inducements to good behavior. . . .

Another ill effect of the exclusion would be the temptation to sordid views, to peculation, and, in some instances, to usurpation. An avaricious man, who might happen to fill the office, looking forward to a time when he must at all events yield up the emoluments he enjoyed, would feel a prospensity, not easy to be resisted by such a man, to make the best use of the opportunity he enjoyed while it lasted, and might not scruple to have recourse to the most corrupt expedients to make the harvest as abundant as it was transitory; though the same man, probably, with a different prospect before him, might content himself with the regular perquisities of his situation, and might even be unwilling to risk the consequences of an abuse of his opportunities. . . .

An ambitious man, too, when he found himself seated on the summit of his country's honors, when he looked forward to the time at which he must descend from the exalted eminence for ever, and reflected that no exertion of merit on his part could save him from the unwelcome reverse; such a man, in such a situation, would be much more violently tempted to embrace a favorable conjuncture for attempting the prolongation of his power, at every personal hazard, than if he had the probability of answering the same end by doing his duty.

Would it promote the peace of the community, or the stability of the government to have half a dozen men who had had credit enough to be raised to the seat of the supreme magistracy, wandering among the people like discontented ghosts, and sighing for a place which they were destined never more to possess?

A third ill effect of the exclusion would be, the depriving the community of the advantage of the experience gained by the chief magistrate in the exercise of his office. That experience is the parent of wisdom, is an adage the truth of which is recognized by the wisest as well as the simplest of mankind. What more desirable or more essential than this quality in the governors of nations? . . .

A fourth ill effect of the exclusion would be the banishing men from stations in which, in certain emergencies of the state, their presence might be of the greatest moment to the public interest or safety. There is no nation which has not, at one period or another, experienced an absolute necessity of the services of particular men in particular situations; perhaps it would not be too strong to say, to the preservation of its political existence. How unwise, therefore, must be every such self-denying ordinance as serves to prohibit a nation from making use of its own citizens in the manner best suited to its exigencies and circumstances! Without supposing the personal essentiality of the man, it is evident that a change of the chief magistrate, at the breaking out of a war, or at any similar crisis, for another, even of equal merit, would at all times be detrimental to the community, inasmuch as it would substitute inexperience to experience, and would tend to unhinge and set afloat the already settled train of the administration.

A fifth ill effect of the exclusion would be, that it would operate as a constitutional interdiction of stability in the administration. By *necessitating* a change of men, in the first office of the nation, it would necessitate a mutability of measures. It is not generally to be expected, that men will vary and measures remain uniform. The contrary is the usual course of things. And we need not be apprehensive that there will be too much stability, while there is even the option of changing; nor need we desire to prohibit the people from continuing their confidence where they think it may be safely placed, and where, by constancy on their part, they may obviate the fatal inconveniences of fluctuating councils and a variable policy. . . .

—*The Federalist* No. 72.

March 21, 1788

The third ingredient towards constituting the vigor of the executive authority, is an adequate provision for its support. It is evident that, without proper attention to this article, the separation of the executive from the legislative department would be merely nominal and nugatory. . . .

It is not easy, therefore, to commend too highly the judicious attention which has been paid to this subject in the proposed Constitution.

It is there provided that "The President of the United States shall, at stated times, receive for his service a compensation *which shall neither be increased nor diminished during the period for which he shall have been elected;* and he *shall not receive within that period any other emolument* from the United States, of any of them." It is impossible to imagine any provision which would have been more eligible than this. The legislature, on the appointment of a President, is once for all to declare what shall be the compensation for his services during the time for which he shall have been elected. This done, they will have no power to alter it, either by increase or diminution, till a new period of service by a new election commences. They can neither weaken his fortitude by operating on his necessities, nor corrupt his integrity by appealing to his avarice. Neither the Union, nor any of its members, will be at liberty to give, nor will he be at liberty to receive, any other emolument than that which may have been determined by the first act. He can, of course, have no pecuniary inducement to renounce or desert the independence intended for him by the Constitution.

The last of the requisites to energy, which have been enumerated, are competent powers. Let us proceed to consider those which are proposed to be vested in the President of the United States.

The first thing that offers itself to our observation, is the qualified negative of the President upon the acts or resolutions of the two houses of the legislature; or, in other words, his power of returning all bills with objections, to have the effect of preventing their becoming laws, unless they should afterwards be ratified by two thirds of each of the component members of the legislative body.

The propensity of the legislative department to intrude upon the rights, and to absorb the powers, of the other departments, has been already suggested and repeated; the insufficiency of a mere parchment delineation of the boundaries of each, has also been remarked upon; and the necessity of furnishing each with constitutional arms for its own defence, has been inferred and proved. From these clear and indubitable principles results the propriety of a negative, either absolute or qualified, in the Executive, upon the acts of the legislative branches. Without the one or the other, the former would be absolutely unable to defend himself against the depredations of the latter. He might gradually be stripped of his authorities by successive resolutions, or annihilated by a single vote. And in one mode or the other, the legislative and executive powers might speedily come to be blended in the same hands. If even no propensity had ever discovered itself in the legislative body to invade the rights of the Executive, the rules of just reasoning and theoretic propriety would of themselves teach us, that the one ought not to be left to the mercy of the other, but ought to possess a constitutional and effectual power of self-defence.

But the power in question has a further use. It not only serves as a shield to the Executive, but it furnishes an additional security against the enaction of improper laws. It establishes a salutary check upon the legislative body, calculated to guard the community against the effects of faction, precipitancy, or of any impulse unfriendly to the public good, which may happen to influence a majority of that body.

The propriety of a negative has, upon some occasions, been combated by an observation, that it was not to be presumed a single man would possess more virtue and wisdom than a number of men; and that unless this presumption should be entertained, it would be improper to give the executive magistrate any species of control over the legislative body.

But this observation, when examined, will appear rather specious than solid. The propriety of the thing does not turn upon the supposition of superior wisdom or virtue in the Executive, but upon the supposition that the legislature will not be infallible; that the love of power may sometimes betray it into a disposition to encroach upon the rights of other members of the government; that a spirit of faction may sometimes pervert its deliberations; that impressions of the moment may sometimes hurry it into measures which itself, on maturer reflection, would condemn. The primary inducement to conferring the power in question upon the Executive is, to enable him to defend himself; the secondary one is to increase the chances in favor of the community against the passing of bad news, through haste, inadvertence, or design. . . .

The superior weight and influence of the legislative body in a free government, and the hazard to the Executive in a trial of strength with that body, afford a satisfactory security that the negative would generally be employed with great caution; and there would oftener be room for a charge of timidity than of rashness in the exercise of it. A king of Great Britain, with all his train of sovereign attributes, and with all the influence he draws from a thousand sources, would, at this day, hesitate to put a negative upon the joint resolutions of the two houses of Parliament. . . .

If a magistrate so powerful and so well fortified as a British monarch, would have scruples about the exercise of the power under consideration, how much greater caution may be reasonably expected in a President of the United States, clothed for the short period of four years with the executive authority of a government wholly and purely republican? . . .

But the convention have pursued a mean in this business, which will both facilitate the exercise of the power vested in this respect in the executive magistrate, and make its efficacy to depend on the sense of a considerable part of the legislative body. Instead of an absolute negative, it is proposed to give the Executive the qualified negative already described. This is a power which would be much more readily exercised than the other. A man who might be afraid to defeat a law by his single VETO, might not scruple to return it for reconsideration; subject to being finally rejected only in the event of more than one third of each house concurring in the sufficiency of his objections. He would be encouraged by the reflection, that if his opposition should prevail, it would embark in it a very respectable proportion of the legislative body, whose influence would be united with his in supporting the propriety of his conduct in the public opinion.

—*The Federalist* No. 73.

April 1, 1788

The President is "to *nominate*, and, by and with the advice and consent of the Senate, to appoint ambassadors, other public ministers and consuls, judges of the Supreme Court, and all other officers of the United States whose appointments are not otherwise provided for in the Constitution. But the Congress may by law vest the appointment of such inferior officers as they think proper, in the President alone, or in the courts of law, or in the heads of departments. The President shall have power to fill up *all vacancies* which may happen *during the recess of the Senate*, by granting commissions which shall *expire* at the end of their next session." . . .

But might not his nomination be overruled? I grant it might, yet this could only be to make place for another nomination by himself. The person ultimately appointed must be the object of his preference, though perhaps not in the first degree. It is also not very probable that his nomination would often be overruled. The Senate could not be tempted, by the preference they might feel to another, to reject the one proposed; because they could not assure themselves, that the person they might wish would be brought forward by a second or by any subsequent nomination. They could not even be certain, that a future nomination would present a candidate in any degree more acceptable to them; and as their dissent might cast a kind of stigma upon the individual rejected, and might have the appearance of a reflection upon the judgment of the chief magistrate, it is not likely that their sanction would often be refused, where there were not special and strong reasons for the refusal.

To what purpose then require the cooperation of the Senate? I answer, that the necessity of their concurrence would have a powerful, though, in general, a silent operation. It would be an excellent check upon a spirit of favoritism in the President, and would tend greatly to prevent the appointment of unfit characters from State prejudice, from family connection, from personal attachment, or from a view to popularity. In addition to this, it would be an efficacious source of stability in the administration. . . .

—*The Federalist* No. 76.

April 4, 1788

. . . We have now completed a survey of the structure and powers of the executive department, which, I have endeavored to show, combines, as far as republican principles will admit, all the requisites to energy. The remaining inquiry is: Does it also combine the requisites to safety, in a republican sense,—a due dependence on the people, a due responsibility? The answer to this question has been anticipated in the investigation of its other characteristics, and is satisfactorily deducible from these circumstances; from the election of the President once in four years by persons immediately chosen by the people for that purpose; and from his being at all times liable to impeachment, trial, dismission from office, incapacity to serve in any other, and to forfeiture of life and estate by subsequent prosecution in the common course of law. But these precautions, great as they are, are not the only ones which the plan of the convention has provided in favor of the public security. In the only instances in which the abuse of the executive authority was materially to be feared, the Chief Magistrate of the United States would, by that plan, be subjected to the control of a branch of the legislative body. What more could be desired by an enlightened and reasonable people?

—*The Federalist* No. 77.

The Treaty-making Power of the President

Although Hamilton advocated a separation of powers between the executive and the legislature, he warmly endorsed the constitutional provision authorizing the President to make treaties "by and with the advice and consent of the Senate." The initiative in treaty-making, as he saw it, was to rest with the executive, and so, too, the initiative in proclaiming neutrality.

[March, 1788]

THE President is to have power, "by and with the advice and consent of the Senate, to make treaties, provided two thirds of the senators present concur."

Though this provision has been assailed, on different grounds, with no small degree of vehemence, I scruple not to declare my firm persuasion, that it is one of the best digested and most unexceptionable parts of the plan. One ground of objection is the trite topic of the intermixture of powers: some contending that the President ought alone to possess the power of making treaties; others, that it ought to have been exclusively deposited in the Senate. Another source of objection is derived from the small number of persons by whom a treaty may be made. . . .

With regard to the intermixture of powers, I shall rely upon the explanations already given in other places, of the true sense of the rule upon which that objection is founded; and shall take it for granted, as an inference from them, that the union of the Executive with the Senate, in the article of treaties, is no infringement of that rule. I venture to add, that the particular nature of the power of making treaties indicates a peculiar propriety in that union. Though several writers on the subject of government place that power in the class of executive authorities, yet this is evidently an arbitrary disposition; for if we attend carefully to its operation, it will be found to partake more of the legislative than of the executive character, though it does not seem strictly to fall within the definition of either of them. The essence of the legislative authority is to enact laws, or, in other words, to prescribe rules for the regulation of the society; while the execution of the laws, and the employment of the common strength, either for this purpose or for the common defence, seem to comprise all the functions of the executive magistrate. The power of making treaties is, plainly, neither the one nor the other. It relates neither to the execution of the subsisting laws, nor to the enaction of new ones; and still less to an exertion of the common strength. Its objects are CONTRACTS with foreign nations, which have the force of law, but derive it from obligations of good faith. They are not rules prescribed by the sovereign to the subject, but agreements between sovereign and sovereign. The power in question seems threrefore to form a distinct department, and to belong, properly, neither to the legislative nor to the executive. The qualities elsewhere detailed as indispensable in the management of foreign negotiations, point out the Executive as the most fit agent in those transactions; while the vast importance of the trust, and the operation of treaties as laws, plead strongly for the participation of the whole or a portion of the legislative body in the office of making them.

However proper or safe it may be in governments where the executive magistrate is an hereditary monarch, to commit to him the entire power of making treaties, it would be utterly unsafe and improper to intrust that power to an elective magistrate of four years' duration. . . .

The history of human conduct does not warrant that exalted opinion of human virtue which would make it wise in a nation to commit interests of so delicate and momentous a kind, as those which concern its intercourse with the rest of the world, to the sole disposal of a magistrate created and circumstanced as would be a President of the United States.

To have intrusted the power of making treaties to the Senate alone, would have been to relinquish the benefits of the constitutional agency of the President in the conduct of foreign negotiations. . . . It *must* indeed be clear to a demonstration that the joint possession of the power in question, by the President and Senate, would afford a greater prospect of security, than the separate possession of it by either of them. And whoever has maturely weighed the circumstances which must concur in the appointment of a President, will be satisfied that the office will always bid fair to be filled by men of such characters as to render their concurrence in the formation of treaties peculiarly desirable, as well on the score of wisdom, as on that of integrity.

The remarks made in a former number, which have been alluded to in another part of this paper, will apply with conclusive force against the admission of the House of Representatives to a share in the formation of treaties. The fluctuating and, taking its future increase into the account, the multitudinous composition of that body, forbid us to expect in it those qualities which are essential to the proper execution of such a trust. Accurate and comprehensive knowledge of foreign politics; a steady and systematic adherence to the same views; a nice and uniform sensibility to national character; decision, secrecy, and despatch, are incompatible with the genius of a body so variable and so numerous. . . .

The only objection which remains to be canvassed, is that which would substitute the proportion of two thirds of all the members composing the senatorial body, to that of two thirds of the members *present*. It has been shown, under the second head of our inquiries, that all provisions which require more than the majority of any body to its resolutions, have a direct tendency to embarrass the operations of the government, and an indirect one to subject the sense of the majority to that of the minority. This consideration seems sufficient to determine our opinion, that the convention have gone as far in the endeavor to secure the advantage of numbers in the formation of treaties as could have been reconciled either with the activity of the public councils or with a reasonable regard to the major sense of the community. If two thirds of the whole number of members had been required, it would, in many cases, from the non-attendance of a part, amount in practice to a necessity of unanimity. And the history of every political establishment in which this principle has prevailed, is a history of impotence, perplexity, and disorder. Proofs of this position might be adduced from the examples of the Roman Tribuneship, the Polish Diet, and the States-General of the Netherlands, did not an example at home render foreign precedents, unnecessary. . . .

And when we . . . look forward to the probable augmentation of the Senate, by the erection of new States, we shall not only perceive ample ground of confidence in the sufficiency of the members to whose agency that power will be intrusted, but we shall probably be led to conclude that a body more numerous than the Senate would be likely to become, would be very little fit for the proper discharge of the trust.

—*The Federalist* No. 75

March, 1792

Will it not be necessary to add an instruction that the usual stipulation respecting the ratification of the treaty by the United States be varied, so as to be adapted to the participation of the Senate?

—To Jefferson. *Works*, IV, 362.

June 29, 1793

It will not be disputed that the management of the affairs of this country with foreign nations is confided to the Government of the United States.

It can as little be disputed that a proclamation of neutrality, when a nation is at liberty to keep out of a war in which other nations are engaged, and means to do so, is a *usual* and a *proper* measure. *Its main object and effect are to prevent the nation's being immediately responsible for acts done by its citizens, without the privity or connivance of the government, in contravention of the principles of neutrality;*[1] an object of the greatest importance to a country whose true interest lies in the preservation of peace.

The inquiry then is: What department of the government of the United States is the proper one to make a declaration of neutrality in the cases in which the engagements of the nation permit and its interests require such a declaration?

A correct and well-informed mind will discern at once, that it can belong neither to the legislative nor judicial department, and of course must belong to the executive. . . .

It appears to be connected with that department in various capacities:—As the *organ* of intercourse between the nation and foreign nations; as the *interpreter* of the national treaties, in those cases in which the judiciary is not competent—that is, in the cases between government and government; as that *power* which is charged with the execution of the laws, of which treaties form a part; as that *power* which is charged with the command and application of the public force. . . .

The general doctrine, then, is that the *executive power* of the nation is vested in the President; subject only to the *exceptions* and *qualifications* which are expressed in the instrument.

[1] See Vattel, Book III, chap. 7, sec. 113.

Two of these have been already noticed: the participation of the Senate in the appointment of offices, and the making of treaties. A third remains to be mentioned: the right of the Legislature "to declare war, and grant letters of marque and reprisal."

With these exceptions, the *executive power* of the Union is completely lodged in the President. This mode of construing the Constitution has indeed been recognized by Congress in formal acts, upon full consideration and debate. The power of removal from office is an important instance. And since upon general principles, for reasons already given, the issuing of a proclamation of neutrality is merely an Executive Act; since, also the general Executive Power of the Union is vested in the President, the conclusion is, that the step, which has been taken by him, is liable to no just exception on the score of authority.[2] . . .

If the Legislature have a right to make war on the one hand, it is, on the other, the duty of the executive to preserve peace till the war is declared; and in fulfilling this duty, it must necessarily possess a right of judging what is the nature of the obligations which the treaties of the country impose on the government; and when in pursuance of this right it has concluded that there is nothing in them inconsistent with a state of neutrality, it becomes both its province and its duty to enforce the laws incident to that state of the nation. The executive is charged with the execution of all laws, the law of nations, as well as the municipal law, which recognizes and adopts those laws. It is consequently bound by faithfully executing the laws of neutrality, when that is the state of the Nation, to avoid giving a cause of war to foreign Powers. . . .

The right of the executive to receive ambassadors and other public ministers may serve to illustrate the relative duties of the executive and legislative departments. This right includes that of judging, in the case of a revolution of government in a foreign country, whether the new rulers are competent organs of the national will, and ought to be recognized or not; and, where a treaty antecedently exists between the United States and such a nation, that right involves the power of giving operation or not to such treaty. For until the new government is *acknowledged*, the treaties between the nations, so far at least as regards *public* rights, are of course suspended. . . .

This serves as an example of the right of the Executive, in certain cases, to determine the condition of the nation, though it may consequently affect the proper or improper exercise of the power of the Legislature to declare war. The Executive indeed cannot control the exercise of that power further than by the exercise of its general right of objecting to all acts of the Legislature, liable to being overruled by

[2] Lodge, *Works,* IV, 425 *et seq.,* gives a variant version which omits here and elsewhere significant clauses.

two thirds of both houses of Congress. The Legislature is still free to perform its own duties, according to its own sense of them; though the Executive, in the exercise of its constitutional powers, may establish an antecendent state of things, which ought to weigh in the legislative decisions.

From the division of the executive power there results in reference to it a *concurrent* authority in the distributed cases.

Hence, in the case stated, though treaties can only be made by the President and Senate, their activity may be continued or suspended by the President alone. . . .

The President is the Constitutional EXECUTOR of the laws. Our treaties, and the laws of nations, form a part of the law of the land. He who is to execute the laws must first judge for himself of their meaning. . . .

The proclamation has been represented as enacting some new law. This is a view of it entirely erroneous. It only proclaims a *fact*, with regard to the *existing state* of the nation; informs the citizens of what the laws previously established require of them in that state, and warns them that these laws will be put in execution against the infractors of them.

—*Letters of Pacificus: Written in Justification of the President's Proclamation of Neutrality* (Philadelphia: Samuel H. Smith, 1796); Hamilton Papers, 1st ser.

July 20, 1793

The words, "make known the disposition of the United States," have also given a pretext for cavil. It has been asked, how could the President undertake to declare the disposition of the United States? The people, for aught he knew, may have a very different sentiment. Thus, a conformity with republican propriety and modesty is turned into a topic of accusation.

Had the President announced his own disposition, he would have been chargeable with egotism, if not presumption. The constitutional organ of intercourse between the United States and foreign nations, whenever he speaks to them, it is in that capacity; it is in the name and on the behalf of the United States. It must, therefore, be with greater propriety that he speaks of their disposition than of his own. . . .

Kings and princes speak of their own dispositions, the magistrates of republics of the dispositions of their nations. The President, therefore, has evidently used the style adapted to his situation, and the criticism upon it is plainly a cavil.

—"Pacificus," VII. Draft in Hamilton's hand. Hamilton Papers, 1st ser.

The ratification and implementing of Jay's Treaty, which Hamilton defended in the notable series of Camillus *letters, raised a moot constitutional issue. What was the role of the House of Representatives in carrying out the provisions of treaties? Once the Senate had ratified the treaty after a bitter and sustained battle, the House called upon President Washington to submit all the papers relating to the negotiations. Washington asked Hamilton to suggest a procedure which would involve "the least bad consequences." Previously Hamilton had advised the President as to the best way of phrasing the treaty to avoid the necessity of action by both houses of Congress. He insisted that the House was bound to carry out the terms of the treaty. This view he enlarged in his draft of Washington's message to the House refusing the papers. In several* Camillus *letters he also dealt with aspects of this same problem.*

June 22, 1794

Though the form of only giving the *opinion* of the President that it was *incumbent upon* the United States to make compensation in the case has been used, yet between nation and nation this is equivalent to a *virtual* engagement that compensation will be made: and we were *all* sensible in advising the President to give that opinion (which advice was unanimous), that a non-compliance with it would be a serious commitment of the character of the nation, the government, and *the President*. Indeed, if the Legislature should not do its part, under such circumstances, it would necessarily give birth to considerations very embarrassing to the delicacy of the President.

In such a posture of things is it not advisable to narrow the obstacles to a right issue of the business? If Mr. Jay is instructed to insert a formal *stipulation* in a *general arrangement*, the Senate only will have to concur. If provision is to be made by law, *both Houses* must concur. The difference is easily seen. And it is a case where the *point of honor* is too materially concerned not to dictate the expediency of leaving as little hazard as possible upon the issue. It is impossible that any question can arise about the *propriety* of giving this course to the business. When we are demanding compensation for our captured vessels and goods, it is the simplest thing in the world, to stipulate compensation for those of Great Britain, which we acknowledge to have been unlawfully made within our territory, or by the use of our means.

—To Washington (Cabinet Paper). Copy by J. A. Hamilton. Hamilton Papers, 1st ser.

March 10, 1796

So, likewise, the constitution says that the President and Senate shall make treaties, and that these treaties shall be supreme laws. It is a contradiction to call a thing a law which is not binding. It follows that by constitutional injunction the House of Representatives quoad the stipulations of treaties, as in the case cited, respecting the judges, are not deliberative, but merely executive, *except as to the means of executing*.

Any other doctrine would vest the Legislature and each House with unlimited discretion, and destroy the very idea of a constitution limiting its discretion. The constitution would at once vanish.

Besides, the *legal* power to refuse the execution of a law is a *power to repeal it*. Thus, the House of Representatives must, as to treaties, concentre in itself the whole legislative power, and undertake, without the Senate, to repeal a law. For the law is complete by the action of the President and Senate.

—To William Smith. *Hamilton*, VI, 92-93.

March 20, 1796

I have received your resolution, and have considered it with the attention always due to a request of the House of Representatives. I feel a consciousness (not contradicted I trust by any part of my conduct) of a sincere disposition to respect the rights, privileges, and authorities of Congress, collectively and in its separate branches—to pay just deference to their opinions and wishes—to avoid intrusion on their province—to communicate freely information pertinent to the subjects of their deliberation. But this disposition, keeping steadily in view the public good, must likewise be limited and directed by the duty incumbent upon us all, of preserving inviolate the constitutional boundary between the several departments of the government; a duty enjoined by the very nature of a Constitution which defines the powers delegated, and distributes them among different depositories; enforced by the solemn sanction of an oath; and only to be fulfilled by a regard no less scrupulous for the rights of the Executive than for those of every other department. . . .

It is contrary to the general practice of governments to promulge the intermediate transactions of a foreign negotiation, without weighty and special reasons. The motives for great delicacy and reserve on this point are powerful. . . .

These reasons explain the grounds of a prevailing rule of conduct among prudent governments, namely, not to promulge without weighty cause, nor without due reserves, the particulars of a foreign negotiation. It so happens indeed that many of them have no immediate application to the case of the present treaty. And it would be unadvisable to discriminate here between such as may and such as may not so apply. But it would be very extraordinary, situated as the United States were in relation to Great Britain at the commencement of the negotiation, if some of them did not operate against a full disclosure of the papers in which it is recorded. . . .

The Constitution of the United States empowers the President, with the advice and consent of the Senate, two thirds concurring, to MAKE treaties. It nowhere professes to authorize the House of Representatives or any other branch of the government to partake with the President and Senate in the making of treaties. The whole power of making treaties is therefore by the Constitution vested in the President and Senate. . . .

[From these different views of the subject it results that the position —that the power of legislation acting in one sphere, and the power of treaty acting in another sphere, may embrace in their action the same objects—involves no interference of constitutional powers; and, of course, that the latter may reach and comprehend objects which the former is authorized to act upon; which it is necessary to suppose it does do, since the contrary supposition would essentially destroy the power of treaty: whereas the stipulations of treaties being only particular exceptions to the discretion of the legislative power, this power will always still have a wide field of action beyond and out of the exceptions. . . .

This inquiry suggests a truth fundamental to the principles of our government, and all important to the security of the people of the United States—namely, that the legislative body is not deliberative in all cases; that it is only deliberative and discretionary where the Constitution and the laws lay it under no command nor prohibition; that where they command, it can only execute; where they prohibit, it cannot act. If the thing be commanded and the means of execution are undefined, it may then deliberate on the choice of the means, but it is obliged to devise some means. It is true that the Constitution provides no method of compelling the legislative body to act, but it is not the less under a constitutional, legal, and moral obligation to act, where action is prescribed, and in conformity with the rule of action prescribed.

In asserting the authority of laws as well as of the Constitution to direct and restrain the legislative action, the position is to be understood with this difference. The Constitution obliges always—the laws till they are annulled or repealed by the proper authority; but till then they oblige the legislative body as well as individuals, and all their antecedent effects are valid and binding. And the abrogation or repeal of a law must be by an act of the regular organ of the national will for that purpose, in the forms of the Constitution,—not by a mere refusal to give effect to its injunctions and requisitions; especially by a part of the legislative body. A legal discretion to refuse the execution of a pre-existing law is virtually a power to repeal it, and to attribute this discretion to a part of the legislative body is to attribute to it the whole, instead of a part, of the legislative power in the given case. . . .

Hence it follows that the House of Representatives have no moral power to refuse the execution of a treaty which is not contrary to the Constitution, because it pledges the public faith; and have no legal power to refuse its execution, because it is a law, until at least it ceases to be a law by a regular act of revocation of the competent authority].[1] . . .

But, under all the circumstances of the present request (circumstances which I forbear to particularize), and in its present indefinite form, I adopt with reluctance and regret, but with entire conviction, the opinion, that a just regard to the Constitution and to the duty of my office forbids on my part a compliance with that request.

—Message from Washington to the House of Representatives. Draft in Hamilton's hand; date in later hand. Hamilton Papers, 1st ser.

1796

1. As to the theory of the Constitution. . . .

The second article, which organizes and regulates the executive department, declares that the "EXECUTIVE POWER shall be vested in a President of the United States of America"; and proceeding to detail particular authorities of the executive, it declares that the "President shall have power, by and with the advice and consent of the Senate, TO MAKE TREATIES, provided two-thirds of the senators present concur." There is in no part of the Constitution any explanation of this power to make treaties, any definition of its objects, or delineation of its bounds. The only other provision in the Constitution respecting it is in the sixth article, which provides, as already noticed, that all treaties made, or which shall be made, under the authority of the United States, shall be the supreme law of the land!—and this notwithstanding any thing in the Constitution or laws of any State to the contrary.

It was impossible for words more comprehensive to be used than those which grant the power to make treaties. They are such as would naturally be employed to confer a *plenipotentiary* authority. A power "to make treaties," granted in these indefinite terms, extends to all kinds of treaties, and with all the latitude which such a power, under any form of government, can possess; the power "*to make*" implies a power to act *authoritatively* and *conclusively*, independent of the after-clause which expressly places treaties among the supreme laws of the land. The thing to be made is a treaty.

With regard to the objects of the treaty, there being no specification, there is, of course, a *carte blanche*. The general proposition must, therefore, be, that whatever is a proper subject of compact, between nation and nation, may be embraced by a treaty between the President of the United States, with the advice and consent of the Senate, and the correspondent organ of a foreign state.

[1] Section in brackets not in Hamilton's hand.

The authority being general, it comprises, of course, whatever cannot be shown to be necessarily an exception to it.

The only constitutional exception to the power of making treaties is, that it shall not change the Constitution; which results from this fundamental maxim, that a delegated authority cannot rightfully transcend the constituting act, unless so expressly authorized by the constituting power. A treaty, for example, cannot transfer the legislative power to the executive department, nor the power of this last department to the judiciary; in other words, it cannot stipulate that the President, and not Congress, shall make laws for the United States,—that the judges, and not the President, shall command the national forces.

Again, there is also a *national* exception to the power of making treaties, as there is to every other delegated power, which respects abuses of authority in palpable and extreme cases. On natural principles, a treaty, which should manifestly betray or sacrifice primary interests of the state, would be null. But this presents a question foreign from that of the modification or distribution of constitutional powers. It applies to the case of the pernicious exercise of a power, where there is legal competency. Thus the power of treaty, though extending to the right of making alliances offensive and defensive, may yet not be exercised in making an alliance so obviously repugnant to the safety of the state as to justify the non-observance of the contract.

Beyond these exceptions to the power, none occurs that can be supported.

Those which have been insisted upon, towards invalidating the treaty with Great Britain, are not even plausible. They amount to this: that a treaty can establish nothing between the United States and a foreign nation, which it is the province of the legislative authority to regulate in reference to the United States alone. It cannot, for instance, establish a particular rule of commercial intercourse between the United States and Great Britain; because it is provided in the Constitution, that Congress "*shall have power to regulate commerce with foreign nations.*" This is equivalent to affirming that all the objects upon which the legislative power may act, in relation to our country, are excepted out of the power to make treaties.

Two obvious considerations refute this doctrine: one, that the power to make treaties, and the power to make laws, are different things, operating by different means, upon different subjects; the other, that the construction resulting from such a doctrine would defeat the power to make treaties, while its opposite reconciles this power with the power of making laws.

The power to make laws is "the power of pronouncing authoritatively the will of the nation as to all persons and things over which it has jurisdiction"; or it may be defined to be "the power of prescribing rules binding upon all persons and things over which the nation has jurisdiction." It acts compulsively upon all persons, whether foreigners or citizens, and upon all things within its territory, and it acts in like manner upon its own citizens and their property without its territory in certain cases and under certain limitations. But it can have no obligatory action whatsoever upon a foreign nation, or upon any person or thing within the jurisdiction of such foreign nation.

The power of treaty, on the other hand, is the power by *agreement, convention,* or *compact,* to establish rules binding upon *two* or *more* nations, their respective citizens and property. The rule established derives its reciprocal obligation from promise, from the faith which the contracting parties pledge to each other, not from the power of either to prescribe a rule for the other. It is not here the will of a SUPERIOR that commands; it is the consent of two independent parties that contract.

The *means* which the power of legislation employs are *laws* which it enacts, or rules which it enjoins; the subject upon which it acts is *the nation of whom it is,* the persons and property within the jurisdiction of the nation. The means which the power of treaty employs are *contracts* with other nations, who may or may not enter into them; the subject upon which it acts are the *nations contracting,* and those persons and things *of each* to which the contract relates. Though a treaty may effect what a law can, yet a law cannot effect what a treaty may. These discriminations are obvious and decisive; and however the operation of a treaty may, in some things, resemble that of a law, no two ideas are more distinct than that of *legislating* and that of *contracting.*

It follows that there is no ground for the inference pretended to be drawn, that the legislative powers of Congress are excepted out of the power of making treaties. It is the province of the latter to do what the former cannot do. . . .

The Constitution accordingly considers the power of treaty as different from that of legislation. This is proved in two ways: 1. That while the Constitution declares that all the *legislative* powers which it grants shall be vested *in Congress,* it vests the power of making treaties in *the President* with consent of the Senate. 2. That the same article by which it is declared that the EXECUTIVE power shall be vested in a President, and in which sundry executive powers are detailed, gives the power to make treaties to the President, with the auxiliary agency of the Senate. Thus the power of making treaties is placed in the class of executive authorities; while the force of laws is annexed to its results. This agrees with the distribution commonly made by theoretical writers, though perhaps the power of treaty, from its peculiar nature, ought to form a class by itself.

—"Camillus," No. 36. Draft in Hamilton's hand. Hamilton Papers, 1st ser.

1796

. . . But the construction which is combated would cause the legislative power to destroy the power of making treaties. Moreover, if the power of the executive department be inadequate to the making of the several kinds of treaties which have been mentioned, there is, then, no power in the Government to make them; for there is not a syllable in the Constitution which authorizes either the legislative or judiciary departments to make a treaty with a foreign nation. And our Constitution would then exhibit the ridiculous spectacle of a government without a power to make treaties with foreign nations; a result as inadmissible as it is absurd; since, in fact, our Constitution grants the power of making treaties, in the most explicit and ample terms, to the President, with the advice and consent of the Senate. On the contrary, all difficulty is avoided, by distinguishing the province of the two powers, according to ideas which have been always familiar to us, and which were never exposed to any question till the treaty with Great Britain gave exercise to the subtilties of party spirit.

By confining the power to make laws within its proper sphere, and restricting its actions to the establishment of rules for our own nation and those foreigners who come within our jurisdiction, and by assigning to the power of treaty the office of concerting those rules of mutual intercourse and connection, between us and foreign nations, which require their consent as well as our own, allowing to it the latitude necessary for this purpose, a harmonious agreement is preserved between the different powers of the Government—that to make laws, and that to make treaties; between the authority of the legislative and the authority of the executive department. . . .

In all these cases, the power to make laws and the power to make treaties are concurrent and co-ordinate. The latter, and not the former, must act, where the co-operation of the other nations is requisite. . . .

So far then it is from being true, that the power of treaty can extend to nothing upon which, in relation to ourselves, the legislative power may act, that it may rather be laid down as a general rule, that a treaty may do between different nations whatever the legislative power of each may do with regard to itself. The exceptions to this rule are to be deduced from the unfitness and inconvenience of its application to particular cases, and are of the nature of abuses of a general principle.

—"Camillus," No. 37. *Works*, VI, 178-182.

1796

The manner in which the power of treaty, as it exists in the Constitution, was understood by the convention in framing it, and by the people in adopting it, is the point next to be considered.

As to the sense of the convention, the secrecy with which their deliberations were conducted does not permit any formal proof of the opinions and views which prevailed in digesting the power of treaty. But from the *best opportunity of knowing the fact,* I aver, that it was understood *by all* to be the intent of the provision to give to that power the most ample latitude—to render it competent to all the stipulations which the exigencies of national affairs might require; competent to the making of treaties of alliance, treaties of commerce, treaties of peace, and every other species of convention usual among nations; and competent, in the course of its exercise for these purposes, to control and bind the legislative power of Congress. And it was emphatically for this reason that it was so carefully guarded; the co-operation of two thirds of the Senate, with the President, being required to make any treaty whatever. I appeal for this, with confidence, to every member of the convention—particularly to those in the two houses of Congress. Two of these are in the House of Representatives, Mr. Madison, and Mr. Baldwin. It is expected by the adversaries of the treaty, that these gentlemen will, in their places, obstruct its execution. However this may be, I feel a confidence that neither of them will deny the assertion I have made. To suppose them capable of such a denial were to suppose them utterly regardless of truth. But though direct proof of the views of the convention on the point cannot be produced, yet we are not wholly without proof on this head. . . .

As to the sense of the community in the adoption of the Constitution, this can only be ascertained from two sources: the writings for and against it, and the debates in the several State conventions, while it was under consideration.

I possess not, at this moment, materials for an investigation, which would enable me to present the evidence they afford; but I refer to them, with confidence, for proof of the fact, that the organization of the power of treaty in the Constitution was attacked and defended with an admission on both sides, of its being of a character which I have assigned to it. Its great extent and importance—its effect to control, by its stipulations, the legislative authority, were mutually taken for granted, and upon this basis it was insisted, by way of objection, that there were not adequate guards for the safe exercise of so vast a power; that there ought to have been reservations of certain rights, a better disposition of the power to impeach, and a participation, general or special, of the House of Representatives in the making of treaties.

The reply to these objections, acknowledging the delicacy and magnitude of the power, was directed to show that its organization was a proper one, and that it was sufficiently guarded.[1] . . .

[1] *The Federalist,* No. 42 [Madison], has these passages: "The power to make treaties and to receive and send ambassadors, speak their own propriety; both of them are comprised in the articles of confederation, *with the difference only* that the former is *disembarrassed* by the plan of the convention, of an exception by which treaties might be substantially frustrated by regulations of the States." This plainly alludes to the *proviso* which has been cited and commented upon. "It is true that

How happens it, that all these invasions of the Constitution, if they were such, were never discovered, and that all the departments of the government, and all parties in the public councils, should have co-operated in giving them a sanction? Does it not prove that *all* were convinced, that the power of treaty applied in our exterior relations to objects which, in the ordinary course of internal administration and in reference to ourselves, were of the cognizance of the legislative power? and particularly that the former was competent to bind the latter in the delicate points of raising and appropriating money? If competent to this, what legislative power can be more sacred, more out of its reach?

—"Camillus," No. 38 (N.Y.) *American Minerva*, Jan. 8, 1796.

Treaties as the Supreme Law of the Land

1784

Does not the act of Confederation place the exclusive right of war and peace in the United States in Congress? Have they not the sole power of making treaties with foreign nations? Are not these among the first rights of sovereignty? And does not the delegation of them to the general Confederacy so far abridge the sovereignty of each particular State? Would not a different doctrine involve the contradiction of *imperium in imperio?*

—*A Letter from Phocion*, p. 10.

---

when treaties of commerce stipulate for the nominal appointment of consuls, the admission of foreign consuls may fall within the power of making commercial treaties." And in No. 64 [Jay] are these passages: "The power of making treaties is an important one, especially *as it relates to war, peace, and commerce*; and it should not be delegated but in such a mode and with such precautions as will afford the *highest security*, that it will be exercised by men the best qualified for the purpose, and in the manner most conducive to the public good." "There are few who will not admit, that the affairs of *trade* and *navigation* should be regulated by a system cautiously formed and steadily pursued, and that both our treaties and our laws should correspond with and be made to promote it." "Some are displeased with it (that is, the power of treaty), not on account of any errors or defects in it, but because, as the treaties, when made, are to have the force of laws, they should be made only by men invested with legislative authority; others, though content that treaties should be made in the mode proposed, are averse to their being the *supreme law of the land*."

It is generally understood that two persons were concerned in the writings of these papers, who, from having been members of the convention, had a good opportunity of knowing its views—and were under no temptation at that time, in this particular, to misrepresent them. . . .

In the 2d volume of the Debates of the Convention of Virginia, which is the the only part I possess, there are many passages that show the great extent of the power of treaty in the opinion of the speakers on both sides. As quotations would be tedious, I will content myself with referring to the papers where they will be found, viz., 91, 99, 131, 137, 143, 147, 150, 186. It will, in particular, appear, that while the opposers of the Constitution denied the power of the House of Representatives to break in upon or control the power of treaties, the friends of the Constitution did not affirm the contrary, but merely contended that the House of Representatives might check by its *influence* the President and Senate—on the subject of treaties.

[1796]

The same reasoning, too, would extend the power of treaties to those objects which are consigned to the legislation of individual States; but here the Constitution has announced its meaning in express terms, by declaring, that the treaties which have been and shall be made under the authority of the United States, shall be the supreme law of the land, *any thing in the Constitution* or *laws of any State to the contrary notwithstanding*. This manifestly recognizes the supremacy of the power of treaties over the laws of particular States, and goes even a step farther.

The obvious reason for this special provision, in regard to the laws of individual states, is, that there might otherwise have been room for question—whether a treaty of the Union could embrace objects, the internal regulation of which belonged to the separate authorities of the States. But with regard to the United States there was no room for a similar question.

The power of treaty could not but be supposed commensurate with all those objects to which the legislative power of the Union extended.

It is a question among some theoretical writers—whether a treaty can repeal *pre-existing laws?* This question must always be answered by the particular form of government of each nation. In our Constitution, which gives, *ipso facto*, the force of law to treaties, making them equally with the acts of Congress, the supreme law of the land, a treaty must necessarily repeal an antecedent law contrary to it; according to the legal maxim that "*leges posteriores priores contrarias abrogant.*"

But even in those forms of government, in which there may be room for such a question, it is not understood that a treaty containing stipulations which require the repeal of antecedent laws, is, on that account, unconstitutional and null. The true meaning is, that the antecedent laws are not, *ispso facto*, abrogated by the treaty; but the Legislature is, nevertheless, bound in good faith, under the general limitation stated in another place, to lend its authority to remove obstacles which previous laws might oppose to a fair execution of a treaty.

—"Camillus," No. 37. Draft in Hamilton's hand; undated. Hamilton Papers, 1st ser.

The President's Power to Declare War

May 17, 1798

In so delicate a case, in one which involves so important a consequence as that of war, my opinion is that no doubtful authority ought to be exercised by the President; but, that as different opinions about his power have been expressed in the House of Representatives, and no special power has been given by the law, it will be expedient for him, and his duty, and the true policy of the conjuncture, to come forward by a message to the two houses of Congress, declaring that "*so far* and *no farther*" he feels himself *confident* of his authority to go in the employment of the naval force; that as, in his opinion, the depredations on our trade demand a more extensive protection, he has thought it his duty to bring the subject under the review of Congress by a communication of his opinion of his own powers, having no desire to exceed the constitutional limits.

This course will remove all clouds as to what the President will do; will gain him credit for frankness and an unwillingness to chicane the Constitution, and will return upon Congress the question in a shape which cannot be eluded.

—To James McHenry. Hamilton Papers, 1st ser.

December 17, 1801

The message of the President,[1] by whatever motives it may have been dictated, is a performance which ought to alarm all who are anxious for the safety of our government, for the respectability and welfare of our nation. It makes, or aims at making, a most prodigal sacrifice of constitutional energy, of sound principle, and of public interest, to the popuuarity of one man.

The first thing in it, which excites our surprise, is the very extraordinary position, that though *Tripoli had declared war in form* against the United States, and had enforced it by actual hostility, yet that there was not power, for want of *the sanction of Congress*, to capture and detain her cruisers with their crews.

—"Lucius Crassus," No. 1. *Hamilton*, VII, 745.

A Code of Presidential Etiquette

Hamilton insisted on upholding the dignity of the Presidential office. Although Jeffersonian Republicans criticized Washington's formal weekly levees as "anti-republican," the prestige of the Chief Executive was firmly established at the conclusion of Washington's administration.

May 5, 1789

. . . Men's minds are prepared for a pretty high tone in the demeanor of the Executive, but I doubt whether for so high a one as in the abstract might be desirable. The notions of equality are yet, in my opinion, too general and too strong to admit of such a distance being placed between the President and other branches of the government as might even be consistent with a due proportion. The following plan will, I think, steer clear of extremes, and involve no very material inconveniences.

I. The President to have a levee day once a week for receiving visits;

[1] Jefferson's Message to Congress of Dec. 7, 1801.

an hour to be fixed at which it shall be understood that he will appear, and consequently that the visitors are to be previously assembled.

The President to remain half an hour, in which time he may converse cursorily on indifferent subjects, with such persons as shall invite his attention, and at the end of that half hour disappear. Some regulation will be hereafter necessary to designate those who may visit.

A mode of introduction through particular officers will be indispensable. No visits to be returned.

II. The President to accept no invitations, and to give formal entertainments only twice or four times a year, the anniversaries of important events in the Revolution. If twice, the day of the declaration of independence, and that of the inauguration of the President, which completed the organization of the Constitution, to be preferred; of four times, the day of the treaty of alliance with France, and that of the definitive treaty with Britain to be added. The members of the two houses of the legislature, principal officers of the government, foreign ministers and other distinguished strangers only to be invited. The numbers form in my mind an objection; but there may be separate tables in separate rooms. This is practised in some European courts. I see no other method in which foreign ministers can, with propriety, be included in any attentions of the table which the President may think fit to pay.

III. The President, on the levee days, either by himself or some gentleman of his household, to give informal invitations to family dinners on the days of invitation. Not more than six or eight to be invited at a time, and the matter to be confined essentially to members of the Legislature and other official characters. The President never to remain long at table.

I think it probable that the last article will not correspond with the ideas of most of those with whom your Excellency may converse; but on pretty mature reflection, I believe it will be necessary to remove the idea of too immense an inequality, which I fear would excite dissatisfaction and cabal. The thing may be so managed as neither to occasion much waste of time nor to infringe on dignity.

It is an important point to consider what persons may have access to your Excellency on business. The heads of departments will, of course, have this privilege. Foreign ministers of some descriptions will also be entitled to it. In Europe, I am informed, ambassadors only have direct access to the chief magistrate. Something very near what prevails there would, in my opinion, be right. The distinction of rank between diplomatic characters requires attention, and the door of access ought not to be too wide to that class of persons. I have thought that the members of the Senate should also have a right of *individual* access on matters relative to the *public administration*. In England and France, peers of the realm have this right. We have none such in this country, but I believe that it will be satisfactory to the people to know that there is some body of men in the state who have a right of continual communication with the President. It will be considered a safeguard against secret combinations to deceive him.

I have also asked myself, Will not the Representatives expect the same privilege, and be offended if they are not allowed to participate with the Senate? There is sufficient danger of this to merit consideration. But there is reason for the distinction in the Constitution. The Senate are coupled with the President in certain executive functions, treaties, and appointments. This makes them in a degree his constitutional counsellors, and gives them a *peculiar* claim to the right of access. On the whole, I think the discrimination will be proper and may be hazarded.

I have chosen this method of communication because I understood your Excellency that it would be most convenient to you. The unstudied and unceremonious manner of it will, I hope, not render it the less acceptable. And if, in the execution of your commands, at any time I consult frankness and simplicity more than ceremony or profession, I flatter myself you will not on that account distrust the sincerity of my cordial wishes for your personal happiness, and the success of your administration.

—To Washington. *Hamilton*, IV, 1-3.

The Structure and Powers of Congress

February 22, 1788

The natural order of the subject leads us to consider, in this place, that provision of the Constitution which authorizes the national legislature to regulate, in the last resort, the election of its own members . . . Its propriety rests upon the evidence of this plain proposition, that *every government ought to contain in itself the means of its own preservation*. . . .

Nothing can be more evident than that an exclusive power of regulating elections for the national government in the hands of the state legislatures would leave the existence of the Union entirely at their mercy. They could at any moment annihilate it, by neglecting to provide for the choice of persons to administer its affairs. . . .

—*The Federalist* No. 59.

March 11, 1788

A review of the principal objections that have appeared against the proposed court for the trial of impeachments, will not improbably eradicate the remains of any unfavorable impressions which may still exist in regard to this matter.

The *first* of these objections is, that the provision in question confounds legislative and judiciary authorities in the same body, in violation of that important and well-established maxim which requires a separation between the different departments of power. The true meaning of this maxim has been discussed and ascertained in another place, and has been shown to be entirely compatible with a partial intermixture of those departments for special purposes, preserving them, in the main, distinct and unconnected. This partial intermixture is even, in some cases, not only proper but necessary to the mutual defense of the several members of the government against each other. An absolute or qualified negative in the executive upon the acts of the legislative body is admitted by the ablest adepts in political science to be an indispensable barrier against the encroachments of the latter upon the former. And it may, perhaps, with no less reason be contended, that the powers relating to impeachments are, as before intimated, an essential check in the hands of that body upon the encroachments of the executive. . . .

—*The Federalist* No. 66.

June 20, 1788

The first thing objected to is that clause which allows a representation for three fifths of the Negroes. Much has been said of the impropriety of representing men who have no will of their own. Whether this be reasoning or declamation, I will not presume to say. It is the unfortunate situation of the Southern States to have a great part of their population as well as property in blacks. The regulation complained of was one result of the spirit of accommodation which governed the Convention; and without this indulgence no union could possibly have been formed. But, Sir, considering some peculiar advantages which we derive from them, it is entirely just that they should be gratified. The Southern States possess certain staples—tobacco, rice, indigo, etc.—which must be capital objects in treaties of commerce with foreign nations; and the advantage which they necessarily procure in these treaties will be felt throughout all the States. But the justice of this plan will appear in another view. The best writers on government have held that representation should be compounded of persons and property. This rule has been adopted, as far as it could be, in the Constitution of New York. It will, however, be by no means admitted that the slaves are considered altogether as property. They are men, though degraded to the condition of slavery. They are persons known to the municipal laws of the states which they inhabit, as well as to the laws of nature. But representation and taxation go together, and one uniform rule ought to apply to both. Would it be just to compute these slaves in the assessment of taxes, and discard them from the estimate in the apportionment of representatives? Would it be just to impose a singular burthen without confering some adequate advantage?

Another circumstance ought to be considered. The rule we have been speaking of is a general rule, and applies to all the States. You have a great number of people in your State which are not represented at all, and have no voice in your government. These will be included in the enumeration, not two fifths, or three fifths, but the whole. This proves that the advantages of the plan are not confined to the Southern States, but extend to other parts of the Union.

. . . The Congress is to consist at first of ninety-one members. This to a reasonable man, may appear to be as near the proper medium as any number whatever; at least, for the present. There is one source of increase, also, which does not depend upon any constructions of the Constitution: it is the creation of new States. Vermont, Kentucky, and Franklin will probably soon become independent. New members of the Union will also be formed from the unsettled tracts of Western Territory. These must be represented, and will all contribute to swell the federal legislature. . . . We may, therefore, safely calculate upon a growing representation, according to the advance of population and the circumstances of the country.

—Speech on the Compromises of the Constitution, *Debates of the N. Y. Convention*, pp. 25-27.

June 21, 1788

Notwithstanding the cry of corruption that has been perpetually raised against the House of Commons, it has been found that that House, sitting at first without any constitutional authority, became at length an essential member of the legislature, and have since, by regular gradations, acquired new and important accessions of privileges; that they have, on numerous occasions, impaired the overgrown prerogative and limited the incroachments of monarchy.

—Speech on the Constitution, *Debates of the N.Y. Convention*, p. 45.

The Senate

Hamilton's speech at the Poughkeepsie Convention on the powers of the Senate was one of his most logical and persuasive efforts. It was delivered in response to a motion of Gilbert Livingston restricting the eligibility of Senators for reelection and giving to the state legislatures the power to recall their senators. Hamilton won the war but lost this battle, as Livingston's amendment was included among the recommendatory amendments finally adopted by the New York Convention.

June 24, 1788

In the commencement of a revolution, which received its birth from the usurpations of tyranny, nothing was more natural than that the public mind should be influenced by an extreme spirit of jealousy. To resist these encroachments, and to nourish this spirit, was the great object of all our public and private institutions. The zeal for liberty became predominant and excessive. In forming our Confederation, this passion alone seemed to actuate us, and we appear to have had no other view than to secure ourselves from despotism. The object certainly was a valuable one, and deserved our utmost attention. But, Sir, there is another object, equally important, and which our enthusiasm rendered us little capable of regarding. I mean a principle of strength and stability in the organization of our government, and of vigor in its operations. This purpose could never be accomplished but by the establishment of some select body, formed peculiarly on this principle. There are few positions more demonstrable than that there should be in every republic some permanent body, to correct the prejudices, check the intemperate passions, and regulate the fluctuations of a popular assembly. It is evident that a body instituted for these purposes must be so formed as to exclude as much as possible from its own character those infirmities and that mutability which it is designed to remedy. It is, therefore, necessary that it should be small, that it should hold its authority during a considerable period, and that it should have such an independence in the exercise of its powers, as will divest it, as much as possible of local prejudices. . . .

. . . The history of ancient and modern republics had taught them that many of the evils which those republic suffered arose from the want of a certain balance, and that mutual control indispensable to a wise administration. They were convinced that popular assemblies are frequently misguided by ignorance, by sudden impulses, and the intrigues of ambitious men; and that some firm barrier against these operations was necessary. They, therefore, instituted your Senate; and the benefits we have experienced have fully justified their conceptions. . . .

Sir, if you consider but a moment the purposes for which the Senate was instituted, and the nature of the business which they are to transact, you will see the necessity of giving them duration. They, together with the President, are to manage all our concerns with foreign nations. They must understand all their interests and their political systems. This knowledge is not soon acquired—but a very small part is gained in the closet.

. . . Considering the Senate, therefore, with a view to responsibility, duration is a very interesting and essential quality. There is another view in which duration in the Senate appears necessary; a government changeable in its policy must soon lose its sense of national character and forfeit the respect of foreigners. Senators will not be solicitous for the reputation of public measures in which they have had but a temporary concern, and will feel lightly the burthen of public disapprobation in proportion to the number of those who partake of the censure.

June 25, 1788

. . . Look through their history: what factions have arisen from the most trifling causes! What intrigues have been practised for the most illiberal purposes! Is not the State of Rhode Island at this moment struggling under difficulties and distresses, for having been led blindly by the spirit of the multitude? What is her legislature but the picture of a mob? In this state, we have a senate, possessed of the proper qualities of a permanent body. Virginia, Maryland, and a few other States are in the same situation. The rest are either governed by a single democratic assembly, or have a senate constituted entirely upon democratic principles. These have been more or less embroiled in factions, and have generally been the image and echo of the multitude. It is difficult to reason on this point, without touching on certain delicate chords. I could refer you to periods and conjunctures when the people have been governed by improper passions, and led by factious and designing men. I could show that the same passions have infected their representatives. Let us beware that we do not make the state legislatures a vehicle in which the evil humors may be conveyed into the national system. To prevent this, it is necessary that the Senate should be so formed, as in some measure to check the state governments, and preclude the communication of the false impressions which they receive from the people. It has been often repeated, that the legislatures of the states can have only a partial and confined view of national affairs; that they can form no proper estimate of great objects which are not in the sphere of their interests. The observation of the gentleman, therefore, cannot take off the force of the argument.

—Speech on the United States Senate, *Debates of the N.Y. Convention*, pp. 71-75, 81, 82.

The Courts and Judicial Review

No legislative act . . . contrary to the Constitution can be valid.

In no area of constitutional government has the authority of Hamilton been more influential than in his insistence on the supremacy of the Constitution and on the right of the courts to declare acts in violation of the Constitution and of national treaties null and void. His was the first powerful voice to be raised in behalf of the principle of judicial review. It was raised as early as 1784, when he was associated as defense counsel in the case of Rutgers v. Waddington. *In March, 1783, the New York legislature, in a blow against the Loyalists, passed an act providing that any citizen whose property, while within British lines, had been occupied by any person other than its lawful owner, might sue such occupant for damages in trespass. When the British occupied New York they took possession of a brewery which belonged to a widow, Elizabeth Rutgers, and her son. This was under military control until June, 1778. Then the British commissary-general licensed the premises to two British merchants. On recovering the premises after New York was surrendeded, the Patriot owners brought suit against one of the two lessees who had been so imprudent as to remain behind after the British quit New York. A galaxy of lawyers, headed by Robert Troup, Hamilton's bosom friend, appeared in the widow's behalf. Hamilton, along with Brockholst Livingston and Morgan Lewis, appeared for the defendant.*

Hamilton interposed a demurrer to the complaint. This consisted of two distinct pleas. First, he insisted that the British army had a right to license the property under international law. Secondly, he argued that after the passage of the Trespass Act the peace treaty had been signed and ratified with Great Britian, whereby all claims for damages arising out of the war were mutually renounced. In other words, the treaty made the act of the legislature null and void. This is an excerpt from his notes in arguing the case:

[August, 1784]

. . . it would be a breach of the Confederation.—Congress have made a treaty. A breach of that would be a breach of their constitutional authority.

Power of Treaty legislative. Proclamation a law. Sovereign authority may violate treaties.

Bold ground admits the intention; but within, each state has no such power, having delegated the management of its foreign concerns to Congress, to whom alone the consideration of these, reason of state belongs.

As well a county may alter the laws of the state as the state those of the Confederation.

It has been said, legislature may alter laws of nations.

Not true in theory. . . .

If such a power does exist in our government 'tis in Congress.

Accession to Confederation was act of legislature. Why may not another act alter it?

UNION preexisted.

Act of accession not a law but a CONTRACT which one part cannot release itself from.

One part of an empire may dismember itself, but this supposes dissolution of the original contract.

While Confederation exists its constitutional authority paramount.

But how are the JUDGES to decide?

Answer: Constitution giving independent power only in prize causes; in all others judges of each state must of necessity be judges of United States—

And the law of each state must adopt the laws of Congress.

Though in relation to its own citizens local laws might govern; yet in relation to foreigners those of United States must prevail.

It must be conceded legislature of one state cannot repeal law of United States.

All must be construed to stand together! . . .

Many of these argument(s) suppose trespass as repugnant to the law of nations. It may, however, receive a construction consistent with all. And to give it this construction is the duty of the court.

We have seen that to make the defendant liable would be TO VIOLATE the laws of nations and forfeit character, to violate a solemn treaty of peace and revive state of hostility, to infringe Confederation and endanger peace of the union.

CAN we suppose all this to have been intended by the legislature?

The LAW cannot suppose it,

And if it was intended the act is void!

—Hamilton Papers, 2nd ser.

Hamilton scored a partial victory. James Duane, the conservative judge who presided over the case, and a good friend of Hamilton, straddled the major question: Was an act of the legislature in derogation of international treaty obligations valid? Instead, he seized upon a technicality to render a compromise decision. Damages were allowed the plaintiff for the period, 1778-80, on the ground that the commissary-general acted beyond his authority, but denied for the subsequent period when the defendant had occupied the property under license from the British commander-in-chief. Hence, the decision was not a square ruling on the question of judicial review. The court declared that statutes contrary to the law of nations as embodied in treaties are void, but also insisted that it could not override the express wishes of the legislature. However, in determining legislative intent, Duane accepted Hamilton's line of argument on statutory interpretation, and held that the court might assume that it was the intent of the legislature to conform to international law. As Hamilton pointed out years later in a Cabinet Paper to President Washington, this decision did not bring about conformity to the Treaty of 1783 in New York. It was necessary for Hamilton and other moderates to fight hard to have the

Trespass Act repealed. In 1788, when the Federalists won control of the legislature, all statutes inconsistent with the treaty were repealed.

[March, 1787]

It had been said, that the judges would have too much power;—this was a misapprehension. He stated the powers of the judges with great clearness and precision. He insisted that their powers would be the same, whether this law was passed or not. For, as all treaties were known by the Constitution as the laws of the land, so must the judges act on the same, any law to the contrary notwithstanding.

Cicero, the great Roman orator and lawyer, lays it down as a rule, that when two laws clash, that which relates to the most important matters ought to be preferred. If this rule prevails, who can doubt what would be the conduct of the judges, should any laws exist inconsistent with the treaty of peace? But it would be impolitic to leave them to the dilemma, either of infringing the treaty to enforce the particular laws of the State, or to explain away the laws of the State to give effect to the treaty.

He declared that the full operation of the bill would be no more than merely to declare the treaty the law of the land; and that the judges, viewing it as such, shall do away all laws that may appear in direct contravention of it. Treaties were known constitutionally to be the law of the land, and why be afraid to leave the interpretation of those laws to the judges? The Constitution knows them as the interpreters of the law. He asked if there was any member of the committee who would be willing to see the first treaty of peace ever made by this country violated. This he did not believe. He could not think that any member on that floor harbored such sentiments.

—Speech in the New York Assembly. *Works,* IV, 293-294.

March 21, 1787

Col. Hamilton said that this amendment to the trespass law was only to repeal that part which was in violation of the public treaty. The courts of justice were at present in a delicate dilemma, obliged either to explain away a positive law of the State, or openly violate the national faith by counteracting the very words and spirit of the treaties now in existence. Because the treaty declares a general amnesty, and this State, by this law declares that no person shall plead any military order for a trespass committed during the war. He said no State was so much interested in the due observance of the treaty as the State of New York, the British having possession of its western frontiers, and which they hold under the sanction of our not having complied with our national engagements. He hoped the House would have too much wisdom not to do away this exception, and indeed he expected the bill would be readily agreed to.

—Speech in the New York Assembly. *Works*, VIII, 39.

[July 9, 1795]

An act of New York for granting a more effectual relief in cases of certain trespasses, passed the 17th of March, 1783.

This act takes away from any person within the British lines who had occupied, injured, or destroyed the property, real or personal, of an inhabitant without the lines, the plea of a military order for so doing; consequently, the justification which he might derive from the laws and usages of war, in contravention of the treaty of peace.

It is true, it preceded for a short time the arrival of the provisional treaty in this country; but it is notorious that it was in expectation and contemplation of the event. . . .

It hardly appears a satisfactory answer to this to say, as Mr. Jefferson has done, that the courts did not sanction the principle of the act; that in one instance, the case of Rutgers and Waddington, the mayor's court overruled it.

The fact is, that from the very express terms of the act, a general opinion was entertained, embracing almost our whole bar, as well as the public, that it was useless to attempt a defence; and, accordingly, many suits were brought, and many judgments given, without the point being regularly raised, and many compromises were made, and large sums paid, under the despair of a successful defence. I was for a long time the only practiser who pursued a different course, and opposed the treaty to the act; and though I was never overruled in the Supreme Court, I never got my point established there. I effected many easy compromises to my clients, afraid myself of the event in the Supreme Court, and produced delays till the exceptionable part of the act was repealed. The Supreme Court frequently, in a studied manner, evaded the main question, and turned their decision upon the forms of pleading.

'Tis perhaps enough for the other party to say that here was a positive law of a State, unrepealed, and acted upon so as in fact to defeat, in a material degree, the operation of the treaty. The injury was suffered, and there ought never to have existed so critical a conflict between the treaty and the statute law of a State.

—To Washington (Cabinet Paper). Draft in Hamilton's hand; date in later hand. Hamilton Papers, 1st ser.

The Constitution is silent on the power of the federal courts to pass upon the constitutionality of acts of Congress. Various opinions had been expressed in the Convention. Hamilton had no doubts whatsoever. In his Federalist *letter No. 78 he asserted that the Constitution is the supreme law of the land, that in any conflict between the Constitution and an act of Congress the former should prevail, and that it was the proper function of the courts to interpret the laws. Hamilton's formula was later embodied by Chief Justice Marshall in the epochal case of* Marbury v. Madison, *decided in the Supreme Court in 1803.*

Hamilton believed strongly in judicial independence. This would attract the best qualified lawyers to the bench and protect minority rights in times of crisis. He believed that the judges should be appointed for good behavior and that the legislature should be restrained from reducing their compensation. Such an independent judiciary, in his opinion, would not dangerously encroach on the legislative authority. What would restrain the actions of the judiciary? Hamilton felt that the power of impeachment would serve as a check on the courts, but time has shown that impeachment by Congress has been a less effective weapon than executive pressure and the Presidential authority to fill vacancies on the bench.

Since in only one instance did the Supreme Court prior to the Dred Scott decision of 1857 set aside an act of Congress as unconstitutional, Hamilton's vision of the ultimate relationship between courts and Congress was remarkably prophetic.

[May, 1788]

We proceed now to an examination of the judiciary department of the proposed government. . . .

As to the tenure by which the judges are to hold their places: this chiefly concerns their duration in office; the provisions for their support; the precautions for their responsibility.

According to the plan of the convention, all judges who may be appointed by the United States are to hold their offices *during good behavior*; which is conformable to the most approved of the State constitutions, and among the rest, to that of this State. Its propriety having been drawn into question by the adversaries of that plan, is no light symptom of the rage for objection, which disorders their imaginations and judgments. The standard of good behavior for the continuance in office of the judicial magistracy, is certainly one of the most valuable of the modern improvements in the practice of government. In a monarchy it is an excellent barrier to the despotism of the prince; in a republic it is a no less excellent barrier to the encroachments and oppressions of the representative body. And it is the best expedient which can be devised in any government, to secure a steady, upright, and impartial administration of the laws.

Whoever attentively considers the different departments of power must perceive, that, in a government in which they are separated from each other, the judiciary, from the nature of its functions, will always be the least dangerous to the political rights of the Constitution; because it will be least in a capacity to annoy or injure them. The Executive not only dispenses the honors, but holds the sword of the community. The legislature not only commands the purse, but prescribes the rules by which the duties and rights of every citizen are to be regulated. The judiciary, on the contrary, has no influence over either the sword or the purse; no direction either of the strength or of the wealth of the society; and can take no active resolution whatever. It may truly be said to have neither FORCE nor WILL, but merely judgment; and must ultimately depend upon the aid of the executive arm even for the efficacy of its judgments.

This simple view of the matter suggests several important consequences. It proves incontestably, that the judiciary is beyond comparison the weakest of the three departments of power*; that it can never attack with success either of the other two; and that all possible care is requisite to enable it to defend itself against their attacks. It equally proves, that though individual oppression may now and then proceed from the courts of justice, the general liberty of the people can never be endangered from that quarter; I mean so long as the judiciary remains truly distinct from both the legislature and the Executive. For I agree, that "there is no liberty, if the power of judging be not separated from the legislative and executive powers."† And it proves, in the last place, that as liberty can have nothing to fear from the judiciary alone, but would have every thing to fear from its union with either of the other departments; that as all the effects of such a union must ensue from a dependence of the former on the latter, notwithstanding a nominal and apparent separation; that as, from the natural feebleness of the judiciary, it is in continual jeopardy of being overpowered, awed, or influenced by its coördinate branches; and that as nothing can contribute so much to its firmness and independence as permanency in office, this quality may therefore be justly regarded as an indispensable ingredient in its constitution, and, in a great measure, as the citadel of the public justice and the public security.

The complete independence of the courts of justice is peculiarly essential in a limited Constitution. By a limited Constitution, I understand one which contains certain specified exceptions to the legislative authority; such, for instance, as that it shall pass no bills of attainder, no *ex-post-facto* laws, and the like. Limitations of this kind can be preserved in practice no other way than through the medium of courts of justice, whose duty it must be to declare all acts contrary to the

* The celebrated Montesquieu, speaking of them says: "Of the three powers above mentioned, the judiciary is next to nothing."—"Spirit of Laws," vol. i., page 186.—PUBLIUS

† *Idem*, page 181.—PUBLIUS

manifest tenor of the Constitution void. Without this, all the reservations of particular rights or privileges would amount to nothing.

Some perplexity respecting the rights of the courts to pronounce legislative acts void, because contrary to the constitution, has arisen from an imagination that the doctrine would imply a superiority of the judiciary to the legislative power. It is urged that the authority which can declare the acts of another void, must necessarily be superior to the one whose acts may be declared void. As this doctrine is of great importance in all the American constitutions, a brief discussion of the ground on which it rests cannot be unacceptable.

There is no position which depends on clearer principles, than that every act of a delegated authority, contrary to the tenor of the commission under which it is exercised, is void. No legislative act, therefore, contrary to the Constitution, can be valid. To deny this, would be to affirm, that the deputy is greater than his principal; that the servant is above his master; that the representatives of the people are superior to the people themselves; that men acting by virtue of powers, may do not only what their powers do not authorize, but what they forbid.

If it be said that the legislative body are themselves the constitutional judges of their own powers, and that the construction they put upon them is conclusive upon the other departments, it may be answered, that this cannot be the natural presumption, where it is not to be collected from any particular provisions in the Constitution. It is not otherwise to be supposed, that the Constitution could intend to enable the representatives of the people to substitute their *will* to that of their constituents. It is far more rational to suppose, that the courts were designed to be an intermediate body between the people and the legislature, in order, among other things, to keep the latter within the limits assigned to their authority. The interpretation of the laws is the proper and peculiar province of the courts. A constitution is, in fact, and must be regarded by the judges, as a fundamental law. It therefore belongs to them to ascertain its meaning, as well as the meaning of any particular act proceeding from the legislative body. If there should happen to be an irreconcilable variance between the two, that which has the superior obligation and validity ought, of course, to be preferred; or, in other words, the Constitution ought to be preferred to the statute, the intention of the people to the intention of their agents.

Nor does this conclusion by any means suppose a superiority of the judicial to the legislative power. It only supposes that the power of the people is superior to both; and that where the will of the legislature, declared in its statutes, stands in opposition to that of the people, declared in the Constitution, the judges ought to be governed by the latter rather than the former. They ought to regulate their decisions by the fundamental laws, rather than by those which are not fundamental. . . .

If, then, the courts of justice are to be considered as the bulwarks of a limited Constitution against legislative encroachments, this consideration will afford a strong argument for the permanent tenure of judicial offices, since nothing will contribute so much as this to that independent spirit in the judges which must be essential to the faithful performance of so arduous a duty.

This independence of the judges is equally requisite to guard the Constitution and the rights of individuals from the effects of those ill humors, which the arts of designing men, or the influence of particular conjunctures, sometimes disseminate among the people themselves, and which, though they speedily give place to better information, and more deliberate reflection, have a tendency, in the meantime, to occasion dangerous innovations in the government, and serious oppressions of the minor party in the community. Though I trust the friends of the proposed Constitution will never concur with its enemies,* in questioning that fundamental principle of republican government, which admits the right of the people to alter or abolish the established Constitution, whenever they find it inconsistent with their happiness, yet it is not to be inferred from this principle, that the representatives of the people, whenever a momentary inclination happens to lay hold of a majority of their constituents, incompatible with the provisions in the existing Constitution, would, on that account, be justifiable in a violation of those provisions; or that the courts would be under a greater obligation to connive at infractions in this shape, than when they had proceeded wholly from the cabals of the representative body. . . .

But it is not with a view to infractions of the Constitution only, that the independence of the judges may be an essential safeguard against the effects of occasional ill humors in the society. These sometimes extend no farther than to the injury of the private rights of particular classes of citizens, by unjust and partial laws. Here also the firmness of the judicial magistracy is of vast importance in mitigating the severity and confining the operation of such laws. It not only serves to moderate immediate mischiefs of those which may have been passed, but it operates as a check upon the legislative body in passing them; who, perceiving that obstacles to the success of iniquitous intention are to be expected from the scruples of the courts, are in a manner compelled, by the very motives of the injustice they meditate, to qualify their attempts. This is a circumstance calculated to have more influence upon the character of our governments, than but few may be aware of. . . . Considerate men, of every description, ought to prize what-

* *Vide* "Protest of the Minority of the Convention of Pennsylvania," Martin's Speech, etc.—Publius

ever will tend to beget or fortify that temper in the courts; as no man can be sure that he may not be to-morrow the victim of a spirit of injustice, by which he may be a gainer today. . . .

That inflexible and uniform adherence to the rights of the Constitution, and of individuals, which we perceive to be indispensable in the courts of justice, can certainly not be expected from judges who hold their offices by a temporary commission. Periodical appointments, however regulated, or by whomsoever made, would, in some way or other, be fatal to their necessary independence. If the power of making them was committed either to the Executive or legislature, there would be danger of an improper complaisance to the branch which possessed it; if to both, there would be an unwillingness to hazard the displeasure of either; if to the people, or to persons chosen by them for the special purpose, there would be too great a disposition to consult popularity, to justify a reliance that nothing would be consulted but the Constitution and the laws.

There is yet a further and a weightier reason for the permanency of the judicial offices, which is deducible from the nature of the qualifications they require. It has been frequently remarked, with great propriety, that a voluminous code of laws is one of the inconveniences necessarily connected with the advantages of a free government. To avoid an arbitrary discretion in the courts, it is indispensable that they should be bound down by strict rules and precedents, which serve to define and point out their duty in every particular case that comes before them; and it will readily be conceived from the variety of controversies which grow out of the folly and wickedness of mankind, that the records of those precedents must unavoidably swell to a very considerable bulk, and must demand long and laborious study to acquire a competent knowledge of them. Hence it is, that there can be but a few men in the society who will have sufficient skill in the laws to qualify them for the stations of judges. And making the proper deductions for the ordinary depravity of human nature, the number must be still smaller of those who unite the requisite integrity with the requisite knowledge. These considerations apprise us, that the government can have no great option between fit character; and that a temporary duration in office, which would naturally discourage such characters from quitting a lucrative line of practice to accept a seat on the bench, would have a tendency to throw the administration of justice into hands less able, and less well qualified, to conduct it with utility and dignity. . . .

Upon the whole, there can be no room to doubt that the convention acted wisely in copying from the models of those constitutions which have established *good behavior* as the tenure of their judicial offices, in point of duration; and that so far from being blamable on this account, their plan would have been inexcusably defective, if it had wanted this important feature of good government. The experience of Great Britain affords an illustrious comment on the excellence of the institution.

—*The Federalist* No. 78.

[May, 1788]

Next to permanency in office, nothing can contribute more to the independence of the judges than a fixed provision for their support. The remark made in relation to the President is equally applicable here. In the general course of human nature, *a power over a man's subsistence amounts to a power over his will*. . . . The plan of the convention accordingly has provided that the judges of the United States "shall at *stated times* receive for their services a compensation which shall not be *diminished* during their continuance in office."

This, all circumstances considered, is the most eligible provision that could have been devised. It will readily be understood that the fluctuations in the value of money and in the state of society rendered a fixed rate of compensation in the Constitution inadmissible. What might be extravagant to-day, might in half a century become penurious and inadequate. It was therefore necessary to leave it to the discretion of the legislature to vary its provisions in conformity to the variations in circumstances, yet under such restrictions as to put it out of the power of that body to change the condition of the individual for the worse. A man may then be sure of the ground upon which he stands, and can never be deterred from his duty by the apprehension of being placed in a less eligible situation. . . .

The want of a provision for removing the judges on account of inability has been a subject of complaint. But all considerate men will be sensible that such a provision would either not be practised upon or would be more liable to abuse than calculated to answer any good purpose. The mensuration of the faculties of the mind has, I believe, no place in the catalogue of known arts. . . .

The Constitution of New York, to avoid investigations that must forever be vague and dangerous, has taken a particular age as the criterion of inability. No man can be a judge beyond sixty. I believe there are few at present who do not disapprove of this provision. There is no station, in relation to which it is less proper than to that of a judge. The deliberating and comparing faculties generally preserve their strength much beyond that period in men who survive it; and when, in addition to this circumstance, we consider how few there are who outlive the season of intellectual vigor, and how improbable it is that any considerable portion of the bench, whether more or less numerous, should be in such a situation at the same time, we shall be ready to conclude that limitations of this sort have little to recommend them. In a republic, where fortunes are not affluent, and pensions not expedient, the dismission of men from stations in which they have served their country long and usefully, on which they depend for subsistence, and from which it will be too late to resort to any other occupation for a livelihood, ought to have some better apology to humanity than is to be found in the imaginary danger of a superannuated bench.

—*The Federalist* No. 79.

[May, 1788]

To JUDGE with accuracy of the proper extent of the federal judicature, it will be necessary to consider, in the first place, what are its proper objects.

It seems scarcely to admit of controversy, that the judiciary authority of the Union ought to extend to these several descriptions of cases: 1st, to all those which arise out of the laws of the United States, passed in pursuance of their just and constitutional powers of legislation; 2nd, to all those which concern the execution of the provisions expressly contained in the articles of Union; 3d, to all those in which the United States are a party; 4th, to all those which involve the PEACE of the CONFEDERACY, whether they relate to the intercourse between the United States and foreign nations, or to that between the States themselves; 5th, to all those which originate on the high seas, and are of admiralty or maritime jurisdiction; and, lastly, to all those in which the State tribunals cannot be supposed to be impartial and unbiased.

The first point depends upon this obvious consideration, that there ought always to be a constitutional method of giving efficacy to constitutional provisions. What, for instance, would avail restrictions on the authority of the State legislatures, without some constitutional mode of enforcing the observance of them? The States, by the plan of the convention, are prohibited from doing a variety of things, some of which are incompatible with the interests of the Union, and others with the principles of good government. The imposition of duties on imported articles, and the emission of paper money, are specimens of each kind. No man of sense will believe, that such prohibitions would be scrupulously regarded, without some effectual power in the government to restrain or correct the infractions of them. This power must either be a direct negative on the State laws, or an authority in the federal courts to overrule such as might be in manifest contravention of the articles of Union. There is no third course that I can imagine. The latter appears to have been thought by the convention preferable to the former, and, I presume, will be most agreeable to the States.

As to the second point, it is impossible, by any argument or comment, to make it clearer than it is in itself. If there are such things as political axioms, the propriety of the judicial power of a government being coextensive with its legislative, may be ranked among the number. The mere necessity of uniformity in the interpretation of the national laws, decides the question. Thirteen independent courts of final jurisdiction over the same causes, arising upon the same laws, is a hydra in government from which nothing but contradiction and confusion can proceed.

Still less need be said in regard to the third point. Controversies between the nation and its members or citizens, can only be properly referred to the national tribunals. Any other plan would be contrary to reason, to precedent, and to decorum.

The fourth point rests on this plain proposition, that the peace of the WHOLE ought not to be left at the disposal of a PART. The Union will undoubtedly be answerable to foreign powers for the conduct of its members. And the responsibility for an injury ought ever to be accompanied with the faculty of preventing it. As the denial or perversion of justice by the sentences of courts, as well as in any other manner, is with reason classed among the just causes of war, it will follow that the federal judiciary ought to have cognizance of all causes in which the citizens of other countries are concerned. . . .

The power of determining causes between two States, between one State and the citizens of another, and between the citizens of different States, is perhaps not less essential to the peace of the Union than that which has been just examined. . . .

It may be esteemed the basis of the Union, that "the citizens of each State shall be entitled to all the privileges and immunities of citizens of the several States." And if it be a just principle that every government *ought to possess the means of executing its own provisions by its own authority*, it will follow, that in order to the inviolable maintenance of that equality of privileges and immunities to which the citizens of the Union will be entitled, the national judiciary ought to preside in all cases in which one State or its citizens are opposed to another State or its citizens. To secure the full effect of so fundamental a provision against all evasion and subterfuge, it is necessary that its construction should be committed to that tribunal which, having no local attachments, will be likely to be impartial between the different States and their citizens, and which, owing its official existence to the Union, will never be likely to feel any bias inauspicious to the principles on which it is founded.

The fifth point will demand little animadversion. The most bigoted idolizers of State authority have not thus far shown a disposition to deny the national judiciary the cognizances of maritime causes. These so generally depend on the laws of nations, and so commonly affect the rights of foreigners, that they fall within the considerations which are relative to the public peace. The most important part of them are, by the present Confederation, submitted to federal jurisdiction. . . .

Having thus laid down and discussed the principles which ought to regulate the constitution of the federal judiciary, we will proceed to test, by these principles, the particular powers of which, according to the plan of the convention, it is to be composed. It is to comprehend "all cases in law and equity arising under the Constitution, the laws of the United States, and treaties made, or which shall be made, under their authority; to all cases affecting ambassadors, other public ministers, and consuls; to all cases of admiralty and maritime jurisdiction; to controversies to which the United States shall be a party; to controversies between two or more States; between a State and citizens of another State; between citizens of different States; between citizens of the same State claiming lands and grants of different States; and between a State or the citizens thereof and foreign states, citizens, and subjects." This constitutes the entire mass of the judicial authority of the Union. Let us now review it in detail. It is, then, to extend:

First. To all cases in law and equity, *arising under the Constitution* and *the laws of the United States*. This corresponds with the two first classes of causes, which have been enumerated, as proper for the jurisdiction of the United States. It has been asked, what is meant by "cases arising under the Constitution," in contradistinction from those "arising under the laws of the United States"? The difference has been already explained. All the restrictions upon the authority of the State legislatures furnish examples of it. They are not, for instance, to emit paper money; but the interdiction results from the Constitution, and will have no connection with any law of the United States. Should paper money, notwithstanding, be emitted, the controversies concerning it would be cases arising under the Constitution and not the laws of the United States, in the ordinary signification of the terms. This may serve as a sample of the whole.

It has also been asked, what need of the word "equity"? What equitable causes can grow out of the Constitution and laws of the United States? There is hardly a subject of litigation between individuals, which may not involve those ingredients of *fraud, accident, trust,* or *hardship,* which would render the matter an object of equitable rather than of legal jurisdiction, as the distinction is known and established in several of the States. It is the peculiar province, for instance, of a court of equity to relieve against what are called hard bargains: these are contracts in which, though there may have been no direct fraud or deceit, sufficient to invalidate them in a court of law, yet there may have been some undue and unconscionable advantage taken of the necessities or misfortunes of one of the parties, which a court of equity would not tolerate. . . .

—*The Federalist* No. 80.

[May, 1788]

LET us now return to the partition of the judiciary authority between different courts, and their relations to each other.

"The judicial power of the United States is" (by the plan of the convention) "to be vested in one Supreme Court, and in such inferior courts as the Congress may, from time to time, ordain and establish."

That there ought to be one court of supreme and final jurisdiction, is a proposition which is not likely to be contested. The reasons for it have been assigned in another place, and are too obvious to need repetition. The only question that seems to have been raised concerning it, is, whether it ought to be a distinct body or a branch of the legislature. The same contradiction is observable in regard to this matter which has been remarked in several other cases. The very men who object to the Senate as a court of impeachments, on the ground of an improper intermixture of powers, advocate, by implication at least, the propriety of vesting the ultimate decision of all causes, in the whole or in a part of the legislative body.

The arguments, or rather suggestions, upon which this charge is founded, are to this effect: "The authority of the proposed Supreme Court of the United States, which is to be a separate and independent body, will be superior to that of the legislature. The power of construing the laws according to the *spirit* of the Constitution, will enable that court to mould them into whatever shape it may think proper; especially as its decisions will not be in any matter subject to the revision or correction of the legislative body. This is as unprecedented as it is dangerous. In Britain, the judicial power, in the last resort, resides in the House of Lords, which is a branch of the legislature; and this part of the British government has been imitated in the State constitutions in general. The Parliament of Great Britain, and the legislatures of the several States, can at any time rectify, by law, the exceptionable decisions of their respective courts. But the errors and usurpations of the Supreme Court of the United States will be uncontrollable and remediless." This, upon examination, will be found to be made up altogether of false reasoning upon misconceived fact.

In the first place, there is not a syllable in the plan under consideration which *directly* empowers the national courts to construe the laws according to the spirit of the Constitution, or which gives them any greater latitude in this respect than may be claimed by the courts of every State. I admit, however, that the Constitution ought to be the standard of construction for the laws, and that wherever there is an evident opposition, the laws ought to give place to the Constitution. But this doctrine is not deducible from any circumstance peculiar to the plan of the convention, but from the general theory of a limited Constitution; and as far as it is true, is equally applicable to most, if not to all the State governments. There can be no objection, therefore, on this account, to the federal judicature which will not lie against the local judicatures in general, and which will not serve to condemn every constitution that attempts to set bounds to legislative discretion.

But perhaps the force of the objection may be thought to consist in the particular organization of the Supreme Court; in its being composed of a distinct body of magistrates, instead of being one of the branches of the legislature, as in the government of Great Britain and that of the State. To insist upon this point, the authors of the objection must renounce the meaning they have labored to annex to the celebrated maxim, requiring a separation of the departments of power. . . .

It is not true, in the second place, that the Parliament of Great Britain, or the legislatures of the particular States, can rectify the exceptionable decisions of their respective courts, in any other sense than might be done by a future legislature of the United States. The theory, neither of the British, nor the State constitutions, authorizes the revisal of a judicial sentence by a legislative act. Nor is there any thing in the proposed Constitution, more than in either of them, by which it is forbidden. In the former, as well as in the latter, the impropriety of the thing, on the general principles of law and reason, is the sole obstacle. A legislature, without exceeding its province, cannot reverse a determination once made in a particular case; though it may prescribe a new rule for future cases. This is the principle, and it applies in all its consequences, exactly in the same manner and extent, to the State governments, as to the national government now under consideration. Nor the least difference can be pointed out in any view of the subject.

It may in the last place be observed that the supposed danger of judiciary encroachments on the legislative authority, which has been upon many occasions reiterated, is in reality a phantom. Particular misconstructions and contraventions of the will of the legislature may now and then happen; but they can never be so extensive as to amount to an inconvenience, or in any sensible degree to affect the order of the political system. This may be inferred with certainty, from the general nature of the judicial power, from the objects to which it relates, from the manner in which it is exercised, from its comparative weakness, and from its total incapacity to support its usurpations by force. And the inference is greatly fortified by the consideration of the important constitutional check which the power of instituting impeachments in one part of the legislative body, and of determining upon them in the other, would give to that body upon the members of the judicial department. This is alone a complete security. There never can be danger that the judges, by a series of deliberate usurpations on the authority of the legislature, would hazard the united resentment of the body intrusted with it, while this body was possessed of the means of punishing their presumption, by degrading them from their stations. While this ought to remove all apprehensions on the subject, it affords, at the same time, a cogent argument for constituting the Senate a court for the trial of impeachments. . . .

Though it may rather be a digression from the immediate subject of this paper, I shall take occasion to mention here a supposition which has excited some alarm upon very mistaken grounds. It has been suggested that an assignment of the public securities of one State to the citizens of another, would enable them to prosecute that State in the federal courts for the amount of those securities; a suggestion which the following considerations prove to be without foundation.

It is inherent in the nature of sovereignty not to be amenable to the suit of an individual *without its consent*. This is the general sense, and the general practice of mankind; and the exemption, as one of the attributes of sovereignty, is now enjoyed by the government of every State in the Union. Unless, therefore, there is a surrender of this immunity in the plan of the convention, it will remain with the States, and the danger intimated must be merely ideal. The circumstances which are necessary to produce an alienation of State sovereignty were discussed in considering the article of taxation, and need not be repeated here. A recurrence to the principles there established will satisfy us, that there is no color to pretend that the State governments would, by the adoption of that plan, be divested of the privilege of paying their own debts in their own way, free from every constraint but that which flows from the obligations of good faith. The contracts between a nation and individuals are only binding on the conscience of the sovereign, and have no pretensions to a compulsive force. . . . To what purpose would it be to authorize suits against States for the debts they owe? How could recoveries be enforced? It is evident, it could not be done without waging war against the contracting State; and to ascribe to the federal courts, by mere implication, and in destruction of a preëxisting right of the State governments, a power which would involve such a consequence, would be altogether forced and unwarrantable. . . .

The amount of the observations hitherto made on the authority of the judicial department is this: that it has been carefully restricted to those causes which are manifestly proper for the cognizance of the national judicature; that in the partition of this authority a very small portion of original jurisdiction has been preserved to the Supreme Court, and the rest consigned to the subordinate tribunals; that the Supreme Court will possess an appellate jurisdiction, both as to law and fact, in all cases referred to them, both subject to any *exceptions* and *regulations* which may be thought advisable; that this appellate jurisdiction does, in no case, *abolish* the trial by jury; and that an ordinary degree of prudence and integrity in the national councils will insure us solid advantages from the establishment of the proposed judiciary, without exposing us to any of the inconveniences which have been predicted from that source.

—*The Federalist* No. 81

[May, 1788]

The objection to the plan of the convention, which has met with most success in this State, and perhaps in several of the other States, is *that relative to the want of a constitutional provision* for the trial by jury in civil cases. The disingenuous form in which this objection is usually stated has been repeatedly adverted to and exposed, but continues to be pursued in all the conversations and writings of the opponents of the plan. The mere silence of the Constitution in regard to *civil causes*, is represented as an abolition of the trial by jury, and the declamations to which it has afforded a pretext are artfully calculated to induce a persuasion that this pretended abolition is complete and universal, extending not only to every species of civil, but even to *criminal, causes*. . . .

With regard to civil causes, subtleties almost too contemptible for refutation have been employed to countenance the surmise that a thing which is only *not provided for*, is entirely *abolished*. Every man of discernment must at once perceive the wide difference between *silence* and *abolition*. . . .

The rules of legal interpretation are rules of *common-sense*, adopted by the courts in the construction of the laws. The true test, therefore, of a just application of them is its conformity to the source from which they are derived. This being the case, let me ask if it is consistent with common-sense to suppose that a provision obliging the legislative power to commit the trial of criminal causes to juries, is a privation of its right to authorize or permit that mode of trial in other cases? Is it natural to suppose, that a command to do one thing is a prohibition to the doing of another, which there was a previous power to do, and which is not incompatible with the thing commanded to be done? If such a supposition would be unnatural and unreasonable, it cannot be rational to maintain that an injunction of the trial by jury in certain cases is an interdiction of it in others.

A power to constitute courts is a power to prescribe the mode of trial; and consequently, if nothing was said in the Constitution on the subject of juries, the legislature would be at liberty either to adopt that institution or to let it alone. This discretion, in regard to criminal causes, is abridged by the express injunction of trial by jury in all such cases; but it is, of course, left at large in relation to civil causes, there being a total silence on this head. The specification of an obligation to try all criminal causes in a particular mode, excludes indeed the obligation or necessity of employing the same mode in civil causes, but does not abridge *the power* of the legislature to exercise that mode if it should be thought proper. The pretence, therefore, that the national legislature would not be at full liberty to submit all the civil causes of federal cognizance to the determination of juries, is a pretence destitute of all just foundation. . . .

The friends and adversaries of the plan of the convention, if they agree in nothing else, concur at least in the value they set upon the trial by jury; or if there is any difference between them it consists in this: the former regard it as a valuable safeguard to liberty; the latter represent it as the very palladium of free government. For my own part, the more the operation of the institution has fallen under my observation, the more reason I have discovered for holding it in high estimation; and it would be altogether superfluous to examine to what extent it deserves to be esteemed useful or essential in a representative republic, or how much more merit it may be entitled to, as a defence against the oppressions of an hereditary monarch, than as a barrier to the tyranny of popular magistrates in a popular government. . . . But I must acknowledge that I cannot readily discern the inseparable connection between the existence of liberty, and the trial by jury in civil cases. Arbitrary impeachments, arbitrary methods of prosecuting pretended offences, and arbitrary punishments upon arbitrary convictions, have ever appeared to me to be the great engines of judicial despotism; and these have all relation to criminal proceedings. The trial by jury in criminal cases, aided by the *habeas-corpus* act, seems therefore to be alone concerned in the question. And both of these are provided for, in the most ample manner, in the plan of the convention. . . . The excellence of the trial by jury in civil cases appears to depend on circumstances foreign to the preservation of liberty. The strongest argument in its favor is, that it is a security against corruption. As there is always more time and better opportunity to tamper with a standing body of magistrates than with a jury summoned for the occasion, there is room to suppose that a corrupt influence would more easily find its way to the former than to the latter. The force of this consideration is, however, diminished by others. The sheriff, who is the summoner of ordinary juries, and the clerks of courts, who have the nomination of special juries, are themselves standing officers, and, acting individually, may be supposed more accessible to the touch of corruption than the judges, who are a collective body. It is not difficult to see, that it would be in the power of those officers to select jurors who would serve the purpose of the party as well as a corrupted bench. In the next place, it may fairly be supposed, that there would be less difficulty in gaining some of the jurors promiscuously taken from the public mass, than in gaining men who had been chosen by the government for their probity and good character. But making every deduction for these considerations, the trial by jury must still be a valuable check upon corruption. It greatly multiplies the impediments to its success. As matters now stand, it would be necessary to corrupt both court and jury; for where the jury have gone evidently wrong, the court will generally grant a new trial, and it would be in most cases of little use to practise upon the jury, unless the court could be likewise gained. Here then is a double security; and it will readily be perceived that this complicated agency tends to preserve the purity of both institutions. By increasing the obstacles to success, it discourages attempts to seduce the integrity of either. . . .

Notwithstanding, therefore, the doubts I have expressed, as to the essentiality of trial by jury in civil cases to liberty, I admit that it is in most cases, under proper regulations, an excellent method of determining questions of property; and that on this account alone it would be entitled to a constitutional provision in its favor if it were possible to fix the limits within which it ought to be comprehended. There is, however, in all cases, great difficulty in this; and men not blinded by enthusiasm must be sensible that in a federal government, which is a composition of societies whose ideas and institutions in relation to the matter materially vary from each other, that difficulty must be not a little augmented. . . .

From this sketch it appears that there is a material diversity, as well in the modification as in the extent of the institution of trial by jury in civil cases in the several States; and from this fact these obvious reflections flow: first, that no general rule could have been fixed upon by the convention which would have corresponded with the circumstances of all the States; and secondly, that more or at least as much might have been hazarded by taking the system of any one State for a standard, as by omitting a provision altogether and leaving the matter, as has been done, to legislative regulation. . . .

But this is not, in my estimation, the greatest objection. I feel a deep and deliberate conviction that there are many cases in which the trial by jury is an ineligible one. I think it so particularly in cases which concern the public peace with foreign nations—that is in most cases where the question turns wholly on the laws of nations. Of this nature, among others, are all prize causes. . . .

My convictions are equally strong that great advantages result from the separation of the equity from the law jurisdiction, and that the causes which belong to the former would be improperly committed to juries. . . .

The examples of innovations which contract its ancient limits, as well in these States as in Great Britain, afford a strong presumption that its former extent has been found inconvenient, and give room to suppose that future experience may discover the propriety and utility of other exceptions. I suspect it to be impossible in the nature of the thing to fix the salutary point at which the operation of the institution ought to stop, and this is with me a strong argument for leaving the matter to the discretion of the legislature. . . .

—*The Federalist* No. 83.

December 29, 1801

In the rage for change, or under the stimulus of a deep-rooted animosity against the former administrations, or for the sake of gaining popular favor by a profuse display of extraordinary zeal for economy, even our judiciary system has not passed unassailed. . . .

No bad thermometer of the capacity of our Chief Magistrate for government is furnished by the rule which he offers for judging of the utility of the Federal Courts; namely, the exact *number* of causes which have been by them decided. There is hardly any stronger symptom of a pigmy mind, than a propensity to allow greater weight to *secondary* than to *primary* considerations. . . .

January, 1802

Weighing maturely all the very important and very delicate considerations which appertain to the subject, would a wise or prudent statesman hazard the consequences of immediately unmaking, at one session, courts and judges, which had only been called into being at the one preceding? Delectable indeed must be the work of disorganization to a mind which can thus rashly advance in its prosecution!—Infatuated must that people be who do not open their eyes to projects so intemperate—so mischievous!—Who does not see what is the ultimate object? *Delenda est Carthago*—Ill-fated Constitution, which Americans had fondly hoped would continue for ages, the guardian of public liberty, the source of national prosperity!

—"Lucius Crassus," Nos. 5 and 6, *Hamilton*, VII, 762-763, 771.

February 23, 1802

From the manner in which the subject was treated in the fifth and sixth numbers of the Examination, it has been doubted whether the writer did or did not entertain a decided opinion as to the power of Congress to abolish the offices and compensations of judges, once instituted and appointed, pursuant to a law of the United States. In a matter of such high constitutional moment, it is a sacred duty to be explicit. . . .

The words of the Constitution are, "The judges *both* of the supreme and inferior courts *shall hold their offices during good behavior*, and shall at stated times receive for their services a compensation which *shall not be diminished during their continuance in office*."

Taking the literal import of the terms as a criterion of their true meaning, it is clear that the *tenure* or *duration* of the office is limited by no other condition than the *good behavior* of the incumbent. The words are imperative, simple, and unqualified: "The judges *shall hold their offices during good behavior.*" Independent therefore of any artificial reasoning to vary the natural and obvious sense of the words, the provision must be understood to vest in the judge a right to the office, indefeasible but by his own misconduct. . . .

From the injunction, that the compensation of the judges shall not be diminished, it is manifest that the Constitution intends to guard the independence of those officers against the legislative department; because, to this department *alone* would have belonged the power of diminishing their compensations.

When the Constitution is thus careful to tie up the Legislature from taking away *part* of the compensation, is it possible to suppose that it can mean to leave that body at full liberty to take away the *whole?* . . .

It is therefore plain to a demonstration, that the doctrine which affirms the right of Congress to abolish the judges of the inferior courts is absolutely fatal to the independence of the judiciary department.

—"Lucius Crassus," No. 12. *Hamilton*, VII, 792, 793-794, 799.

February 27, 1802

A very strong confirmation of the true intent of the provision respecting the tenure of judicial office, results from an argument by analogy. In each of the articles which establishes any branch of the government, the duration of office is a prominent feature. Two years for the House of Representatives, six for the Senate, four for the President and Vice-President, are the respective terms of duration; and for the judges, the term of good behavior is allotted. It is presumable, that each was established in the same spirit, as a point material in the organization of the government and of a nature to be properly fundamental. It will not be pretended that the duration of office prescribed as to any other department, is within the reach of legislative discretion. And why shall that of judicial officers form an exception? Why shall the Constitution be supposed less tenacious of securing to this organ of the sovereign power a fixed duration than to any other? If there be any thing which ought to be supposed to be peculiarly excepted out of the power of the ordinary Legislature, it is emphatically the organization of the several constituent departments of the government; which in our system are the *Legislative, Executive,* and *Judicial.* Reasons of the most cogent nature recommend that the stability and independence of the last of these three branches should be guarded with particular circumspection and care.

—"Lucius Crassus," No. 13. *Hamilton*, VII, 803-804.

March 2, 1802

This character of the judiciary clearly indicates that it is not only the weakest of the three departments of power, but, also, as it regards the security and preservation of civil liberty, by far the safest. In a conflict with the other departments, it will be happy if it can defend itself—to annoy them is beyond its power. In vain would it singly attempt enterprises against the rights of the citizen. The other departments could quickly arrest its arm and punish its temerity. It can only, then, become an effectual instrument of oppression, when it is combined with one of the more active and powerful organs; and against a combination of this sort, the true and best guard is a complete independence of each and both of them. Its dependence on either will imply and involve a subserviency to the views of the department on which it shall depend. Its independence of both will render it a powerful check upon the others, and a precious shield to the rights of persons and property. Safety, liberty, are therefore inseparably connected with the real and substantial independence of the courts and judges.

—"Lucius Crassus," No. 14. *Hamilton*, VII, 808.

Separation of Powers—Checks and Balances

How could the government maintain liberty and at the same time guarantee security? Were not these basic objectives in conflict? Would not a powerful federal government oppress the people, or the states? In Federalist *47-51, now generally ascribed to Madison, the answer was provided by the principle of separation of powers. The* Federalist *acknowledges that Montesquieu had exaggerated the extent of this separation under the British Constitution and demonstrates that there was a good deal of overlapping between departments under the state constitutions. Under the new federal system the powers yielded by the people are divided between two distinct governments, and in turn the portion allotted to each subdivided between departments. The Constitution recognizes the principle of separation of powers among the legislative, executive, and judicial departments, and provides that each of them will be protected against the other, and the people against all, by a system of checks and balances, whereby the approval of one department is required for certain acts of another. In this way, as Madison saw it, one group or class could be guarded against oppression by other groups or classes. These views accorded with Hamilton's own, and were expounded by him on a number of occasions.*

June 27, 1788

After all our doubts, our suspicions, and speculations on the subject of government, we must return at last to the important truth, that when we have formed a Constitution upon free principles, when we have given a proper balance to the different branches of administration, and fixed representation upon pure and equal principles, we may with safety furnish it with all the powers necessary to answer in the most ample manner the purposes of government. The great desiderata are a free representation and mutual checks. . . . Now, what do gentlemen mean by coming forward and declaiming against this government? Why do they say we ought to limit its powers, to disable it, and to destroy its capacity of blessing the people? Has philosophy suggested, has experience taught, that such a government ought not to be trusted with everything necessary for the good of society? Sir, when you have divided and nicely balanced the departments of government, when you have strongly connected the virtue of your rulers with their interest, when, in short, you have rendered your system as perfect as human forms can be, you must place confidence, you must give power.

We have heard a great deal of the sword and the purse. It is said our liberties are in danger if both are possessed by Congress. Let us see what is the true meaning of this maxim, which has been so much used and so little understood. It is, that you shall not place these powers in either the legislative or executive, singly; neither one nor the other shall have both; because this would destroy that division of powers on which political liberty is founded, and would furnish one body with all the means of tyranny. But where the purse is lodged in one branch, and the sword in another, there can be no danger.

June 27, 1788

. . . The true principle of government is this: Make the system complete in its structure; give a perfect proportion and balance to its parts, and the powers you give it will never affect your security. The question, then, of the division of powers between the general and state governments, is a question of convenience. It becomes a prudential inquiry, what powers are proper to be reserved to the latter, and this immediately involves another enquiry into the proper objects of the two governments. This is the criterion by which we shall determine the just distribution of powers.

The great leading objects of the federal government, in which revenue is concerned, are to maintain domestic peace, and provide for the common defence. In these are comprehended the regulation of commerce—that is, the whole system of foreign intercourse, the support of armies and navies, and of the civil administration. It is useless to go into detail. Every one knows that the objects of the general government are numerous, extensive, and important. Every one must acknowledge the necessity of giving powers, in all respects, and in every degree, equal to these objects. This principle assented to, let us inquire what are the objects of the state governments. Have they to provide against foreign invasion? Have they to maintain fleets and armies? Have they any concern in the regulation of commerce, the procuring alliances, or forming treaties of peace? No. Their objects are merely civil and domestic, to support the legislative establishment, and to provide for the administration of the laws.

—Speech on the United States Senate, *Debates of the N.Y. Convention*, pp. 103-105.

March 2, 1802

It is a fundamental maxim of free government, that the three great departments of power, *legislative*, *executive*, and *judiciary*, shall be essentially distinct and independent, the one of the other. This principle, very influential in most of our State constitutions, has been particularly attended to in the Constitution of the United States; which, in order to give effect to it, has adopted a precaution peculiar to itself, in the provisions that forbid the Legislature to vary in any way the compensation of the *President*, or to diminish that of a *judge*.

—"Lucius Crassus," No. 14. *Hamilton*, VII, 807.

The Power to Tax

Hamilton was among the first to urge granting to the federal government full power to tax. In the Pay Book of the artillery company he commanded, which bears the date of August 31, 1776, we find this entry in his own handwriting, probably written a few years later:

Quare? Would it not be advisable to let all taxes, even those imposed by the states, be collected by persons of Congressional appointment, and would it not be advisable to pay the collectors so much per cent on the sums collected?

—Pay Book of the New York State Company of Artillery in Hamilton's hand. Hamilton Papers.

Hamilton's Continentalist *essays, published in 1781 and 1782, advocated enlarging federal powers, including that of taxation. In January, 1783, in the course of a debate in Congress recorded by Madison, Hamilton favored having the tax collectors appointed by Congress. In his enthusiasm for the cause he let the cat out of the bag and revealed that his real reason for wanting Continentally-appointed tax collectors was to increase the power and prestige of Congress. This frank but indiscreet remark alerted the antifederalists to the true objective of the Hamiltonian program.*

January 27, 1783

Mr. Hamilton went extensively into the subject; the sum of it was as follows: He observed that funds considered as permanent sources of revenue were of two kinds: first, such as would extend generally and uniformly throughout the United States, and would be collected under the authority of Congress; secondly, such as might be established separately within each State, and might consist of any objects which were chosen by the States, and might be collected either under the authority of the States or of Congress. Funds of the first kind, he contended, were preferable; as being, first, more simple, the difficulties attending the mode of fixing the quotas laid down in the Confederation rendering it extremely complicated, and in a manner insuperable; secondly, as being more certain, since the States, according to the said plan, would probably retain the collection of the revenue, and a vicious system of collection prevailed generally throughout the United States, a system by which the collectors were chosen by the people, and made their offices more subservient to their popularity than to the public revenue; thirdly, as being more economical, since the collection would be effected with fewer officers under the management of Congress than under that of the States.

—Debates in the Congress of the Confederation.
Hunt, ed., *Writings of Madison*, I, 332.

January 28, 1783

Mr. Hamilton, in reply to Mr. Ellsworth, dwelt long on the inefficiency of State funds. He supposed, too, that greater obstacles would arise to the execution of the plan than to that of a general revenue. As an additional reason for the latter to be collected by officers under the appointment of Congress, he signified that as the energy of the Federal Government was evidently short of the degree necessary for pervading and uniting the States, it was expedient to introduce the influence of officers deriving their emoluments from, and consequently interested in supporting the power of, Congress.

—Debates in the Congress of the Confederation.
Writings of Madison, I, 336.

In The Federalist *Hamilton insisted that direct taxation of the people by the federal government was the only substitute for the inadequate system of quotas and requisitions, that the taxing power sustained public credit, and that "a government ought to contain in itself every power requisite to the full accomplishment of the objects committed to its care."*

December 28, 1787

It has been already observed that the federal government ought to possess the power of providing for the support of the national forces;

in which proposition was intended to be included the expense of raising troops, of building and equipping fleets, and all other expenses in any wise connected with military arrangements and operations. But these are not the only objects to which the jurisdiction of the Union, in respect to revenue, must necessarily be empowered to extend. It must embrace a provision for the support of the national civil list; for the payment of the national debts contracted, or that may be contracted; and, in general, for all those matters which will call for disbursements out of the national treasury. The conclusion is, that there must be interwoven in the frame of the government a general power of taxation in one shape or another. . . .

What remedy can there be for this situation, but in a change of the system which has produced it—in a change of the fallacious and delusive system of quotas and requisitions? What substitute can there be imagined for this *ignis fatuus* in finance, but that of permitting the national government to raise its own revenues by the ordinary methods of taxation authorized in every well-ordered constitution of civil government? Ingenious men may declaim with plausibility on any subject; but no human ingenuity can point out any other expedient to rescue us from the inconveniences and embarrassments naturally resulting from defective supplies of the public treasury.

The more intelligent adversaries of the new Constitution admit the force of this reasoning; but they qualify their admission by a distinction between what they call *internal* and *external* taxation. The former they would reserve to the state governments; the latter, which thy explain into commercial imposts, or rather duties on imported articles, they declare themselves willing to concede to the federal head. This distinction, however, would violate the maxim of good sense and sound policy, which dictates that every POWER ought to be in proportion to its OBJECT; and would still leave the general government in a kind of tutelage to the state governments, inconsistent with every idea of vigor or efficiency. Who can pretend that commercial imposts are, or would be, alone equal to the present and future exigencies of the Union? Taking into the account the existing debt, foreign and domestic, upon any plan of extinguishment which a man moderately impressed with the importance of public justice and public credit could approve, in addition to the establishments which all parties will acknowledge to be necessary, we could not reasonably flatter ourselves, that this resource alone, upon the most improved scale, would even suffice for its present necessities. Its future necessities admit not of calculation or limitation; and upon the principle, more than once adverted to, the power of making provision for them as they arise ought to be equally unconfined. I believe it may be regarded as a position warranted by the history of mankind, that, *in the usual progress of things, the necessities of a nation, in every stage of its existence, will be found at least equal to its resources.*

—*The Federalist* No. 30.

January 1, 1788

A government ought to contain in itself every power requisite to the full accomplishment of the objects committed to its care, and to the complete execution of the trusts for which it is responsible, free from every other control but a regard to the public good and to the sense of the people.

As the duties of superintending the national defence and of securing the public peace against foreign or domestic violence involve a provision for casualties and dangers to which no possible limits can be assigned, the power of making that provision ought to know no other bounds than the exigencies of the nation and the resources of the community.

As revenue is the essential engine by which the means of answering the national exigencies must be procured, the power of procuring that article in its full extent must necessarily be comprehended in that of providing for those exigencies.

As theory and practice conspire to prove that the power of procuring revenue is unavailing when exercised over the States in their collective capacities, the federal government must of necessity be invested with an unqualified power of taxation in the ordinary modes. . . .

—*The Federalist* No. 31.

January 3, 1788

ALTHOUGH I am of opinion that there would be no real danger of the consequences which seem to be apprehended to the State governments from a power in the Union to control them in the levies of money, because I am persuaded that the sense of the people, the extreme hazard of provoking the resentments of the State governments, and a conviction of the utility and necessity of local administrations for local purposes, would be a complete barrier against the oppressive use of such a power; yet I am willing here to allow, in its full extent, the justness of the reasoning which requires that the individual States should possess an independent and uncontrollable authority to raise their own revenues for the supply of their own wants. And making this concession, I affirm that (with the sole exception of duties on imports and exports) they would, under the plan of the convention, retain that authority in the most absolute and unqualified sense; and that an attempt on the part of the national government to abridge them in the exercise of it, would be a violent assumption of power, unwarranted by any article or clause of its Constitution. . . .

As the plan of the convention aims only at a partial union or consolidation, the State governments would clearly retain all the rights of sovereignty which they before had, and which were not, by that act, *exclusively* delegated to the United States. This exclusive delegation, or rather this alienation, of State sovereignty, would only exist in three cases: where the Constitution in express terms granted an exclusive authority to the Union; where it granted in one instance an authority to the Union, and in another prohibited the States from exercising the like authority; and where it granted an authority to the Union, to which a similar authority in the States would be absolutely and totally *contradictory* and *repugnant*. . . . These three cases of exclusive jurisdiction in the federal government may be exemplified by the following instances: The last clause but one in the eighth section of the first article provides expressly that Congress shall exercise "*exclusive legislation*" over the district to be appropriated as the seat of government. This answers to the first case. The first clause of the same section empowers Congress "*to lay and collect taxes, duties, imposts, and excises*"; and the second clause of the tenth section of the same article declares that, "*no State shall,* without the consent of Congress, *lay any imposts or duties on imports or exports,* except for the purpose of executing its inspection laws." Hence would result an exclusive power in the Union to lay duties on imports and exports, with the particular exception mentioned; but this power is abridged by another clause, which declares that no tax or duty shall be laid on articles exported from any State; in consequence of which qualification, it now only extends to the *duties on imports.* This answers to the second case. The third will be found in that clause which declares that Congress shall have power "to establish an UNIFORM RULE of naturalization throughout the United States." This must necessarily be exclusive; because if each State had power to prescribe a DISTINCT RULE, there could not be a UNIFORM RULE.

A case which may perhaps be thought to resemble the latter, but which is in fact widely different, affects the question immediately under consideration. I mean the power of imposing taxes on all articles other than exports and imports. This, I contend, is manifestly a concurrent and coequal authority in the United States and in the individual States. There is plainly no expression in the granting clause which makes that power *exclusive* in the Union. There is no independent clause or sentence which prohibits the States from exercising it. . . .

As to a supposition of repugnancy between the power of taxation in the States and in the Union, it cannot be supported in that sense which would be requisite to work an exclusion of the States. It is, indeed, possible that a tax might be laid on a particular article by a State which might render it *inexpedient* that thus a further tax should be laid on the same article by the Union; but it would not imply a constitutional inability to impose a further tax. The quantity of the imposition, the expediency or inexpediency of an increase on either side, would be mutually questions of prudence; but there would be involved no direct contradiction of power. The particular policy of the national and of the State systems of finance might now and then not exactly coincide, and might require reciprocal forbearances. It is not, however, a mere possibility of inconvenience in the exercise of powers, but an immediate constitutional repugnancy that can by implication alienate and extinguish a preëxisting right of sovereignty.

The necessity of a concurrent jurisdiction in certain cases results from the division of the sovereign power; and the rule that all authorities, of which the States are not explicitly divested in favor of the Union, remain with them in full vigor, is not a theoretical consequence of that division, but is clearly admitted by the whole tenor of the instrument which contains the articles of the proposed Constitution. We there find that, notwithstanding the affirmative grants of general authorities, there has been the most pointed care in those cases where it was deemed improper that the like authorities should reside in the States, to insert negative clauses prohibiting the exercise of them by the States. The tenth section of the first article consists altogether of such provisions. This circumstance is a clear indication of the sense of the convention, and furnishes a rule of interpretation out of the body of the act, which justifies the position I have advanced and refutes every hypothesis to the contrary.

—*The Federalist* No. 32.

January 3, 1788

THE residue of the argument against the provisions of the Constitution in respect to taxation is ingrafted upon the following clauses.* The last clause of the eighth section of the first article of the plan under consideration authorizes the national legislature "to make all laws which shall be *necessary* and *proper* for carrying into execution *the powers* by that Constitution vested in the government of the United States, or in any department or officer thereof"; and the second clause of the sixth article declares, "that the Constitution and the laws of the United States made *in pursuance thereof*, and the treaties made by their authority shall be the *supreme law* of the land, any thing in the constitution or laws of any State to the contrary notwithstanding."

These two clauses have been the source of much virulent invective and petulant declamation against the proposed Constitution. . . . They are only declaratory of a truth which would have resulted by necessary and unavoidable implication from the very act of constituting a federal government, and vesting it with certain specified powers. . . .

* The original newspaper essays were divided at this point. The opening sentence first appeared in the McLean edition of 1788.

What is a power, but the ability or faculty of doing a thing? What is the ability to do a thing, but the power of employing the *means* necessary to its execution? What is a LEGISLATIVE power, but a power of making LAWS? What are the *means* to execute a LEGISLATIVE power, but LAWS? What is the power of laying and collecting taxes, but a *legislative power*, or a power of *making laws*, to lay and collect taxes? What are the proper means of executing such a power, but *necessary* and *proper laws?*

This simple train of inquiry furnishes us at once with a test by which to judge of the true nature of the clause complained of. It conducts us to this palpable truth, that a power to lay and collect taxes must be a power to pass all laws *necessary* and *proper* for the execution of that power; and what does the unfortunate and calumniated provision in question do more than declare the same truth, to wit, that the national legislature, to whom the power of laying and collecting taxes had been previously given, might, in the execution of that power, pass all laws *necessary* and *proper* to carry it into effect? . . .

But it may be again asked, Who is to judge of the *necessity* and *propriety* of the laws to be passed for executing the powers of the Union? I answer, first that this question arises as well and as fully upon the simple grant of those powers as upon the declaratory clause; and I answer, in the second place, that the national government, like every other, must judge, in the first instance, of the proper exercise of its powers, and its constituents in the last. . . . Suppose by some forced constructions of its authority (which, indeed, cannot easily be imagined), the Federal legislature should attempt to vary the law of descent in any State, would it not be evident that, in making such an attempt, it had exceeded its jurisdiction, and infringed upon that of the State? Suppose, again, that upon the pretence of an interference with its revenues, it should undertake to abrogate a land-tax imposed by the authority of a State; would it not be equally evident that this was an invasion of that concurrent jurisdiction in respect to this species of tax, which its Constitution plainly supposes to exist in the State governments?

But it is said that the laws of the Union are to be the *supreme law* of the land. But what inference can be drawn from this, or what would they amount to, if they were not to be supreme? It is evident they would amount to nothing. A LAW, by the very meaning of the term, includes supremacy. It is a rule which those to whom it is prescribed are bound to observe. This results from every political association. If individuals enter into a state of society, the laws of that society must be the supreme regulator of their conduct. If a number of political societies enter into a larger political society, the laws which the latter may enact, pursuant to the powers intrusted to it by its constitution, must necessarily be supreme over those societies, and the individuals of whom they are composed. It would otherwise be a mere treaty, dependent on the good faith of the parties, and not a government, which is only another word for POLITICAL POWER AND SUPREMACY. But it will not follow from this doctrine that acts of the larger society which are *not pursuant* to its constitutional powers, but which are invasions of the residuary authorities of the smaller societies, will become the supreme law of the land. These will be merely acts of usurpation, and will deserve to be treated as such. . . .

The inference from the whole is, that the individual States would, under the proposed Constitution, retain an independent and uncontrollable authority to raise revenue to any extent of which they may stand in need, by every kind of taxation, except duties on imports and exports.

—*The Federalist* No. 33.

January 4, 1788

To form a more precise judgment of the true merits of this question, it will be well to advert to the proportion between the objects that will require a federal provision in respect to revenue, and those which will require a State provision. We shall discover that the former are altogether unlimited, and that the latter are circumscribed within very moderate bounds. In pursuing this inquiry, we must bear in mind that we are not to confine our view to the present period, but to look forward to remote futurity. Constitutions of civil government are not to be framed upon a calculation of existing exigencies, but upon a combination of these with the probable exigencies of ages, according to the natural and tried course of human affairs. Nothing, therefore, can be more fallacious than to infer the extent of any power, proper to be lodged in the national government, from an estimate of its immediate necessities. There ought to be a CAPACITY to provide for future contingencies as they may happen; and as these are illimitable in their nature, it is impossible safely to limit that capacity. It is true, perhaps, that a computation might be made with sufficient accuracy to answer the purpose of the quantity of revenue requisite to discharge the subsisting engagements of the Union, and to maintain those establishments which, for some time to come, would suffice in time of peace. But would it be wise, or would it not rather be the extreme of folly to stop at this point, and to leave the government intrusted with the care of the national defence in a state of absolute incapacity to provide for the protection of the community against future invasions of the public peace, by foreign war or domestic convulsions? If, on the contrary, we ought to exceed this point, where can we stop, short of an indefinite power of providing for emergencies as they may arise? . . . Let us recollect that peace or war will not always be left to our option; that however moderate or unambitious we may be, we cannot count upon the moderation, or hope to extinguish the ambition of others. Who could have imagined at the conclusion of the last war that France and Britain, wearied and exhausted as they both were, would so soon have looked with so hostile an aspect upon each other? To judge from the history of mankind, we shall be compelled to conclude that the fiery and destructive passions of war reign in the human breast with much more powerful sway than the mild and beneficent sentiments of peace; and that to model our political systems upon speculations of lasting tranquillity, is to calculate on the weaker spring of the human character. . . .

—*The Federalist* No. 34.

[January, 1788]

Before we proceed to examine any other objections to an indefinite power of taxation in the Union, I shall make one general remark; which is, that if the jurisdiction of the national government in the article of revenue should be restricted to particular objects, it would naturally occasion an undue proportion of the public burdens to fall upon those objects. Two evils would spring from this source: the oppression of particular branches of industry; and an unequal distribution of the taxes, as well among the several states as among the citizens of the same state.

Suppose, as has been contended for, the federal power of taxation were to be confined to duties on imports, it is evident that the government for want of being able to command other resources, would frequently be tempted to extend these duties to an injurious excess. There are persons who imagine that they can never be carried to too great a length; since the higher they are, the more it is alleged they will tend to discourage an extravagant consumption, to produce a favorable balance of trade, and to promote domestic manufactures. But all extremes are pernicious in various ways. Exorbitant duties on imported articles would beget a general spirit of smuggling; which is always prejudicial to the fair trader, and eventually to the revenue itself: they tend to render other classes of the community tributary, in an improper degree, to the manufacturing classes, to whom they give a premature monopoly of the markets: they sometimes force industry out of its more natural channels into others in which it flows with less advantage; and in the last place, they oppress the merchant, who is often obliged to pay them himself without any retribution from the consumer. When the demand is equal to the quantity of goods at market, the consumer generally pays the duty; but when the markets happen to be overstocked, a great proportion falls upon the merchant, and sometimes not only exhausts his profits, but breaks in upon his capital. I am apt to think that a division of the duty between the seller and the buyer more often happens than is commonly imagined. It is not always possible to raise the price of a commodity in exact proportion to every additional imposition laid upon it. The merchant, especially in a country of small commercial capital, is often under a necessity of keeping prices down in order to a more expeditious sale.

. . . Let us now return to the examination of objections.

One which, if we may judge from the frequency of its repetition, seems most to be relied on, is, that the House of Representatives is not sufficiently numerous for the reception of all the different classes of citizens, in order to combine the interests and feelings of every part of the community, and to produce a due sympathy between the representative body and its constituents. This argument presents itself under a very specious and seducing form; and is well calculated to lay hold of the prejudices of those to whom it is addressed. But when we come to dissect it with attention, it will appear to be made up of nothing but fair-sounding words. The object it seems to aim at is, in the first place, impracticable, and in the sense in which it is contended for, is unnecessary. I reserve for another place the discussion of the question which relates to the sufficiency of the representative body in respect to numbers, and shall content myself with examining here the particular use which has been made of a contrary supposition, in reference to the immediate subject of our inquiries.

The idea of an actual representation of all classes of the people, by persons of each class, is altogether visionary. Unless it were expressly provided in the Constitution, that each different occupation should send one or more members, the thing would never take place in practice. Mechanics and manufacturers will always be inclined, with few exceptions, to give their votes to merchants, in preference to persons of their own professions or trades. Those discerning citizens are well aware that the mechanic and manufacturing arts furnish the materials of mercantile enterprise and industry. Many of them, indeed, are immediately connected with the operations of commerce. They know that the merchant is their natural patron and friend; and they are aware, that however great the confidence they may justly feel in their own good sense, their interests can be more effectually promoted by the merchant than by themselves. They are sensible that their habits in life have not been such as to give them those acquired endowments, without which, in a deliberative assembly, the greatest natural abilities are for the most part useless; and that the influence and weight, and superior acquirements of the merchants render them more equal to a contest with any spirit which might happen to infuse itself into the public councils, unfriendly to the manufacturing and trading interests. . . .

With regard to the learned professions, little need be observed; they truly form no distinct interest in society, and according to their situation and talents, will be indiscriminately the objects of the confidence and choice of each other, and of other parts of the community.

Nothing remains but the landed interest; and this, in a political view, and particularly in relation to taxes, I take to be perfectly united, from the wealthiest landlord down to the poorest tenant. No tax can be laid on land which will not affect the proprietor of millions of acres as well as the proprietor of a single acre. Every landholder will therefore have a common interest to keep the taxes on land as low as possible; and common interest may always be reckoned upon as the surest bond of sympathy. But if we even suppose a distinction of interest between the opulent landholder and the middling farmer, what reason is there to conclude, that the first would stand a better chance of being deputed to the national legislature than the last? If we take fact as our guide, and look into our own senate and assembly, we shall find that moderate proprietors of land prevail in both; nor is this less the case in the senate, which consists of a smaller number, than in the assembly, which is composed of a greater number. Where the qualifications of the electors are the same, whether they have to choose a small or a large number, their votes will fall upon those in whom they have most confidence; whether these happen to be men of large fortunes, or of moderate property, or of no property at all.

It is said to be necessary, that all classes of citizens should have some of their own number in the representative body, in order that their feelings and interests may be the better understood and attended to. But we have seen that this will never happen under any arrangement that leaves the votes of the people free. Where this is the case, the representative body, with too few exceptions to have any influence on the spirit of the government, will be composed of landholders, merchants, and men of the learned professions. But where is the danger that the interests and feelings of the different classes of citizens will not be understood or attended to by these three descriptions of men? Will not the landholder know and feel whatever will promote or insure the interests of landed property? And will he not, from his own interest in that species of property, be sufficiently prone to resist every attempt to prejudice or encumber it? Will not the merchant understand and be disposed to cultivate, as far as may be proper, the interests of the mechanic and manufacturing arts, to which his commerce is so nearly allied? Will not the man of the learned profession, who will feel a neutrality to the rivalships between the different branches of industry, be likely to prove an impartial arbiter between them, ready to promote either, so far as it shall appear to him conducive to the general interests of the society?

If we take into the account the momentary humors or dispositions which may happen to prevail in particular parts of the society, and to which a wise administration will never be inattentive, is the man whose situation leads to extensive inquiry and information less likely to be a competent judge of their nature, extent, and foundation than one whose observation does not travel beyond the circle of his neighbors and acquaintances? Is it not natural that a man who is a candidate for the favor of the people, and who is dependent on the suffrages of his fellow-citizens for the continuance of his public honors, should take care to inform himself of their dispositions and inclinations, and should be willing to allow them their proper degree of influence upon his conduct? This dependence, and the necessity of being bound himself, and his posterity, by the laws to which he gives his assent, are the true, and they are the strong chords of sympathy between the representative and the constituent.

There is no part of the administration of government that requires extensive information and a thorough knowledge of the principles of political economy, so much as the business of taxation. The man who understands those principles best will be least likely to resort to oppressive expedients, or to sacrifice any particular class of citizens to the procurement of revenue. It might be demonstrated that the most productive system of finance will always be the least burdensome. There can be no doubt that in order to a judicious exercise of the power of taxation, it is necessary that the person in whose hands it is should be acquainted with the general genius, habits, and modes of thinking of the people at large, and with the resources of the country. And this is all that can be reasonably meant by a knowledge of the interests and feelings of the people. In any other sense the proposition has either no meaning, or an absurd one. And in that sense let every considerate citizen judge for himself where the requisite qualification is most likely to be found.

—*The Federalist* No. 35.

January 8, 1788

As to the suggestion of double taxation, the answer is plain. The wants of the Union are to be supplied in one way or another; if to be done by the authority of the federal government, it will not be to be done by that of the state government. The quantity of taxes to be paid by the community must be the same in either case; with this advantage, if the provision is to be made by the Union—that the capital resource of commercial imposts, which is the most convenient branch of revenue, can be prudently improved to a much greater extent under federal than under state regulation, and of course will render it less necessary to recur to more inconvenient methods; and with this further advantage, that as far as there may be any real difficulty in the exercise of the power of internal taxation, it will impose a disposition to greater care in the choice and arrangement of the means; and must naturally tend to make it a fixed point of policy in the national administration to go as far as may be practicable in making the luxury of the rich tributary to the public treasury, in order to diminish the necessity of those impositions which create dissatisfaction in the poorer and most numerous classes of the society. Happy it is when the interest which the government has in the preservation of its own power, coincides with a proper distribution of the public burdens, and tends to guard the least wealthy part of the community from oppression!

As to poll taxes, I, without scruple, confess my disapprobation of them; and though they have prevailed from an early period in those states[1] which have uniformly been the most tenacious of their rights, I should lament to see them introduced into practice under the national government. . . .

—*The Federalist* No. 36.

[c. 1790]

Yet experience had demonstrated that a power in the general head to tax the States only in their collective capacities—that is, by the system of requisitions, was a system of imbecility and injustice: imbecility, because it did not produce to the common treasury the requisite supplies; injustice, because the separate efforts of the States under such a system were, and from the nature of things, would ever be unequal, and consequently their contributions disproportionate.

Hence, all those who agreed in the necessity of a union of the States under a common head, felt and acknowledged that a change in the plan was an essential feature in a new arrangement of the constitution of General Government. . . .

The subordination of the State power of taxation to that of the General Government, or the confining it to particular objects, would probably have been an insuperable obstacle to the adoption of the Constitution. The division of the power between the Union and the States could not have been regulated upon any plan which would not either have left the General Government more restricted than was compatible with a due provision for the exigencies of the Union, or would have so confined the State Government as would have been equally an impediment to the success of the Constitution. Besides that, a truly eligible division, which consulted all the cases possible by the general principles of the Constitution, was intrinsically very difficult if not impracticable.

But though it is admitted that the course pursued by the Convention was the most expedient, yet it is not the less true that the plan involved inherent and great difficulties.

It may not unaptly be styled the Gordian-knot of our political situation.

To me there appeared but one way of untying or severing it, which was in practice to leave the States under as little necessity as possible

[1] The New England states.—PUBLIUS

of exercising the power of taxation. The narrowness of the limits of its exercise on one side left the field more free and unembarrassed to the other, and avoided essentially the interference and collisions to be apprehended *inherent* in the plan of concurrent jurisdiction.

Thus, to give a clear field to the Government of the United States was so manifestly founded in good policy that the time must come when a man of sense would blush to dispute it.

—"Defence of the Funding System," II. Draft in Hamilton's hand. Hamilton Papers, 1st ser.

[c. 1790]

Nothing could be more revolting than that the citizens of one State should live at ease free from taxes and the citizens of a neighboring State be overburthened with taxes growing out of a war which had given equal political advantages to the citizens of both States.

This condition of things previous to the assumption was remarkably exemplified between New York and Massachusetts, between New York and Connecticut. The citizens of New York scarcely paid any taxes, those of Massachusetts and Connecticut were heavily burthened. A like comparison though different in degree might be extended to other States.

—"Defence of the Funding System," II. Hamilton Papers, 1st ser.

July 27, 1791

. . . I feel myself called upon by the occasion to express an opinion that every thing in the nature of a direct tax on property in the funds of the United States is contrary to the true principles of public credit, and tends to disparage the value of the public stock. If any law of the State of Massachusetts, therefore, gives sanction to such a tax, it is presumed that it must have been passed without an advertence to this important idea; and it is not doubted that in the execution of it there will be all the care and moderation which the delicacy of the operation requires. It is desirable on every account that no occasion should be given to a discussion concerning the regularity of the proceeding.

—To Supervisors of Boston. *Hamilton,* IV, 167.

January 16, 1795

Is there a right in a government to tax its own funds?

The pretence of this right is deduced from the general right of the legislative power to make all the property of the state contributory to its own exigencies.

But this right is obviously liable to be restricted by the *engagements* of the *Government;* it cannot be justly exercised in contravention of them; they must form an exception. It will not be denied, that the general right in question could, and would, be abridged, by an express promise not to tax the funds. This promise, indeed, has not been given in terms, but it has been given in substance. When an individual lends money to the state, the state stipulates to repay him the principal lent, with a certain interest, or to pay a certain interest, indefinitely, till the principal is reimbursed; or it stipulates something equivalent, in another form. In our case, the stipulation is in the second form.

To tax the funds, is manifestly either to *take* or to *keep back* a portion of the principal or interest *stipulated to be paid.*

To do this, on whatever pretext, is *not to do what is expressly promised;* it is not to pay that precise principal, or that precise interest, which has been engaged to be paid; it is, therefore, to violate the promise given to the lender. . . .

Public debt can scarcely, in legal phrase, be defined either as *property* in possession or in *action*. It is evidently not the first, till it is reduced to possession by payment. To be the second, would suppose a *legal power* to *compel* payment by *suit*. Does such a power exist? The true definition of public debt is *a property subsisting in the faith of the government. Its* essence is *promise*. Its definite value depends upon the reliance that the promise will be definitely fulfilled. Can the government rightfully tax its promises? Can it put its faith under contribution? Where or *what* is the value of the debt, if such a right exists? . . .

When a government enters into contract with an individual, it deposes as to the matter of the contract its constituional authority, and exchanges the character of legislator for that of a moral agent, with the same rights and obligations as an individual. Its promises may be justly considered as excepted out of its *power to legislate,* unless in aid of them. It is, in theory, impossible to reconcile the two ideas of a *promise which obliges* with a *power to make a law which can vary the effect of it*. This is the great principle that governs the question, and abridges the general right of the government to lay taxes, excepting out of it a species of property which subsists only in its promise.

—To the U.S. Senate. *American State Papers,* V, 334-335.

The first time the Supreme Court passed upon the constitutionality of an act of Congress Hamilton appeared in behalf of the government. In 1794, *at Hamilton's behest, Congress enacted a tax on carriages "for the conveyance of persons," which exempted carriages used in agriculture or to transport freight. It was aimed to be a tax on the rich, since only the well-to-do in those days kept carriages merely for pleasure and personal transportation. Madison objected to the tax as unconstitutional, and a test case was instituted in the United States circuit court in Virginia. That court divided on the constitutional question, and the defendant, Hylton, preferred to pay the small judgment against him rather than undergo the expense of appeal, but the government felt it advisable to have a full argument on the issue before the Supreme Court. There the Attorney General was supported by special counsel in the person of Alexander Hamilton, who had recently resigned as Secretary of the Treasury. Hamilton made a deep impression on the court, which upheld his argument that the carriage tax was an indirect tax. This decision was an important victory for Hamilton's tax program. It left the door open for the imposition of excise taxes by the federal government so long as they were uniformly applied.*

February 24, 1795

What is the distinction between *direct* and *indirect* taxes? It is a matter of regret that terms so uncertain and vague in so important a point are to be found in the Constitution. We shall seek in vain for any *antecedent* settled legal meaning to the respective terms—there is none. . . .

Shall we call an indirect tax, a tax which is ultimately paid by a person, *different* from the one who pays it in the *first instance?*

Truly speaking, there is no such tax—those on imported articles best claim the character. But in many instances the merchant cannot transfer the tax to the buyer; in numerous cases it falls on himself, partly or wholly. . . .

Shall it be said that an indirect tax is that of which a man *is not conscious* when he pays? Neither is there any such tax. The ignorant may not see the tax in the enhanced price of the commodity—but the man of reflection knows it is there. . . .

Now, if a duty on carriages is to be considered as a *direct tax,* to be apportioned according to the rates of representation, very absurd consequences must ensue.

'T is *possible* that a particular State may have no carriages of the description intended to be taxed, or a very small number.

But each State would have to pay a proportion of the sum to be laid, according to its relative numbers; yet, while the State would have to pay a quota, it might have no carriages upon which its quota could be assessed, or so few, as to render it ruinous to the owners to pay the tax. To consider then a duty on carriages as a direct tax, may be to defeat the power of laying such a duty. This is a consequence which ought not to ensue from construction. . . .

The following are presumed to be the only direct taxes.

Capitation or poll taxes.

Taxes on lands and buildings.

General assessments, whether on the whole property of individuals, or on their whole real or personal estate; all else must of necessity be considered as indirect taxes.

To apply a rule of apportionment according to numbers to taxes of the above description, has some *rationale* in it; but to extend an apportionment of that kind to other cases, would, in many instances, produce, as has been seen, preposterous consequences, and would greatly embarrass the operations of the government. Nothing could be more capricious or outré, than the application of quotas in such cases.

The Constitution gives power to Congress to lay and collect the taxes, duties, imposts, and excises, requiring that all duties, imposts, and excises shall be uniform throughout the United States.

Here *duties, imposts,* and *excises* appear to be contradistinguished from *taxes,* and while the latter is left to apportionment, the former are enjoined to be uniform.

But, unfortunately, there is equally here a want of criterion to distinguish *duties, imposts,* and *excises* from taxes.

If the meaning of the word *excise* is to be sought in the British statutes, it will be found to include the duty on carriages, which is there considered as an *excise,* and then must necessarily be uniform and not liable to apportionment; consequently not a direct tax.

An argument results from this, though not perhaps a conclusive one: yet where so important a distinction in the Constitution is to be realized, it is fair to seek the meaning of terms in the statutory language of that country from which our jurisprudence is derived.

—Brief in *Hylton v. U.S.* Hamilton Papers, 1st ser. See also 3 Dallas 171.

The Government and National Security

> To model our political systems upon speculations of lasting tranquillity, is to calculate on the weaker springs of the human character . . .

Believing as he did that the powers of the government should be adequate to the needs of a stable union, Hamilton urged Congress as early as 1783 to take steps to place the national defense under federal control.

[1783]

The committee are of opinion, that as soon as the situation of public affairs will permit, it ought to be made a serious object of policy, to be able to supply ourselves with all the articles of first necessity in war; and in this view, to establish foundries, manufactories of arms, powder, etc.

There are two reasons which appear to them conclusive for this. The first is, that every country ought to have within itself all the essential means of defence, for to depend on foreign supplies is to render its security precarious; the second, that as it will be indispensable to keep up a corps of artillery, and some other troops, the labor of a part of these, bestowed upon the manufactories, will enable the public to supply itself on better terms than by importation. The committee propose that the Secretary at War be directed to lay before Congress a plan, in detail, for this purpose; designating the places where those foundries and manufactories can be erected with advantage, the means to be employed, and the expense to be incurred in the execution of the plan.

—Draft Report of a Committee on a Peace Establishment in Hamilton's hand—marked "incomplete." Hamilton Papers, 1st ser.

[1783]

Notes to be recollected

An absurdity, that Congress are empowered to build and equip a navy; and yet, in time of peace, the States are to keep up one for their own defence.

There must be a navy formed in time of peace; it ought to be proportioned to our defence; and will then be all in the hands of certain States.

Congress, constituted as they are, can't have time for usurpation. Usurpation in such an extensive empire requires long previous preparation, etc.

A people seldom reform with moderation. Men, accustomed to read of usurpation suddenly effected in small cities, look upon such a thing as a work of a day.

The weak side of democracies, is danger of foreign corruption. No individual has sufficient interest in the State, to be proof against the seduction.

The want of an army lost the liberty of Athens—*vide* Demosthenes.

—Hamilton Papers, 1st ser.

Hamilton's views on national security and the problems arising from the control by the federal government of the military and naval forces were expounded in The Federalist.

December 18, 1787

The necessity of a Constitution, at least equally energetic with the one proposed, to the preservation of the Union, is the point at the examination of which we are now arrived.

This inquiry will naturally divide itself into three branches—the objects to be provided for by the federal government, the quantity of power necessary to the accomplishment of those objects, the persons upon whom that power ought to operate. Its distribution and organization will more properly claim our attention under the succeeding head.

The principal purposes to be answered by union are these—the common defence of the members; the preservation of the public peace, as well against internal convulsions as external attacks; the regulation of commerce with other nations and between the States; the superintendence of our intercourse, political and commercial, with foreign countries.

The authorities essential to the common defence are these: to raise armies; to build and equip fleets; to prescribe rules for the government of both; to direct their operations; to provide for their support. These powers ought to exist without limitation, because it is impossible to foresee or define the extent and variety of national exigencies, or the correspondent extent and variety of the means which may be necessary to satisfy them. The circumstances that endanger the safety of nations are infinite, and for this reason no constitutional shackles can wisely be imposed on the power to which the care of it is committed. This power ought to be co-extensive with all the possible combinations of such circumstances; and ought to be under the direction of the same councils which are appointed to preside over the common defence.

This is one of those truths which, to a correct and unprejudiced mind, carries its own evidence along with it; and may be obscured, but cannot be made plainer by argument or reasoning. It rests upon axioms as simple as they are universal; the *means* ought to be proportioned to the *end;* the persons, from whose agency the attainment of any *end* is expected, ought to possess the *means* by which it is to be attained.

Whether there ought to be a federal government intrusted with the care of the common defence, is a question in the first instance, open for discussion; but the moment it is decided in the affirmative, it will follow, that that government ought to be clothed with all the powers requisite to complete execution of its trust. And unless it can be shown that the circumstances which may affect the public safety are reducible within certain determinate limits; unless the contrary of this position can be fairly and rationally disputed, it must be admitted, as a necessary consequence, that there can be no limitation of that authority which is to provide for the defence and protection of the community, in any matter essential to its efficacy—that is, in any matter essential to the *formation, direction,* or *support* of the NATIONAL FORCES.

Defective as the present Confederation has been proved to be, this principle appears to have been fully recognized by the framers of it; though they have not made proper or adequate provision for its exercise. Congress have an unlimited discretion to make requisitions of men and money; to govern the army and navy; to direct their operations. As their requisitions are made constitutionally binding upon the States, who are in fact under the most solemn obligations to furnish the supplies required of them, the intention evidently was, that the United States should command whatever resources were by them judged requisite to the "common defence and general welfare." It was presumed that a sense of their true interests, and a regard to the dictates of good faith, would be found sufficient pledges for the punctual performance of the duty of the members to the federal head.

The experiment has, however, demonstrated that this expectation was ill-founded and illusory; and the observations, made under the last head, will, I imagine, have sufficed to convince the impartial and discerning, that there is an absolute necessity for an entire change in the first principles of the system; that if we are in earnest about giving the Union energy and duration, we must abandon the vain project of legislating upon the States in their collective capacities; we must extend the laws of the federal government to the individual citizens of America; we must discard the fallacious scheme of quotas and requisitions, as equally impracticable and unjust. The result from all this is that the Union ought to be invested with full power to levy troops; to build and equip fleets; and to raise the revenues which will be required for the formation and support of an army and navy, in the customary and ordinary modes practised in other governments. . . .

Shall the Union be constituted the guardian of the common safety? Are fleets and armies and revenues necessary to this purpose? The government of the Union must be empowered to pass all laws, and to make all regulations which have relation to them. The same must be the case in respect to commerce, and to every other matter to which its jurisdiction is permitted to extend. Is the administration of justice between the citizens of the same State the proper department of the local governments? These must possess all the authorities which are connected with this object, and with every other that may be allotted to their particular cognizance and direction. Not to confer in each case a degree of power commensurate to the end, would be to violate the most obvious rules of prudence and propriety, and improvidently to trust the great interests of the nation to hands which are disabled from managing them with vigor and success.

Who so likely to make suitable provisions for the public defence, as that body to which the guardianship of the public safety is confided; which, as the centre of information, will best understand the extent and urgency of the dangers that threaten; as the representative of the

WHOLE, will feel itself most deeply interested in the preservation of every part; which, from the responsibility implied in the duty assigned to it, will be most sensibly impressed with the necessity of proper exertions; and which, by the extension of its authority throughout the States, can alone establish uniformity and concert in the plans and measures by which the common safety is to be secured? Is there not a manifest inconsistency in devolving upon the federal government the care of the general defence, and leaving in the State governments the *effective* powers by which it is to be provided for? Is not a want of co-operation the infallible consequence of such a system? And will not weakness, disorder, and undue distribution of the burdens and calamities of war, an unnecessary and intolerable increase of expense, be its natural and inevitable concomitants? Have we not had unequivocal experience of its effects in the course of the revolution which we have just accomplished?

Every view we may take of the subject, as candid inquirers after truth, will serve to convince us, that it is both unwise and dangerous to deny the federal government an unconfined authority, as to all those objects which are intrusted to its management. It will indeed deserve the most vigilant and careful attention of the people, to see that it be modelled in such a manner as to admit of its being safely vested with the requisite powers. If any plan which has been, or may be, offered to our consideration, should not, upon a dispassionate inspection, be found to answer this description, it ought to be rejected. A government, the constitution of which renders it unfit to be trusted with all the powers which a free people *ought to delegate to any government*, would be an unsafe and improper depository of the NATIONAL INTERESTS. Wherever THESE can with propriety be confided, the coincident powers may safely accompany them. This is the true result of all just reasoning upon the subject. . . .

I trust, however, that the impracticability of one general system cannot be shown. I am greatly mistaken, if any thing of weight has yet been advanced of this tendency; and I flatter myself, that the observations which have been made in the course of these papers have served to place the reverse of that position in as clear a light as any matter still in the womb of time and experience can be susceptible of. This, at all events, must be evident, that the very difficulty itself, drawn from the extent of the country, is the strongest argument in favor of an energetic government; for any other can certainly never preserve the Union of so large an empire. If we embrace the tenets of those who oppose the adoption of the proposed Constitution, as the standard of our political creed, we cannot fail to verify the gloomy doctrines which predict the impracticability of a national system pervading entire limits of the present Confederacy.

The Federalist No. 23.

[December, 1787]

. . . From a close examination it will appear that restraints upon the discretion of the legislature in respect to military establishments in time of peace would be improper to be imposed, and if imposed, from the necessities of society, would be unlikely to be observed.

Though a wide ocean separates the United States from Europe, yet there are various considerations that warn us against an excess of confidence or security. On one side of us, and stretching far into our rear, are growing settlements subject to the dominion of Britain. On the other side, and extending to meet the British settlements, are colonies and establishments subject to the dominion of Spain. This situation and the vicinity of the West India Islands, belonging to these two powers, create between them, in respect to their American possessions and in relation to us, a common interest. The savage tribes on our Western frontier ought to be regarded as our natural enemies, their natural allies, because they have most to fear from us, and most to hope from them. . . .

If we mean to be a commercial people, or even to be secure on our Atlantic side, we must endeavor, as soon as possible, to have a navy. To this purpose there must be dock-yards and arsenals; and for the defense of these, fortifications, and probably garrisons. When a nation has become so powerful by sea that it can protect its dock-yards by its fleets, this supersedes the necessity of garrisons for that purpose; but where naval establishments are in their infancy, moderate garrisons will, in all likelihood, be found an indispensable security against descents for the destruction of the arsenals and dock-yards, and sometimes of the fleet itself.

—*The Federalist* No. 24.

December 21, 1787

The framers of the existing Confederation, fully aware of the danger to the Union from the separate possession of military forces by the states, have, in express terms, prohibited them from having either ships or troops, unless with the consent of Congress. The truth is, that the existence of a federal government and military establishments under state authority are not less at variance with each other than a due supply of the federal treasury and the system of quotas and requisitions.

There are other lights besides those already taken notice of, in which the impropriety of restraints on the discretion of the national legislature will be equally manifest. The design of the objection, which has been mentioned, is to preclude standing armies in times of peace, though we have never been informed how far it is designed the prohibition should extend: whether to raising armies as well as to *keeping them up* in a season of tranquillity or not. . . .

If, to obviate this consequence, it should be resolved to extend the prohibition to the *raising* of armies in time of peace, the United States would then exhibit the most extraordinary spectacle which the world has yet seen,—that of a nation incapacitated by its Constitution to prepare for defense before it was actually invaded. As the ceremony of a formal denunciation of war has of late fallen into disuse, the presence of an enemy within our territories must be waited for, as the legal warrant to the government to begin its levies of men for the protection of the state. . . . All that kind of policy by which nations anticipate distant danger and meet the gathering storm must be abstained from, as contrary to the genuine maxims of a free government. We must expose our property and liberty to the mercy of foreign invaders, and invite them by our weakness to seize the naked and defenseless prey, because we are afraid that rulers, created by our choice, dependent on our will, might endanger that liberty, by an abuse of the means necessary to its preservation.

Here I expect we shall be told that the militia of the country is its natural bulwark, and would be at all times equal to the national defense. This doctrine, in substance, had like to have lost us our independence. It cost millions to the United States that might have been saved.

The Federalist No. 25.

[December, 1787]

. . . Schemes to subvert the liberties of a great community *require time* to mature them for execution. An army, so large as seriously to menace those liberties, could only be formed by progressive augmentations; which would suppose, not merely a temporary combination between the legislature and executive, but a continued conspiracy for a series of time. Is it probable that such a combination would exist at all? Is it probable that it would be persevered in, and transmitted along through all the successive variations in a representative body, which biennial elections would naturally produce in both houses? Is it presumable, that every man, the instant he took his seat in the national Senate or House of Representatives, would commence a traitor to his constituents and to his country? Can it be supposed that there would not be found one man, discerning enough to detect so atrocious a conspiracy, or bold or honest enough to apprise his constituents of their danger? If such presumptions can fairly be made, there ought at once to be an end of all delegated authority. The people should resolve to recall all the powers they have heretofore parted with out of their own hands, and to divide themselves into as many States as there are counties, in order that they may be able to manage their own concerns in person. . . .

It has been said that the provision which limits the appropriation of money for the support of an army to the period of two years would be unavailing, because the Executive, when once possessed of a force large enough to awe the people into submission, would find resources in that very force sufficient to enable him to dispense with supplies from the acts of the legislature. But the question again recurs, upon what pretence could he be put in possession of a force of that magnitude in time of peace? If we suppose it to have been created in consequence of some domestic insurrection or foreign war, then it becomes a case not within the principles of the objection; for this is levelled against the power of keeping up troops in time of peace. Few persons will be so visionary as seriously to contend that military forces ought not to be raised to quell a rebellion or resist an invasion; and if the defence of the community under such circumstances should make it necessary to have an army so numerous as to hazard its liberty, this is one of those calamities for which there is neither preventative nor cure. It cannot be provided against by any possible form of government; it might even result from a simple league offensive and defensive, if it should ever be necessary for the confederates or allies to form an army for common defence.

But it is an evil infinitely less likely to attend us in a united than in a disunited state; nay, it may be safely asserted that it is an evil altogether unlikely to attend us in the latter situation. It is not easy to conceive a possibility that dangers so formidable can assail the whole Union, as to demand a force considerable enough to place our liberties in the least jeopardy, especially if we take into our view the aid to be derived from the militia, which ought always to be counted upon as a valuable and powerful auxiliary. But in a state of disunion (as has been fully shown in another place), the contrary of this supposition would become not only probable, but almost unavoidable.

—*The Federalist* No. 26.

January 10, 1788

There is something so far-fetched and so extravagant in the idea of danger to liberty from the militia, that one is at a loss whether to treat it with gravity or with raillery; whether to consider it as a mere trial of skill, like the paradoxes of rhetoricians; as a disingenuous artifice to instil prejudices at any price; or as the serious offspring of political fanaticism. Where, in the name of common sense, are our fears to end if we may not trust our sons, our brothers, our neighbors, our fellow-citizens? What shadow of danger can there be from men who are daily mingling with the rest of their countrymen, and who participate with them in the same feelings, sentiments, habits, and interests? What reasonable cause of apprehension can be inferred from a power in the Union to prescribe regulations for the militia, and to command its services when necessary, while the particular states are to have the *sole and exclusive appointment of officers?*

—*The Federalist* No. 29.

The Doctrine of Implied Powers

No state paper written by Hamilton had larger consequences than his opinion on the constitutionality of the bank. Hamilton's proposal for a national bank passed both houses of Congress despite the opposition of Madison in the House of Representatives. Before signing the bill President Washington considered Madison's contention that the bill was unconstitutional, a position in which he was supported by Edmund Randolph, the Attorney General, and by Secretary of State Jefferson. The latter argued that the power to establish a national bank was not among the express powers of the Constitution. He denied that the power "to make all laws necessary and proper for carrying into execution the enumerated powers" could be legitimately interpreted to support such a measure.

Washington then asked Hamilton for his opinion, and his answer has become the classic exposition of the doctrine of implied powers. Hamilton won the argument, and the President signed the bill. His views were adopted almost word for word by Chief Justice Marshall in 1819, when, in McCulloch v. Maryland, *he upheld the power of Congress to charter a bank.*

February 23, 1791

In entering upon the argument, it ought to be premised that the Objections of the Secretary of State and the Attorney General are founded on a general denial of the authority of the United States to erect corporations. The latter, indeed, expressly admits, that if there be anything in the bill which is not warranted by the Constitution, it is the clause of incorporation.

Now it appears to the Secretary of the Treasury that this *general principle* is *inherent* in the very *definition* of government, and *essential to* every step of the progress to be made by that of the United States, namely: That every power vested in a government is in its nature *sovereign*, and includes, by *force* of the *term*, a right to employ all the *means* requisite and fairly applicable to the attainment of the *ends* of such power, and which are not precluded by restrictions and exceptions specified in the Constitution, or not immoral, or not contrary to the *essential ends* of political society. . . .

If it would be necessary to bring proof to a proposition so clear, as that which affirms that the powers of the Federal Government, as to *its objects*, are sovereign, there is a clause of its Constitution which would be decisive. It is that which declares that the Constitution, and the laws of the United States made in pursuance of it, and all treaties made, or which shall be made, under their authority, shall be the *supreme law of the land*. The power which can create the su-

preme law of the land in any case, is doubtless sovereign as to such case.

This general and indisputable principle puts at once an end to the abstract question, whether the United States have power to erect a *corporation;* that is to say, to give a *legal* or *artificial Capacity* to one or more persons, distinct from the *natural.* For it is unquestionably incident to *Sovereign Power* to erect corporations, and consequently to that of the United States, in *relation* to the *objects* intrusted to the management of the government. The difference is this: where the authority of the government is general, it can create corporations in *all* cases; where it is confined to certain branches of legislation, it can create corporations only in those cases. . . .

It is not denied that there are *implied,* as well as *express* powers, and that the former are as effectually delegated as the latter. And for the sake of accuracy it shall be mentioned that there is another class of powers, which may be properly denominated resulting powers. It will not be doubted that if the United States should make a conquest of any of the territories of its neighbors, they would possess sovereign jurisdiction over the conquered territory. This would rather be a result from the whole mass of the powers of the government, and from the nature of political society, than a consequence of either of the powers specially enumerated. . . .

It is conceded that *implied powers* are to be considered as delegated equally with *express ones.* Then it follows, that as a power of erecting a corporation may as well be *implied* as any other thing, it may as well be employed as an *instrument* or *means* of carrying into execution any of the specified powers, as any other *instrument* or *mean* whatever. The only question must be in this, as in every other case, whether the *mean* to be employed, or, in this instance, the corporation to be erected, has a natural relation to any of the acknowledged objects or lawful ends of the government. Thus a corporation may not be erected by Congress for superintending the police of the city of Philadelphia, because they are not authorized to *regulate* the *police* of that city. But one may be erected in relation to the collection of taxes, or to the trade with foreign countries, or to the trade between the States, or with the Indian tribes, because it is the province of the Federal Government to *regulate* those objects, and because it is incident to a general *sovereign* or legislative power to *regulate* a thing, to employ all the means which relate to its regulation to the best and greatest advantage. . . .

To this mode of reasoning respecting the right of employing all the means requisite to the execution of the specified powers of the government, it is objected, that none but necessary and proper means are to be employed; and the Secretary of State maintains, that no means are to be considered *necessary* but those without which the grant of the power would be *nugatory.* . . .

It is essential to the being of the national government, that so erroneous a conception of the meaning of the word *necessary* should be exploded. It is certain, that neither the grammatical nor popular sense of the term requires that construction. According to both, *necessary* often means no more than *needful, requisite, incidental, useful,* or *conducive to.* It is a common mode of expression to say, that it is *necessary* for a government or a person to do this or that thing, when nothing more is intended or understood, than that the interests of the government or person require, or will be promoted by, the doing of this or that thing. The imagination can be at no loss for exemplifications of the use of the word in this sense. And it is the true one in which it is to be understood as used in the Constitution. The whole turn of the clause containing it indicates, that it was the intent of the Convention, by that clause, to give a liberal latitude to the exercise of the specified powers. The expressions have peculiar comprehensiveness. They are, "to make all *laws* necessary and proper for *carrying into execution* the foregoing powers, and all *other powers* vested by the Constitution in the *Government* of the United States, or in any *department* or *Officer* thereof."

To understand the word as the Secretary of State does, would be to depart from its obvious and popular sense, and to give it a *restrictive* operation, an idea never before entertained. It would be to give it the same force as if the word *absolutely* or *indispensably* had been prefixed to it. . . .

The *degree* in which a measure is necessary can never be a *test* of the legal right to adopt it; that must be a matter of opinion, and can only be a *test* of expediency. The *relation* between the *measure* and the *end;* between the *nature* of the *mean* employed towards the execution of a power, and the object of that power, must be the criterion of constitutionality, not the more or less of *necessity* or *utility.* . . .

This restrictive interpretation of the word *necessary* is also contrary to this sound maxim of construction; namely, that the powers contained in a constitution of government, especially those which concern the general administration of the affairs of a country, its finances, trade, defence, etc., ought to be construed liberally in advancement of the public good. This rule does not depend on the particular form of a government, or on the particular demarcation of the boundaries of its powers, but on the nature and objects of government itself. The means by which national exigencies are to be provided for, national inconveniences obviated, national prosperity promoted, are of such infinite variety, extent, and complexity, that there must of necessity be great latitude of discretion in the selection and application of those means. Hence, consequently, the necessity and propriety of exercising the authorities intrusted to a government on principles of liberal construction. . . .

But the doctrine which is contended for is not chargeable with the consequences imputed to it. It does not affirm that the National Government is sovereign in all respects, but that it is sovereign to a certain extent—that is, to the extent of the objects of its specified powers.

It leaves, therefore, a criterion of what is constitutional, and of what is not so. This criterion is the *end,* to which the measure relates as a *mean.* If the *end* be clearly comprehended within any of the specified powers, and if the measure have an obvious relation to that *end,* and is not forbidden by any particular provision of the Constitution, it may safely be deemed to come within the compass of the national authority. There is also this further criterion, which may materially assist the decision: Does the proposed measure abridge a pre-existing right of any State or of any individual? If it does not, there is a strong presumption in favor of its constitutionality, and slighter relations to any declared object of the Constitution may be permitted to turn the scale. . . .

It is presumed to have been satisfactorily shown in the Course of the preceding observations:

1. That the power of the government, as to the objects intrusted to its management, is, in its nature, sovereign.

2. That the right of erecting corporations is one inherent in, and inseparable from, the idea of sovereign power.

3. That the position, that the government of the United States can exercise no power but such as is delegated to it by its Constitution, does not militate against this principle.

4. That the word *necessary,* in the general clause, can have no *restrictive* operation derogating from the force of this principle; indeed, that the degree in which a measure is or is not *necessary,* cannot be a *test* of *constitutional right,* but of *expediency* only.

5. That the power to erect corporations is not to be considered as an *independent* and *substantive* power, but as an *incidental* and *auxiliary* one, and was therefore more properly left to implication, than expressly granted.

6. That the principle in question does not extend the power of the government beyond the prescribed limits, because it only affirms a power to *incorporate* for purposes within the *sphere* of the *specified powers.*

And lastly, that the right to exercise such a power in certain cases is unequivocally granted in the most *positive* and *comprehensive* terms. . . .

To establish such a right, it remains to show the relation of such an institution to one or more of the specified powers of the government. Accordingly it is affirmed that it has a relation, more or less direct, to the power of collecting taxes, to that of borrowing money, to that of regulating trade between the States, and to those of raising and maintaining fleets and armies. To the two former, the relation may be said to be immediate; and in the last place it will be argued, that it is clearly within the provision which authorizes the making of all *needful rules* and *regulations* concerning the *property* of the United States, as the same has been practised upon by the government.

A bank relates to the collection of taxes in two ways—*indirectly*, by increasing the quantity of circulating medium and quickening circulation, which facilitates the means of paying directly, by creating a *convenient species* of medium in which they are to be paid.

To designate or appoint the *money* or *thing* in which taxes are to be paid, is not only a proper but a *necessary* exercise of the power of collecting them. Accordingly Congress, in the law concerning the collection of the duties on imposts and tonnage, have provided that they shall be paid in gold and silver. But while it was an indispensable part of the work to say in what they should be paid, the choice of the specific thing was mere matter of discretion. The payment might have been required in the commodities themselves. Taxes in kind, however ill-judged, are not without precedents, even in the United States; or it might have been in the paper money of the several States, or in the bills of the Bank of North America, New York, and Massachusetts, all or either of them; or it might have been in bills issued under the authority of the United States.

No part of this can, it is presumed, be disputed. The appointment, then, of the *money* or *thing* in which the taxes are to be paid, is an incident to the power of collection. And among the expedients which may be adopted, is that of bills issued under the authority of the United States. . . .

A bank has a direct relation to the power of borrowing money, because it is an usual, and in sudden emergencies an essential, instrument in the obtaining of loans to government.

A nation is threatened with war; large sums are wanted on a sudden to make the requisite preparations. Taxes are laid for the purpose, but it requires time to obtain the benefit of them. Anticipation is indispensable. If there be a bank the supply can at once be had. If there be none, loans from individuals must be sought. The progress of these is often too slow for the exigency; in some situations they are not practicable at all. Frequently, when they are, it is of great consequence to be able to anticipate the product of them by advance from a bank.

The essentiality of such an institution as an instrument of loans, is exemplified at this very moment. An Indian expedition is to be prosecuted. The only fund out of which the money can arise, consistently with the public engagements, is a tax, which only begins to be collected in July next. The preparations, however, are instantly to be made. The money must, therefore, be borrowed—and of whom could it be borrowed if there were no public banks?

It happens that there are institutions of this kind, but if there were none, it would be indispensable to create one.

Let it then be supposed that the necessity existed (as but for a casualty would be the case), that proposals were made for obtaining a loan; that a number of individuals came forward and said, we are willing to accommodate the government with the money; with what we have in hand, and the credit we can raise upon it, we doubt not of being able to furnish the sum required, but in order to do this it is indispensable that we should be incorporated as a bank. This is essential towards putting it in our power to do what is desired, and we are obliged on that account to make it the *consideration* or *condition* of the loan.

Can it be believed that a compliance with this proposition would be unconstitutional? Does not this alone evince the contrary? It is a necessary part of a power to borrow, to be able to stipulate the consideration or conditions of a loan. It is evident, as has been remarked elsewhere, that this is not confined to the mere stipulation of a *franchise*. If it may, and it is not perceived why it may not, then the grant of a corporate capacity may be stipulated as a consideration of the loan. There seems to be nothing unfit or foreign from the nature of the thing in giving individuality, or a corporate capacity, to a number of persons, who are willing to lend a sum of money to the government, the better to enable them to do it, and make them an ordinary instrument of loans in future emergencies of the state. But the more general view of the subject is still more satisfactory. The legislative power of borrowing money, and of making all laws necessary and proper for carrying into execution that power, seems obviously competent to the appointment of the *organ*, through which the abilities and wills of individuals may be most efficaciously exerted for the accommodation of the government by loans. . . .

A hope is entertained that, by this time, it has been made to appear, to the satisfaction of the President, that a bank has a natural relation to the power of collecting taxes—to that of regulating trade—to that of providing for the common defence—and that, as the bill under consideration contemplates the government in the light of a joint proprietor of the stock of the bank, it brings the case within the provision of the clause of the Constitution which immediately respects the property of the United States.

Under a conviction that such a relation subsists, the Secretary of the Treasury, with all deference, conceives that it will result as a necessary consequence from the position, that all the specified powers of government are sovereign, as to the proper objects; that the incorporation of a bank is a constitutional measure; and that the objections taken to the bill, in this respect, are ill-founded.

—To Washington—Hamilton's Opinion on the Constitutionality of the Bank. Draft in Hamilton's hand in Special Collections, Columbia

Univ. Lib. Another draft, not in Hamilton's hand, is in Hamilton Papers, 1st ser.

The Welfare Clause

Hamilton believed that the government should not be fettered, that the powers enumerated in the Constitution should be broadly construed, and that the government should have full powers to act for the general welfare. His views have at long last prevailed and have been expanded to cover probelms which none of the founding fathers could possibly have envisioned. In Helvering v. Davis (1937) *which upheld the Social Security Act, Justice Cardozo for the majority asserted: "The conception of the spending power advocated by Hamilton and strongly reinforced by Story has prevailed over that of Madison, which has not been lacking in adherents." In view of recent federal grants to states in aid of education and road construction, Hamilton's forthright advocacy of federal activity in the fields of education and internal improvements takes on special significance.*

December 21, 1787

Wise politicians will be cautious about fettering the government with restrictions that cannot be observed, because they know that every breach of the fundamental laws, though dictated by necessity, impairs that sacred reverence which ought to be maintained in the breast of rulers towards the constitution of a country, and forms a precedent for other breaches where the same plea of necessity does not exist at all, or is less urgent and palpable.

—*The Federalist* No. 25.

December 5, 1791

A question has been made concerning the constitutional right of the Government of the United States to apply this species of encouragement,[1] but there is certainly no good foundation for such a question. The National Legislature has express authority "to lay and collect taxes, duties, imposts, and excises, to pay the debts, and provide for the common defence and general welfare," with no other qualifications than that "all duties, imposts, and excises shall be uniform throughout the United States; and that no capitation or other direct tax shall be laid, unless in proportion to numbers ascertained by a census or enumeration, taken on the principles prescribed in the Constitution," and that "no tax or duty shall be laid on articles exported from any State."

These three qualifications excepted, the power to raise money is plenary and indefinite, and the objects to which it may be appropriated

[1] Protective tariffs and bounties.

are no less comprehensive than the payment of the public debts, and the providing for the common defence and general welfare. The terms "general welfare" were doubtless intended to signify more than was expressed or imported in those which preceded; otherwise, numerous exigencies incident to the affairs of a nation would have been left without a provision. The phrase is as comprehensive as any that could have been used, because it was not fit that the constitutional authority of the Union to appropriate its revenues should have been restricted within narrower limits than the "general welfare," and because this necessarily embraces a vast variety of particulars, which are susceptible neither of specification nor of definition.

It is, therefore, of necessity, left to the discretion of the National Legislature to pronounce upon the objects which concern the general welfare, and for which, under that description, an appropriation of money is requisite and proper. And there seems to be no room for a doubt that whatever concerns the general interests of learning, of agriculture, of manufactures, and of commerce, are within the sphere of the national councils, as far as regards an application of money.

The only qualification of the generality of the phrase in question, which seems to be admissible, is this: That the object to which an appropriation of money is to be made be general, and not local; its operation extending in fact or by possibility throughout the Union, and not being confined to a particular spot.

—Report on Manufacturers. Hamilton Papers, 2nd ser.

December 7, 1796

. . . can it be doubted that the general government would with peculiar propriety occupy itself in affording nutriment to those higher branches of science, which, though not within the reach of general acquisition, are in their consequences and relations productive of general advantage? Or can it be doubted that this great object would be materially advanced by a university erected on that broad basis to which the national resources are most adequate, and so liberally endowed, as to command the ablest professors in the several branches of liberal knowledge? It is true, and to the honor of our country, that it offers many colleges and academies, highly respectable and useful, but the funds upon which they are established are too narrow to permit any of them to be an adequate substitute for such an institution as is contemplated, and to which they would be excellent auxiliaries. Amongst the motives to such an institution, the assimilation of the principles, opinions, manners, and habits of our countrymen, by drawing from all quarters our youth to participate in a common education, well deserves the attention of government. To render the people of this country as homogeneous as possible, must tend as much as any other circumstance to the permanency of their union and prosperity.

—Part of Washington's Speech to Congress. Draft in Hamilton's hand. Hamilton Papers, 1st ser.

The Bill of Rights

Why declare that things shall not be done which there is no power to do?

Hamilton's argument supporting ratification of the Constitution despite its failure to include a bill of rights cannot be fairly adduced to prove that he was unsympathetic to civil liberties. He was a stanch advocate of freedom of the press, trial by jury, and minority rights.

[May, 1788]

. . . The most considerable of the remaining objections is that the plan of the convention contains no bill of rights. Among other answers given to this, it has been upon different occasions remarked that the constitutions of several of the States are in a similar predicament. I add that New York is of the number. And yet the opposers of the new system, in this State, who profess an unlimited admiration for its constitution, are among the most intemperate partisans of a bill of rights. To justify their zeal in this matter, they allege two things: one is that, though the constitution of New York has no bill of rights prefixed to it, yet it contains, in the body of it, various provisions in favor of particular privileges and rights, which, in substance, amount to the same thing; the other is, that the Constitution adopts, in their full extent, the common and statute law of Great Britain, by which many other rights, not expressed in it, are equally secured.

To the first I answer, that the Constitution proposed by the convention contains, as well as the constitution of this State, a number of such provisions.

Independent of those which relate to the structure of the government, we find the following: Article 1, section 3, clause 7—"Judgment in cases of impeachment shall not extend further than to removal from office, and disqualification to hold and enjoy any office of honor, trust, or profit under the United States; but the party convicted shall, nevertheless, be liable and subject to indictment, trial, judgment, and punishment according to law." Section 9, of the same article, clause 2—"The privilege of the writ of *habeas corpus* shall not be suspended, unless when in cases of rebellion or invasion the public safety may require it." Clause 3—"No bill of attainder or *ex-post-facto* law shall be passed." Clause 7—"No title of nobility shall be granted by the United States; and no person holding any office of profit or trust under them, shall, without the consent of the Congress, accept of any present, emolument, office, or title of any kind whatever, from any king, prince, or foreign state." Article 3, section 2, clause 3—"The trial of all crimes, except in cases of impeachment, shall be by jury; and such trial shall be held in the State where the said crimes shall have been committed; but when not committed within any State, the trial shall be at such place or places as the Congress may by law have directed." Section 3, of the same article—"Treason against the United States shall consist only in levying war against them, or in adhering to their enemies, giving them aid and comfort. No person shall be convicted of treason, unless on the testimony of two witnesses to the same overt act, or on confession in open court." And clause 3, of the same section—"The Congress shall have power to declare the punishment of treason; but no attainder of treason shall work corruption of blood, or forfeiture, except during the life of the person attainted."

It may well be a question, whether these are not, upon the whole, of equal importance with any which are to be found in the constitution of this State. The establishment of the writ of *habeas corpus*, the prohibition of *ex-post-facto* laws, and of TITLES OF NOBILITY, *to which we have no corresponding provision in our Constitution*, are perhaps greater securities to liberty and republicanism than any it contains. The creation of crimes after the commission of the fact, or, in other words, the subjecting of men to punishment for things which, when they were done, were breaches of no law, and the practice of arbitrary imprisonments, have been, in all ages, the favorite and most formidable instruments of tyranny. The observations of the judicious Blackstone,[1] in reference to the latter, are well worthy of recital: "To bereave a man of life [says he,] or by violence to confiscate his estate, without accusation or trial, would be so gross and notorious an act of despotism, as must at once convey the alarm of tyranny throughout the whole nation; but confinement of the person, by secretly hurrying him to jail, where his sufferings are unknown or forgotten, is a less public, a less striking, and therefore *a more dangerous engine* of arbitrary government." And as a remedy for this fatal evil he is everywhere peculiarly emphatical in his encomiums on the *habeas-corpus* act, which in one place he calls "the BULWARK of the British Constitution."[2]

Nothing need be said to illustrate the importance of the prohibition of titles of nobility. This may truly be denominated the cornerstone of republican government; for so long as they are excluded, there can never be serious danger that the government will be any other than that of the people.

[1] Vide Blackstone's *Commentaries*, vol 1, p. 136—Publius.
[2] *Idem*, vol. 4, p. 438—Publius.

To the second—that is, to the pretended establishment of the common and statute law by the Constitution, I answer, that they are expressly made subject "to such alterations and provisions as the legislature shall from time to time make concerning the same." They are therefore at any moment liable to repeal by the ordinary legislative power, and of course have no constitutional sanction. The only use of the declaration was to recognize the ancient law, and to remove doubts which might have been occasioned by the Revolution. This consequently can be considered as no part of a declaration of rights, which under our constitutions must be intended as limitations of the power of the government itself.

It has been several times truly remarked that bills of rights are, in their origin, stipulations between kings and their subjects, abridgments of prerogative in favor of privilege, reservations of rights not surrendered to the prince. Such was MAGNA CHARTA, obtained by the barons, sword in hand, from King John. Such were the subsequent confirmations of that charter by succeeding princes. Such was the *Petition of Right* assented to by Charles I., in the beginning of his reign. Such, also, was the Declaration of Right presented by the Lords and Commons to the Prince of Orange in 1688, and afterwards thrown into the form of an act of parliament called the Bill of Rights. It is evident, therefore, that, according to their primitive signification, they have no application to constitutions, professedly founded upon the power of the people, and executed by their immediate representatives and servants. Here, in strictness, the people surrender nothing; and as they retain every thing they have no need of particular reservations. "WE, THE PEOPLE of the United States, to secure the blessings of liberty to ourselves and our posterity, do *ordain* and *establish* this Constitution for the United States of America." Here is a better recognition of popular rights, than volumes of those aphorisms which make the principal figure in several of our State bills of rights, and which would sound much better in a treatise of ethics than in a constitution of government.

But a minute detail of particular rights is certainly far less applicable to a Constitution like that under consideration, which is merely intended to regulate the general political interests of the nation, than to a constitution which has the regulation of every species of personal and private concerns. If, therefore, the loud clamors against the plan for the convention, on this score, are well founded, no epithets of reprobation will be too strong for the constitution of this State. But the truth is, that both of them contain all which, in relation to their objects, is reasonably to be desired.

I go further, and affirm that bills of rights, in the sense and to the extent in which they are contended for, are not only unnecessary in the proposed Constitution, but would even be dangerous. They would contain various exceptions to powers not granted; and, on this very account, would afford a colorable pretext to claim more than were granted. For why declare that things shall not be done which there is no power to do? Why, for instance, should it be said that the liberty of the press shall not be restrained, when no power is given by which restrictions may be imposed? I will not contend that such a provision would confer a regulating power; but it is evident that it would furnish, to men disposed to usurp, a plausible pretence for claiming that power. They might urge with a semblance of reason, that the Constitution ought not to be charged with the absurdity of providing against the abuse of an authority which was not given, and that the provision against restraining the liberty of the press afforded a clear implication that a power to prescribe proper regulations concerning it was intended to be vested in the national government. This may serve as a specimen of the numerous handles which would be given to the doctrine of constructive powers, by the indulgence of an injudicious zeal for bills of rights.

On the subject of the liberty of the press, as much as has been said, I cannot forbear adding a remark or two: in the first place, I observe, that there is not a syllable concerning it in the constitution of this State; in the next, I contend, that whatever has been said about it in that of any other State, amounts to nothing. What signifies a declaration, that "the liberty of the press shall be inviolably preserved"? What is the liberty of the press? Who can give it any definition which would not leave the utmost latitude for evasion? I hold it to be impracticable; and from this I infer, that its security, whatever fine declarations may be inserted in any constitution respecting it, must altogther depend on public opinion, and on the general spirit of the people and of the government. And here, after all, as is intimated upon another occasion, must we seek for the only solid basis of all our rights.

There remains but one other view of this matter to conclude the point. The truth is, after all the declamations we have heard, that the Constitution is itself, in every rational sense, and to every useful purpose, A BILL OF RIGHTS. The several bills of rights in Great Britain form its Constitution, and conversely the constitution of each State is its bill of rights. And the proposed Constitution, if adopted, will be the bill of rights of the Union. Is it one object of a bill of rights to declare and specify the political privileges of the citizens in the structure and administration of the government? This is done in the most ample and precise manner in the plan of the convention; comprehending various precautions for the public security, which are not to be found in any of the State constitutions. Is another object of a bill of rights to define certain immunities and modes of proceeding, which are relative to personal and private concerns? This we have seen has also been attended to, in a variety of cases, in the same plan. Adverting therefore to the substantial meaning of a bill of rights, it is absurd to allege that it is not to be found in the work of the convention. It may be said that it does not go far enough, though it will not be easy to make this appear; but it can with no propriety be contended that there is no such thing. It certainly must be immaterial what mode is observed as to the order of declaring the rights of the citizens, if they are to be found in any part of the instrument which establishes the government. And hence it must be apparent, that much of what has been said on this subject rests merely on verbal and nominal distinctions, entirely foreign from the substance of the thing. . . .

The great bulk of citizens of America are with reason convinced, that Union is the basis of their political happiness. Men of sense of all parties now, with few exceptions, agree that it cannot be preserved under the present system, nor without radical alterations; that new and extensive powers ought to be granted to the national head, and that these require a different organization of the federal government—a single body being an unsafe depositary of such ample authorities. In conceding all this, the question of expense must be given up; for it is impossible, with any degree of safety, to narrow the foundation upon which the system is to stand. . . .

—*The Federalist* No. 84.

Nationalism, Federalism, and States Rights

The Federalist *papers reflect a certain divergence of opinion between Hamilton and Madison on the role of the states in the new federal government. Hamilton saw the proposed Constitution as designed to establish a "consolidated system," one in which the states would be subordinated to the authority of the union. In* Federalist *No. 22 he asserts: "The fabric of American empire ought to rest on the solid basis of* THE CONSENT OF THE PEOPLE." *Madison, on the other hand, felt that the people's assent to the Constitution was to be given not as individuals but through their respective states, and that the act establishing the Constitution would be "federal" rather than "national." Hamilton believed that the powerful states and state machines menaced popular liberty and that the federal government was the bulwark of the people's rights. However, he could not afford to be too blunt in expressing his views during the contest over ratification, and he constantly sought to reassure the states-rights politicians that state sovereignty would not be jeopardized and that the first loyalty of the citizens would be to their own states.*

[1787]

The first ground of the objection is deduced from that clause of the constitution which declares "that no power shall be exercised over the people of this State but such as is granted by or derived from them."

This, it is plain, amounts to nothing more than a declaration of that fundamental maxim of republican government, "that all power, mediately or immediately, is derived from the consent of the people," in opposition to those doctrines of despotism which uphold the divine right of kings, or lay the foundations of government in force, conquest, or necessity. It does not at all affect the question how far the Legislature may go in granting power to the United States. A power conferred by the representatives of the people, if warranted by the constitution under which they act, is a power derived from the people. . . .

The next clause of the constitution relied upon, is that which declares that "the supreme legislative power *within this State* shall be vested in a Senate and Assembly." This, it is said, excludes the idea of any other legislative power operating within the State. But the more obvious construction of this clause, and *that* which best consists with the situation and views of the country at this time, with what has been done before and since the formation of our constitution, and with those parts of the constitution itself which acknowledge the Federal Government, is this: "In the distribution of the different parts of the sovereignty in the *particular* government of this State, the legislative authority shall reside in a Senate and Assembly"; or, in other words, "the legislative authority of the particular government of the State of New York shall be vested in a Senate and Assembly." The framers of the constitution could have had nothing more in view than to delineate the different departments of power in our own State government, and never could have intended to interfere with the formation of such a Constitution for the Union as the safety of the whole might require. The justness of this construction will be further elucidated by that part of the constitution which prescribes, "that the supreme executive authority *of the State* shall be vested in a governor." If the former clause excludes the grant of legislative power, this must equally exclude the grant of the executive power, and the consequence would be that there could be no Federal Government at all.

—Speech on the Revenue System before the New York Assembly. *Works*, 194-196.

December 25, 1787

It has been urged, in different shapes, that a Constitution of the kind proposed by the convention cannot operate without the aid of a military force to execute its laws. This, however, like most other things that have been alleged on that side, rests on mere general assertion, unsupported by any precise or intelligible designation of the reasons upon which it is founded. As far as I have been able to divine the latent meaning of the objectors, it seems to originate in a presupposition that the people will be disinclined to the exercise of federal authority in any matter of an internal nature. Waiving any exception that might be taken to the inaccuracy or inexplicitness of the distinction between internal and external, let us inquire what ground there is to presuppose that disinclination in the people. Unless we presume at the same time that the powers of the general government will be worse administered than those of the State governments, there seems to be no room for the presumption of ill-will, disaffection, or opposition in the people. I believe it may be laid down as a general rule that their confidence in and obedience to a government will commonly be proportioned to the goodness or badness of its administration. . . .

The hope of impunity is a strong incitement to sedition; the dread of punishment, a proportionably strong discouragement to it. Will not the government of the Union, which, if possessed of a due degree of power, can call to its aid the collective resources of the whole Confederacy, be more likely to repress the *former* sentiment and to inspire the *latter*, than that of a single State, which can only command the resources within itself? A turbulent faction in a State may easily suppose itself able to contend with the friends to the government in that State; but it can hardly be so infatuated as to imagine itself a match for the combined efforts of the Union. If this reflection be just, there is less danger of resistance from irregular combinations of individuals to the authority of the Confederacy than to that of a single member.

I will, in this place, hazard an observation, which will not be the less just because to some it may appear new; which is, that the more the operations of the national authority are intermingled in the ordinary exercise of government, the more the citizens are accustomed to meet with it in the common occurrences of their poltical life, the more it is familiarized to their sight and to their feelings, the further it enters into those objects which touch the most sensible chords and put in motion the most active springs of the human heart, the greater will be the probability that it will conciliate the respect and attachment of the community. Man is very much a creature of habit. A thing that rarely strikes his senses will generally have but little influence upon his mind. A government continually at a distance and out of sight can hardly be expected to interest the sensations of the people. The inference is, that the authority of the Union, and the affections of the citizens towards it, will be strengthened, rather than weakened, by its extension to what are called matters of internal concern; and will have less occasion to recur to force, in proportion to the familiarity and comprehensiveness of its agency. The more it circulates through those channels and currents in which the passions of mankind naturally flow, the less will it require the aid of the violent and perilous expedients of compulsion. . . .

The plan reported by the convention, by extending the authority of the federal head to the individual citizens of the several States, will enable the government to employ the ordinary magistracy of each, in the execution of its laws. It is easy to perceive that this will tend to destroy, in the common apprehension, all distinction between the sources from which they might proceed; and will give the federal government the same advantage for securing a due obedience to its authority which is enjoyed by the government of each State, in addition to the influence on public opinion which will result from the important consideration of its having power to call to its assistance and support the resources of the whole Union. It merits particular attention in this place, that the laws of the Confederacy, as to the *enumerated* and *legitimate* objects of its jurisdiction, will become the SUPREME LAW of the land; to the observance of which all officers, legislative, executive, and judicial, in each State, will be bound by the sanctity of an oath. Thus the legislatures, courts, and magistrates, of the respective members, will be incorporated into the operations of the national government *as far as its just and constitutional authority extends*; and will be rendered auxiliary to the enforcement of its laws. Any man who will pursue, by his own reflections, the consequences of this situation, will perceive that there is good ground to calculate upon a regular and peaceable execution of the laws of the Union, if its powers are administered with a common share of prudence. . . .

—*The Federalist* No. 27.

January 1, 1788

The moment we launch into conjectures about the usurpations of the federal government, we get into an unfathomable abyss, and fairly put ourselves out of the reach of all reasoning. Imagination may range at pleasure till it gets bewildered amidst the labyrinths of an enchanted castle, and knows not on which side to turn to extricate itself from the perplexities into which it has so rashly adventured. Whatever may be the limits or modifications of the powers of the Union, it is easy to imagine an endless train of possible dangers; and by indulging an excess of jealousy and timidity, we may bring ourselves to a state of absolute scepticism and irresolution. . . .

It should not be forgotten that a disposition in the State governments to encroach upon the rights of the Union is quite as probable as a disposition in the Union to encroach upon the rights of the State governments. What side would be likely to prevail in such a conflict, must depend on the means which the contending parties could employ towards insuring success. As in republics strength is always on the side of the people, and as there are weighty reasons to induce a belief that the State governments will commonly possess most influence over them, the natural conclusion is that such contests will be most apt to end to the disadvantage of the Union; and that there is greater probability of encroachments by the members upon the federal head, than by the federal head upon the members. . . .

—*The Federalist* No. 31.

June 20, 1788

. . . Sir, if we have national objects to pursue, we must have national revenues. If you make requisitions and they are not complied with, what is to be done? It has been well observed, that to coerce the States is one of the maddest projects that was ever devised. A failure of compliance will never be confined to a single State; this being the case, can we suppose it wise to hazard a civil war? Suppose Massachusetts or any large State should refuse, and Congress should attempt to compel them, would they not have influence to procure assistance, especially from those States who are in the same situation as themselves? What a picture does this idea present to our view! A complying State at war with a non-complying State; Congress marching the troops of one State into the bosom of another; this State collecting auxiliaries and forming perhaps a majority against its federal head. Here is a nation at war with itself! A government that can exist only by the sword! Every such war must involve the innocent with the guilty. This single consideration should be sufficient to dispose every peaceable citizen against such a government.

But can we believe that one State will ever suffer itself to be used as an instrument of coercion? It is a dream. It is impossible. We are brought to this dilemma: Either a federal standing army is to enforce the requisitions, or the federal treasury is left without supplies, and the government without support. What is the cure for this great evil? Nothing but to enable the national laws to operate on individuals, in the same manner as those of the states do.

—Speech on the Compromises of the Constitution, *Debates of N.Y. Convention*, pp. 22-23.

June 28, 1788

. . . I maintain that the word *supreme* imports no more than this—that the Constitution and laws made in pursuance thereof cannot be controlled or defeated by any other law. The acts of the United States, therefore, will be absolutely obligatory as to all the proper objects and powers of the general government. The states, as well as individuals, are bound by these laws; but the laws of Congress are restricted to a certain sphere, and when they depart from this sphere, they are no longer supreme or binding. In the same manner the states have certain independent powers, in which their laws are supreme; for example, in making and executing laws concerning the punishment of certain crimes, such as murder, theft, etc., the states cannot be controlled.

With respect to certain other objects, the powers of the two governments are concurrent yet supreme.

—Speech on the United States Senate, *Debates of the N.Y. Convention*, p. 113.

Nullification, Interposition, and Secession

With Hamilton the Union was ever paramount. He regarded the excise tax as a test of the national authority, and was quick to react when the tax was denounced in the central counties of North Carolina and in western Pennsylvania. At a convention at Pittsburgh on August 21, 1792, to which Hamilton alludes, a series of resolves were drawn up declaring that the collection of the tax would be blocked by legal means. Acting on Hamilton's advice, Washington issued a proclamation warning against unlawful combinations and stating his intention to enforce the excise tax. Two years later Washington had to call out troops to suppress the Whisky uprising. Hamilton accompanied Henry Lee, who commanded the government forces.

The next threat to the national authority was posed by the adoption in 1798 by the Kentucky and Virginia legislatures of sets of resolutions denouncing the Alien and Sedition laws. The Kentucky resolves, drawn up by Jefferson, asserted that each state "should judge for itself, as well of infractions as of the mode and measure of redress." The Virginia resolves, drafted by Madison, insisted that the states "had the right and are in duty bound to interpose for arresting the progress of the evil." This doctrine of interposition was the basis of Calhoun's later concept of nullification. Hamilton regarded these ideas as constitutional aberrations—a point of view which a non-Hamiltonian president, Andrew Jackson, later adopted. Hamilton's solution: an increase in the prestige and power of the federal government, even if it meant breaking up the large states.

April 10, 1791

. . . It is to be lamented that our system is such as still to leave the public peace of the Union at the mercy of each State government. This is not only the case as it regards direct interferences, but as it regards the inability of the national government, in many particulars, to take those direct measures for carrying into execution its views and engagements which exigencies require. For example: a party comes from a county of Virginia into Pennsylvania and wantonly murders some friendly Indians. The national government, instead of having power to apprehend murderers and bring them to justice, is obliged to make a representation to that of Pennsylvania; that of Pennsylvania again is to make a representation to that of Virginia. And whether the murderers shall be brought to justice at all, must depend upon the particular policy and energy and good disposition of two State governments and the efficacy of the provisions of their respective laws; and the security of other States, and the money of all, are at the discretion of one. These things require a remedy.

—To Washington. *Hamilton,* IV, 149.

August 18, 1792

It is certainly much to be regretted that party discriminations are so far geographical as they have been, and that ideas of a severance of the Union are creeping in both North and South. In the South, it is supposed that more government than is expedient is desired by the North. In the North, it is believed that the prejudices of the South are incompatible with the necessary degree of government, and with the attainment of the essential ends of national union. In both quarters there are respectable men, who talk of separation as a thing dictated by the different geniuses and different prejudices of the parts. But happily their number is not considerable, and the prevailing sentiment of the people is in favor of their true interest, UNION. And it is to be hoped that the efforts of wise men will be able to prevent a schism which would be injurious in different degrees to different portions of the Union, but would seriously wound the prosperity of all.

As to the sacrifice of Southern to Northern prejudices—if the conflict has been between *prejudices* and *prejudices,* it is certainly to be wished, for mutual gratification, that there had been mutual concession; but if the conflict has been between great and substantial national objects on the one hand, and theoretical prejudices on the other, it is difficult to desire that the former should in any instance have yielded.

—To Washington, "Objections and Answers Respecting the Administration of the Government." Hamilton Papers, 1st ser.

September 3, 1792

The proceedings at Pittsburgh which you will find stated in the inclosed papers and other incidents in the western parts of this State announce so determined and persevering a spirit of opposition to the laws, as in my opinion to render a vigorous exertion of the powers of government indispensable. . . .

Would a proclamation from the President be advisable, stating the criminality of such proceedings, and warning all persons to abstain from them as the laws will be strictly enforced against all offenders?

If the plot should thicken and the application of force should appear to be unavoidable, will it be expedient for the President to repair in person to the scene of commotion?

—To John Jay. (Private) Hamilton Papers, 1st ser.

February 2, 1799

What, my dear sir, are you going to do in Virginia? This is a very serious business, which will call for all the wisdom and firmness of the government. The following are the ideas which occur to me on the occasion. The first thing in all great operations of such a government as ours is to secure the opinion of the people. To this end the proceedings of Virginia and Kentucky, with the two laws complained of, should be referred to a special committee. That committee should make a report, exhibiting with great luminousness and particularity the reasons which support the constitutionality and expediency of those laws, the tendency of the doctrines advanced by Virginia and Kentucky to destroy the Constitution of the United States, and with calm dignity united with pathos, the full evidence which they afford of a regular conspiracy to overturn the government. And the report should likewise dwell upon the inevitable effect, and probably the intention, of the proceedings to encourage hostile foreign powers to decline accommodation and proceed in hostility.

The government must not merely defend itself, it must attack and arraign its enemies. But in all this there should be great care to distinguish the people of Virginia from their Legislature, and even the greater part of those who may have concurred in the Legislature from their chiefs, manifesting, indeed, a strong confidence in the good sense and patriotism of the people that they will not be the dupes of an insidious plan to disunite the people of America, to break down their Constitution, and expose them to the enterprise of a foreign power.

—To Theodore Sedgwick. *Works*, X, 340-341.

[1799]

. . . it is admitted by close observers that some of the parts of the Union which, in times past, have been the soundest, have of late exhibited signs of a gangrene begun and progressive.

It is likewise apparent that opposition to the government has acquired more system than formerly, is bolder in the avowal of its designs, less solicitous than it was to discriminate between the Constitution and the administration, and more open and more enterprising in its projects. The late attempt of Virginia and Kentucky to unite the State Legislatures in a direct resistance to certain laws of the Union can be considered in no other light than as an attempt to change the government. . . .

Amidst such serious indications of hostility, the safety and the duty of the supporters of the government call upon them to adopt vigorous measures of counteraction. . . . Possessing, as they now do, all the constitutional powers, it will be an unpardonable mistake on their part if they do not exert them to surround the Constitution with more ramparts and to disconcert the schemes of its enemies.

The measures proper to be adopted may be classed under [ ] heads.

FIRST.—Establishments which will extend the influence and promote the popularity of the government. Under this head three important expedients occur. First. The extension of the judiciary system. Second. The improvement of the great communications, as well interiorly as coastwise, by turnpike roads. Third. The institution of a society with funds to be employed in premiums for new inventions, discoveries, and improvements in agriculture and in the arts. . . .

SECOND.—Provision for augmenting the means and consolidating the strength of the government. A million of dollars may without difficulty be added to the revenue, by increasing the rates of some existing indirect taxes, and by the addition of some new items of a similar character. . . .

THIRD.—Arrangements for confirming and enlarging the legal powers of the government. There are several temporary laws which, in this view, ought to be rendered permanent, particularly that which authorizes the calling out of the militia to suppress unlawful combinations and insurrections.

An article ought to be proposed, to be added to the Constitution, for empowering Congress to open canals in all cases in which it may be necessary to conduct them through the territory of two or more states, or through the territory of a State and that of the United States. . . . Happy would it be if a clause could be added to the Constitution, enabling Congress, on the application of any considerable portion of a State, containing not less than a hundred thousand persons, to erect it into a separate State, on the condition of fixing the quota of contributions which it shall make toward antecedent debts, if any there shall be, reserving to Congress the authority to levy within such State the taxes necessary to the payment of such quota, in case of neglect on the part of the State. *The subdivision of the great States is indispensable to the security of the general government, and with it of the Union.*

Great States will always feel a rivalship with the common head; will often be supposed to machinate against it, and in certain situations will be able to do it with decisive effect. The subdivision of such States ought to be a cardinal point in the federal policy, and small States are doubtless best adapted to the purposes of local regulation and to the preservation of the republican spirit. . . .

FOURTH.—Laws for restraining and punishing incendiary and seditious practices. It will be useful to declare that all such writings, etc., which at common law are libels, if levelled against any officer whatsoever of the United States, shall be cognizable in the courts of the United States.

—To Jonathan Dayton. Draft in Hamilton's hand. Date in later hand. Hamilton Papers, 1st ser.

January 5, 1800

The spirit of faction is abated nowhere. In Virginia it is more violent than ever. It seems demonstrated that the leaders there, who possess completely all the powers of the local government, are resolved to possess those of the national, by the most dangerous combinations; and, if they cannot effect this, to resort to the employment of physical force. The want of disposition in the people to second them will be the only preventive. It is believed that it will be an effectual one.

—To Rufus King. *Hamilton,* VI, 415-417.

Ideas of nullification and secession were contagious. After Jefferson's accession to power the extremists among the Federalists seriously considered severing New England from the Union. In one of his last letters Hamilton repudiated the notion of secession. The next day he was killed by Burr.

July 10, 1804

. . . I have had on hand for some time a long letter to you, explaining my view of the course and tendency of our politics, and my intentions as to my own future conduct. But my plan embraced so large a range that, owing to much avocation, some indifferent health, and a growing distaste to politics, the letter is still considerably short of being finished. I write this now to satisfy you that want of regard for you has not been the cause of my silence.

I will here express but one sentiment, which is, that dismemberment of our empire will be a clear sacrifice of great positive advantages without any counterbalancing good, administering no relief to our real disease, which is *democracy,* the poison of which, by a subdivision, will only be the more concentrated in each part, and consequently the more virulent. King is on his way for Boston, where you may chance to see him, and hear from himself his sentiments. God bless you.

—To Theodore Sedgwick. *Hamilton,* VI, 567-568.

8

Economic Program

While not an original economic thinker, Hamilton's gift for creative economic planning has never been surpassed in American history. He was familiar with the older European economists, the mercantilists and the bullionists, and borrowed heavily from Postlethwayt, excerpts from whose Universal Dictionary of Trade and Commerce *are scattered through his Army Pay Book. He also showed familiarity with Adam Smith. In essence, Hamilton was an economic nationalist, who believed that the government should take an active part in promoting and sustaining trade, manufacturing, and agriculture by sound credit, tax, and currency policies. More immediately, his views foreshadowed those of Henry Clay and the Whig nationalists of the ante-bellum period.*

Hamilton's economic ideas were years ahead of his time. In 1790 America was a land of farmers. The Jeffersonians lacked the vision of American capitalism which fired Hamilton's imagination. The fact that both Big Business Republicans and Big Government New and Fair Dealers can find most of their arguments about the government's role in economic affairs in Hamilton's words and deeds constitutes a tribute to their durable content. A multi-billion dollar road-building program is straight Hamiltonianism.

Hamilton came into Washington's cabinet with a seven-point program: (1) the restoration of public credit; (2) a sound system of taxation; (3) a national bank; (4) a sound currency; (5) the promotion of commerce; (6) the encouragement of manufactures; and (7) a liberal immigration policy. In his public papers he made it clear that the carrying out of this program was not to be at the expense of agriculture, but would result in the building of a balanced economy which would benefit all economic groups. His program was brilliantly presented to the nation in a series of bold and masterful reports.

Restoration of Public Credit

> A national debt, if it is not excessive, will be to us a national blessing.
>
> . . . The creation of debt should always be accompanied with the means of extinguishment.

As early as 1779-80 Hamilton had urged the Federal government to set up a sound system of public finance, and a few years later he pointed out to the New York state legislature the necessity of building "a solid financial system." His thinking was shared by Robert Morris, Superintendent of Finance, who unsuccessfully urged Congress to do very much what Hamilton accomplished when he became Secretary of the Treasury. The issue was precipitated when Morris quit. Hamilton felt that the two principal groups of public creditors—the army and businessmen—should join forces to get action from Congress, and he pointed out to Washington how difficult it was to "keep a complaining and suffering army within the bounds of moderation." In his courageous speech at Newburgh on March 15, 1783, Washington reassured the army that their just demands for back pay and half pay would be met by Congress. This was considered a sacred pledge, and Hamilton felt honor bound to carry it out.

Hamilton's notable state paper, his Report on Public Credit, constitutes a watershed in American history. It marked the end of an era of bankruptcy and repudiation. At the same time it exposed a deepening cleavage between the Hamiltonian nationalists on the one hand and the proponents of states rights, now championed by Madison, a cleavage which led to the formation of the Federalist and Republican parties.

Opponents of the plan objected on two grounds. They regarded the proposal to fund the domestic debt as furnishing unfair profits to speculators and as discriminating against those original holders whose circumstances had forced them to part with their securities. James Madison proposed an alternative plan which would have discriminated between original and present holders, each to get one-half of the face amount. Some opposed Madison's plan because of its impracticality, as the record books in many cases did not list the original holder. Others who held or had recently acquired certificates of indebtedness opposed it out of self-interest. Still others felt that Hamilton's plan of scaling down the interest and deferring final payment of the debt amounted in fact to a compromise settlement in the public interest. Hamilton's funding plan was carried overwhelmingly.

Madison's charges had considerable basis in fact. Since 1787 there had been much speculative buying and selling of Continental and Confederation certificates of indebtedness and bills of credit on the prospect that they might be redeemed by the new Federal government. Speculation reached its climax while the funding program was under debate. Only two weeks before Hamilton's report was made to Congress Assistant Secretary of the Treasury William Duer had entered into a private contract with William Constable, Robert Morris's New York partner, to speculate in government securities and to buy up certificates in the Southern states. Jeremiah Wadsworth and others were also heavily involved in trading in government paper. Duer did what would be considered unconscionable today. He took advantage of his official position to use inside information to benefit himself and his associates. Hamilton was in no way involved in these speculations, but must have been aware of them. In the light of the clear evidence of conflict of interest which is now available but was not known to Madison at the time, it is indeed regrettable that Hamilton and Madison, two men of the highest personal integrity who were both above the speculative orgy of the moment, could not have worked out a compromise proposal that would have distinguished between legitimate creditors and short-term operators. Hamilton's speculatively-minded and greedy associates unfairly besmirched his reputation. Madison's inept handling of the opposition lost him his political leadership in Congress.

The heaviest guns of the opposition were kept in reserve for the second part of Hamilton's plan—the assumption scheme. The New England states, with the largest total of unpaid state debts, generally favored assumption. But the Southern states, most of whom had already made arrangements for discharging their indebtedness, were hostile to an immense increase in the national debt for which their inhabitants would be taxed seemingly without reciprocal benefits. They feared that assumption would magnify Federal power at the expense of the states.

Madison, who had proposed that the Confederation assume the state debts back in 1783, now viewed the matter quite differently. Under his leadership Virginia led the opposition to the plan and succeeded in defeating it by a narrow vote when it first was proposed in April, 1790. Hamilton's resourceful negotiations kept the assumption measure alive, and differences were finally settled by a compromise between Hamilton and Jefferson on the location of the permanent seat of the national government. Hamilton agreed to exert his influence to secure enough Northern votes to assure location of the National Capital along the Potomac, instead of in Philadelphia, in return for Madison's pledge to obtain a sufficient number of Southern votes to effect passage of assumption. Many years later Jefferson declared that he had been "duped by Hamilton." But the evidence indicates that Jefferson knew just what he was doing, but did not realize at the time the momentous political issue which was raised by funding and assumption.

Hamilton's strong financial program provided public credit where *there had been none before, gave the nation a circulating medium and financial machinery. It was a major stroke in the development of American capitalism. But Hamilton's own vindication of his program constitutes its most brilliant defense.*

December 16, 1782

THE UNITED STATES have already contracted a debt in Europe and in this country, for which their faith is pledged. The capital of this debt can only be discharged by degrees; but a fund for this purpose, and for paying the interest annually, on every principle of policy and justice, ought to be provided. The omission will be the deepest ingratitude and cruelty to a large number of meritorious individuals, who, in the most critical periods of the war, have adventured their fortunes in support of our independence. It would stamp the national character with indelible disgrace.

—Report on Impost Duty. *Works*, II, 188.

January 29, 1783

Mr. Hamilton disliked every plan that made but partial provision for the public debts, as an inconsistent and dishonorable departure from the declaration made by Congress on that subject. He said the domestic creditors would take the alarm at any distinctions unfavorable to their claims; that they would withhold their influence from any such measures recommended by Congress; and that it must be principally from their influence on their respective Legislatures that success could be expected to any application from Congress for a general revenue.

—Debates of the Congress of the Confederation. *Writings of Madison*, I, 351.

February 12, 1783

[*Resolved*,] That it is the opinion of Congress that complete justice cannot be done to the creditors of the United States, nor the restoration of public credit be effected, nor the future exigencies of the war provided for, but by the establishment of permanent and adequate funds to operate generally throughout the United States, to be collected by Congress.

—*Journals of Continental Congress*, XXIV, 127n.

February 18, 1783

Whereas it is the desire of Congress that the motives of their deliberations and measures (as far as they can be disclosed consistently with the public safety) should be fully known to their constituents,

Therefore, Resolved, That when the establishment of funds for paying the principal and interest of the public debt shall be under the consideration of this House, the doors shall be opened.

—*Journals of the Continental Congress*, XXIV, 140.

February 19, 1783

Mr. Hamilton opposed the motion[1] strenuously; declared that, as a friend to the army as well as to the other creditors and to the public at large, he would never assent to such a partial distribution of justice; that the different States, being differently attached to different branches of the public debt, would never concur in establishing a fund which was not extended to every branch; that it was impolitic to divide the interests of the civil and military creditors, whose joint efforts in the States would be necessary to prevail on them to adopt a general revenue.

—Debates in the Congress of the Confederation. *Writings of Madison*, I, 374.

October 7, 1789

In this state of things you will readily perceive that I can say nothing very precise with regard to the provision to be made for discharging the arrearages due to France. I am, however, desirous that it should be understood that proper attention will be paid to the subject on my part; and I take it for granted that the national legislature will not fail to sanction the measures which the faith and credit of the United States require in reference to it. In addition to this I shall only remark that it would be a valuable accommodation to the government of this country if the court of France should think fit to suspend the payment of the instalments of the principal due and to become due, for five or six years from this period, on the condition of effectual arrangements for the punctual discharge of the interest which has accrued and shall accrue.

—To William Short (Cabinet Paper). *Hamilton*, IV, 5.

Hamilton's Report on the Public Credit

January 9, 1790[2]

In the discharge of this duty, [the Secretary of the Treasury] has felt, in no small degree, the anxieties which naturally flow from a just estimate of the difficulty of the task, from a well-founded diffidence of his own qualifications for executing it with success, and from a deep and solemn conviction of the momentous nature of the truth contained in the resolution under which his investigations have been conducted, "That an *adequate* provision for the support of the Public Credit is a matter of high importance to the honor and prosperity of the United States." . . .

In the opinion of the Secretary, the wisdom of the House, in giving explicit sanction to the proposition which has been stated, cannot but

[1] By Rutledge, to appropriate the impost to the army exclusively; seconded by Lee.
[2] Submitted to Congress January 14.

be applauded by all, who will seriously consider, and trace through their obvious consequences, these plain and undeniable truths:

That exigencies are to be expected to occur, in the affairs of nations, in which there will be a necessity for borrowing.

That loans in time of public danger, especially from foreign war, are found an indispensable resource, even to the wealthiest of them.

And that, in a country which, like this, is possessed of little active wealth, or, in other words, little moneyed capital, the necessity for that resource must, in such emergencies, be proportionably urgent.

And as, on the one hand, the necessity for borrowing in particular emergencies cannot be doubted, so, on the other, it is equally evident that, to be able to borrow upon good terms, it is essential that the credit of a nation should be well established.

For, when the credit of a country is in any degree questionable, it never fails to give an extravagant premium, in one shape or another, upon all the loans it has occasion to make. Nor does the evil end here; the same disadvantage must be sustained on whatever is to be bought on terms of future payment.

From this constant necessity of borrowing and buying dear, it is easy to conceive how immensely the expenses of a nation, in a course of time, will be augmented by an unsound state of the public credit....

If the maintenance of public credit, then, be truly so important, the next inquiry which suggests itself is: By what means is it to be effected? The ready answer to which question is, by good faith; by a punctual performance of contracts. States, like individuals, who observe their engagements are respected and trusted, while the reverse is the fate of those who pursue an opposite conduct.

Every breach of the public engagements, whether from choice or necessity, is, in different degrees, hurtful to public credit. When such a necessity does truly exist, the evils of it are only to be palliated by a scrupulous attention, on the part of the Government, to carry the violation no further than the necessity absolutely requires, and to manifest, if the nature of the case admit of it, a sincere disposition to make reparation whenever circumstances shall permit. . . .

While the observance of that good faith, which is the basis of public credit, is recommended by the strongest inducements of political expediency, it is enforced by considerations of still greater authority. There are arguments for it which rest on the immutable principles of moral obligation. And in proportion as the mind is disposed to contemplate, in the order of Providence, an intimate connection between public virtue and public happiness, will be its repugnancy to a violation of those principles.

This reflection derives additional strength from the nature of the debt of the United States. It was the price of liberty. The faith of America has been repeatedly pledged for it, and with solemnities that give peculiar force to the obligation. There is, indeed, reason to regret that it has not hitherto been kept; that the necessities of the war, conspiring with inexperience in the subjects of finance, produced direct infractions; and that the subsequent period has been a continued scene of negative violation or non-compliance. But a diminution of this regret arises from the reflection, that the last seven years have exhibited an earnest and uniform effort, on the part of the Government of the Union, to retrieve the national credit, by doing justice to the creditors of the nation; and that the embarrassments of a defective Constitution, which defeated this laudable effort, have ceased.

From this evidence of a favorable disposition given by the former Government, the institution of a new one, clothed with powers competent to calling forth the resources of the community, has excited correspondent expectations. A general belief accordingly prevails, that the credit of the United States will quickly be established on the firm foundation of an effectual provision for the existing debt. The influence which this has had at home is witnessed by the rapid increase that has taken place in the market value of the public securities. From January to November, they rose thirty-three and a third per cent.; and, from that period to this time, they have risen fifty per cent. more; and the intelligence from abroad announces effects proportionably favorable to our national credit and consequence. . . .

To justify and preserve their confidence; to promote the increasing respectability of the American name; to answer the calls of justice; to restore landed property to its due value; to furnish new resources, both to agriculture and commerce; to cement more closely the union of the States; to add to their security against foreign attack; to establish public order on the basis of an upright and liberal policy;—these are the great and invaluable ends to be secured by a proper and adequate provision, at the present period, for the support of public credit.

To this provision we are invited, not only by the general considerations which have been noticed, but by others of a more particular nature. It will procure, to every class of the community, some important advantages, and remove some no less important disadvantages.

The advantage to the public creditors, from the increased value of that part of their property which constitutes the public debt, needs no explanation.

But there is a consequence of this, less obvious, though not less true, in which every other citizen is interested. It is a well-known fact, that, in countries in which the national debt is properly funded, and an object of established confidence, it answers most of the purposes of money. Transfers of stock or public debt are there equivalent to payments in specie; or, in other words, stock, in the principal transactions of business, passes current as specie. The same thing would, in all probability, happen here under the like circumstances.

The benefits of this are various and obvious:

First.—Trade is extended by it, because there is a larger capital to carry it on, and the merchant can, at the same time, afford to trade for smaller profits; as his stock, which, when unemployed, brings him an interest from the Government, serves him also as money when he has a call for it in his commercial operations.

Secondly.—Agriculture and manufacturers are also promoted by it, for the like reason, that more capital can be commanded to be employed in both; and because the merchant whose enterprise in foreign trade gives to them activity and extension, has greater means for enterprise.

Thirdly.—The interest of money will be lowered by it; for this is always in a ratio to the quantity of money, and to the quickness of circulation. This circumstance will enable both the public and individuals to borrow on easier and cheaper terms.

And from the combination of these effects, additional aids will be furnished to labor, to industry, and to arts of every kind. But these good effects of a public debt are only to be looked for, when, by being well funded, it has acquired an adequate and stable value; till then, it has rather a contrary tendency. The fluctuation and insecurity incident to it, in an unfunded state, render it a mere commodity, and a precarious one. As such, being only an object of occasional and particular speculation, all the money applied to it is so much diverted from the more useful channels of circulation, for which the thing itself affords no substitute; so that, in fact, one serious inconvenience of an unfunded debt is, that it contributes to the scarcity of money. . . .

The effect which the funding of the public debt, on right principles, would have upon landed property, is one of the circumstances attending such an arrangement, which has been least adverted to, though it deserves the most particular attention. The present depreciated state of that species of property is a serious calamity. The value of cultivated lands, in most of the States, has fallen, since the Revolution, from twenty-five to fifty per cent. In those farther south, the decrease is still more considerable. Indeed, if the representations continually received from that quarter may be credited, lands there will command no price which may not be deemed an almost total sacrifice. This decrease in the value of lands ought, in a great measure, to be attributed to the scarcity of money; consequently, whatever produces an augmentation of the moneyed capital of the country must have a proportional effect in raising that value. The beneficial tendency of a funded debt, in this respect, has been manifested by the most decisive experience in Great Britain.

The proprietors of lands would not only feel the benefit of this increase in the value of their property, and of a more prompt and better sale, when they had occasion to sell, but the necessity of selling would be itself greatly diminished. As the same cause would contribute to the facility of loans, there is reason to believe that such of them as are indebted would be able, through that resource, to satisfy their more urgent creditors. . . .

Having now taken a concise view of the inducements to a proper provision for the public debt, the next inquiry which presents itself is: What ought to be the nature of such a provision? This requires some preliminary discussions.

It is agreed, on all hands, that the part of the debt which has been contracted abroad, and is denominated the foreign debt, ought to be provided for according to the precise terms of the contracts relating to it. The discussions which can arise, therefore, will have reference essentially to the domestic part of it, or to that which has been contracted at home. It is to be regretted that there is not the same unanimity of sentiment on this part as on the other.

The Secretary has too much deference for the opinions of every part of the community not to have observed one, which has more than once made its appearance in the public prints, and which is occasionally to be met with in conversation. It involves this question: Whether a discrimination ought not to be made between original holders of the public securities, and present possessors, by purchase? Those who advocate a discrimination are for making a full provision for the securities of the former at their nominal value, but contend that the latter ought to receive no more than the cost to them, and the interest. And the idea is sometimes suggested of making good the difference to the primitive possessor.

In favor of this scheme it is alleged that it would be unreasonable to pay twenty shillings in the pound to one who had not given more for it than three or four. And it is added that it would be hard to aggravate the misfortune of the first owner, who, probably through necessity, parted with his property at so great a loss, by obliging him to contribute to the profit of the person who had speculated on his distresses.

The Secretary, after the most mature reflection on the force of this argument, is induced to reject the doctrine it contains, as equally unjust and impolitic; as highly injurious, even to the original holders of public securities; as ruinous to public credit.

It is inconsistent with justice, because, in the first place, it is a breach of contract—a violation of the rights of a fair purchaser.

The nature of the contract, in its origin, is that the public will pay the sum expressed in the security, to the first holder or his assignee. The intent in making the security assignable is, that the proprietor may be able to make use of his property, by selling it for as much as it may be worth in the market, and that the buyer may be safe in the purchase.

Every buyer, therefore, stands exactly in the place of the seller; has the same right with him to the identical sum expressed in the security;

and, having acquired that right by fair purchase and in conformity to the original agreement and intention of the Government, his claim cannot be disputed without manifest injustice.

That he is to be considered as a fair purchaser, results from this: whatever necessity the seller may have been under, was occasioned by the Government, in not making a proper provision for its debts. The buyer had no agency in it, and therefore ought not to suffer. He is not even chargeable with having taken an undue advantage. He paid what the commodity was worth in the market, and took the risks of reimbursement upon himself. He, of course, gave a fair equivalent, and ought to reap the benefit of his hazard—a hazard which was far from inconsiderable, and which, perhaps, turned on little less than a revolution in government.

That the case of those who parted with their securities from necessity is a hard one, cannot be denied. But, whatever complaint of injury, or claim of redress, they may have, respects the Government solely. They have not only nothing to object to the persons who relieved their necessities, by giving them the current price of their property, but they are even under an implied condition to contribute to the reimbursement of those persons. They knew that, by the terms of the contract with themselves, the public were bound to pay to those to whom they should convey their title the sums stipulated to be paid to them; and that, as citizens of the United States, they were to bear their proportion of the contribution for that purpose. This, by the act of assignment, they tacitly engage to do; and, if they had an option, they could not, with integrity or good faith, refuse to do it, without the consent of those to whom they sold.

But, though many of the original holders sold from necessity, it does not follow that this was the case with all of them. It may well be supposed that some of them did it either through want of confidence in an eventual provision, or from the allurements of some profitable speculation. How shall these different classes be discriminated from each other? How shall it be ascertained, in any case, that the money which the original holder obtained for his security was not more beneficial to him, than if he had held it to the present time, to avail himself of the provision which shall be made? How shall it be known whether, if the purchaser had employed his money in some other way, he would not be in a better situation than by having applied it in the purchase of securities, though he should now receive their full amount? And, if neither of these things can be known, how shall it be determined, whether a discrimination, independent of the breach of contract, would not do a real injury to purchasers; and, if it included a compensation to the primitive proprietors, would not give them an advantage to which they had no equitable pretension?

It may well be imagined, also, that there are not wanting instances in which individuals, urged by a present necessity, parted with the securities received by them from the public, and shortly after replaced them with others, as an indemnity for their first loss. Shall they be deprived of the indemnity which they have endeavored to secure by so provident an arrangement?

Questions of this sort, on a close inspection, multiply themselves without end, and demonstrate the injustice of a discrimination, even on the most subtile calculations of equity, abstracted from the obligation of contract.

The difficulties, too, of regulating the details of a plan for that purpose, which would have even the semblance of equity, would be found immense. It may well be doubted, whether they would not be insurmountable, and replete with such absurd as well as inequitable consequences, as to disgust even the proposers of the measure. . . .

It will be perceived, at first sight, that the transferable quality of stock is essential to its operation as money, and that this depends on the idea of complete security to the transferee, and a firm persuasion that no distinction can, in any circumstances, be made between him and the original proprietor.

The precedent of an invasion of this fundamental principle would, of course, tend to deprive the community of an advantage with which no temporary saving could bear the least comparison.

And it will as readily be perceived that the same cause would operate a diminution of the value of stock in the hands of the first as well as of every other holder. The price which any man who should incline to purchase would be willing to give for it, would be in a compound ratio to the immediate profit it afforded, and the chance of the continuance of his profit. If there was supposed to be any hazard of the latter, the risk would be taken into the calculation, and either there would be no purchase at all, or it would be at a proportionably less price.

For this diminution of the value of stock every person who should be about to lend to the Government would demand a compensation, and would add to the actual difference between the nominal and the market value an equivalent for the chance of greater decrease, which, in a precarious state of public credit, is always to be taken into the account. Every compensation of this sort, it is evident, would be an absolute loss to the Government. . . .

It would be repugnant to an express provision of the Constitution of the United States. This provision is that "all debts contracted and engagements entered into before the adoption of that Constitution, shall be as valid against the United States under it as under the Confederation"; which amounts to a constitutional ratification of the contracts respecting the debt in the state in which they existed under the Confederation. And, resorting to that standard, there can be no doubt that the rights of assignees and original holders must be considered as equal. In exploding thus fully the principle of discrimination, the Secretary is happy in reflecting that he is only the advocate of what has been already sanctioned by the formal and express authority of the Government of the Union in these emphatic terms: "The remaining class of creditors," says Congress, in their circular address to the States of the 26th April, 1783, "is composed of such of our fellow-citizens as originally lent to the public the use of their funds, or have since manifested most confidence in their country by receiving transfers from the lenders; and partly of those whose property has been either advanced or assumed for the public service. To discriminate the merits of these several descriptions of creditors would be a task equally unnecessary and invidious. If the voice of humanity pleads more loudly in favor of some than of others, the voice of policy, no less than of justice, pleads in favor of all. A wise nation will never permit those who relieve the wants of their country, or who rely most on its faith, its firmness, and its resources, when either of them is distrusted, to suffer by the event."

The Secretary, concluding that a discrimination between the different classes of creditors of the United States cannot, with propriety, be made, proceeds to examine whether a difference ought to be permitted to remain between them and another description of public creditors—those of the States individually. The Secretary, after mature reflection on this point, entertains a full conviction that an assumption of the debts of the particular States by the Union, and a like provision for them as for those of the Union, will be a measure of sound policy and substantial justice.

It would, in the opinion of the Secretary, contribute, in an eminent degree, to an orderly, stable, and satisfactory arrangement of the national finances. Admitting, as ought to be the case, that a provision must be made, in some way or other, for the entire debt, it will follow that no greater revenues will be required whether that provision be made wholly by the United States, or partly by them and partly by the States separately.

The principal question, then, must be whether such a provision cannot be more conveniently and effectually made by one general plan, issuing from one authority, than by different plans, originating in different authorities? In the first case there can be no competition for resources; in the last there must be such a competition. The consequences of this, without the greatest caution on both sides, might be interfering regulations, and thence collision and confusion. Particular branches of industry might also be oppressed by it. The most productive objects of revenue are not numerous. Either these must be wholly engrossed by one side, which might lessen the efficacy of the provisions by the other, or both must have recourse to the same objects, in different modes, which might occasion an accumulation upon them beyond what they could properly bear. If this should not happen, the caution requisite to avoiding it would prevent the revenue's deriving the full benefit of each object. The danger of interference and of excess would be apt to impose restraints very unfriendly to the complete command of those resources which are the most convenient, and to compel the having recourse to others, less eligible in themselves and less agreeable to the community. The difficulty of an effectual command of the public resources, in case of separate provisions for the debt, may be seen in another, and, perhaps, more striking light. It would naturally happen that different States, from local considerations, would, in some instances, have recourse to different objects, in others to the same objects, in different degrees, for procuring the funds of which they stood in need. It is easy to conceive how this diversity would affect the aggregate revenue of the country. By the supposition, articles which yielded a full supply in some States would yield nothing, or an insufficient product, in others. And hence, the public revenue would not derive the full benefit of those articles from State regulations; neither could the deficiencies be made good by those of the Union. It is a provision of the national Constitution that "all duties, imposts, and excises shall be uniform throughout the United States." And, as the General Government would be under a necessity, from motives of policy, of paying regard to the duty which may have been previously imposed upon any article, though but in a single State, it would be constrained either to refrain wholly from any further imposition upon such article, where it had been already rated as high as was proper, or to confine itself to the difference between the existing rate and what the article would reasonably bear. Thus the preoccupancy of an article by a single State would tend to arrest or abridge the impositions of the Union on that article. And as it is supposable that a great variety of articles might be placed in this situation, by dissimilar arrangements of the particular States, it is evident that the aggregate revenue of the country would be likely to be very materially contracted by the plan of separate provisions.

If all the public creditors receive their dues from one source, distributed with an equal hand, their interest will be the same. And, having the same interests, they will unite in the support of the fiscal arrangements of the Government—as these, too, can be made with more convenience where there is no competition. These circumstances combined will insure to the revenue laws a more ready and more satisfactory execution. . . .

There is an objection, however, to an assumption of the State debts, which deserves particular notice. It may be supposed that it would increase the difficulty of an equitable settlement between them and the United States.

The principles of that settlement, whenever they shall be discussed, will require all the moderation and wisdom of the Government. In the opinion of the Secretary, that discussion, till further lights are obtained, would be premature. All, therefore, which he would now think advisable on the point in question would be that the amount of the debts assumed and provided for should be charged to the respective States to abide an eventual arrangement. This the United States, as assignees to the creditors, would have an indisputable right to do. . . .

The only discussion of a preliminary kind which remains, relates to the distinctions of the debt into principal and interest. It is well known that the arrears of the latter bear a large proportion to the amount of the former. The immediate payment of these arrears is evidently impracticable; and a question arises, What ought to be done with them?

There is good reason to conclude, that the impressions of many are more favorable to the claim of the principal, than to that of the interest; at least so far as to produce an opinion, that an inferior provision might suffice for the latter.

But, to the Secretary, this opinion does not appear to be well founded. His investigations of the subject have led him to a conclusion, that the arrears of interest have pretensions at least equal to the principal. . . .

The result of the foregoing discussion is this: That there ought to be no discrimination between the original holders of the debt, and present possessors by purchase; that it is expedient there should be an assumption of the State debts by the Union; and that the arrears of interest should be provided for on an equal footing with the principal. . . .

The interesting problem now occurs: Is it in the power of the United States, consistently with those prudential considerations which ought not to be overlooked, to make a provision equal to the purpose of funding the whole debt, at the rates of interest which it now bears, in addition to the sum which will be necessary for the current service of the Government?

The Secretary will not say that such a provison would exceed the abilities of the country, but he is clearly of opinion that to make it would require the extension of taxation to a degree and to objects which the true interest of the public creditors forbids. It is, therefore, to be hoped, and even to be expected, that they will cheerfully concur in such modifications of their claims, on fair and equitable principles, as will facilitate to the Government an arrangement substantial, durable, and satisfactory to the community. The importance of the last characteristic will strike every discerning mind. No plan, however flattering in appearance, to which it did not belong, could be truly entitled to confidence. . . .

The Secretary conceives that there is good reason to believe, if effectual measures are taken to establish public credit, that the Government rate of interest in the United States will, in a very short time, fall at least as low as five per cent.; and that, in a period not exceeding twenty years, it will sink still lower, probably to four. There are two principal causes which will be likely to produce this effect: one, the low rate of interest in Europe; the other, the increase of the moneyed capital of the nation by the funding of the public debt. . . .

Premising these things, the Secretary submits to the House the expediency of proposing a loan, to the full amount of the debt, as well of the particular States as of the Union, upon the following terms:

First. That, for every hundred dollars subscribed payable in the debt (as well interest as principal), the subscriber be entitled, at his option, either to have two thirds funded at an annuity or yearly interest of six per cent., redeemable at the pleasure of the Government by payment of the principal, and to receive the other third in lands in the Western territory, at the rate of twenty cents per acre; or to have the whole sum funded at an annuity or yearly interest of four per cent., irredeemable by any payment exceeding five dollars per annum, on account both of principal and interest, and to receive, as a compensation for the reduction of interest, fifteen dollars and eighty cents, payable in lands, as in the preceding case; or to have sixty-six dollars and two thirds of a dollar funded immediately, at an annuity or yearly interest of six per cent., irredeemable by any payment exceeding four dollars and two thirds of a dollar per annum, on account both of principal and interest, and to have, at the end of ten years, twenty-six dollars and eighty-eight cents funded at the like interest and rate of redemption; or to have an annuity, for the remainder of life, upon the contingency of fixing to a given age, not less distant than ten years, computing interest at four per cent.; or to have an annuity for the remainder of life, upon the contingency of the survivorship of the youngest of two persons, computing interest in this case also at four per cent.

In addition to the foregoing loan, payable wholly in the debt, the Secretary would propose that one should be opened for ten millions of dollars, on the following plan:

That, for every hundred dollars subscribed, payable one half in specie and the other half in debt (as well principal as interest), the subscriber be entitled to an annuity or yearly interest of five per cent., irredeemable by any payment exceeding six dollars per annum, on account both of principal and interest. . . .

The general price at which the Western lands have been heretofore sold, has been a dollar per acre in public securities; but, at the time the principal purchases were made, these securities were worth, in the market, less than three shillings in the pound. The nominal price, therefore, would not be the proper standard, under present circumstances, nor would the precise specie value then given be a just rule; because, as the payments were to be made by instalments, and the securities were, at the times of the purchases, extremely low, the probability of a moderate rise must be presumed to have been taken into the account.

Twenty cents, therefore, seems to bear an equitable proportion to the two considerations of value at the time and likelihood of increase.

It will be understood that, upon this plan, the public retains the advantage of availing itself of any fall in the market rate of interest, for reducing that upon the debt; which is perfectly just, as no present sacrifice, either in the quantum of the principal, or in the rate of interest, is required from the creditor. . . .

The Secretary thinks it advisable to hold out various propositions, all of them compatible with the public interest, because it is, in his opinion, of the greatest consequence that the debt should, with the consent of the creditors, be remoulded into such a shape as will bring the expenditure of the nation to a level with its income. Till this shall be accomplished the finances of the United States will never wear a proper countenance. Arrears of interest, continually accruing, will be as continual a monument, either of inability or of ill faith, and will not cease to have an evil influence on public credit. In nothing are appearances of greater moment than in whatever regards credit. Opinion is the soul of it; and this is affected by appearances as well as realities. By offering an option to the creditors between a number of plans, the change meditated will be more likely to be accomplished. Different tempers will be governed by different views of the subject.

But while the Secretary would endeavor to effect a change in the form of the debt by new loans, in order to render it more susceptible of an adequate provision, he would not think it proper to aim at procuring the concurrence of the creditors by operating upon their necessities.

Hence, whatever surplus of revenue might remain, after satisfying the interest of the new loans and the demand for the current service, ought to be divided among those creditors, if any, who may not think fit to subscribe to them. But for this purpose, under the circumstance of depending propositions, a temporary appropriation will be most advisable, and the sum must be limited to four per cent., as the revenues will only be calculated to produce in that proportion to the entire debt. . . .

This sum may, in the opinion of the Secretary, be obtained from the present duties on imports and tonnage, with the additions which, without any possible disadvantage, either to trade or agriculture, may be made on wines, spirits (including those distilled within the United States), teas, and coffee.

The Secretary conceives that it will be sound policy to carry the duties upon articles of this kind as high as will be consistent with the practicability of a safe collection. This will lessen the necessity, both of having recourse to direct taxation, and of accumulating duties where they would be more inconvenient to trade and upon objects which are more to be regarded as necessaries of life.

That the articles which have been enumerated will, better than most others, bear high duties, can hardly be a question. They are all of them in reality luxuries; the greatest part of them foreign luxuries; some of them, in the excess in which they are used, pernicious luxuries. And there is, perhaps, none of them which is not consumed in so great abundance as may justly denominate it a source of national extravagance and impoverishment. The consumption of ardent spirits, particularly, no doubt very much on account of their cheapness, is carried to an extreme which is truly to be regretted, as well in regard to the health and morals as to the economy of the community.

Should the increase of duties tend to a decrease of the consumption of those articles, the effect would be in every respect desirable. The saving which it would occasion would leave individuals more at their ease, and promote a favorable balance of trade. As far as this decrease might be applicable to distilled spirits, it would encourage the substitution of cider and malt liquors, benefit agriculture, and open a new and productive source of revenue.

It is not, however, probable that this decrease would be in a degree which would frustrate the expected benefit to the revenue from raising the duties. Experience has shown that luxuries of every kind lay the strongest hold on the attachments of mankind, which, especially when confirmed by habit, are not easily alienated from them....

With regard to such of them as will be brought from abroad, a duty on importation recommends itself by two leading considerations: one is, that meeting the object at its first entrance into the country, the collection is drawn to a point, and, so far, simplified; the other is, that it avoids the possibility of interference between the regulations of the United States and those of the particular States.

But a duty, the precautions for the collection of which should terminate with the landing of the goods, as is essentially the case in the existing system, could not, with safety, be carried to the extent which is contemplated.

In that system, the evasion of the duty depends, as it were, on a single risk. To land the goods in defiance of the vigilance of the officers of the customs, is almost the sole difficulty. No future pursuit is materially to be apprehended. And where the inducement is equivalent to the risk, there will be found too many who are willing to run it.

Consequently, there will be extensive frauds of the revenue, against which the utmost rigor of penal laws has proved, as often as it has been tried, an ineffectual guard.

The only expedient which has been discovered, for conciliating high duties with a safe collection, is the establishment of a *second* or interior scrutiny.

By pursuing the article, from its importation in to the hands of the dealers in it, the risk of detection is so greatly enhanced, that few, in comparison, will venture to incur it. Indeed, every dealer who is not himself the fraudulent importer, then becomes in some sort a sentinel upon him.

The introduction of a system founded on this principle in some shape or other, is, in the opinion of the Secretary, essential to the efficacy of every attempt to render the revenues of the United States equal to their exigencies, their safety, their prosperity, their honor.

Nor is it less essential to the interest of the honest and fair trader. It might even be added, that every individual citizen, besides his share in the general weal, has a particular interest in it. The practice of smuggling never fails to have one of two effects, and sometimes unites them both. Either the smuggler undersells the fair trader, as, by saving the *duty*, he can afford to do, and makes *it* a charge upon him, or he sells at the increased price occasioned by the duty, and defrauds every man who buys of him, of his share of what the public ought to receive; for it is evident that the loss falls ultimately upon the citizens, who must be charged with other taxes to make good the deficiency and supply the wants of the State. . . .

Persuaded, as the Secretary is, that the proper funding of the present debt will render it a national blessing, yet he is so far from acceding to the position, in the latitude in which it is sometimes laid down, that "public debts are public benefits"—a position inviting to prodigality and liable to dangerous abuse—that he ardently wishes to see it incorporated as a fundamental maxim in the system of public credit of the United States, that the creation of debt should always be accompanied with the means of extinguishment. This he regards as the true secret for rendering public credit immortal. And he presumes that it is difficult to conceive a situation in which there may not be an adherence to the maxim. At least, he feels an unfeigned solicitude that this may be attempted by the United States, and that they may commence their measures for the establishment of credit with the observance of it. . . .

Deeply impressed, as the Secretary is, with a full and deliberate conviction that the establishment of the public credit, upon the basis of a satisfactory provision for the public debt, is, under the present circumstances of this country, the true desideratum toward relief from individual and national embarrassments; that without it these embarrassments will be likely to press still more severely upon the community; he cannot but indulge an anxious wish that an effectual plan for that purpose may during the present session be the result of the united wisdom of the Legislature.

He is fully convinced that it is of the greatest importance that no further delay should attend the making of the requisite provision: not only because it will give a better impression of the good faith of the country, and will bring earlier relief to the creditors, both which circumstances are of great moment to public credit, but because the advantages to the community, from raising stock, as speedily as possible, to its natural value, will be incomparably greater than any that can result from its continuance below that standard. No profit which could be derived from purchases in the market, on account of the Government, to any practicable extent, would be an equivalent for the loss which would be sustained by the purchases of foreigners at a low value. Not to repeat, that governmental purchases to be honorable ought to be preceded by a provision. Delay, by disseminating doubt, would sink the price of stock; and, as the temptation to foreign speculations, from the lowness of the price, would be too great to be neglected, millions would probably be lost to the United States.

All of which is humbly submitted.

ALEXANDER HAMILTON,
Secretary of the Treasury.

—Report of the Secretary of the Treasury to the House of Representatives relative to a provision for the support of the Public Credit of the United States in conformity to a Resolution of the 21 Day of September 1789. Presented to the House of Representatives the 14 January 1790. New York: Francis Childs and John Swaine, 1790.

Arguments against Discrimination

May 28, 1790

It is, perhaps, too questionable whether an assignee, however equitable his pretensions were, could, under the operation of the provision which has been recited, have any remedy whatever for the recovery of the money or value which he may have paid to the assignor.

It is not certain that a legislative act decreeing payment to a different person, would not be a legal bar; but if the existence of such a remedy were certain, it would be but a very inconclusive consideration. The assignment may have been a security for a precarious or desperate debt, which security will be wrested from the assignee; or it may have been a composition between an insolvent debtor and his creditor, and the only resource of the latter; or the assignor may be absent and incapable either of benefiting by the provision, or of being called to an account. And in every case the assignee would be left to the casualty of the ability of the assignor to repay; to the perplexity, trouble, and expense of a suit at law. In respect to the soldiers, the presumption would be, in the greater number of cases, that the pursuit of redress would be worse than acquiescence in the loss. To vary the risks of parties, to supersede the contracts between them, to turn over a creditor without his consent from one *debtor* to *another*, to take away a right to a *spectific thing*, leaving only the chance of a remedy for retribution, are not less positive violations of property than a direct confiscation.

It appears from the debates in the House of Representatives, and it may be inferred from the nature of the proceeding, that a suggestion of fraud has been the occasion of it. Fraud is certainly a good objection to any contract, and where it is properly ascertained invalidates it. But the power of ascertaining it is the peculiar province of the Judiciary Department. The principles of good government conspire with those of justice to place it there. 'Tis there only that such an investigation of the fact can be had as ought to precede a decision. 'Tis there only the parties can be heard, and evidence on both sides produced; without which *surmise* must be substituted to *proof*, and *conjecture* to *fact*.

This, then, is the dilemma incident to legislative interference. Either the legislature must erect itself into a court of justice and determine each case upon its own merits, after a full hearing of the allegations and proofs of the parties; or it must proceed upon vague suggestions, loose reports, or at best upon partial and problematical testimony, to condemn, in the gross and in the dark, the fairest and most unexceptionable claims, as well as those which may happen to be fraudulent and exceptionable. The first would be an usurpation of the judiciary authority, the last is at variance with the rules of property, the dictates of equity, and the maxims of good government.

All admit the truth of these positions as general rules. But, when a departure from it is advocated for any particular purpose, it is usually alleged that there are exceptions to it, that there are certain extraordinary cases in which the public good demands and justifies an extraordinary interposition of the legislature.

This doctrine in relation to extraordinary cases is not to be denied; but it is highly important that the nature of those cases should be carefully distinguished.

It is evident that every such interposition deviating from the usual course of law and justice, and infringing the established rules of property, which ought as far as possible to be held sacred and inviolable, is an overleaping of the ordinary and regular bounds of legislative discretion; and is in the nature of a resort to first principles.

Nothing, therefore, but some urgent public necessity, some impending national calamity, something that threatens direct and general mischief to society, for which there is no adequate redress in the established course of things, can, it is presumed, be a sufficient cause for the employment of so extraordinary a remedy. An accommodation to the interests of a small part of the community, in a case of inconsiderable magnitude, on a national scale, cannot in the judgment of the Secretary, be entitled to that character.

If partial inconveniences and hardships occasion legislative interferences in private contracts, the intercourses of business become uncertain, the security of property is lessened, the confidence in government destroyed or weakened.

The Constitution of the United States interdicts the states individually from passing any law impairing the obligation of contracts. This, to the more enlightened part of the community, was not one of the least recommendations of that Constitution. The too frequent intermeddlings of the state legislatures, in relation to private contracts, were extensively felt, and seriously lamented; and a constitution which promises a preventive, was, by those who felt and thought in that manner, eagerly embraced. Precedents of similar interferences by the legislature of the United States cannot fail to alarm the same class of persons, and at the same time to diminish the respect of the state legislatures for the interdiction alluded to. The *example* of the national government in a matter of this kind may be expected to have a far more powerful influence than the precepts of the Constitution.

The present case is that of a particular class of men, highly meritorious indeed, but inconsiderable in point of numbers, and the whole of the property in question less than fifty thousand dollars, which, when distributed among those who are principally to be benefited by the regulation, does not exceed twenty-five dollars per man. The relief of the individuals who may have been subjects of imposition, in so limited a case, seems a very inadequate cause for a measure which breaks in upon those great principles that constitute the foundations of property.

The eligibility of the measure is more doubtful, as the courts of justice are competent to the relief which it is the object of the resolution to give, as far as the fact of fraud or imposition or undue advantage can be substantiated. It is true that many of the individuals would probably not be in a condition to seek that relief from their own resources; but the aid of government may in this respect be afforded, in a way which will be consistent with the established order of things. The Secretary, from the information communicated to him, believing it to be probable that undue advantages had been taken, had conceived a plan for the purpose, of the following kind: That measures should be adopted for procuring the appointment of an agent or attorney, by the original claimants, or if deceased, by their legal representatives; that payment of the money should be deferred until this had been effected; that the amount of the sums due should then be placed in the hands of the proper officer for the purpose of payment; that a demand should be made upon him, on behalf of the original claimants, by their agent, and as a like demand would of course be made by the assignees, that the parties should be informed that a legal adjudication was necessary to ascertain the validity of their respective pretensions; and that in this state of things the Attorney-General should be directed either to prosecute or defend for the original claimants, as should appear to him most likely to insure justice. A step of this kind appeared to the Secretary to be warranted and dictated, as well by a due regard to the defenceless situation of the parties who may have been prejudiced, as by considerations resulting from the propriety of discouraging similar practices.

—To Washington, On Arrears of Pay. *Hamilton*, IV, 16-20.

Hamilton explicitly advised the public not to part with their securities by selling to speculators and he utilized the private Bank of New York to support government bonds, to encourage the bulls and punish the bears.

ADDRESS TO THE PUBLIC CREDITORS
By A Friend

September 1, 1790

It is probable that many of you are not sufficiently apprised of the advantages of your own situation, and that for want of judging rightly of it, and of your future prospects, you may be tempted to part with your securities much below their true value, and considerably below what it is probable they will sell for in eight or nine months from his time.

To guard you against an unnecessary sacrifice of your interests by a precipitate sale, I will now state to you, in a plain and concise way, what has been done for you in the course of the last session of Congress, and what you may reasonably expect. . . .

I return to the subject of the value of your securities. Their present price, if compared with that at which they were current before the establishment of the new Constitution, will be deemed to be *high*, and is as great as at this time could reasonably have been expected; but compared with their true value, and the solidity of footing on which they stand, is still far too low. The rise which has already taken place is an earnest to you of their probable future rise. Such of you who do not incline to be permanent holders will at least do well to postpone a sale till after March, when the first payment of interest is to be made. The effect of this on the price of securities must undoubtedly be very favorable, and you may then calculate on a better market.

The holders of State securities have still stronger reasons for keeping those they have, the price of which, in most of the States, is out of all proportion lower than that of the present securities of the United States, and must, in all probability, undergo a considerable change for the better, as soon as funds are actually appropriated for them, which is not now the case, but which must of course be so at the ensuing session of December. The present debt of the United States having been provided for out of the duties on imposts and tonnage only, seems to leave no doubt of the facility of devising the means of providing for the amount which has been assumed of the State debts.

—Address to the Public Creditors. *Hamilton,* VI, 632, 635.

August 7, 1791

I observe what you say respecting the quotation of my opinion. I was not unaware of the delicacy of giving any, and was sufficiently reserved until I perceived the extreme to which bank scrip, and with it other stock, was tending. But when I saw this I thought it advisable to speak out—for a bubble connected with any operation is, of all the enemies I have to fear, in my judgment the most formidable; and not only not to promote, but, as far as depends on me, to counteract, delusions, appears to me to be the only secure foundation on which to stand. I thought it expedient, therefore, to risk some thing in contributing to dissolve the charm.

—To Rufus King. *Hamilton,* V, 475-477.

August 15, 1791

Inclosed is a resolution of the Trustees of the Sinking Fund, appropriating a certain sum for the purchase of public debt, within certain limits therein specified; in consequence of that resolution I have concluded to apply one hundred and fifty thousand dollars towards purchases in the city of New York, and to ask you to undertake the execution of the business. In thus forbearing to employ some officer of the United States, and having recourse to your aid, I am governed by the consideration that your situation would lead to such an execution of the business as might at the same time best consist with the accommodation of the Bank of New York.

—To William Seton. Hamilton Papers, 1st ser.

August 16, 1791

. . . When you make a purchase, therefore, it will be proper that it should be understood that it is on account of the United States, but this need not precede the purchase; and it will be best that there should be no unnecessary demonstration, lest it should raise hopes beyond what will be realized. . . .

If there are any gentlemen who support the *funds* and others who *depress* them, I shall be pleased that your purchases may aid the *former*, —this in great confidence.

—To William Seton (Private) *Works*, IX, 492.

In Defense of Funding and Assumption

[1791]

There is yet another class of men, who, in all the stages of our republican system, either from desperate circumstances, or irregular ambition, or a mixture of both, will labor incessantly to keep the government in a troubled and unsettled state, to sow disquietudes in the minds of the people, and to promote confusion and change. Every republic at all times has its Catilines and its Caesars.

Men of this stamp, while in their hearts they scoff at the principles of liberty, while in their real characters they are arbitrary, persecuting, and intolerant, are in all their harangues and professions the most zealous; nay, if they are to be believed, the only friends to liberty. Mercenary and corrupt themselves, they are continually making a parade of their purity and disinterestedness, and heaping upon others charges of peculation and corruption. Extravagant and dissipated in their own affairs, they are always prating about public economy, and railing at the government for its pretended profusion. Conscious that as long as the confidence of the people shall be maintained in their tried and faithful servants, in men of real integrity and patriotism, their ambitious projects can never succeed, they leave no artifice unessayed, they spare no pains to destroy that confidence, and blacken the characters that stand in their way.

Convinced that as long as order and system in the public affairs can be maintained, their schemes can never be realized, they are constantly representing the means of that order and system as chains forged for the people. Themselves the only plotters and conspirators, they are for ever spreading tales of plots and conspiracies; always talking of the republican cause, and meaning nothing but the cause of themselves and their party; virtue and liberty constantly on their lips, fraud, usurpation, and tyranny in their hearts.

There is yet another class of opponents to the government and its administration, who are of too much consequence not to be mentioned: a sect of political doctors; a kind of POPES in government; standards of political orthodoxy, who brand with heresy all opinions but their own; men of sublimated imaginations and weak judgments; pretenders to profound knowledge, yet ignorant of the most useful of all sciences—the science of human nature; men who dignify themselves with the appellation of philosophers, yet are destitute of the first elements of true philosophy; lovers of paradoxes; men who maintain expressly that religion is not necessary to society, and very nearly that government itself is a nuisance; that priests and clergymen of all descriptions are worse than useless. Such men, the ridicule of any cause that they espouse, and the best witnesses to the goodness of that which they oppose, have no small share in the clamors which are raised, and in the dissatisfactions which are excited. . . .

Suspicions of the most flagitious prostitution and corruption in office, of improper connections with brokers and speculators to fleece the community, of the horrid depravity of promoting wars, and the shedding of human blood, for the sake of sharing collusively the emoluments of lucrative contracts, suspicions like these are, if possible, to be thrown upon men, the whole tenor of whose lives gives the lie to them; who, before they came into office, were never either *land*-jobbers, or stock-jobbers, or jobbers of any other kind; who can appeal to their fellow-citizens of every other party and description to attest that their reputations for probity are unsullied, that their conduct in all pecuniary concerns has been nicely correct and even exemplarily disinterested; who, it is notorious, have sacrificed and are sacrificing the interests of their families to their public zeal; who, whenever the necessity of resisting the machinations of the enemies of the public quiet will permit them to retire, will retire poorer than they came into office, and will have to resume under numerous disadvantages the pursuits which they before followed under every advantage. Shame, where is thy blush—if detraction so malignant as this can affront the public ear. Integrity, where is thy shield, where thy reward—if the poisonous breath of an unprincipled cabal can pollute that good name which thou incessantly toiled to deserve.

—"Vindication of the Funding System," No. 1. Draft in Hamilton's hand. Hamilton Papers, 1st ser.

[1791]

It is a curious phenomenon in political history (not easy to be paralleled), that a measure which has elevated the credit of the country from a state of absolute prostration to a state of exalted pre-eminence, should bring upon the authors of it reprobation and censure.

—"Vindication of the Funding System," No. 2. Draft in Hamilton's hand. Hamilton Papers, 1st ser.

[1791]

And yet this is the simple and exact state of the business. The whole of the debt embraced by the provisions of the funding system consisted of the unextinguished principal and arrears of interest of the debt which had been contracted by the United States in the course of the late war with Great Britain, and which remained uncancelled, and the principal and arrears of interest of the separate debts of the respective States contracted during the same period, which remained out-

standing and unsatisfied, relating to services and supplies for carrying on the war. Nothing more was done by that system than to incorporate these two species of debt into the mass, and to make for the whole one general, comprehensive provision.

There is, therefore, no arithmetic, no logic, by which it can be shown that the funding system has augmented the aggregate debt of the country. The sum total is manifestly the same; though the parts which were before divided are now united.

There is, consequently, no color for an assertion that the system in question either created any *new* debt, or made any addition to the *old.*

And it follows that the collective burthen upon the people of the United States must have been as great *without* as *with* the union of the different portions and descriptions of the debt. The only difference can be, that without it that burthen would have been otherwise distributed, and would have fallen with unequal weight instead of being equally borne as it now is.

These conclusions which have been drawn respecting the non-increase of the debt proceed upon the presumption that every part of the public debt, as well that of the States individually as that of the United States, was to have been honestly paid. . . .

Charity itself cannot avoid concluding from the language and conduct of some men (and some of them of no inconsiderable importance), that in their vocabularies *creditor* and *enemy* are synonymous terms, and that they have a laudable antipathy against every man to whom they owe money, either as individuals or as members of the society.

—"Vindication of the Funding System," No. 2.
Hamilton Papers, 1st ser.

[1791]

The principle which shall be assumed here is this, that the established *rules of morality and justice are applicable to nations as well as to individuals;* that the *former* as well as the *latter* are bound *to keep their promises; to fulfil their engagements to respect the rights of property* which others have acquired under contracts with them. Without this there is an end of all distinct ideas of right or wrong, justice or injustice, in relation to society or government. There can be no such thing as rights, no such thing as property or liberty; all the boasted advantages of a constitution of government vanish into air. Every thing must float on the variable and vague opinions of the governing party, of whomsoever composed. . . .

The treaties of the United States, the sacred rights of private property, have been too frequently sported with, from a too great facility in admitting exceptions to the maxims of public faith and the general rules of property. A desire to escape from this evil was a principal cause of the union which took place among good men to establish the national government. . . .

A nation is alike excusable in certain extraordinary cases for not observing a right or performing a duty, if the one or the other would involve a *manifest* and *great* national calamity. But here, also, an extreme case is intended; the calamity to be avoided must not only be evident and considerable—it must be such an one as is like to prove fatal to the nation, as threatens its existence, or at least its permanent welfare.

War, for instance, is almost always a national calamity, of a serious kind; but it ought often to be encountered in protection *even* of a *part* of the community injured or annoyed; or in performance of the condition of a defensive alliance with some other nation.

But if such special circumstances exist in either case, that the going to war would eminently endanger the existence or permanent welfare of the nation, it may excusably be forborne.

Of the second class of exceptions, the case of certain feudal rights, which once oppressed all Europe, and still oppress too great a part of it, may serve as an example; rights which made absolute slaves of a part of the community, and rendered the condition of the greatest proportion of the remainder not much more eligible.

These rights, though involving that of property, being contrary to the social order, and to the permanent welfare of society, were justifiably abolished in the instances in which abolitions have taken place, and may be abolished in all the remaining vestiges.

Wherever, indeed, a right of property is infringed for the general good, if the nature of the case admits of compensation, it ought to be made; but if compensation be impracticable, that impracticability ought not to be an obstacle to a clearly essential reform. . . .

A single glance will suffice to convince that the case of the debt of the United States was not one of those cases which could justify a clear infraction of the fundamental rules of good faith, and a clear invasion of rights of property acquired under the most unequivocal national stipulations.

—"Vindication of the Funding System," No. 3.
Hamilton, VII, 644-646.

January 23, 1792

. . . The equalizing of the condition of the citizens of every State, and exonerating those of the States most indebted, from partial burthens which would press upon them, in consequence of exertions in a common cause, is not completely fulfilled until the entire debt of every State, contracted in relation to the war, is embraced in one general and comprehensive plan. The inconvenience to the United States of disburthening the States which are still encumbered with considerable debts, would bear no proportion to the inconvenience which they would feel, if left to struggle with those debts, unaided. . . .

But there is a further reason of material weight for an immediate general assumption. Moneyed men, as well foreigners as citizens, through the expectation of an eventual assumption, or that, in some shape or other, a substantial provision will be made for the unassumed residue of the State debts, will be induced to speculate in the purchase of them. In proportion as the event is unsettled, or uncertain, the price of the article will be low, and the present proprietors will be under disadvantage in the sale. The loss to them in favor of the purchasers is to be regarded as an evil; and as far as it is connected with a transfer to foreigners, at an undervalue, it will be a national evil. By whatsoever authority an ultimate provision may be made, there will be an absolute loss to the community, equal to the total amount of such undervalue.

—"Loans." *Hamilton,* III, 291.

May 26, 1792

. . . When I accepted the office I now hold, it was under full persuasion, that from similarity of thinking, conspiring with personal goodwill, I should have the firm support of Mr. Madison, in the general course of my administration. Aware of the intrinsic difficulties of the situation, and of the powers of Mr. Madison, I do not believe I should have accepted under a different supposition. I have mentioned the similarity of thinking between that gentleman and myself. This was relative, not merely to the general principles of national policy and government, but to the leading points, which were likely to constitute questions in the administration of the finances. I mean, first, the expediency of funding the debt; second, the inexpediency of discrimination between original and present holders; third, the expediency of assuming the State debts.

As to the first point, the evidence of Mr. Madison's sentiments, at one period, is to be found in the address of Congress, of April twenty-sixth, seventeen hundred and eighty-three, which was planned by him, in conformity to his own ideas, and without any previous suggestions from the committee, and with his hearty co-operation in every part of the business. His conversations upon various occasions since have been expressive of a continuance in the same sentiment; nor, indeed, has he yet contradicted it, by any part of his official conduct. How far there is reason to apprehend a change in this particular, will be stated hereafter. As to the second part, the same address is an evidence of Mr. Madison's sentiments at the same period. And I had been informed that at a later period he had been, in the Legislature of Virginia, a strenuous and successful opponent of the principle of discrimination. Add to this, that a variety of conversations had taken place between him and myself, respecting the public debt, down to the commencement of the new government, in none of which had he glanced at the idea of a change of opinion. I wrote him a letter after my appointment, in the recess of Congress, to obtain his sentiments on the subject of the finances. In his answer, there is not a lisp of his new system.

As to the third point, the question of an assumption of the State debts by the United States was in discussion when the convention that framed the present government was sitting at Philadelphia, and in a long conversation which I had with Mr. Madison in an afternoon's walk, I well remember that we were perfectly agreed in the expediency and propriety of such a measure; though we were both of opinion that it would be more advisable to make it a measure of administration than an article of Constitution, from the impolicy of multiplying obstacles to its reception on collateral details.

Under these circumstances you will naturally imagine that it must have been matter of surprise to me when I was apprised that it was Mr. Madison's intention to oppose my plan on both the last-mentioned points. Before the debate commenced, I had a conversation with him on my report; in the course of which I alluded to the calculation I had made of his sentiments, and the grounds of that calculation. He did not deny them; but alleged in his justification that the very considerable alienation of the debt, subsequent to the periods at which he had opposed a discrimination, had essentially changed the state of the question; and that as to the assumption, he had contemplated it to take place as matters stood at the peace. . . .

It was not till the last session that I became unequivocally convinced of the following truth: "that Mr. Madison, co-operating with Mr. Jefferson, is at the head of a faction decidedly hostile to me and my administration; and actuated by views, in my judgment, subversive of the principles of good government and dangerous to the Union, peace, and happiness of the country."

—To Colonel Edward Carrington. *Works*, IX, 513-517.

[1795-98]

The true politician, on the contrary, takes human nature (and human society its aggregate) as he finds it, a compound of good and ill qualities, of good and ill tendencies, endued with powers and actuated by passions and propensities which blend enjoyment with suffering and make the causes of welfare the causes of misfortune.

With this view of human nature he will not attempt to warp or disturb from its natural direction, he will not attempt to promote its happiness by means to which it is not suited, he will not reject the employment of the means which constitute its bliss because they necessarily involve alloy and danger, but he will seek to promote his action according to the bias of his nature, to lead him to the development of his energies according to the scope of his passions, and erecting the social organization on this basis he will favor all those institutions and plans which tend to make men happy according to their natural bent, which multiply the sources of individual enjoyment and increase of national resources and strength, taking care to infuse in each case all the ingredients which can be devised as preventives or correctives of the evil which is the eternal concomitant of temporal blessing.

Thus, observing the immense importance of credit to the strength and security of nations, he will endeavor to obtain it for his own country in its highest perfection, by the most efficient means; yet not overlooking the abuses to which, like all other good things, it is liable, he will seek to guard against them by prompting a spirit of true national economy, by pursuing steadily, especially in a country which has no need of external acquisition, the maxims of justice, moderation, and peace, and by endeavoring to establish, as far as human inconstancy allows, certain fixed principles in the administration of the finances calculated to secure efficaciously the extinguishment of debt as fast at least as the public exigencies of the nation is [*sic*] likely to occasion the contracting of it. These, I can truly say, are the principles which have regulated every part of my conduct in my late office.

And as a first step to this great result, I proposed the *funding* of the public debt.

—"Defence of the Funding System." Draft in Hamilton's hand; dated in later hand. Hamilton Papers, 1st ser.

[1795-98]

It is the part of wisdom in a government, as well as in an individual, to guard against its own infirmities; and, having taken beforehand a comprehensive view of its duty and interest, to tie itself down by every constitutional precaution to the steady pursuit of them.

—"Defence of the Funding System." Hamilton Papers, 1st ser.

[1795-98]

It may be remarked that it is now a considerable time since the public stock has reached the desirable point and put an end to the excessive spirit of speculation. This, for some time past, has been far more active, even to intemperateness in other pursuits, in trading adventures and in lands. And it is curious to observe how little clamor there is against the spirit of speculation in its present direction; though it were not difficult to demonstrate that it were not less extravagant or as pernicious in the shape of land-jobbing than in that of stock-jobbing. But many of the noisy patriots who were not in condition to be stock-jobbers are land-jobbers, and have a becoming tenderness for this species of extravagance. And virtuous, sensible men, lamenting the partialities of all over-driven speculation, know at the same time that they are inseparable from the spirit and freedom of commerce and that the cure must result from the disease.

—"Defence of the Funding System." Hamilton Papers, 1st ser.

[1795-98]

But it has been contended that the case of our public debt was an extraordinary and peculiar case, justifying, on great principles of national justice and policy, a departure from common rules. The quantity of alloy in its original concoction, the extensive alienations at undervalues, the extreme point of depreciation for a certain period, the confused state of the debt by antecedent violations of contract and by the concession of partial advantages to particular descriptions of it, the impossibility of reinstating the primitive contracts which had been formerly violated, and the inequality of a full provision according to the new,—all these were urged or espoused as reasons for an arbitrary provision for the debt according to certain abstract notions of equity and right. It has been intimated that these heretics were divided into two principal classes: one which advocated a provision for the debt on the ground of a discrimination between original holders and alienees; another which advocated an equal provision for all at some arbitrary rate of interest inferior to the stipulated rates. . . .

There never was a doubt that if the idea of discrimination had obtained it would have resulted in a fraud on alienees without benefit to their alienors. A large proportion of those who supported the principle of discrimination clearly manifested that they meant to leave the difference in the public pocket.

—"Defence of the Funding System." Hamilton Papers, 1st ser.

[1795-98]

The assumption would tend to consolidate and secure public credit. This would happen from various causes.

If it had not taken place, there would have been a conflict of interests and feelings among the public creditors.

The creditors of certain States, from the impracticality, admitting a disposition, of making for them a provision equal to that which was made for the creditors of the United States, would naturally have felt jealousy and dissatisfaction. They would have considered it as unjust that their claims, equally meritorious, should be worse treated, and the sensibility in certain cases would have been aggravated by the reflection that the most productive resources, before exclusively enjoyed by the State Government and applied to their benefit, had been devoted to the General Government, and applied by it to the sole benefit of the national creditors.

This jealousy and dissatisfaction would have augmented the mass of dissatisfaction from other causes which would exist against an adequate provision for the general debt. The sources of such dissatisfaction have been stated, and it was certain that enmity to the government in some and the spirit of faction in others would make them engines for agitating the public mind. Such dissatisfactions in a popular government especially tend to jeopardize the security of the public creditors, and, consequently, of the public credit.

The assumption, by uniting the interests of public creditors of all descriptions, was calculated to produce an opposite effect. It brought into the field an anxiety to fortify the public opinion in opposition to the efforts of faction and of the *anti-proprietary* spirit, in favor of a just and reasonable provision for the debt and for the support of credit.

—"Defence of the Funding System," No. 2. Draft in Hamilton's hand. Hamilton Papers, 1st ser.

It is known that the relaxed conduct of the State Governments in regard to property and credit was one of the most serious diseases under which the body politic labored prior to the adoption of our present Constitution, and was a material cause of that state of public opinion which led to its adoption.

The Constitution of the United States contained guards against this evil. Its provisions inhibit to the State Governments [the power to make any thing but gold and silver coin a tender in payment of debts, or to pass any law impairing the obligation of contracts, which had been great engines of violating property,][1] destroying confidence and credit, and propagating public dishonor and private distress.

In the practice of the Federal Government it was wise to second the spirit of those provisions: [1, by avoiding examples of those very practices which were meant to be guarded against in the States; 2, by removing, as far as it could be constitutionally done, out of the way of the States, whatever would oblige or tempt to further tampering with faith, credit, and property.

The assumption was calculated to do this, and it is not one of its least merits.]

—"Defence of the Funding System," No. 2. Hamilton Papers, 1st ser.

The effect of energy and system is to vulgar and feeble minds a kind of magic which they do not comprehend, and thus they make false interpretation of the most obvious facts. The people of several parts of the State, relieved and happy by the effects of the assumption, execrate the measure and its authors, to which they owe the blessing.

—"Defence of the Funding System", No. 2. Hamilton Papers, 1st ser.

[1] Text in brackets not in draft. See *Works*, IX, 17-18.

1801

What is this funding system? It is nothing more nor less than the *pledging of adequate funds or revenues for paying the interest and for the gradual redemption of the principal* of that very debt which was the sacred price of independence. The country being unable to pay off the principal, what better could have been done? . . .

What have been the effects of this system? An extension of commerce and manufactures, the rapid growth of our cities and towns, the consequent prosperity of agriculture, and the advancement of the farming interest. All this was effected by giving life and activity to a capital in the public obligations, which was before dead, and by converting it into a powerful instrument of mercantile and other industrious enterprise.

—Address to the Electors of the State of New York. *Hamilton,* VII, 735, 736.

Reassurance to Washington

August 18, 1792

SIR:

I am happy to be able, at length, to send you answers to the objections which were communicated in your letter of the 29th of July.

They have unavoidably been drawn in haste, too much so, to do perfect justice to the subject, and have been copied just as they flowed from my heart and pen, without revision or correction. You will observe that here and there some severity appears. I have not fortitude enough always to hear with calmness, calumnies, which necessarily include me, as a principal agent in the measures censured, of the falsehood of which I have the most unqualified consciousness. I trust I shall always be able to bear, as I ought, imputations of errors of judgment; but I acknowledge that I cannot be entirely patient under charges which impeach the integrity of my public motives or conduct. I feel that I merit them in no degree; and expressions of indignation sometimes escape me, in spite of every effort to suppress them. I rely on your goodness for the proper allowances.

With the highest respect and the most affectionate attachment, I have the honor to be, sir, etc.

—To Washington. Hamilton Papers, 1st ser.

August 18, 1792

But whether the public debt shall be extinguished or not, within a moderate period, depends on the temper of the people. If they are rendered dissatisfied by misrepresentations of the measures of the government, the government will be deprived of an efficient command of the resources of the community toward extinguishing the debt. And thus those who clamor are likely to be the principal causes of protracting the existence of the debt. . . .

But if the Northern people who were originally greater creditors than the Southern, have become still more so as purchasers, is it any reason that an honorable provision should not be made for their debt? Or is the government to blame for having made it? Did the Northern people take their property by violence from the Southern, or did they purchase and pay for it?

It may be answered that they obtained considerable part of it by speculation, taking advantage of superior opportunities of information.

But admitting this to be true in all the latitude in which it is commonly stated, is a government to bend the general maxims of policy and to mould its measures according to the accidental course of private speculations? Is it to do this, or omit that, in cases of great national importance, because one set of individuals may gain, another lose, from unequal opportunities of information, from unequal degrees of resource, craft, confidence, or enterprise?

Moreover, there is much exaggeration in stating the manner of the alienation of the debt. The principal speculations in State debts, whatever may be pretended, certainly began after the promulgation of the plan for assuming by the report of the Secretary of the Treasury to the House of Representatives. The resources of individuals in this country are too limited to have admitted of much progress in purchases before the knowledge of that plan was diffused throughout the country. After that, purchasers and sellers were upon equal ground. If the purchasers speculated upon the sellers, in many instances the sellers speculated upon the purchasers. Each made his calculation of chances, and founded upon it an exchange of money for certificates. It has turned out generally that the buyer had the best of the bargain, but the seller got the value of his commodity according to his estimate of it, and probably in a great number of instances more. This shall be explained.

It happened that Mr. Madison and some other distinguished characters of the South started in opposition to the assumption. The high opinion entertained of them made it be taken for granted in that quarter that the opposition would be successful. The securities quickly rose, by means of purchases, beyond their former prices. It was imagined that they would soon return to their old station by a rejection of the proposition for assuming. And the certificate-holders were eager to part with them at their current prices, calculating on a loss to the purchasers from their future fall. This representation is not conjectural; it is founded on information from respectable and intelligent Southern characters, and may be ascertained by inquiry.

Hence it happened that the inhabitants of the Southern States sustained a considerable loss by the opposition to the assumption from Southern gentlemen, and their too great confidence in the efficacy of that opposition.

Further, a great part of the debt which has been purchased by

Northern and Southern citizens has been at higher prices—in numerous instances beyond the true value. In the late delirium of speculation large sums were purchased at twenty-five per cent. above par and upward.

The Southern people, upon the whole, have not parted with their property for nothing. They parted with it voluntarily, in most cases, upon fair terms, without surprise or deception—in many cases for more than its value. 'Tis their own fault if the purchase money has not been beneficial to them; and the presumption is, that it has been so in a material degree.

—To Washington, "Objections and Answers Respecting the Administration of the Government." Hamilton Papers, 1st ser.

Avoiding an Excessive Public Debt

September 15, 1792

Much declamation has been indulged against certain characters, who are charged with advocating the pernicious doctrine, that "*public debts are public blessings*," and with being friends to a perpetuation of the public debt of the country. Among these characters, if the Secretary of the Treasury has not been named, he has been pretty plainly alluded to. It is proper to examine what foundation there is, then, for those charges.

That officer, it is very certain, explicitly maintained, that the *funding* of the existing debt of the United States would render it a national blessing; and a man has only to travel through the United States with his eyes open, and to observe the invigoration of industry in every branch, to be convinced that the position is well founded. But, whether right or wrong, it is quite a different thing from maintaining, as a general proposition, that a public debt is a blessing. Particular and temporary circumstances might render that advantageous at one time, which at another might be hurtful.

It is known that prior to the Revolution, a great part of the circulation was carried on by paper money; that in consequence of the events of the Revolution, that resource was in a great measure destroyed, by being discredited, and that the same events had destroyed a large proportion of the moneyed and mercantile capital of the country, and of personal property generally. It was natural to think that the chasm created by these circumstances required to be supplied, and a just theory was sufficient to demonstrate, that a funded debt would answer the end.

To infer that it would have such an effect, was no more to maintain the general doctrine of "*public debts being public blessings*," than the saying, that paper emissions, by the authority of Government, were useful in the early periods of the country, was the maintaining that they would be useful in all the future stages of its progress.

—"Fact", in *Gazette of the U. S.*, Sept. 15, 1792.

September 15, 1792

Extracts from a report of the Secretary of the Treasury relative to additional supplies for carrying on the Indian war, presented the 16th of March, 1792.

"The result of mature reflection is, in the mind of the Secretary, a strong conviction that the last of the three expedients which have been mentioned (that was the raising of the sum required by taxes) is to be preferred to either of the other two."

"Nothing can more interest the national credit and prosperity than a constant and systematic attention to husband all the means previously possessed for extinguishing the present debt, and to avoid, as much as possible, the incurring of any new debt." . . . A certain description of men are for getting out of debt, yet are against all taxes for raising money to pay it off; they are among the foremost for carrying on war, and yet will have neither loans nor taxes. They are alike opposed to what creates debt and to what avoids it.

In the first case their meaning is not difficult to be divined; in the last it would puzzle any man, not endowed with the gift of second sight, to find it out, unless it be to quarrel with and pull down every man who will not consent to walk in their leading strings; or to throw all things into confusion.

—"Fact," in *Gazette of the U. S.*, Sept. 15, 1792.

January 16, 1795

On the first point it has been argued that, supposing a steady preservation of its faith by the Government, it is indifferent to the creditor whether his demand stands upon the basis of an annual provision, or upon that of mortgaged funds.

This is to substitute theory to fact. As well with regard to a government as to an individual, there is, in the nature of things, an *intrinsic* difference between the value of a debt bottomed on mortgaged funds, and that of a debt resting on what is called, in the one case, and may be called in the other, personal security. The degree of this difference, and some of the circumstances on which it depends, may be different in the two cases, but the reality of its existence can be denied in neither.

Government, being administered by men, is naturally, like individuals, subject to particular impulses, passions, prejudices, vices; of course to inconstancy of views and mutability of conduct.

A kind of property, of which the essence is contract, must necessarily, therefore, be more or less valuable, because more or less secure, in proportion as it is little or much exposed to the influence of that inconstancy or that mutability.

If a provision is to be made by a new resolution every year, that resolution, being always liable to be affected by momentary circumstances, is always casual.

If made once for all, it continues, of course, unless revoked by some positive act, and has for that reason a moral certainty of stability.

But why, it might be asked, if a disposition unfaithful to the public engagements, or unfriendly to the public credit, should exist, would it not operate to produce a violation of a provision made, as well as to prevent the making of one?

The two things are widely different. To *undo*, which is to *act*, and in such a case *to act with violence*, requires more enterprise and vigor, and presupposes greater energy, or a stronger impulse, than *not to do* or to forbear to act. This is particulraly true where a number of wills is to concur. Many men who will not rouse to the effort, or encounter the responsibility of doing mischief by positive acts, will readily enough slide into it by a negative conduct—that is, by omitting to act. Many men, merely from easiness of temper or want of active fortitude, will suffer evil to take place which they neither desire nor would themselves commit. In collective bodies, votes are necessary to ACTION: absences may produce INACTION. It often happens that a majority of voices could not be had to a resolution to undo or reverse a thing once done, which there would not be a majority of voices *to do*.

This reasoning acquires tenfold force when applied to a complex government like ours; that is, to a government distributed into departments, acting through different organs, which must concur to give it motion; as, in our Constitution, the HOUSE OF REPRESENTATIVES, the SENATE, and the PRESIDENT.

In delicate and difficult cases, whether to issue in good or ill, a suspension of action is far more natural to such a government than action. . . .

Hence the value of property in public debt, which rests on specified and competent funds, firmly pledged for the satisfaction of the creditor, is intrinsically greater, and to a considerable extent, than that of property in public debt, which depends on annual provision. Hence, too, a creditor to whom such a pledge was not stipulated, may be justly said to have received a compensation for the relinquishment of a portion of his interest. . . .

There is no sentiment which can better deserve the serious attention of the legislators of a country than the one expressed in the speech of the President, which indicates the danger to every government from the progressive accumulation of debt. A tendency to it is, perhaps, the natural disease of all governments; and it is not easy to conceive any thing more likely than this to lead to great and convulsive revolutions of empire.

On the one hand, the exigencies of a nation, creating new causes of expenditure, as well from its own, as from the ambition, rapacity, injustice, intemperance, and folly of other nations, proceed in increasing and rapid succession. On the other, there is a general propensity in those who administer the affairs of a government, founded in the constitution of man, to shift off the burden from the present to a future day—a propensity which may be expected to be strong in proportion as the form of a state is popular.

To extinguish a debt which exists, and to avoid the contracting more, are ideas always favored by public feeling and opinion: but to pay taxes for the one or the other purpose, which are the only means of avoiding the evil, is always, more or less, unpopular. These contradictions are in human nature; and happy, indeed, would be the lot of a country that should ever want men ready to turn them to the account of their own popularity, or to some other sinister account.

Hence, it is no uncommon spectacle to see the same men clamoring for occasions of expense, when they happen to be in unison with the present humor of the community, whether well or ill directed, declaiming against a public debt, and for the reduction of it as an abstract thesis; yet vehement against every plan of taxation which is proposed to discharge old debts, or to avoid new, by the defraying expenses of exigencies as they emerge. . . .

True patriotism and genuine policy cannot, it is respectfully presumed, be better demonstrated by those of the United States, at the present juncture, than by improving efficaciously, the very favorable situation in which they stand, for extinguishing, with reasonable celerity, the actual debt of the country, and for laying the foundation of a system which may shield posterity from the consequences of the usual improvidence and selfishness of its ancestors, and which, if possible, may give IMMORTALITY TO PUBLIC CREDIT. . . .

The first report of the Secretary on the subject of the public debt, of the 9th of January, 1790, suggests the idea of "incorporating, as a *fundamental maxim* in the system of public credit of the United States, that the *creation* of debt should *always* be *accompanied with the means of extinguishment;* that this is the *true secret for rendering public credit immortal,* and that it is difficult to conceive a situation in which there may not be *an adherence to the maxim*"; and it expresses "an unfeigned solicitude, that *this* may be attempted by the United States, and that they may commence their measures for the establishment of credit with the observance of it."[1]

[1] It is understood that the Parliament of Great Britain has, within the last four years, formally adopted, as a *standing rule,* the principle of *incorporating, with the creation of debt, the means of extinguishment.* How much easier must the execution of this important principle be to the United States, than to a nation which, before it began, had so deeply mortgaged its resources. Let the United States never have to regret, hereafter, that they postponed too long so provident a precaution.

No opportunity has been lost by the Secretary, as far as he could contribute to the event, to reduce this principle to practice; and important steps towards it have been, from time to time, taken by the Legislature.

. . . The *inviolable* application of an adequate sinking fund is the only practicable security against an excessive accumulation of debt, and the essential basis of a permanent national credit.

Experience has shown, in countries the most attentive to the principles of credit, that a simple appropriation of the sinking fund is not a complete barrier against its being diverted, when immediate exigencies press. The causes which have been stated with another view, tempt the administrators of government to lay hold of this resource rather than to resort to new taxes. This indicates the utility of endeavoring to give, by additional sanctions, inviolability to the fund. . . .

If a nation can find embarrassment in creating the revenues requisite on this scale, it must arise from her having reached a stage when, from the neglect of the principle now inculcated, the mass of her debt has become so enormous as to strain her faculties in order to make a provision for it.

The United States are in a situation altogether different. An inspection of the list of their revenues discovers that they have a large field of resource unexplored. Their youth, and large tracts of unsettled lands, and land in the infancy of improvement, assure them a great and rapid increase of means. Even their actual revenues, without additions, must, with the progress of the country, considerably increase. And, though war may interrupt, the temporary interruption being removed by the restoration of peace, their increasing productiveness, suspended for a time, must resume its vigor and growth. In a given number of years a considerable augmentation is certain.

The government of this country may, therefore, adopt, fearless of future embarrassment, a principle which, being adopted, will ultimately furnish resources for future exigencies, without an increase of burthen to the community.

To explain this last idea: It will readily be perceived that the funds pledged for paying the interest and sinking the principal of a portion of the debt existing or created at a particular time, will, within a certain period, extinguish that portion of debt.

They will then be liberated, and will be ready for any future use, either to defray current expenditures, or be the basis of new loans, as circumstances may dictate. And, after a course of time, it is a reasonable presumption, that the funds, so successively liberated, will be adequate to new exigencies, as they occur. . . .

Credit, public and private, is of the greatest consequence to every country. Of this, it might be emphatically called the invigorating principle. No well-informed man can cast a retrospective eye over the progress of the United States, from their infancy to the present period, without being convinced that they owe, in a great degree, to the fostering influence of credit, their present mature growth. This credit has been of a mixed nature, mercantile and public, foreign and domestic. . . .

There can be no time, no state of things, in which credit is not essential to a nation, especially as long as nations in general continue to use it as a resource in war. It is impossible for a country to contend, on equal terms, or to be secure against the enterprises of other nations, without being able equally with them to avail itself of this important resource; and to a young country, with moderate pecuniary capital, and not a very various industry, it is still more necessary than to countries more advanced in both. A truth not less weighty for being obvious and frequently noticed. . . .

But credit is not only one of the main pillars of the public safety; it is among the principal engines of useful enterprise and internal improvement. As a substitute for capital, it is a little less useful than gold or silver, in agriculture, in commerce, in the manufacturing and mechanic arts.

If the individual capital of this country has become more adequate to its exigencies than formerly, it is because individuals have found new resources in the public *credit*—in the funds to which that has given value and activity. Let public credit be prostrated, and the deficiency will be greater than before. Public and private credit are closely allied, if not inseparable. There is, perhaps, no example of the one being in a flourishing, where the other was in a bad state. A shock to public credit would, therefore, not only take away the additional means which it has furnished, but by the derangements, disorders, distrusts, and false principles which it would engender and disseminate, would diminish the antecedent resources of private credit.

If the United States observe, with delicate caution, the maxims of credit, as well toward foreigners as their own citizens, in connection with the general principles of an upright, stable, and systematic administration, the strong attractions which they present to foreign capital will be likely to insure them the command of as much as they may want, in addition to their own, for every species of internal amelioration. . . .

Credit is an *entire* thing. Every part of it has the nicest sympathy with every other part; wound one limb, and the whole tree shrinks and decays. . . .

It is in vain to attempt to disparage credit by objecting to its abuses. What is there not liable to abuse or misuse? The precious metals, those great springs of labor and industry, are also the ministers of extravagance, luxury, and corruption. Commerce, the nurse of agriculture and manufactures, if overdriven, leads to bankruptcy and distress. A fertile soil, the principal source of human comfort, not unfrequently begets indolence and effeminacy. Even liberty itself, degenerating into licentiousness, produces a frightful complication of ills, and works its own destruction.

It is wisdom, in every case, to cherish whatever is useful, and guard against its abuse. It will be the truest policy of the United States to give all possible energy to public credit, by a firm adherence to its strictest maxims; and yet to avoid the ills of an excessive employment of it by true economy and system in the public expenditures; by steadily cultivating peace; and by using sincere, efficient, and persevering endeavors to diminish present debts, prevent the accumulation of new, and secure the discharge, within a reasonable period, of such as it may be at any time matter of necessity to contract.

—Final, or Second, Report on the Public Credit —to the U. S. Senate. *American State Papers* V, 329-338.

April 10, 1795

. . . The opinion which some entertain is altogether a false one—that it is more important to maintain our credit abroad than at home. The latter is far the most important nursery of resources, and, consequently, far the most important to be inviolably maintained. A failure here would be the more material, because it would argue want of means, and could not shelter itself under the plea of temporary embarrassments from external causes, and because it would derange our whole internal economy.

—To Oliver Wolcott. Hamilton Papers, 1st ser.

Hamilton regarded the fiscal policies of Jefferson and his Secretary of the Treasury, Albert Gallatin, as a repudiation of his own program. Jefferson was committed to retrenchment. His administration cut taxes to the bone and reduced the national debt by almost fifty per cent. Once more Hamilton took up his pen to warn of the dangers of this course.

December 26, 1801

What, then, are we to think of the ostentatious assurance in the Inaugural Speech as to the preservation of PUBLIC FAITH? Was it given merely to amuse with agreeable but deceptive sounds? Is it possible that it could have been intended to conceal the insidious design of aiming a deadly blow at a system which was opposed in its origin, and has been calumniated in every stage of its progress?

Alas! how deplorable will it be, should it ever become proverbial, that a President of the United States, like the *Weird Sisters* in *Macbeth*, "*Keeps his word of promise to our ear, but breaks it to our hope!*"[1]

—"Lucius Crassus," No. IV. Works, VIII, 270.

[1] *Hamilton*, VII, 761-762, renders it, "but breaks it to the sense."

A Sound Tax Program

From the early years of the Revolution Hamilton advocated conferring upon the Federal government both the power to tax and to collect taxes. To him, this was the keystone of the national structure.

Principles and Objectives of Taxation

December 16, 1782

The Committee, consisting of Mr. Hamilton, Mr. Madison, and Mr. Fitzsimmons, to whom was referred the letter of the thirtieth of November, from the Honorable William Bradford, Speaker of the lower House of Assembly of the State of Rhode Island, containing, under three heads, the reasons of that State for refusing their compliance with the recommendation of Congress for a duty on imports and prize goods, report:

That they flatter themselves the State, on a reconsideration of the objections they have offered, with a candid attention to the arguments which stand in opposition to them, will be induced to retract their dissent, convinced that the measure is supported on the most solid grounds of equal justice, policy, and general utility. The following observations, contrasted with each head of the objections successively, will furnish a satisfactory answer to the whole.

First Objection.—"That the proposed duty would be unequal in its operation, bearing hardest upon the most commercial States, and so would press peculiarly hard upon that State which draws its chief support from commerce."

The most common experience, joined to the concurrent opinions of the ablest commercial and political observers, have established, beyond controversy, this general principle: "That every duty on imports is incorporated with the price of the commodity, and ultimately paid by the consumer, with a profit on the duty itself as a compensation to the merchant for the advance of his money."

The merchant considers the duty demanded by the State on the imported article in the same light with freight or any similar charge, and, adding it to the original cost, calculates his profit on the aggregate sum. It may happen that, at particular conjunctures, where the markets are overstocked, and there is a competition among the sellers, this may not be practicable; but, in the general course of trade, the demand for consumption preponderates; and the merchant can with ease indemnify himself, and even obtain a profit on the advance. As a consumer, he pays his share of the duty, but it is no further a burthen upon him. The consequence of the principle laid down is that every class of the community bears its share of the duty in proportion to its consumption; which last is regulated by the comparative wealth of the respective classes, in conjunction with their habits of expense or frugality. The rich and luxurious pay in proportion to their riches and luxury; the poor and parsimonious, in proportion to their poverty and parsimony. A chief excellence of this mode of revenue is that it preserves a just measure to the abilities of individuals, promotes frugality, and taxes extravagance. The same reasoning, in our situation, applies to the intercourse between two States: if one imports and the other does not, the latter must be supplied by the former. The duty, being transferred to the price of the commodity, is no more a charge on the importing State for what is consumed in the other, than it is a charge on the merchant for what is consumed by the farmer or artificer.

—Report on Impost Duty. *Works*, II, 179-181.

December 16, 1782

The principal thing to be consulted for the advancement of commerce is to promote exports. All impediments to these, either by way of prohibition, or by increasing the prices of native commodities, decreasing by that means their sale and consumption at foreign markets, are injurious. Duties on exports have this operation. For the same reason taxes on possessions and the articles of our own growth or manufacture, whether in the form of a land-tax, excise, or any other, are more hurtful to trade than impost duties. The tendency of all such taxes is to increase the prices of those articles which are the objects of exportation, and to enable others to undersell us abroad. The farmer, if he pays a heavy land-tax, must endeavor to get more for the products of his farm; the mechanic and laborer, if they find the necessaries of life grow dearer by an excise, must endeavor to exact higher wages: and these causes will produce an increase of prices within, and operate against foreign commerce.

It is not, however, to be inferred that the whole revenue ought to be drawn from imports; all extremes are to be rejected. The chief thing to be attended to is that the weight of the taxes fall not too heavily, in the first instance, upon particular parts of the community. A judicious distribution to all kinds of taxable property, is a first principle in taxation. The tendency of these observations is only to show that taxes on possessions, on articles of our own growth and manufacture, are more prejudicial to trade than duties on imports.

—Report on Impost Duty. *Works*, II, 190-191.

February 24, 1783

I am of opinion that the article of the Confederation[1] itself was ill-judged. In the first place I do not believe there is any general repre-

[1] The 8th article provided that expenses for war, defense, or general welfare were to be defrayed out of a common treasury from taxes levied by the state legislatures, the proportion each state was to pay to be based upon the value of granted or surveyed land.—Ed.

sentative of the wealth of a nation, the criterion of its ability to pay taxes. There are only two that can be thought of—*land* and *numbers*.

The revenues of the United Provinces (general and particular) were computed, before the present war, to more than half as much as those of Great Britain. The extent of their territory is not one fourth part as great, their population less than a third. The comparison is still more striking between those provinces and the Swiss Cantons, in both of which extent of territory and population are nearly the same, and yet the revenues of the former are five times as large as those of the latter; nor could any efforts of taxation bring them to any thing like a level. . . .

The truth is, the ability of a country to pay taxes depends on infinite combinations of physical and moral causes which can never be accommodated to any general rule—climate, soil, productions, advantages for navigation, government, genius of the people, progress of arts and industry, and an endless variety of circumstances. The diversities are sufficiently great in these States to make an infinite difference in their relative wealth, the proportion of which can never be found by any common measure whatever.

The only possible way, then, of making them contribute to the general expense in an equal proportion to their means, is by general taxes imposed under Continental authority.

—To Governor Clinton. Hamilton's hand. Hamilton Papers, 1st ser.

February 17, 1787

Theoretical and practical financiers have agreed in condemning the arbitrary in taxation. By the arbitrary is meant the leaving the amount of tax to be paid by each person to the discretion of the officers employed in the management of the revenue. It is indeed another word for assessment, where all is left to the *discretion* of the assessors. . . .

He would not say that the practice was contrary to the provisions of our Constitution; but it was certainly repugnant to the genius of our government. What is the power of the supervisors and assessors, but a power to tax in detail, while the Legislature taxes in gross? Is it proper to transfer so important a trust from the hands of the Legislature to the officers of the particular districts? Equality and certainty are the two great objects to be aimed at in taxation.

—Speech in the New York Assembly. *Works*, VIII, 34-35.

March 22, 1787

(Motion for laying £13,000 tax on New York County.)

. . . He asked if it was justice that city and county of New York, which was not a tenth part of the value or population of the State, should bear one fourth of its burdens. He hoped this would be considered, and no partiality exhibited by the Legislature.

—Speech in the New York Assembly. *Works*, VIII, 40.

[c. 1791]

In Massachusetts taxation was carried still further, even to a degree too burdensome for the comfortable condition of the citizens. This may have been partly owing to that unskilfulness [*sic*] which was the common attribute of the State administration of finance, but it was still more owing to the real weight of the taxes. The insurrection[1] was in a great degree the offspring of this pressure.

—"Defence of the Funding System", II. Hamilton Papers, 1st ser.

December 5, 1791

There are certain species of taxes, which are apt to be oppressive to different parts of the community, and, among other ill effects, have a very unfriendly aspect towards manufactures. All poll or capitation taxes are of this nature. They either proceed according to a fixed rate, which operates unequally and injuriously to the industrious poor, or they vest a discretion, in certain officers, to make estimates and assessments, which are necessarily vague, conjectural, and liable to abuse. They ought, therefore, to be abstained from in all but cases of distressing emergency.

All such taxes (including all taxes on occupations) which proceed according to the amount of capital supposed to be employed in a business, or of profits supposed to be made in it, are unavoidably hurtful to industry.

—Report on Manufactures. Hamilton Papers, 2nd ser.

Hamilton's Tax Program

While Hamilton favored a national debt, he also believed that so far as practicable the operating expenses of the government should be paid out of taxes. In his Report on the Public Credit (December 13, 1790) the Secretary of the Treasury recommended various excise taxes, including a tax on the domestic manufacture of distilled liquor, as a means of supplementing the revenues obtained from the tariff. Earlier he had recommended a variety of excise taxes, including one on tobacco, a tax on auction sales, and a license tax to practice law.

March 4, 1790

. . . [Tobacco] being an absolute superfluity, is the fairest object of

[1] Shays' Rebellion.—Ed.

revenue that can be imagined, and may be so regulated as, in no degree, to injure either the growth or manufacture of the commodity.

—To House of Representatives. *Hamilton,* III, 51.

December 13, 1790

The Secretary, however, begs leave to remark, that there appear to him two leading principles, one or the other of which must necessarily characterize whatever plan may be adopted. One of them makes the *security* of the *revenue* to depend chiefly on the *vigilance* of the *public officers;* the other rests it essentially on the *integrity* of the *individuals* interested to avoid the payment of it.

The first is the basis of the plan submitted by the Secretary; the last has pervaded most if not all the systems which have been hitherto practised upon in different parts of the United States. The oaths of the dealers have been almost the only security for their compliance with the laws.

It cannot be too much lamented that these have been found an inadequate dependence. But experience has, on every trial, manifested them to be such. Taxes or duties relying for their collection on that security wholly, or almost wholly, are uniformly unproductive. And they cannot fail to be unequal, as long as men continue to be discriminated by unequal portions of rectitude. The most conscientious will pay most; the least conscientious least.

The impulse of interest, always sufficiently strong, acts with peculiar force in matters of this kind, in respect to which a loose mode of thinking is too apt to prevail. The want of a habit of appreciating properly the nature of the public rights renders that impulse in such cases too frequently an overmatch for the sense of obligation, and the evasions which are perceived, or suspected to be practised by some, prompt others to imitation, by the powerful motive of self-defence. They infer that they must follow the example, or be unable to maintain an advantageous competition in the business—an alternative very perplexing to all but men of exact probity, who are thereby rendered, in a great measure, victims to a principle of legislation which does not sufficiently accord with the bias of human nature. And thus the laws become sources of discouragement and loss to honest industry, and of profit and advantage to perjury and fraud. It is a truth that cannot be kept too constantly in view, that all revenue laws which are so constructed as to involve a lax and defective execution, are instruments of oppression to the most meritorious part of those on whom they immediately operate, and of additional burthens on the community at large. . . .

Among other substantial reasons which recommend, as a provision for the public debt, duties upon articles on consumption, in preference to taxes on houses and lands, is this: It is very desirable, if practicable, to reserve the latter fund for objects and occasions which will more immediately interest the sensibility of the whole community, and more directly affect the public safety.

—Report on the Public Credit, Hamilton Papers, 1st ser.

From time to time Hamilton was called upon to justify both the whisky tax, which at its inception and again within a few years, was defied by western distillers, as well as his basic program of keeping the national debt within moderate dimensions and relying as much as possible on taxes.

March 6, 1792

Duties on articles of internal production and manufacture form in every country the principal sources of revenue. Those on imported articles can only be carried to a certain extent, without defeating their object, by operating either as prohibitions, or as bounties upon smuggling. They are, moreover, in some degree temporary; for, as the growth of manufactures diminishes the quantum of duty on imports, the public revenue, ceasing to arise from that source, must be derived from articles which the national industry has substituted for those previously imported. If the Government cannot then resort to internal means for the additional supplies which the exigencies of every nation call for, it will be unable to perform its duty, or, even to preserve its existence. The community must be unprotected, and the social compact be dissolved. . . .

As to the circumstance of equality, it may safely be affirmed to be impracticable to devise a tax which shall operate with exact equality upon every part of the community. Local and other circumstances will inevitably create disparities, more or less great.

Taxes on consumable articles have, upon the whole, better pretensions to equality than any other. If some of them fall more heavily on particular parts of the community, others of them are chiefly borne by other parts. And the result is an equalization of the burthen as far as it is attainable. Of this class of taxes it is not easy to conceive one which can operate with greater equality than a tax on distilled spirits. There appears to be no article, as far as the information of the Secretary goes, which is an object of more equal consumption throughout the United States. . . .

As far as habits of less moderation, in the use of distilled spirits, should produce inequality anywhere, it would certainly not be a reason with the Legislature either to repeal or lessen a tax, which, by rendering the article dearer, might tend to restrain too free an indulgence of such habits.

It is certainly not obvious how this tax can operate particularly unequally upon the part of the country in question. As a general rule it is a true one, that duties on articles of consumption fall on the consumers, by being added to the price of the commodity. This is illustrated, in the present instance, by facts. Previous to the law laying a duty on homemade spirits, the price of whiskey was about thirty-eight cents; it is now about fifty-six cents. Other causes may have contributed in some degree to this effect, but it is evidently to be ascribed chiefly to the duty.

Unless, therefore, the inhabitants of the counties which have been mentioned are greater consumers of spirits than those of other parts of the country, they cannot pay a greater proportion of the tax. If they are, it is their interest to become less so. It depends on themselves, by diminishing the consumption, to restore equality.

The argument that they are obliged to convert their grain into spirits, in order to transportation to distant markets, does not prove the point alleged. The duty on all they send to those markets will be paid by the purchasers. They will still pay only upon their own consumption. . . .

It is unnecessary to urge to the House of Representatives how essential it must be to the execution of the law, in a manner effectual to the purposes of the Government and satisfactory to the community, to secure by competent though moderate rewards the *diligent services* of respectable and trustworthy characters.

—Original Signed Report of the Secretary of the Treasury on the difficulties in the Execution of the Act laying duties on distilled Spirits. (Endorsed: "Ordered to lie on the table"). Hamilton Papers, 2nd ser.

March 16, 1792

Nothing can more interest the national credit and prosperity than a constant and systematic attention to husband all the means previously possessed for extinguishing the present debt, and to avoid as much as possible the incurring of any new debt.

Necessity alone, therefore, can justify the application of any of the public property, other than the annual revenues, to the current service, or to the temporary and casual exigencies of the country, or the contracting of an additional debt, by loans, to provide for those exigencies.

Great emergencies, indeed, might exist, in which loans would be indispensable. But the occasions which will justify them must be truly of that description.

The present is not of such a nature. The sum to be provided is not of magnitude enough to furnish the plea of necessity.

Taxes are never welcome to a community. They seldom fail to excite uneasy sensations, more or less extensive. Hence, a too strong propensity in the governments of nations to anticipate and mortgage the resources of posterity, rather than encounter the inconveniences of an increase of taxes.

—Original Report of the Secretary of the Treasury relative to the additional supplies for the ensuing year. (Endorsed: 17 March, 1792, Committed to a Committee of the Whole House on Friday Next. 7th April 1792, Resolutions agreed to and Bill ordered). Hamilton Papers, 2nd ser.

November 30, 1792

Loans, from time to time, equal to the sums annually redeemable, and bottomed on the same revenues, which are now appropriated to pay the interest upon those sums, offer themselves as one expedient which may be employed with a degree of advantage. As there is a probability of borrowing at a lower rate of interest, a material saving would result; and even this resource, if none better could be devised, ought not to be neglected.

But it is obvious that to rely upon this resource alone would be to do little towards the final exoneration of the nation. To stop at that point would consequently be neither provident nor satisfactory. The interests as well as the expectations of the Union require something more effectual.

The establishment of additional revenues is the remaining resource. This, if the business is to be undertaken in earnest, is unavoidable. And a full confidence may reasonably be entertained, that the community will see with satisfaction the employment of those means which alone can be effectual for accomplishing an end in itself so important and so much an object of general desire. It cannot fail to be universally felt that, if the end is to be attained, the necessary means must be employed.

—To the House of Representatives. *Hamilton*, III, 339-340.

The Jeffersonian Republicans were committed to economies. Increasing customs receipts made it possible to repeal all excises in 1802 except a tax on salt, which was later dropped. Hamilton viewed with alarm the abandonment of his tax program. The new military commitments of the nation by 1812 clearly vindicated Hamilton's prudence and foresight.

December 21, 1801

The next most prominent feature in the message [of President Jefferson] is the proposal to abandon at once all the internal revenue of the country. The motives avowed for this astonishing scheme are, that "There is *reasonable ground of confidence* that this part of the revenue may now be safely dispensed with. . . .

How is this reconcilable with the wanton and unjust clamors heretofore vented against those who projected and established our present system of public credit; charging them with a design to perpetuate the debt, under the pretext that a *public debt was a public blessing?* It is not to be forgotten, that in these clamors Mr. Jefferson liberally participated! Now, it seems, the tone is entirely changed. The past administrations, who had so long been calumniated by the imputation of that pernicious design, are of a sudden discovered to have done too much for the speedy discharge of the debt, and its duration is to be prolonged, by throwing away a part of the fund destined for its prompt redemption. Wonderful union of consistency and wisdom?

—"Lucius Crassus," No. 2. *Hamilton*, VII, 749, 752.

December 24, 1801

Had our laws been less provident than they have been, yet must it give us a very humble idea of the talents of our President as a statesman, to find him embarrassed between an absolute abandonment of revenue, and an inconvenient accumulation of treasure. Pursuing the doctrine professed by his *sect*, that our public debt is a national *curse*, which cannot too promptly be removed, and adhering to the assurance which he has virtually given,[1] that a sponge, *the favorite instrument*, shall not be employed for the purpose, how has it happened that he should have overlooked the simple and obvious expedient of using the supposed excess of income as a remedy for so great a mischief? . . .

But admitting it to be clearly ascertained, that the fund is greater than is requisite to extinguish the debt with convenient celerity, does it follow that the excess, if retained, must be suffered to accumulate, and that no different method could have been found to employ it which would have been productive of adequate utility?

Whatever diversity of opinion there may be with regard to military and naval preparations, for the defence and security of the country, there are some things in which all well-informed and reflecting men unite. In order that upon the breaking out of a war there may be a sufficient supply of warlike implements, together with the means of speedily creating a navy, arsenals, foundries, dock-yards, magazines (especially of materials for the construction and equipment of ships), are by all deemed eligible objects of public care. To provide for these objects upon a competent, though moderate scale, will be attended with expense so considerable, as to leave nothing to spare from the amount of our present income. . . .

In addition to objects of national security, there are many purposes of great public utility to which the revenues in question might be applied. The improvement of the communications between the different parts of our country is an object well worthy of the national

[1] One of the essential principles of government is, "*the honest payment of our debts and the sacred preservation of the public faith*."—Inaugural Speech.

purse, and one which would abundantly repay *to labor* the portion of its *earnings*, which may have been borrowed for the purpose. To provide roads, and bridges is within the direct purview of the Constitution. In many parts of the country, especially in the Western Territory, a matter in which the Atlantic states are equally interested, aqueducts and canals would also be fit subjects of pecuniary aid from the general government. In France, England, and other parts of Europe, institutions exist supported by public contributions, which eminently promote agriculture and the arts. Such institutions merit imitation by our government; they are of the number of those which directly and sensibly recompense *labor* for what it lends to their agency.

To suggestions of the last kind, the adepts of the new school have a ready answer: *Industry will succeed and prosper in proportion as it is left to the exertions of individual enterprise.* This favorite dogma, when taken as a general rule, is true; but as an exclusive one, it is false, and leads to error in the administration of public affairs. In matters of industry, human enterprise ought, doubtless, to be left free in the main; not fettered by too much regulation; but practical politicians know that it may be beneficially stimulated by prudent aids and encouragements on the part of the government. . . .

But admitting the position, that there is an excess of income which ought to be relinquished, still the proposal to surrender the *internal* revenue is impolitic. It ought to be carefully preserved, as not being exposed to the casualties incident to our intercourse with foreign nations, and therefore the most certain. It ought to be preserved, as reaching to descriptions of persons who are not proportionately affected by the impost, and as tending, for this reason, to distribute the public burden more equitably. It ought to be preserved, because if revenue can really be spared, it is best to do it in such a manner as will conduce to the relief or advancement of our navigation and commerce.

—"Lucius Crassus", No. 3. *Hamilton*, VII, 753, 755-756, 757.

A National Bank

The only plan that can preserve the currency is one that will make it the *immediate* interest of the moneyed men to cooperate with government in its support.

The financial crisis to which the government was heading in the closing years of the Revolution impelled Washington's youthful military aide to draw up a series of proposals to expedite financing the war effort. He suggested that a foreign loan be procured which would be convertible into merchandise and imported on public account. In addition, to obtain the full support of the moneyed men behind the government, he recommended setting up a national bank, the ownership of which was to be evenly divided between the government and private capital. Others were advocating a central bank at this time, including Pelatiah Webster, the economist, and Gouverneur Morris. Hamilton took up the matter again when Robert Morris became Superintendent of Finance. Actually his project was far more comprehensive than the scheme for the Bank of North American sponsored by Morris. Hamilton's bank was not only to perform the functions of discount and deposit, but also to coin money, issue paper currency, and have allotted to it all the contracts for supplying the armed forces.

Hamilton brought forth a new plan for a national bank when he became Secretary of the Treasury. It was less grandiose in conception than the earlier plan, and provided that the government might acquire one-fifth of the shares and could name five out of the twenty-five directors. It was, therefore, much more clearly under private control than was the first proposal. It was really a private bank with semi-public functions, patterned after the Bank of England.

Hamilton's report of December 13, 1790 raised a storm of opposition in Congress, but his masterly economic reasoning and his persuasive constitutional arguments on the implied powers of the constitution (excerpted above) carried the day. In February, 1791, Congress chartered the Bank of the United States, fixing its life at twenty years. The bank's opponents were horrified. Senator Maclay of Pennsylvania, who regarded the bank as "an aristocratic engine," was moved to exclaim: "Would to God this same General Washington were in heaven! We would not then have him brought forth as the constant cover to every unconstitutional and irrepublican act." But the operations of the Bank in its early years provided the Jeffersonians with comparatively little ammunition. In the 1790's the Bank admirably performed its dual functions as a depository for the funds of individuals and the government and as a lender to businessmen and government.

Hamilton's interest in banking was not confined to the national bank. In 1784 he rallied New York business men behind his successful effort to defeat a proposal of Chancellor Livingston to establish a land bank. He countered with a commercial bank, which was organized as the Bank of New York. Hamilton was active in formulating the policies of the bank, both through its cashier, William Seton, and through Jeremiah Wadsworth, his representative on the board of directors, who became its president in 1785. As Secretary of the Treasury Hamilton used the bank as a fiscal agent of the government and continued to advise the officers on the conduct of their operations.

[1780][1]

The present conjuncture is by all allowed to be peculiarly critical.

[1] Date in later hand. Schachner suggests Nov., 1779 as the correct date.

. . . The object of principal concern is the state of our currency. In my opinion, all our speculations on this head have been founded in error. Most people think that the depreciation might have been avoided by provident arrangements in the beginning, without [any aid][1] from abroad; and a great many of our [sanguine] politicians, till very lately, imagined the money might still be restored by expedients with[in our]selves. Hence the delay in attempting to procure a foreign loan.

This idea proceeded from [an igno]rance of the real extent of our resources. The war, particularly in the first periods, [required] exertions beyond our strength, to which [neither] our population nor riches were equal. [We] have the fullest proof of this in the const[ant thin]ness of our armies, the impossibility, at [this time,] of recruiting them otherwise than by [compulsion,] the scarcity of hands in husbandry and [other oc]cupations, the decrease of our staple [commodi]ties, and the difficulty of every species [of supply.] I am aware that the badness of the [money] has its influence; but it [was ori]ginally an effect, not a cause, tho[ugh it] now partakes of the nature of both. A part of those [evils] would appear [were] our finances in a more flourishing cond[ition.] We experienced them before the [money] was materially depreciated; and they [contri]buted to its depreciation. The want [of men] soon obliged the public to pay extrav[agant] wages for them in every department. [Agri]culture languished from a defect [of] [hands.] The mechanic arts did the same. [The price] of every kind of labor increased, [and the] articles of foreign commerce, from the [interrup]tion it received, more than kept pace [with] other things.

The relative value of m[oney] being determined by the greater or less [portion] of labor and commodities which it [will pur]chase; whatever these gained in price, [that of] course lost in value.

The public expenditures, from the dearness of everything, necessarily became immense; great[er] in proportion than in other countries; and much beyond any revenues which the best concreted scheme of finance could have extracted from the natural funds of the State. No taxes, which the people were capable of bearing, on that quantity of money which is deemed a proper medium for this country (had it been gold instead of paper), would have been sufficient for the current exigencies of government.

The most opulent states of Europe, in a war of any duration, are commonly obliged to have recourse to foreign loans or subsidies.[2] How, then, could we expect to do without them, and not augment the quantity of our artificial wealth beyond those bounds which were proper to preserve its credit? The idea was chimerical.

[1] Words in brackets are illegible.
[2] In a long footnote Hamilton cites the huge debts of foreign nations.—Ed.

The quantity of money formerly in circulation among us is estimated at about thirty millions of dollars. This was barely sufficient for our interior commerce. Our exterior commerce was chiefly carried on by barter. We sent our commodities abroad, and brought back others in return. The balance of the principal branch was against us, and the little *specie* derived from others was transferred directly to the payment of that balance, without passing into home circulation. It would have been impracticable, by loans and taxes, to bring such a portion of the forementioned sum into the public coffers as would have answered the purposes of the war; nor could it have spared so considerable a part, without obstructing the operations of domestic commerce. Taxes are limited, not only by the quantity of wealth in a state, but by the temper, habits, and genius of the people; all which, in this country, conspired to render them moderate; and as to loans, men will not be prevailed upon to lend money to the public when there is a scarcity, and they can find a more profitable way of employing it otherwise, as was our case. . . .

From these reasonings it results, that it was not in the power of Congress, when their emissions had arrived at the thirty millions of dollars, to put a stop to them.[1] They were obliged, in order to keep up the supplies, to go on creating artificial revenues by new emissions; and as these multiplied, their value declined. The progress of the depreciation might have been retarded, but it could not have been prevented. It was, in a great degree, necessary.

There was but one remedy; a foreign loan. All other expedients should rather have been considered as auxiliary. Could a loan have been obtained, and judiciously applied, assisted by a vigorous system of taxation, we might have avoided that excess of emissions which has ruined the paper. The credit of such a fund would have procured loans from the moneyed and trading men within ourselves; because it might have been so directed, as to have been beneficial to them in their commercial transactions abroad.[2]

The necessity for a foreign loan is now greater than ever. Nothing else will retrieve our affairs. . . .

How this loan is to be employed is now the question; and its difficulty equal to its importance. Two plans have been proposed: one, to purchase up at once, in specie or sterling bills, all superfluous paper; and to endeavor, by taxes, loans, and economy, to hinder its returning into circulation. The remainder, it is supposed, would then recover its value. This, it is said, will reduce our public debt to the sterling cost of the paper. . . .

A great source of error in disquisitions of this nature, is the judging

[1] This is meant, without employing the assistance of a foreign loan, and of other expedients beside borrowing and taxing.

[2] This will appear from the plan which will be proposed.

of events by abstract calculations; which, though geometrically true, are false as they relate to the concerns of beings governed more by passion and prejudice than by an enlightened sense of their interests. A degree of illusion mixes itself in all the affairs of society. The opinion of objects has more influence than their real nature. The quantity of money in circulation is certainly a chief cause of its decline; but we find it is depreciated more than five times as much as it ought to be by this rule. The excess is derived from opinion; a want of confidence. In like manner we deceive ourselves, when we suppose the value will increase in proportion as the quantity is lessened. Opinion will operate here also; and a thousand circumstances may promote or counteract the principle.

The other plan proposed is to convert the loan into merchandise, and import it on public account. This plan is incomparably better than the former. Instead of losing on the sale of its specie or bills, the public would gain a considerable profit on the commodities imported. The loan would go much further this way, towards supplying the expenses of the war; and a large stock of valuable commodities, useful to the army and to the country, would be introduced. This would affect the prices of things in general, and assist the currency. But the arts of monopolize[r]s would prevent its having so extensive and durable an influence as it ought to have.

A great impediment to the success of this, as well as the former scheme, will be the vast sums requisite for the current expenses. . . .

The farmers have the game in their own hands, and will make it very difficult to lower the price of their commodities. . . .

One measure, alone, can counterbalance these advantages of the farmers, and oblige them to contribute their proper quota to the support of government: a tax in kind.

This ought instantly to begin throughout the States. The present quantity of cash, though nominally enormous, would, in reality, be found incompetent to domestic circulation, were it not that a great part of our internal commerce is carried on by barter. For this reason, it is impossible, by pecuniary taxes, to raise a sum proportioned to the wants of the State. The money is no longer a general representative; and when it ceases to be so, the State ought to call for a portion of the thing represented; or, in other words, to tax in kind. This will greatly facilitate whatever plan of finance is adopted; because it will lessen the expenditures in cash, and make it the easier to retain what is drawn in. . . .

The only plan that can preserve the currency is one that will make it the *immediate* interest of the moneyed men to cooperate with government in its support. The country is in the same predicament in which France was previous to the famous Mississippi scheme, projected by Mr. Law. Its paper money, like ours, had dwindled to nothing;

and no efforts of the government could revive it, because the people had lost all confidence in its ability. Mr. Law, who had much more penetration than integrity, readily perceived that no plan could succeed which did not unite the interest and credit of rich individuals with those of the state; and upon this he framed the idea of his project, which, so far, agreed in principle with the Bank of England. The foundation was good, but the superstructure too vast. The proprietors aimed at unlimited wealth, and the government itself expected too much; which was the cause of the ultimate miscarriage of the scheme, and of all the mischiefs that befell the kingdom in consequence.

It will be our wisdom to select what is good in this plan, and in any others that have gone before us, avoiding their defects and excesses. Something on a similar principle in America will alone accomplish the restoration of paper credit, and establish a permanent fund for the future exigencies of government.

Article 1st. The plan I would propose is that of an American bank, instituted by authority of Congress for ten years, under the denomination of The Bank of the United States. . . .

I have confined the bank to the space of ten years, because this will be long enough to judge of its advantages and disadvantages; and the latter may be rectified by giving it a new form. I do not suppose it will ever be discontinued; because it seems to be founded on principles that must always operate well, and make it the interest, both of government and the company, to uphold it. But I suppose the plan capable of improvement, which experience will suggest.

I give one half of the whole property of the bank to the United States; because it is not only just but desirable to both parties. The United States contribute a great part of the stock; their auhority is essential to the existence of the bank; their credit is pledged for its support. The plan would ultimately fail, if the terms were too favorable to the company, and too hard upon government. It might be encumbered with a debt which it could never pay, and be obliged to take refuge in a bankruptcy. The share which the State has in the profits will induce it to grant more ample privileges, without which the trade of the company might often be under restrictions injurious to its success. . . .

It may be objected that this plan will be prejudicial to trade, by making the government a party with a trading company; which may be a temptation to arrogate exclusive privileges, and thereby fetter that spirit of enterprise and competition on which the prosperity of commerce depends. But Congress may satisfy the jealousies on this head, by a solemn resolution not to grant exclusive privileges, which alone can make the objection valid. Large trading companies must be beneficial to the commerce of a nation, when they are not invested with these, because they furnish a capital with which the most extensive enterprises may be undertaken. There is no doubt the establishment proposed would be very serviceable at this juncture, merely in a commercial view; for private adventurers are not a match for the numerous obstacles resulting from the present posture of affairs.

—To a Member of Congress.[1] Probably in Hamilton's hand. Hamilton Papers, 1st ser.

April 30, 1781

. . . 'Tis by introducing order into our finances—by restoring public credit—not by gaining battles, that we are finally to gain our object. 'Tis by putting ourselves in a condition to continue the war—not by temporary, violent, and unnatural efforts to bring it to a decisive issue, that we shall, in reality, bring it to a speedy and successful one. In the frankness of truth I believe, sir, you are the man best capable of performing this great work. . . .

The first step towards determining what ought to be done in the finances of this country, is to estimate, in the best manner we can, its capacity for revenue; and the proportion between what it is able to afford, and what it stands in need of, for the expenses of its civil and military establishments. . . .

From a comparison of the several estimates I have seen, [of the quantity of current cash][2] in this country previous to the war (specie and paper), I have settled my opinion of the amount at thirty millions of dollars, of which about eight might have been in specie: one fourth of this, by analogy, was at that time the proper revenue of these States; that is, seven and a half millions of dollars.

As taxation, however, has, by slow gradations, been carried to an extreme in those countries which I have chosen as examples, that would not be, but in a course of time, practicable in this, where the people have been so little accustomed to taxes, it may be doubted whether it would be possible to raise the same proportion of revenue here. The object of the war, I imagine, would supply the want of habit, and reconcile the minds of the people to paying to the utmost of their abilities, provided the taxes were judiciously imposed, and the revenues wisely administered. Besides this, there is a circumstance in our favor, which puts it in the power of government to raise an equal proportion of revenue without burthening the lower classes of the people in the same degree as in Europe. This circumstance is the much greater equality of fortunes, by which means men, in this country, may be made to contribute to the public exigencies in a much juster proportion to their property; and this is in fact the case. . . .

[1] Lodge names Robert Morris as the addressee, although he was not in Congress at this time. Schachner suggests General John Sullivan, who was active in Congress in financial measures.

[2] Not legible in MS.

The diminution of our circulating cash is principally artificial. It is true, our foreign commerce has declined by the war, but our domestic commerce has increased. I know of no good reason to believe, that the quantity of labor and commodities have been materially diminished. Our exports have lessened, but our internal consumption has augmented. . . .

We may infer from all this, that [we] stand in need now of nearly the same quantity of medium for our circulation as before the war. The depreciation of the money below the standard is to be attributed to a want of confidence rather than to a decay of resources. We find the people, in some of the States, distressed to pay their taxes for want of money, with ample means otherwise; which is a proof, that our current cash is not a competent representative of the labor and commodities of the country. Another proof of the same nature is, that particular States which have found no small difficulty in collecting their pecuniary taxes, have been successful in raising contributions to a large amount in kind. . . .

In the present system of things, the health of a State, particularly a commercial one, depends on a due quantity and regular circulation of cash, as much as the health of an animal body depends upon the due quantity and regular circulation of the blood. There are indisputable indications that we have not a sufficient medium; and what we have is in continual fluctuation. The only cure to our public disorders, is to fix the value of the currency we now have, and increase it to a proper standard, in a species that will have the requisite stability.

The error of those who would explode paper money altogether, originates in not making proper distinctions. Our paper was, in its nature, liable to depreciation, because it had no funds for its support, and was not upheld by private credit. The emissions under the resolution of March, '80, have partly the former advantage, but are destitute of the latter, which is equally essential. No paper credit can be substantial, or durable, which has not funds, and which does not unite, immediately, the interest and influence of the moneyed men, in its establishment and preservation. A credit begun on this basis, will, in process of time, greatly exceed its funds: but this requires time and a well-settled opinion in its favor. 'Tis in a national bank, alone, that we can find the ingredients to constitute a wholesome, solid, and beneficial credit. . . .

The plan I propose requires a stock of three millions of pounds, lawful money; but if one half the sum could be obtained, I should entertain no doubt of its full success. It now remains to submit my plan, which I rather offer as an outline, than as a finished plan. It contains, however, the general principles. . . .

We shall find good models in the different European banks, which we can accommodate to our circumstances. Great care, in particular, should be employed to guard against counterfeits; and I think methods may be devised that would be effectual.

I see nothing to prevent the practicability of a plan of this kind, but a distrust of the final success of the war, which may make men afraid to risk any considerable part of their fortunes in the public funds; but, without being an enthusiast, I will venture to assert, that, with such a resource as is here proposed, the loss of our independence is impossible. All we have to fear is, that the want of money may disband the army, or so perplex and enfeeble our operations as to create in the people a general disgust and alarm, which may make them clamor for peace on any terms. But if a judicious administration of our finances, assisted by a bank, takes place, and the ancient security of property is restored, no convulsion is to be apprehended. . . .

Never did a nation unite more circumstances in its favor than we do; we have nothing against us but our own misconduct. . . .

Speaking within moderate bounds, our population will be doubled in thirty years; there will be a confluence of emigrants from all parts of the world, our commerce will have a proportionable progress, and of course our wealth and capacity for revenue. It will be a matter of choice if we are not out of debt in twenty years, without at all encumbering the people.

A national debt, if it is not excessive, will be to us a national blessing. It will be a powerful cement of our Union. It will also create a necessity for keeping up taxation to a degree which, without being oppressive, will be a spur to industry, remote as we are from Europe, and shall be from danger. It were otherwise to be feared our popular maxims would incline us to too great parsimony and indulgence. We labor less now than any civilized nation of Europe; and a habit of labor in the people is as essential to the health and vigor of their minds and bodies, as it is conducive to the welfare of the state. We ought not to suffer our self-love to deceive us in a comparison upon these points.

—To Robert Morris. Hamilton Papers, 1st ser.

Report on a National Bank

December 13, 1790

The following are among the principal advantages of a bank:

First.—The augmentation of the active or productive capital of a country. Gold and silver, when they are employed merely as the instruments of exchange and alienation, have not been improperly denominated dead stock; but when deposited in banks, to become the basis of a paper circulation, which takes their character and place, as the signs or representatives of value, they then acquire life, or, in other words, an active and productive quality. . . .

It is a well-established fact, that banks in good credit can circulate a far greater sum than the actual quantum of their capital in gold and silver. The extent of the possible excess seems indeterminate; though it has been conjecturally stated at the proportions of two and three to one. This faculty is produced in various ways. 1st. A great proportion of the notes which are issued, and pass current as cash, are indefinitely suspended in circulation, from the confidence which each holder has, that he can, at any moment, turn them into gold and silver. 2dly. Every loan which a bank makes, is, in its first shape, a credit given to the borrower on its books, the amount of which it stands ready to pay, either in its own notes, or in gold or silver, at his option. But, in a great number of cases, no actual payment is made in either. The borrower, frequently, by a check or order, transfers his credit to some other person, to whom he has a payment to make; who, in his turn, is as often content with a similar credit, because he is satisfied that he can, whenever he pleases, either convert it into cash, or pass it to some other hand, as an equivalent for it. And in this manner the credit keeps circulating, performing in every stage the office of money, till it is extinguished by a discount with some person who has a payment to make to the bank, to an equal or greater amount. Thus large sums are lent and paid, frequently through a variety of hands, without the intervention of a single piece of coin. 3dly. There is always a large quantity of gold and silver in the repositories of the bank, besides its own stock, which is placed there, with a view partly to its safe-keeping, and partly to the accommodation of an institution which is itself a source of general accommodation. These deposits are of immense consequence in the operations of a bank. Though liable to be redrawn at any moment, experience proves, that the money so much oftener changes proprietors than place, and that what is drawn out is generally so speedily replaced, as to authorize the counting upon the sums deposited, as an *effective fund*, which, concurring with the stock of the bank, enables it to extend its loans, and to answer all the demands for coin, whether in consequence of those loans, or arising from the occasional return of its notes.

These different circumstances explain the manner in which the ability of a bank to circulate a greater sum than its actual capital in coin is acquired. This, however, must be gradual, and must be preceded by a firm establishment of confidence—a confidence which may be bestowed on the most rational grounds, since the excess in question will always be bottomed on good security of one kind or another. . . .

The same circumstances illustrate the truth of the position, that it is one of the properties of banks to increase the active capital of a country. This, in other words, is the sum of them: the money of one individual, while he is waiting for an opportunity to employ it, by being either deposited in the bank for safe-keeping, or invested in its stock, is in a condition to administer to the wants of others, without being put out of his own reach when occasion presents. This yields an extra profit, arising from what is paid for the use of his money by others, when he could not himself make use of it, and keeps the money itself in a state of incessant activity. . . .

Secondly.—Greater facility as to the government in obtaining pecuniary aids, especially in sudden emergencies. This is another and an undisputed advantage of public banks—one which, as already remarked, has been realized in signal instances among ourselves. The reason is obvious: the capitals of a great number of individuals are, by this operation, collected to a point, and placed under one direction. The mass formed by this union, is, in a certain sense, magnified by the credit attached to it; and while this mass is always ready, and can at once be put in motion, in aid of the government, the interest of the bank to afford that aid, independent of regard to the public safety and welfare, is a sure pledge for its disposition to go as far in its compliances as can in prudence be desired. There is, in the nature of things, as will be more particularly noticed in another place, an intimate connection of interest between the government and the bank of a nation.

Thirdly.—The facilitating of the payment of taxes. This advantage is produced in two ways. Those who are in a situation to have access to the bank, can have the assistance of loans, to answer, with punctuality, the public calls upon them. This accommodation has been sensibly felt in the payment of the duties heretofore laid by those who reside where establishments of this nature exist. This, however, though an extensive, is not a universal, benefit. The other way in which the effect here contemplated is produced, and in which the benefit is general, is the increasing of the quantity of circulating medium, and the quickening of circulation. . . .

It would be to intrude too much on the patience of the House, to prolong the details of the advantages of banks; especially as all those which might still be particularized are readily to be inferred as consequences from those which have been enumerated. Their disadvantages, real or supposed, are now to be reviewed. The most serious of the charges which have been brought against them are:

That they serve to increase usury;

That they tend to prevent other kinds of lending;

That they furnish temptations to overtrading;

That they afford aid to ignorant adventurers, who disturb the natural and beneficial course of trade;

That they give to bankrupt and fraudulent traders a fictitious credit, which enables them to maintain false appearances and to extend their impositions; and, lastly,

That they have a tendency to banish gold and silver from the country.

There is great reason to believe, that, on a close and candid survey, it will be discovered that these charges are either destitute of foundation, or that, as far as the evils they suggest have been found to exist, they have proceeded from other, or partial, or temporary causes, are not inherent in the nature and pemanent tendency of such institutions, or are more than counterbalanced by opposite advantages. . . .

The capital of every public bank will, of course, be restricted within a certain defined limit. It is the province of legislative prudence so to adjust this limit, that, while it will not be too contracted for the demand which the course of business may create, and for the security which the public ought to have for the solidity of the paper which may be issued by the bank, it will still be within the compass of the pecuniary resources of the community; so that there may be an easy practicability of completing the subscriptions to it. When this is once done, the supposed effect, of necessity, ceases. There is then no longer room for the investment of any additional capital. Stock may, indeed, change hands, by one person selling and another buying; but the money which the buyer takes out of the common mass to purchase the stock, the seller receives and restores to it. Hence, the future surpluses which may accumulate must take their natural course. and lending at interest must go on as if there were no such institution.

It must, indeed, flow in a more copious stream. The bank furnishes an extraordinary supply for borrowers, within its immediate sphere. A larger supply consequently remains for borrowers elsewhere. In proportion as the circulation of the bank is extended, there is an augmentation of the aggregate mass of money for answering the aggregate mass of demand. Hence greater facility in obtaining it for every purpose.

It ought not to escape without a remark, that, as far as the citizens of other countries become adventurers in the bank, there is a positive increase of the gold and silver of the country. It is true, that, from this, a half yearly rent is drawn back, accruing from the dividends upon the stock. But as this rent arises from the employment of the capital by our own citizens, it is probable that it is more than replaced by the profits of that employment. It is also likely that a part of it is, in the course of trade, converted into the products of our country; and it may even prove an incentive, in some cases, to emigration to a country in which the character of citizen is as easy to be acquired as it is estimable and important. This view of the subject furnishes an answer to an objection which has been deduced from the circumstance here taken notice of, namely, the income resulting to foreigners from the part of the stock owned by them, which has been represented as tending to drain the country of its specie. In this objection the original investment of the capital, and the constant use of it afterwards, seem both to have been overlooked. . . .

If banks, in spite of every precaution, are sometimes betrayed into giving a false credit to the persons described, they more frequently enable honest and industrious men, of small, or, perhaps, of no capital, to undertake and prosecute business with advantage to themselves and to the community; and assist merchants, of both capital and credit, who meet with fortuitous and unforseen shocks, which might, without such helps, prove fatal to them and to others, to make head against their misfortunes, and finally to retrieve their affairs—circumstances which form no inconsiderable encomium on the utility of banks.

But the last and heaviest charge is still to be examined: this is, that banks tend to banish the gold and silver of the country.

The force of this objection rests upon their being an engine of paper credit, which, by furnishing a substitute for the metals, is supposed to promote their exportation. It is an objection which, if it has any foundation, lies not against banks peculiarly, but against every species of paper credit.

The most common answer given to it is, that the thing supposed is of little or of no consequence; that it is immaterial what serves the purpose of money, whether paper, or gold and silver; that the effect of both upon industry is the same; and that the intrinsic wealth of a nation is to be measured, not by the abundance of the precious metals contained in it, but by the quantity of the productions of its labor and industry.

This answer is not destitute of solidity, though not entirely satisfactory. It is certain that the vivification of industry, by a full circulation, with the aid of a proper and well-regulated paper credit, may more than compensate for the loss of a part of the gold and silver of a nation, if the consequence of avoiding that loss should be a scanty or defective circulation.

But the positive and permanent increase or decrease of the precious metals in the country can hardly ever be a matter of indifference. As the commodity taken in lieu of every other, it is a species of the most effective wealth; and as the money of the world, it is of great concern to the state, that it possess a sufficiency of it to face any demands which the protection of its external interest may create.

The objection seems to admit of another and a more conclusive answer, which controverts the fact itself. A nation that has no mines of its own must derive the precious metals from others; generally speaking, in exchange for the products of its labor and industry. The quantity it will possess will, therefore, in the ordinary course of things, be regulated by the favorable or unfavorable balance of its trade; that is, by the proportion between its abilities to supply foreigners, and its wants of them—between the amount of its exportations and that of its importations. Hence, the state of its agriculture and manufactures, the quantity and quality of its labor and industry, must, in the main, influence and determine the increase or decrease of its gold and silver.

If this be true, the inference seems to be, that well-constituted banks favor the increase of the precious metals. It has been shown that they augment, in different ways, the active capital of a country. This it is which generates employment—which animates and expands labor and industry. Every addition which is made to it, by contributing to put in motion a greater quantity of both, tends to create a greater quantity of the products of both; and, by furnishing more materials for exportation, conduces to a favorable balance of trade, and, consequently, to the introduction and increase of gold and silver. . . .

The judgment of many concerning them has, no doubt, been perplexed by the misinterpretation of appearances which were to be ascribed to other causes. The general devastation of personal property, occasioned by the late war, naturally produced, on the one hand, a great demand for money, and, on the other, a great deficiency of it to answer the demand. Some injudicious laws, which grew out of the public distresses, by impairing confidence, and causing a part of the inadequate sum in the country to be locked up, aggravated the evil. The dissipated habits contracted by many individuals during the war, which, after the peace, plunged them into expenses beyond their incomes; the number of adventurers without capital, and, in many instances, without information, who at that epoch rushed into trade, and were obliged to make any sacrifice to support a transient credit; the employment of considerable sums in speculations upon the public debt, which, from its unsettled state, was incapable of becoming itself a substitute; all these circumstances concurring, necessarily led to usurious borrowing, produced most of the inconveniences, and were the true causes of most of the appearances which, where banks were established, have been by some erroneously placed to their account—a mistake which they might easily have avoided by turning their eyes toward places where there were none, and where, nevertheless, the same evils would have been perceived to exist, even in a greater degree than where those institutions had obtained.

These evils have either ceased or been greatly mitigated. Their more complete extinction may be looked for from that additional security to property which the Constitution of the United States happily gives (a circumstance of prodigious moment in the scale both of public and private prosperity); from the attraction of foreign capital, under the auspices of that security, to be employed upon objects and in enterprises for which the state of this country opens a wide and inviting field; from the consistency and stability which the public debt is fast acquiring, as well in the public opinion at home and abroad, as in fact; from the augmentation of capital which that circumstance and the quarter-yearly payment of interest will afford; and from the more copious circulation which will be likely to be created by a well-constituted national bank.

The establishment of banks in this country seems to be recommended by reasons of a peculiar nature. Previously to the Revolution, circulation was in a great measure carried on by paper emitted by the several local governments. In Pennsylvania alone the quantity of it was near a million and a half of dollars. This auxiliary may be said to be now at an end. And it is generally supposed that there has been, for some time past, a deficiency of circulating medium. How far that deficiency is to be considered as real or imaginary, is not susceptible of demonstration; but there are circumstances and appearances which, in relation to the country at large, countenance the supposition of its reality.

The circumstances are, besides the fact just mentioned respecting paper emissions, the vast tracts of waste land, and the little advanced state of manufactures. The progressive settlement of the former, while it promises ample retribution in the generation of future resources, diminishes or obstructs, in the meantime, the *active* wealth of the country. It not only draws off a part of the circulating money, and places it in a more passive state, but it diverts into its own channels a portion of that species of labor and industry which would otherwise be employed in furnishing materials for foreign trade, and which, by contributing to a favorable balance, would assist the introduction of specie. In the early periods of new settlements, the settlers not only furnish no surplus for exportation, but they consume a part of that which is produced by the labor of others. The same thing is a cause that manufacturers do not advance, or advance slowly. And notwithstanding some hypotheses to the contrary, there are many things to induce a suspicion that the precious metals will not abound in any country which has not mines, or variety of manufactures. They have been sometimes acquired by the sword; but the modern system of war has expelled this resource, and it is one upon which it is to be hoped the United States will never be inclined to rely.

The appearances alluded to are: Greater prevalency of direct barter, in the more interior districts of the country, which, however, has been for some time past gradually lessening; and greater difficulty generally in the advantageous alienation of improved real estate, which also has of late diminished, but is still seriously felt in different parts of the Union. The difficulty of getting money, which has been a general complaint, is not added to the number, because it is the complaint of all times, and one in which imagination must ever have too great scope to permit an appeal to it.

If the supposition of such a deficiency be in any degree well founded, and some aid to circulation be desirable, it remains to inquire what ought to be the nature of that aid.

The emitting of paper money by the authority of the government is wisely prohibited to the individual States by the National Constitution; and the spirit of that prohibition ought not to be disregarded by the Government of the United States. Though paper emissions, under a general authority, might have some advantages not applicable, and be free from some disadvantages which are applicable, to the like emissions by the States, separately, yet they are of a nature so liable to abuse—and, it may even be affirmed, so certain of being abused,—that the wisdom of the government will be shown in never trusting itself with the use of so seducing and dangerous an expedient. In times of tranquillity it might have no ill consequence,—it might even perhaps be managed in a way to be productive of good; but in great and trying emergencies there is almost a moral certainty of its becoming mischievous. The stamping of paper is an operation so much easier than the laying of taxes, that a government in the practice of paper emissions would rarely fail, in any such emergency, to indulge itself too far in the employment of that resource, to avoid as much as possible, one less auspicious to present popularity. If it should not even be carried so far as to be rendered an absolute bubble, it would at least be likely to be extended to a degree which would occasion an inflated and artificial state of things, incompatible with the regular and prosperous course of the political economy.

Among other material differences between a paper currency, issued by the mere authority of government, and one issued by a bank, payable in coin, is this: That, in the first case, there is no standard to which an appeal can be made, as to the quantity which will only satisfy, or which will surcharge, the circulation; in the last, that standard results from the demand. If more should be issued than is necessary, it will return upon the bank. Its emissions, as elsewhere intimated, must always be in a compound ratio to the fund and the demand: whence it is evident that there is a limitation in the nature of the thing; while the discretion of the government is the only measure of the extent of the emissions, by its own authority. . . .

The want of a principle of rotation in the constitution of the Bank of North America is another argument for a variation of the establishment. Scarcely one of the reasons which militate against this principle in the constitution of a country, is applicable to that of a bank; while there are strong reasons in favor of it, in relation to the one, which do not apply to the other. The knowledge to be derived from experience is the only circumstance common to both, which pleads against rotation in the directing officers of a bank.

But the objects of the government of a nation, and those of the government of a bank, are so widely different, as greatly to weaken the force of that consideration in reference to the latter. Almost every important case in legislation requires, toward a right decision, a general and accurate acquaintance with the affairs of the State, and habits of thinking seldom acquired but from a familiarity with public concerns. The administration of a bank, on the contrary, is regulated by a few simple fixed maxims, the application of which is not difficult to any man of judgment, especially if instructed in the principles of trade. It is, in general, a constant succession of the same details. . . .

The argument in favor of the principle of rotation is this: that by lessening the danger of combinations among the directors, to make the institution subservient to party views, or to the accommodation, preferably, of any particular set of men, it will render the public confidence more firm, stable, and unqualified. . . .

The situation of the United States naturally inspires a wish that the form of the institution could admit of a plurality of branches. . . .

The argument against it is, that each branch must be under a distinct, though subordinate direction, to which a considerable latitude of discretion must, of necessity, be intrusted. And, as the property of the whole institution would be liable for the engagements of each part, that and its credit would be at stake, upon the prudence of the directors of every part. The mismanagement of either branch might hazard serious disorder in the whole. . . .

Considerations of public advantage suggest a further wish, which is—that the bank could be established upon principles that would cause the profits of it to redound to the immediate benefit of the State. This is contemplated by many who speak of a national bank, but the idea seems liable to insuperable objections. To attach full confidence to an institution of this nature, it appears to be an essential ingredient in its structure, that it shall be under a *private* not a *public* direction—under the guidance of *individual interest*, not of *public policy;* which would be supposed to be, and, in certain emergencies, under a feeble or too sanguine administration, would really be, liable to being too much influenced by *public necessity*. The suspicion of this would, most probably, be a canker that would continually corrode the vitals of the credit of the bank, and would be most likely to prove fatal in those situations in which the public good would require that they should be most sound and vigorous. It would, indeed, be little less than a miracle, should the credit of the bank be at the disposal of the government, if, in a long series of time, there was not experienced a calamitous abuse of it. It is true, that it would be the real interest of the government not to abuse it; its genuine policy to husband and cherish it with the most guarded circumspection, as an inestimable treasure. But what government ever uniformly consulted its true interests in opposition to the temptations of momentary exigencies? What nation was ever blessed with a constant succession of upright and wise administrators?

The keen, steady, and, as it were, magnetic sense of their own interest as proprietors, in the directors of a bank, pointing invariably to its true pole—the prosperity of the institution,—is the only security that can always be relied upon for a careful and prudent administration. It is, therefore, the only basis on which an enlightened, unqualified, and permanent confidence can be expected to be erected and maintained. . . .

It will not follow, from what has been said, that the state may not be a holder of a part of the stock of a bank, and consequently a sharer in the profits of it. It will only follow that it ought not to desire any participation in the direction of it, and, therefore, ought not to own the whole or a principal part of the stock; for, if the mass of the property should belong to the public, and if the direction of it should be in private hands, this would be to commit the interests of the state to persons not interested, or not enough interested, in their proper management.

There is one thing, however, which the government owes to itself and the community—at least, to all that part of it who are not stockholders—which is, to reserve to itself a right of ascertaining, as often as may be necessary, the state of the bank; excluding, however, all pretension to control. This right forms an article in the primitive constitution of the Bank of North America; and its propriety stands upon the clearest reasons. If the paper of a bank is to be permitted to insinuate itself into all the revenues and receipts of a country, if it is even to be tolerated as a substitute for gold and silver in all the transactions of business, it becomes, in either view, a national concern of the first magnitude. As such, the ordinary rules of prudence require that the government should possess the means of ascertaining, whenever it thinks fit, that so delicate a trust is executed with fidelity and care. A right of this nature is not only desirable, as it respects the government, but it ought to be equally so to all those concerned in the institution, as an additional title to public and private confidence, and as a thing which can only be formidable to practices that imply mismanagement. . . .

The confining of the right of the bank to contract debts to the amount of its capital is an important precaution, which is not to be found in the constitution of the Bank of North America, and which while the fund consists wholly of coin, would be a restriction attended with inconveniences, but would be free from any, if the composition of it should be such as is now proposed. The restriction exists in the establishment of the Bank of England, and, as a source of security, is worthy of imitation. The consequence of exceeding the limit, there, is, that each stockholder is liable for the excess, in proportion to his interest in the bank. When it is considered that the directors owe their appointments to the choice of the stockholders, a responsibility of this kind, on the part of the latter, does not appear unreasonable; but, on the other hand, it may be deemed a hardship upon those who may have dissented from the choice. And there are many among us, whom it might perhaps discourage from becoming concerned in the institution. These reasons have induced the placing of the responsibility upon the directors by whom the limit prescribed should be transgressed.

The interdiction of loans on account of the United States, or of any particular State, beyond the moderate sum specified, or of any foreign Power, will serve as a barrier to Executive encroachments, and to combinations inauspicious to the safety, or contrary to the policy, of the Union. . . .

The last thing which requires any explanatory remark is, the authority proposed to be given to the President, to subscribe the amount of two millions of dollars on account of the public. The main design of this is, to enlarge the specie fund of the bank, and to enable it to give a more early extension to its operations. Though it is proposed to borrow with one hand what is lent with the other, yet the disbursement of what is borrowed will be progressive, and bank-notes may be thrown into circulation, instead of the gold and silver. Besides, there is to be an annual reimbursement of a part of the sum borrowed, which will finally operate as an actual investment of so much specie. In addition to the inducements to this measure, which result from the general interest of the government to enlarge the sphere of the utility of the bank, there is this more particular consideration, to wit: That, as far as the dividend on the stock shall exceed the interest paid on the loan, there is a positive profit.

—Secretary of the Treasury to the House of Representatives: Report on a National Bank. Hamilton Papers, 2nd ser.

February 19, 1793

I am not sure but that I owe an apology to the House for taking up so much of its time in obviating the imputation of partiality or favoritism towards the banks; the aspect under which I view it admonishes me, that I may have annexed to it greater importance than was intended to be given to it by its authors.

That a disposition friendly to the accommodation of those institutions, as far as might be consistent with official duty and the public interest, has characterized the conduct of the Department, will not be denied.

No man, placed in the office of the Secretary of the Treasury, whatever theoretic doubts he may have brought into it, would be a single month without surrendering those doubts to a full conviction, that banks are essential to the pecuniary operations of the Government.

No man, having a practical knowledge of the probable resources of the country, in the article of specie (which he would with caution rate beyond the actual revenues of the Government), would rely upon the annual collection of four millions and a half dollars, without the instrumentality of institutions that give a continual impulse to circulation, and prevent the stagnation to be otherwise expected from locking up from time to time large sums for periodical disbursements; to say nothing of the accommodations, which facilitate to the merchant the payment of the considerable demands made upon him by the Treasury.

No man, practically acquainted with the pecuniary ability of individuals, in this country, would count upon finding the means of those anticipations of the current revenue for the current service, which have been, and will be necessary, from any other source than that of the banks.

No prudent administrator of the finances of the country, therefore, but would yield to the disposition, which has been acknowledged, as alike essential to the interest of the Government, and to the satisfactory discharge of his trust; a disposition which would naturally lead to good offices, within the proper and justifiable bounds.

After the explanation which has been offered, to manifest the necessity and propriety of the loans made of the bank, it can scarcely be requisite to enter into a refutation of the process by which it has been endeavored to establish that Government pays seventeen per cent. upon these loans. The state of the Treasury rendered it expedient to borrow the sums which were borrowed; they have been duly received, and the rate of interest stipulated upon them is five per cent. The Government then pays upon them five per cent. and no more.

—To the House of Representatives. *Hamilton*, III, 433-434.

A Sound but Flexible Currency

Hamilton believed that a sound credit rested upon a sound currency, and that both were essential to the growth of the economy. However, he did not advocate a hard money policy at the expense of urgent government fiscal needs. The program embodied in his report of January 28, 1791 was carried out in the Mint Act of April 2, 1792, which provided for a decimal system of coinage, fixed the value of the U. S. gold dollar, established a system of bimetallism, with silver and gold legal tender at a ratio of 15 to 1, and set up a mint at Philadelphia. The ratio proposed by Hamilton was based on current European practice, but new discoveries of silver in Mexico resulted in silver being somewhat overvalued at this ratio. In 1834 it was changed to 16 to 1. Hamilton's letter to Secretary of the Treasury Wolcott which he wrote during the quasi-war emergency in 1798 sounds very much like the kind of economic thinking we would expect to hear from the proponents of a managed currency today.

January 28, 1791

The unequal values allowed in different parts of the Union to coins of the same intrinsic worth, the defective species of them which embarrass the circulation of some of the States, and the dissimilarity in their several moneys of account, are inconveniences which, if not to be ascribed to the want of a national coinage, will at least be most effectually remedied by the establishment of one—a measure that will, at the same time, give additional security against impositions by counterfeit as well as by base currencies. . . .

The next inquiry towards a right determination of what ought to be the future money unit of the United States turns upon these questions: Whether it ought to be peculiarly attached to either of the metals, in preference to the other, or not; and, if to either, to which of them? . . .

Contrary to the ideas which have heretofore prevailed, in the suggestions concerning a coinage for the United States, though not without much hesitation, arising from a deference for those ideas, the Secretary is, upon the whole, strongly inclined to the opinion, that a preference ought to be given to neither of the metals, for the money unit. Perhaps, if either were to be preferred, it ought to be gold rather than silver.

The reasons are these:

The inducement to such a preference is to render the unit as little variable as possible; because on this depends the steady value of all contracts, and, in a certain sense, of all other property. And, it is truly observed, that if the unit belong indiscriminately to both the metals, it is subject to all the fluctuations that happen in the relative value which they bear to each other. But the same reason would lead to annexing it to that particular one, which is itself the least liable to variation, if there be, in this respect, any discernible difference between the two.

Gold may, perhaps in certain senses, be said to have greater stability than silver: as, being of superior value, less liberties have been taken with it, in the regulations of different countries. Its standard has remained more uniform, and it has, in other respects, undergone fewer changes: as, being not so much an article of merchandise, owing to the use made of silver in the trade with the East Indies and China, it is less liable to be influenced by circumstances of commercial demand. And if, reasoning by analogy, it could be affirmed that there is a physical probability of greater proportional increase in the quantity of silver than in that of gold, it would afford an additional reason for calculating on greater steadiness in the value of the latter.

As long as gold, either from its intrinsic superiority as a metal, from its greater rarity, or from the prejudices of mankind, retains so considerable a preeminence in value over silver, as it has hitherto had, a natural consequence of this seems to be that its condition will be more stationary. The revolutions, therefore, which may take place in the comparative value of gold and silver, will be changes in the state of the latter, rather than in that of the former. . . .

One consequence of overvaluing either metal, in respect to the other, is the banishment of that which is undervalued. If two countries are supposed, in one of which the proportion of gold to silver is as 1 to 16, in the other as 1 to 15, gold being worth more, silver less, in one than in the other, it is manifest that, in their reciprocal payments, each will select that species which it values least, to pay to the other, where it is valued most. Besides this, the dealers in money will, from the same cause, often find a profitable traffic in an exchange of the metals between the two countries. And hence it would come to pass, if other things were equal, that the greatest part of the gold would be collected in one, and the greatest part of the silver in the other. . . .

In establishing a proportion between the metals, there seems to be an option of one of two things:

To approach, as nearly as can be ascertained, the mean or average proportion, in what may be called the commercial world; or,

To retain that which now exists in the United States.

As far as these happen to coincide, they will render the course to be pursued more plain and more certain.

To ascertain the first, with precision, would require better materials than are possessed, or than could be obtained, without an inconvenient delay.

Sir Isaac Newton, in a representation to the treasury of Great Britain, in the year 1717, after stating the particular proportions in the different countries of Europe, concludes thus:—"By the course of trade and exchange between nation and nation, in all Europe, fine gold is to fine silver as 14 4/5 or 15 to 1."

But however accurate and decisive this authority may be deemed, in relation to the period to which it applies, it cannot be taken, at the distance of more than seventy years, as a rule for determining the existing proportion. . . .

It has been seen that the existing proportion between the two metals, in this country, is about as 1 to 15.

It is fortunate, in this respect, that the innovations of the Spanish mint have imperceptibly introduced a proportion so analogous, as this is, to that which prevails among the principal commercial nations, as it greatly facilitates a proper regulation of the matter.

This proportion of 1 to 15 is recommended by the particular situation of our trade, as being very nearly that which obtains in the market of Great Britain, to which nation our specie is principally exported. A lower rate for either of the metals, in our market, than in hers, might not only afford a motive the more, in certain cases, to remit in specie rather than in commodities; but it might, in some others, cause us to pay a greater quantity of it for a given sum that we should otherwise do. If the effect should rather be to occasion a premium to be given for the metal which was underrated, this would obviate those disadvantages, but it would involve another—a customary difference between the market and legal proportions, which would amount to a species of disorder in the national coinage.

—Secretary of the Treasury to the House of Representatives: Original Report on the Establishment of a Mint. Hamilton Papers, 2nd ser.

June 21, 1791

It has occurred to me that it would be productive of very useful information, if some officer of the United States, in each foreign country where there is one, were instructed to transmit occasionally a state of the coins of the country, specifying their respective standards, weights, and values; and, periodically, a state of the market prices of gold and silver in coin and bullion, and of the rates of foreign exchange; and of the rates of the different kinds of labor, as well that employed in manufactures and in tillage.

—To Jefferson. *Hamilton*, IV, 162.

New York August 22, 1798

No one knows better than yourself how difficult and oppressive is the collection even of taxes very moderate in their amount, if there be a defective circulation. According to all the phenomena which fall under my notice, this is our case in the interior parts of the country.

Again, individual capitalists, and consequently the facility of direct loans, are not very extensive in the United States. The banks can only go a certain length, and must not be forced. Yet government will stand in need of large anticipations.

For these and other reasons which I have thought well of, I have come to a conclusion that our Treasury ought to raise up a circulation of its own. I mean by the issuing of Treasury-notes payable, some on demand, others at different periods, from very short to pretty considerable—at first having but little time to run.

This appears to me an expedient equally necessary to keep the circulation full and to facilitate the anticipations which government will certainly need. By beginning early the public eye will be familiarized, and as emergencies press it will be easy to enlarge without hazard to credit. . . .

—To Oliver Wolcott. (Copy) Hamilton Papers, 1st ser.

Encouragement of Trade

From the earliest years of the Confederation Hamilton had taken a strong stand in favor of enlarging the powers of the federal government to regulate trade. This was the immediate reason for the calling of the Annapolis Convention, in which Hamilton played a major role. There is little doubt that Hamilton favored a broad interpretation of the commerce clause of the Constitution. He did not agree with those who felt that trade should not be subject to regulation. He insisted that there must be "a common directing power." When a member of Washington's cabinet Hamilton favored reciprocal trade agreements with foreign nations.

April 18, 1782

The vesting Congress with the power of regulating trade ought to have been a principal object of the Confederation for a variety of reasons. It is as necessary for the purposes of commerce as of revenue. There are some who maintain that trade will regulate itself, and is not to be benefited by the encouragements or restraints of government. Such persons will imagine that there is no need of a common directing power. This is one of those wild speculative paradoxes, which have grown into credit among us, contrary to the uniform practice and sense of the most enlightened nations.

Contradicted by the numerous institutions and laws that exist everywhere for the benefit of trade, by the pains taken to cultivate particular branches and to discourage others, by the known advantages derived from those measures, and by the palpable evils that would attend their discontinuance, it must be rejected by every man acquainted with commercial history. Commerce, like other things, has its fixed principles, according to which it must be regulated. If these are understood and observed, it will be promoted by the attention of government; if unknown, or violated, it will be injured—but it is the same with every other part of administration.

To preserve the balance of trade in favor of a nation ought to be a leading aim of its policy. The avarice of individuals may frequently find its account in pursuing channels of traffic prejudicial to that balance, to which the government may be able to oppose effectual impediments. . . .

The contrary opinion, which has grown into a degree of vogue among us, has originated in the injudicious attempts made at different times to effect a REGULATION OF PRICES. It became a cant phrase among the opposers of these attempts, that TRADE MUST REGULATE ITSELF; by which at first was only meant that it had its fundamental laws, agreeable to which its general operations must be directed, and that any violent attempts in opposition to these would commonly miscarry. In this sense the maxim was reasonable, but it has since been extended to militate against all interference by the sovereign; an extreme as little reconcilable with experience or common sense as the practice it was first framed to discredit. . . .

Trade may be said to have taken its rise in England under the auspices of Elizabeth, and its rapid progress there is in a great measure to be ascribed to the fostering care of government in that and succeeding reigns. . . .

Perhaps it may be thought that the power of regulation will be best placed in the governments of the several states, and that a general superintendence is unnecessary. If the States had distinct interests, were unconnected with each other, their own governments would then be the proper, and could be the only, depositories of such a power; but as they are parts of a whole, with a common interest in trade, as in other things, there ought to be a common direction in that as in all other matters. It is easy to conceive that many cases may occur in which it would be beneficial to all the States to encourage or suppress a particular branch of trade, while it would be detrimental to either to attempt it without the concurrence of the rest, and where the experiment would probably be left untried for fear of a want of that concurrence.

No mode can be so convenient as a source of revenue to the United States. It is agreed that imposts on trade, when not immoderate, or improperly laid, are one of the most eligible species of taxation. They fall in a great measure upon articles not of absolute necessity, and being partly transferred to the price of the commodity, are so far imperceptibly paid by the consumer. It is therefore that mode which may be exercised by the Federal government with least exception or disgust. Congress can easily possess all the information necessary to impose the duties with judgment, and the collection can without difficulty be made by their own officers. . . .

The maxim, that the consumer pays the duty, has been admitted in theory with too little reserve; frequently contradicted in practice. It is true, the merchant will be unwilling to let the duty be a deduction from his profits, if the state of the market will permit him to incorporate it with the price of his commodity. But this is often not practicable. It turns upon the quantity of goods at market in proportion to the demand. When the latter exceeds the former, and the competition is among the buyers, the merchant can easily increase his price, and make his customers pay the duty. When the reverse is the case, and the competition is among the sellers, he must then content himself with smaller profits and lose the value of the duty, or at least a part of it. When a nation has a flourishing and well-settled trade, this more commonly happens than may be imagined, and it will, many times, be found that the duty is divided between the merchant and the consumer.

—"The Continentalist," No. 5. *N.Y. Packet*, April 18, 1782.

January 13, 1791

. . . I have doubts of the eligibility of *ex parte* concessions, liable to be resumed at pleasure. I had rather endeavor, by a new treaty of commerce with France, to extend reciprocal advantages, and fix them on a permanent basis. This would not only be more solid, but it would, perhaps, be less likely, than apparently gratuitous and voluntary exemptions, to beget discontents elsewhere, especially (as ought to be the case) if each party should be at liberty, for equivalent considerations, to grant like privileges to others. My commercial system turns very much on giving a free course to trade, and cultivating good humor with all the world. And I feel a particular reluctance to hazard any thing, in the present state of our affairs, which may lead to a commercial warfare with any power; which, as far as my knowledge of examples extends, is commonly productive of mutual inconvenience and injury, and of dispositions tending to a worse kind of warfare. Exemptions and preferences which are not the effect of treaty are apt to be regarded by those who do not partake in them as proofs of an unfriendly temper towards them.

—To Jefferson (Cabinet Paper). *Hamilton*, IV. 98-99.

Encouragement of Manufactures

Of all Hamilton's economic papers, his Report on the Subject of Manufacturers (December 5, 1791) was by far his most constructive and far-sighted, certainly his best informed. As background for the report Hamilton carried on a voluminous correspondence with key men throughout the country, collecting data on the status of manufacturing. In addition he sent local Treasury agents to visit factories, however small, and report to him on their scope and operations.

Hamilton's report stands as the Bible of whose who have advocated government aid to encourage industry. He presented the classical arguments in support of protective duties, but was more inclined to using government bounties than to relying upon a high tariff. This report gives remarkable expression to the idea which came to be known as "the harmony of interests" principle. Hamilton argued that a government-supported industry would strengthen rather than weaken agriculture, create opportunities for enterprise and investment, make jobs for workers, and attract immigrants. These ideas were far ahead of the age and most of the recommendations were not adopted at that time.

Hamilton personally promoted a large enterprise known as The Society for Establishing Useful Manufactures, which was founded in Paterson, N.J., in 1791. But few of the products planned for in that ambitious project were ever manufactured. While Hamilton's own business associates were not successful as industrial entrepreneurs, others were encouraged by his program, and there was a significant expansion of the factory system in this period.

December 5, 1791

The Secretary of the Treasury, in obedience to the order of the House of Representatives, of the 15th day of January, 1790, has applied his attention, at as early a period as his other duties would permit, to the subject of Manufactures, and particularly to the means of promoting such as will tend to render the United States independent on [*sic*] foreign nations for military and other essential supplies; . . .

It ought readily be conceded that the cultivation of the earth, as the primary and most certain source of national supply, as the immediate and chief source of subsistence to a man, as the principal source of those materials which constitute the nutriment of other kinds of labor, as including a state most favorable to the freedom and independence of the human mind—one, perhaps, most conducive to the multiplication of the human species, has intrinsically a strong claim to pre-eminence over every other kind of industry.

But, that it has a title to any thing like an exclusive predilection, in any country, ought to be admitted with great caution; that it is even more productive than every other branch of industry, requires more evidence than has yet been given in support of the position. That its real interests, precious and important as, without the help of exaggeration, they truly are, will be advanced, rather than injured, by the due encouragement of manufactures, may, it is believed, be satisfactorily demonstrated. And it is also believed that the expediency of such encouragement, in a general view, may be shown to be recommended by the most cogent and persuasive motives of national policy. . . .

But, without contending for the superior productiveness of manufacturing industry, it may conduce to a better judgment of the policy which ought to be pursued respecting its encouragement, to contemplate the subject under some additional aspects, tending not only to confirm the idea that this kind of industry has been improperly represented as unproductive in itself, but to evince, in addition, that the establishment and diffusion of manufactures have the effect of rendering the total mass of useful and productive labor, in a community, greater than it would otherwise be. . . .

To affirm that the labor of the manufacturer is unproductive, because he consumes as much of the produce of land as he adds value to the raw material which he manufactures, is not better founded than it would be to affirm that the labor of the farmer, which furnishes materials to the manufacturer, is unproductive, because he consumes an equal value of manufactured articles. Each furnishes a certain portion of the produce of his labor to the other, and each destroys a corresponding portion of the produce of the labor of the other. In the meantime, the maintenance of two citizens, instead of one, is going on; the State has two members instead of one; and they, together, consume twice the value of what is produced from the land.

If, instead of a farmer and artificer, there were a farmer only, he would be under the necessity of devoting a part of his labor to the fabrication of clothing and other articles, which he would procure of the artificer, in the case of there being such a person; and of course he would be able to devote less labor to the cultivation of his farm, and would draw from it a proportionately less product. The whole quantity of production, in this state of things, in provisions, raw materials, and manufactures, would certainly not exceed in value the amount of what would be produced in provisions and raw materials only, if there were an artificer as well as a farmer.

Again, if there were both an artificer and a farmer, the latter would be left at liberty to pursue exclusively the cultivation of his farm. A greater quantity of provisions and raw materials would, of course, be produced, equal, at least, as has been already observed, to the whole amount of the provisions, raw materials, and manufactures, which would exist on a contrary supposition. The artificer, at the same time, would be going on in the production of manufactured commodities, to an amount sufficient, not only to repay the farmer, in those commodities, for the provisions and materials which were procured from him, but to furnish the artificer himself with a supply of similar commodies for his own use. Thus, then, there would be two quantities or values in existence, instead of one; and the revenue and consumption would be double, in one case, what it would be in the other.

If, in place of both of these suppositions, there were supposed to be two farmers and no artificer, each of whom applied a part of his labor to the culture of land and another part to the fabrication of manufactures; in this case, the portion of the labor of both, bestowed upon land, would produce the same quantity of provisions and raw materials only, as would be produced by the entire sum of the labor of one, applied in the same manner; and the portion of the labor of both, bestowed upon manufactures, would produce the same quantity of manufactures only, as would be produced by the entire sum of the labor of one, applied in the same manner. Hence, the produce of the labor of the two farmers would not be greater than the produce of the labor of the farmer and artificer; and hence it results, that the labor of the artificer is as positively productive as that of the farmer, and as positively augments the revenue of the society.

The labor of the artificer replaces to the farmer that portion of his labor with which he provides the materials of exchange with the artificer, and which he would otherwise have been compelled to apply to manufactures; and while the artificer thus enables the farmer to enlarge his stock of agricultural industry, a portion of which he purchases for his own use, he also supplies himself with the manufactured articles of which he stands in need. He does still more. Besides this equivalent, which he gives for the portion of agricultural labor consumed by him, and this supply of manufactured commodities for his own consumption, he furnishes still a surplus, which compensates for the use of the capital advanced, either by himself or some other person, for carrying on the business. This is the ordinary profit of the stock employed in the manufactory, and is, in every sense, as effective an addition to the income of the society as the rent of the land.

The produce of the labor of the artificer, consequently, may be regarded as composed of three parts: one, by which the provisions for his subsistence and the materials for his work are purchased of the farmer; one, by which he supplies himself with manufactured necessaries; and a third, which constitutes the profit on the stock employed. The two last portions seem to have been overlooked in the system which represents manufacturing industry as barren and unproductive.

In the course of the preceding illustrations, the products of equal quantities of the labor of the farmer and artificer have been treated as if equal to each other. But this is not to be understood as intending to assert any such precise equality. It is merely a manner of expression, adopted for the sake of simplicity and perspicuity. Whether the value of the produce of the labor of the farmer be somewhat more or less than that of the artificer, is not material to the main scope of the argument, which, hitherto, has only aimed at showing that the one, as well as the other, occasions a positive augmentation of the total produce and revenue of the society.

It is now proper to proceed a step further, and to enumerate the principal circumstances from which it may be inferred that manufacturing establishments not only occasion a positive augmentation of the produce and revenue of the society, but that they contribute essentially to rendering them greater than they could possibly be without such establishments. These circumstances are:

1. The division of labor.
2. An extension of the use of machinery.
3. Additional employment to classes of the community not ordinarily engaged in the business.
4. The promoting of emigration from foreign countries.
5. The furnishing greater scope for the diversity of talents and dispositions, which discriminate men from each other.
6. The affording a more ample and various field for enterprise.

7. The creating, in some instances, a new, and securing, in all, a more certain and steady demand for the surplus produce of the soil.

Each of these circumstances has a considerable influence upon the total mass of industrious effort in a community; together, they add to it a degree of energy and effect which is not easily conceived. Some comments upon each of them, in the order in which they have been stated, may serve to explain their importance.

1. *As to the division of labor.*

It has justly been observed, that there is scarcely any thing of greater moment in the economy of a nation than the proper division of labor. The separation of occupations causes each to be carried to a much greater perfection than it could possibly acquire if they were blended. This arises principally from three circumstances:

1st. The greater skill and dexterity naturally resulting from a constant and undivided application to a single object. It is evident that these properties must increase in proportion to the separation and simplification of objects, and the steadiness of the attention devoted to each; and must be less in proportion to the complication of objects, and the number among which the attention is distracted.

2d. The economy of time, by avoiding the loss of it, incident to a frequent transition from one operation to another of a different nature. This depends on various circumstances: the transition itself, the orderly disposition of the implements, machines, and materials employed in the operation to be relinquished, the preparatory steps to the commencement of a new one, the interruption of the impulse which the mind of the workman acquires from being engaged in a particular operation, the distractions, hesitations, and reluctances which attend the passage from one kind of business to another.

3d. An extension of the use of machinery. A man occupied on a single object will have it more in his power, and will be more naturally led to exert his imagination, in devising methods to facilitate and abridge labor, than if he were perplexed by a variety of independent and dissimilar operations. Besides this the fabrication of machines, in numerous instances, becoming itself a distinct trade, the artist who follows it has all the advantages which have been enumerated, for improvement in his particular art; and, in both ways, the invention and application of machinery are extended.

And from these causes united, the mere separation of the occupation of the cultivator from that of the artificer, has the effect of augmenting the productive powers of labor, and with them, the total mass of the produce or revenue of a country. In this single view of the subject, therefore, the utility of artificers or manufacturers, towards producing an increase of productive industry, is apparent.

2. *As to an extension of the use of machinery, a point which, though partly anticipated, requires to be placed in one or two additional lights.*

The employment of machinery forms an item of great importance in the general mass of national industry. It is an artificial force brought in aid of the natural force of man; and, to all the purposes of labor, is an increase of hands, an accession of strength, unencumbered too by the expense of maintaining the laborer. May it not, therefore, be fairly inferred, that those occupations which give greatest scope to the use of this auxiliary, contribute most to the general stock of industrious effort, and, in consequence, to the general product of industry?

It shall be taken for granted, and the truth of the position referred to observation, that manufacturing pursuits are susceptible, in a greater degree, of the application of machinery, than those of agriculture. If so, all the difference is lost to a community which, instead of manufacturing for itself, procures the fabrics requisite to its supply from other countries. The substitution of foreign for domestic manufactures is a transfer to foreign nations of the advantages accruing from the employment of machinery, in the modes in which it is capable of being employed with most utility and to the greatest extent.

The cotton-mill, invented in England, within the last twenty years, is a signal illustration of the general proposition which has been just advanced. In consequence of it, all the different processes for spinning cotton are performed by means of machines, which are put in motion by water, and attended chiefly by women and children—and by a smaller number of persons, in the whole, than are requisite in the ordinary mode of spinning. And it is an advantage of great moment, that the operations of this mill continue with convenience during the night as well as through the day. The prodigious effect of such a machine is easily conceived. To this invention is to be attributed, essentially, the immense progress which has been so suddenly made in Great Britain, in the various fabrics of cotton.

3. *As to the additional employment of classes of the community not originally engaged in the particular business.*

This is not among the least valuable of the means by which manufacturing institutions contribute to augment the general stock of industry and production. In places where those institutions prevail, besides the persons regularly engaged in them, they afford occasional and extra employment to industrious individuals and families, who are willing to devote the leisure resulting from the intermissions of their ordinary pursuits to collateral labors, as a resource for multiplying their acquisitions or their enjoyments. The husbandman himself experiences a new source of profit and support from the increased industry of his wife and daughters, invited and stimulated by the demands of the neighboring manufactories.

Besides this advantage of occasional employment to classes having different occupations, there is another, of a nature allied to it, and of a similar tendency. This is the employment of persons who would otherwise be idle, and in many cases a burthen on the community, either from the bias of temper, habit, infirmity of body, or some other cause, indisposing or disqualifying them for the toils of the country. It is worthy of particular remark that, in general, women and children are rendered more useful, and the latter more early useful, by manufacturing establishments, than they would otherwise be. Of the number of persons employed in the cotton manufactories of Great Britain, it is computed that four sevenths, nearly, are women and children, of whom the greatest proportion are children, and many of them of a tender age.

And thus it appears to be one of the attributes of manufactures, and one of no small consequence, to give occasion to the exertion of a greater quantity of industry, even by the same number of persons, where they happen to prevail, than would exist if there were no such establishments.

4. *As to the promoting of emigration from foreign countries.*

Men reluctantly quit one course of occupation and livelihood for another, unless invited to it by very apparent and proximate advantages. Many who would go from one country to another, if they had a prospect of continuing with more benefit the callings to which they have been educated, will often not be tempted to change their situation by the hope of doing better in some other way. Manufacturers who, listening to the powerful invitations of a better price for their fabrics or their labor, of greater cheapness of provisions and raw materials, of an exemption from the chief part of the taxes, burthens, and restraints which they endure in the Old World, of greater personal independence and consequence, under the operation of a more equal government, and of what is far more precious than mere religious toleration, a perfect equality of religious privileges, would probably flock from Europe to the United States, to pursue their own trades or professions, if they were once made sensible of the advantages they would enjoy, and were inspired with an assurance of encouragement and employment, will, with difficulty, be induced to transplant themselves, with a view to becoming cultivators of the land.

If it be true, then, that it is the interest of the United States to open every possible avenue to emigration from abroad, it affords a weighty argument for the encouragement of manufactures; which, for the reasons just assigned, will have the strongest tendency to multiply the inducements to it.

Here is perceived an important resource, not only for extending the population, and with it the useful and productive labor of the country, but likewise for the prosecution of manufactures, without deducting from the number of hands which might otherwise be drawn to tillage, and even for the indemnification of agriculture for such as might happen to be diverted from it. Many, whom manufacturing views would induce to emigrate, would, afterwards, yield to the temptations which the particular situation of this country holds out to agricultural pursuits. And while agriculture would, in other respects, derive many signal and unmingled advantages from the growth of manufactures, it is a problem whether it would gain or lose, as to the article of the number of persons employed in carrying it on.

5. *As to the furnishing greater scope for the diversity of talents and dispositions, which discriminate men from each other.*

This is a much more powerful means of augmenting the fund of national industry, than may at first sight appear. It is a just observation, that minds of the strongest and most active powers for their proper objects, fall below mediocrity, and labor without effect, if confined to uncongenial pursuits. And it is thence to be inferred, that the results of human exertion may be immensely increased by diversifying its objects. When all the different kinds of industry obtain in a community, each individual can find his proper element, and can call into activity the whole vigor of his nature. And the community is benefited by the services of its respective members, in the manner in which each can serve it with most effect.

If there be any thing in a remark often to be met with, namely, that there is, in the genius of the people of this country, a peculiar aptitude for mechanic improvements, it would operate as a forcible reason for giving opportunities to the exercise of that species of talent, by the propagation of manufactures.

6. *As to the affording a more ample and various field for enterprise.*

This also is of greater consequence in the general scale of national exertion than might, perhaps, on a superficial view be supposed, and has effects not altogether dissimilar from those of the circumstance last noticed. To cherish and stimulate the activity of the human mind, by multiplying the objects of enterprise, is not among the least considerable of the expedients by which the wealth of a nation may be promoted. Even things in themselves not positively advantageous sometimes become so, by their tendency to provoke exertion. Every new scene which is opened to the busy nature of man to rouse and exert itself, is the addition of a new energy to the general stock of effort.

The spirit of enterprise, useful and prolific as it is, must necessarily be contracted or expanded, in proportion to the simplicity or variety of the occupations and productions which are to be found in a society. It must be less in a nation of mere cultivators, than in a nation of cultivators and merchants; less in a nation of cultivators and merchants, than in a nation of cultivators, artificers, and merchants.

7. *As to the creating, in some instances, a new, and securing, in all, a more certain and steady demand for the surplus produce of the soil.*

This is among the most important of the circumstances which have been indicated. It is a principal means by which the establishment of manufactures contributes to an augmentation of the produce or revenue of a country, and has an immediate and direct relation to the prosperity of agriculture.

It is evident that the exertions of the husbandman will be steady or fluctuating, vigorous or feeble, in proportion to the steadiness or fluctuation, adequateness or inadequateness, of the markets on which he must depend for the vent of the surplus which may be produced by his labor; and that such surplus, in the ordinary course of things, will be greater or less in the same proportion.

For the purpose of this vent, a domestic market is greatly to be preferred to a foreign one; because it is, in the nature of things, far more to be relied upon.

It is a primary object of the policy of nations, to be able to supply themselves with subsistence from their own soils; and manufacturing nations, as far as circumstances permit, endeavor to procure from the same source the raw materials necessary for their own fabrics. This disposition, urged by the spirit of monopoly, is sometimes even carried to an injudicious extreme. It seems not always to be recollected, that nations who have neither mines nor manufactures can only obtain the manufactured articles of which they stand in need, by an exchange of the products of their soils; and that if those who can best furnish them with such articles are unwilling to give a due course to this exchange, they must, of necessity, make every possible effort to manufacture for themselves; the effect of which is, that the manufacturing nations abridge the natural advantages of their situation, through an unwillingness to permit the agricultural countries to enjoy the advantages of theirs, and sacrifice the interests of a mutually beneficial intercourse to the vain project of selling every thing and buying nothing.

But it is also a consequence of the policy which has been noted, that the foreign demand for the products of agricultural countries is, in a great degree, rather casual and occasional, than certain or constant. To what extent injurious interruptions of the demand for some of the staple commodities of the United States may have been experienced from that cause, must be referred to the judgment of those who are engaged in carrying on the commerce of the country; but it may be safely affirmed that such interruptions are, at times, very inconveniently felt, and that cases not unfrequently occur, in which markets are so confined and restricted as to render the demand very unequal to the supply.

Independently, likewise, of the artificial impediments which are created by the policy in question, there are natural causes tending to render the external demand for the surplus of agricultural nations a precarious reliance. The differences of seasons in the countries which are the consumers, make immense differences in the produce of their own soils, in different years; and consequently in the degrees of their necessity for foreign supply. Plentiful harvests with them, especially if similar ones occur at the same time in the countries which are the furnishers, occasion, of course, a glut in the markets of the latter.

Considering how fast and how much the progress of new settlements in the United States must increase the surplus produce of the soil, and weighing seriously the tendency of the system which prevails among most of the commercial nations of Europe, whatever dependence may be placed on the force of natural circumstances to counteract the effects of an artificial policy, there appear strong reasons to regard the foreign demand for that surplus as too uncertain a reliance, and to desire a substitute for it in an extensive domestic market.

To secure such a market there is no other expedient than to promote manufacturing establishments. Manufacturers, who constitute the most numerous class, after the cultivators of land, are for that reason the principal consumers of the surplus of their labor.

This idea of an extensive domestic market for the surplus produce of the soil, is of the first consequence. It is, of all things, that which most effectually conduces to a flourishing state of agriculture. If the effect of manufactories should be to detach a portion of the hands which would otherwise be engaged in tillage, it might possibly cause a smaller quantity of lands to be under cultivation; but, by their tendency to procure a more certain demand for the surplus produce of the soil, they would, at the same time, cause the lands which were in cultivation to be better improved and more productive. And while, by their influence, the condition of each individual farmer would be meliorated, the total mass of agricultural production would probably be increased. For this must evidently depend as much upon the degree of improvement, if not more, than upon the number of acres under culture.

It merits particular observation, that the multiplication of manufactories not only furnishes a market for those articles which have been accustomed to be produced in abundance in a country, but it likewise creates a demand for such as were either unknown or produced in inconsiderable quantities. The bowels as well as the surface of the earth are ransacked for articles which were before neglected. Animals, plants, and minerals acquire a utility and a value which were before unexplored.

The foregoing considerations seem sufficient to establish, as general propositions, that it is the interest of nations to diversify the industrious pursuits of the individuals who compose them; that the establishment of manufactures is calculated not only to increase the general stock of useful and productive labor, but even to improve the state of agriculture in particular,—certainly to advance the interests of those who are engaged in it. There are other views that will be hereafter taken of the subject, which it is conceived will serve to confirm these inferences. . . .

The objections to the pursuit of manufactures in the United States which next present themselves to discussion, represent an impracticability of success, arising from three causes: scarcity of hands, dearness of labor, want of capital.

The two first circumstances are, to a certain extent, real; and, within due limits, ought to be admitted as obstacles to the success of manufacturing enterprise in the United States. But there are various considerations which lessen their force, and tend to afford an assurance that they are not sufficient to prevent the advantageous prosecution of many very useful and extensive manufactories. . . .

But there are circumstances which have been already noticed, with another view, that materially diminish, everywhere, the effect of a scarcity of hands. These circumstances are: the great use which can be made of women and children, on which point a very pregnant and instructive fact has been mentioned—the vast extension given by late improvements to the employment of machines—which, substituting the agency of fire and water, has prodigiously lessened the necessity for manual labor; the employment of persons ordinarily engaged in other occupations, during the seasons or hours of leisure, which, besides giving occasion to the exertion of a greater quantity of labor, by the same number of persons, and thereby increasing the general stock of labor as has been elsewhere remarked, may also be taken into the calculation, as a resource for obviating the scarcity of hands; lastly, the attraction of foreign emigrants. Whoever inspects, with a careful eye, the composition of our towns, will be made sensible to what an extent this resource may be relied upon. This exhibits a large proportion of ingenious and valuable workmen, in different arts and trades, who, by expatriating from Europe, have improved their own condition, and added to the industry and wealth of the United States. It is a natural inference, from the experience we have already had, that, as soon as the United States shall present the countenance of a serious prosecution of manufactures, as soon as foreign artists shall be made sensible that the state of things here affords a moral certainty of employment and encouragement, competent numbers of European workmen will transplant themselves, effectually to insure the success of the design. How, indeed, can it otherwise happen, considering the various and powerful inducements which the situation of this country offers —addressing themselves to so many strong passions and feelings, to so many general and particular interests. . . .

The supposed want of capital for the prosecution of manufactures in the United States, is the most indefinite of the objections which are usually opposed to it. . . .

The following considerations are of a nature to remove all inquietude on the score of the want of capital:

The introduction of banks, as has been shown on another occasion, has a powerful tendency to extend the active capital of a country. Experience of the utility of these institutions is multiplying them in the United States. It is probable that they will be established wherever they can exist with advantage; and wherever they can be supported, if administered with prudence, they will add new energies to all pecuniary operations.

The aid of foreign capital may safely, and with considerable latitude, be taken into calculation. Its instrumentality has been long experienced in our external commerce; and it has begun to be felt in various other modes. Not only our funds, but our agriculture, and other internal improvements, have been animated by it. It has already, in a few instances, extended even to our manufactures. . . .

When the manufacturing capitalist of Europe shall advert to the many important advantages which have been intimated in the course of this report, he cannot but perceive very powerful inducements to a transfer of himself and his capital to the United States. Among the reflections which a most interesting peculiarity of situation is calculated to suggest, it cannot escape his observation, as a circumstance of moment in the calculation, that the progressive population and improvement of the United States insure a continually increasing domestic demand for the fabrics which he shall produce, not to be affected by any external casualties or vicissitudes. . . .

. . . The sum of the debt in circulation is continually at the command of any useful enterprise; the coin itself, which circulates it, is never more than momentarily suspended from its ordinary functions. It experiences an incessant and rapid flux and reflux, to and from the channels of industry, to those of speculations in the funds.

There are strong circumstances in confirmation of this theory. The force of moneyed capital which has been displayed in Great Britain, and the height to which every species of industry has grown up under it, defy a solution, from the quantity of coin which that kingdom has ever possessed. Accordingly, it has been, coeval with its funding system, the prevailing opinion of men of business, and of the generality of the most sagacious theorists of that country, that the operation of the public funds, as capital, has contributed to the effect in question. Among ourselves, appearances, thus far, favor the same conclusion.

Industry, in general, seems to have been reanimated. There are symptoms indicating an extension of our commerce. Our navigation has certainly, of late, had a considerable spring; and there appears to be, in many parts of the Union, a command of capital which till lately, since the Revolution at least, was unknown. But it is, at the same time, to be acknowledged, that other circumstances have concurred (and in a great degree) in producing the present state of things, and that the appearances are not yet sufficiently decisive to be entirely relied upon. . . .

It is not an unreasonable supposition, that measures which serve to abridge the free competition of foreign articles, have a tendency to occasion an enhancement of prices; and it is not to be denied that such is the effect, in a number of cases; but the fact does not uniformly correspond with the theory. . . .

But, though it were true that the immediate and certain effect of regulations controlling the competition of foreign with domestic fabrics was an increase of price, it is universally true that the contrary is the ultimate effect with every successful manufacture. When a domestic manufacture has attained to perfection, and has engaged in the prosecution of it a competent number of persons, it invariably becomes cheaper. Being free from the heavy charges which attend the importation of foreign commodities, it can be afforded, and accordingly seldom or never fails to be sold, cheaper, in process of time, than was the foreign article for which it is a substitute. The internal competition which takes place soon does away with every thing like monopoly, and by degrees reduces the price of the article to the minimum of a reasonable profit on the capital employed. This accords with the reason of the thing, and with experience.

Whence it follows, that it is the interest of a community, with a view to eventual and permanent economy, to encourage the growth of manufactures. In a national view, a temporary enhancement of price must always be well compensated by a permanent reduction of it. . . .

The want of a navy, to protect our external commerce, as long as it shall continue, must render it a peculiarly precarious reliance for the supply of essential articles, and must serve to strengthen prodigiously the arguments in favor of manufactures. . . .

As in most countries, domestic supplies maintain a very considerable competition with such foreign productions of the soil as are imported for sale, if the extensive establishment of manufactories in the United States does not create a similar competition in respect to manufactured articles, it appears to be clearly deducible, from the considerations which have been mentioned, that they must sustain a double loss in their exchanges with foreign nations, strongly conducive to an unfavorable balance of trade, and very prejudicial to their interests. . . .

Ideas of a contrariety of interests between the Northern and Southern regions of the Union are, in the main, as unfounded as they are mischievous. The diversity of circumstances, on which such contrariety is usually predicated, authorizes a directly contrary conclusion. Mutual wants constitute one of the strongest links of political connection; and the extent of these bears a natural proportion to the diversity in the means of mutual supply. . . .

There is, at the present juncture, a certain fermentation of mind, a certain activity of speculation and enterprise which, if properly directed, may be made subservient to useful purposes; but which, if left entirely to itself, may be attended with pernicious effects. . . .

Except the simple and ordinary kinds of household manufacture or those for which there are very commanding local advantages, pecuniary bounties are, in most cases, indispensable to the introduction of a new branch. A stimulus and a support, not less powerful and direct, is, generally speaking, essential to the overcoming of the obstacles which arise from the competitions of superior skill and maturity elsewhere. Bounties are especially essential in regard to articles upon which those foreigners, who have been accustomed to supply a country, are in the practice of granting them.

The continuance of bounties on manufactures long established must almost always be of questionable policy; because a presumption would arise, in every such case, that there were natural and inherent impediments to success. But, in new undertakings, they are as justifiable as they are oftentimes necessary.

There is a degree of prejudice against bounties, from an appearance of giving away the public money without an immediate consideration, and from a supposition that they serve to enrich particular classes at the expense of the community.

But neither of these sources of dislike will bear a serious examination. There is no purpose to which public money can be more beneficially applied than to the acquisition of a new and useful branch of industry; no consideration more valuable than a permanent addition to the general stock of productive labor. . . .

But it may, hereafter, deserve legislative consideration, whether manufactories of all the necessary weapons of war ought not to be established on account of the government itself. Such establishments are agreeable to the usual practice of nations, and that practice seems founded on sufficient reason.

There appears to be an improvidence in leaving these essential implements of national defence to the casual speculations of individual adventure—a resource which can less be relied upon, in this case, than in most others; the articles in question not being objects of ordinary and indispensable private consumption or use. As a general rule, manufactories on the immediate account of government are to be avoided; but this seems to be one of the few exceptions which that rule admits, depending on very special reasons. . . .

The measures, however, which have been submitted, taken aggregately, will, for a long time to come, rather augment than decrease the public revenue. . . .

This surplus will serve:

First. To constitute a fund for paying the bounties which shall have been decreed.

Secondly. To constitute a fund for the operations of a board to be established, for promoting arts, agriculture, manufactures, and commerce.

—Secretary of the Treasury to the House of Representatives. Original Report on the Subject of Manufactures. Hamilton Papers, 2nd ser.

November 10, 1796

I have been employed in making, and have actually completed a rough draft on the following heads: "*National University; Military Academy; Board of Agriculture; establishment of such manufactories* on *public account* as are relative to the equipment of army and navy, *to the extent of the public demand for supply*, and excluding all the branches already well established in the country; the *gradual* and *successive* creation of a navy; compensations to public officers; *reinforcement* of provision for public debt." I send you this enumeration, that you may see the objects which I shall prepare for.

—To Washington. Hamilton's hand. Hamilton Papers, 1st ser.

December 7, 1796

. . . As a general rule, manufactories carried on upon public account are to be avoided. But every general rule may admit of exceptions. Where the state of things in our country leaves little expectation that certain branches of manufacture will, for a great length of time, be sufficiently cultivated—when these are of a nature to be essential to the furnishing and equipping of the troops and ships of war of which we stand in need—are not establishments on the public account, to the *extent of the public demand* for supply, recommended by very strong considerations of national policy? Ought our country to be dependent in such cases upon foreign supply, precarious because liable to be interrupted? [If the necessary supplies should be procured in this mode, at great expense—in time of peace—will not the security and independence arising from it very amply compensate? . . .

If adopted, the plan ought, of course, to exclude all those branches which may be considered as already established in our country, and to which the efforts of individuals appear already, or likely to be, speedily adequate.]

—Part of Washington's Speech to Congress. Draft in Hamilton's hand except for bracketed section. Hamilton Papers, 1st ser.

Encouragement of Labor

To Hamilton the workingman had an important place in the economy. He differed from Jefferson in his early recognition of the essential need for factory labor as well as farmhands. He was seeking not purely an agrarian state, but a balanced economy. His Report on the Subject of Manufactures reveals him to be a proponent of high wages. He sought to reassure industrial enterpreneurs that they could afford to pay higher wages than the prevailing European scale. Along with Washington and Franklin, he took a liberal attitude toward emigration of industrious persons and favored giving financial assistance to foreign skilled workmen to help them emigrate to America. In a period of labor shortage Hamilton regarded the employment of women and children as necessary to expanding industry and as providing the farmers with supplementary income. But the factory owners did not need this encouragement from Hamilton. At the very time when Hamilton was drafting his report Moses Brown was relying chiefly on the labor of children between eight and fourteen years of age to operate his textile mill in Rhode Island.

December 5, 1791

As to the dearness of labor (another of the obstacles alleged), this has relation principally to two circumstances: one, that which has been just discussed, of the scarcity of hands; the other, the greatness of profits.

As far as it is a consequence of the scarcity of hands, it is mitigated by all the considerations which have been adduced as lessening that deficiency. It is certain, too, that the disparity in this respect, between some of the most manufacturing parts of Europe and a large proportion of the United States, is not nearly so great as is commonly imagined. It is also much less in regard to artificers and manufacturers, than in regard to country laborers; and while a careful comparison shows that there is, in this particular, much exaggeration, it is also evident that the effect of the degree of disparity which does truly exist, is diminished in proportion to the use which can be made of machinery. . . .

So far as the dearness of labor may be a consequence of the greatness of profits in any branch of business, it is no obstacle to its success. The undertaker can afford to pay the price.

There are grounds to conclude, that undertakers of manufactures in this country can, at this time, afford to pay higher wages to the workmen they may employ, than are paid to similar workmen in Europe. . . .

The disturbed state of Europe inclining its citizens to emigration, the requisite workmen will be more easily acquired than at another time; and the effect of multiplying the opportunities of employment to those who emigrate, may be an increase of the number and extent of valuable acquisitions to the population, arts, and industry of the country.

To find pleasure in the calamities of other nations would be criminal; but to benefit ourselves, by opening an asylum to those who suffer in consequence of them, is as justifiable as it is politic. . .

There is reason to believe that the progress of particular manufactures has been much retarded by the want of skilful workmen. And it often happens, that the capitals employed are not equal to the purposes of bringing from abroad workmen of a superior kind. Here, in cases worthy of it, the auxiliary agency of government would, in all probability, be useful. There are also valuable workmen in every branch, who are prevented from emigrating, solely, by the want of means. Occasional aids to such persons, properly administered, might be a source of valuable acquisitions to the country.

—Report on Manufactures. Hamilton Papers, 2nd ser.

November 6, 1793

In execution of the authority given by the Legislature, measures have been taken for engaging some artists from abroad to aid in the establishment of our mint; others have been employed at home.

—Speech of President Washington (Draft by Hamilton). *Works*, VIII, 106-107.

Encouragement of Agriculture

December 7, 1796

That, among the objects of labor and industry, agriculture, considered with reference either to individual or national welfare, is first in importance, may safely be affirmed, without derogating from the just and real value of any other branch. It is, indeed, the best basis of the prosperity of every other. . .

Nothing appears to be so unexceptionable, and likely to be more efficacious, than the institution of a Board of Agriculture, with the views I have mentioned, and with a moderate fund towards executing them.

—Part of Washington's Speech to Congress. Draft in Hamilton's hand. Hamilton Papers, 1st ser.

9

War and Peace

Foreign influence is truly the Grecian horse to a republic.

Peace and trade with all nations; beyond our present engagements, political connections with none.

Alexander Hamilton was a major architect of American foreign policy. As virtual prime minister under Washington he was in fact more influential in the administration than was Secretary of State Jefferson or his successor, Edmund Randolph, in determining the course of our relations with the great powers of Europe. The young nation was confronted with grave international issues. As the French Revolution became a general European war, all powers were expected to take sides. Jefferson and Hamilton agreed on one point. They did not want war. Jefferson was pro-French; Hamilton was accused of bias toward Britain. But both put America's sovereignty and independence above the interests of other powers. The watchwords of Hamilton's foreign policy were national self-interest, integrity, and avoidance of dangerous entanglements.

Some Maxims for the Conduct of Foreign Relations

[December, 1787]

There is nothing absurd or impracticable in the idea of a league or alliance between independent nations for certain defined purposes precisely stated in a treaty regulating all the details of time, place, circumstance, and quantity; leaving nothing to future discretion; and depending for its execution on the good faith of the parties. Compacts of this kind exist among all civilised nations, subject to the usual vicissitudes of peace and war, of observance and non-observance, as the interests or passions of the contracting powers dictate. In the early part of the present century there was an epidemical rage in Europe for this species of compacts, from which the politicians of the times fondly hoped for benefits which were never realised. With a view to establishing the equilibrium of power and the peace of that part of the world, all the resources of negotiation were exhausted, and triple and quadruple alliances were formed; but they were scarcely formed before they were broken, giving an instructive but afflicting lesson to mankind, how little dependence is to be placed on treaties which have no other sanction than the obligations of good faith, and which oppose general considerations of peace and justice to the impulse of any immediate interest or passion. . . .

—*The Federalist* No. 15

September 15, 1790

Gratitude is a word, the very sound of which imposes something like respect. Where there is even an appearance upon which the claim to it can be founded, it can seldom be a pleasing task to dispute that claim. But where a word may become the basis of a political system, affecting the essential interests of the state, it is incumbent upon those who have any concern in the public administration, to appreciate its true import and application.

It is necessary, then, to reflect, however painful the reflection, that gratitude is a duty, or sentiment, which between nations can rarely have any solid foundation. . . .

For it is a *sound maxim*, that a state had better hazard any calamities than submit tamely to absolute disgrace.

—To Washington (Cabinet Paper). Hamilton Papers, 1st ser.

July 17, 1793

. . . Foreign influence is truly the Grecian horse to a republic. We cannot be too careful to exclude its entrance. Nor ought we to imagine that it can only make its approaches in the gross form of direct bribery. It is then most dangerous when it comes under the patronage of our passions, under the auspices of national prejudice and partiality.

—"Pacificus," No. 6. *Works*, IV, 481-482.

April 27, 1794

. . . Energy, without asperity, seems best to comport with the dignity of national language. Force ought to be more in the idea than in the expression or manner.

—To Randolph. Hamilton Papers, 1st ser.

December 8, 1795

Contemplating the situation of the United States in their internal as well as external relations, we find equal cause for contentment and satisfaction, while the greater part of the nations of Europe, with their American dependencies, have been, and several of them continue to be, involved in a contest unusually bloody, exhausting, and calamitous; in which the ordinary evils of foreign war are aggravated by domestic convulsion, riot, and insurrection; in which many of the arts most useful to society are exposed to decay or exile; and in which scarcity of subsistence embitters other sufferings, while even the anticipations of the blessings of peace and repose are alloyed by the sense of heavy and accumulating burthens, which press upon all the departments of industry, and threaten to clog the future springs of government;—our favored country, happy in a striking contrast, enjoys universal peace—a peace the more satisfactory because preserved at the expense of no duty.

—Washington's Speech to Congress. Draft in Hamilton's hand. Hamilton Papers, 1st ser.

British-American Relations

Hamilton believed that the terms of the treaty of peace with Great Britain should be faithfully observed. He warned that Britain might see fit to use violations by the American states as a ground for holding on to the Western posts.

June 1, 1783

I observe with great regret the intemperate proceedings among the people in different parts of the State, in violation of a treaty, the faithful observance of which so deeply interests the United States.

Surely the State of New York, with its capital and its frontier posts (on which its important fur trade depends), in the hands of the British troops, ought to take care that nothing is done to furnish a pretext on the other side, even for delaying, much less for refusing, the execution of the treaty. We may imagine that the situation of Great Britain puts her under a necessity, at all events, of fulfilling her engagements and cultivating the good-will of this country.

This is, no doubt, her true policy: but when we feel that passion makes us depart from the dictates of reason; when we have seen that passion has had so much influence in the conduct of the British councils in the whole course of the war; when we recollect that those who govern them are men like ourselves, and alike subject to passions and resentments; when we reflect also that all the great men in England are not united in the liberal scheme of policy with respect to this country, and that in the anarchy which prevails there is no knowing to whom the reins of government may be committed; when we recollect how little in a condition we are to enforce a compliance with our claims we ought certainly to be cautious in what manner we act, especially when we in particular have so much at stake, and should not openly provoke a breach of faith on the other side by setting the example. . . .

But if I am not misinformed, there are violations going on in form of law. I am told that indictments continue to be brought under the former confiscation laws. A palpable infraction, if true, of the sixth article of the treaty,[1] to which an immediate stop ought no doubt to be put. . . .

I am not, indeed, apprehensive of the renewal of the war, for peace is necessary to Great Britain. I think it also most probable her disposition to conciliate this country will outweigh the resentments which a breach of our engagements is calculated to inspire. But with a treaty which has exceeded the hopes of the most sanguine; which, in the articles of boundary and the fisheries, is even better than we asked; circumstanced, too, as this counry is with respect to the means of making war, I think it the height of imprudence to run any risk. Great Britain, without recommencing hostilities, may evade parts of the treaty. She may keep possession of the frontier posts; she may obstruct the free enjoyment of the fisheries; she may be indisposed to such extensive concessions in matters of commerce as it is our interest to aim at. In all this she would find no opposition from any foreign power, and we are not in a condition to oblige her to any thing.

—To Governor Clinton. Draft in Hamilton's hand. Hamilton Papers, 1st ser.

American neutrality was first threatened in the year 1790, when Great Britain and Spain were at the point of war following a collision of British and Spanish subjects at Nootka Sound off southwest British Columbia. Recognizing the danger that Britain might attempt to march troops from Canada across United States territory, Washington requested his cabinet for opinions on such an eventuality. Hamilton's answer:

September 15, 1790

As to the first point, if it were to be determined upon principle only, without regard to precedents or opinions, there would seem to be no room for hesitation about the right to refuse. The exclusive jurisdiction which every independent nation has over its own territory, appears to involve in it the right of prohibiting to all others the use to that territory in any way disagreeable to itself, and more especially for any purpose of war, which always implies a degree of danger and inconvenience, with the exception only of cases of necessity.

[1] Forbidding future confiscations of Loyalist property or prosecutions of Loyalists.—Ed.

And if the United States were in a condition to do it without material hazard, there would be strong inducements to their adopting it as a general rule never to grant a passage for a voluntary expedition of one power against another, unless obliged to it by treaty.

But the present situation of the United States is too little favorable to encountering hazards, to authorize attempts to establish rules, however eligible in themselves, which are repugnant to the received maxims or usages of nations. . . .

. . . The support of public opinion (perhaps more essential to our government than to any other) could only be looked for in a war evidently resulting from necessity. . . .

But the reality of such an interest is a thing about which the best and the ablest men of this country are far from being agreed. There are of this number, who, if the United States were at perfect liberty, would prefer an intimate connection between them and Great Britain as most conducive to their security and advantage; and who are of the opinion that it will be wise to cultivate friendship between that country and this, to the utmost extent which is reconcilable with the faith of existing engagements; while the most general opinion is, that it is our true policy to steer as clear as possible of all foreign connection, other than commercial and in this respect to cultivate intercourse with all the world on the broadest basis of reciprocal privilege.

—To Washington (Cabinet Paper). Hamilton Papers, 1st ser.

Jay's Treaty

An old source of American grievance against England was the British refusal to conform to the provisions of the peace treaty of 1783 requiring her to evacuate the Northwest military posts. Britain, in turn, charged that the American states had, in violation of that same treaty, raised legal obstacles against the recovery of pre-Revolutionary debts owed to British merchants and of Loyalist property which had been confiscated. By holding on to the posts Britain discouraged Western settlement and kept the profitable fur trade in her own hands. Anglo-American friction was intensified when the British issued Orders in Council in 1793 interfering with neutral shipping. American vessels were seized and American seamen impressed and imprisoned.

Indignation swept the country. The Jeffersonian Republicans, in retaliation, proposed a bill which would have prohibited the importation of goods not the growth, product, or manufacture of the country under whose flag they were shipped—a proposal aimed at ending the British carrying trade with the United States. This proposal alarmed Hamilton, who believed that British exports to the United States were the chief source of tariff revenue, the main prop of his fiscal system. To have upset commercial relations, in his opinion, would have cut our credit to the roots.

Washington agreed with Hamilton and planned to send him to England as a special envoy to negotiate a settlement of differences. The Jeffersonians protested so vehemently that Hamilton withdrew and proposed in his place John Jay, the chief justice. Hamilton, with Washington's approval, drew up instructions to Jay. Whether the results might have been different had Hamilton gone abroad is a subject of fair speculation, for Jay certainly proved no match for the skillful British diplomats. But the basic notion that peace was essential at that time to the growth of the American nation was Hamilton's, and it would be just as proper, then, to call it Hamilton's Treaty as Jay's Treaty.

April 14, 1794[1]

It seems advisable, then, that the President should come to a conclusion whether the plan ought to be preparation for war, and negotiation unincumbered by measures which forbid the expectation of success, or immediate measures of a coercive tendency, to be accompanied with the ceremony of a demand of redress. For I believe there is no middle plan between those two courses.

If the former appears to him to be the true policy of the country, I submit it as my conviction, that it is *urgent* for him to demonstrate that opinion as a preventive of wrong measures and future embarrassment.

The mode of doing it which occurs is this: to nominate a person who will have the confidence of those who think peace still within our reach, and who may be thought qualified for the mission as Envoy Extraordinary to Great Britain; to announce this to the one as well as the other House of Congress, with an observation that it is done with an intention to make a solemn appeal to the justice and good sense of the British Government, to avoid if possible an ulterior rupture, and adjust the causes of misunderstanding between the two countries, and with an earnest recommendation that vigorous and effectual measures may be adopted to be prepared for war, should it become inevitable, abstaining for the present from measures which may be contrary to the spirit of an attempt to adjust existing differences by negotiation.

Knowing as I do, sir, that I am among the persons who have been in your contemplation to be employed in the capacity I have mentioned, I should not have taken the present step, had I not been resolved at the same time to advise you with decision to drop me from the consideration, and to fix upon another character. I am not unapprised of what has been the bias of your opinion on the subject. I am well aware

[1] Endorsement in Washington's hand. Hamilton dated it "April 1794."

of all the collateral obstacles which exist; and I assure you in the utmost sincerity that I shall be completely and entirely satisfied with the election of another.

I beg leave to add, that of the persons whom you would deem free from any constitutional objections, Mr. Jay is the only man in whose qualifications for success there would be thorough confidence, and him whom alone it would be advisable to send. I think the business would have the best chance possible in his hands, and I flatter myself that his mission would issue in a manner that would produce the most important good to the nation.

—To Washington (Cabinet Paper). Draft in Hamilton's hand. Hamilton Papers, 1st ser.

May 6, 1794

The navigation of the Mississippi is to us an object of immense consequence. Besides other considerations connected with it, if the Government of the United States can procure and secure the enjoyment of it to our Western country, it will be an infinitely strong link of union between that country and the Atlantic States. As its preservation will depend on the naval resources of the Atlantic States, the western country cannot but feel that this essential interest depends on its remaining firmly united with them.

If any thing could be done with Great Britain to increase our chances for the speedy enjoyment of this right, it would be, in my judgment, a very valuable ingredient in any arrangement you could make. Nor is Great Britain without a great interest in the question, if the arrangement shall give to her a participation in that navigation, and a treaty of commerce shall admit her advantageously into this large field of commercial adventure.

May it not be possible to obtain a guaranty of our right in this particular from Great Britain, on the condition of mutual enjoyment and a trade on the same terms as to our Atlantic ports?

—To Jay (Cabinet Paper). Draft in Hamilton's hand. Hamilton Papers, 1st ser.

Jay's bargaining position with England's foreign minister, Lord Grenville, was weakened when Hammond, the British minister to the United States, relayed to Grenville the assurance Hamilton had indiscreetly given him that the United States would never ally itself with the European neutrals for the defense of its rights against Great Britain. Thereafter the British negotiators stiffened perceptibly, and Jay won disappointingly few concessions.

Hamilton was doubtless dismayed when he read the confidential text of the treaty. Jefferson quoted a remark of Talleyrand that Hamilton dubbed the treaty "an execrable one" and called Jay "an old woman."

If Hamilton felt this way he was careful not to let his sentiments be made known to the public. Under the terms of the treaty the British agreed to withdraw from the Northwest posts and to open the East Indian trade to America on fairly liberal terms. Debts, boundary disputes, and compensation for maritime seizures were referred to joint commissions. The United States was placed on a most-favored nation basis in trade with the British Isles, but no provision was made for the issues of impressment, slaves removed by the British, or Loyalist claims.

A storm broke out when the treaty's terms were published in March, 1795. Southern planters were annoyed at the treaty's provision for settlement of the debts and its silence concerning slaves not returned to them. Friends of France were chagrined because the treaty gave the same privilege to British ships-of-war and privateers as France enjoyed under the treaty of amity and commerce of 1778. Hamilton had retired to private life, but at Washington's urgent request he entered the controversy with the publication, beginning on July 22, 1795 of his masterly Camillus essays, among his most notable polemical efforts. Previously, in a letter to Washington dated July 9th he had defended the treaty as in "no way inconsistent with national honor." However, it is significant that on September 4th he urged the President to press for a stipulation by England against impressing American seamen, a glaring omission of Jay's Treaty.

July 9, 1795

To these particular views of the different articles of the treaty, the following general views may be added.

The truly important side of this treaty is, that it closes, and upon the whole as reasonably as could have been expected, the controverted points between the two countries; and thereby gives us the prospect of repossessing our Western posts, an object of primary consequence in our affairs, of escaping finally from being implicated in the dreadful war which is ruining Europe, and of preserving ourselves in a state of peace for a considerable time to come.

Well considered, the greatest interest of this country in its external relations, is that of peace. The more or less of commercial advantages which we may acquire by particular treaties, are of far less moment. With peace, the force of circumstances will enable us to make our way sufficiently fast in trade. War, at this time, would give a serious wound to our growth and prosperity. Can we escape it for ten or twelve years more, we may then meet it without much inquietude, and may advance and support with energy and effect any just pretensions to greater commercial advantages than we may enjoy.

It follows that the objects contained in the permanent articles are of real and great value to us. The price they will cost us in the articles of compensation for the debts, is not likely to bear any proportion to the expenses of a single campaign to enforce our rights. The calculation is therefore a simple and a plain one. The terms are no way inconsistent with national honor.

—To Washington (Cabinet Paper). Draft in Hamilton's hand; date in later hand. Hamilton Papers, 1st ser.

September 4, 1795

Some provision for the protection of our seamen is infinitely desirable. At least Great Britain ought to agree that no seaman shall be impressed out of any of our vessels at sea, and that none shall be taken out of such vessel in any of her colonies which were in the vessel *at the time of her arrival at such colony*. This provision ought to be pressed with energy as one unexceptionably just, and at the same time safe for Great Britain.

—To Washington. Draft in Hamilton's hand. Hamilton Papers, 1st ser.

The Camillus *Letters*

1795-96

It is only to know the vanity and vindictiveness of human nature, to be convinced, that while this generation lasts there will always exist among us men irreconcilable to our present national Constitution; embittered in their animosity in proportion to the success of its operations, and the disappointment of their inauspicious predictions. It is a material inference from this, that such men will watch, with lynx's eyes, for opportunities of discrediting the proceedings of the government, and will display a hostile and malignant zeal upon every occasion, where they think there are any prepossessions of the community to favor their enterprises. A treaty with Great Britain was too fruitful an occasion not to call forth all their activity.

—"Camillus", No. 1. (N.Y.) *Argus*, July 22, 1795.

If we can avoid a war for ten or twelve years more, we shall then have acquired a maturity, which will make it no more than a common calamity, and will authorize us, in our national discussions, to take a higher and more imposing tone.

This is a consideration of the greatest weight to determine us to exert all our prudence and address to keep out of war as long as it shall be possible; to defer, to a state of manhood, a struggle to which infancy is ill adapted. This is the most effectual way to disappoint the enemies of our welfare; to pursue a contrary conduct may be to play into their hands, and to gratify their wishes. If there be a foreign power which sees with envy or ill-will our growing prosperity, that power must discern that our infancy is the time for clipping our wings. We ought to be wise enough to see that this is not a time for trying our strength.

Should we be able to escape the storm which at this juncture agitates Europe, our disputes with Great Britain terminated, we may hope to postpone war to a distant period. This, at least, will greatly diminish the chances of it. For then there will remain only one power with whom we have any embarrassing discussions. I allude to Spain, and the question of the Mississippi; and there is reason to hope that this question, by the natural progress of things, and perseverance in an amicable course, will finally be arranged to our satisfaction without the necessity of the *dernier resort*. . . .

I proceed now to observe summarily that the objects of the mission, contrary to what has been asserted, have been substantially obtained. What were these? They were principally:

1. To adjust the matters of controversy concerning the inexecution of the treaty of peace, and especially to obtain restitution of our Western posts.

2. To obtain reparation for the captures and spoliations of our property in the course of the existing war.

Both these objects have been provided for, and it will be shown, when we come to comment upon the articles which make the provisions in each case, that it is a reasonable one, as good a one as ought to have been expected; as good a one as there is any prospect of obtaining hereafter; one which it is consistent with our honor to to accept, and which our interest bids us to close with.

—"Camillus," No. 2. Draft in Hamilton's hand; dated in later hand, July, 1795. Hamilton Papers, 1st ser.

Nations, no more than individuals, ought to persist in error, especially at the sacrifice of their peace and prosperity; besides, nothing is more common, in disputes between nations, than each side to charge the other with being the aggressor or delinquent. This mutual crimination, either from the nature of circumstances, or from the illusions of the passions, is sometimes sincere; at other times it is dictated by pride or policy. But in all such cases, where one party is now powerful enough to dictate to the other, and where there is a mutual disposition to avoid war, the natural retreat for both is in compromise, which waives the question of first aggression or delinquency. This is the salvo for national pride; the escape for mutual error; the bridge by which nations, arrayed against each other, are enabled to retire with honor, and without bloodshed, from the field of contest. . . .

But our dilemma is this, if the delay of orders for evacuating the Western posts, previous to the ratification of the definitive treaty, was, on the part of Great Britain, a breach of treaty, our delay to act upon the points stipulated by us, till after that ratification, must have been equally a breach of treaty; and it must have been at least contemporary with any breach that could have been committed by Great Britain.

—"Camillus," No. 3. (N.Y.) *American Minerva*, July 30, 1795.

True honor is a rational thing. It is as distinguishable from Quixotism as true courage from the spirit of a bravo. It is possible for one nation to commit so undisguised and unqualified an outrage upon another as to render a negotiation of the question dishonorable. But this seldom, if ever, happens. In most cases, it is consistent with honor to precede rupture by negotiation, and whenever it is, reason and humanity demand it. Honor cannot be wounded by consulting moderation. . . .

So likewise, when it is asserted that war is preferable to the sacrifice of our rights and interests, this to be true, to be rational, must be understood of such rights and interests as are certain, as are important, such as regard the honor, security, or prosperity of our country. It is not a right disputable, or of small consequence, it is not an interest temporary, partial, and inconsiderable, which will justify, in our situation, an appeal to arms.

Nations ought to calculate as well as individuals, to compare evils, and to prefer the lesser to the greater; to act otherwise, is to act unreasonably; those who counsel it are impostors or madmen.

—"Camillus," No. 5. (N.Y.) *American Minerva*, Aug. 7, 1795.

There is one more objection to the treaty for what it does not do, which requires to be noticed. This is an omission to provide against the impressment of our seamen.

It is certain that our trade has suffered embarrassments in this respect, and that there have been abuses which have operated very oppressively upon our seamen; and all will join in the wish that they could have been guarded against in future by the treaty.

But it is easier to desire this, than to see how it could have been done. A general stipulation against the impressment of our seamen would have been nugatory, if not derogatory. Our right to an exemption is perfect by the laws of nations, and a contrary right is not even pretended by Great Britain. The difficulty has been, and is, to fix a rule of evidence, by which to discriminate our seamen from theirs, and by the discrimination to give ours protection, without covering theirs in our service. It happens that the two nations speak the same language, and in every exterior circumstance closely resemble each other; that many of the natives of Great Britain and Ireland are among our citizens, and that others, without being properly our citizens, are employed in our vessels. . . .

When we consider candidly the peculiar difficulties which various circumstances of similitude between the people of the two countries oppose to a satisfactory arrangement, and that to the belligerent party it is a question of *national safety*, to the neutral party a question of commercial convenience and individual security, we shall be the less disposed to think the want of such a provision as our wishes would dictate a blemish in the treaty.

The truth seems to be, that, from the nature of the thing, it is matter of necessity to leave it to occasional and temporary expedients—to the effects of special interpositions from time to time, to procure the correction of abuses; and if the abuse becomes intolerable, to the *ultima ratio*; the good faith of the parties, and the motives which they have to respect the rights of each other and to avoid causes of offence, and vigilance in noting and remonstrating against the irregularities which are committed, are probably the only peaceable securities of which the case is susceptible.

—"Camillus," No. 6. Hamilton Papers, 1st ser.

Mutual charges of breach of faith are not uncommon between nations; yet this does not prevent their making new stipulations with each other, and relying upon their performance. The argument from the breach of one promise, if real, to the breach of every other, is not supported by experience; and if adopted as a general rule, would multiply, infinitely, the impediments to accord and agreement among nations. . . .

In estimating the plan which the treaty adopts for the settlement of the old controversy, it is an important reflection that, from the course of things, there will be nothing to be performed by us before the period for the restitution of the posts will have elapsed; and that, if this restitution should be evaded, we shall be free to put an end to the whole treaty, about which there could not be a moment's hesitation. We should then be where we were before the treaty, with the advantage of having strengthened the justice of our cause, by removing every occasion of reproach which the infractions of the treaty of peace may have furnished against us. . . .

Why did we not insist on indemnification for the expenses of our Revolution war? Surely, not because it was less reasonable, but because it was evident that it could not have been obtained, and because peace was necessary to us as well as to our enemy.

This likewise would be the end of a war undertaken to enforce the claim of indemnification for the detention of the posts. We should at length be glad to make peace, either without the indemnification sought, or at best at an expense to carry on the war, without a chance of reimbursement, with which the thing gained would bear no comparison.

—"Camillus," No. 8. Draft in Hamilton's hand. Hamilton Papers, 1st ser.

. . . The surrender of the posts naturally drew with it an arrangement with regard to inland trade and navigation. Such an arrangement, convenient in several respects, appears to be in some respects necessary. To restrain the Indians on either side of the line from trading with the one party or the other, at discretion, besides the questionableness of the right, could not be attempted without rendering them disgusted and hostile. The truth of this seems to have influenced the conduct of Great Britain and France, while the latter was in possession of Canada. . . .

. . . the expediency of some arrangement was indicated by the circumstance of the boundary line between the parties, running for an extent of sixteen hundred miles through the middle of the same rivers, lakes and waters. It may be deemed impossible, from the varying course of winds and currents, for the ships of one party to keep themselves constantly within their own limits, without passing or transgressing those of the other. How, indeed, was the precise middle line of those great lakes to be always known?

It appears evident, that to render the navigation of these waters useful to, and safe for, both parties, it was requisite that they should be common. Without this, frequent forfeitures to enforce interdictions of intercourse might be incurred, and there would be constant danger of interference and controversy. It is probable, too, that when those waters are better explored in their whole extent, it will be found that the best navigation of those lakes is sometimes on the one side, sometimes on the other, and that common convenience will, in this respect, also be promoted by community of right.

Again, it is almost always mutually beneficial for bordering territories to have free and friendly intercourse with each other. This relates not only to the advantages of an interchange of commodities for the supply of mutual wants, and to those of the reciprocal reaction of industry connected with that interchange, but also to those of avoiding jealousy, collision, and contest, of preserving friendship and harmony. . . . Perhaps it may be safely affirmed, that freedom of intercourse, or violent hatred and enmity, is the alternative in every case of contiguity of territory. . . .

The maxims of the United States have hitherto favored a free intercourse with all the world. They have conceived that they had nothing to fear from the unrestrained competition of commercial enterprise, and have only desired to be admitted to it on equal terms. . . .

New ideas seem of late to have made their way among us. The extremes of commercial jealousy are inculcated. Regulation, restriction, exclusion, are now with many the favorite topics; instead of feeling pleasure that new avenues of trade are opened, a thousand dangers and mischiefs are portrayed when the occasion occurs. Free trade with all the world seems to have dwindled into trade with France and her dominions. That country, in the eyes of a certain party, appears to be an epitome of the universe.[1]

—"Camillus," No. 10. Draft in Hamilton's hand. Hamilton Papers, 1st ser.

The facts demonstrate that a trade between us and the British territories in our neighborhood, upon equal terms as to privilege, must afford a balance of advantages on our side. As to the fur trade, for a participation in one eighth of the whole, which we concede, we gain a participation in seven eighths, which is conceded to us. As to the European and East India trade, we acquire the right of competition upon equal terms of privilege, with real and considerable advantages of situation. . . .

. . . . In fact, under the circumstance of common privileges, there is every possible link of common interest between us and Great Britain in the preservation of peace with the Indians.

In this question of danger to our peace by the British participation in the trade with our Indians, the difficulty of restraining the Indians from trading with whom they please (which is admitted by the argument of both sides) is a very material consideration. Would there not be greater hazard to our peace from the attempts of the British to participate in a trade from which we endeavored to exclude them, seconded by the discontents of the Indians, than from any dispositions to supplant us, when allowed a free competition, when no cause of dissatisfaction was given to the Indians, and when it was certain, that war must interfere with their means of carrying on the trade? The security for our peace appears to be much greater in the latter than in the former state of things.

—"Camillus," No. 11. Draft in Hamilton's hand. Hamilton Papers, 1st ser.

. . . The treaty of peace established between us and Great Britain, a common interest in the Mississippi; the present treaty strengthens that common interest. Every body knows that the use of the river is denied to us by Spain, and that it is an indispensable outlet to our western country. Is it an inconvenient thing to us that the interest of

[1] For variant text, see *Works*, V, 291-293.

Great Britain has, in this particular, been more completely separated from that of Spain and more closely connected with ours? . . .

Can any good reason be given why one side of a country should not be accessible to foreigners, for purposes of trade, equally with another? Might not the cultivators on the side from which they were excluded, have cause to complain that the carriage of their productions was subject to an increased charge, by a monopoly of the national navigation; while the cultivators in other quarters enjoyed the benefit of a competition between that and foreign navigation? And might not all the inhabitants have a right to demand a reason, why their commerce should be less open and free, than that of other parts of the country?

—"Camillus," No. 12. (N.Y.) *American Minerva.* Sept. 9, 1795.

Is there any good objection to the mode of the arbitration?[1] It seems impossible that any one more fair or convenient could have been devised, and it is recommended by its analogy to what is common among individuals. . . .

The submission of this question to arbitration has been represented as an eventual dismemberment of empire, which, it has been said, cannot rightfully be agreed to, but in a case of extreme necessity. This rule of extreme necessity is manifestly only applicable to a cession or relinquishment of a part of a country, held by a clear and acknowledged title; not to a case of disputed boundary.

It would be a horrid and destructive principle that nations could not terminate a dispute about the title to a particular parcel of territory, by amicable agreement, or by submission to arbitration as its substitute; but would be under an indispensable obligation to prosecute the dispute by arms, till real danger to the existence of one of the parties should justify, by the plea of extreme necessity, a surrender of its pretensions. . . .

The question is not, in this case, Shall we cede a tract of our country to another power? It is this—To whom does this tract of country truly belong? . . .

It has been asked, among other things, whether the United States were competent to the adjustment of the matter without the special consent of the State of Massachusetts. Reserving a more particular solution of this question to a separate discussion of the constitutionality of the treaty, I shall content myself with remarking that our treaty of peace with Great Britain, by settling the boundaries of the United States without the special consent or authority of any State, assumes the principle that the Government of the United States was of itself competent to the regulation of boundaries with foreign powers—that

[1] Provided for in Jay's Treaty to determine what was meant by the St. Croix River mentioned in the Treaty of 1783 as forming a part of the Northern boundary. —Ed.

the actual government of the Union has even more plenary authority with regard to treaties than was possessed under the confederation, and that acts, both of the former and of the present government, presuppose the competency of the national authority to decide the question in the very instance under consideration. I am informed, also, that the State of Massachusetts has, by repeated acts, manifested a corresponding sense on the subject.

—"Camillus," No. 13. Draft in Hamilton's hand.
Hamilton Papers, 1st ser.

To a man who has a due sense of the sacred obligation of a just debt, a proper conception of the pernicious influence of laws which infringe the rights of creditors, upon morals, upon the general security of property, upon public as well as private credit, upon the spirit and principles of good government; who has an adequate idea of the sanctity of the national faith, explicitly pledged—of the ignominy attendant upon a violation of it in so delicate a particular as that of private pecuniary contracts—of the evil tendency of a precedent of this kind to the political and commercial interests of the nation generally—every law which has existed in this country, interfering with the recovery of the debts in question, must have afforded matter of serious regret and real affliction. To such a man, it must be among the most welcome features of the present treaty, that it stipulates reparation for the injuries which laws of that description may have occasioned to individuals, and that, as far as is now practicable, it wipes away from the national reputation the strain which they have cast upon it. . . .

It is an established principle of the laws of nations, that, on the return of peace between nations which have been at war, a free and undisturbed course shall be given to the recovery of private debts on both sides.[1] . . .

With regard to the reference to commissioners to settle the quantum of the compensation to be made, this course was dictated by the nature of the case. The tribunals of neither country were competent to retrospective adjustment of losses and damages, in many cases which might require it. It is for this very reason of the incompetency of the ordinary tribunals to do complete justice, that a special stipulation of compensation, and a special mode of obtaining it, became necessary. In constructing a tribunal to liquidate the quantum of reparation, in the case of a breach of treaty, it was natural and just to devise one likely to be more certainly impartial than the established courts of either party. Without impeaching the integrity of those courts, it was morally impossible that they should not feel a bias towards the nation to which they belonged, and for that very reason they were

[1] Grotius, Bk. III, ch. XX, sec. xvi.

unfit arbitrators. In the case of the spoliations of our property, we should undoubtedly have been unwilling to leave the adjustment in the last resort to the British courts; and by parity of reason, they could not be expected to refer the liquidation of compensation in the case of the debts to our courts. To have pressed this would have been to weaken our argument for a different course in regard to the spoliations. We should have been puzzled to find a substantial principle of discrimination. . . .

Nations acknowledging no common judge on earth, when they are willing to submit the question between them to a judicial decision, must of necessity constitute a special tribunal for the purpose. The mode by commissioners, as being the most unexceptionable, has been repeatedly adopted.

—"Camillus," No. 14. Draft in Hamilton's hand.
Hamilton Papers, 1st ser.

As to the revival of the claims of traitors or exiles, if property, *confiscated* and *taken* away, is property *holden* by those who have been deprived of it, then there may be ground for alarm on this score. How painful is it to behold such gross attempts to deceive a whole people on so momentous a question! How afflicting, that imposture and fraud should be so often able to assume with success the garb of patriotism? And that this sublime virtue should be so frequently discredited by the usurpation and abuse of its name!

—"Camillus," No. 17. Draft in Hamilton's hand.
Hamilton Papers, 1st ser.

A question may be raised—Does this customary law of nations, as established in Europe, bind the United States? An affirmative answer to this is warranted by conclusive reasons.

1. The United States, when a member of the British Empire, were, in this capacity, a party to that law, and not having dissented from it, when they became independent, they are to be considered as having continued a party to it. 2. The common law of England, which was and is in force in each of these States, adopts the law of nations, the positive equally with the natural, as a part of itself. 3. Ever since we have been an independent nation, we have appealed to and acted upon the modern law of nations as understood in Europe—various resolutions of Congress during our revolution, the correspondence of executive officers, the decisions of our courts of admiralty, all recognized this standard. 4. Executive and legislative acts, and the proceedings of our courts, under the present government, speak a similar language. The President's proclamation of neutrality, refers expressly to the *modern* law of nations, which must necessarily be understood as that prevailing in Europe, and acceded to by this country; and the

general voice of our nation, together with the very arguments used against the treaty, accord in the same point. It is indubitable, that the customary law of European nations is [as] a part of the common law, and, by adoption, that of the United States.

But let it not be forgotten, that I derive the vindication of the article from a higher source, from the natural or necessary law of nature—from the eternal principles of morality and good faith.

—"Camillus," No. 20. Draft in Hamilton's hand. Hamilton Papers, 1st ser.

The truth unfortunately is, that the passions of men stifle calculation; that nations the most attentive to pecuniary considerations, easily surrender them to ambition, to jealousy, to anger, or to revenge. . . .

Besides (as, if requisite, might be proved from the records of history), in national controversies, it is of real importance to conciliate the good opinion of mankind; and it is even useful to preserve or gain that of our enemy. The latter facilitates accommodation and peace; the former attracts good offices, friendly interventions, sometimes direct support, from others. The exemplary conduct, in general, of our country, in our contest for independence, was probably not a little serviceable to us in this way; it secured to the intrinsic goodness of our cause every collateral advantage, and gave it a popularity among nations, unalloyed and unimpaired, which even stole into the cabinets of princes. A contrary policy tends to contrary consequences. . . . Moreover, the measures of war ought ever to look forward to peace. The confiscation or sequestration of the private property of an enemy must always be a point of serious discussion, when interest or necessity leads to negotiations for peace.

—"Camillus," No. 21. Draft in Hamilton's hand. Hamilton Papers, 1st ser.

The inviolability of the principles of the navigation act had become a kind of axiom, incorporated in the habits of thinking of the British Government and nation. Precedent, it is known, has great influence, as well upon the councils as upon the popular opinions of nations!—and there is, perhaps, no country in which it has greater force than that of Great Britain. The precedent of a serious and unequivocal innovation upon the system of the navigation act dissolved, as it were, the spell by which the public prejudices had been chained to it.

—"Camillus," No. 25. *The American Remembrancer* (Philadelphia, 1795-96).

. . . The law of nations was against the rule which it is desired to introduce. The United States could not have insisted upon it as matter of right; and in point of policy it would have been madness in them to go to war, to support an innovation upon the pre-established law. It was not honorable to claim a right, and suffer it to be infracted without resistance. It is not for young and weak nations to attempt to enforce novelties or pretensions of equivocal validity. It is still less proper for them to contend, at the hazard of their peace, against the clear right of others. The object was truly not of moment enough to risk much upon it. To use the French proverb, "*The play was not worth the candle.*" In every view, therefore, it was wise to desert the pretension. . . .

I confess, however, that I entertain much doubt as to the probability of a speedy general establishment of the rule, that friendly ships shall make friendly goods, and enemy ships enemy goods. It is a rule against which, it is to be feared, the preponderant maritime power, to whatever nation this character may belong, will be apt to struggle with perseverance and effect, since it would tend to contract materially the means of that power to annoy and distress her enemies, whose inferiority on the sea would naturally cause their commerce, during war, to be carried on in neutral bottoms. This consideration will account for the resistance of Great Britain to the principle, and for the endeavors of some other powers to promote it . . .

—"Camillus," No. 31. Draft in Hamilton's hand. Hamilton Papers, 1st ser.

No one nation can make a law of nations; no positive regulation of one state, or of a partial combination of states, can pretend to this character. A law of nations is a law which nature, agreement, or usage, has established between nations . . .

—"Camillus," No. 32. Draft in Hamilton's hand. Hamilton Papers, 1st ser.

The remainder of the article,[1] which gives an option to each party, either to request the recall, or *immediately to send home*, the ambassador of the other without prejudice to their mutual friendship and good understanding, is a valuable feature. The power "*immediately to send home*," without giving offence, avoids much delicate embarrassment connected with an application to recall; it renders it easier to arrest an intriguing minister in the midst of a dangerous intrigue, and it is a check upon the minister by placing him more completely in the power of the government with which he resides. These last circumstances are particularly important to a republic, one of the chief dangers of which arises from its exposure to foreign intrigue and corruption.

—"Camillus," No. 35. Draft in Hamilton's hand. Hamilton Papers, 1st ser.

[1] The 26th Article, relating to severance of relations between the contracting parties.—Ed.

Deteriorating Relations

The effects of the Camillus letters upon the opposition to Jay's Treaty were devastating. In despair Jefferson wrote to Madison that Hamilton was "really a colossus to the anti-republican party. Without numbers, he is an host within themselves. . . . In truth, when he comes forward, there is nobody but yourself who can meet him." "For God's sake," he enjoined, "take up your pen, and give a fundamental reply to Curtius and Camillus."

The treaty was finally ratified by the Senate, but hit a snag in the House, when, upon Washington's refusal to turn over confidential papers relating to the negotiations, that body refused to grant funds to carry the treaty into effect. Hamilton was exasperated with the House, which finally yielded, and equally so with the British who continued their high-handed behavior on the seas while the issue of ratification seemed touch-and-go.

April 15, 1796

A letter by yesterday's post from our friend Ames, informed me that the majority (fifty-seven concurring) had resolved in a private meeting to refuse appropriation for the treaty. A most important crisis ensues. Great evils may result, unless good men play their card well and with promptitude and decision. For we must seize and carry along with us the public opinion, and loss of time may be loss of every thing.

To me our true plan appears to be the following (I presuppose that a certain communication has been made):

1st. The President ought, immediately after the House has taken the ground of refusal, to send them a solemn protest. This protest ought to contain reasons in detail against the claim of the House in point of constitutional right, and ought to suggest summarily, but with solemnity and energy, the danger to the interest and peace of the country from the measures of the House, the certainty of a deep wound to our character with foreign nations, and essential destruction of their confidence in the government, concluding with an intimation that in such a state of things he must experience extreme embarrassment in proceeding in any pending or future negotiations which the affairs of the United States may require, inasmuch as he cannot look for due confidence from others, nor give them the requisite expectation that stipulations will be fulfilled on our part.

A copy of this protest to be sent to the Senate for their information. The Senate, by resolutions to express strongly their approbation of his principles, to assure him of their firm support, and to advise him to proceed in the execution of the treaty on his part in the confidence that he will derive from the virtue and good sense of the people, constitutionally exerted, eventual and effectual support, and may still be the instrument of preserving the Constitution, the peace, and the honor of the nation.

Then the merchants to meet in the cities, and second by their resolutions the measures of the President and Senate, further addressing their fellow-citizens to co-operate with them. Petitions afterwards to be handed throughout the United States.

The Senate to hold fast, and consent to no adjournment till the expiration of the term of service of the present House, unless provision made.

The President to cause a confidential communication to be made to the British minister, stating candidly what has happened, his regrets, his adherence nevertheless to the treaty, his resolution to persist in the execution, as far as depends on the Executive, and his hope that the faith of the country will be eventually preserved. . . .

But in all this business, celerity, decision, and an imposing attitude are indispensable. The glory of the President, the safety of the Constitution—the greatest interests—depend upon it. Nothing will be wanting here. I do not write to the President on the subject.

An idea has come from Cooper of an intention in our friends in the House of Representatives to resist the execution of the other treaties—the Spanish and Algerine—unless coupled with the British. But this will be altogether wrong and impolitic. The misconduct of the other party cannot justify in us an imitation of their principles. . . .

Let us be *right*, because to do right is intrinsically proper, and I verily believe it is the best means of securing final success. Let our adversaries have the whole glory of sacrificing the interests of the nation.

P. S.—If the treaty is not executed, the President will be called upon, by regard to his character and the public good, to *keep his post* till another House of Representatives has pronounced.

—To Rufus King. *Hamilton*, VI, 103-105.

April 20, 1796

The British ministry are as great fools or as great rascals as our Jacobins, else our commerce would not continue to be distressed as it is by their cruisers; nor would the Executive be embarrassed as it now is by the new proposition.

. . . the government must take care not to appear pusillanimous. I hope a *very serious* remonstrance has long since gone against the wanton impressment of our seamen. It will be an error to be too tame with this overbearing Cabinet.

—To Oliver Wolcott. Hamilton Papers, 1st ser.

The policy of avoiding foreign entanglements and maintaining neutrality, which Washington, in language refurbished by Hamilton, had expressed in 1796 in his Farewell Address, was as much Hamilton's as

Washington's. When the country seemed to be drifting into war with France Hamilton opposed a formal alliance with England, but did not reject naval cooperation. However, he was as much disturbed about England's violations of American neutrality as about France's. Toward both nations, he counselled Secretary of State Pickering, one of his close followers, the United States should act "with spirit and energy," even if it meant going to war with two nations already at war with each other.

March 27, 1798

. . . I am against going immediately into alliance with Great Britain. It is my opinion that her interests will insure us her co-operation to the extent of her power, and that a treaty will not secure her further. On the other hand, a treaty might entangle us. Public opinion is not prepared for it. . . .

The *desideratum* is that Britain could be engaged to lodge with her *minister here* powers commensurate with such arrangement as exigencies may require and the progress of opinion permit. I see no good objection on her part to this plan.

It would be good policy in her to send to this country a dozen frigates to pursue the directions of this government.

—To Timothy Pickering. Hamilton's hand. Hamilton Papers, 1st ser.

May, 1798

But, in this posture of things, how unfortunate is it that the new instructions offered by Great Britain, which appear, according to the reports of the day, to be giving rise to many abusive captures of our vessels, are likely to produce a counter-current, and to distract the public dissatisfaction between two powers, who, it will be said, are equally disposed to plunder and oppress. In vain will it be urged that the British Government cannot be so absurd as at such a juncture to intend us injury. The effects will be alone considered, and they will make the worst possible impression. By what fatality has the British Cabinet been led to spring any new mine, by new regulations, at such a crisis of affairs? What can be gained to counteract the mischievous tendency of abuses? Why are weapons to be furnished to our Jacobins?

—To Rufus King. *Hamilton*, VI, 287-288.

June 6, 1798

How vexatious that at such a juncture there should be officers of Great Britain, who, actuated by a spirit of plunder, are doing the most violent things, calculated to check the proper amount of popular feeling, and to furnish weapons to the enemies of government. Combauld at the Mole is acting a part quite as bad as the Directory and their instruments. I have seen several of his condemnations. They are wanton beyond measure. It is not enough that his acts are disavowed, and a late and defective redress given through the channels of the regular courts. Justice, and the policy of the crisis, demand that he be decisively punished and disgraced.

—To Rufus King. *Hamilton,* VI, 298-299.

June 8, 1798

. . . I take the liberty to express to you my opinion that it is of the true policy as well as of the dignity of our government, to act with spirit and energy as well toward Great Britain as France. I would *mete* the same measure to both of them, though it should ever furnish the extraordinary spectacle of a nation at war with two nations at war with each other. One of them will quickly court us, and by this course of conduct our citizens will be enthusiastically united to the government. It will evince that we are neither *Greeks* nor *Trojans.*

—To Timothy Pickering. *Works,* X, 294.

October 12, 1799

A firm occupation of the straits which connect Lake Erie with the Huron and Ontario, appears to me a material point. . . . It would seem to me desirable erelong to have on each strait, a work suited to about a thousand men, with an interior work in the nature of a citadel, adapted to about two hundred. . . . The good understanding which at this time subsists between the United States and Great Britain, justifies an arrangement less efficient than that just intimated. But the permanency of friendship between nations is too little to be relied upon not to render it prudent to look forward to more substantial precautions than are immediately meditated.

—To McHenry. Draft in Hamilton's hand. Hamilton Papers, 1st ser.

[1800]

I never advised any connection[1] with Great Britain other than a commercial one; and in this I never advocated the giving to her any privilege or advantage which was not to be imparted to other nations. With regard to her pretensions as a belligerent power in relation to neutrals, my opinions, while in the administration, to the best of my recollection, coincided with those of Mr. JEFFERSON. When, in the year 1793, her depredations on our commerce discovered a hostile spirit, I recommended one definitive effort to terminate differences by negotiation, to be followed, if unsuccessful, by a declaration of war. . . .

[1] I mean a lasting connection. From what I recollect of the train of my ideas, it is possible I may at some time have suggested a *temporary* connection for the purpose of co-operating against France, in the event of a definitive rupture; but of this I am not certain, as I well remember that the expediency of the measure was always problematical in my mind, and that I have occasionally discouraged it.

After the rejection of Mr. PINCKNEY by the government of France, immediately after the instalment of Mr. ADAMS as President, and long before the measure was taken, I urged a member of Congress, then high in the confidence of the President, to propose to him the immediate appointment of three commissioners, of whom Mr. *Jefferson* or Mr. *Madison* to be one, to make another attempt to negotiate. And when afterwards commissioners were appointed, I expressly gave it as my opinion, that indemnification for spoliations should not be a *sine qua non* of accommodation. In fine, I have been disposed to go greater lengths to avoid rupture with France than with Great Britain; to make greater sacrifices for reconciliation with the former than with the latter.

In making this avowal, I owe it to my own character to say, that the disposition I have confessed, did not proceed from predilection for France (revolutionary France, after her early beginnings, has been always to me an object of horror), nor from the supposition that more was to be feared from France, as an enemy, than from Great Britain (I thought that the maritime power of the latter could do us most mischief), but from the persuasion that the sentiments and prejudices of our country would render war with France a more unmanageable business than war with Great Britain.

—*The Public Conduct and Character of John Adams, Esq.*, pp. 47, 49-50.

January 5, 1800

The recent depredations of British cruisers, sanctioned in various instances by the courts, have rekindled in many hearts an animosity which was fast being extinguished. Such persons think they see in this circumstance a new proof that friendship towards this country on the part of Great Britain will always be measured by the scale of her success. A very perplexing conflict of sensations is the result of this impression.

—To Rufus King. *Hamilton*, VI, 415-417.

Franco-American Relations

Hamilton spoke and wrote French fluently and was employed by Washington on numerous missions to officers of the French army and navy stationed in America. His friendship with Lafayette was deep and abiding and he was extremely popular with other French officers. This did not prevent him, however, from sharing with Washington some sense of disappointment that so many of the French officers who were coming to America had ambitions for rank which far outdistanced their actual ability. Hamilton was sensitive to anti-French actions by

American officers which might jeopardize the alliance. Hence, his chagrin at the indiscreet criticism by General Sullivan of Count D'Estaing, the French admiral, whose fleet had been scattered by a storm off Newport in the joint Franco-American expedition against the British in mid-summer of '78, and his criticism on the floor of Congress of the American peace commissioners for ignoring their specific instructions and signing the treaty with Britain without first showing the terms to the French.

HEADQUARTERS, MORRISTOWN May 6, 1777

We are already greatly embarrassed with the Frenchmen among us, and, from the genius of the people, shall continue to be so. It were to be wished that our agents in France, instead of courting them to come out, were instructed to give no encouragement but where they could not help it; that is, where applications were made to them by persons, countenanced and supported by great men, whom it would be impolitic to disoblige. Be assured, sir, we shall never be able to satisfy them; and they can be of no use to us, at least for some time. Their ignorance of our language, of the disposition of the people, the resources and deficiencies of the country—their own habits and tempers; all these are disqualifications that put it out of their power to be of any real use or service to us. You will consider what I have said entirely as my own sentiments.

—To William Duer. Hamilton's hand. Hamilton Papers, 1st ser.

September 1778

You know the feuds and discontents which have attended the departure of the French fleet from Rhode Island. You are probably not uninformed of the imprudence of General Sullivan on the occasion, particularly in the orders he issued charging our allies with refusing to assist us. This procedure was the summit of folly, and has made a very deep impression upon the minds of the Frenchmen in general, who naturally consider it as an unjust and ungenerous reflection on their nation. The stigmatizing an ally in public orders, and one with whom we meant to continue in amity, was certainly a piece of absurdity without parallel. . . . The credit universally given him[1] for a happy and well-conducted retreat, will strengthen the sentiments in his favor, and give an air of cruelty to any species of disgrace which might be thrown upon a man, who will be thought rather to deserve the esteem and applause of his country. To know how to strike the proper string will require more skill than I am master of; but I would offer this general hint, that there should be a proper mixture of the sweet and bitter in the potion which may be administered.

—To Elias Boudinot. Works, IX, 149-151.

[1] Major General John Sullivan.—Ed.

March 17, 1783

. . . I am really apprehensive if peace does not take place that the negotiations will tend to sow distrusts among the allies and weaken the force of the common league. We have, I fear, men among us, and men in trust, who have a hankering after British connection. We have others whose confidence in France savors of credulity. The intrigues of the former and the incautiousness of the latter may be both, thought in different degrees, injurious to the American interests, and make it difficult for prudent men to steer a proper course.

—To Washington. Draft in Hamilton's hand. Hamilton Papers, 1st ser.

March 19, 1783

With respect to the instructions submitting our ministers to the advice of France, he had disapproved it uniformly since it had come to his knowledge, but he had always judged it improper to repeal it. He disapproved highly of the conduct of our ministers in not showing the preliminary articles to our ally before they signed them, and still more so of their agreeing to the separate article. This conduct gave an advantage to the enemy, which they would not fail to improve for the purpose of inspiring France with indignation and distrust of the United States. He did not apprehend (with Mr. Mercer) any danger of a coalition between France and Great Britain against America, but foresaw the destruction of mutual confidence between France and the United States which would be likely to ensue, and the danger which would result from it in case the war should be continued.

. . . He observed, particularly with respect to Mr. Jay, that, although he was a man of profound sagacity and pure integrity, yet he was of a suspicious temper, and that this trait might explain the extraordinary jealousies which he professed. He finally proposed that the ministers should be commended, and the separate article communicated. This motion was seconded by Mr. Osgood, as compared, however, with the proposition of the Secretary for Foreign Affairs, and so far only as to be referred to a committee.

—Speech in Congress on the Treaty of Paris. G. Hunt, ed., *Writings of Madison* (New York and London, 1900), I, 415, 426-427.

March 24, 1783

Mr. Hamilton said that whilst he despised the man who would enslave himself to the policy even of our friends, he could not but lament the overweening readiness which appeared in many to suspect every thing on that side, and to throw themselves into the bosom of our enemies. He urged the necessity of vindicating our public honor by renouncing that concealment to which it was the wish of so many to make us parties.

—Speech in Congress on the Treaty of Paris. *Writings of Madison*, I, 415-46.

The French Revolution came as a shock to Hamilton and prompted him to reexamine America's relations with France and to reevaluate the French contribution to American independence. During the first few years of the Revolution he adopted a policy of watchful waiting.

September 15, 1790

It is not to be doubted, that the part which the courts of France and Spain took in our quarrel with Great Britain, is to be attributed, not to an attachment to our independence and liberty, but to a desire of diminishing the power of Great Britain by severing the British Empire. This they considered as an interest of very great magnitude to them. In this their calculations and their passions conspired. For this, they united their arms with ours and encountered the expenses and perils of war. This has been accomplished; the advantages of it are mutual; and so far the account is balanced. . . .

France is the only weight which can be thrown into the scale, capable of producing an equilibrium. . . .

It is possible indeed, that the enthusiasm which the transition from slavery to liberty may inspire, may be a substitute for the energy of a good administration, and the spring of great exertions. But the ebullitions of enthusiasm must ever be a precarious reliance. And it is quite as possible that the greatness, and perhaps immaturity, of that transition, may prolong licentiousness and disorder. Calculations of what may happen in France must be unusually fallible, not merely from the yet unsettled state of things in that kingdom, but from the extreme violence of the change which has been wrought in the situation of the people.

—To Washington (Cabinet Paper). Hamilton Papers, 1st ser.

His dispassionate judgment of the actual French contribution to American victory is disclosed in these comments on a report submitted to him by Secretary of State Jefferson dealing with negotiations with Spain for the free navigation of the Mississippi.

March, 1792

The general tenor of the report[1] appears solid and proper.

The following observations, however, on a hasty perusal occur.

[1] *These notes are in the hand of Jefferson:* "The report is amended in conformity with this observation."

Page 2. Is it to put our revolution upon the *true* or the best footing, to say that the circumstances which obliged us to discontinue our foreign magistrate *brought upon us the war?* Did not the war previously exist and bring on the *discontinuance?* Was it not rather the *cause* than the effect?

Is it *accurate* to say that France aided us in capturing the *whole* army of the enemy? Does this not imply that there was no other enemy-army in the country; though there were in fact two others, one in New York, another in South Carolina? This last is a mere criticism as to the accuracy of expression. The sense is clear enough.[2] . . .

—To Jefferson. *Works,* IV, 359-360.

Swift-moving events in France and the injection of the French issue into American politics caused the administration much concern. On September 21, 1792, the French monarchy was abolished; in January of '93 Louis XVI was executed. The years 1793-94 came to be known as the Reign of Terror. As the French Revolution was rapidly turning into a war against all of Europe, the First Coalition of the French Republic hoped to secure aid from the United States, not direct intervention but rather to convert America into a transatlantic base of operations against enemy colonies and commerce. Hamilton advocated strict neutrality and also felt that this was an appropriate time to repeal the treaties concluded with France in 1778, but Washington followed him only so far as to proclaim neutrality (April 22, 1793).

April 9, 1793

I have already written you by this post. A further question occurs—Would not a proclamation prohibiting our citizens from taking commissions on either side be proper? Would it be well that it should include a declaration of neutrality? If you think the measure prudent, could you draught such a thing as you would deem proper? I wish much you could.

—To John Jay. *Works,* X, 39.

April, 1793

. . . the late king of France has been tried and condemned by the convention, and has suffered death.

Whether he has suffered justly or unjustly, whether he has been a guilty tyrant or an unfortunate victim, is at least a problem. There certainly can be no hazard in affirming that no proof has yet come to light sufficient to establish a belief that the death of Louis is an act of national justice.

It appears to be regarded in a different light throughout Europe,

[2] "The capture of the army struck out" (Jefferson).

and by a numerous and respectable part, if not by a majority, of the people of the United States.

Almost all Europe is or seems likely to be armed in opposition to the present rulers of France, with the declared or implied intention of restoring, if possible, the royalty in the successor of the deceased monarch. . . .

They have been stated, not with a view to indicate a definitive opinion concerning the propriety of the conduct of the present rulers of France, but to show that the course of the revolution there has been attended with circumstances, which militate against a full conviction of its having been brought to its present stage by such a *free, regular* and *deliberate* act of the nation, and with such a spirit of justice and humanity, as ought to silence all scruples about the validity of what has been done, and the morality of aiding it, if consistent with policy.

This great and important question arises out of the facts which have been stated:

Are the United States bound, by the principles of the laws of nations, to consider the treaties heretofore made with France as in present force and operation between them and the actual governing powers of the French nation? or may they elect to consider their operations as suspended, reserving also a right to judge finally whether any such changes have happened in the political affairs of France as may justify a renunciation of those treaties?

It is believed that they have an option to consider the operation of the treaties as suspended, and will have eventually a right to renounce them, if such changes shall take place as can *bona fide* be pronounced *to render* a continuance of the connections which result from them disadvantageous or dangerous. . . .

If, then, a nation thinks fit to make changes in its government, which render treaties that before subsisted between it and another nation useless, or dangerous, or hurtful to that other nation, it is a plain dictate of reason, that the *latter* will have a right to renounce those treaties; because *it* also has a right to take care of its own happiness, and cannot be obliged to suffer this to be impaired by the means which its neighbor or ally may have adopted for its own advantage, contrary to the ancient state of things. . . .

Nothing can be more evident than that the existing forms of government of two nations may enter far into the motives of a real treaty. Two republics may contract an alliance, the principal inducement to which may be a similarity of constitutions, producing a common interest to defend their mutual rights and liberties. A change of the government of one of them into a monarchy or despotism may destroy the inducement and the main link of common interest. . . .

A treaty *pernicious* to the state is of itself void, where no change in the situation of either of the parties takes place. By a much stronger reason it must become *voidable* at the option of the other party, when the voluntary act of one of the allies has made so material a change in the condition of things as is always implied in a radical revolution of government. . . .

The character of the United States may also be concerned in keeping clear of any connection with the present government of France in other views.

A struggle for liberty is in itself respectable and glorious; when conducted with magnanimity, justice, and humanity, it ought to command the admiration of every friend to human nature; but if sullied by crimes and extravagances, it loses its respectability. Though success may rescue it from infamy, it cannot, in the opinion of the sober part of mankind, attach to it much positive merit or praise. But in the event of a want of success, a general execration must attend it.

It appears, thus far, but too probable, that the pending revolution of France has sustained some serious blemishes. There is too much ground to anticipate that a sentence uncommonly severe will be passed upon it if it fails. . . .

It may likewise be asked whether we are not too late for the ground proposed to be taken—whether the payment on account of the debt to France, subsequent to the last change, be not an acknowledgment that all engagements to the former government are to be fulfilled to the present.

The two objects of a debt in money, and a treaty of alliance, have no necessary connection. They are governed by considerations altogether different and irrelative.

The payment of a debt is a matter of perfect and strict obligation. It must be done at all events. It is to be regulated by circumstances of time and place, and ought to be done with precise punctuality. . . .

Treaties between nations are capable of being affected by a great variety of considerations, casualties, and contingencies. Forms of government, it is evident, may be the considerations of them. Revolutions of government, by changing those forms, may consequently vary the obligations of parties.

—To Washington (Cabinet Paper). Hamilton Papers, 1st ser.

The cause of France in America was seriously damaged by the rash acts of its diplomatic agents. Citizen Genêt, the French minister, commissioned privateers and organized an expedition against Spanish and British territories. When he was rebuked by Washington, he threatened to appeal over the President's head to the people. The antifederalist press and the newly-established pro-French Democratic societies attacked Washington's neutrality policy. Hamilton, writing under the pseudonym, Pacificus, *defended the proclamation of neutrality and the President's constitutional right to proclaim it.*

[May, 1793] (?)

. . . The cause of France is compared with that of America during its late revolution. Would to Heaven that the comparison were just. Would to Heaven we could discern in the mirror of French affairs the same humanity, the same decorum, the same gravity, the same order, the same dignity, the same solemnity, which distinguished the cause of the American Revolution. Clouds and darkness would not then rest upon the issue as they now do. I own I do not like the comparison.

—To ——. Works, X, 45.

[May 2, 1793]

The Convention, on the 19th of November, passed a decree in these words:

"The National Convention declare, in the name of the French nation, that they will grant FRATERNITY and ASSISTANCE TO EVERY PEOPLE who wish to recover their liberty; and they charge the executive power to send the necessary orders to the generals to give assistance to such people, and to *defend* those citizens *who may have been* or *who may be vexed for the cause of liberty.*" Which decree was ordered to be printed IN ALL LANGUAGES.

This decree ought justly to be regarded in an exceptionable light by the government of every country. For though it be lawful and meritorious to assist a people in a virtuous and rational struggle for liberty, *when the particular* case *happens,* yet it is not justifiable in any government or nation to hold out to the world a *general invitation* and *encouragement* to *revolution* and insurrection, under a promise of *fraternity* and assistance. . . .

Her decree of the 15th of December is one of them. This decree, extraordinary in every respect, which contemplates the total subversion of all the ancient establishments of every country into which the arms of France should be carried, has the following article:

"The French nation declare—'That it *will treat* as *enemies,* the *people who, refusing* or *renouncing liberty and equality,* are *desirous* of *preserving their prince and privileged* castes, or of *entering into an accommodation with them.* The nation promises and engages not to lay down its arms until the sovereignty and liberty of the people, on whose territories the French armies *shall have entered,* shall be established, and not to consent to any *arrangement* or *treaty with the prince* and *privileged persons* so dispossessed, with whom the republic is at war.'"

This decree cannot but be regarded as an outrage little short of a declaration of war against every government of Europe, and as a violent attack upon the *freedom of opinion of all mankind.*

The *incorporation* of the territories conquered by the arms of France with France herself, is another of the acts alluded to, as giving just cause of umbrage and alarm to neutral nations in general. It is a principle well established by the laws of nations, that the property and dominion of conquered places do not become *absolute* in the conquerors, until they have been ceded or relinquished by a treaty of peace or some equivalent termination of the war. . . .

That *incorporation,* therefore, changed entirely the principle of the war on the part of France. It ceased to be a war for the defence of her rights, for the preservation of her liberty. It became a war of acquisition, of extension of territory and dominion, and in a manner altogether subversive of the laws and usages of nations, and tending to the aggrandizement of France, to a degree dangerous to the independence and safety of every country in the world. . . .

The pretext of propagating liberty can make no difference. Every nation has a right to carve out its own happiness in its own way, and it is the height of presumption in another to attempt to fashion its political creed.

—To Washington. Draft in Hamilton's hand, undated. Hamilton Papers, 1st ser.

May 15, 1793

The equipping, manning, and commissioning of vessels of war—the enlisting, levying, or raising of men for military service, whether by land or sea, all which are essentially of the same nature, are among the highest and most important exercises of sovereignty.

It is, therefore, an injury and an affront of a very serious kind, for one nation to do acts of the above description within the territories of another, without its consent or permission. . . .

It is manifestly contrary to the duty of a neutral nation to suffer itself to be made the instrument of hostility by one Power at war against another. In doing it, such nation becomes an associate, a party.

The United States would become effectually an instrument of hostility to France against the other Powers at war, if France could, ad libitum, build, equip, and commission, in their ports, vessels of war—man those vessels with their seamen—send them out of their ports to cruise against the enemies of France—bring or send the vessels and property taken from those enemies *into* their ports—dispose of them there; with a right to repeat these expeditions as often as she should find it expedient.

By the same rule, that France could do these things, she could issue commissions among us at pleasure for raising any number of troops—

could march those troops toward our frontiers—attack from thence the territories of Spain or England—return with the plunder which had been taken within our territories—go again on new expeditions, and repeat them as often as was found advantageous.

—To Washington (Cabinet Paper). Hamilton Papers, 1st ser.

July 3, 1793

Whatever partiality may be entertained for the general object of the French Revolution, it is impossible for any well-informed or sober-minded man not to condemn the proceedings which have been stated, as repugnant to the rights of nations, to the true principles of liberty, to the freedom of opinion of mankind; or not to acknowledge as a consequence of this, that the justice of the war on the part of France, with regard to some of the Powers with which she is engaged, is from those causes questionable enough to free the United States from all embarrassment on that score, if it be at all incumbent upon them to go into the inquiry.

—"Pacificus," No. 2. Draft in Hamilton's hand. Hamilton Papers, 1st ser.

July 6, 1793

. . . All contracts are to receive a reasonable construction. Self-preservation is the first duty of a nation; and though in the performance of stipulations relating to war, good faith requires that its *ordinary hazards* of war should be fairly encountered, because they are directly contemplated by such stipulations, yet it does not require that *extraordinary* and *extreme* hazards should be run, especially where the object, for which they are to be run, is only a *partial* and *particular* interest of the ally, for whom they are to be run.

As in the present instance, good faith does not require that the United States should put in jeopardy their essential interests, perhaps their very existence, in one of the most unequal contests in which a nation could be engaged, to secure to France—what? Her West India islands and other less important possessions in America. . . .

The revolution in France is the primitive source of the war in which she is engaged. The restoration of the monarchy is the avowed object of some of her enemies, and the implied one of all. That question, then, is essentially involved in the principle of the war, a question certainly never in the contemplation of the government with which our treaty was made, and it may thence be fairly inferred, never intended to be embraced by it.

—"Pacificus," No. 3. Draft in Hamilton's hand. Hamilton Papers, 1st ser.

When Genêt undertook to equip the brigantine Little Sarah as a privateer in the port of Philadelphia, Hamilton and Knox advocated erecting a battery on Mud Island and sinking the ship if she tried to depart. Jefferson resisted and the ship went to sea. Among the reasons advanced by the Secretary of the Treasury and the Secretary of War were the following:

July 8, 1793

Because there is satisfactory evidence of a regular system in the pursuit of that object, to endeavor to control the government itself by creating, if possible, a schism between it and the people, and enlisting them on the side of France in opposition to their own constitutional authorities. This is deducible not only from a great variety of collateral incidents, but from direct written and verbal declarations of the French Minister.

The memorial lately presented by him to the Secretary of State, the most offensive paper perhaps that was ever offered by a foreign minister to a friendly power with which he resided, announces unequivocally the system which is alleged to exist.

Besides the exorbitant pretensions which that paper advances, of a right in defiance of the declared sense of the government to fit out armed vessels from the ports of the United States, and even to enlist our citizens in their own territories in the service of France; to hold courts within their jurisdiction for the condemnation of prizes unsanctioned by compact, contrary to the rights of neutrality, contrary even to the spirit of the regulations of France for her own consulate establishment, besides the loose and unfounded charges of breach of treaty rudely urged;—that paper more than insinuates the imputation on the President of *ill will* to France *under the instigation of foreign influence*, of having gone beyond his duty and his authority by the decision of matters not within his province, and sufficiently implies an appeal from him to Congress, if not to the people, whose disposition is at least indelicately put in contrast with his. Language of this sort, if even better founded than it is in the present instance, can never be used by a diplomatic character without a culpable violation of decorum. He has nothing to do but with the constitutional organ of the government for foreign intercourse. In his official communication he ought never to look beyond him—nor can he do it without disrespect to the government and to the nation.

The declaration of the Minister of France to Mr. Dallas, Secretary of the Commonwealth of Pennsylvania, as related by him to the Governor of that Commonwealth and to the Secretary of State, is a further confirmation of the same system. That declaration, among other exceptionable things, expressed, "That he, the French Minister, would appeal from the President to the people."

It would be a fatal blindness not to perceive the spirit which inspires such language, and ill-omened passiveness not to resolve to withstand it with energy.

—Cabinet Opinion—Hamilton and Knox. Draft in Hamilton's hand. Hamilton Papers, 1st ser.

July 10, 1793

Whence it follows that an individual may, on numerous occasions, meritoriously indulge the emotions of generosity and benevolence, not only without an eye to, but even at the expense of, his own interest. But a Nation can rarely be justifiable [in pursuing a similar co][1]urse; and, when it does so, ought to confine itself within much stricter bounds.[2] . . .

It is not here meant to recommend a policy absolutely selfish or interested in nations; but to show, that a policy regulated by their own interest, as far as justice and good faith permit, *is*, and ought to be, their prevailing policy; and that either to ascribe to them a different principle of action, or to deduce, from the supposition of it, arguments for a self-denying and self-sacrificing gratitude on the part of a nation which may have received from another good offices, is to misconceive or misstate what usually are, and ought to be, the springs of national conduct.

—"Pacificus," No. 4. Draft in Hamilton's hand. Hamilton Papers, 1st ser.

July 13, 1793

The victories of Saratoga, the capture of an army, which went a great way toward deciding the issue of the contest, decided also the hesitations of France. They established in the government of that country a confidence of our ability to accomplish our purpose, and, as a consequence of it, produced the treaties of alliance and commerce.

It is impossible [to see][3] in all this any thing more than the co[ndu]ct, of a rival nation,[4] e[mb]racing a most promising opportunity to repress the pride and diminish the power of a dangerous rival, by seconding a successful resistance to its authority, and by lopping off a valuable portion of its dominions. The dismemberment of this country from Great Britain was an obvious and a very important interest of France. It cannot be doubted that it was both the determining motive and an adequate compensation for the assistance afforded to us. . . .

Louis the XVI. no doubt took par[t in] our contest from reasons of

[1] Illegible in MS.

[2] This conclusion derives confirmation from the reflection, that under every form of government rulers are only trustees for the happiness and interest of their nation, and cannot, consistently with their trust, follow the suggestions of kindness or humanity toward others, to the prejudice of their constituents. [Footnote not in draft.]

[3] Words in brackets obliterated by wear, tear, and damage.

[4] "Jealous competitor" in published version in *Gazette of the United States.*

state; but Louis the XVI. was a humane and kind-hearted man. The acts of his early youth had entitled him to this character. It is natural for a man of such a disposition to become interested in the cause of those whom he protects or aids; and if the concurrent testi[mony] of the period may be credited, there was no man in France more personally friendly to the cause of this country than Louis XVI. I am much misinformed if repeated declarations of the venerable Franklin did not attest this fact. . . .

The preachers of gratitude are not ashamed to brand *Louis* the XVI. as a tyrant, *La Fayette* as a traitor. But how can we wonder at this, when they insinuate a distrust even of [a] ——!!!

—"Pacificus," No. 5. Draft in Hamilton's hand. Hamilton Papers, 1st ser.

Jefferson recognized that the Pacificus *series bore the inimitable Hamiltonian stamp. "For God's sake, my dear sir," he wrote Madison, "take up your pen. Select the most striking heresies and cut him to pieces in the face of the public." But Madison's* Helvidius *letters could not atone for the outrageous behavior of Citizen Genêt. In his* No Jacobin[1] *series Hamilton castigated the French minister, and in correspondence with Federalist friends elaborated on the threat of Genêt to appeal from the President to the people, a threat which Jefferson had endeavored to withhold from the public.*

[July 31, 1793]

It is publicly rumored in this city that the minister of the French republic has *threatened to appeal from the President of the United States to the people*. . . .

Let us now see in what manner the heavy charges of breach of treaty, which are brought against the executive of the general government, are supported. . . .

All advantages relating to war, which are stipulated in favor of one nation, so as to be incommunicable to another, include more or less of hazard. They are apt to produce irritations, which produce war. In every case of doubt, therefore, upon the construction of treaties, the rule is against the concession of such advantages. The principles of interpretation favor nothing that tends to put the peace of a nation in jeopardy. It is incumbent on a power at war, claiming of a neutral nation, on the ground of treaty, particular privileges of a military nature, to rest his pretensions upon clear and definite, not upon doubtful or obscure, expressions. When founded upon expressions of the latter kind, this claim is always to be rejected.

Hence, consequently, the pretension even to fit or arm in our ports

[1] In answer to letters supporting Genêt published in the *National Gazette* and the *General Advertiser* under the pseudonyms of "Juba" and "A Jacobin," respectively. —Ed.

privateers antecedently commissioned in the ports of France, beyond the mere point of reparation, is inadmissible. It is not necessary to admit it for the sake of finding a useful object of the clause in question. That clause will have a very natural and a very useful application, when it is understood as merely a prohibition to each party to permit a power at war with the other to fit or arm its privateers in the ports of the party at peace. For without it each party would have been at liberty to grant by treaty such a right to other powers, which is now prevented.

—"No Jacobin," No. 1. Draft in Hamilton's hand (dated in later hand). Hamilton Papers, 1st ser.

[August 5, 1793]

. . . But if there had been a disposition to proceed with strictness and rigor, it will be shown in the sequel that it was fully warranted by the very disrespectful treatment we have experienced from the agents of France, who have acted towards us from the beginning more like a dependent colony than an independent nation,—a state of degradation, to which I trust the freedom of the American mind will never deign to submit.

—"No Jacobin," No. 2. Draft in Hamilton's hand (dated in later hand). Hamilton Papers, 1st ser.

August 8, 1793

An established rule of the law of nations can only be deemed to be altered by agreements between all the civilized powers, or a new usage generally adopted and sanctioned by time.

—"No Jacobin," No. 3. Draft in Hamilton's hand (dated in later hand). Hamilton Papers, 1st ser.

August 13, 1793

I have, I believe, sufficiently answered charges which the Jacobin has brought against the Executive of the United States.

In doing this, it has been shown that the claim of a right on the part of France to fit out privateers in the ports of the United States, as derived from treaty, is without foundation. As this is the basis on which it has been rested, and indeed it is the only one upon which it could rest if at all to be supported, it is not necessary, by way of answer to the Jacobin, to discuss how the claim of such a right would stand independent of treaty. But a few remarks on this point, for the information of those who may not be familiar with subjects of the kind, may not be without use.

It is a plain dictate of reason and an established principle of the law of nations that a neutral state in any matter relating to war (not specially promised by some treaty made prior to the commencement of the war and without reference to it) cannot lawfully succor, aid, countenance, or support either of the parties at war with each other; cannot make itself, or suffer itself to be made, with its own consent, permission, or connivance, an instrument of the hostility of one party against the other, and as a consequence of these general principles cannot allow one party to prepare within its territories the means of annoying the other, or to carry on from thence against the other, with means prepared there, military expeditions of any sort by land or water.

To allow such practices is manifestly to associate with one party against the other. The state which does it, ceases thereby to be a neutral state, becomes an enemy, and may be justly treated as such. In common life it is readily understood that whoever knowingly assists my enemy to injure me becomes himself, by doing so, my enemy also; and the reason being the same, the case cannot be different between nations.

—"No Jacobin," No. 4 (New York) *The Daily Advertiser*, August 13, 1793.

August 13, 1793

The facts with regard to Mr. Genet's threat, to appeal from the President to the people, stand thus:

On Saturday, the 6th of July last, the warden of this port reported to Governor Mifflin that the brig Little Sarah, since called the Petit Democrat (an English merchant vessel, mounting from two to four guns, taken off our coast by the French frigate the Ambuscade, and brought into this port), had very materially altered her military equipments, having then fourteen iron cannon and six swivels mounted, and it being understood that her crew was to consist of one hundred and twenty men.

Governor Mifflin, in consequence of this information, sent Mr. Dallas to Mr. Genet to endeavor to prevail upon him to enter into an arrangement for detaining the vessel in port, without the necessity of employing for that purpose military force.

Mr. Dallas reported to Governor Mifflin that Mr. Genet had absolutely refused to do what had been requested of him, that he had been very angry and intemperate, that he had complained of ill-treatment from the government, and had declared that "he would appeal from the President to the people"; mentioned his expectation of the arrival of three ships of the line, observing that he would know how to do justice to his country, or, at least, he had a frigate at his command, and could easily withdraw himself from this; *said that he would not advise an attempt to take possession of the vessel, as it would be resisted.*

The refusal was so peremptory that Governor Mifflin, in consequence of it, ordered out 120 men for the purpose of taking possession of the vessel.

This conversation between Genet and Dallas was *in toto* repeated by General Mifflin to General Knox the day following, and the day after that the governor confirmed to me the declaration with regard to appealing to the people, owned that something like the threat to do justice to his country by means of the ships of the line was thrown out by Mr. Genet, but showed an unwillingness to be explicit on this point, objecting to a more particular disclosure, that it would tend to bring Mr. Dallas into a scrape.

Mr. Jefferson, on Sunday, went to Mr. Genet, to endeavor to prevail upon him to detain the Petit Democrat until the president could return and decide upon his case, but, as Mr. Jefferson afterwards communicated, he absolutely refused to give a promise of the kind, saying only that she would not probably be ready to depart before the succeeding Wednesday, the day of the President's expected return. This, however, Mr. Jefferson construed into an intimation that she would remain. (Mr. Jefferson also informed that Mr. Genet had been very unreasonable and intemperate in his conversation [though he did not descend to particulars], *and that Dallas had likewise told him* [Mr. Jefferson] *that Genet had declared he would appeal from the President to the people.)*

The Petit Democrat, instead of remaining, as Mr. Jefferson had concluded, fell down to Chester previous to the Wednesday referred to, where she was when the President returned. A letter was written to Mr. Genet, by order of the President, informing him that the case of the vessel, among others, was under consideration, and desiring that she might be detained until he should come to a decision about her, but this requisition was disregarded. She departed in defiance of it.

—To Rufus King. Draft in Hamilton's hand. Hamilton Papers, 1st ser.

August 16, 1793

The observations hitherto made have been designed to vindicate the Executive of the United States from the aspersions cast upon it by the Jacobin. Let us now examine what has been the conduct of the agents of France.

Mr. Genet, charged with the commission of Minister Plenipotentiary from the French Republic to the United States, arrived first at Charleston, South Carolina. Instead of coming immediately on to the seat of government, as in propriety he ought to have done, he continued at that place and on the road so long as to excite no small degree of observation and surprise.

Here, at once, the system of electrifying the people (to use a favorite phrase of the agents of France) began to be put in execution. Discerning men saw, from this first opening of the scene, what was to be the progress of the drama. They perceived that negotiation with the constitutional organs of the nation was not the only means to be relied upon for carrying the points with which the representative of France was charged—that popular intrigue was at least to second, if not to enforce, the efforts of negotiation.

During the stay of Mr. Genet at Charleston, without a possibility of sounding or knowing the disposition of our government on the point, he causes to be fitted out two privateers, under French colors, and commissions to cruise from our ports against the enemies of France. Citizens of the United States are engaged to serve on board these privateers, contrary to the natural duties of humanity between nations at peace, and contrary to the positive stipulations of our treaties with some of the powers at war with France. One of these privateers makes a prize of an English vessel, brings her into the port of Charleston, where a Consul of France proceeds to try, condemn, and sell her; unwarranted by usage, by treaty, by precedent, by permission.

It is impossible for a conduct less friendly or less respectful than this to have been observed. To direct violations of our sovereignty, amounting to a serious aggression, was added a dangerous commitment of our peace, without even the ceremony of previously feeling the pulse of our government. The incidents that attended Mr. Genet's arrival here, previous to his reception, though justly subject to criticism, shall be passed over in silence. Breaches of decorum lose their importance when mingled with injuries and outrages. . . .

We read of cases in which one nation has raised men for military service in the dominions of another, with the consent of the nation in whose territories they were raised; but the raising of men, not only without the consent but against the will of the government of the country in which they are raised, is a novelty reserved for the present day, to display the height of arrogance on one side and the depth of humiliation on the other. This is but a part of the picture.

—"No Jacobin," No. 5. (New York) *The Daily Advertiser*, August 16, 1793.

Genêt was recalled. In fact, the Jacobin government had already replaced him with Joseph Fauchet, who arrived in 1794. By this time the constant series of purges in France had aroused in the minds of Federalists like Hamilton the spectre of anarchy and atheism. A shriller note appears in Hamilton's writings, for example in his Americanus *and* Horatius *essays. Fauchet was scarcely an improvement over Genêt. Hamilton was chagrined at Secretary of State Randolph's indiscretion in revealing confidential information to the French minister about the course of Jay's negotiations with Great Britain. In his series of* France *essays Hamilton denounced Fauchet for his intervention in American domestic politics.*

February 1, 1794

. . . There was a time when all men in this country entertained the same favorable view of the French Revolution. At the present time, they all still unite in the wish that the troubles of France may terminate in the establishment of a free and good government; and dispassionate, well-informed men must equally unite in the doubt whether this be likely to take place under the auspices of those who now govern the affairs of that country. But agreeing in these two points, there is a great and serious diversity of opinion as to the real merits and probable issue of the French Revolution.

None can deny that the cause of France has been stained by excesses and extravagances, for which it is not easy, if possible, to find a parallel in the history of human affairs, and from which reason and humanity recoil. Yet many find apologies and extenuations with which they satisfy themselves; they still see in the cause of France the cause of liberty; they are still sanguine in the hope that it will be crowned with success; that the French nation will establish for themselves not only a free but a republican government, capable of promoting solidly, their happiness. Others, on the contrary, discern no adequate apology for the horrid and disgusting scenes which have been, and continue to be, acted. They conceive that the excesses which have been committed, transcend greatly the measure of those which, with every due allowance for circumstances, were reasonably to have been expected. They perceive in them proofs of atrocious depravity in the most influential leaders of the revolution. They observe that among these, a MARAT[1] and a ROBESPIERRE, assassins still reeking with the blood of their fellow-citizens, monsters who outdo the fabled enormities of a *Busiris* and a *Procrustes*, are predominant in influence as in iniquity. They find everywhere marks of an unexampled dissolution of all the social and moral ties. They see nowhere anything but principles and opinions so wild, so extreme, passions so turbulent, so tempestuous, as almost to forbid the hope of agreement in any rational or well-organized system of government. They conclude, that a state of things like this is calculated to extend disgust and disaffection throughout the nation, to nourish more and more a spirit of insurrection and mutiny, facilitating the progress of the invading armies, and exciting in the bowels of France commotions, of which it is impossible to compute the mischiefs, the duration, or the end; that if by the energy of the national character and the intrinsic difficulty of the enterprise, the enemies of France shall be compelled to leave her to herself, this era may only prove the commencement of greater misfortunes; that after wading through seas of blood, in a furious and sanguinary civil war, France

[1] This man has lately met a fate which, though the essential principles of society will not permit us to approve, loses its odium in the contemplation of the character.

may find herself at length the slave of some victorious Sylla,[1] or Marius, or Caesar: and they draw this afflicting inference from the whole view of the subject, that there is more reason to fear that the CAUSE OF TRUE LIBERTY has received a deep wound in the mismanagements of it, by those who, unfortunately for the French nation, have for a considerable time past maintained an ascendant in its affairs, than to regard the revolution of France in the form it has lately worn, as entitled to the honors due to that sacred and all-important cause, or as a safe bark on which to freight the fortunes, the liberties, and the reputation of this now respectable and happy land. . . .

Though it is not to be doubted, that the people of the United States would hereafter, as heretofore, throw their whole property into a common stock for their common defence against internal invasion or an unprovoked attack, who is there sanguine enough to believe, that large contributions of any kind, could be extracted from them to carry on an external war, voluntarily undertaken for a foreign and speculative purpose?

—"Americanus," No. 1. Hamilton Papers, 1st ser.

May, 1795

If Mr. Randolph showed Fauchet any part of the instructions to Mr. Jay, I do not much regret that he manifests displeasure at the withholding of a part. When shall we cease to consider ourselves as a colony of France? To assure her minister that the instructions to Mr. Jay contained nothing which could interfere with our engagements to France might, under all the circumstances, have been expedient; but to communicate specifically any part of the instructions to our envoy, was, in my judgment, improper in principle and precedent.

—To William Bradford. *Works*, X, 99.

May, 1795

But, that any of your countrymen—that men who have been honored with your suffrages—should be the supple instruments of this crooked policy; that they should stoop to nourish and foster this exotic plant, and should exchange the pure and holy love of their own country for a meretricious foreign amour; that they should be willing to sacrifice your interests to their animosity against one foreign nation and their devotion for another, is justly matter of surprise and indignation. No terms of reprobation are too severe for so faithless and so unworthy a conduct.

Reason, religion, philosophy, policy, disavow the spurious and odious doctrine, that we ought to cherish and cultivate enmity with any nation whatever.

In reference to a nation with whom we have such extensive relations of commerce as with Great Britain—to a power, from her maritime

[1] Or Sulla.—Ed.

strength so capable of annoying us—it must be the offspring of treachery or extreme folly. If you consult your true interest your motto cannot fail to be: "PEACE and TRADE with ALL NATIONS; beyond our present engagements, POLITICAL CONNECTION with NONE." You ought to spurn from you, as the box of Pandora, the fatal heresy of a CLOSE ALLIANCE, or in the language of *Genêt*, a true *family compact*, with France. This would at once make you a mere satellite of France, and entangle you in all the contests, broils, and wars of Europe.

'Tis evident that the controversies of Europe must often grow out of causes and interests foreign to this country. Why then should we, by a close political connection with any power of Europe, expose our peace and interest, as a matter of course, to all the shocks with which their mad rivalships and wicked ambition so frequently convulse the earth? 'Twere insanity to embrace such a system. The avowed and secret partisans of it merit our contempt for their folly, or our execration for their depravity.

—"Horatius." Draft in Hamilton's hand. Hamilton Papers, 1st ser.

[1796]

. . . It is time for plain truths, which can only be unacceptable to the hirelings or dupes of that nation.

France, in our revolution-war, took part with us. At first she afforded us secret and rather scanty succors, which wore more the complexion of a disposition to nourish a temporary disturbance in the dominions of a rival power, than of an intention to second a revolution.

The capture of Burgoyne and his army decided the till then hesitating councils of France; produced the acknowledgment of our independence, and treaties of commerce and defensive alliance. These again produced the war which ensued between France and Great Britain.

The co-operation and succor of France after this period were efficient and liberal. They were extremely useful to our cause, and no doubt contributed materially to its success.

The primary motive of France for the assistance she gave us, was obviously to enfeeble a hated and powerful rival, by breaking in pieces the British Empire. A secondary motive was to extend her relations of commerce in the New World, and to acquire additional security for her possessions there, by forming a connection with this country when detached from Great Britain. To ascribe to her any other motives—to suppose that she was actuated by friendship towards us, or by a regard for our particular advantage, is to be ignorant of the springs of action which invariably regulate the cabinets of princes. . . .

It is certain that in the progress and towards the close of our revolution-war, the views of France, in several important particulars, did not accord with our interests. She manifestly favored and intrigued to effect the sacrifice of our pretensions on the Mississippi to Spain; she looked coldly upon our claim to the privileges we enjoy in the cod fisheries; and she patronized our negotiation with Great Britain, *without* the previous *acknowledgment of our independence*;—a conduct which, whatever color of moderation may be attempted to be given to it, can only be rationally explained into *the desire of leaving us in such a state of half peace, half hostility with Great Britain,* as *would necessarily render us dependent upon France*. . . .

Fauchet succeeded Genet. It was a *meteor* following a comet. No very marked *phenomena* distinguish his course. But the little twinkling appearances which are here and there discern[ible], indicate the same general spirit in him which gov[erned] his predecessor. The Executive of our country, in consequence of an insurrection, to which one of them had materially contributed, had publicly arraigned political clubs. *Fauchet*, in opposition, openly patronizes them. At the festivals of these clubs he is always a guest, swallowing toasts full of sedition and hostility to the government. Without examining what is the real tendency of these clubs, without examining even the policy of what is called the President's denunciation of them, it was enough for a foreign minister that the Chief Magistrate of our country had declared them to be occasions of calamity to it. It was neither friendly nor decent in a foreign minister after this to countenance these institutions. This conduct discovered towards us not only unkindness but contempt. . . .

. . . Can it be any thing else than a part of that policy which deems it useful to France, that there should perpetually exist between us and Great Britain [germs] of discord and quarrel? . . .

Those who can justify displeasure in France on this account, are not *Americans*, but *Frenchmen*. They are not fit for being members of an independent nation, but are prepared for the abject state of colonists. If our government could not without the permission of France terminate its controversies with another foreign power, and settle with it a treaty of commerce, to endure three or four years, our boasted independence is a name. We have only transferred our allegiance! we are slaves!

—"France." Draft in Hamilton's hand. Hamilton Papers, 1st ser.

Evidence uncovered in the French archives in more recent years supports Hamilton and discloses that France outrageously interfered in American domestic policies. Delacroix, in charge of foreign affairs under the new Directory, insisted that Washington be overthrown by "the right kind of revolution." The Farewell Address struck a powerful blow against French interference in American affairs. The French government hoped that Jefferson's party would start a pro-French popular revolution, but they were quickly disabused. Adet, who succeeded Fauchet, observed that Jefferson was an American and "as such, he cannot sincerely be our friend. An American is the born enemy of all the people of Europe."

Jay's Treaty and the Farewell Address provoked a violent reaction in France. The Directory refused to receive Charles C. Pinckney as American minister and President John Adams appointed a commission consisting of two Federalists, Pinckney and John Marshall, and one Republican, Elbridge Gerry. Three agents of the Directory, designated in the mission's dispatches as X, Y, and Z, proposed a loan to France and demanded a bribe. The X Y Z affair aroused America to fever heat. Adams avoided a declaration of war, but the years 1798-1800 are marked by an undeclared naval war with France. It is against this background that Hamilton's writings must be placed, notably his shrill exhortations against France in The Warning *and* The Stand.

November 4, 1796

I have lately been honored with two letters from you, one from Mount Vernon, the other from Philadelphia, which came to hand yesterday. I immediately sent the last to Mr. Jay, and conferred with him last night. We settled our opinion on one point, viz.: that whether Mr. Adet acted with or without instruction from his government in publishing his communication, he committed a disrespect towards our government, which ought not to pass *unnoticed*, and would most properly be *noticed* to him as the representative or agent. That the manner of noticing it, in the first instance, at least, ought to be *negative*; that is, by the personal conduct of the President towards the Minister. That the true rule on this point would be to receive the Minister at your levees with a *dignified* reserve, holding an exact *medium* between an *offensive* coldness and *cordiality*. The point is a nice one to be hit, but no one will know better how to do it than the President. . . .

But whatever be the mode adopted, it is certain that the reply will be one of the most delicate papers that has proceeded from our government, in which it will require much care and nicety to steer between *sufficient* and too *much justification*, between *self-respect* and *provocation* of further insult or injury; and that will at the same time save a great political interest which this step of the French Government opens to us. Did I not know how guarded you will yourself be, I should be afraid of Mr. Pickering's *warmth*. We must, if possible, avoid a rupture with France, who, if not effectually checked, will, in the insolence of power, become no less troublesome to us than to the rest of the world.

—To Washington. *Hamilton*, VI, 161-162.

November 11, 1796

I think it is to be regretted that answers were not given to the preceding communications of Mr. Adet. For silence commonly carries with it the appearance of *hauteur* and *contempt*. And even if the paper to be answered is offensive, 'tis better and less hazardous to harmony to say so, with calmness and moderation, than to say nothing. Silence is only then to be adopted when things have come to such a state with a minister, that it is the intention to break with him. And even in this case, if there is still a disposition to maintain harmony with his government, a reply ought to go through our own organ to it, so as to distinguish between the minister and the government.

—To Washington. Hamilton's hand. Hamilton Papers, 1st ser.

November 22, 1796

The alliance, in its future operation, must be against our interest. The door to escape from it is opened. Though we ought to maintain with good faith our engagements, if the conduct of the other party releases us, we should not refuse the release, so far as we may accept without compromitting our peace. This idea is very important.

—To Oliver Wolcott. Hamilton Papers, 1st ser.

[c. 1796]

Facts, numerous and unequivocal, demonstrate that the present AERA is among the most extraordinary which have occurred in the history of human affairs. Opinions, for a long time, have been gradually gaining ground, which threaten the foundations of religion, morality, and society. An attack was first made upon the Christian revelation, for which natural religion was offered as the substitute. The Gospel was to be discarded as a gross imposture, but the being and attributes of GOD, the obligations of piety, even the doctrine of a future state of rewards and punishments, were to be retained and cherished.

In proportion as success has appeared to attend the plan, a bolder project has been unfolded. The very existence of a Deity has been questioned and in some instances denied. The duty of piety has been ridiculed, the perishable nature of man asserted, and his hopes bounded to the short span of his earthly state. DEATH has been proclaimed an ETERNAL SLEEP; "the dogma of the *immortality* of the soul a *cheat*, invented to torment the living for the benefit of the dead." Irreligion, no longer confined to the closets of conceited sophists, nor to the haunts of wealthy riot, has more or less displayed its hideous front among all classes. . . .

A league has at length been cemented between the apostles and disciples of irreligion and of anarchy. Religion and government have both been stigmatized as abuses; as unwarrantable restraints upon the freedom of man; as causes of the corruption of his nature, intrinsically good; as sources of an artificial and false morality which tyrannically robs him of the enjoyments for which his passions fit him, and as clogs upon his progress to the perfection for which he was destined.

As a corollary from these premises, it is a favorite tenet of the sect that religious opinion of any sort is unnecessary to society; that the maxims of a genuine morality and the authority of the magistracy and the laws are a sufficient and ought to be the only security for civil rights and private happiness.

—Fragment on the French Revolution. *Works*, VIII, 425-427.

December 6, 1796

The generosity of France and the gratitude of the United States have been often suggested by some of our own citizens, and we are now *reproached* with it by France herself. Gratitude is due for favors received; and this virtue may exist among nations as well as among individuals; but the motive of the benefit must be solely the advantage of the party on whom it was conferred, else it ceases to be a favor. There is positive proof that France did not enter into the alliance with us in 1778 *for our advantage*, but for her own. The whole course of the investigation, as well as a positive knowledge of the fact, proves this. She resisted all of our solicitations for effectual assistance for war three years, and rose in her demand during the campaign of 1777, when our affairs presented the most threatening aspect. Memorials were presented in August and September of that year, while General Burgoyne's army arrived in December;[1] fearing we might be able to do the business without them, the French court began to change its tone. . . . In the interval between the declaration of independence and the alliance with France, that court sometimes ordered away our privateers, and sometimes restored their prizes. They refused to receive an ambassador or acknowledge our independence; all of which was for fear of bringing France prematurely into the war. The fact is, that the French spoke of very different terms, as the condition of their assistance, before the capture of Burgoyne, from those actually agreed on afterwards.

—"The Answer." *Hamilton*, VII, 609-610.

January 19, 1797

Our merchants here are becoming very uneasy on the subject of the French captures and seizures. They are certainly very perplexing and alarming, and present an evil of a magnitude to be intolerable, if not shortly remedied. My anxiety to preserve peace with France is known to you, and it must be the wish of every prudent man that no honorable expedient for avoiding a rupture be omitted. Yet there are bounds

[1] Burgoyne surrendered at Saratoga on Oct. 17, 1777, but the bulk of his troops were held as prisoners in America until the end of the war.—Ed.

to all things. This country cannot see its trade an absolute prey to France without resistance. We seem to be where we were with Great Britain when Mr. Jay was sent there, and I cannot discern but that the spirit of the policy, then pursued with regard to England, will be the proper one now in respect to France—viz.: a solemn and final appeal to the justice and interest of France, and if this will not do, measures of self-defence. Any thing is better than absolute humiliation. France has already gone much further than Great Britain ever did.

—To Washington. *Works*, X, 229-230.

January 20, 1797

. . . I believe *erelong* an embargo on *our own vessels* will be advisable—to last till the conduct of France changes, or till it is ascertained it will not change. In the last event, the following system may be adopted: to grant special letters of *mark*, with authority to repel aggressors and capture *assailants;* to equip our frigates; to arm a number of *sloops-of-war* of existing vessels to convoy our merchantmen. This may be a middle term to general hostility, though it may slide into the latter. Yet, in this case, it may be well to let France make the progress. But at all events we must protect our commerce and save our honor.

—To Theodore Sedgwick. Hamilton's hand. Hamilton Papers, 1st ser.

January 27, 1797

The complaints of France may be regarded principally as weapons furnished to her adherents to defend her cause, notwithstanding the blows she inflicts. Her aim has been, in every instance, to seduce the people from their government, and, by dividing, to conquer and oppress. Hitherto, happily, the potent spells of this political sorcery have, in most countries, been counteracted and dissipated by the sacred flame of patriotism. One melancholy exception serves as a warning to the rest of mankind to shun the fatal snare. It is, nevertheless, humiliating, that there are men among us depraved enough to make use of the arms she has furnished in her service, and to vindicate her aggressions as the effect of a just resentment, provoked by the ill conduct of our government. But the artifice will not succeed. The eyes of the people of this country are, every day, more and more opened to the true character of the politics of France; and the period is fast approaching when it will be universally seen in all its intrinsic deformity.

The desire of a power at war to destroy the commerce of its enemy, is a natural effect of the state of war, and while exercised within bounds, consistent with the rights of nations who are not engaged in the contest, entirely justifiable; but when it manifestly overleaps these bounds, and indulges in palpable violations of neutral rights, without even the color of justification in the usages of war, it becomes an intolerable tyranny, wounds the sovereignty of nations, and calls them to resistance by every motive of self-preservation and self-respect. . . .

It is now indispensable that the disagreeable and menacing truth should be exposed in full day to the people of America; that they should contemplate it seriously, and prepare their minds for extremities, which nothing short of abject submission may be able to avert. This will serve them as an armor against the machinations of traitorous men, who may wish to make them instruments of the ambition of a foreign power, to persuade them to concur in forging chains for mankind, and to accept, as their reward, the despicable privilege of wearing them a day later than others.

—"The Warning," I. Draft in Hamilton's hand.
Hamilton Papers, 1st ser.

February 7, 1797

. . . If France can finally realize her present plan of aggrandizement, she will attain to a degree of greatness and power which, if not counteracted by internal disorder, will tend to make her the terror and the scourge of nations. The spirit of moderation in a state of overbearing power is a phenomenon which has not yet appeared, and which no wise man will expect ever to see. It is certain that a very different spirit has hitherto marked the career of the new republic; and it is due to truth to add, that the ardent, impetuous, and military genius of the French affords perhaps less prospect of such a spirit in them than in any other people. . . .

When it was the opinion, that France was defending the cause of liberty, it was a decisive argument against embarking with her in the contest, that it would expose us to hazards and evils infinitely disproportioned to the assistance we could render. Now that question plainly is, whether France shall give the law to mankind. . . .

No! let this never be doubted! the servile minions of France—those who have no sensibility to injury but when it comes from Great Britain, who are unconscious of any rights to be protected against France; who, at a moment when the public safety more than ever demands a strict union between the people and their government, traitorously labor to detach them from it, and to turn against the government, for pretended faults, the resentment which the real oppressions of France ought to inspire;—these wretched men will discover in the end, that they are as insignificant as they are unprincipled. They will find that they have vainly flattered themselves with the co-operation of the great body of those men with whom the spirit of party has hitherto associated them. In such an extremity the adventitious discriminations of party will be lost in the patriotism and pride of the American character. Good citizens of every political denomination will remember that they are Americans; that when their country is in danger, the merit or demerit of particular measures is no longer a question; that it is the duty of all to unite their efforts to guard the national rights, to avert national humiliation, and to withstand the imposition of a foreign yoke. The true and genuine spirit of 1776, not the vile counterfeits of in which so often disgust our eyes and our ears, will warm every truly American heart, and light up in it a noble emulation to maintain inviolate the rights and unsullied the honor of the nation. It will be proved, to the confusion of all false patriots, that we did not break the fetters of one foreign tyranny to put on those of another. It will be again proved to the world that we understand our rights, and have the courage to defend them.

—"Americus", in *The Warning,* Part II. Draft in Hamilton's hand. Hamilton Papers, 1st ser.

February 26, 1797

The commission should be charged to make explanations, to remonstrate, to ask indemnification, and they should be empowered to make a new treaty of commerce, not inconsistent with our other treaties, and perhaps to abrogate or remodify the treaty of alliance.

That treaty can only be inconvenient to us in the future. The guaranty of our sovereignty and independence henceforth is nominal. The guaranty of the West India Islands of France, as we advance in strength, will be more and more real. In future, and in a truly defensive war, I think we shall be bound to comply efficaciously with our guaranty. Nor have I been able to see that it means less than obligation to take part in such a war with our whole force. I have no idea of treaties which are not executed.

Hence, I want to get rid of that treaty by mutual CONSENT, or to liquidate its meaning to a treaty of *definite* succor, in a clearly *defensive* war; so many men, so many ships, so much money, etc. to be furnished by one ally to the other. This, of course, must be so managed as to exclude unequivocally the present war in all its possible mutations. The idea of a definite duration would also be useful.

—To Theodore Sedgwick. Hamilton's hand. Hamilton Papers, 1st ser.

March 22, 1797

. . . I would appoint a day of humiliation and prayer. In such a crisis this appears to me proper in itself, and it will be politically useful to impress our nation that there is a serious state of things—to strengthen religious ideas in a contest, which in its progress may require that our people may consider themselves as the defenders of their country against atheism, conquest, and anarchy.

—To Timothy Pickering. *Hamilton,* VI, 213-215.

March 27, 1797

The man who, after this mass of evidence, shall be the apologist of France, and the calumniator of his own government, is not an American. The choice for him lies between being deemed a fool, a madman, or a traitor.

—"Americus", in *The Warning,* Part VI. Draft in Hamilton's hand. Hamilton Papers, 1st ser.

April 5, 1797

The situation of our country, my dear sir, is singularly critical. The map of Europe is every way discouraging. There is too much reason to apprehend that the Emperor of Germany, in danger from Russia and Prussia, perhaps from the Porte, as well as from France, may be compelled to yield to the views of the latter. England, standing alone, may be driven to a similar issue. It is certain that great consternation in court and country attended the intelligence of Bonaparte's last victories. Either to be in rupture with France, united with England alone, or singly, as is possible, would be a most unwelcome situation. Divided as we are, who can say what would be hazarded by it?

In such a situation, it appeared to me we should rather err on the side of condescension than on the opposite side. We ought to do every thing to avoid rupture, without unworthy sacrifices, and to keep in view, as a primary object, union at home.

No measure can tend more to this than an extraordinary mission. And it is certain to fulfil the ends proposed.

—To Oliver Wolcott. Hamilton Papers, 1st ser.

April 8, 1797

The conduct of France has been a very powerful medicine for the political disease of our country. I think the community improves in soundness.

—To Rufus King. *Hamilton,* VI, 236.

June 6, 1797

I like very well the course of Executive conduct in regard to the controversy with France, and I like the answer of the Senate in regard to the President's speech.

But I confess, I have not been well satisfied with the answer reported in the House. It contains too many hard expressions; and *hard words* are very rarely useful in public proceedings. Mr. *Jay* and other friends here have been struck in the same manner with myself. We shall not regret to see the answer softened down. *Real firmness* is good for every thing. *Strut* is good for nothing.

—To Oliver Wolcott. Hamilton Papers, 1st ser.

[1798]

Every day brings fresh confirmations of the truth of the prediction to our envoys that the French faction in America would go all lengths with their imperious and unprincipled masters. . . . After all that has happened, there is no other solution of the indefatigable and malignant exertions which they are making to propagate disaffection to our own government, and to justify or extenuate the conduct of France. . . .

It may serve as an index to the affair to understand that *Beaumarchais* is one of the most cunning and intriguing men of Europe; that he was employed under the royal government as a secret confidential agent, in which capacity he acted between the United States and France, before the acknowledgment of our independence, and that he is known to be in intimate connection with the present French Minister for Foreign Relations.

In the capacity of confidential agent a considerable part of the monies advanced by France for the use of the United States passed through his hands. There was a sum of a million of livres which Dr. Franklin, in the carelessness of confidence, acknowledged to have been received, of which the application could not be traced. When inquiry on behalf of our government was made of the French Minister concerning the appropriation of this million, the only answer to be obtained was that it was a "*secret du cabinet.*" But the Revolution has unravelled this secret. During the reign of Robespierre, *Beaumarchais* was in disgrace and a fugitive. The ministry of that period, not scrupling to unveil the corruptions of the old government, charged the receipt of the missing million upon *Beaumarchais,* and furnished a copy of *the receipt*[1] *which he is alleged to have* given for it.

This transaction proves that *Beaumarchais,* besides being the confidential political agent of the then administration of France, was the instrument or accomplice of its cupidity. What but the participation of the Minister in a scheme of embezzlement could have induced him to make a *cabinet secret* of the application of this million?

Who a more likely, a more fit instrument of the avidity of the present government than this same *Beaumarchais?* When men apparently in close connection with him take bribes from foreign ministers, professedly for the use of the Directory, what more probable than that they are truly for that use—that Beaumarchais is the link between the Directory and the ostensible agents?

If afterwards expedient or necessary to disavow, what more easy to be managed? *Beaumarchais* is no doubt too adroit to transact such business in a manner that can admit of proof of his agency. If inculpated by his agents he has only boldly to deny the charge and to treat it as a part of the imposture. The all sufficient patronage of the Directory could not fail to ensure credit to his denial and to shield him from detection.

—"Detector." Draft in Hamilton's hand. Hamilton Papers, 1st ser.

[1] This copy of the receipt is in the Gouverneur Morris Papers. Special Collections, Columbia Univ. Lib.

April 16, 1798

In acknowledging the republic, the United States preceded every other nation. It was not till a long time after, that any of the neutral powers followed the example. Had prudence been exclusively consulted, our government might not have done all that it did at this juncture, when the case was very nearly EUROPE in arms against FRANCE. . . .

It ought to have no small merit in the eyes of France, that at so critical a period of her affairs, we were willing to run risks so imminent. The fact is, that it had nearly implicated us in the war on her side, at a juncture when all calculations were against her, and when it was certain she could have afforded us no protection or assistance.

What was the return? *Genet* came with neutrality on his lips, but war in his heart. The instructions published by himself, and his practice upon them, demonstrate that it was the premeditated plan to involve us in the contest; not by a candid appeal to the judgment, friendship, or interest of our country but by alluring the avarice of bad citizens into acts of predatory hostility, by instituting within our territory military expeditions against nations with whom we were at peace. And when it was found that our Executive would not connive at this insidious plan, bold attempts were made to create a schism between the people and the government, and, consequently, to sow the seeds of civil discord, insurrection, and revolution. Thus began the republic.

—"Titus Manlius," in *The Stand,* Part V. Draft in Hamilton's hand; date in later hand. Hamilton Papers, 1st ser.

March 10, 1798

With an immense ocean rolling between the United States and France; with ample materials for ship-building, and a body of hardy seamen more numerous and more expert than France can boast; with a population exceeding five millions, spread over a wide extent of country, offering no one point, the seizure of which, as of the great capitals of Europe, might decide the issue; with a soil liberal of all the productions that give strength and resource; with the rudiments of the most essential manufactures, capable of being developed in proportion to our want; with a numerous and, in many quarters, well-appointed militia; with respectable revenues and a flourishing credit; with many of the principal sources of taxation yet untouched; with considerable arsenals, and the means of extending them; with experienced officers ready to form an army under the command of the same illustrious chief who before lead them to victory and glory, and who, if the occasion should require it, could not hesitate to obey the summons of his country;—what a striking and encouraging contrast does this situation in many respects present, to that in which we defied the thunder of

Britain! What is there in it to excuse or palliate the cowardice and baseness of a tame surrender of our rights to France?

The question is unnecessary. The people of America are neither idiots nor dastards. They did not break one yoke to put on another. Though a portion of them have been hitherto misled; yet not even these, still less the great body of the nation, can be long unaware of the true situation, or blind to the treacherous arts by which they are attempted to be hoodwinked. The unfaithful and guilty leaders of a foreign faction, unmasked in all their intrinsic deformity, must quickly shrink from the scene appalled and confounded. The virtuous whom they have led astray will renounce their exotic standard. Honest men of all parties will unite to maintain and defend the honor and the sovereignty of their country.

—"The Stand," Part I. *Hamilton,* VII, 642-643.

March 17, 1798

I wish to see a *temperate,* but *grave, solemn,* and *firm* communication from the President to the two houses on the result of the advices from our commissioners. . . .

The measures to be advocated by our friends in Congress to be these:

I.—Permission to our merchant vessels to arm and to capture those which may attack them.

II.—The completion of our frigates, and the provision of a considerable number of sloops-of-war not exceeding twenty guns. Authority to capture all attacking, and privateers found within twenty leagues of our coast.

III.—Power to the President, in general terms, to provide and equip ten ships of the line in case of open rupture with any foreign power.

IV.—The increase of our military establishment to twenty thousand, and a provisional army of thirty thousand, besides the militia.

V.—The efficacious fortification of our principal ports, say Portsmouth, Boston, Newport, New London, New York, Philadelphia, Norfolk, Baltimore, Wilmington, N. C., Charleston, Savannah. It is a waste of money to be more diffusive.

VI.—The extension of our revenue to all the principal objects of taxation, and a loan commensurate with the contemplated expenditures.

VII.—The *suspension* of our treaties with France till a basis of connection shall be re-established by treaty.

In my opinion, bold language and bold measures are indispensable. The attitude of *calm defiance* suits us. It is vain to talk of peace with a power with which we are actually in hostility.

—To Timothy Pickering. *Hamilton,* VI, 269-271.

April 7, 1798

In reviewing the disgusting spectacle of the French Revolution, it is difficult to avert the eye entirely from those features of it which betray a plan to disorganize the human mind itself, as well as to undermine the venerable pillars that support the edifice of civilized society. The attempt by the rulers of a nation to destroy all religious opinion, and to pervert a whole nation to atheism, is a phenomenon of profligacy reserved to consummate the infamy of the unprincipled reformers of France. . . .

Equal pains have been taken to deprave the morals as to extinguish the religion of the country, if indeed morality in a community can be separated from religion. It is among the singular and fantastic vagaries of the French Revolution, that while the Duke of Brunswick was marching to Paris a new law of divorce was passed, which makes it as easy for a husband to get rid of his wife, and a wife of her husband, as to discard a worn-out habit.[1] To complete the dissolution of those ties, which are the chief links of domestic and ultimately of social attachment, the journals of the convention record with guilty applause the accusations preferred by children against their parents. . . .

In these transactions we discover ambition and fanaticism marching hand in hand—bearing the ensigns of hypocrisy, treachery, and rapine. The dogmas of a false and fatal creed second the weapons of ambition. Like the prophet of Mecca, the tyrants of France press forward with the alcoran of their faith in one hand and the sword in the other. They proselyte, subjugate, and debase; no distinction is made between republic and monarchy; all must alike yield to the aggrandizement of the "*great nation*"—the distinctive, the arrogant appellation lately assumed by France to assert in the face of nations her superiority and ascendancy. Nor is it a mere title with which vanity decorates itself—it is the substantial claim of dominion. France, swelled to a gigantic size, and aping ancient Rome, except in her virtues, plainly meditates the control of mankind, and is actually giving the law to nations. Unless they quickly rouse and compel her to abdicate her insolent claim, they will verify the truth of that philosophy, which makes man in his natural state a quadruped, and it will only remain for the miserable animal, converting his hands into paws in the attitude of prone submission, to offer his patient and servile back to whatever burthens the *lordly* tyrants of France may think fit to impose.

—"The Stand," Part III. *Hamilton*, VII, 650-651, 654-655.

[1] This law, it was understood, had been lately modified in consequence of its manifest pernicious tendency; but upon a plan which, according to the opinions of the best men in the two councils lately banished, would leave the evil in full force.

April 19, 1798

Our true policy is, in the attitude of calm defiance, to meet the aggressions upon us by proportionate resistance, and to prepare vigorously for further resistance. To this end, the chief measures requisite are—to invigorate our treasury by calling into activity the principal untouched resources of revenue—to fortify in earnest our chief seaports—to establish foundries, and increase our arsenals—to create a respectable naval force, and to raise with the utmost diligence a considerable army. Our merchant vessels ought to be permitted not only to arm themselves, but to sink or capture their assailants. . . .

This course, it will be objected, implies a state of war. Let it be so. But it will be a limited, a mitigated state of war, to grow into a general war or not at the election of France.

—"Titus Manlius," in "The Stand," Part VI. Draft in Hamilton's hand. Hamilton Papers, 1st ser.

April 21, 1798

To pay such a price for peace, is to prefer peace to independence. The nation which becomes tributary takes a master. Peace is doubtless precious, but it is a bauble compared with national independence, which includes national liberty.

—"The Stand," Part VII. *Hamilton*, VII, 678.

December 13, 1798

Though it may be true, that some late occurrences have rendered the prospect of invasion by France less probable or more remote, yet, duly considering the rapid vicissitudes, at all times, of political and military events, the extraordinary fluctuations, which have been peculiarly characteristic of the still subsisting contest in Europe, and the more extraordinary position of most of the principal nations of that quarter of the globe, it can never be wise to vary our measures of security with the continually varying aspect of European affairs. A very obvious policy dictates to us a strenuous endeavor, as far as may be practicable, to place our safety out of the reach of the casualties which may befall the contending parties and the powers more immediately within their vortex. The way to effect this is to pursue a steady system, to organize all our resources, and put them in a state of preparation for prompt action. Regarding the overthrow of Europe at large as a matter not entirely chimerical, it will be our prudence to cultivate a spirit of self-dependence and to endeavor by unanimity, vigilance, and exertion, under the blessing of Providence, to hold the scales of our destiny in our own hands. Standing as it were in the midst of falling empires, it should be our aim to assume a station and attitude which will preserve us from being overwhelmed in their ruins.

—Washington to Secretary of War McHenry (Draft by Hamilton). *Hamilton*, V, 157-158.

On February 18, 1799 President Adams dropped a thunderbolt on the heads of the High Federalists who wanted war with France. He announced his intention of reopening negotiations with France and nominated William Vans Murray as minister to that country. He had already received assurances from Talleyrand that the American minister would be received with respect. Hamilton did not go along with the extremists in his party who would have blocked the mission entirely. He proposed adding two members to the mission, and the Senate followed his advice. He also favored ratification of the Convention of 1800 which formally released the United States from its defensive alliance with France.

January 6, 1799

I join with you in regretting the misunderstanding between our two countries. You will have seen by the President's speech that a door is again opened for terminating them amicably. And you may be assured that we are sincere, and that it is in the power of France, by reparation to our merchants for past injury, and the stipulation of justice in future, to put an end to the controversy.

But I do not much like the idea of your being any way implicated in the affair, lest you should be compromitted in the opinion of one or the other of the parties. It is my opinion that it is best for you to stand aloof.

—To Lafayette. Copy. Hamilton Papers, 1st ser.

February 21, 1799

The step announced in your letter just received, in all its circumstances, would astonish, if any thing from that quarter could astonish.

But as it has happened, my present impression is that the measure must go into effect with the additional idea of a commission of three.

The mode must be accommodated with the President. Murray is certainly not strong enough for so immensely important a mission.

—To Theodore Sedgwick. *Hamilton*, VI, 397.

February 21, 1799

How is the sending an agent to Toussaint to encourage the independency of St. Domingo, and a minister to France to negotiate an accommodation reconcilable to consistency or good faith?

—To Timothy Pickering. *Works*, X, 345.

December 24, 1800

Several friends at Washington inform me that there is likely to be much hesitation in the Senate about ratifying the convention with France. I do not wonder at it, and yet I should be sorry that it should mature itself into a disagreement to the instrument. Having received its present form, I think it should be ratified.

In my opinion, there is nothing in it contrary to our treaty with Great Britain. The annulling of our former treaties with France was an act of reprisal in consequence of hostile differences, of which no other power had a right to benefit, and which, upon an accommodation, might have been rescinded, even to the restoration of the *status quo*. Great Britain is now, in this respect, in a better situation than she was when she made the treaty. She has, so far, no good cause to complain.

—To Gouverneur Morris. *Hamilton*, VI, 496-497.

Policy toward Spain and Latin-America

We ought to squint at South America.

Hamilton was an expansionist, but chiefly from considerations of trade rather than settlement. He was more interested in obtaining the free navigation of the Mississippi than in the trans-Mississippi lands. Pinckney's Treaty with Spain (1795) granted the United States the right of free navigation of the Mississippi, but the undeclared naval war with France prompted High Federalists, chief among them Hamilton, to propose military measures against Spanish territory in the Americas. As senior field general Hamilton encouraged the liberation movement in Latin America and was in regular correspondence with Francisco Miranda, the Venezuelan revolutionist, whom he later repudiated. Hamilton unsuccessfully sought to win Adams over to his South American project. He himself had command over the troops in the North and West, and dreamed dreams of military glory and liberation.

September 15, 1790

Spain therefore must be regarded, upon the whole, as having slender claims to peculiar good-will from us. There is certainly nothing that authorizes her to expect we should expose ourselves to any extraordinary jeopardy for her sake. And to conceive that any considerations relative to France ought to be extended to her, would be to set up a doctrine altogether new in politics. The ally of our ally has no claim, as such, to our friendship. We may have substantial grounds of dissatisfaction against him, and act in consequence of them, even to open hostility, without derogating in any degree from what we owe to our ally. . . .

. . . An explicit recognition of our right to navigate the Mississippi to and from the ocean, with the possession of New Orleans, would greatly mitigate the causes of apprehension from the conquest of the Floridas by the British. . . .

We have objects which, in such a conjuncture, are not to be neglected. The western posts, on one side, and the navigation of the Mississippi, on the other, call for a vigilant attention to what is going on. They are both of importance. The securing of the latter may be regarded in its consequences as essential to the unity of the empire. . . .

In regard to the possessions of Great Britain on our left, it is at least problematical, whether the acquisition of them will ever be desirable to the United States. It is certain that they are in no shape essential to our prosperity. Except, therefore, the detention of our western posts (an object, too, of far less consequence than the navigation of the Mississippi), there appears no necessary source of future collision with that power.

This view of the subject manifests that we may have a more urgent interest to differ with Spain, than with Britain; and that conclusion will become the stronger, if it be admitted that when we are able to make good our pretensions, we ought not to leave in the possession of any foreign power the *territories* at the mouth of the Mississippi, which are to be regarded as the key to it.

—To Washington (Cabinet Paper). Hamilton Papers, 1st ser.

August 22, 1798

The plan in my opinion ought to be: A fleet of Great Britain, an army of the United States, a government for the liberated territory agreeable to both co-operators, about which there will be no difficulty. To arrange the plan a competent authority from Great Britain to some person here is the best expedient. Your presence here will, in this case, be extremely essential.

—To Francisco Miranda. Hamilton Papers, 1st ser.

August 22, 1798

I have received several letters from General Miranda. I have written an answer to some of them, which I send you to deliver or not, according to your estimate of what is passing in the scene where you are. Should you deem it expedient to suppress my letter you may do it, and say as much as you think fit on my part in the nature of a communication through you.

With regard to the enterprise in question, I wish it much to be undertaken, but I should be glad that the principal agency was in the United States,—they to furnish the whole land force if necessary. The command in this case would very naturally fall upon me, and I hope I shall disappoint no favorable anticipation. The independence of the separate territory under a moderate government, with the joint guaranty of the co-operating powers, stipulating equal privileges in commerce, would be the sum of the results to be accomplished.

—To Rufus King. Hamilton Papers, 1st ser.

January 26, 1799

As it is every moment possible that the project of taking possession of the Floridas and Louisiana, long since attributed to France, may be attempted to be put in execution, it is very important that the Executive should be clothed with power to meet and defeat so dangerous an enterprise. Indeed, if it is the policy of France to leave us in a state of semi-hostility, 'tis preferable to terminate it, and by taking possession of those countries for ourselves, to obviate the mischief of their falling into the hands of an active foreign power, and at the same time to secure to the United States the advantage of keeping the key to the Western country. I have been long in the habit of considering the acquisition of those countries as essential to the permanency of the Union which I consider as very important to the welfare of the whole.

If universal empire is still to be the pursuit of France, what can tend to defeat the purpose better than to detach South America from Spain, which is only the channel through which the riches of *Mexico and Peru* are conveyed to France? The Executive ought to be put in a situation to embrace favorable conjunctures for effecting that separation. 'Tis to be regretted that the preparation of an adequate military force does not advance more rapidly. There is some sad nonsense on this subject in some good heads. The reveries of some of the friends of the government are more injurious to it than the attacks of its declared enemies.

When will men learn to profit by experience?

—To Harrison Gray Otis. Copy. Hamilton Papers, 1st ser.

NEW YORK, June 27, 1799

It is a pity, my dear sir, and a reproach, that our administration have no general plan. Certainly there ought to be one formed without delay. If the chief is too desultory, his ministry ought to be more united and steady, and well-settled in some reasonable system of measures.

Among other things, it should be agreed what precise force should be created, *naval* and *land*, and this proportioned to the state of our finances. It will be ridiculous to raise troops, and immediately after disband them. Six ships of the line and twenty frigates and sloops of war are desirable. More would not now be comparatively expedient. It is desirable to complete and prepare the land force which has been provided for by law. Besides eventual security against invasion, we ought certainly to look to the possession of the Floridas and Louisiana, and we ought to squint at South America.

Is it possible that the accomplishment of these objects can be attended with financial difficulty? I deny the possibility. Our revenue can be considerably reinforced. The progress of the country will quickly supply small deficiencies, and these can be temporarily satisfied by loans, provided our loans are made on the principle that we require the aliment of European capital,—that lenders are to gain, and their gains to be facilitated, not obstructed. . . .

—To McHenry. Hamilton Papers. Special Collections, Columbia Univ. Lib.

October 12, 1799

In the event of an invasion from below, our reserved force placed on the *Ohio*, reinforced by the militia, to which it would be a rallying point, can descend to meet it with effect, or can take such other measures as circumstances may dictate. If a rupture with Spain should induce us to become the invaders, the force assigned to the undertaking can rapidly descend the Mississippi, and, being at a great distance, will have a better chance of making its approach and of arriving unexpectedly, than if stationed at a place which by its nearness would excite jealousy and vigilance.

But I agree in opinion with General Wilkinson, that a strongly fortified post ought to guard our Southern extremity on the Mississippi. It will not only serve as an impediment to invasion by the Spaniards, but will have an impressive influence on the powerful tribes of Indians in our Southwestern Territory.

—To McHenry. Draft in Hamilton's hand. Hamilton Papers, 1st ser.

The expedition never materialized, and Hamilton became despondent. In an ironic note to William Smith in 1800 he remarked: "You see I am in a humor to laugh. What can we do better in this best of all possible worlds? Should you even be shut up in the seven towers, or get the plague, if you are a true philosopher you will consider this only a laughing matter."

Administration of the Army

During Washington's administration Hamilton was concerned about putting the army and navy in a strong posture for defense. When war clouds gathered Adams named Washington as commanding general, and, at Washington's request, Hamilton as inspector general, second in command. Hamilton's correspondence for the next few years was largely concerned with military matters—problems of recruitment of personnel, training, promotion, and discipline. He favored national conscription in the event of attack.

March 8, 1794

The present situation of the United States is undoubtedly critical, and demands measures vigorous, though prudent. We ought to be in a respectable military posture, because war may come upon us, whether we choose it or not; and because, to be in a condition to defend ourselves, and annoy any who may attack us, will be the best method of securing our peace. If it is known that our principal maritime points are out of the reach of any but formal serious operations, and that the government has an efficient active force in its disposal for defence or offence on an emergency, there will be much less temptation to attack us, and much more hesitation to provoke us.

—To Washington. Hamilton Papers, 1st ser.

December 7, 1796

I have, heretofore, suggested the expediency of establishing a National University, and a Military Academy. The vast utility of both these measures presses so seriously and so constantly upon my mind, that I cannot forbear with earnestness to repeat the recommendation. . . .

The eligibleness of a military academy depends on that evident maxim of policy which requires every nation to be prepared for war while cultivating peace, and warns it against suffering the military spirit and military knowledge wholly to decay. . . .

A systematic plan for the creation of a moderate navy appears to me recommended by very weighty considerations. An active external commerce demands a naval power to protect it, besides the dangers from wars, in which a maritime state is a party. It is a truth, which our own experience has confirmed, that the most equitable and sincere neutrality is not sufficient to exempt a state from the depredations of other nations at war with each other. It is essential to induce them to respect that neutrality, that there shall be an organized force ready to vindicate the national flag.

—Part of Washington's Speech to Congress. Draft in Hamilton's hand. Hamilton Papers, 1st ser.

June 2, 1798

It is a great satisfaction to me to ascertain what I had anticipated in hope, that you are not determined in an *adequate emergency* against affording once more your military services. There is no one but yourself that would unite the public confidence in such an emergency, independent of other considerations, and it is of the last importance that this confidence should be *full* and *complete*. As to the wish of the country, it is certain that it will be *ardent and universal*. You intimate a desire to be informed what would be my part in such an event as to entering into military service. I have no scruple about opening myself to you on this point. If I am invited to a *station in which the service I may render may be proportionate to the sacrifice I am to make*, I shall be willing to go into the army. If you command, the place in which I should hope to be most useful is that of Inspector-General, with a command in the line. This I would accept. The public must judge for itself as to whom it will employ, but every individual must judge for himself as to the terms on which he will serve, and consequently must estimate his own pretensions.

—To Washington. Hamilton Papers, 1st ser.

July 30, 1798

But you will perceive that ideas of this sort presuppose an abandonment of the plan of suspending the emoluments of these officers. They cannot afford to give their time and attention without compensation. As to myself, I must be free to confess that this is utterly impossible. I have the less embarrassment in making the declaration, because it must be obvious that the plan is against my pecuniary interest. Serious occupation in my military office must involve the relinquishment substantially of my profession; and the exchange of from three to four thousand pounds for the compensation of Inspector-General, is evidently but a sorry bargain.

—To McHenry. Draft in Hamilton's hand. Hamilton Papers, 1st ser.

December 13, 1798

It is deeply to be lamented, that a very precious period of leisure was not improved towards forming among ourselves engineers and artillerists; and that, owing to this neglect, we are in danger of being overtaken by war, without competent characters of these descriptions. To form them suddenly is impossible. Much previous study and experiment are essential. If possible to avoid it, a war ought not to find us wholly unprovided.

—Washington to McHenry (Draft by Hamilton). *Hamilton,* V, 174.

December 22, 1798

It will likewise deserve consideration, whether provision ought not to be made for classing all persons from eighteen to forty-five inclusively, and for draughting out of them by lot *in case of invasion,* the number necessary to complete the entire army of fifty thousand. In the case of invasion, the expedient of draughting must be resorted to, and it will greatly expedite it if there be a previous classing with a view to such an event. The measure, too, will place the country in a very imposing attitude, and will add to the motives of caution on the part of our enemies.

—To James Gunn. Hamilton Papers, 1st ser.

[1799]

Tacticians agree that a proper regulation of the length and speed of the step is of primary importance in a system of tactics.

Upon this depends essentially the exactness of all evolutions, the attainment of the best results with the least inconvenience to the soldier. Yet, in the theories of military writers, and in the establishments of military nations, there is great diversity in this important article. For example: while our step is two feet English, that of France (and it is believed of Russia) is two feet French, or about twenty-six inches English; that of Great Britain, two feet six inches English. There is also some, though less, difference as to the velocity of the step: that of France being 76, 100, 120 in a minute; that of Great Britain, 75, 108, and 120 in a minute.

This diversity is a reason against adopting implicitly any foreign standard, and a motive to investigation of the principles on which the step ought to be predicated. It is desirable, if possible, to find a standard in nature.

As to length, the step ought to be accommodated to men of the smaller sizes. A tall man can abridge easier than a short man extend his natural pace. And yet, perhaps neither extreme ought to govern; a short man may, by habit, somewhat lengthen his usual step without fatigue, while a tall man may be too much constrained, if obliged to contract his step to the measure of a very short man. The man of middle stature may be the proper criterion, or perhaps the average of a number of men of different sizes marching together, may furnish a still better rule. In such case, a kind of compromise naturally takes place, by the mutual effort of all to move in unison.

—"Guide in Making Tactical Experiments Relative to the Step." Date in later hand. Hamilton Papers, 1st ser.

[1799]

Further measures to be taken without delay:

I.—To authorize the President to proceed forthwith to raise the 10,000 men already ordered.

II.—To establish an academy for military and naval instruction. This is a very important measure and ought to be permanent.

III.—To provide for the immediate raising of a corps of non-commissioned officers, viz., sergeants and corporals, sufficient with the present establishment for an army of 50,000 men. The having these men prepared and disciplined will accelerate extremely the disciplining of an additional force.

IV.—To provide before Congress rise that in case it shall appear that an invasion of this country by a large army is actually on foot, there shall be a draft from the militia to be classed, of a number sufficient to complete the army of 30,000 men. Provision for volunteers in lieu of drafts. A bounty to be given.

V.—To authorize the President to provide a further naval force of six ships of the line, and twelve frigates, with twenty small vessels not exceeding sixteen guns. It is possible the ships of the line and frigates may be purchased of Great Britain, to be paid for in stock. We ought to be ready to cut up all the small privateers and gun-boats in the West Indies, so as at the same time to distress the French islands as much as possible and protect our trade.

VI.—Is not the independence of the French colonies under the guaranty of the United States to be aimed at? If it is, there cannot be too much promptness in opening negotiations for the purpose. . . .

VIII.—It is essential the Executive should have half a million of secret-service money. If the measure cannot be carried without it, the expenditure may be with the approbation of three members of each House of Congress.

VIII.—Revenue in addition to the $2,000,000 of land tax, say:

Probable Produce		
$500,000		A stamp duty on hats, as well manufactured at home as imported, distributed into three classes—10, 15, 25 cents.
$100,000		Saddle-horses, one dollar each, excluding those engaged in agriculture.
		Salt, so as to raise the present duty to 25 cents per bushel.
$500,000	In lieu of tax on slaves, which is liable to much objection.	Male servants of the capacities by whatever name: Maitre d'hôtel, house-steward, valet de chambre, butler, under-butler, confectioner, cook, house-porter, waiter, footman, coachman, groom, postilions, stable-boy,—for one such servant, $1; for two such servants, and not more, $2 each; for three such servants, $3 each; above three, $4 each; one dollar additional by bachelors.
$100,000		New modifications with greater diversity of licenses for sale of wines.
$100,000		One per cent on all successions by descent or devise.

IX.—A loan of $10,000,000. The interest to be such as will insure the loan at par. It is better to give high interest, redeemable at pleasure, than low interest with accumulation of capital as in England.

—"Measures of Defence." *Works*, VII, 48-50.

January 30, 1799

I cannot let this first opportunity pass, without calling your attention in an official manner to the discipline of the troops. The cursory observation which I have been hitherto able to make, has been sufficient to satisfy that there exists in this respect too general a relaxation;

an evil which must at all events, be corrected by the union of care, prudence and energy.

No argument is necessary to prove how essential is discipline to the respectability and success of the service, and consequently to the honor, interest, and individual importance of every officer of the army. To the exertions for maintaining it, my firm support at all times may be absolutely counted upon, as it will be my steady aim, on the one hand, to promote, to every reasonable extent, the comfort of the troops; on the other, to secure a strict observance of their duty.

—To the Comamnding Officer at West Point and its dependencies (Circular). Draft in Hamilton's hand. Hamilton Papers, 1st ser.

February 6, 1799

I object,[1] also, that the objection against anti-federalism has been carried so far as to exclude several of the characters proposed by us. We were very attentive to the importance of appointing friends of the government to military stations; but we thought it well to relax the rule in favor of particular merit in a few instances, and especially in reference to the inferior grades. It does not seem advisable to exclude all hope, and to give to appointments too absolute a party feature. Military situations, on young minds particularly, are of all others best calculated to inspire a zeal for the service and the cause in which the incumbents are employed. When the President thinks of his son-in-law, he should be moderate in this respect.

—To McHenry. Hamilton Papers, 1st ser.

April 20, 1799

Inclosed are the proceedings of a general court-martial, of which Major Wilcocks is president. . . .

As I do not conceive the United States to be now at war, in the legal import of that term (which I construe to be a state not of *partial* but of *general* hostility), I consider it as beyond my power to approve or execute such sentences as by the articles of war are referred to the President in time of peace. But while I think it my duty on this ground to transmit the sentence without acting upon it, I feel myself called upon by a profound conviction of the necessity of some severe examples to check a spirit of desertion which, for want of them in time past, has become too prevalent, and to respectfully declare my opinion that the confirmation and execution of the sentence are of material consequence to the prosperous course of the military service. The crime of desertion is in this instance aggravated by the condition of the offender, who is a sergeant, and by the breach of trust, in purloining the money which was in his hands for the pay of his company.

—To McHenry. Hamilton Papers, 1st ser.

[1] "Regret" in *Works*, VII, 63-64.

May 18, 1799

Nothing is more necesary than to stimulate the vanity of soldiers. To this end, a smart dress is essential. When not attended to, the soldier is exposed to ridicule and humiliation. If the articles promised to him are defective in quality or appearance, he becomes dissatisfied, and the necessity of excusing the public delinquency towards him, is a serious bar to the enforcement of discipline. The government of the country is not now in the indigent situation in which it was during our revolutionary war. It possesses, amply, the means of placing its military on a respectable footing, and its dignity and its interest equally require that it shall act in conformity with this situation. This course is indeed indispensable, if a faithful, zealous, and well-regulated army is thought necessary to the security or defense of the country.

—To McHenry. Draft in Hamilton's hand. Hamilton Papers, 1st ser.

May 27, 1799

The returns from every quarter show that desertion prevails to a ruinous extent. For this the natural remedies are: 1st, greater attention to discipline; 2d, additional care in furnishing the supplies due to the soldiery, of such quality and with such exactness as will leave no real cause for dissatisfaction; 3d, the forbearance to enlist foreigners; and lastly, energy in the punishment of offenders.

—To McHenry. Draft in Hamilton's hand. Hamilton Papers, 1st ser.

July 2, 1799

The service of the cavalry in this country has never been but imperfectly understood. Even in Europe, ideas about the formation and tactics of that species of troops appear to be less well settled than about the other branches of military service. It is, in my opinion, very important to possess the means of making an experiment of the different principles in order to the formation of a good system, adapted to the geographical circumstances of the country. For this purpose alone a small body of cavalry is indispensable.

—To McHenry. *Hamilton*, V, 284.

July 29, 1799

I have the honor to acknowledge the receipt of your letter of the 25th instant, inclosing a warrant for the execution of Sergeant Hunt.

I have reflected carefully on the point submitted to our joint consideration, and, upon the whole, I incline to the side of forbearance.

The temper of our country is not a little opposed to the frequency of capital punishment. Public opinion, in this respect, though it must not have too much influence, is not wholly to be disregarded. There must be some caution not to render our military system odious by giving it the appearance of being sanguinary.

Considering, too, the extreme lenity in time past, there may be danger of shocking even the opinion of the army by too violent a change. The idea of cruelty inspires disgust, and ultimately is not much more favorable to authority than the excess of lenity.

Neither is it clear that one example, so quickly following upon the heels of another, in the same corps, will materially increase the impression intended to be made, or answer any valuable purpose.

If, for any or all of these reasons, the utility of the measure be doubtful, in favor of life it ought to be forborne. It is the true policy of the government to maintain an attitude which shall express a reluctance to strike, united with a determination to do it whenever it shall be essential. . . .

Under these impressions, if I hear nothing to the contrary from you by the return of the post, I shall issue an order to the following effect: "That, though the President has fully approved the sentence of Sergeant Hunt, and, from the heinous nature of his conduct, considers him a very fit subject for punishment; yet, being unwilling to multiply examples of severity, however just, beyond what experience may show to be indispensable, and hoping that the good faith and patriotism of the soldiery will spare him the painful necessity of frequently resorting to them, he has thought fit to authorize a remission of the punishment; directing, nevertheless, that Sergeant Hunt be degraded from his station."

I request to be speedily instructed.

—To Secretary at War. Draft in Hamilton's hand. Hamilton Papers, 1st ser.

August 27, 1799

In military service it is essential that each individual should move within his proper sphere, according to a just gradation and the relations which subsist between him and others. It is a consequence of this principle that a regular chain of communication should be preserved, and that, *in all matters relating to service*, each person should address him[self] for information or direction to his immediate superior, and should not step beyond him to a higher authority. This observation of course excepts the case where an individual, having received an injury from his immediate superior, is disposed to seek redress from the superior of both; but in other cases the principle ought to be rigidly observed.

—"Circular." Hamilton Papers, 1st ser.

September 2, 1799

You add that nothing is more common among officers, than complaints about everything furnished by the public. I am inclined to believe with you, that the spirit of complaining is apt to be carried to an excess. But it is important, when it is observed to prevail, to inquire with candor and calmness whether it has not been produced in whole or in part from real causes of complaint, [sic] If it has, it is then essential that any defects in the public plan which may have occasioned them, should be corrected.

This is essential for two reasons: one, that justice, the success of the service, and the public good require that right should be done to the troops; the other, that the doing of it will most certainly and effectually remedy the evil.

In a new army especially, the force of discipline can hardly be expected to stifle complaint if material ground for it truly exist. To be frank on this point is a duty. . . .

—To McHenry. Draft in Hamilton's hand. Hamilton Papers, 1st ser.

September 17, 1799

I remark, incidentally, that it is to be wished that a corps of invalids, and an establishment for the maintenance and education of the children of persons in the army and navy, were provided for by law. Policy, justice, and humanity forbid the abandoning to want and misery men who have spent their best years in the military service of a country, or who, in that service, have contracted infirmities which disqualify them to earn their bread in other modes.

Employment might be found for such a corps which would indemnify the public for the mere maintenance of its members in *clothing, lodging,* and *food.* The United States is perhaps the only country in which an institution of this nature is not to be found—a circumstance, which, if continued, will be discreditable. The establishment as to children is recommended by similar motives, with the additional consideration that they may be rendered by it useful members of society, and acquisitions to the army and navy as musicians, etc. I shall wait for your opinion as to the abolition of issues to children.

—To McHenry. Draft in Hamilton's hand. Hamilton Papers, 1st ser.

November 23, 1799

One which I have always thought of primary importance, is a military academy. This object has repeatedly engaged the favorable attention of the administration, and some steps toward it have been taken. But these, as yet, are very inadequate. A more perfect plan is in a high degree desirable.

No sentiment is more just than this, that in proportion as the circumstances and policy of a country forbid a large military establishment, it is important that as much perfection as possible should be given to that which may at any time exist. Since it is agreed that we are not to keep on foot numerous forces instructed and disciplined, military science in its various branches ought to be cultivated with peculiar care, in proper nurseries, so that there may always exist a sufficient body of it ready to be imparted and diffused, and a competent number of persons on condition to act as instructors to the additional troops which events may successively require to be raised.

This will be to substitute the elements of an army to the thing itself, and it will greatly tend to enable the government to dispense with a large body of standing forces, from the facility which it will give of forming officers and soldiers promptly upon emergencies.

No sound mind can doubt the essentiality of military science in time of war, any more than the moral certainty that the most pacific policy on the part of a government will not preserve it from being engaged in war more or less frequently.

To avoid great evils, it must either have a respectable force prepared for service, or the means of preparing such a force with expedition. The latter, most agreeable to the genius of our government and nation, is the object of a military academy.

—To McHenry, Hamilton Papers, 1st ser.

December, 1799

The proper mode of treating the crime of desertion has been, in most cases, an embarrassing subject. In ours it is particularly so. The punishment of death, except in time of war, is contrary to the popular habits of thinking. Whipping is found ineffectual. I have a hope that confinement and labor would prove more effectual. Believing this punishment to be within the discretion of courts-martial, I encourage its adoption. But as the matter now stands, the confinement would not exceed the term of service, and when this is nearly expired, it would be inadequate. Some auxiliary provisions are desirable to give a fair chance to the experiment. It is not, however, my idea to abolish death, which in some aggravated cases would be proper even in time of peace, and in time of war ought invariably to ensue. I incline even to the opinion, that the power of pardoning ought to be taken away in this case, certainly in every instance of desertion, or an attempt to desert to enemies or traitors.

—Hamilton to McHenry. *Hamilton*, V, 392-393.

[June, 1800]

Major-General Hamilton has it in command from the President of the United States, to assure the officers and men of the corps which are about to retire from the service, that he entertains a strong sense of the laudable zeal by which they were induced to take the field at the appearance of danger to their country, and of their good conduct in every respect, since they have been in the service; and that he deeply regrets any inconvenience which may result to any of them from an anticipated dissolution of their services; that he doubts not their patriotism will lead them to make a just construction of the motives of the government; and that he relies firmly upon them as the zealous defenders of their country in any future emergency.

The Major-General is happy to be the organ of this expression of the sentiments of the President. To add the assurance of his high sense of their merits, is a tribute due to them and to justice. He cherishes a deep sympathy in the feelings which naturally actuate them at so interesting a moment, and he entreats them to be pursuaded that his warm affection will follow them, wheresoever they may be.

—"General Order." Draft in Hamilton's hand; date in later hand. Hamilton Papers, 1st ser.

July 28, 1800

North has since set on foot criminal prosecutions against Captain Stille and several of his men for riot and theft. A hot-headed magistrate, without the decency of a previous resort to higher authority, issued a warrant, upon which the captain and those men were apprehended, and after a refusal to bail them, committed them to the common jail of the county. On a representation of the district-attorney, a habeas corpus was issued by our Supreme Court, and the prisoners have all been liberated on easy bail. The honor and success of the service require absolutely that this affair should be probed with all possible attention. I have expressed this opinion; you may perhaps think it [expedient to confirm the sentiment.][1]

—To McHenry. Draft and date in Hamilton's hand. Hamilton Papers, 1st ser.

Treatment of the Indians

November 6, 1792

I cannot dismiss the subject of Indian affairs without recalling to your attention the necessity of more adequate provision for giving energy to the laws throughout our interior frontiers, so as effectually to restrain depredations upon the Indians, without which every pacific system must prove abortive; and also for enabling the employment of qualified persons to reside as agents among the Indians, an expedient of material importance in the successful management of Indian affairs.

If some efficacious plan could be devised for carrying on trade with the Indians, upon a scale adequate to their wants, and under regulations calculated to protect them from extortion and imposition, it would prove hereafter a powerful means of preserving peace and a good understanding with them.

—4th Annual Address to Congress of President Washington (Draft by Hamilton). *Hamilton*, IV, 324-325.

[1] Not in draft; see Works, VII, 223.

10

Liberty and Security

Wise men have thought that even there they have carried the business of oaths to an exceptionable length.

Why should we wound the tender conscience of any man?

I contend for the liberty of publishing truth, for good motives and justifiable ends.

Let us not establish a tyranny.

Human Rights and Due Process

Hamilton's reading in political thought and his studies in the common law deepened his attachment to civil liberties and the principle of due process of law. These principles were put to a stern test late in the Revolution, when a proposal was before Washington to execute a captured British officer in retaliation for the murder by a Tory military unit of the Patriot Captain Huddy. Hamilton was outraged, and Washington never authorized the execution.

ALBANY June 7, 1782

WE ARE told here that there is a British officer coming on from Cornwallis' army to be executed by way of retaliation for the murder of Capt. Huddy. As this appears to me clearly to be an ill-timed proceeding, and if persisted in will be derogatory to the national character, I cannot forbear communicating to you my ideas upon the subject. A sacrifice of this sort is entirely repugnant to the genius of the age we live in, and is without example in modern history, nor can it fail to be considered in Europe as wanton and unnecessary. It appears that the enemy (from necessity, I grant, but the operation is the same) have changed their system and adopted a more humane one; and, therefore, the only justifying motive of retaliation—the preventing a repetition of cruelty—ceases. But if this were not the case, so solemn and deliberate a sacrifice of the innocent for the guilty must be condemned on the present received notions of humanity, and encourage an opinion that we are, in a certain degree, in a state of barbarism. Our affairs are now in a prosperous train, and so vigorous—I would rather say so violent—a measure would want the plea of necessity. It would argue meanness in us that at this late stage of the war, in the midst of success, we should suddenly depart from that temper with which we have all along borne with a great and more frequent provocation. The death of André could not have been dispensed with, but it must still be viewed at a distance as an act of *rigid justice*. If we wreak our resentment on an innocent person, it will be suspected that we are too fond of executions. I am persuaded it will have an influence peculiarly unfavorable to the General's character.

If it is seriously believed that in this advanced stage of affairs retaliation is necessary, let another mode be chosen. Let under actors be employed, and let the authority by which it is done be wrapt in obscurity and doubt. Let us endeavor to make it fall upon those who have had a direct or indirect share in the guilt. Let not the Commander-in-Chief—considered as the first and most respectable character among us—come forward in person and be the avowed author of an act at which every humane feeling revolts. Let us at least have as much address as the enemy; and, if we must have victims, appoint some obscure agents to perform the ceremony and bear the odium which must always attend even justice itself when directed by extreme severity.

For my own part, my dear sir, I think a business of this complexion entirely out of season. The time for it, if there every was one, is past.

But it is said that the Commander-in-Chief has pledged himself for it and cannot recede. Inconsistency in this case would be better than consistency. But pretexts may be found and will be readily admitted in favor of humanity. Carleton will in all probability do something like apology and concession. He will give appearances of preventing everything of the kind in future. Let the General appear to be satisfied with these appearances. The steps Carleton is said to have taken to suppress the refugee incursions will give the better color to lenity.

I address myself to you upon this occasion, because I know your liberality and your influence with the General. If you are of my opinion, I am sure you will employ it, if it should not be too late. I would not think a letter necessary, but I know how apt men are to be actuated by the circumstances which immediately surround them, and to be led into an approbation of measures which, in another situation, they would disapprove. Mrs. Hamilton joins me in compliments to Mrs. Knox.

—To General Knox. *Works*, IX, 256-258.

When Hamilton penned the letter about the Huddy case he was already busily engaged in the study of the law in the Albany office of his old friend Robert Troup. It was during this period that he drew up a handbook of practice before the New York Supreme Court, the groundwork for several subsequent treatises on a larger scale. Like his undergraduate work at King's College, Hamilton's professional studies were accelerated. After three months of intensive study he was admitted to the bar in July of 1783. Then came a stint in Congress, and immediately upon the evacuation of the British army from New York City he opened law offices at 57 Wall Street.

One of the first cases which he handled involved the defense of the property rights of a Loyalist during the period of British military occupation. Hamilton enunciated in the public press his views on due process to which every person was entitled, Whig or Tory.

[1784]

The principles of all the arguments I have used, or shall use, lie within the compass of a few simple propositions which, to be assented to, need only to be stated.

FIRST. That no man can forfeit, or be justly deprived, without his consent, of any right to which as a member of the community, he is entitled, but for some crime incurring the forfeiture.

SECONDLY. That no man ought to be condemned unheard, or punished for supposed offences, without having an opportunity of making his defence.[1]

THIRDLY. That a crime is *an act* committed or omitted, in violation of a public law, either forbidding or commanding it.[2]

FOURTHLY. That a prosecution is, in its most precise signification, an *inquiry* or *mode of ascertaining*, whether a particular person has committed or omitted such *act*.

FIFTHLY. That *duties* and *rights*, as applied to subjects, are reciprocal; or, in other words, that a man cannot be a *citizen* for the purpose of punishment, and not a *citizen* for the purpose of privilege. . . .

To place this matter in a still clearer light, let it be supposed, that instead of the mode of indictment and trial by jury, the Legislature was to declare, that every citizen who did not swear he had never adhered to the King of Great Britain, should incur all the penalties which our treason laws prescribe. Would this not be a palpable evasion of the treaty, and a direct infringement of the Constitution? . . .

Let us not forget, that the Constitution declares, that trial by jury, in all cases in which it has been formerly used, should remain inviolate for ever; and that the Legislature should, at no time, erect any new jurisdiction which should not proceed according to the courses of the

[1] *Vide* Address of Congress to the people of Great Britain, September 5, 1774.
[2] Blackstone, vol. iv, page 5.

common law. Nothing can be more repugnant to the true genius of the common law, than such an inquisition as has been mentioned into the consciences of men.

A share in the sovereignty of the state, which is exercised by the citizens at large, in voting at elections, is one of the most important rights of the subject, and, in a republic, ought to stand foremost in the estimation of the law. It is that right by which we exist a free people; and it certainly, therefore, will never be admitted, that less ceremony ought to be used in divesting any citizen of that right than in depriving him of his property. Such a doctrine would ill suit the principles of the Revolution, which taught the inhabitants of this country to risk their lives and fortunes in asserting their *liberty*; or, in other words, their *right* to a *share* in the government. That portion of the sovereignty to which each individual is entitled, can never be too highly prized. It is that for which we have fought and bled; and we should cautiously guard against any precedents, however they may be immediately directed against those we hate, which may, in their consequences, render our title to this great privilege precarious. Here we may find the criterion to distinguish the genuine from the pretended Whig. The man that would attack that right, in whatever shape, is an enemy to Whiggism.

If any oath, with retrospect to past conduct, were to be made the condition on which individuals who have resided within the British lines should hold their estates, we should immediately see that this proceeding would be tyrannical, and a violation of the treaty; and yet, when the same mode is employed to divest that right, which ought to be deemed still more sacred, many of us are so infatuated as to overlook the mischief. . . .

It has been urged, in support of the doctrines under consideration, that every government has a right to take precautions for its own security, and to prescribe the terms on which its rights shall be enjoyed. . . .

In the first formation of a government, the society may multiply its precautions as much, and annex as many conditions to the enjoyment of its rights, as it shall judge expedient; but when it has once adopted a Constitution that Constitution must be the measure of its discretion in providing for its own safety, and in prescribing the conditions upon which its privileges are to be enjoyed. If the Constitution declares that persons possessing certain qualifications shall be entitled to certain rights while that Constitution remains in force, the government, which is the mere creature of the Constitution, can divest no citizen, who has the requisite qualifications, of his corresponding rights. . . .

The rights, too, of a republican government are to be modified and regulated by the principles of such a government. These principles dictate that no man shall lose his rights without a hearing and conviction before the proper tribunal; that, previous to his disfranchisement, he shall have the full benefit of the laws to make his defence; and that his innocence shall be presumed until his guilt has been proved. These, with many other maxims, never to be forgotten in any but tyrannical governments, oppose the aims of those who quarrel with the principles of Phocion.

—*A Second Letter from Phocion to the Considerate Citizens of New York Containing Remarks on Mentor's Reply* (New York: Samuel Loudon, 1784), pp. 6, 23-25, 29, 31.

When the New York state legislature debated a bill to disfranchise all those who had engaged in privateering for the British side during the Revolution, Hamilton reiterated the principles he had earlier advanced. Such a law, he argued, would violate the bill of rights.

February 6, 1787

. . . He would not repeat what he had said, but he hoped to be indulged by the House in explaining a sentence in the Constitution, which seems not well understood by these gentlemen. In one article it says, that no man shall be disfranchised or deprived of any right he enjoys under the Constitution, but by the law of the land or the judgment of his peers.

Some gentlemen hold that the law of the land will include an act of the Legislature. But Lord Coke, that great luminary of the law, in his comment upon a similar clause in Magna Charta, interprets the law of the land to mean presentment and indictment and process of outlawry, as contradistinguished from trial by jury. But if there were any doubt upon the Constitution, the bill of rights enacted in this very session removes it. It is there declared that no man shall be disfranchised or deprived of any right but by due process of law, or the judgment of his peers. The words "due process" have a precise technical import, and are only applicable to the process and proceedings of courts of justice; they can never be referred to an act of the Legislature.

Are we willing, then, to endure the inconsistency of passing a bill of rights and committing a direct violation of it in the same session? In short, are we ready to destroy its foundations at the moment they are laid?

—Speech in the New York Assembly. *Works*, VIII, 28-29.

Hamilton believed in due process for lawyers as well as for their clients. In the state legislature he criticized a proposal to fix lawyer's fees, insisting on the safeguard that attorneys should be permitted "reasonable allowances." His own fees were modest, but he was sensitive to criticisms of lawyers by laymen. In one instance he turned down a client on the ground that the latter had made "an unjustifiable reflection on the profession to which I belong, and of a nature to put it out of my power to render you any service in the line of that profession." He added: "I really believe that you did not attend to the full force of the expression when you told Mr. Lewis, 'Attorneys like to make the most of their bills of cost;' but it contains in it other insinuations which cannot be pleasing to any man in the profession, and which must oblige anyone that has the proper delicacy to decline the business of a person who professedly entertains such an idea of the conduct of this profession." In that case, Le Guen v. Gouverneur and Kemble, *Hamilton's fee was considered by the victorious plaintiff to be much too "moderate." Burr, who was associated with Hamilton for the plaintiff, submitted a much bigger bill.*

February 21, 1787

Col. Hamilton expressed a hope that the House would not carry matters to an extreme. It would be, he thought, as improper to make the fees of the profession too low as to make them too high. Gentlemen who practised the law, if they were men of ability, would be paid for the services required of them; and if the law did not allow a proper compensation, it would be evaded. Names might be given to things and charges made; against which there would be no guard. In Pennsylvania and Jersey attempts had been made to reduce the emoluments of the profession below the proper standard. This had afforded no relief; on the contrary, the expenses of the law and the profits of the practisers had increased since the experiment, the only effect of which had been to transfer the expense from the delinquent debtor to the injured creditor. If the legal fees amount to a compensation, in most cases the practiser would content himself with them; if they did not, he would consider himself justified in making the best bargain he could,—the consequences of which were obvious. While differences would arise among mankind, and that there would be differences was certain, lawyers would be necessary, and for their services they would be paid. He, therefore, was of the opinion, that in going through the bill, the House should agree that reasonable allowances should be made for the services mentioned in the bill, or they would defeat their own object.

—Speech in the New York Assembly. *Works*, VIII, 36-37.

One of the great issues on the eve of the Revolution was the issuance of writs of assistance, or general search warrants, to customs officers.

Such writs were specifically condemned in the Virginia Bill of Rights of 1776 and declared illegal in the Fourth Amendment to the Constitution. Hamilton took pains to convince Congress that his tax bill did not violate due process.

December 13, 1790

It may not be improper further to remark, that the two great objections to the class of duties denominated excises are inapplicable to the plan suggested. These objections are: first, the *summary jurisdiction* confided to the officers of excise, in derogation from the course of the common law and the right of trial by jury; and, secondly, the general power vested in the same officers, of *visiting and searching, indiscriminately*, the houses, stores, and other buildings of the dealers in excised articles. But, by the plan proposed, the officers to be employed are to be clothed with no such *summary* jurisdiction, and their *discretionary* power of visiting and searching is to be restricted to those places which the dealers themselves shall designate by public insignia or marks as the depositories of the articles on which the duties are to be laid. Hence, it is one of the recommendations of the plan, that it is not liable to those objections.

—Report on the Public Credit. Hamilton Papers, 1st ser.

Freedom and Bondage

As a friend of freedom and an opponent of prejudice Hamilton might well be expected to take an advanced stand on the Negro question. He saw the advantages of utilizing Negro slaves in the war effort against Britain and rewarding them with their liberation. Although he himself later in life owned a few slaves, he was active in the organization and operations of the New York Society for Promoting the Manumission of Slaves, which carried through the legislature a program of gradual emancipation. One of the criticisms against Jay's Treaty was that Jay had not obtained satisfaction for slaves who had been freed by the British army. Hamilton had no sympathy for the stand taken by the Southern planters on this issue.

HEADQUARTERS March 14, 1779

Colonel Laurens, who will have the honor of delivering you this letter, is on his way to South Carolina, on a project which I think, in the present situation of affairs there, is a very good one, and deserves every kind of support and encouragement. This is to raise two, three, or four battalions of Negroes, with the assistance of the government of that State, by contributions from the owners, in proportion to the number they possess. If you should think proper to enter upon the subject with him, he will give you a detail of his plan. He wishes to have it recommended by Congress to the State; and, as an inducement, that they would engage to take their battalions into Continental pay.

It appears to me that an expedient of this kind, in the present state of Southern affairs, is the most rational that can be adopted, and promises very important advantages. Indeed, I hardly see how a sufficient force can be collected in that quarter without it; and the enemy's operations there are growing infinitely serious and formidable. I have not the least doubt that the Negroes will make very excellent soldiers, with proper management; and I will venture to pronounce, that they cannot be put in better hands than those of Mr. Laurens. He has all the zeal, intelligence, enterprise, and every other qualification requisite to succeed in such an undertaking. It is a maxim with some great military judges, that, with sensible officers, soldiers can hardly be too stupid; and, on this principle, it is thought that the Russians would make the best soldiers in the world, if they were under other officers than their own. The king of Prussia is among the number who maintains this doctrine, and has a very emphatic saying on the occasion, which I do not exactly recollect. I mention this because I have frequently heard it objected to the scheme of embodying Negroes, that they are too stupid to make soldiers. This is so far from appearing to me a valid objection, that I think their want of cultivation (for their natural faculties are as good as ours), joined to that habit of subordination which they acquire from a life of servitude, will enable them sooner to become soldiers than our white inhabitants. Let officers be men of sense and sentiment; and the nearer the soldiers approach to machines, perhaps the better.

I foresee that this project will have to combat much opposition from prejudice and self-interest. The contempt we have been taught to entertain for the blacks, makes us fancy many things that are founded neither in reason nor experience; and an unwillingness to part with property of so valuable a kind, will furnish a thousand arguments to show the impracticability, or pernicious tendency, of a scheme which requires such sacrifices. But it should be considered, that if we do not make use of them in this way, the enemy probably will; and that the best way to counteract the temptations they will hold out, will be to offer them ourselves. An essential part of the plan is to give them their freedom with their swords. This will secure their fidelity, animate their courage, and, I believe, will have a good influence upon those who remain, by opening a door to their emancipation. This circumstance, I confess, has no small weight in inducing me to wish the success of the project; for the dictates of humanity, and true policy, equally interest me in favor of this unfortunate class of men.

—To John Jay, President of Congress. *Hamilton*, I, 76-78.

July 30, 1795

In the interpretation of treaties, things *odious* or *immoral* are not to be presumed. The abandonment of Negroes, who had been induced to quit their masters on the faith of official proclamations, promising them liberty, to fall again under the yoke of their masters, and into slavery, is as *odious* and *immoral* a thing as can be conceived. It is odious, not only as it imposes an act of perfidy on one of the contracting parties, but as it tends to bring back to servitude men once made free. The general interests of humanity conspire with the obligation which Great Britain had contracted towards the Negroes, to repel this construction of the treaty, if another can be found.

—"Camillus," No. 3. (N.Y.) *American Minerva*, July 30, 1795.

Minority Rights and the Tories

As a hot-blooded Patriot Hamilton yielded to no one in his detestation of the Loyalists and his awareness of their political intrigues. But he believed that a large portion of them were not beyond redemption, and that serious punishment should be reserved for the flagrant offenders. "Tenderness to the innocent," caution in dispensing punishment, a stern stand toward "atrocious offenders," and the avoidance of inflicting trivial penalties which would not deter—these principles determined his attitude toward Toryism.

April, 1777

. . . I have transmitted you a bundle of papers, in which you will find the information and evidence that support the charges against them, and the confession they made in the court of inquiry. Many of them have nothing against them but what is to be found in their own acknowledgments. How far these may operate in fixing their guilt you can best determine. Several of them have been taken in arms, and others were beyond a doubt employed in enlisting men for the service of the enemy. You will readily concur with his Excellency in the obvious necessity of inflicting exemplary punishment on such daring offenders, to repress that insolent spirit of open and avowed enmity to the American cause, which, unhappily, is too prevalent in this and some of the States. The examination, in this instance, is somewhat irregular and out of the common order of things. But in the present unsettled state of government, the distinction between the civil and military powers cannot be upheld with that exactness which every friend to society must wish. His Excellency desires to avoid nothing more, I flatter myself you will believe me, than deviations from the strict rules of propriety in this respect, or the least encroachments either upon the rights of the citizens or of the magistrate. It was necessary to make inquiry for the sake of the discrimination before mentioned, and tenderness to the innocent, to save them from long and unmerited confinement, commended the measure.

—To William Livingston. *Works*, IX, 60-61.

HEADQUARTERS, MORRIS TOWN, April 20, 1777

Gentlemen:

The disposition of the Convention with respect to the disaffected among you is highly commendable, and justified by every principle of equity and policy. The necessity of exemplary punishment throughout the States is become evident beyond a doubt, and it were to be wished every one of the thirteen would imitate the judicious conduct of New York. Lenity and forbearance have been tried too long to no purpose: it is high time to discard what the dearest experience has shown to be ineffectual.

But in dispensing punishments the utmost care and caution ought to be used. The power of doing it, or even of bringing the guilty to trial, should be placed in hands that know well how to use it. I believe it would be a prudent rule to meddle with none but those whose crimes are supported by very sufficient evidence, and are of a pretty deep die [sic]. The apprehending innocent persons, or those whose offenses are of so slender a nature as to make it prudent to dismiss them, furnishes an occasion of triumph, and a foundation for a species of animadversion which is very injurious to the public cause. Persons so apprehended generally return home worse than they were; and by expatiating on their sufferings first excite the pity towards themselves and afterwards the abhorrence towards their persecutors, of those with whom they converse.

I believe it would also be a general good rule, either to pardon offenders intirely or to inflict capital and severe punishments. The advice given by a certain general to his son when the latter had the Roman army in his power was certainly very politic. He advised him either to destroy them utterly or to dismiss them with every mark of honour and respect. By the first method, says he, you disable the Romans from being your enemies, by the last you make them your friends. So with respect to thes[e] Tories, I would either disable them from doing us any injury, or I would endeavor to gain their friendship by clemency. Inflicting trifling punishments only imbitters the minds of those on which they fall, and increases their disposition to do mischief without taking away the power of doing it.

I shall communicate your additional resolves to the General and consult him on what you mention; and shall let you know his opinion in my next. Mine however is that those who appear to be of such a character as to be susceptible of reformation should be employed, but it is a delicate point. . . .

—To Messrs. Gouverneur Morris, R. R. Livingston, and William Allison, Committee of the New York Convention, Kingston. Robert R. Livingston Collection, N. Y. Hist. Soc.

HEADQUARTERS, MORRISTOWN April 29, 1777

. . . I send you a second list of four others that have been lately committed to jail. These are high offenders, and among the number of those who it were to be wished could have an immediate trial and punishment. Isaac Ogden, in particular, is one of the most barefaced, impudent fellows that ever came under my observation. He openly acknowledged himself a subject of the king of Great Britain; and flatly refused to give any satisfaction to some questions that were put to him respecting one Moses Nichols, an emissary from the enemy; assigning no other reason for his refusal, than that he had given his word to be silent.

A spirit of disaffection shows itself with so much boldness and violence in different parts of this State, that it is the ardent wish of his Excellency, that no delay, which can be avoided, might be used in making examples of some of the most atrocious offenders. If something be not speedily done, to strike a terror into the disaffected, the consequences must be very disagreeable.

Among others, all security to the friends of the American cause will be destroyed; and the natural effect of this, will be an extinction of zeal in seconding and promoting it. Their attachment, if it remain, will be a dead, inactive, useless principle. And the disaffected, emboldened by impunity, will be encouraged to proceed to the most dangerous and pernicious lengths.

—To William Livingston. Hamilton Papers, 1st ser.

HEADQUARTERS, MORRIS TOWN May 12, 1777

I have received the pleasure of your favor of yesterday's date. The reasons you assign for the interval of silence on your part are admitted as sufficient, though I regret that the principal one exists—the combination of the Tories for a general insurrection. But, perhaps, on the scale of policy, I ought rather to congratulate you on the event. That there are too many Tories in your State, as well as in several others, is a fact too well known. That they should confederate themselves for active purposes of revolt and disaffection, when once discovered, is desirable, because it arms the vindictive justice of the state, and will justify, in the eyes of all the world, a radical blow at the faction. Were it not that we have seen so many similar instances, that only prove the temerity and folly of the Tories, I should consider this as a presumptive argument, that the enemy intend your way.

—To Gouverneur Morris. Robert R. Livingston Collection, N. Y. Hist. Soc.

As the war drew to a close Hamilton was desirous of letting bygones be bygones and of permitting the respectable and industrious Loyalists to remain in America. He opposed discriminatory taxation and policies which would discourage moderate Loyalists possessing capital from staying in America.

ALBANY August 13, 1782

. . . I gave you, in a former letter, a sketch of our plan of taxation, but I will now be more particular.

The general principle of it is apparent, according to *circumstances* and *abilities collectively considered*. The ostensible reason for adopting this vague basis was a desire of equality. It was pretended that this could not be obtained so well by any fixed tariff of taxable property, as by leaving it to the discretion of persons chosen by the people themselves to determine the ability of each citizen. But perhaps the true reason was a desire to discriminate between the *Whigs* and *Tories*. This chimerical attempt at perfect equality has resulted in total inequality, or rather this narrow disposition to overburthen a particular class of citizens (living under the protection of the government) has been retorted upon the contrivers or their friends, wherever that class has been numerous enough to preponderate in the election of the officers who were to execute the law. The exterior figure a man makes, the decency and meanness of his manner of living, the personal friendships or dislikes of the assessors, have much more share in determining what individuals shall pay, than the proportion of property.

The Legislature first assesses or quotas the several counties. Here the evil begins—the members cabal and intrigue to throw the *burthen* off their respective constituents. Address and influence, more than considerations of real ability, prevail. A great deal of time is lost, and a great deal of expense incurred, before the juggle is ended and the necessary compromise made.

—To Robert Morris. Hamilton Papers, 1st ser.

August 13, 1783

. . . I do not think the British will take leave before the *ides* of October.

The spirit of emigration is greatly increased of late. Some violent papers sent into the city have determined many to depart, who hitherto have intended to remain. Many merchants of second class, characters of no political consequence, each of whom may carry eight or ten thousand guineas, have, I am told, lately applied for shipping to convoy them away. Our State will feel for twenty years at least the effects of the popular phrenzy.

—To Robert R. Livingston. Robert R. Livingston Collection, N. Y. Hist. Soc.

Once the treaty was ratified Hamilton advocated strict and honorable compliance with its terms. He risked his political future by insisting that reprisals against the Tories should cease and that the lawful debts due to British and Loyalists creditors be recovered, and, most of all, by his defense of the Loyalist Waddington in the suit under the Trespass Act brought by the widow Rutgers. Under the pseudonym of Phocion *Hamilton wrote a letter to the press in which he pleaded for justice and moderation for ex-Tories and observance of the terms of the treaty. The faction behind Governor Clinton seized upon the situation to make as much political capital as they could from anti-Tory prejudice. Writing as* Mentor, *Isaac Ledyard denied Hamilton's arguments and insisted on the unrestricted sovereignty of the state of New York. Hamilton answered with his second* Phocion *letter. Some of his hotheaded opponents were so infuriated by his stand that they actually concocted a plot to challenge him successively to a series of duels until this champion of Tory rights would be liquidated. Hamilton's courageous stand did not hurt his law practice one bit. Conservative businessmen now rushed to him with their cases. As he wrote Gouverneur Morris, "a legislative folly has afforded so plentiful a harvest to us lawyers that we have scarcely a moment to spare from the substantial business of reaping."*

December 8, 1783

Being concerned as counsel for a number of persons who have been, since the annunciation of the provisional treaty, indicted under the confiscation laws of this State for the part they are supposed to have taken in the late war, we are induced, at the desire of our clients and in their behalf, to apply to Congress, through your Excellency, for an exemplification of the definitive treaty. We take it for granted that ere this it will have been [done under the][1] direction of the United States. We have found a great strictness in the courts in this State. It will, we apprehend, be necessary to be able to produce an exemplification of the treaty under the seal of the United States. In a matter so interesting to a great number of individuals (for it does not belong to us to urge considerations of national honor) we hope we shall be excused when we observe that there appears to be no probability that the Legislature of this State will interpose its authority to put a stop

[1] Bracketed material torn or undecipherable.

to prosecutions till the definitive treaty is announced in [ ] form. In the mean time a period is limited for the appearance of the indicted persons to plead to their indictments, and if they neglect to appear, judgment by default will be entered against them. It is therefore of great consequence to them that we should have in our possession as speedily as possible an authentic document of the treaty and of its ratification by Congress; and we, on this account, pray an exemplification of both.

We persuade ourselves that the justice and liberality of Congress will induce a ready compliance with our prayer, which will conduce to the security of a great number of individuals who derive their hopes of safety from the national faith.

—To Thomas Mifflin, President of Congress.
Hamilton's hand. Hamilton Papers, 1st ser.

[1784]

The persons alluded to pretend to appeal to the spirit of Whiggism; while they endeavor to put in motion all the furious and dark passions of the human mind. The spirit of Whiggism is generous, humane, beneficent, and just. These men inculcate revenge, cruelty, persecution, and perfidy. The spirit of Whiggism cherishes legal liberty, holds the rights of every individual sacred, condemns or punishes no man without regular trial and conviction of some crime declared by antecedent laws; reprobates equally the punishment of the citizen by arbitrary acts of legislation, as by the lawless combinations of unauthorized individuals; while these men are advocates for expelling a large number of their fellow-citizens unheard, untried; or, if they cannot effect this, are for disfranchising them, in the face of the Constitution, without the judgment of their peers, and contrary to the law of the land.

The 13th article of the Constitution declares, "that no member of the State shall be *disfranchised*, or *defrauded of any of the rights* or *privileges* sacred to the subjects of this State by the Constitution, unless *by the law of the land or the judgment of his peers.*" If we inquire what is meant by the law of the land, the best commentators will tell us, that it means *due process of law; that is by indictment or presentment of good and lawful men,*[1] and trial and conviction in consequence.

It is true, that in *England*, on extraordinary occasions, attainders for high treason, by act of Parliament, have been practised; but many of the ablest advocates for civil liberty have condemned this practice; and it has commonly been exercised with great caution upon individuals only by name, never against *general descriptions* of men. The sense of our Constitution on this practice, we may gather from the 41st article, where all attainders, other than for crimes committed during the late war, are forbidden.

[1] Coke upon Magna Charta, Chap. 29, p. 50.

If there had been no treaty in the way, the Legislature might, by *name*, have attainted particular persons of high treason for crimes committed during the war; but, independent of the treaty, it could not, and cannot, without tyranny, disfranchise or punish whole classes of citizens by general descriptions, without trial and conviction of offences known by laws previously established, declaring the offence and prescribing the penalty.

This is a dictate of natural justice, and a fundamental principle of law and liberty.

Nothing is more common than for a free people, in times of heat and violence, to gratify momentary passions, by letting into the government, principles and precedents which afterwards prove fatal to themselves. Of this kind is the doctrine of disqualification, disfranchisement, and banishment, by acts of Legislature. The dangerous consequences of this power are manifest. If the Legislature can disfranchise any number of citizens at pleasure, by general descriptions, it may soon confine all the votes to a small number of partisans, and establish an aristocracy or an oligarchy. If it may banish at discretion all those whom particular circumstances render obnoxious, without hearing or trial, no man can be safe, nor know when he may be the innocent victim of a prevailing faction. The name of liberty applied to such a government would be a mockery of common sense. . . .

The sound and ingenious construction of the two articles, taken collectively, is this: That where the property of any persons, other than those who have been in arms against the United States, had been actually confiscated, and themselves prescribed, then Congress are to recommend a restoration of estates, rights, and properties; and, with respect to those who had been in arms, they are to recommend permission for them to remain a twelvemonth in the country, to solicit a like restoration; but with respect to all those who were not in this situation, and who had not already been the objects of confiscation and banishment, they were to be absolutely secured from all future injury, to person, liberty, or property.

To say that this exemption from positive injury, does not imply a right to live among us as citizens, is a pitiful sophistry; it is to say that the banishment of a person from his country, connections, and resources (one of the greatest punishments that can befall a man), is no punishment at all.

The meaning of the word *liberty* has been contested. Its true sense must be, the enjoyment of the common privileges of subjects under the same government. There is no middle line of just construction between this sense and a mere exemption from personal imprisonment! . . .

There is a very simple and conclusive point of view in which this subject may be placed. No citizen can be deprived of any right which the citizens in general are entitled to, unless forfeited by some offence. It has been seen that the regular and constitutional mode of ascertaining whether this forfeiture has been incurred, is by legal process, trial, and conviction. This *ex vi termini* supposes prosecution. Now, consistent with the treaty, there can be no future prosecution for any thing done on account of the war. Can we then do, by act of Legislature, what the treaty disables us from doing by due course of law? This would be to imitate the Roman general, who, having promised Antiochus to restore half his vessels, caused them to be sawed in two before their delivery; or the Platœaens, who, having promised the Thebans to restore their prisoners, had them first put to death, and returned them dead.

Such fraudulent subterfuges are justly considered more odious than an open and avowed violation of treaty. . . .

The *uti possidetis, each party to hold what it possesses,* is the point from which nations set out in framing a treaty of peace. If one side gives up a part of its acquisitions, the other side renders an equivalent in some other way. What is the equivalent given to Great Britain for all the important concessions she has made? She has surrendered the capital of this State and its large dependencies. She is to surrender our immensely valuable posts on the frontier; and to yield to us a vast tract of western territory, with one half of the lakes, by which we shall command almost the whole fur trade. She renounces to us her claim to the navigation of the Mississippi, and admits us to share in the fisheries, even on better terms than we formerly enjoyed it. As she was in possession, by right of war, of all these objects, whatever may have been our original pretensions to them, they are, by the laws of nations, to be considered as so much given up on her part. And what do we give in return? We stipulate—that there shall be no future injury to her adherents among us. How insignificant the equivalent in comparison with the acquisition! . . .

The men who are at the head of the party which contends for disqualification and expulsion, endeavor to enlist a number of people on their side by holding out motives of private advantage to them. To the trader they say: "You will be overborne by the large capitals of the Tory merchants"; to the mechanic: "Your business will be less profitable, your wages less considerable, by the interference of Tory workmen." A man, the least acquainted with trade, will indeed laugh at such suggestions. . . .

These arguments, if they were understood, would be conclusive with the mechanic: "There is already employment enough for all the workmen in the city, and wages are sufficiently high. If you could raise them by expelling those who remained in the city, and whom you consider as rivals, the extravagant price of wages would have two effects; it would draw persons to settle here, not only from other parts of this

State, but from the neighboring States. Those classes of the community who are to employ you, will make a great many shifts rather than pay the exorbitant prices you demand; a man will wear his old clothes so much longer, before he gets a new suit; he will buy imported shoes cheap rather than those made here at so dear a rate; the owner of a house will defer the repairs as long as possible; he will only have those which are absolutely necessary made; he will not attend to elegant improvement: and the like will happen in other branches. These circumstances will give less employment, and in a very little time bring back your wages to what they now are, and even sink them lower. But this is not all. You are not required merely to expel your rival mechanics, but you must drive away the rich merchants and others who are called Tories, to please your leaders, who will persuade you they are dangerous to your liberty (though, in fact, they only mean their own consequence). By this conduct you will drive away the principal part of those who have the means of becoming large undertakers. The carpenters and masons, in particular, must be content with patching up the houses already built, and building little huts upon the vacant lots, instead of having profitable and durable employment in erecting large and elegant edifices."

. . . The safest reliance of every government is on men's interests. This is a principle of human nature, on which all political speculation, to be just, must be founded. Make it the interest of those citizens who, during the Revolution, were opposed to us, to be friends to the new government, by affording them not only protection, but a participation in its privileges, and they will undoubtedly become its friends.

—*A Letter from Phocion to the Considerate Citizens of New York on the Politics of the Times in Consequence of the Peace.* (New York: Samuel Loudon, 1784), pp. 4, 5, 7-9, 14, 16.

[1784]

It was the policy of the Revolution, to inculcate upon every citizen the obligation of renouncing his habitation, property, and every private concern for the service of his country; and many of us have scarcely yet learned to consider it as less than treason to have acted in a different manner. But it is time we should correct the exuberances of opinions propagated through policy and embraced from enthusiasm; and while we admit, that those who did act so disinterested and noble a part deserve the applause and, wherever they can be bestowed with propriety, the rewards of the country, we should cease to impute indiscriminate guilt to those who, submitting to the accidents of war, remained with their habitations and property. . . . Shall we go into an inquiry to ascertain the crime of each person? *This would be a prosecution;* and the treaty forbids all future prosecutions. Shall the Legislature take the map, and make a geographical delineation of the rights and disqualifications of its citizens? This would be to measure innocence and guilt by latitude and longitude. It would be to *condemn* and *punish*, not one man but thousands, for *supposed offenses*, without giving them an opportunity of making their defence. God forbid that such an act of barefaced tyranny should ever disgrace our history! God forbid that the body of the people should be corrupt enough to wish it, or even to submit to it! . . .

The common interests of humanity, and the general tranquility of the world, require that the power of making peace, wherever lodged, should be construed and exercised liberally; and even in cases where its extent may be doubtful, it is the policy of all wise nations to give it latitude rather than confine it. The exigencies of a community, in time of war, are so various, and often so critical, that it would be extremely dangerous to prescribe narrow bounds to that power by which it is to be restored. The consequence might frequently be a diffidence of our engagements, and a prolongation of the calamities of war. . . .

The Constitution is the compact made between the society at large and each individual. The society, therefore, cannot without breach of faith and injustice refuse to any individual a single advantage which he derives under that compact, no more than one man can refuse to perform his agreement with another. If the community have good reasons for abrogating the old compact and establishing a new one, it undoubtedly has a right to do it; but until the compact is dissolved with the same solemnity and certainty with which it was made, the society as well as individuals are bound by it. . . .

The danger from the corruption of the principles of our government is more plausible, but not more solid. It is an axiom, that governments form manners, as well as manners form governments. The body of the people of this state are too firmly attached to the democracy to permit the principles of a small number to give a different tone to that spirit. The present law of inheritance, making an equal division among the children of the parents' property, will soon melt down those great estates, which, if they continued, might favor the power of the *few*. The number of the disaffected, who are so from speculative notions of government, is small. The great majority of those who took part against us did it from accident, from the dread of the British power, and from the influence of others to whom they had been accustomed to look up. Most of the men who had that kind of influence are already gone: the residue and their adherents must be carried along by the torrent, and, with a very few exceptions, if the government is mild and just, will soon come to view it with approbation and attachment. . . .

There is a bigotry in politics as well as in religions, equally pernicious in both. The zealots, of either description, are ignorant of the advantage of a spirit of toleration. It was a long time before the kingdoms of Europe were convinced of the folly of persecution with respect to those who were schismatics from the established church. The cry was, these men will be equally the disturbers of the hierarchy and of the state. While some kingdoms were impoverishing and depopulating themselves by their severities to the non-conformists, their wiser neighbors were reaping the fruits of their folly, and augmenting their own numbers, industry, and wealth, by receiving, with open arms, the persecuted fugitives. Time and experience have taught a different lesson: and there is not an enlightened nation which does not now acknowledge the force of this truth, that whatever speculative notions of religion may be entertained, men will not on that account, be enemies to a government that affords them protection and security. . . .

If we set out with justice, moderation, liberality, and a scrupulous regard to the Constitution, the government will acquire a spirit and tone productive of permanent blessings to the community. If, on the contrary, the public councils are guided by humor, passion, and prejudice; if from resentment to individuals, or a dread of partial inconveniences, the Constitution is slighted, or explained away, upon every frivolous pretext, the future spirit of government will be feeble, distracted, and arbitrary. The rights of the subjects will be the sport of every party vicissitude. There will be no settled rule of conduct, but every thing will fluctuate with the alternate prevalency of contending factions.

—*A Second Letter from Phocion*, pp. 8-10, 17, 33, 36-38.

A few years later Hamilton managed to push through the legislature a bill repealing the Trespass Act. The very same issues arose again during the debate in the public press over Jay's Treaty. Again Hamilton insisted upon honest compliance with the provisions of the Treaty of 1783 regarding the property rights both of Loyalists and British subjects.

January 16, 1795

The right of a government to sequester or confiscate property, in its funds, in time of war, involves considerations analogous to those which regard the right of taxing them. Whether the foreigner be, himself, the original lender, or the proprietor of stock, in its constitution *transferable without discrimination,* he stands upon equal ground with the citizen. He has an equal claim upon the faith of the government. . . .

To sequester or confiscate the stock, is as effectually a breach of the contract to pay, as to absorb it by a tax. It is to annihilate the promise, under the sanction of which the foreigner became a proprietor.

But, does not the general right of war, to seize and confiscate enemy property, extend to the property of the citizens of one nation in the funds of another—the two nations being at war with each other? . . .

Though politically right, that, in wars between nations, the property of private persons which depend on the *laws of their own country*, or on *circumstances foreign to the nation with which their own is at war*, should be subject to seizure and confiscation by the enemy nation; yet it is both politically and morally wrong, that this should extend to property acquired under the faith of the government, and the laws of that enemy nation.

When the government enters into a contract with the citizen of a foreign country, it considers him as *an individual in a state of nature, and contracts with him as such*. It does not contract with him as *the member of another society*.

The contracts, therefore, with him, cannot be affected by his political relations to that society. War, whatever right it may give over his other property, can give none over that which he derives from those contracts. The character in which they are made with him, the faith pledged to him personally, virtually exempt it. . . .

The usages of war, still savor too much of the ferocious maxims of the times, when war was the chief occupation of man. Enlightened reason would never have pronounced that the persons or property of foreigners, found in a country at the breaking out of a war between that country and their own, were liable to any of the rigors which a state of war authorizes against the persons and goods of the enemy. It would have decreed to them, an inviolable sanctuary in the faith of those permissions and those laws, by which themselves and their property had come under the jurisdiction where they were found. It would have rejected the treachery of converting the indulgences, and even rights of a previous state of amity, into snares for innocent individuals.

—To the U. S. Senate. *American State Papers*, V, 336.

[July 9, 1795]

It was ever my opinion that no adjustment of the controversy on the inexecution of the former treaty was ever likely to be made, which would not embrace an indemnification for losses sustained, in consequence of legal impediments to the recovery of debts; and indeed it always appeared to me just that an indemnification should be embraced.

The article of the former treaty on this head was, as I conceive, nothing more than the formal sanction of a doctrine which makes part of the modern law or usage of nations. The *confiscation* of private debts in time of war is reprobated by the most approved writers on the laws of nations, and by the negative practice of civilized nations, during the present century. The free recovery of them, therefore, on the return of peace, was a matter of course, and ought not to have been impeded, had there been no article.

Admitting that the first breaches of the treaty were committed, as we alleged, by Great Britain, still it would not follow that the impediments which the laws of certain States opposed to the recovery of debts were justifiable. . . .

Two breaches of treaty are imputed to Great Britain; one respecting the carrying away of the Negroes, and the other respecting the retention of the posts.

As to the first, Great Britain has much to say with truth and justice. Her proceedings in seducing away our Negroes during the war were to the last degree infamous, and form an indelible stain on her annals. But having done it, it would have been still more infamous to have surrendered them to their masters.

The reply to this may be, that they ought not then to have stipulated it. This is just; but still the inquiry is, whether they have stipulated it; and here the odiousness of the thing, as applied to them, is an argument of weight against such a construction of general expressions in the treaty as would imply the obligation to restitution. Odious things are not favored in the interpretation of treaties; and though the restoration *of property* is a favored thing, yet the surrender of persons *to slavery* is an odious thing, speaking in the language of the laws of nations.

The words of the article are, that his Britannic Majesty shall, with all convenient speed, and without *causing any destruction or carrying away any Negroes or other property* of the American inhabitants, withdraw all his armies, etc.

There are two constructions of this article: one that the *evacuation should be made without depredation*—that is, without *causing any destruction* or carrying away any *property*, which continued to be *such (having undergone no change by the laws of war)* at the time of the evacuation; the other, that there was to be, besides a forbearance to destroy or carry away, a positive *restitution* of all property *taken in the war*, and, *at the time of the evacuation, which then existed in kind.*

In favor of the last construction is the most obvious sense of the words; and as it applies to the Negroes, merely as an article of property, the justice of restoring what had been taken away in many instances by unwarrantable means.

Against it, and in favor of the first construction, are these considerations.

1. That the expressions are, Negroes and *other property;* which puts Negroes, cows, horses, and all other articles of *property*, on the same footing, and considers them, if at all liable, equally liable to *restitution*, and all as having equally the common quality of *property* of the American inhabitants.

Could any thing be considered as property of the American inhabitants, at the time of the treaty, and in contemplation of the treaty, which, by the ordinary rules of the laws of war, had previously become the absolute *property of the captors?* Is there anything which exempts Negroes, more than other articles of personal property, from capture and confiscation as booty? If there is not, why should Negroes have been claimed under this article, more than the vessels which had been captured and condemned? Is that a probable sense of the treaty which would require such a restitution?

2. If Negroes were objects of capture in war, the captor might proclaim their liberty when in his possession. If once declared free, could the grant be recalled? Could the British Government stipulate the surrender of men made free to slavery? Is it natural to put such a construction upon general words, if they will bear another? Is not this, as it regards the rights of humanity, an odious sense?

3. The treaty will bear another construction—that which is put upon it by the British,—a provision *for greater caution* against depredation or the carrying away of property not changed by the laws of war. It is observable, in confirmation of this, that there is no *stipulation to restore*, but negatively not to carry away; whereas, immediately after, in the same article, there follows a clause which stipulates that "archives, records, etc., shall be *restored* and *delivered up*." This different mode of expression seems to denote a different sense in the two cases.

—To Washington (Cabinet Paper). Draft in Hamilton's hand; date in later hand. Hamilton Papers, 1st ser.

[1795]

As to the third point, it is to be observed, that though there may have been no express formal decision of our courts, enforcing the exceptionable principle of the trespass act, yet there never was a decision of a superior court against it; and it may not be amiss to remark incidentally, that the decision of the mayor's court,[1] from which Mr. Jefferson is glad to derive an exculpation of our conduct, was the object of severe animadversion at a popular meeting in this city, as a judiciary encroachment on the legislative authority of the State.

The truth on this point is, that according to the general opinion of our bar, a defence under a military order was desperate, and it was believed that a majority of our Supreme-Court bench would overrule the plea. Hence, in numerous cases where it might have been used, it was waived; and the endeavor on behalf of the defendants was either to effect, on collateral grounds, a mitigation of damages, or to accomplish the best compromises that could be obtained; even the suit of Rutgers and Waddington, after a partial success in the mayor's court, was terminated by a compromise, according to the advice of the defendant's council, owing to the apprehension of an unfavorable issue in the

[1] *Rutgers v. Waddington* (1784)—Ed.

Supreme Court; and this, notwithstanding the defendant was a British subject. . . .

Under these circumstances, which are faithfully represented, is it possible to doubt, that the act in question operated a breach of our treaty with Great Britain—and this from the very commencement of its existence? Can we reasonably expect that nations with whom we have treaties will allow us to substitute theoretic problems to performances of our engagements, and will be willing to accept them as apologies for actual violations?

—"Camillus," No. 4. Draft in Hamilton's hand. Hamilton Papers, 1st ser.

[1795]

. . . British subjects are now free, by our laws, to reside in all parts of the United States. As to the permission to become citizens, it has been the general policy and practice of our country to facilitate the naturalization of foreigners. And we may safely count on the interest of individuals, and on that desire to enjoy equal rights which is so deeply planted in the human breast, that all who resolve to make their permanent residence with us will become citizens. . . .

Suppose the stipulation had not been made, what would have been the probable policy of the United States? Would it not have been to leave the handful of settlers undisturbed, in quiet enjoyment of their property, and at liberty, if British subjects, to continue such, or become American citizens, on the usual conditions? A system of depopulation, or of coercion to one allegiance or another, would have been little congenial with our modes of thinking, and would not, I am persuaded have been attempted.

. . . it has always been understood, and upon recent and careful inquiry is confirmed, *that the British Government has never, since the peace, made a grant of lands within our limits*. It appears, indeed, to have been its policy to prevent settlements in the vicinity of the posts.

Hence the stipulation, as it affects lands, does nothing more than confirm the property of those which were holden at the treaty of peace; neither is the quantity considerable; and it chiefly, if not altogether, depends on titles acquired under the French Government, while Canada was a province of France.

In giving this confirmation, it only pursues what is a constant rule among civilized nations. When territory is ceded or yielded up by one nation to another, it is a common practice, if not a special condition, to leave the inhabitants in the enjoyment of their property. A contrary conduct would be disgraceful to a nation. . . .

—"Camillus," No. 9. Draft in Hamilton's hand. Hamilton Papers, 1st ser.

[1795-96]

. . . No powers of language at my command can express the abhorrence I feel at the idea of violating the property of individuals, which, in an authorized intercourse, in time of peace, has been confided to the faith of our Government and laws, on account of controversies between nation and nation. In my view, every moral and every political sentiment unite to consign it to execration. . . .

But so degrading an idea will be rejected with disdain, by every man who feels a true and well-informed national pride; by every man who recollects and glories, that in a state of still greater immaturity, we achieved independence without the aid of this dishonorable expedient[1]; that even in a revolutionary war, a war of liberty against usurpation, our national councils were never provoked or tempted to depart so widely from the path of rectitude; by every man, who, though careful not to exaggerate, for rash and extravagant projects, can nevertheless fairly estimate the real resources of the country, for meeting dangers which prudence cannot avert.

Such a man will never endure the base doctrine, that our security is to depend on the tricks of a swindler.

—"Camillus," No. 18. Draft in Hamilton's hand. Hamilton Papers, 1st ser.

[1795-96]

Public debt has been truly defined, "A *property subsisting in the faith of government.*" Its essence is promise. To confiscate or sequester it is emphatically to rescind the promise given, to revoke the faith plighted. It is impossible to separate the two ideas of a breach of faith, and the confiscation or sequestration of a property subsisting only in the faith of the government by which it is made.

When it is considered that the promise made to the foreigner is not made to him in the capacity of member of another society, but in that of citizen of the world, or of an individual in the state of nature, the infraction of it towards him, on account of the fault, real or pretended, of the society to which he belongs, is the more obviously destitute of color.

—"Camillus," No. 19. Draft in Hamilton's hand. Hamilton Papers, 1st ser.

[1] The federal government never resorted to it; and a few only of the State Governments stained themselves with it. It may, perhaps, be said, that the Federal Government had no power on the subject; but the reverse of this is truly the case. The Federal Government alone had power. The State Governments had none, though some of them undertook to exercise it. This position is founded on the solid ground that the confiscation or sequestration of the debts of an enemy is a high act of reprisal and war, necessarily and exclusively incident to the power of making war, which was always in the Federal Government.

Loyalty and Other Oaths

The issue of loyalty oaths in Hamilton's day has a contemporary ring. During the Revolution both sides required persons suspected of disloyalty to take an oath of allegiance. After the war was over it was proposed in New York to require all voters to swear that they had not in the past been guilty of acts of disloyalty. In his second Phocion letter Hamilton opposed the principle of what he called "retrospective oaths." In the state legislature he took a strong stand against imposing an oath on Roman Catholics. But loyalty oaths were in an entirely different category from those required under the revenue laws, he insisted when he became Secretary of the Treasury.

[1784]

It has been said, too, that an oath to determine the qualifications of electors is an usual precaution in free governments; but we may challenge those who make the assertion, to show that retrospective oaths have ever been administered, requiring electors to swear that they have not been guilty of past offences. In all the violence of party which has, at different periods, agitated Great Britain, nothing of this kind has ever been adopted; but even where religious fanaticism has given an edge to political opposition, and in an undecided contest for the crown, they have never gone further than to prescribe oaths for testing present dispositions towards the government, on general principles, without retrospection to particular instances of past mal-conduct. The practical notions of legal liberty established in that country by a series of trials, would make such an experiment too odious to be attempted by the government. Wise men have thought that even there they have carried the business of oaths to an exceptionable length; but we, who pretend a purer zeal for liberty, in a decided contest, after a formal renunciation of claims by the adverse party, are for carrying the matter to a still more blamable extreme.

—*A Second Letter from Phocion*, p. 26.

January 24, 1787

Mr. Hamilton declared the Constitution to be their creed and standard, and ought never to be departed from; but in the present instance it was proper first to examine how far it applied to the subject under consideration: that there were two different bodies in the State to which this has reference; these were the Roman Catholics already citizens and those coming from abroad. Between these two were great distinctions. The foreigner who comes among us and will become a citizen, who wishes a naturalization, may with propriety be asked these terms; it may be necessary he should abjure his former sovereign. For the natural subject, the man born amongst us, educated with us, possessing our manners, with an equally ardent love of his native country, to be required to take the same oath of abjuration—what has he to abjure? He owes no fealty to any other power upon earth; nor is it likely his mind should be led astray by bigotry or the influence of foreign powers. Then, why give him occasion to be dissatisfied with you, by bringing forward a test which will not add to his fidelity? Moreover, the clause in the Constitution confines this test to foreigners, and, if I am not misinformed, it was not till after much debate and warm contention that it got admittance, and then only by a small majority in the convention.

It was a question with him whether it was proper to propose this test in the case before them. But he was decidely against going so far as to extend it to ecclesiastical matters. Why should we wound the tender conscience of any man? and why present oaths to those who are known to be good citizens? Why alarm them? Why set them upon inquiry which is useless and unnecessary? You give them reason to suppose that you expect too much of them, and they cannot but refuse compliance. The Constitution does not require such a criterion to try the fidelity of any citizen. It is solely intended for aliens and foreigners coming from abroad, with manners and habits different from our own, and whose intentions are concealed. . . .

Again, sir, we should be cautious how we carry the principle of requiring and multiplying tests upon our fellow-citizens, so far as to practise it to the exclusion and disfranchisement of any.

—Speech in the New York Assembly. *Works*, VIII, 19-21.

March 6, 1792

It is not easy to conceive what maxim of liberty is violated by requiring persons who carry on particular trades, which are made contributory to the revenue, to designate, by public marks, the places in which they are carried on. There can certainly be nothing more harmless, or less inconvenient, than such a regulation. The thing itself is frequently done by persons of various callings for the information of customers; and why it should become a hardship or grievance, if required for a public purpose, can with difficulty be imagined.

The supposed tendency of the act to injure morals seems to have relation to the oaths, which are, in a variety of cases, required, and which are liable to the objection that they give occasion to perjuries.

The necessity of requiring oaths is, whenever it occurs, matter of regret. It is certainly desirable to avoid them as often and as far as possible; but it is more easy to desire than to find a substitute. The requiring of them is not peculiar to the act in question; they are a common appendage of revenue laws, and are among the usual guards of those laws, as they are of public and private rights in courts of justice. They constantly occur in jury trials, to which the citizens of the United States are so much and so justly attached. The same objection, in different degrees, lies against them in both cases, yet it is not perceivable how they can be dispensed with in either.

It is remarkable that *both* the kinds of security to the revenue, which are to be found in the act, the oaths of parties and the inspection of officers are objected to. If they are both to be abandoned, it is not easy to imagine what security there can be for any species of revenue, which is to be collected from articles of consumption. . . .

There appears to be but one provision in the law, which admits of a question whether the penalty prescribed may not partake of severity. It is that which inflicts the pains of perjury on any person who shall be convicted of "wilfully taking a false oath or affirmation in any of the cases in which oaths or affirmations are required by the act."

Precedents in relation to this particular, vary. In many of them, the penalties are less severe than for perjury, in courts of justice; in others, they are the same. The latter are, generally, of the latest date, and seem to have been the result of experience.

The United States have, in other cases, pursued the same principle as in the law in question. And the practice is certainly founded on strong reasons.

1st. The additional security which it gives to the revenue cannot be doubted. Many who would risk pecuniary forfeitures and penalties would not encounter the more disgraceful punishment annexed to perjury.

2d. There seems to be no solid distinction between one false oath in violation of law and right and another false oath in violation of law and right. A distinction in the punishments of different species of false swearing is calculated to beget false opinions concerning the sanctity of an oath; and by countenancing an impression, that a violation of it is less heinous in the cases in which it is less punished, it tends to impair in the mind that scrupulous veneration for the obligation of an oath which ought always to prevail, and not only to facilitate a breach of it in the cases which the laws have marked with less odium, but to prepare the mind for committing the crime in other cases. . . .

There are other provisions of the act which mark the scrupulous attention of the Government to protect the parties concerned from inconvenience and injury, and which conspire to vindicate the law from imputations of severity or oppression.

—"Spirits, Foreign and Domestic." Hamilton Papers, 2d ser.

Freedom of the Press

Hamilton's most enduring contribution to civil liberties is found in the area of freedom of the press. His views first received an acid test on the eve of the Revolution, when hot-headed Patriots used strong-arm measures to suppress Tory newspapers. The most notorious incident was the raid of Connecticut Minute Men led by Isaac Sears, a veteran of the New York Sons of Liberty, upon the shop of the notorious royalist printer, James Rivington. Hamilton protested immediately. Again, at the end of the war, when Rivington chose to stay on in New York, the printer was once more a target of mob action. Again Hamilton came to his defense.

NEW YORK November 26, 1775

Dear Sir:

I take the liberty to trouble you with some remarks on a matter which to me appears of not a little importance; doubting not that you will use your influence in Congress to procure a remedy for the evil I shall mention, if you think the considerations I shall urge are of that weight they seem in my judgment to possess.

You will probably ere this reaches you have heard of the late incursion made into this city by a number of horsemen from New England under the command of Capt. Sears, who took away Mr. Rivington's types and a Couteau or two. Though I am fully sensible how dangerous and pernicious Rivington's press has been, and how detestable the character of the man is in every respect, yet I cannot help disapproving and condemning this step.

In times of such commotion as the present, while the passions of men are worked up to an uncommon pitch, there is a great danger of fatal extremes. The same state of the passions which fits the multitude, who have not a sufficient stock of reason and knowledge to guide them, for opposition to tyranny and oppression, very naturally leads them to a contempt and disregard of all authority. The due medium is hardly to be found among the more intelligent; it is almost [im]possible among the unthinking populace. When the minds of these are loosened from their attachment to ancient establishments and courses, they seem to grow giddy and are apt more or less to run into anarchy. These principles, too true in themselves, and confirmed to me both by reading and my own experience, deserve extremely the attention of those who have the direction of public affairs. In such tempestuous times, it requires the greatest skill in the political pilots to keep men steady and within proper bounds, on which account I am always more or less alarmed at every thing which is done of mere will and pleasure without any proper authority. Irregularities, I know, are to be expected, but they are nevertheless dangerous and ought to be checked by every prudent and moderate mean. From these general maxims, I disapprove of the irruption in question, as serving to cherish a spirit of disorder at a season when men are too prone to it of themselves.

Moreover, New England is very populous and powerful. It is not safe to trust to the virtue of any people. Such proceedings will serve to produce and encourage a spirit of encroachment and arrogance in them. I like not to see potent neighbors indulged in the practice of making inroads at pleasure into this or any other province.

You well know too, Sir, that antipathies and prejudices have long subsisted between this province and New England. To this may be attributed a principal part of the disaffection now prevalent among us. Measures of the present nature, however they may serve to intimidate, will secretly revive and increase those ancient animosities, which, though smothered for a while, will break out when there is a favorable opportunity.

Besides this, men coming from a neighboring province to chastise the notorious friends of the ministry here, will hold up an idea to our enemies not very advantageous to our affairs. They will imagine that the New Yorkers are totally, or a majority of them, disaffected to the American cause, which makes the interposal of their neighbors necessary; or that such violences will breed differences and effect that which they have been so eagerly wishing, a division and quarreling among ourselves. Everything of such an aspect must encourage their hopes.

Upon the whole the measure is condemned, by all the cautious and prudent among the Whigs, and will evidently be productive of secret jealously and ill blood if a stop is not put to things of this kind for the future.

All the good purposes that could be expected from such a step will be answered; and many ill consequences will be prevented if your body gently interposes a check for the future. Rivington will be intimidated and the Tories will be convinced that the other colonies will not tamely see the general cause betrayed by the Yorkers. A favorable idea will be impressed of your justice and impartiality in discouraging the encroachments of any one province on another; and the apprehensions of prudent men respecting the ill-effects of an ungoverned spirit in the people of New England will be quieted. Believe me, Sir, it is a matter of consequence and deserves serious attention.

The Tories, it is objected by some, are growing insolent and clamorous. It is necessary to repress and overawe them. There is truth in this; but the present remedy is a bad one. Let your body station in different parts of the province most tainted with the ministerial infection a few regiments of troops raised in Philadelphia, the Jerseys or any other province except New England. These will suffice to strengthen and support the Whigs who are still, I flatter myself, a large majority and to suppress the efforts of the Tories. The pretense for this would be plausible. There is no knowing how soon the Ministry may make an attempt upon New York. There is reason to believe they will not be long before they turn their attention to it. In this there will be some order and regularity, and no grounds of alarm to our friends.

I am, Sir, with very great esteem

Your most humble servant

A. HAMILTON

—To John Jay. Hamilton MSS., N. Y. Pub. Lib.

March 18, 1789

Some short time after the evacuation of this City, on the occasion of certain irregularities committed (I think by Sears and others in regard to Rivington) the Council for the temporary government came to some resolution, or agreed upon some proclamation of a spirited nature for discountenancing such proceedings, which was delivered to the Governor to publish. He kept it in his hands and did not publish it, and when the Council met alleged that he had consulted Mr. Lamb and Willet, who thought it would have an ill effect to publish it by exciting ill blood and therefore had not done it. The majority of the Council consented to the suppression. I remember to have understood at the time that Benson and yourself were very angry at the procedure. . . . I will thank you to let me know by the first post after this the particulars of the transaction. A public use has been made of the fact and I understand it is meant to call it in question. It is of great importance that charges when made should be supported and I will therefore be obliged to you for an accurate statement. . . .

—To Robert R. Livingston. Robert R. Livingston Collection, N. Y. Hist. Soc.

March 22, 1789

. . . I will therefore esteem it a favour if you will write me by the next post (if not already done) all the circumstances of the affair, especially as they respect the Governor's conduct on the occasion. Should you wish that your name may not be brought into question, I engage that the matter shall be so managed as to avoid it.

—To Robert R. Livingston. Robert R. Livingston Collection, N. Y. Hist. Soc.

The value of a completely free and irresponsible press was seriously questioned during Washington's administration. Both Jefferson and Hamilton used press agents to disseminate their opposing views. Jefferson put the poet Philip Freneau on the payroll of the State Department, and his later profession of innocence in this matter has never rung true. With a pipeline to the cabinet, Freneau published a series of outrageous attacks on Washington and Hamilton in the columns of the National Gazette. *Hamilton answered in kind through the medium of John Fenno's* United States Gazette. *After he retired from the cabinet Hamilton felt impelled to go into the state courts to vindicate himself from the false accusation of having accepted money from the British minister to the United States for the purpose of buying the* Aurora, *an opposition newspaper, with a view to silencing this anti-Federalist mouthpiece. A printer named David Frothingham was convicted of criminal libel upon Hamilton, fined $100, and imprisoned for four months.*

[September-October, 1799]

Greenleaf's *New Daily Advertiser* of this morning contains a publication entitled, "Extract of a Letter from Philadelphia, dated September 20th," which charges me with being at the "bottom" of an effort recently made to suppress the *Aurora* (a newspaper of that city) by pecuniary means.

It is well known that I have long been the object of the most malignant calumnies of the faction opposed to our government through the medium of the papers devoted to their views. Hitherto I have forborne to resort to the laws for the punishment of the authors or abettors, and were I to consult personal considerations alone, I should continue in this course, repaying hatred with contempt.

But public motives now compel me to a different conduct. The designs of that faction to overturn our government, and with it the great pillars of social security and happiness in this country, become every day more manifest, and have of late acquired a degree of system which renders them formidable.

One principal engine for effecting the scheme is by audacious falsehoods to destroy the confidence of the people in all those who are in any degree conspicuous among the supporters of the government—an engine which has been employed in time past with too much success, and which, unless counteracted in future, is likely to be attended with very fatal consequences.

To counteract it is therefore a duty to the community. Among the specimens of this contrivance, that which is the subject of the present letter demands peculiar attention. A bolder calumny—one more absolutely destitute of foundation—was never propagated, and its dangerous tendency needs no comment; being calculated to inspire the belief that the independence and liberty of the press are endangered by the intrigues of ambitious citizens aided by foreign gold. In so flagrant a case the force of the laws must be tried.

I therefore request that you will take immediate measures towards the prosecution of the persons who conduct the enclosed paper.

—To Josiah O. Hoffman. Draft in Hamilton's hand. Date in later hand. Hamilton Papers, 1st ser; originally published in *Gazette and General Advertiser*, Nov. 8, 1799.

In the Zenger trial back in colonial days Andrew Hamilton urged the right of the jury to inquire into the truth or falsity of a seditious libel and argued that truth was a defense. Although Zenger was acquitted, these principles of law were not established in Anglo-American jurisprudence at that time. The unpopular Sedition Act of the Adams' *administration allowed the truth of the matter in the publication charged as libel to be introduced by the defense, but by its own terms the law expired in two years. Its termination did not bring an end to prosecutions for seditious libel at common law.*

The Jeffersonians were loud in protest when Hamilton successfully prosecuted the printer of the Argus *but upon their accession to national power they used the same weapon to silence the opposition. Much depended on whose ox was gored. Harry Croswell, publisher of the Hudson,* N. Y., Wasp *and an unreconstructed Federalist, made the scurrilous charge in his paper that Jefferson had paid James* T. *Callender, erstwhile Jeffersonian journalist and victim of the Sedition Act who went over to the opposition, for calling Washington a traitor, robber, and perjurer, and for attacking Adams as an incendiary. Croswell was prosecuted for seditious libel. At the trial on the circuit in July,* 1803 *Chief Justice Lewis, a Jeffersonian, charged the jury to confine themselves to the fact of publication, and ruled that the truth could not be given in evidence.*

Croswell's counsel happened to be none other than Alexander Hamilton, who moved for a new trial in the state Supreme Court. Hamilton's argument on the motion was careful and reasoned, one of the last of his career. While condemning "this spirit of abuse and calumny as the pest of society," he contended "for the liberty of publishing truth, with good motives and justifiable ends, even though it reflect on government, magistrates, or private persons." For this insistence on good motives there was no support whatsoever at common law, and Hamilton deserves credit as a notable legal innovator. In his opinion, a judge, appointed by the executive, was not as objective as a jury chosen by lot, and the latter should have power to decide the issue in libel.

Fortunately for Hamilton's client the Supreme Court was just then coming under the intellectual spell of another great New Yorker, James Kent, a man of conservative temper and extraordinary range of erudition. A Federalist, Kent had been silent during the ignominy of the Alien and Sedition laws, but rallied to the defense of the press when opposition party idols were the target for attack. In a learned opinion among the manuscripts in the New York Public Library Kent upheld Hamilton's arguments. However, the court voted on straight party lines and was evenly divided. This division caused Hamilton's motion for a new trial to be lost, but the public prosecutor failed in turn to make a motion for judgment on the verdict. The following year a revised libel bill passed the legislature and incorporated the Hamiltonian formula about good motives and justifiable ends. In consequence of this declaratory act, the Supreme Court in August term of that year unanimously granted Harry Croswell a new trial. Hamilton's principle embodied in the act of 1805 was incorporated into the state constitutions of 1821 and 1846, and serves as a source and model for the press guarantees in many of our present-day state constitutions.

February 13, 1804

The liberty of the press consists, in my idea, in publishing the truth, from good motives and for justifiable ends, though it reflects on the government, on magistrates, or individuals. If it be not allowed, it excludes the privilege of canvassing men, and our rulers. It is in vain to say, you may canvass measures. This is impossible without the right of looking to men. To say that measures can be discussed, and that there shall be no bearing on those who are the authors of those measures, cannot be done. The very end and reason of discussion would be destroyed. Of what consequence to show its object? Why is it to be thus demonstrated, if not to show, too, who is the author? It is essential to say, not only that the measure is bad and deleterious, but to hold up to the people who is the author, that, in this our free and elective government, he may be removed from the seat of power. If this be not to be done, then in vain will the voice of the people be raised against the inroads of tyranny. For, let a party but get into power, they may go on from step to step, and, in spite of canvassing their measures, fix themselves firmly in their seats, especially as they are never to be reproached for what they have done. This abstract mode, in practice, can never be carried into effect. But if, under the qualifications I have mentioned, the power be allowed, the liberty for which I contend will operate as a salutary check. In speaking thus for the freedom of the press, I do not say there ought to be an unbridled license; or that the characters of men who are good will naturally tend eternally to support themselves. I do not stand here to say that no shackles are to be laid on this license.

I consider this spirit of abuse and calumny as the pest of society. I know the best of men are not exempt from the attacks of slander. Though it pleased God to bless us with the first of characters, and though it has pleased God to take him from us and this band of calumniators, I say that falsehood eternally repeated would have affected even his name. Drops of water, in long and continued succession, will wear out adamant. This, therefore, cannot be endured. It would be to put the best and the worst on the same level.

I contend for the liberty of publishing truth, with good motives and for justifiable ends, even though it reflect on government, magistrates, or private persons. I contend for it under the restraint of our tribunals. When this is exceeded, let them interpose and punish. From this will follow none of those consequences so ably depicted. When, however, we do look at consequences, let me ask whether it is right that a permanent body of men, appointed by the executive, and, in some degree, always connected with it, should exclusively have the power of deciding on what shall constitute a libel on our rulers, or that they shall share it, united with a changeable body of men chosen by the people. Let our juries still be selected, as they now are, by lot. But it cannot be denied, that every body of men is, more or less, liable to be influenced by the spirit of the existing administration; that such a body may be liable to corruption, and that they may be inclined to lean over towards party modes. No man can think more highly of our judges, and I may say personally so of those who now preside, than myself; but I must forget what human nature is, and how her history has taught us that permanent bodies may be so corrupted, before I can venture to assert that it cannot be. As then it may be, I do not think it safe thus to compromise our independence. For though, as individuals, the judges may be interested in the general welfare, yet, if once they enter into these views of government, their power may be converted into the engine of oppression. It is in vain to say that allowing them this exclusive right to declare the law, on what the jury has found, can work no ill; for, by this privilege, they can assume and modify the fact, so as to make the most innocent publication libellous. It is therefore not a security to say, that this exclusive power will but follow the law. It must be with the jury to decide on the intent; they must in certain cases be permitted to judge of the law, and pronounce on the combined matter of law and of fact. . . .

What is a libel that it should be otherwise? Why take it out of the rule that allows, in all criminal cases, when the issue is general, the jury to determine upon the whole? . . .

The criminal quality is its maliciousness. The next ingredient is, that it shall have an intent to defame. I ask, then, if the intent be not the very essence of the crime. It is admitted that the word falsity, when the proceedings are on the statute, must be proved to the jury, because it makes the offence. Why not then the malice, when, to constitute the crime, it must necessarily be implied? In reason there can be no difference.

A libel is, then, a complicated matter of fact and law, with certain things and circumstances to give them a character. If so, then the malice is to be proved. The tendency to provoke is its constituent. Must it not be shown how and in what manner? If this is not to be the case, must every one who does not panegyrize be said to be a libeller?

. . . Let it rather be said that crime depends on intent, and intent is one parcel of the fact. Unless, therefore, it can be shown that there is some specific character of libel that will apply in all cases, intent, tendency, and quality must all be matters of fact for a jury. There is therefore, nothing which can be libel, independent of circumstances; nothing which can be so called in opposition to time and circumstances. . . .

. . . I must examine how far truth is to be given in evidence. This depends on the intent being a crime. Its being a truth is a reason to infer that there was no design to injure another. Thus, not to decide on it would be injustice, as it may be material in ascertaining the intent. It is impossible to say that to judge of the quality and nature of an act, the truth is immaterial. It is inherent in the nature of things, that the assertion of truth cannot be a crime. In all systems of law this is a general axiom, but this single instance, it is attempted to assert, creates an exception, and is therefore an anomaly. If, however, we go on to examine what may be the case that shall be so considered, we cannot find it to be this. . . .

Personal defects can be made public only to make a man disliked. Here, then, it will not be excused; it might, however, be given in evidence to show the libellous degree. Still, however, it is a subject of inquiry. There may be a fair and honest exposure. But if he uses the weapon of truth wantonly; if for the purpose of disturbing the peace of families, if for relating that which does not appertain to official conduct, so far we say the doctrine of our opponents is correct. If their expressions are, that libellers may be punished though the matter contained in the libel be true, in these I agree. I confess that the truth is not material as a broad proposition respecting libels. But that the truth cannot be material in any respect, is contrary to the nature of things. No tribunal, no codes, no systems can repeal or impair this law of God, for by his eternal laws it is inherent in the nature of things. . . .

I affirm that, in the general course of things, the disclosure of truth is right and prudent, when liable to the checks I have been willing it should receive as an object of animadversion.

It cannot be dangerous to government, though it may work partial difficulties. If it be not allowed, they will stand liable to encroachments on their rights. It is evident that if you cannot apply this mitigated doctrine, for which I speak, to the cases of libels here, you must forever remain ignorant of what your rulers do. I never can think this ought to be; I never did think the truth was a crime; I am glad the day is come in which it is to be decided, for my soul has ever abhorred the thought that a free man dared not speak the truth; I have forever rejoiced when this question has been brought forward.

I come now to examine the second branch of this inquiry—the different provinces of the court and the jury. I will introduce this subject by observing that the trial by jury has been considered, in the system of English jurisprudence, as the palladium of public and private liberty. In all the political disputes of that country, this has been deemed the barrier to secure the subjects from oppression. If, in that country, juries are to answer this end, if they are to protect from the weight of state prosecutions, they must have this power of judging of the intent, in order to perform their functions; they could not otherwise answer the ends of their institution. . . .

Let us see if any thing in the annals of America will further the argument. Zenger's case has been mentioned as an authority. A decision in a factitious period, and reprobated at the very time.

A single precedent never forms the law. If in England it was fluctuating in an English court, can a colonial judge, of a remote colony, ever settle it? He cannot fix in New York what was not fixed in Great Britain. It was merely one more precedent to a certain course of practice. But because a colonial governor, exercising judicial power, subordinate to the judges of the mother country, decides in this way, can it be said that he can establish the law, and that he has, by a solitary precedent, fixed what his superior could not? The most solemn decisions of the court of king's bench are at one time made and at another time overruled. Why are our courts to be bound down by the weight of only one precedent? Is a precedent, like the laws of the Medes and Persians, never to be changed? This is to make the colonial precedent of more weight than is in England allowed to a precedent of Westminster Hall. To pursue the precedents more emphatically our own, let us advert to the sedition law, branded indeed with epithets the most odious, but which will one day be pronounced a valuable feature in our national character. In this we find not only the intent but the truth may be submitted to the jury, and that even in a justificatory manner. This, I affirm, was on common-law principles. It would, however, be a long detail to investigate the applicability of the common law to the Constitution of the United States. It is evident, however, that parts of it use a language which refers to former principles. The *habeas corpus* is mentioned, and as treason, it adopts the very words of the common law. Not even the Legislature of the Union can change it. Congress itself cannot make constructive or new treasons. Such is the general tenor of the Constitution of the United States, that it evidently looks to antecedent law. What is, on this point, the great body of the common law? Natural law and natural reason applied to the purposes of society. What are the English courts now doing but adopting natural law?

What have the court done here? Applied moral law to constitutional principles, and thus the judges have confirmed this construction of the common law; and therefore, I say, by our Constitution it is said the truth may be given in evidence. . . .

Going on, however, to precedents, I find another in the words of Chief-Justice Jay, when pronouncing the law on this subject. The jury are, in the passage already cited, told the law, and the fact is for their determination; I find him telling them that it is their right. This admits of no qualification. The little, miserable conduct of the judge in Zenger's case, when set against this, will kick the beam; and it will be seen that even the twelve judges do not set up, with deference, however, to their known ability, that system now insisted on. If the doctrine for which we contend is true in regard to treason and murder, it is equally true in respect to libel. For there is the great danger. Never can tyranny be introduced into this country by arms; these can never get rid of a popular spirit of inquiry; the only way to crush it down is by a servile tribunal.[1] It is only by the abuse of the forms of justice that we can be enslaved. An army never can do it. For ages it can never be attempted. The spirit of the country, with arms in their hands, and disciplined as a militia, would render it impossible. Every pretence that liberty can be thus invaded is idle declamation. It is not to be endangered by a few thousand of miserable, pitiful military. It is not thus that the liberty of this country is to be destroyed. It is to be subverted only by a pretence of adhering to all the forms of law, and yet by breaking down the substance of our liberties; by devoting a wretched but honest man as the victim of a nominal trial. . . .

It is important to have it known to the men of our country, to us all, whether it be true or false; it is important to the reputation of him against whom the charge is made, that it should be examined. It will be a glorious triumph for truth; it will be happy to give it a fair chance of being brought forward; an opportunity, in case of another course of things, to say that the truth stands a chance of being the criterion of justice. Notwithstanding, however, the contrary is asserted to be the doctrine of the English courts, I am, I confess, happy to hear that the freedom of the English is allowed; that a nation with king, lords, and commons, can be free. I do not mean to enter into a comparison between the freedom of the two countries.[2] But the attorney-general

[1] "The road to tyranny will be opened by making dependent judges, by packing juries, by stifling the press, by silencing leaders and patriots." Summary of argument in 3 Johns. Cas. (N.Y.) 358.

[2] "That country is free where the people have a representation in the government, so that no law can pass without their consent; and where they are secured in the administration of justice by trial by jury. We have gone further in this country into the popular principle, and he cordially united his prayers with the opposite counsel, that the experiment with us might be successful." 3 Johns. Cas. (N.Y.) 358, 359.

has taken vast pains to celebrate Lord Mansfield's character. Never, till now, did I hear that his reputation was high in republican estimation; never, till now, did I consider him as a model for republican imitation. I do not mean, however, to detract from the fame of that truly great man, but only conceived his sentiments were not those fit for a republic. No man more truly reveres his exalted fame than myself; if he had his faults, he had his virtues; and I would not only tread lightly on his ashes, but drop a tear as I passed by. He, indeed, seems to have been the parent of the doctrines of the other side. Such, however, we trust, will be proved not to be the doctrines of the common law nor of this country, and that in proof of this, a new trial will be granted.

—Speech in *People v. Croswell. Works,* VIII, 389-392, 394-395, 400, 403, 407, 409-410, 419-425; variant summary of Hamilton's argument in 3 Johns. Cas. (N.Y.) 336 at 352.

Sedition and Insurrection

The drift of events in Hamilton's day provided a stern test for creative statesmanship. How could the security of the nation be safeguarded against sedition without sacrificing the right of Americans to criticize, assemble, and form a political opposition? When it came to overt resistance Hamilton's answer was forthright. Demonstrate the full authority of the government at once. That issue was first raised during the so-called Whisky Insurrection, a protest against the enforcement of Hamilton's excise law.

At Washington's solicitation Hamilton drafted an opinion on August 2, 1794, as to what should be done to quell the disorder. The main theme was: The national government should act. Hamilton drafted the warning sent through Secretary of State Randolph to Governor Mifflin of Pennsylvania. In his Tully *essays he sought public backing for the government's course. Temporarily filling the office of Secretary of War on the resignation of Knox in addition to his duties in the Treasury, Hamilton notified Washington of his intention to accompany the troops in the field. He marched with Major-General Lee into western Pennsylvania, where the insurgents put up no resistance. Hamilton had the leading agitators summarily rounded up and turned over to the courts, but those convicted were pardoned by Washington.*

September 1, 1792

My present clear conviction is, that it is indispensable, if competent evidence can be obtained, to exert the full force of the law against the offenders, with every circumstance that can manifest the determination of government to enforce its execution; and if the processes of the courts are resisted, as is rather to be expected, to employ those means which in the last resort are put in the power of the Executive. If this is not done, the spirit of disobedience will naturally extend, and the authority of the government will be prostrated. Moderation enough has been shown; it is time to assume a different tone. The well-disposed part of the community will begin to think the Executive wanting in decision and vigor.

—To Washington. *Hamilton*, IV, 289.

August 2, 1794

Armed collections of men, with the avowed design of opposing the execution of the laws, have attacked the house of the Inspector of the Revenue, burnt and destroyed his property, and shed the blood of persons engaged in its defence; have made prisoner of the marshal of the district, and did not release him till, for the safety of his life, he stipulated to execute no more processes within the disaffected counties; have compelled both him and the Inspector of the Revenue to fly the country by a circuitous route, to avoid personal injury, perhaps assassination; have proposed the assembling of a convention of delegates from those counties and the neighboring ones of Virginia, probably with a view to systematize measures of more effectual opposition; have forcibly seized, opened, and spoliated a mail of the United States.

What in this state of things is proper to be done? The President has, with the advice of the heads of departments and the Attorney-General, caused to be submitted all the evidence of the foregoing facts to the consideration of an associate judge, under the act entitled, "An act to provide for calling forth the militia to execute the laws of the Union, suppress insurrection, and repel invasion."

If the judge shall pronounce that the case described in the second section of that act exists, it will follow that a competent force of militia should be called forth and employed to suppress the insurrection, and support the civil authority in effectuating obedience to the laws and punishment of offenders.

It appears to me that the very existence of government demands this course, and that a duty of the highest nature urges the Chief Magistrate to pursue it. The Constitution and laws of the United States contemplate and provide for it.

What force of militia shall be called out, and from what State or States?

The force ought, if attainable, to be an imposing one, such, if practicable, as will deter from opposition, save the effusion of the blood of citizens, and serve the object to be accomplished.

—To Washington. Copy by J. A. Hamilton. Hamilton Papers, 1st ser.

August 5, 1794[1]

The idea of pursuing *legal* measures to *obstruct* the *operation* of a *law*, needs little comment. Legal measures may be pursued to procure the repeal of a law, but to *obstruct its operation* presents a contradiction in terms. The *operation*, or, what is the same thing, the *execution* of a law, cannot be obstructed after it has been constitutionally enacted without illegality and crime. The expression quoted is one of those phrases which can only be used to conceal a disorderly and culpable intention under forms that may escape the hold of the law.

Neither was it difficult to perceive that the anathema pronounced against the officers of the revenue placed them in a state of virtual outlawry, and operated as a signal to all those who were bold enough to encounter the guilt and the danger to violate both their lives and their properties.

—To Washington. Hamilton Papers, 1st ser.

August 7, 1794

The people of the United States have established a government for the management of their general interests; they have instituted executive organs for administering that government; and their representatives have established the rules by which those organs are to act. When their authority in that of their government is attacked, by lawless combinations of the citizens of part of a State, they could never be expected to approve that the care of vindicating their authority, of enforcing their laws, should be transferred from the officers of their own government to those of a State, and this to wait the issue of a process so indeterminate in its duration as that which it is proposed to pursue. . . .

If there were no other objection to a transfer of this kind, the very important difference which is supposed to exist in the nature and consequences of the offences that have been committed, in the contemplation of the laws of the United States and those of Pennsylvania, would alone be a very serious obstacle. . . .

You are already, sir, advised that the President, yielding to the impressions which have been stated, has determined to take measures for calling forth the militia; and that these measures contemplate the assembling of a body of between twelve and thirteen thousand men, from Pennsylvania and the neighboring States of Virginia, Maryland, and New Jersey. The recourse thus early to the militia of the neighboring States, proceeds from a probability of the insufficiency of that of Pennsylvania alone to accomplish the object. . . .

But, while the President has conceived himself to be under an indispensable obligation to prepare for that eventual resort, he has still consulted the sentiment of regret which he expressed to you, at the

[1] Dated by Hamilton: "Treasury Department 1794."

possible necessity of an appeal to arms; and to avert it, if practicable, as well as to manifest his attention to the principle, that "a firm and energetic conduct does not preclude the exercise of a prudent and humane policy," he has (as you have been also advised) concluded upon the measure of sending himself commissioners to the discontented counties, to make one more experiment of a conciliatory appeal to the reason, virtue, and patriotism of their inhabitants; and has also signified to you how agreeable would be to him your co-operation in the same expedient, which you have been pleased to afford. It can scarcely be requisite to add, that there is nothing he has more at heart than that the issue of this experiment, by establishing the authority of the laws, may preclude the always calamitous necessity of an appeal to arms.

—Edmund Randolph, Secretary of State, to Mifflin. Draft in Hamilton's hand. Hamilton Papers, 1st ser.

August 26, 1794

Let us see then what is this question. It is plainly this—Shall the majority govern or be governed? shall the nation rule or be ruled? shall the general will prevail, or the will of a faction? shall there be government or no government? It is impossible to deny that this is the true and the whole question. No art, no sophistry can involve it in the least obscurity.

The Constitution *you* have ordained for yourselves and your posterity contains this express clause: "The Congress *shall have power* to lay and collect taxes, duties, imposts, and *excises*, to pay the debts, and provide for the common defence and general welfare of the United States." You have, then, by a solemn and deliberate act, the most important and sacred that a nation can perform, pronounced and decreed, that your representatives in Congress shall have power to lay *excises*. You have done nothing since to reverse or impair that decree. . . .

That a fate like this may never await you, let it be deeply imprinted in your minds, and handed down to your latest posterity, that there is no road to *despotism* more sure or more to be dreaded than that which begins at anarchy.

Threats of joining the British are actually thrown out—how far the idea may go is not known.

—"Tully," No. 2. *Hamilton*, VII, 161, 163.

August 28, 1794

If it were to be asked, What is the most sacred duty, and the greatest source of security in a republic? the answer would be, An inviolable respect for the Constitution and laws—the first growing out of the last. It is by this, in a great degree, that the rich and the powerful are to be restrained from enterprises against the common liberty—operated upon by the influence of a general sentiment, by their interest in the principle, and by the obstacles which the habit it produces erects against innovation and encroachment. It is by this, in a still greater degree, that caballers, intriguers, and demagogues are prevented from climbing on the shoulders of faction to the tempting seats of usurpation and tyranny. . . .

Government is frequently and aptly classed under two descriptions—a government of FORCE, and a government of LAWS; the first is the definition of despotism—the last, of liberty. But how can a government of laws exist when the laws are disrespected and disobeyed? Government supposes control. It is that POWER by which individuals in society are kept from doing injury to each other, and are brought to co-operate to a common end. The instruments by which it must act are either the AUTHORITY of the laws or FORCE. If the first be destroyed, the last must be substituted; and where this becomes the ordinary instrument of government, there is an end to liberty!

—"Tully," No. 3. *Hamilton*, VII, 163, 164.

September 19, 1794

Upon full reflection I entertain an opinion that it is advisable for me, on public ground, considering the connection between the immediate ostensible cause of the insurrection in the western country and my department, to go out upon the expedition against the insurgents.

In a government like ours it cannot but have a good effect for the person who is understood to be the adviser or proposer of a measure, which involves danger to his fellow-citizens, to partake in that danger; while not to do it might have a bad effect. I therefore request your permission for the purpose.

—To Washington. Hamilton Papers, 1st ser.

BEDFORD, October 20, 1794

I have it in special instruction from the President of the United States, now at this place, to convey to you the following instructions for the general direction of your conduct in the command of the militia army, with which you are charged.

The objects for which the militia have been called forth are:

1st. To suppress the combinations which exist in some of the western counties in Pennsylvania, in opposition to the laws laying duties upon spirits distilled within the United States, and upon stills.

2d. To cause the laws to be executed.

These objects are to be effected in two ways:

1. By military force.

2. By judiciary process and other civil proceedings.

The objects of the military force are twofold:

1. To overcome any armed opposition which may exist.

2. To countenance and support the civil officers in the means of executing the laws. . . .

You are aware that the judge cannot be controlled in his functions; but I count on his disposition to co-operate in such a general plan as shall appear to you consistent with the policy of the case. But your method of giving a direction to legal proceedings, according to your general plan, will be by instruction to the district attorney.

He ought particularly to be instructed (with due regard to time and circumstances): 1st. To procure to be arrested all influential actors in riots and unlawful assemblies relating to the insurrection, and combinations to resist the laws, or having for object to abet that insurrection and those combinations, and who shall not have complied with the terms offered by the commissioners, or manifested their repentance in some other way which you may deem satisfactory. 2d. To cause process to issue for enforcing penalties on delinquent distillers. 3d. To cause offenders who may be arrested, to be conveyed to jails where there will be no danger of rescue: those for misdemeanors, to the jails of York and Lancaster; those for capital offences, to the jail of Philadelphia, as more secure than the others. 4th. To prosecute indictable offences in the courts of the United States; those for penalties on delinquents, under the laws before mentioned, in the courts of Pennsylvania. . . .

The seizure of stills is the province of the supervisor and other officers of inspection. It is difficult to chalk out the precise line concerning it. There are opposite considerations which will require to be nicely balanced, and which must be judged of by those officers on the spot. It may be found useful to confine the seizures to stills of the most leading and refractory distillers. It may be advisable to extend them far in the most refractory county.

When the insurrection is subdued, and the requisite means have been put in execution to secure obedience to the laws, so as to render it proper for the army to retire (an event which you will accelerate as much as shall be consistent with the object), you will endeavor to make an arrangement for detaching such a force as you deem adequate, to be stationed within the disaffected country, in such a manner as best to afford protection to well-disposed citizens and to the officers of the revenue, and to repress, by their presence, the spirit of riot and opposition to the laws.

But before you withdraw the army, you will promise, on behalf of the President, a general pardon to all such as shall not have been arrested, with such exceptions as you shall deem proper. The promise must be so guarded as not to affect pecuniary claims under the revenue laws. In this measure, it is advisable there should be a co-operation with the Governor of Pennsylvania. . . .

You are to exert yourselves by all possible means to preserve discipline among the troops, particularly a scrupulous regard to the rights of persons and property, and to a respect for the authority of the civil magistrate; taking especial care to inculcate and cause to be observed this principle: that the duties of the army are confined to the attacking and subduing of armed opponents of the laws, and to the supporting and aiding of the civil officers in the execution of their functions.

It has been settled that the Governor of Pennsylvania will be second, the Governor of New Jersey third in command, and that the troops of the several States in line, on the march and upon detachment, are to be posted according to the rule which prevailed in the army during the late war—namely, in moving towards the sea-board, the most southern troops will take the right; in moving westward, the most northern will take the right.

—To Major-General Lee. *Hamilton,* V, 38, 40-42.

November 8, 1794

It appears evident, that to wait for preliminary investigations to apprehend the guilty upon process, would defeat the object, and produce delay beyond the patience of the troops, or the time allowed by the season for operation. With the advice of the district attorney, the Commander-in-Chief has concluded to take hold of all who are worth the trouble in a more summary way—that is, by the military arm, and then to deliver them over to the disposition of the judiciary. In the meantime, all possible means are using to obtain evidence, and accomplices will be turned against the others.

This step is directed by that principle of common law that every man may of right apprehend a traitor.

—To Washington. Copy by J. A. Hamilton. Hamilton Papers, 1st ser.

November 19, 1794. 7 o'clock in the morning

I wrote you the day before yesterday, by express. Nothing material remains to be said. The army is, generally, in motion homeward—the Virginia line, by way of Morgantown, to Winchester, etc.; the Maryland line, by way of Uniontown, to Williamsport, etc.; the Pennsylvania and New Jersey, by the old Pennsylvania route, to Bedford. The judiciary is industrious in prosecuting the examination of prisoners—among whom there is a sufficient number of proper ones for examples, and with sufficient evidence. Col. Gaddis has been brought in.

With perfect respect and true attachment, I have the honor, etc.

P. S.—In five minutes I set out for Philadelphia.

—To Washington. Copy by J. A. Hamilton. Hamilton Papers, 1st ser.

The Whisky Rebellion demonstrated that the United States was not "a rope of sand," that its laws were sovereign, and its taxes had to be paid. Ultimately the shipment of grain westward and down to New Orleans ended western Pennsylvania's dependence upon whisky shipments over the mountains and made local resistance economically unjustifiable. But Hamilton never forgot the lesson he learned on this march, and when Secretary of War McHenry was confronted with some disorders he received from his friend a judicious bit of advice.

March 18, 1799

Beware, my dear sir, of magnifying a riot into an insurrection, by employing in the first instance an inadequate force. 'Tis better far to err on the other side. Whenever the government appears in arms, it ought to appear like a *Hercules*, and inspire respect by the display of strength. The consideration of expense is of no moment compared with the advantages of energy. 'Tis true, this is always a relative question, but 'tis always important to make no mistake. I only offer a *principle* and a *caution*.

—To McHenry (Private). Draft in Hamilton's hand. Hamilton Papers, 1st ser.

The threat of war with France in the summer of 1798 increased the nation's sense of insecurity. Since several of the leading Jeffersonian publicists happened to be European refugees anti-alien feeling mounted in some quarters. The result was a two-pronged attack known as the Alien and Sedition Laws. The former changed from five to fourteen years the period of residence required for admission to citizenship and authorized the president to expel aliens regarded as dangerous to the public peace and safety. The latter made it a high misdemeanor, punishable by fine and imprisonment, for citizens or aliens to enter into unlawful combinations opposing execution of the national laws or attempting "any insurrection, riot, unlawful assembly, or combination." In addition, fine and imprisonment were to be imposed for persons convicted of publishing "any false, scandalous and malicious writing" bringing into disrepute the government or its officials.

Although Hamilton was the guiding spirit in the defensive measures undertaken against France, he had no hand in the Alien and Sedition Laws. "I hope sincerely the thing will not be hurried through," he wrote of the first draft of the Sedition Act. "Let us not establish a tyranny." He found the alien bill less objectionable, but urged his friends to avoid sweeping and unfair discrimination against foreigners. Once the laws were enacted, however, he pressed for their vigorous enforcement. When Jefferson, upon becoming President, favored abolishing all restrictions on naturalization, Hamilton cautioned against impulsive action and urged the five-year residence requirement, which was re-enacted into law.

June 7, 1798

. . . If an alien bill passes, I would like to know what policy, in execution, is likely to govern the *Executive*. My opinion is, that while the mass ought to be obliged to leave the country, the provisions in our treaties in favor of merchants ought to be observed, and there ought to be *guarded* exceptions of characters whose situation would expose them too much if sent away, and whose demeanor amongst us has been unexceptionable. There are a few such. Let us not be cruel or violent.

—To Timothy Pickering. *Hamilton,* VI, 299-300.

June 29, 1798

I have this moment seen a bill[1] brought into the Senate entitled "A Bill to define more particularly the crime of Treason," etc. There are provisions in this bill, which, according to a cursory view, appear to me highly exceptionable, and such as, more than any thing else, may endanger civil war. I have not time to point out my objections by this post, but I will do it tomorrow. I hope sincerely the thing may not be hurried through. Let us not establish a tyranny. Energy is a very different thing from violence. If we make no false step, we shall be essentially united, but if we push things to an extreme, we shall then give to faction *body* and solidity.

—To Oliver Wolcott. (Copy). Hamilton Papers, 1st ser.

January 7, 1802

The next most exceptionable feature in the message is the proposal to abolish all restriction on naturalization, arising from a previous residence. In this the President is not more at variance with the concurrent maxims of all commentators on popular governments, than he is with himself. The Notes on Virginia are in direct contradiction to the message, and furnish us with strong reasons against the policy now recommended. The passage alluded to is here presented. ". . . Civil government being the sole object of forming societies, its administration must be conducted by common consent. Every species of government has its specific principles. Ours, perhaps, are more peculiar than those of any other in the universe. *It is a composition of the freest principles of the English Constitution*, with others, derived from natural right and reason. To these, nothing can be more opposed than the maxims of absolute monarchies. Yet from such, we are to expect the *greatest number of emigrants. . . . Is it not safer to wait with patience*

[1] Draft of the Sedition law.

for the attainment of any degree of population desired or expected? May not our government be more homogeneous, *more peaceable, more durable?* Suppose twenty millions of republican Americans, thrown all of a sudden into France, what would be the condition of that kingdom? If it would be more turbulent, less happy, less strong, we may believe that the addition of half a million of foreigners, to our present numbers, would produce a similar effect here." Thus wrote Mr. Jefferson in 1781.—Behold the reverse of the medal. . . .

The impolicy of admitting foreigners to an immediate and unreserved participation in the right of suffrage, or in the sovereignty of a republic, is as much a received axiom as any thing in the science of politics, and is verified by the experience of all ages.

—"Lucius Crassus," No. 7. *Hamilton,* VII, 776. 773, 774.

January 12, 1802

. . . The present law was merely a temporary measure adopted under peculiar circumstances, and perhaps demands revision. But there is a wide difference between closing the door altogether and throwing it entirely open; between a postponement of fourteen years, and an immediate admission to all the rights of citizenship. Some reasonable term ought to be allowed to enable aliens to get rid of foreign and acquire American attachments; to learn the principles and imbibe the spirit of our government; and to admit of a probability at least, of their feeling a real interest in our affairs. A residence of not less than five years ought to be required.

—"Lucius Crassus," No. 8. *Hamilton,* VII, 776.

11

On Leaders and Leadership

The Washington-Hamilton Relationship

He was an *Aegis* very essential to me.

The intimate friendship of Washington and Hamilton and their complete agreement on major political issues had momentous consequences for building the new nation. That friendship went back to the days when Hamilton was the general's military aide. From the start Hamilton made it scrupulously clear to the New York Patriot leaders that he was speaking for himself alone. In the early years of the war Hamilton was one of Washington's most ardent defenders and a leading denunciator of the so-called Conway Cabal, that much-touted, if inchoate, move to oust Washington after Saratoga and replace him with Gates. Washington's critic, Thomas Conway, previously an Irish colonel in the French army, had been made inspector general by Congress. He later resigned from the army.

March 20, 1777

With cheerfulness I embrace the proposal of corresponding with your convention through you, and shall from time to time, as far as my leisure will permit and my duty warrant, communicate such transactions as shall happen, such pieces of intelligence as shall be received, and such comments upon them as shall appear necessary to convey a true idea of what is going on in the military line. Let me caution you, however, that whatever opinions I shall give in the course of correspondence are to be considered merely as my private sentiments, and are never to be interpreted as an echo of those of the *General;* since they will not be really so, and a construction of the kind may lead into errors and be productive of inconveniences.

—To Gouverneur Morris, Robert Livingston, and William Allison, Esqs. Robert R. Livingston Coll., N. Y. Hist. Soc.

HEADQUARTERS February 13, 1778

. . . You and I had some conversation when I had the pleasure of seeing you last, with respect to the existence of a certain faction. Since I saw you I have discovered such convincing traits of the monster that I cannot doubt its reality in the most extensive sense. I dare say you have heard enough to settle the matter in your own mind. I believe it unmasked its batteries too soon, and begins to hide its head; but as I imagine it will only change the storm to a sap, all the true and sensible friends to their country, and of course to a certain great man, ought to be upon the watch to counterplot the secret machinations of his enemies. Have you heard anything of Conway's history? He is one of the vermin bred in the entrails of his chimera dire, and there does not exist a more villainous calumniator and incendiary. He is gone to Albany on a certain expedition.

—To Governor George Clinton. *Works*, IX, 126-127.

WEST POINT September 11, 1779

Apropos, speaking of a Caesar and a Cromwell, don't you think the Cabal have reported that I declared in a public house in Philadelphia that it was high time for the people to rise, join General Washington, and turn Congress out of doors? I am running the rogues pretty hard. Dana[1] was the first mentioned to me. He has given up Dr. Gordon,[2] of Jamaica Plains. You well remember the old Jesuit. He made us a visit at Fredericksburg, and is writing the history of America. The proverb is verified,—"There never was any mischief, but had a priest or a woman at the bottom." I doubt not subornation and every species of villainy will be made use of to cover the villainy of the attack. I have written to Gordon, and what do you think is his answer?—he will give up his author if I will pledge my honor "neither to give nor accept a challenge, to cause it to be given or accepted, nor to engage in any encounter that may produce a duel." Pleasant terms enough. I am first to be calumniated, and then, if my calumniator takes it into his head, I am to bear a cudgelling from him with Christian patience and forbearance; for the terms required, if pursued to their consequences, come to this. I have ridiculed the proposal, and insisted on the author, on

[1] Francis Dana, of Massachusetts, an intimate of John Adams.

[2] William Gordon, British emigrant to Massachusetts, a notorious gossip, then engaged in gathering material for a history of the American Revolution.—Ed.

the principle of unconditional submission. What the Doctor's impudence will answer, I know not. But you who know my sentiments will know how to join me in despising these miserable detractors. On revising my work, I find several strokes of the true schoolboy sublime. Pray let them pass, and admire them if you can.

—To John Laurens. *Works*, IX, 174-175.

Hamilton, eager to attain military distinction before the war came to an end, became fed up with his post as aide to the general. That February day in 1781 when he broke with Washington he must have been thoroughly insufferable. Written in heat, the letters describing his break with Washington do him little credit. Washington never criticized Hamilton and was happy to revive the friendship and confidential relationship that had existed in the past. After Yorktown Hamilton reappraised the relationship in a more objective light and came to understand Washington's unique role in the attainment of victory.

HEADQUARTERS, NEW WINDSOR February 18, 1781

Since I had the pleasure of writing you last, an unexpected change has taken place in my situation. I am no longer a member of the General's family. This information will surprise you, and the manner of the change will surprise you more. Two days ago, the General and I passed each other on the stairs. He told me he wanted to speak to me. I answered that I would wait upon him immediately. I went below, and delivered Mr. Tilghman a lettter to be sent to the commissary, containing an order of a pressing and interesting nature.

Returning to the General, I was stopped on the way by the Marquis de La Fayette, and we conversed together about a minute on a matter of business. He can testify how impatient I was to get back, and that I left him in a manner which, but for our intimacy, would have been more than abrupt. Instead of finding the General, as is usual, in his room, I met him at the head of the stairs, where, accosting me in an angry tone, "Colonel Hamilton," said he, "you have kept me waiting at the head of the stairs these ten minutes. I must tell you, sir, you treat me with disrespect." I replied, without petulancy, but with decision: "I am not conscious of it, sir; but since you have thought it necessary to tell me so, we part." "Very well, sir," said he, "if it be your choice," or something to this effect, and we separated. I sincerely believe my absence, which gave so much umbrage, did not last two minutes.

In less than an hour after, Tilghman came to me in the General's name, assuring me of his great confidence in my abilities, integrity, usefulness, etc., and of his desire, in a candid conversation, to heal a difference which could not have happened but in a moment of passion.

I requested Mr. Tilghman to tell him—1st. That I had taken my resolution in a manner not to be revoked. 2d. That, as a conversation could serve no other purpose than to produce explanations, mutually disagreeable, though I certainly would not refuse an interview if he desired it, yet I would be happy if he would permit me to decline it. 3d. That, though determined to leave the family, the same principles which had kept me so long in it would continue to direct my conduct towards him when out of it. 4th. That, however, I did not wish to distress him, or the public business, by quitting him before he could derive other assistance by the return of some of the gentlemen who were absent. 5th. And that, in the mean time, it depended on him to let our behavior to each other be the same as if nothing had happened. He consented to decline the conversation, and thanked me for my offer of continuing my aid in the manner I had mentioned. Thus we stand. I wait Mr. Humphrey's return from the eastward, and may be induced to wait the return of Mr. Harrison from Virginia.

I have given you so particular a detail of our difference from the desire I have to justify myself in your opinion. Perhaps you may think I was precipitate in rejecting the overture made by the General to an accommodation. I assure you, my dear sir, it was not the effect of resentment; it was the deliberate result of maxims I had long formed for the government of my own conduct.

I always disliked the office of an aid-de-camp as having in it a kind of personal dependence. I refused to serve in this capacity with two major-generals at an early period of the war. Infected, however, with the enthusiasm of the times, an idea of the General's character which experience taught me to be unfounded overcame my scruples, and induced me to *accept his invitation* to enter into his family. It was not long before I discovered he was neither remarkable for delicacy nor good temper, which revived my former aversion to the station in which I was acting, and it has been increasing ever since. It has been often with great difficulty that I have prevailed upon myself not to renounce it; but while, from motives of public utility, I was doing violence to my feelings, I was always determined, if there should ever happen a breach between us, never to consent to an accommodation. I was persuaded that when once that nice barrier, which marked the boundaries of what we owed to each other, should be thrown down, it might be propped again, but could never be restored.

I resolved, whenever it should happen, not to be in the wrong. I was convinced the concessions the General might make would be dictated by his interest, and that his self-love would never forgive me for what it would regard as a humiliation.

I believe you know the place I held in the General's confidence and counsels, which will make it the more extraordinary to you to learn that for three years past I have felt no friendship for him and have professed none. The truth is, our dispositions are the opposites of each other, and the pride of my temper would not suffer me to profess what I did not feel. Indeed, when advances of this kind have been made to me on his part, they were received in a manner that showed at least that I had no desire to court them, and that I desired to stand rather upon a footing of military confidence than of private attachment.

You are too good a judge of human nature not to be sensible how this conduct in me must have operated on a man to whom all the world is offering incense. With this key you will easily unlock the present mystery.

At the end of the war I may say many things to you concerning which I shall impose upon myself till then an inviolable silence.

The General is a very honest man. His competitors have slender abilities, and less integrity. His popularity has often been essential to the safety of America, and is still of great importance to it. These considerations have influenced my past conduct respecting him, and will influence my future. I think it is necessary he should be supported.

His estimation in your mind, whatever may be its amount, I am persuaded has been formed on principles which a circumstance like this cannot materially affect; but if I thought it could diminish your friendship for him, I should almost forego the motives that urge me to justify myself to you. I wish what I have said to make no other impression than to satisfy you I have not been in the wrong. It is also said in confidence, as a public knowledge of the breach would, in many ways, have an ill effect. It will probably be the policy of both sides to conceal it, and cover the separation with some plausible pretext. I am importuned by such of my friends as are privy to the affair, to listen to a reconciliation; but my resolution is unalterable.

—To Philip Schuyler. *Works*, IX, 232-236.

February, 1781

. . . I am about leaving him to be any thing that fortune may cast up —I mean in the military line. This, my dear General, is not an affair of calculation, but of feeling. You may divine the rest, and I am sure you will keep your divinations to yourself. The enemy have gotten so much in the way of intercepting our mails that I am afraid of seeing whatever I write hung up the week after in *Rivington's Gazette*. This obliges me to be cautious. Adieu. My dear General, let me beg you will believe that whatever change there may be in my situation, there will never be any in my respect, esteem, and affection for you.

P. S.—Let me know if I could find any thing worth my while to do in the southern army. You know I shall hate to be nominally a soldier.

—To General Nathanael Greene. *Works*, IX, 238.

March 24, 1783

. . . I congratulate your Excellency on this happy conclusion of your labors. It now only remains to make solid establishments within, to perpetuate our Union, to prevent our being a ball in the hands of European powers, bandied against each other at their pleasure; in fine to make our independence truly a blessing. This, it is to be lamented, will be an arduous work; for, to borrow a figure from mechanics, the centrifugal is much stronger than the centripetal force in these States,—the seeds of disunion much more numerous than those of union.

—To Washington. Hamilton's hand. Hamilton Papers, 1st ser.

In the years of the Confederation Washington and Hamilton saw eye-to-eye on the need for a strong union. That intimate relationship aroused some jealousy. Washington replied to Hamilton's letter, stating: "I do . . . explicitly declare that both charges are entirely unfounded."

[October, 1787]

It is, however, of some importance to the party to diminish whatever credit or influence I may possess, and to effect this they stick at nothing. Among many contemptible artifices practised by them they have had recourse to an insinuation that I *palmed* myself upon you, and that you *dismissed* me from your family. This I confess hurts my feelings, and if it obtains credit, will require a contradiction.

—To Washington. *Hamilton,* I, 444-445.

Hamilton urged Washington to stand for the Presidency, to run for reelection, and to withhold until the very last moment his decision not to run for a third term.

August 13, 1788

I take it for granted, sir, you have concluded to comply with what will no doubt be the general call of your country in relation to the new government. You will permit me to say that it is indispensable you should lend yourself to its first operations. It is of little purpose to have *introduced* a system, if the weightiest influence is not given to its firm *establishment* in the outset.

—To Washington. Hamilton's hand. Hamilton Papers, 1st ser.

September, 1788

. . . I have, however, reflected maturely on the subject, and have come to a conclusion (in which I feel no hesitation), that every public and personal consideration will demand from you an acquiescence in what will *certainly* be the unanimous wish of your country. The absolute retreat which you meditated at the close of the late war was natural and proper. Had the government produced by the Revolution gone on in a *tolerable* train, it would have been most advisable to have persisted in that retreat. But I am clearly of opinion that the crisis which brought you again into public view left you no alternative but to comply, and I am equally clear in the opinion that you are by that act *pledged* to take a part in the execution of the government. I am not less convinced that the impression of this necessity of your filling the station in question is so universal that you run no risk of any uncandid imputation by submitting to it. But even if this were not the case, a regard to your own reputation, as well as to the public good, calls upon you in the strongest manner to run that risk.

It cannot be considered as a compliment to say that on your acceptance of the office of President the success of the new government in its commencement may materially depend.

—To Washington. Hamilton Papers, 1st ser.

July 30, 1792

I received the most sincere pleasure at finding in our late conversation, that there was some relaxation in the disposition you had before discovered to decline a re-election. Since your departure, I have left no opportunity of sounding the opinions of persons, whose opinions were worth knowing on these two points. 1st. The effect of your declining, upon the public affairs, and upon your own reputation. 2dly. The effect of your continuing, in reference to the declarations you have made of your disinclination to public life; and I can truly say that I have not found the least difference of sentiment on either point. The impression is uniform, that your declining would be to be deplored as the greatest evil that could befall the country at the present juncture, and as critically hazardous to your own reputation; that your continuance will be justified in the mind of every friend to his country, by the evident necessity for it. 'Tis clear, says every one with whom I have conversed, that the affairs of the national government are not yet firmly established—that its enemies, generally speaking, are as inveterate as ever— . . . that if you continue in office nothing materially mischievous is to be apprehended, if you quit, much is to be dreaded—that the same motives which induced you to accept originally ought to decide you to continue till matters have assumed a more determined aspect—that indeed it would have been better, as it regards your own character, that you had never consented to come forward, than now to leave the business unfinished and in danger of being undone—that in the event of storms arising, there would be an imputation either of want of foresight or want of firmness—and, in fine, that on public and personal accounts, on patriotic and prudential considerations, the clear path to be pursued by you will be, again to obey the voice of your country, which, it is not doubted, will be as earnest and as unanimous as ever.

—To Washington. *Hamilton*, IV, 235.

September 9, 1792

I have the pleasure of your private letter of the 26th of August. The feelings and views which are manifested in that letter are such as I expected would exist. And I most sincerely regret the causes of the uneasy sensations you experience. It is my most anxious wish, as far as may depend upon me, to smooth the path of your administration, and to render it prosperous and happy. And if any prospect shall open of healing or terminating the differences which exist, I shall most cheerfully embrace it; though I consider myself as the deeply injured party. . . .

I considered myself as compelled to this conduct by reasons public as well as personal, of the most cogent nature. I *know* that I have been an object of uniform opposition from Mr. Jefferson, from the moment of his coming to the city of New York to enter upon his present office. I *know* from the most authentic sources, that I have been the frequent subject of the most unkind whispers and insinuations from the same quarter. I have long seen a party formed in the Legislature under his auspices, bent upon my subversion. I cannot doubt from the evidence I possess, that the *National Gazette* was instituted by him for political purposes, and that one leading object of it has been to render me, and all the measures connected with my department, as odious as possible. Nevertheless, I can truly say, that, except explanations to confidential friends, I never directly or indirectly retaliated or countenanced retaliation till very lately. I can even assure you, that I was instrumental in preventing a very severe and systematic attack upon Mr. Jefferson by an association of two or three individuals, in consequence of the persecution which he brought upon the Vice-President, by his indiscreet and light letter to the printer, transmitting *Paine's* pamphlet. . . .

But when I no longer doubted that there was a formed party deliberately bent upon the subversion of measures, which in its consequences would subvert the government; when I saw that the undoing of the funding system in particular (which, whatever may be the original merits of that system, would prostrate the credit and the honor of the nation, and bring the government into contempt with that description of men who are in every society the only firm supporters of government) was an avowed object of the party, and that all possible pains were taken to produce that effect, by rendering it odious to the body of the people, I considered it as a duty to endeavor to resist the torrent, and, as an effectual means to this end, to draw aside the veil from the principal actors. To this strong impulse, to this decided conviction, I have yielded. And I think events will prove that I have judged rightly.

Nevertheless, I pledge my honor to you, sir, that if you shall hereafter form a plan to reunite the members of your administration upon some steady principle of cooperation, I will faithfully concur in executing it during my continuance in office; and I will not directly or indirectly say or do a thing that shall endanger a feud.

—To Washington. *Hamilton*, IV, 303-305.

July 5, 1796

As to your resignation, sir, it is not to be regretted that the declaration of your intention should be suspended as long as possible, and suffer me to add that you should really hold the thing undecided to the last moment. I do not think it is in the power of party to throw any slur upon the lateness of your declaration. And you have an obvious justification in the state of things. If a storm gathers, how can you retreat? This is a most serious question. The proper period now for your declaration seems to be two months before the time for the meeting of the electors. This will be sufficient. The parties will in the meantime electioneer conditionally, that is to say, if you decline; for a serious opposition to you will, I think, hardly be risked.

—To Washington. *Works*, X, 181-182.

One of the most shocking and unwarranted incidents in Washington's administration occurred when "A Calm Observer," believed to be John Beckley, clerk of the House and an old enemy of Hamilton's, virtually accused the President of being an embezzler. He asserted that during his first term in office Washington had drawn from the Treasury some five thousand dollars more than the salary fixed by law, although much had since been repaid, and that he had since then overdrawn his quarterly salary allotments. Hamilton rightly regarded this as a reflection on his own integrity as Secretary of the Treasury as well as on Washington's.

November 11, 1795

A very virulent attack has recently been made upon the President of the United States, the present Secretary of the Treasury, and myself, as his predecessor in office, on the ground of extra payments to the President on account of his salary.

The charges against all the three are no less heinous than those of intentional violation of the Constitution, of the laws, of their oaths of office. I use the epithet *intentional*, because though not expressly used in the terms of the attack, it is implied in every line of it, since an involuntary error of construction, if that could ever be made out, would not warrant the imputation "of *contemning* and *despising every principle* which the people have established for the security of their rights, of *setting at defiance* all *law* and *authority*, and of *servile submission* and compliance with the *lawless will* and *pleasure* of a President." . . .

Thus has it been shown that the advances for the use of the President have been governed by a rule of construction which has obtained in analogous cases, or, more truly, which has regulated the general course of disbursements from the Treasury— a rule which, I trust, has been demonstrated to be consonant with the Constitution and the laws.

It is requsite to inquire a little further, whether there has been any improper use or rather abuse of the discretion which is contended for; for here there is likewise an unquestionable responsibility. It is seen that the advances have at no time equalled one quarter's salary.

I ask, Was it unreasonable or unfit, if constitutional and legal, to afford the President of the United States an accommodation of this extent?

I pledge my veracity that I have always understood, and to this moment I have good reason to be satisfied, that the expenses of the President—those of his household and others incident to his official situation—have fully equalled, if not on some occasions exceeded, the allowance made to him by the United States. Under this conviction especially, how could the head of a department hesitate by so *small an accommodation* as the advance of *less than* a quarter's salary, to enable the President of the United States to meet his expenses as they accrued, without being obliged to intrench upon his own private resources, or to resort to the expedient of borrowing, to defray expenses imposed upon him by public situation? I knew that no possible risk could attend the advance, little considerable as it was. The estate of the President was answerable in case of death or other premature vacancy and abundant for the indemnification of the government.

Reasons of a peculiar kind forbade hesitation. The scale of expense was unavoidably such as to render the income even of what is deemed a large landed property in this country, a slender auxiliary; without an advance from the Treasury, it was not improbable borrowing might be necessary. Was it just to compel the President to resort to that expedient, for a purpose in fact public, at his private expense? Was it for the dignity of the nation that he should have been exposed to a necessity, an embarrassment of this sort?

My judgment and feelings answered both these questions in the negative. I entertained no doubt of the constitutionality and legality of the advance, and I thought the making of it due to the situation, due to propriety, due to every public consideration connected with the subject. I can never regret it.

How far the President was privy to the course of advances I cannot say; but it is certain that they have been all made to his private secretaries upon a general arrangement, and not by special directions from him. And I think it proper to add, that very early in the day, and probably before any was made, on an application to Mr. Lear[1] for a sum which would constitute an advance, he qualified it by this observation: "If in your opinion it can be done with legality and perfect propriety." I answered that I had no doubt of either. I shall not attempt to assume any greater responsibility in this transaction than belongs to me; but I have been accustomed to think that the responsibility for the due and regular disbursement of moneys from the Treasury lies exclusively with the officers of the department, and that, except in a very palpable and glaring case, the charge of blamable participation could not fall on any other person.

As between the officers of the Treasury, I take the responsibility to stand thus. The Secretary and Comptroller, in granting warrants upon the Treasury, are both answerable for their *legality*. In this respect, the Comptroller is a check upon the Secretary. With regard to the *expediency* of an advance, in my opinion, the right of judging is exclusively with the head of the department. The Comptroller has no voice in this matter. So far, therefore, as concerns legality in the issues of money while I was in the department, the Comptroller must answer with me; so far as a question of expediency or the due exercise of discretion may be involved, I am solely answerable. And uniformly was the matter so understood between successive comptrollers and myself. So also it is essential to the due administration of the department, that it should be so understood. . . .

Hard would be the condition of public officers if even a misconstruction of constitutional and legal provisions, attended with no symptom of criminal motive, carrying the proof of innocence in the openness and publicity of conduct, could justly expose them to the odious charges which on this occasion are preferred. Harder still would be their condition if, in the management of the great and complicated business of a nation, the fact of misconstruction, which is to constitute their guilt, is to be decided by the narrow and rigid rules of a criticism no less pedantic than malevolent. Pre-eminently hard in such circumstances was the lot of the man who, called to the head of the most arduous department in the public administration in a new government, without the guidance of antecedent practice and precedent, had to trace out his own path, and to adjust for himself the import and bearings of delicate and important provisions in the Constitution and in the laws.

Reposing myself on a consciousness which, in no possible situation,

[1] Tobias Lear, private secretary to Washington, and for a time manager of the President's business affairs.—Ed.

can fail to prove an invulnerable shield to my tranquillity, I leave to a candid public to pronounce the sentence which is due to an attempt, on such a foundation, to erect against the President of the United States, my successor in office, and myself, the heinous charges of violation of the Constitution, violation of the laws, exertion of arbitrary will on the one side, abject submission on the other, misapplication of the public money, and, to complete the newspaper group, intentional PERJURY!

—Letter of explanation. Draft in Hamilton's hand; date in later hand. Hamilton Papers, 1st ser.

Hamilton's "Original Draft" of the Farewell Address

The Farewell Address exemplifies that perfect collaboration on both foreign and domestic issues that obtained between Washington and Hamilton during the former's presidency. Hamilton drafted many of Washington's state papers, speeches to Congress, and proclamations. In some cases they were a vehicle for ideas that originated with Hamilton; in others they were a literary re-phrasing of Washington's own thoughts. The Farewell Address is the most notable example of the latter. Back in February, 1792, Washington asked James Madison to prepare a draft of an address about retirement. Madison sent him a "Form for an Address." When Washington definitely decided to retire at the end of his second term he made a draft of his own, embodying some material from Madison's earlier suggested draft. Then he sent the paper on to Hamilton. Hamilton faithfully followed Washington's ideas, but re-phrased them in a masterly way. Hamilton wrote two drafts, an "Original Draft," herein published from the original manuscript in the Hamilton Papers, with Hamilton's marginal notes appearing as footnotes, and a draft for "incorporation" with the first draft. But Washington preferred Hamilton's original draft.

May 10, 1796

When last in Philadelphia you mentioned to me your wish that I should re-dress a certain paper which you had prepared. As it is important that a thing of this kind should be done with great care, and much at leisure, touched and re-touched, I submit a wish that as soon as you have given it the *body* you mean it to have, it may be sent to me.

—To Washington. *Hamilton*, VI, 119-120.

[August, 1796]

The period for a new election of a citizen to administer the executive government of the United States being not very distant, and the time actually arrived when your thoughts must be employed in designating the person who is to be clothed with that important trust for another term, it appears to me proper, and especially as it may conduce to a more distinct expression of the public voice, that I should now apprise you of the resolution I have formed to decline being considered among the number of those out of whom a choice is to be made.

I beg you, nevertheless,[1] to be assured that the resolution which I announce has not been taken without a strict regard to all the considerations attached to[2] the relation which, as a dutiful citizen, I bear[3] to my[4] country, and that in withdrawing the tender of my service, which silence in my situation might imply, I am influenced by no diminution of zeal for its future interest, nor by any deficiency of grateful respect for its past kindness, but by a full conviction that such a step is compatible with both.

The acceptance of, and the continuance hitherto in the office to which your suffrages have twice called me, has been a uniform sacrifice of private inclination to the opinion of public duty coinciding[5] with what appeared to be your wishes. I had constantly hoped that it would have been much earlier in my power, consistently with motives which I was not at liberty to disregard, to return to that retirement from which *those*[6] *motives* had reluctantly drawn me.

The strength of my desire to withdraw previous to the last election, had even led to the preparation of an address to declare it to you, but deliberate[7] reflection on the very critical and perplexed posture of our affairs with foreign nations, and the unanimous advice of men[8] every way entitled to my confidence, obliged[9] me to abandon the idea.

I rejoice that the state of your national concerns, external as well as internal, no longer renders the pursuit of my inclination incompatible with the sentiment of duty or propriety, and that whatever partiality any portion of you may still retain for my services, they, under the existing circumstances of our country, will not disapprove the[10] resolution[11] I have formed.

The impressions under which I first accepted the arduous trust of Chief Magistrate of the United States, were explained on the proper occasion. In the discharge of this trust, I can only say that I have, with pure intentions, contributed towards the organization and administration of the government the best exertions of which a very fallible judgment was capable; that unconscious at[12] the outset of the inferiority of my qualifications for the station, experience in my own eyes, and perhaps still more in those of others, has not diminished in me the diffidence of myself—and every day the increasing weight of years admonishes me more and more that the shade of retirement is as necessary to me as it will be welcome [to me]. Satisfied that if any

[1] Hamilton's alternative phrasing: at the same time [2] connected with—inseparable from—incident to [3] bears [4] his
[5] combined with a deference for [6] they [7] mature [8] persons [9] impelled
[10] my [11] to retire [12] in

circumstances have given a peculiar value to my services, they were temporary, I have the consolation to believe that while inclination and prudence urge me to recede from the political scene, patriotism does not forbid it. May I also have that of [perceiving] knowing in my retreat,[13] that the involuntary errors which I have probably committed have been the causes of no serious or lasting mischief to my country, and thus be spared the anguish of regrets which would disturb the repose of my retreat and embitter the remnant of my life! I may then expect to realize, without alloy, the pure enjoyment of partaking, in the midst of my fellow-citizens, of the benign influence of good laws under a free government; the ultimate object of all my wishes, and to which I look as the happy reward[14] of our mutual labors and dangers.

In looking forward to the moment which is to terminate the career of my public life, my sensations do not permit me to suspend the deep acknowledgments required by that debt of gratitude, which I owe to my beloved country, for the many honors it has conferred upon me, still more for the distinguished and steadfast confidence it has reposed in me, and for the opportunities *it has thus afforded me*[15] of manifesting my inviolable attachment, by services faithful and persevering—however the inadequateness of my faculties may have ill seconded my[16] zeal. If benefits have resulted to you, my fellow-citizens, from these services, let it always be remembered to your praise, and as an instructive example in our annals, that the constancy of your support amidst appearances[17] sometimes dubious, vicissitudes of fortune often discouraging, and in situations in which, not unfrequently, want of success has seconded the criticisms of malevolence, was the essential prop of the efforts and the guaranty of the measures by which they were achieved.

Profoundly penetrated with this idea, I shall carry it with me to my retirement, and to my grave, as a lively incitement to unceasing vows (the only returns I can henceforth make) that Heaven may continue to you the choicest tokens of its beneficence, merited by national piety and morality; that your union and brotherly affection may be perpetual; that the free Constitution, which is the work of your own hands, may be sacredly maintained; that its administration in every department may be stamped with wisdom and virtue; that, in fine, the happiness of the people of these States under the auspices of liberty may be made complete, by so careful a preservation, and so prudent a use of this blessing, as will acquire them the glorious satisfaction of recommending it to the affection, the praise, and the adoption of every nation which is yet a stranger to it.

Here, perhaps, I ought to stop; but a solicitude for your welfare,

[13] retirement [14] I hope

[15] I have thence enjoyed [16] have rendered their efforts unequal to my—disproportional [17] under circumstances in which the passions, agitated in every direction, were liable to the greatest fluctuations

which cannot end but with my life, and the fear that there may exist projects unfriendly to it, against which it may be necessary you should be guarded, urge me in taking leave of you to offer to your solemn consideration and frequent review, some sentiments, the result of mature reflection confirmed by observation and experience, which appear to me essential to the permanency of your felicity as a people. These will be offered with the more freedom, as you can only see in them the disinterested advice of a parting friend, who can have no personal motive to tincture or bias his counsel.

Interwoven as is the love of liberty with every fibre of your hearts, no recommendation is necessary to fortify your attachment TO IT. Next to this, that unity of government which constitutes you as one people, claims your vigilant care and guardianship—as a main pillar of your real independence, of your peace, safety, freedom, and happiness. This being the point in your political fortress against which the batteries of internal and external enemies will be most constantly and actively, however covertly and insidiously levelled, it is of the utmost importance that you should appreciate, in its full force, the immense value of your political union to your national and individual happiness —that you should cherish towards it an affectionate and immovable attachment, and that you should watch for its preservation with zealous solicitude.

For this, you have every motive of sympathy and interest. Children for the most part of a common country, that country claims and ought to concentrate your affections. The name of American must always gratify and exalt the just pride of patriotism more than any denomination which can be derived from local discriminations. You have, with slight shades of difference, the same religion, manners, habits, and political institutions and principles; you have, in a common cause, fought and triumphed together. The independence and liberty you enjoy are the work of joint councils, efforts, dangers, sufferings, and successes. By your union you have achieved them, by your union you will most effectually maintain them.

The considerations which address themselves to your sensibility are greatly[18] strengthened[19] by those which apply to your interest. Here, every portion of our country will find the most urgent and commanding motives for guarding and preserving the union of the whole.

The North, in a [20] intercourse with the South, under the equal laws of one government, will, in the productions of the latter, many of them peculiar, find vast additional resources of maritime and commercial enterprise.[21] The South, in the same intercourse, will share in the benefits of the agency of the North, will find its agriculture promoted and

[18] even [19] outweighed [20] free and unfettered
[21] and precious materials of their manufacturing industry

its commerce extended by turning into its own channels those means of naviagtion which the North more abundantly affords; and while it contributes to extend the national navigation, will participate in the protection of a maritime strength to which itself is unequally adapted. The East, in a like intercourse with the West, finds[22] a valuable vent for the commodities which it brings from abroad or manufactures at home. The West derives through this channel an essential supply of its wants; and what is far more important to it, it must owe the secure and permanent enjoyment of the indispensable outlets for its own productions to the weight, influence, and maritime resources of the Atlantic States.[23] The tenure by which it could hold this advantage, either from its own separate strength, or by an apostate and unnatural connection with any foreign nation, must be intrinsically and necessarily precarious, at every moment liable to be disturbed by the[24] combinations of those primary[25] interests which constantly regulate the conduct of every portion of Europe—and where every part finds a particular interest in the Union. All the parts of our country will find in their Union[26] strength, proportional security from external danger, less frequent interruption of their peace with foreign nations; and what is far more valuable, an exemption from those broils and wars between the parts if disunited, which, then, our rivalships, fomented by foreign intrigue or the opposite alliances with foreign nations engendered [by] their mutual jealousies, would inevitably produce.[27]

These considerations speak a conclusive language to every virtuous and considerate mind. They place the continuance of our union among the first objects of patriotic desire. Is there a doubt whether a common government can long embrace so extensive a sphere? Let time and experience decide the question. Speculation in such a case ought not to be listened to. And 'tis rational to hope that the auxiliary agency of the governments of the subdivisions, with a proper organization of the whole, will secure a favorable issue to the experiment. 'Tis allowable to believe that the spirit of party, the intrigues of foreign nations, the corruption and the ambition of individuals, are likely to prove more formidable adversaries to the unity of our empire, than any inherent difficulties in the scheme. 'Tis against these that the [mound] guards of national opinion, national sympathy, national prudence and virtue, are to be erected. With such obvious motives to union, there will be always cause from the fact itself to distrust the *patriotism* of those

[22] and in the progressive improvement of internal navigation will more and more find

[23] directed by an indissoluble community of interests

[24] fluctuating [25] European

[26] greater independence from the superior abundance and variety of production incident to the diversity of soil and climate. All the parts of it must find in the aggregate assemblage and reaction of their mutual population—production

[27] consequent exemption from the necessity of those military establishments upon a large scale which bear in every country so menacing an aspect towards liberty

who[28] may endeavor to weaken its bands. And by all the love I bear you, my fellow citizens, I conjure[29] you, as often as it appears, to frown upon the attempt.

Besides the more serious causes which have been hinted at as endangering our Union, there is another less dangerous, but against which it is necessary to be on our guard; I mean the petulance of party[30] differences of opinion. It is not uncommon to hear the irritations which these excite, vent themselves in declarations that the different parts of the Union are ill assorted and cannot remain together—in menaces from the inhabitants of one part to those of another, that it will be dissolved by this or that measure. Intimations of the kind are as indiscreet as they are intemperate. Though frequently made with levity and without being in earnest, they have a tendency to produce the consequence which they indicate. They teach the minds of men to consider the Union as precarious, as an object to which they are not to attach their hopes and fortunes, and thus weaken the sentiment in its favor. By rousing the resentment and alarming the pride of those to whom they are addressed, they set ingenuity to work to deprecate the value of the object, and to discover motives of indifference to it. This is not wise. Prudence demands that we should habituate ourselves in all our words and actions to reverence the Union as a sacred and inviolable palladium of our happiness, and should discountenance whatever can lead to a suspicion that it can in any event be abandoned.

'Tis matter of serious concern that parties in this country for some time past have been too much characterized by geographical discriminations—northern and southern States, Atlantic and western country. These discriminations,[31] which are the mere artifice of the spirit of party (always dexterous to avail itself of every source of sympathy, of every handle by which the passions can be taken hold of, and which has been careful to turn to account the circumstance of territorial vicinity),[32] have furnished an argument against the Union as evidence of a real difference of local interests and views, and serve to hazard it by organizing large districts of country under the direction of[33] different factions whose passions and prejudices, rather than the true interests of the country, will be too apt to regulate the use of their influence. If it be possible to correct this poison in the affairs of our country, it is worthy the best endeavors of moderate and virtuous men to effect it.

One of the expedients which the partisans of faction employ towards strengthening their influence by local discriminations,[34] is to misrepresent the opinions and views of rival districts. The people at large cannot be too much on their guard against the jealousies which grow out of these misrepresentations. They tend to render aliens to each other

[28] in any quarter [29] exhort—(*written first*) [30] collisions and disgusts
[31] of party [32] sympathy of neighborhood [33] the leaders of
[34] within local spheres

those who ought to be tied together by fraternal affection. The western country have lately had a useful lesson on this subject. They have seen in the negotiation by the Executive, and in the unanimous ratification of the treaty with Spain by the Senate, and in the universal satisfaction at that event in all parts of the country, a decisive proof how unfounded have been the suspicions instilled[35] in them of a policy in the Atlantic States, and in the different departments of the general government, hostile to their interests in relation to the Mississippi. They have seen two treaties formed which secure to them every thing that they could desire to confirm their prosperity. Will they not henceforth rely for the preservation of these advantages on that Union by which they were procured? Will they not reject those counsellors who would render them alien to their brethren and connect them with aliens?

To the duration and efficacy of your Union, a government extending over the whole is indispensable. No alliances however strict between the parts could be an adequate substitute. These could not fail to be liable to the infractions and interruptions which all alliances in all times have suffered. Sensible of this important truth, you have lately established a Constitution of general government, better calculated than the former for an intimate union, and more adequate to the direction of your common concerns. This government, the offspring of your own choice, uninfluenced and unawed, completely free in its principles, in the distribution of its powers, uniting energy with safety, and containing in itself a provision for its own amendment, is well entitled to your confidence and support. Respect for its authority, compliance with its laws, acquiescence in its measures,[36] are duties dictated by the fundamental maxims of true liberty. The basis of our political systems is the right of the people to make and to alter their constitutions of government. But the Constitution for the time, and until changed by an explicit and authentic act of the whole people, is sacredly binding upon all. The very idea of the right and power of the people to establish government pre-supposes the duty of every individual to obey the established government.

All obstructions to the execution of the laws—all *combinations* and *associations* under whatever plausible character, with the real design to counteract,[37] control,[38] or awe the regular[39] action of the constituted authorities, are contrary to this fundamental principle, and of the most fatal tendency. They serve to organize faction,[40] and to put in the stead of the delegated will of the whole nation the will of a party, often a small[41] minority of the whole community; and according to the alternate triumph of different parties to make the public adminis-

[35] propagated among
[36] ordinary management of affairs to be left to represent.
[37] direct [38] influence [39] deliberation or [40] to give it an artificial force
[41] but artful and enterprising

tration reflect the[42] schemes and projects of faction rather than the wholesome plans of common councils and deliberations. However combinations or associations of this description may occasionally promote popular ends and purposes, they are likely to produce, in the course of time and things, the most effectual engines by which artful, ambitious, and unprincipled men will be enabled to subvert the power of the people and usurp the reins of government.

Towards the preservation of your government and the permanency of your present happy state, it is not only requisite that you steadily discountenance irregular oppositions to its authority, but that you should be upon your guard against the spirit of innovation upon its principles, however specious the pretexts. One method of assault may be to effect alterations in the forms of the Constitution tending to impair the energy of the system, and so to undermine what cannot be directly overthrown. In all the changes to which you may be invited, remember that time and habit are as necessary to fix the true character of governments as of any other human institution; that experience is the surest standard by which the real tendency of existing constitutions of government can be tried; that changes upon[43] the credit of mere hypothesis and opinion expose you to perpetual change from the successive and endless variety of hypothesis and opinion. And remember also [always], that for the efficacious management of your common interests, in a country so extensive as ours, a government of as much force and strength as is consistent with the perfect security of liberty is indispensable. Liberty itself will find in such a government, with powers properly distributed and arranged, its surest guardian and protector. In my opinion, the real danger in our system is, that the general government, organized as at present, will prove too weak rather than too powerful.

I have already observed the danger to be apprehended from founding our parties on geographical discriminations. Let me now enlarge the view of this point, and caution you in the most solemn manner against the baneful effects of party spirit in general. This spirit unfortunately is inseparable from human nature, and has its root in the strongest passions of the human heart. It exists under different shapes in all governments, but[44] in those of the popular form it is always seen in its utmost vigor and rankness, and is their worst enemy. In republics of narrow extent, it is not difficult for those who at any time possess the reins of administration, or even for partial combinations of men, who from birth, riches, and other sources of distinction have an extraordinary influence, by possessing or acquiring the direction of the military force, or by sudden efforts of partisans and followers, to overturn the established order of things, and effect a usurpation. But in repub-

[42] ill concerted
[43] facility in [44] in different degrees stifled, controlled, or repressed

lics of large extent, the one or the other is scarcely possible. The powers and opportunities of resistance of a numerous and wide-extended nation defy the successful efforts of the ordinary military force, or of any collections[45] which wealth and patronage may call to their aid, especially if there be no city of overbearing force, resources, and influence. In such republics it is perhaps safe to assert that the conflicts of popular faction offer the only avenues to tyranny and usurpation. The domination of one faction over another, stimulated by that spirit of revenge which is apt to be gradually engendered, and which in different ages and countries has produced the greatest enormities, is itself a frightful despotism. But this leads at length to a more formal and permanent despotism. The disorders and miseries which result predispose the minds of men to seek repose and security in the absolute power of a single man. And some leader of a prevailing faction, more able or more fortunate than his competitors, turns this disposition to the purposes of an ambitious and criminal self-aggrandizement.

Without looking forward to such an extremity (which, however, ought not to be out of sight), the ordinary and continual mischiefs of the spirit of party make it the interest and the duty of a wise people, to discountenance and repress it.

It serves always to distract the councils and enfeeble the administration of the government. It agitates the community with ill-founded jealousies and false alarms.[46] It opens inlets for foreign corruption and influence, which find an easy access through the channels of party passions, and causes the true policy and interest of our own country to be made subservient to the policy and interest of one and another foreign nation, sometimes enslaving our own government to the will of a foreign government.

There is an opinion that parties in free countries are salutary checks upon the administration of the government, and serve to invigorate the spirit of liberty. This, within certain limits, is true; and in governments of a monarchical character or bias, patriotism may look with some favor on the spirit of party. But in those of the popular kind, in those purely elective, it is a spirit not to be fostered or encouraged. From the natural tendency of such governments, it is certain there will always be enough of it for every salutary purpose, and there being constant danger of excess, the effort ought to be, by the force of public opinion, to mitigate and correct it. 'Tis a fire which[47] cannot be quenched, but demands[48] a uniform vigilance to prevent its bursting into a flame—lest it should not only warm but consume.

It is important, likewise, that the habits of thinking of the people

[45] assemblages

[46] embittering one part of the community against another, and producing occasionally riot and insurrection

[47] not to [48] demanding

should tend to produce caution in their public agents in the several departments of government, to retain each within its proper sphere, and not to permit one to encroach upon another; that every attempt of the kind, from whatever quarter, should meet with the discountenance[49] of the community, and that, in every case in which a precedent of encroachment shall have been given, a corrective be sought in [revocation be effected by] a careful attention to the next choice[50] of public agents. The spirit of encroachment tends to absorb[51] the powers of the several branches and departments into one, and thus to establish, under whatever forms, a despotism. A just knowledge of the human heart, of that love of power which predominates in it, is alone sufficient to establish this truth. Experiments, ancient and modern, some in our own country, and under our own eyes, serve to confirm it. If, in the public opinion, the distribution of the constitutional powers be in any instance wrong, or inexpedient, let it be corrected by the authority of the people in a legitimate constitutional course. Let there be no change by usurpation, for though this may be the instrument of good in one instance, it is the ordinary[52] instrument of the destruction[53] of free government—and the influence of the precedent is always infinitely more pernicious than any thing which it may achieve can be beneficial.

In all those dispositions which promote political happiness,[54] religion and morality are essential props. In vain does he[55] claim the praise of patriotism, who labors to subvert or undermine these great pillars of human happiness, these firmest foundations of the duties of men and citizens. The mere politician, equally with the pious man, ought to respect and cherish them. A volume could not trace all their connections with private and public happiness.

Let it simply be asked, where is the security for property, for reputation, for life, if the sense of moral and religious obligation deserts the oaths which are administered[56] in courts of justice? Nor ought we to flatter ourselves that morality can be separated from religion. Concede as much as may be asked to the effect of refined education in minds of peculiar structure, can we believe, can we in prudence suppose, that national morality can be maintained in exclusion of religious principles? Does it not require the aid of a generally received and divinely authoritative religion?

'Tis essentially true that virtue or morality is a main and necessary spring of popular or republican governments. The rule, indeed, extends with more or less force to all free governments. Who that is a prudent and sincere friend to them, can look with indifference on the ravages which are making in the foundation of the fabric?—religion?

[49] reprobation [50] election [51] and consolidate [52] and natural [53] death
[54] prosperity [55] that man [56] instruments of investigation

The uncommon means which of late have been directed to this fatal end, seem to make it in a particular manner the duty of a retiring chief of a nation to warn his country against tasting of the poisonous draught.

Cultivate, also, industry and frugality. They are auxiliaries of good morals, and great sources of private and national prosperity. Is there not room for regret, that our propensity to expense exceeds the maturity of our country for expense? Is there not more luxury among us, in various classes, than suits the actual period of our national progress? Whatever may be the apology for luxury in a country mature in all the arts which are its ministers and the means of national opulence—can it promote the advantage of a young agricultural country, little advanced in manufactures, and not much advanced in wealth?[57]

Cherish public credit as a means of strength and security. As one method of preserving it, use it as little as possible. Avoid occasions of expense by cultivating peace—remembering always that the preparation against danger, by timely and provident disbursements, is often a mean of avoiding greater disbursements to repel it. Avoid the accumulation of debt by avoiding occasions of expense, and by vigorous exertions in time of peace to discharge the debts which unavoidable wars may have occasioned, not transferring to posterity the burthen which we ought to bear ourselves. Recollect, that towards the payment of debts there must be revenue, that to have revenue there must be taxes, that it is impossible to devise taxes which are not more or less inconvenient and unpleasant—that they are always a choice of difficulties, that the intrinsic embarrassment which never fails to attend a selection of objects ought to be a motive for a candid construction of the conduct of the government in making it, and that a spirit of acquiescence in those measures for obtaining revenue which the public exigencies dictate, is, in an especial manner, the duty and interest of the citizens of every state.

Cherish good faith and justice towards, and peace and harmony with, all nations. Religion and morality enjoin this conduct, and it cannot be but that true policy equally demands it. It will be worthy of a free, enlightened, and at no distant period, a great nation, to give to mankind the magnanimous and too novel example of a people invariably governed by[58] those exalted views. Who can doubt that in a long course of time and events the fruits of such a conduct would richly repay any temporary advantages which might be lost by a steady adherence to the plan? Can it be that Providence has not connected the permanent felicity of a nation with its virtue? The experiment is recommended by every sentiment which ennobles human nature. Alas! is it rendered impossible by its vices?

[57] in the infancy of the arts, and certainly not in the manhood of wealth
[58] exalted justice and benevolence

Towards the execution of such a plan,[59] nothing is more essential than that antipathies against particular nations and passionate attachments for others should be avoided, and that instead of them we should cultivate just and amicable feelings towards all. * * * That nation which indulges towards another an habitual hatred or an habitual fondness, is in some degree a slave. * * * It is a slave to its animosity, or to its affection—either of which is sufficient to lead it astray from its duty and interest. Antipathy against one nation, which never fails to beget a similar sentiment in the other, disposes each more readily to offer injury and insult to the other, to lay hold of slight causes of umbrage, and to be haughty and untractable when accidental or trifling differences arise. Hence frequent quarrels[60] and bitter and obstinate contests. The nation urged by resentment and rage, sometimes compels the government to war, contrary to its own calculations of policy. The government sometimes participates in this propensity, and does through passion what reason would forbid at other times; it makes the animosity of the nations subservient to hostile projects which originate in ambition and other sinister motives. The peace, often, and sometimes the liberty of nations, has been the victim of this cause.

In like manner[61] a passionate attachment of the one nation to another produces multiplied ills. Sympathy for the favorite nation, promoting[62] the illusion of a supposed common interest, in cases where it does not exist,[63] the enmities of the one betray the other into a participation in its quarrels and wars, without adequate inducements or justifications. It leads to the concession of privileges to one nation, and to the denial of them to others, which is apt doubly to injure the nation making the concession by an unnecessary yielding of what ought to have been retained, and by exciting jealousy, ill-will, and retaliation in the party from whom an equal privilege is withheld. And it gives to ambitious, corrupted[64] citizens, who devote themselves to the views of the favorite foreign power, facility in betraying or sacrificing the interests of their own country,[65] even with popularity, gilding with[66] [*sic*]

As avenues to foreign influence in innumerable ways, such attachments are peculiarly alarming to the enlightened independent patriot. How many opportunities do they afford to intrigue with domestic

[59] it is very material that while we entertain proper impressions of particular cases—of friendly or unfriendly conduct of different foreign nations towards us, we nevertheless avoid fixed and rooted antipathies against any, or passionate attachments for any, instead of these cultivating, as a general rule, just and amicable feelings towards all

[60] broils [61] So likewise [62] facilitating [63] and communicating to one

[64] or deluded [65] without odium

[66] the appearance of a virtuous impulse, the base yieldings of ambition or corruption

factions, to practise with success the arts of seduction, to mislead the public opinion—to influence or awe the public councils? Such an attachment of a small or weak towards a great and powerful nation, destines the former to revolve round the latter as its satellite.

Against the mischiefs of foreign influence all the jealousy of a free people ought to be constantly[67] exerted[68]; but the jealousy of it to be useful must be impartial, else it becomes an instrument of the very influence to be avoided, instead of a defence[69] against it.

Excessive partiality for one foreign nation, and excessive dislike of another, leads to see [sic] danger only on one side, and serves to veil[70] the arts of influence on the other. Real patriots, who resist the intrigues of the favorite, become suspected and odious. Its tools and dupes usurp the applause and confidence of the people to betray their interests.

The great rule of conduct for us in regard to foreign nations ought to be to have as little *political* connection with them as possible. So far as we have already formed engagements, let them be fulfilled with circumspection, indeed, but with perfect good faith; here let it stop.

Europe has a set of primary interests, which have none or a very remote relation to us. Hence she must be involved in frequent contests, the causes of which will be essentially foreign to us. Hence therefore, it must necessarily be unwise on our part to implicate ourselves by an artificial connection in the ordinary vicissitudes of European politics—in the combination and collisions of her friendships or enmities.

Our detached and distant situation invites us to a different course, and enables us to pursue it. If we remain a united people, under an efficient government, the period is not distant when we may defy material injury from external annoyance—when we may take such an attitude as will cause the neutrality we shall at any time resolve to observe, to be violated with caution—when it will be the interest of belligerent nations, under the impossibility of making acquisitions upon us, to be very careful how either forced us to throw our weight into the opposite scale—when we may choose peace or war, as our interest, guided by justice, shall dictate.

Why should we forego the advantages of so felicitous a situation? Why quit our own ground to stand upon foreign ground? Why, by interweaving our destiny with any part of Europe, should we entangle our prosperity and peace in the nets of European ambition, rivalship, interest, or caprice?

Permanent alliance, intimate connection with any part of the foreign world is to be avoided; so far, (I mean) as we are now at liberty to do it; for let me never be understood as patronizing infidelity to

[67] continually

[68] all history and experience in different ages and nations have proved that foreign influence is one of the most baneful foes of republican government

[69] guard [70] and second

pre-existing engagements. These must be observed in their true and genuine sense.[71]

Harmony, liberal intercourse, and commerce with all nations are recommended by justice, humanity, and interest. But even our commercial policy should hold an equal hand, neither seeking nor granting exclusive favors or preferences—consulting the natural course of things —*diffusing* and *diversifying* by gentle means the streams of commerce, but forcing nothing—establishing with powers so disposed[72] temporary[73] rules of intercourse, the best that present circumstances and mutual opinion of interest will permit, but temporary, and liable to be abandoned or varied, as time, experience, and future circumstances may dictate—remembering[74] that it is folly in one nation to expect disinterested favor in another, that to accept[75] is to part with a portion of its independence, and that it may find itself in the condition of having given equivalents for nominal favors, and of being reproached with ingratitude in the bargain. There can be no greater error in national policy than to desire, expect, or calculate upon real favors. 'Tis an illusion that experience must cure, that a just pride ought to discard.

In offering to you, my countrymen, these counsels of an old and affectionate friend—counsels suggested by laborious reflection, and matured by a various experience, I dare not hope that they will make the strong and lasting impressions I wish—that they will control the current of the passions, or prevent our nation from running the course which has hitherto marked the destiny of all nations.

But[76] if they may even produce partial benefit, some occasional good * * * that they sometimes recur to moderate the violence of party spirit, to warn against the evils of foreign intrigue, to guard against the impositions of pretended patriotism, the having offered them must always afford me a precious consolation.

How far in the execution of my present office I have been guided by the principles which have been inculcated, the public records and the external evidences of my conduct must witness. My conscience assures me that I have at least believed myself to be guided by them.

In reference to the present war of Europe, my proclamation of the 22d April, 1793, is the key to my plan, sanctioned by your approving voice, and that of your Representatives in Congress—the spirit of that measure has continually governed me—uninfluenced and unawed by the attempts of any of the warring powers, their agents, or partisans, to deter or divert from it.

[71] But 'tis not necessary, nor will it be prudent, to extend them. 'Tis our true policy, as a general principle, to avoid permanent or close alliances. Taking care always to keep ourselves by suitable establishments in a respectably defensive position, we may safely trust to occasional alliances for extraordinary emergencies.

[72] In order to give to trade a stable course, to define the rights of our merchants, and enable the government to support them

[73] and conventional [74] always [75] any thing under that character [76] I may flatter myself

After deliberate consideration, and the best lights I could obtain (and from men who did not agree in their views of the origin, progress, and nature of that war), I was satisfied that our country, under all the circumstances of the case, had a right and was bound in propriety and interest to take a neutral position. And having taken it, I determined as[77] should depend on me to maintain it steadily and firmly.

Though in reviewing the incidents of my administration I am unconscious of intentional error, I am yet too sensible of my own deficiencies, not to think it possible[78] that I have committed many errors; I deprecate the evils to which they may tend, and fervently implore the Almighty to avert or mitigate them. I shall carry with me, nevertheless, the hope that my motives will continue to be viewed by my country with indulgence, and that after forty-five years of my life, devoted with an upright zeal to the public service, the faults of inadequate abilities will be consigned to oblivion, as myself must soon be to the mansions of rest.

Neither ambition nor interest has been the impelling cause of my actions. I never designedly misused any power confided in me. The fortune with which I came into office, is not bettered otherwise than by that improvement in the value of property which the natural progress and peculiar prosperity of our country have produced. I retire[79] with a pure heart,[80] with undefiled hands, and with ardent vows for the happiness of a country, the native soil of himself and his progenitors for four generations.

—"Original Draft" in Hamilton's hand. Date in later hand. Hamilton Papers, 1st ser.

The Death of Washington

December, 1799

The death of our beloved Commander-in-Chief was known to you before it was to me. I can be at no loss to anticipate what have been your feelings. I need not tell you what have been mine. Perhaps no friend of his has more cause to lament on personal account than myself. The public misfortune is one which all the friends of our government will view in the same light. I will not dwell on the subject. My imagination is gloomy—my heart is sad.

Inclosed is an order relative to the occasion which speaks its own object.

With the sincerest esteem, etc., etc. . . .

[77] as far as

[78] "probable" for "possible" [79] without cause for a blush

[80] with no alien sentiment to the ardor of those vows for the happiness of his country, which is so natural to a citizen who sees in it

If the sad privilege [of] pre-eminence in sorrow may justly be claimed [from the] companions in arms of our lamented chief, their affections will spontaneously perform the dear though painful duty. 'Tis only for me to mingle my tears with theirs, embittered by recollection that in mourning the loss of the "MAN OF THE AGE," I equally mourn that of the long-tried patron—the kind and unchanging [frie]nd.

—Hamilton to General Pinckney, and "General Order for the Ceremonial to be Used on the Interment of Washington." Draft of letter and document in Hamilton's hand. Hamilton Papers, 1st ser.

January 2, 1800

Your letter of the 15th of December last was delayed in getting to hand by circumstance of its having gone to New York while I was at Philadelphia, and of its having arrived at Philadelphia after I had set out on my return to New York.

The very painful event which it announces had, previous to the receipt of it, filled my heart with bitterness. Perhaps no man in this community has equal cause with myself to deplore the loss. I have been much indebted to the kindness of the General, and he was an *AEgis very essential to me*. But regrets are unavailing. For great misfortunes it is the business of reason to seek consolation. The friends of General Washington have very noble ones. If virtue can secure happiness in another world, he is happy. In this the seal is now put upon *his* glory. It is no longer in jeopardy from the fickleness of fortune.

P. S.—In whose hands are his papers gone? Our very confidential situation will not permit this to be a point of indifference to me.

—To Tobias Lear. Copy. Hamilton Papers, 1st ser.

On Thomas Jefferson

. . . a man of sublimated and paradoxical imagination.

. . . there is no fair reason to suppose him capable of being corrupted.

The cleavage between Hamilton and Jefferson occurred early in the administration of Washington and led to the two-party system. As early as 1792 Hamilton felt that Jefferson had long-range aspirations for the presidency. In 1796 Hamilton favored the Adams-Pinckney ticket, actually preferring Pinckney to Adams for the presidency. Jefferson's conciliatory moves at the outset of his administration were hailed by Hamilton, but the old divergence in ideas appeared once more.

May 26, 1792

. . . In respect to foreign politics, the views of these gentlemen are, in my judgment, equally unsound and dangerous. They have a womanish attachment to France and a womanish resentment against Great Britain. They would draw us into the closest embrace of the former, and involve us in all the consequences of her politics; and they would risk the peace of the country in their endeavors to keep us at the greatest possible distance from the latter.

Whether any peculiar opinions of Mr. Jefferson's concerning the public debt wrought a change in the sentiments of Mr. Madison (for it is certain that the former is more radically wrong than the latter), or whether Mr. Madison, seduced by the expectation of popularity, and possibly by the calculation of advantage to the State of Virginia, was led to change his own opinion, certain it is that a very material change took place, and that the two gentlemen were united in the new ideas. . . .

These causes, and perhaps some others, created, much sooner than I was aware of it, a systematic opposition to me, on the part of these gentlemen. My subversion, I am now satisfied, has been long an object with them. . . .

Another circumstance has contributed to widening the breach, 'Tis evident, beyond a question, from every movement, that Mr. Jefferson aims with ardent desire at the Presidential chair. This, too, is an important object of the party-politics. It is supposed, from the nature of my former personal and political connections, that I may favor some other candidate more than Mr. Jefferson, when the question shall occur by the retreat of the present gentleman. My influence, therefore, with the community becomes a thing, on ambitious and personal grounds, to be resisted and destroyed.

—To Colonel Edward Carrington. *Works*, IX, 527, 529-530.

July 25, 1792

Mr. Fenno:

The editor of the *National Gazette*[1] receives a salary from the government.

Quere.—Whether this salary is paid him for *translations*, or for *publications*, the design of which is to vilify those to whom the voice of the people has committed the administration of our public affairs—to oppose the measures of government, and, by false insinuations, to disturb the public peace?

In common life it is thought ungrateful for a man to bite the hand

[1] Philip Freneau, who was induced by Jefferson and Madison to start the *National Gazette* in opposition to the Hamiltonian organ, the *United States Gazette* edited by John Fenno.

that puts bread in his mouth; but if the man is hired to do it, the case is altered.

T. L.

—*Gazette of the U. S.*, July 25, 1792.

August 11, 1792

It is impossible for a correct mind not to pronounce that, in the abstract, a connection like that which is acknowledged to subsist between you and Mr. Jefferson, between the *editor of a newspaper* and the head of a department of the government, is *indelicate* and *unfit*, and consequently of a nature to justify suspicion.

A connection of that sort in a free country is a pernicious precedent, inconsistent with those pretensions to extraordinary republican purity, of which so suspicious a parade is upon every occasion exhibited.

—"An American"—for the *Gazette of the United States*. Hamilton Papers, 1st ser.

September 15, 1792

We find the head of a department taking the editor of a gazette into his employment, as a clerk, with a stated salary—not for any special purpose, which could not have been accomplished otherwise; for he had, at the time, in his department, a clerk who was capable of performing the very service required, and could without difficulty have procured others similarly qualified; nor from any particular necessity arising from a too limited allowance, or any other cause; for he had it in his power to allow an adequate compensation to a character who might have been regularly attached to the department.

The very existence of such a connection, then, is alone a sufficient foundation for believing that the design of the arrangement was to secure an influence over the paper, the editor of which was so employed. But the circumstances which attend it explain the nature of it beyond a doubt. That which has been just mentioned, namely, there having been previously a clerk in the department qualified to render the service, is a weighty one. The coming of a *new* printer, from another State, to institute a *new* paper—his having been appointed clerk in the department *prior* to his removal to this city—his having been compensated *before* he was even present, to satisfy the *appearance* of his rendering service,—these circumstances give a point and energy to the language of the transaction which render it unequivocal. There perhaps never was a more flimsy covering for the pensioning of a printer. Some ostensible ground for giving him the public money was necessary to be contrived—the clerkship of foreign languages was deemed a plausible pretext. But no man acquainted with human nature, or with the ordinary expedients of political intrigue, can be deceived by it. . . .

These facts prove, to the satisfaction of every impartial mind, that Mr. Jefferson is the INSTITUTOR and PATRON of the *National Gazette*.

—"Catullus to Aristides." Draft in Hamilton's hand. Hamilton Papers, 1st ser.

September 29, 1792

The first volume of the *Rights of Man* makes its appearance. The opportunity is eagerly seized to answer the double purpose of wounding a competitor, and of laying in an additional stock of popularity, by associating and circulating the name of Thomas Jefferson with a popular production of a favorite writer on a favorite subject.

—"Catullus to Aristides." *Gazette of the U. S.*, Sept. 29, 1792.

October 10, 1792

. . . 'Tis suspected by some that the plan is only to divide the votes of the Northern and the Middle States, to let in Mr. Jefferson by the votes of the South. I will not scruple to say to you, in confidence, that this also would be a serious misfortune to the government. That gentleman whom I once *very much esteemed*, but who does not permit me to retain that sentiment for him, is certainly a man of sublimated and paradoxical imagination, entertaining and propagating opinions inconsistent with dignified and orderly government. Mr. Adams, whatever objections may lie against some of his theoretic opinions, is a firm, honest, and independent politician.

—To Gen. C. C. Pinckney. *Hamilton*, V, 532-533.

October 24, 1792

What! (it will probably be asked) is a man to sacrifice his conscience and his judgment to an office? Is he to be a dumb spectator of measures which he deems subversive of the rights or interests of his fellow-citizens? Is he to postpone to the frivolous rules of a false complaisance, or the arbitrary dictates of a tyrannical decorum, the higher duty which he owes to the community?

I answer, No! he is to do none of these things. If he cannot coalesce with those with whom he is associated, as far as the rules of official decorum, propriety, and obligation may require, without abandoning what he conceives to be the true interest of the community, let him place himself in a situation in which he will experience no collision of opposite duties. Let him not cling to the honor or emolument of an office, whichever it may be that attracts him, and content himself with defending the injured rights of the people by obscure or indirect means. Let him renounce a situation which is a clog upon his patriotism; tell the people that he could no longer continue in it without forfeiting his duty to them, and that he had quitted it to be more at liberty to afford them his best services.

Such is the course which would be indicated by a firm and virtuous independence of character. Such the course that would be pursued by a man attentive to unite the sense of delicacy with the sense of duty, in earnest about the pernicious tendency of public measures, and more solicitous to act the disinterested friend of the people, than the interested, ambitious, and intriguing head of a party.

—"Metellus." *Hamilton*, VII, 63-64.

[1796]

Our excellent President, as you have seen, has declined a re-election. 'Tis all-important to our country that his successor shall be a safe man. But it is far less important who of many men that may be named shall be the person, than that it shall not be Jefferson. We have every thing to fear if this man comes in, and from what I believe to be an accurate view of our political map I conclude that he has too good a chance of success, and that good calculation, prudence, and exertion were never more necessary to the Federal cause than at this very critical juncture. All personal and partial considerations must be discarded, and every thing must give way to the great object of excluding Jefferson. It appears to be a common opinion (and I think it a judicious one), that Mr. Adams and Mr. Pinckney (late minister to England) are to be supported on our side for President and Vice-President. New York will be unanimous for both. I hope New England will be so too. Yet I have some apprehensions on this point, lest the fear that he may outrun Mr. Adams should withhold votes from Pinckney. Should this happen, it will be, in my opinion, a most unfortunate policy. . . . At foot, is my calculation of chances between Adams and Jefferson. 'Tis too precarious. Pinckney has the chance of some votes southward and westward, which Adams has not. This will render our prospect in the main point, the exclusion of Jefferson, far better.

—To ——————. *Works*, 195-196.

[1801]

In the speech of the new President upon assuming the exercise of his office, we find among the articles of his creed,—"the honest *payment of our* DEBT, *and sacred preservation of the* PUBLIC FAITH."

The funding system, the national debt, the British treaty, are not therefore in his conception abuses, which, if no longer to be tolerated, would be of course to be abolished.

But we think ourselves warranted to derive from the same source, a condemnation still more extensive of the opinions of our adversaries. The speech characterizes our present government "as a republican in the *full tide* of successful *experiment*." Success in the *experiment* of a government is success in the *practice* of it, and this is but another phrase for an administration, in the main, wise and good. That administration has been hitherto in the hands of the Federalists.

Here then, fellow-citizens, is an open and solemn protest against the principles and opinions of our opponents, from a quarter which as yet they dare not arraign.

In referring to this speech, we think it proper to make a public declaration of our approbation of its contents. We view it as virtually a candid retraction of past misapprehensions, and a pledge to the community, that the new President will not lend himself to dangerous innovations, but in essential points will tread in the steps of his predecessors.

In doing this, he prudently anticipates the loss of a great portion of that favor which has elevated him to his present station. Doubtless, it is a just foresight. Adhering to the professions he has made, it will not be long before the body of the Anti-Federalists will raise their croaking and ill-omened voices against him. But in the talents, the patriotism, and the firmness of the Federalists, he will find more than an equivalent for all that he shall lose.

—Address to the Electors of the State of New York. *Hamilton,* VII, 739-740.

[December 17, 1801]

. . . It is impossible to conceive the idea, that one nation can be in full war with another, and this other not in the same state with respect to its adversary. The moment that two nations are, in an absolute sense, at war, the public force of each may exercise every act of hostility, which the general laws of war authorize, against the persons and property of the other. . . .

"The Congress shall have power to declare war"; the plain meaning of which is, that it is the peculiar and exclusive province of Congress, *when the nation is at peace,* to change that state into a state of war; whether from calculations of policy, or from provocations or injuries received; in other words, it belongs to Congress only, *to go to war.* But when a foreign nation declares or openly and avowedly makes war upon the United States, they are then by the very fact *already at war,* and any declaration on the part of Congress is nugatory; it is at least unnecessary. . . .

Till the Congress should assemble and declare war, which would require time, our ships might, according to the hypothesis of the message, be sent by the President to fight those of the enemy as often as they should be attacked, but not to capture and detain them; if beaten, both vessels and crews would be lost to the United States; if successful, they could only disarm those they had overcome, and must suffer them to return to the place of common rendezvous, there to equip anew, for the purpose of resuming their depredations on our towns and our trade.

Who could restrain the laugh of derision at positions so preposterous, were it not for the reflection that in the first magistrate of our country they cast a blemish on our national character? What will the world think of the fold when such is the shepherd?

—"Lucius Crassus," No. I. *Hamilton*, VII, 746-747, 748.

June 3, 1802

Truly, my dear sir, the prospects of our country are not brilliant. The mass is far from sound. At headquarters a most visionary theory presides. Depend upon it, this is the fact to a great extreme. No army, no navy, no *active* commerce; national defence, not by arms, but by embargoes, prohibitions of trade, etc.; as little government as possible within;—these are the pernicious dreams which, as far and as fast as possible, will be attempted to be realized. Mr. Jefferson is distressed at the codfish having latterly emigrated to the southern coast, lest the people there should be tempted to catch them, and commerce, of which we have already too much, receive an accession. Be assured this is no pleasantry, but a very sober anecdote.

—To Rufus King. *Hamilton*, VI, 546-549.

On John Adams

"He is always honest, sometimes great, but often mad" . . . as far as a man excessively vain and jealous and ignobly attached to place can be.

Since Adams made no secret of his lack of admiration for Washington, Hamilton was never one of the New Englander's ardent admirers. Yet he came to Adams' defense in 1792 when the Vice President's pamphlet, The Discourses on Davila, *was construed as favoring the establishment of an aristocracy in America. Adams never forgave Hamilton for preferring Pinckney to him in 1796. The ouster of Hamilton's supporters from Adams' cabinet was the last straw.*

The election of 1800 showed how maladroit a politician Hamilton could be. With the Federalists facing a formidable fight for the presidency, Hamilton contributed to dividing his party by preferring Pinckney to Adams. In the late summer of 1800 he committed an unpardonable indiscretion. He published a lengthy attack on Adams under his own name, but meant it for private circulation to top party leaders. Burr got his hands on it and had it widely distributed. As his friend Troup asserted, Hamilton preferred anyone to Adams, even Jefferson. If Hamilton had hit below the belt, Adams did not disdain to use the same tactics. In private correspondence he referred to Hamilton as "the Creole bastard." Hamilton had called Adams an ordinary man who dreams himself to be a Frederick. "To this," Adams wrote, "I shall make but a short answer. When a Miss of the street shall print a pamphlet in London, and call the Queen of England an ordinary woman who dreams herself a Catherine of Russia, no Englishman will have the less esteem for his queen for that impudent libel."

October 9, 1788

On the subject of Vice-President, my ideas have concurred with yours, and I believe Mr. Adams will have the votes of this State. He will certainly, I think, be preferred to the other gentleman. Yet *certainly* is perhaps too strong a word. I can conceive that the other, who is supposed to be a more pliable man, may command Anti-federal influence.

The only hesitation in my mind with regard to Mr. Adams has arisen within a day or two from a suggestion by a particular gentleman that he is unfriendly in his sentiments to General Washington. Richard H. Lee, who will probably, as rumor now runs, come from Virginia, is also in this style. The Lees and Adamses have been in the habit of uniting, and hence may spring up a cabal very embarrassing to the Executive, and of course to the administration of the government. Consider this—sound the reality of it, and let me hear from you.

What think you of Lincoln or Knox? This is a flying thought.

—To Theodore Sedgwick. Hamilton's hand. Hamilton Papers, 1st ser.

November 9, 1788

On the question between Mr. H.[1] and Mr. A.,[2] Mr. King will probably have informed you that I have, upon the whole, concluded that the latter ought to be supported. My measures will be taken accordingly. I had but one scruple, but after mature consideration, I have relinquished it. Mr. A., to a sound understanding, has always appeared to me to add an ardent love for the public good, and, as his further knowledge of the world seems to have corrected those jealousies which he is represented to have once been influenced by, I trust nothing of the kind suggested in my former letter will disturb the harmony of the administration.

—To Theodore Sedgwick. Hamilton's hand. Hamilton Papers, 1st ser.

September 29, 1792

Some time since there appeared in print certain speculations, which have been construed into an advocation of hereditary distinctions in

[1] John Hancock—Ed.
[2] John Adams—Ed.

government. These (whether with or without foundation, is to this moment matter of conjecture) were ascribed to a particular character, pre-eminent for his early intrepid, faithful, persevering, and comprehensively useful services to his country—a man, pure and unspotted in private life, a citizen having a high and solid title to the esteem, the gratitude, and the confidence of his fellow-citizens.

—"Catullus to Aristides." *Gazette of the U. S.*, Sept. 29, 1792.

February 15, 1797

Mr. Adams is President, Mr. Jefferson is Vice-President. Our Jacobins say they are well pleased, and that the *lion* and the *lamb* are to lie down together. Mr. Adams' PERSONAL friends talk a little in the same way. "Mr. Jefferson is not half so ill a man as we have been accustomed to think him. There is to be a united and a vigorous administration." Skeptics like me quietly look forward to the event, willing to hope, but not prepared to believe. If Mr. Adams has *vanity*, 'tis plain a plot has been laid to take hold of it. We trust his real good sense and integrity will be a sufficient shield.

—To Rufus King. *Hamilton*, VI, 206.

May 4, 1800

You have heard of the loss of our election in the city of New York. This renders it too probable that the electors of President for this State will be anti-federal. If so, the policy which I was desirous of pursuing at the last election is now recommended by motives of additional cogency.

To support *Adams* and *Pinckney* equally is the only thing that can possibly save us from the fangs of *Jefferson*.

It is, therefore, essential that the Federalists should not separate without coming to a distinct and solemn concert to pursue this course *bona fide*.

Pray attend to this, and let me speedily hear from you that it is done.

—To Theodore Sedgwick. Draft in Hamilton's hand. Hamilton Papers, 1st ser.

May 10, 1800

If we must have an *enemy* at the head of the government, let it be one whom we can oppose, and for whom we are not responsible, who will not involve our party in the disgrace of his foolish and bad measures. Under *Adams*, as under *Jefferson*, the government will sink. The party in the hands of whose chief it shall sink will sink with it, and the advantage will all be on the side of his adversaries.

—To Theodore Sedgwick. Draft in Hamilton's hand. Hamilton Papers, 1st ser.

July 1, 1800

. . . In the meantime, it is not advisable that Maryland should be too deeply pledged to the support of Mr. Adams.

That this gentleman ought not to be the object of the federal wish is, with me, reduced to demonstration. His administration has already very materially disgraced and sunk the government. There are defects in his character which must inevitably continue to do this more and more. And if he is supported by the federal party, his party must, in the issue, fall with him. Every other calculation will, in my judgment, prove illusory.

Doctor *Franklin*, a sagacious observer of human nature, drew this portrait of Mr. Adams: "He is always honest, *sometimes* great, but *often mad*." I subscribe to the justness of this picture, adding, as to the first trait of it, this qualification: "as far as a man excessively *vain* and *jealous* and *ignobly* attached *to place* can be."

—To Charles Carroll. *Hamilton*, VI, 445-447.

August 1, 1800

It has been repeatedly mentioned to me that you have on different occasions asserted the existence of a British faction in this country, embracing a number of leading or influential characters of the federal party (as usually denominated) and that you have sometimes named me, at others plainly alluded to me, as one of this description of persons. And I have likewise been assured that of late some of your warm adherents, for electioneering purposes, have employed a corresponding language.

I must, sir, take it for granted that you cannot have made such assertions or insinuations without being willing to avow them, and to assign the reasons to a party who may conceive himself injured by them. I therefore trust that you will not deem it improper, that I apply directly to yourself, to ascertain from you, in reference to your own declarations, whether the information I have received is correct or not, and if correct, what are the grounds upon which you have founded the suggestion.

—To John Adams. Draft in Hamilton's hand. Hamilton Papers, 1st ser.

[October 1, 1800]

The time which has elapsed since my letter of the 1st Aug. was delivered to you precludes the further expectation of an answer.

From this silence I will draw no inference, nor will I presume to judge of the fitness of silence on such an occasion on the part of the chief magistrate of a republic towards a citizen who, without a stain, has discharged so many important public trusts.

But this much I will affirm, that by whomsoever a charge of the kind mentioned in my former letter may at any time have been made or insinuated against me, it is a base, wicked, and cruel calumny, destitute even of a plausible pretext to excuse the folly or mask the depravity which must have dictated it.

—To John Adams. Draft in Hamilton's hand. Hamilton Papers, 1st ser.

[1800]

Some of the warm personal friends of Mr. ADAMS are taking unwearied pains to disparage the motives of those Federalists who advocate the equal support of Gen. PINCKNEY at the approaching election of President and Vice-President.

. . . Not denying to Mr. ADAMS patriotism and integrity, and even talents of a certain kind, I should be deficient in candor, were I to conceal the conviction that he does not possess the talents adapted to the *administration* of government, and that there are great and intrinsic defects in his character, which unfit him for the office of chief magistrate. . . .

Upon my first going into Congress, I discovered symptoms of a party already formed, too well disposed to subject the interests of the United States to the management of France. Though I felt, in common with those who had participated in our revolution, a lively sentiment of good will toward a power whose co-operation, however it was and ought to have been dictated by its own interest, had been extremely useful to us, and had been afforded in a liberal and handsome manner; yet, tenacious of the real independence of our country, and dreading the preponderance of foreign influence, as the natural disease of popular government, I was struck with disgust at the appearance, in the very cradle of our republic, of a party actuated by an undue complaisance to a foreign power; and I resolved at once to resist this bias in our affairs—a resolution which has been the chief cause of the persecution I have endured in the subsequent stages of my political life.

Among the fruits of the bias I have mentioned, were the celebrated instructions to our commissioners, for treating of peace with Great Britain; which, not only as to final measures, but also as to preliminary and intermediate negotiations, placed them in a state of dependence on the French ministry, humiliating to themselves, and unsafe for the interests of the country. This was the more exceptionable, as there was cause to suspect, that in regard to the two cardinal points of the fisheries and the navigation of the Mississippi, the policy of the cabinet of Versailles did not accord with the wishes of the United States.

The commissioners, of whom Mr. ADAMS was one, had the fortitude to break through the fetters which were laid upon them by those instructions; and there is reason to believe that, by doing it, they both accelerated the peace with Great Britain, and improved the terms, while they preserved our faith with France.

. . . This scrutiny enhanced my esteem in the main for his moral qualifications, but lessened my respect for his intellectual endowments. I then adopted an opinion, which all my subsequent experience has confirmed, that he is a man of an imagination sublimated and eccentric; propitious neither to the regular display of sound judgment, nor to steady perserverance in a systematic plan of conduct; and I began to perceive what has been since too manifest, that to this defect are added the unfortunate foibles of a vanity without bounds, and a jealousy capable of discoloring every object. . . .

Great was my astonishment, and equally great my regret, when, afterwards, I learned from persons of unquestionable veracity that Mr. ADAMS had complained of unfair treatment, in not having been permitted to take an equal chance with General WASHINGTON, by leaving the votes to an uninfluenced current.

The extreme egotism of the temper, which could blind a man to considerations so obvious as those that had recommended the course pursued, cannot be enforced by my comment. It exceeded all that I had imagined, and showed, in too strong a light, that the vanity which I have ascribed to him existed to a degree that rendered it more than a harmless foible. . . .

Well-informed men knew that the event of the election[1] was extremely problematical; and while the friends of Mr. Jefferson predicted his success with sanguine confidence, his opposers feared that he might have at least an equal chance with any Federal candidate.

To exclude him was deemed, by the Federalists, a primary object. Those of them who possessed the best means of judging were of opinion that it was far less important whether Mr. Adams or Mr. Pinckney was the successful candidate, than that Mr. Jefferson should not be the person; and on this principle, it was understood among them, that the two first-mentioned gentlemen should be equally supported, leaving to casual accessions of votes in favor of the one or the other to turn the scale between them.

In this plan I united with good faith, in the resolution, to which I scrupulously adhere, of giving to each candidate an equal support. This was done wherever my influence extended, as was more particularly manifested in the State of New York, where all the electors were my warm personal or political friends, and all gave a concurrent vote for the two Federal candidates.

It is true that a faithful execution of this plan would have given Mr. Pinckney a somewhat better chance than Mr. Adams; nor shall it be concealed, that an issue favorable to the former would not have been disagreeable to me; as indeed I declared at the time, in the circles of

[1] Of 1796.—Ed.

my confidential friends. My position was, that if the chance should decide in favor of Mr. Pinckney, it probably would not be a misfortune; since he, to every essential qualification for the office, added a temper far more discreet and conciliatory than that of Mr. Adams. . . .

It is a fact, which ought not to be forgotten, that Mr. Adams, who had evinced discontent, because he had not been permitted to take an equal chance with General Washington, was enraged with all those who had thought that Mr. Pinckney ought to have had an equal chance with him. But in this there is perfect consistency. The same turn of temper is the solution of the displeasure in both cases.

It is to this circumstance of the equal support of Mr. Pinckney, that we are in a great measure to refer the serious schism which has since grown up in the Federal party. . . .

It is in regard to our foreign relations, that the public measures of Mr. Adams first attract criticism.

It will be recollected that General Pinckney, the brother of Thomas, and the gentleman now supported together with Mr. Adams, had been deputed by President Washington as successor to Mr. Monroe, and had been refused to be received by the French Government in his quality of Minister Plenipotentiary. . . .

As a final effort for accommodation, and as a means, in case of failure, of enlightening and combining public opinion, it was resolved to make another, and a more solemn, experiment, in the form of a commission of three. . . .

The event of this experiment is fresh in our recollection. Our envoys, like our minister were rejected. Tribute was demanded as a preliminary to negotiation. To their immortal honor, though Farnce at the time was proudly triumphant, they repelled the disgraceful pretension. Americans will never forget that General Pinckney was a member, and an efficient member, of this commission. . . .

Without imitating the flatterers of Mr. Adams, who, in derogation from the intrinsic force of circumstances, and from the magnanimity of the nation, ascribe to him the whole merit of producing the spirit which appeared in the community, it shall with cheerfulness be acknowledged that he took upon the occasion a manly and courageous lead—that he did all in his power to rouse the pride of the nation—to inspire it with a just sense of the injuries and outrages which it had experienced, and to dispose it to a firm and magnanimous resistance; and that his efforts contributed materially to that end. . . .

When the President pledged himself in his speech to send a minister, if satisfactory assurances of a proper reception were given, he must have been understood to mean such as were direct and official, not such as were both informal and destitute of a competent sanction.

Yet upon this loose and vague foundation, Mr. Adams precipitately nominated Mr. Murray as Envoy to the French Republic, without previous consultation with any of his ministers. The nomination itself was to each of them, even to the Secretary of State, his constitutional counsellor in similar affairs, the first notice of the project.

Thus was the measure wrong, both as to mode and substance.

A PRESIDENT is not bound to conform to the advice of his ministers. He is even under no positive injunction to ask or require it. But the Constitution presumes that he will consult them; and the genius of our government and the public good recommend the practice. . . .

Yet with this opinion of Mr. ADAMS, I have finally resolved not to advise the withholding from him a single vote. The body of Federalists, for want of sufficient knowledge of facts, are not convinced of the expediency of relinquishing him. It is even apparent, that a large proportion still retain the attachment which was once a common sentiment. Those of them, therefore, who are dissatisfied, as far as my information goes, are, generally speaking willing to forbear opposition, and to acquiesce in the equal support of Mr. ADAMS with Mr. PINCKNEY, whom they prefer. . . .

To refrain from a decided opposition to Mr. ADAMS's re-election has been reluctantly sanctioned by my judgment; which has been not a little perplexed between the unqualified conviction of his unfitness for the station contemplated, and a sense of the great importance of cultivating harmony among the supporters of the government; on whose firm union hereafter will probably depend the preservation of order, tranquillity, liberty, property; the security of every social and domestic blessing.

—*Letter from Alexander Hamilton, concerning the Public Conduct and Character of John Adams, Esq., President of the United States* (New York: printed for John Lang by Geo. G. Hopkins, 1800), pp. 3-52. *passim.*

On Aaron Burr

I feel it a religious duty to oppose his career.

Hamilton and Jefferson disagreed on many issues, but were in complete accord on one subject—that scoundrel Burr. Jefferson looked upon Burr "as a crooked gun, or other perverted machine, whose aim or shot you could never be sure of." Hamilton met Burr at the Battle of Brooklyn Heights, and their paths crossed on numerous occasions thereafter. He admired him as an attorney, but distrusted him as a politician. Superficially, Hamilton and Burr had much in common. Young, brilliant, with a flair for military strategy and an instinctive knowledge of men and politics, they were slight in stature, handsome and vivacious, dynamic personalities, devastating with the ladies, and politically ambitious. But there was at least one important difference. Hamilton had integrity.

As a result of the inept provisions of the election laws, Burr was tied in votes with Jefferson in the presidential election of 1800, although there was no question that the latter was the choice of the people. The final vote was thrown into the lap of the lame-duck House of Representatives, strongly Federalist in character. One of Hamilton's greatest contributions was his perception of the peril to the country from the accession of Burr to the presidency and his forthright advice to his political supporters to vote for Jefferson. Hamilton wrote a number of such letters to Senator Bayard of Delaware, whose switch to Jefferson decided the election.

Dissatisfied with the vice-presidency, Burr sought the governorship of New York. When he failed to get the Republican nomination, he solicited the aid of embittered Federalists. Again Hamilton denounced him and thwarted his ambitions. The denouement will be treated in the section on The Duel.

September 21, 1792

I take the liberty to inclose you the copy of a letter from a very respectable friend in New York. The contents surprised me—nor am I quite persuaded that the appearance of Mr. Burr on the stage is not a diversion in favor of Mr. Clinton.

Mr. Clinton's success I should think very unfortunate; I am not for trusting the government too much in the hands of its enemies. But still Mr. C. is a man of property, and in private life, as far as I know, of probity. I fear the other gentleman is unprincipled, both as a public and a private man. When the Constitution was in deliberation, his conduct was equivocal, but its enemies, who, I believe, best understood him, considered him as with them. In fact, I take it, he is for or against nothing, but as it suits his interest or ambition. He is determined, as I conceive, to make his way to be the head of the popular party, and to climb *per fas et nefas* to the highest honors of the State, and as much higher as circumstances may permit. Embarrassed, as I understand, in his circumstances, with an extravagant family, bold, enterprising, and intriguing, I am mistaken if it be not his object to play the game of confusion, and I feel it a religious duty to oppose his career.

—To ———— Hamilton's hand. Hamilton Papers, 1st ser.

September 26, 1792

Mr. Burr's integrity as an individual is not unimpeached. As a public man, he is one of the worst sort—a friend to nothing but as it suits his interest and ambition. Determined to climb to the highest honors of the State, and as much higher as circumstances may permit, he cares nothing about the means of effecting his purpose. 'Tis evident that he aims at putting himself at the head of what he calls the "popular party" as affording the best tools for an ambitious man to work with, secretly turning liberty into ridicule. He knows as well as most men how to make use of the name. In a word, if we have an embryo-Caesar in the United States, 'tis Burr.

—To ———— Hamilton's hand. Hamilton Papers, 1st ser.

August 6, 1800

. . . There seems to be too much probability that Jefferson or Burr will be President. The latter is intriguing with all his might in New Jersey, Rhode Island, and Vermont, and there is a possibility of some success in his intrigues. He counts positively on the universal support of the Antifederalists, and that, by some adventitious aid from other quarters, he will overtop his friend Jefferson. Admitting the first point, the conclusion may be realized; and if it is so, Burr will certainly attempt to reform the government *a la Bonaparte*. He is as unprincipled and dangerous a man as any country can boast—as true a Catiline as ever met in midnight conclave.

—To James A. Bayard. Copy. Hamilton Papers, 1st ser.

December 1800

'Tis enough for us to know that Mr. Burr is one of the most unprincipled men in the United States, to determine us to decline being responsible for the precarious issues of his calculations of interest. You cannot, in my opinion, render a greater service to your country than by exerting your influence to counteract the impolitic and impure idea of raising Mr. Burr to the chief magistracy.

—To John Rutledge. *Works*, X, 405.

December 17, 1800

There is no circumstance which has occurred in the course of our political affairs that has given me so much pain as the idea that Mr. Burr might be elevated to the Presidency by the means of the Federalists. I am of opinion that this party has hitherto solid claims of merit with the public, and so long as it does nothing to forfeit its title to confidence, I shall continue to hope that our misfortunes are temporary, and that the party will erelong emerge from its depression. But if it shall act a foolish or unworthy part in any capital instance, I shall then despair.

Such, without doubt, will be the part it will act, if it shall seriously attempt to support Mr. Burr, in opposition to Mr. Jefferson. If it fails, as, after all, is not improbable, it will have riveted the animosity of that person; will have destroyed or weakened the motives to moderation which he must at present feel, and it will expose them to the disgrace of a defeat, in an attempt to elevate to the first place of the government one of the worst men in the community. . . .

Adieu to the Federal Troy, if they once introduce this Grecian horse into their citadel.

Trust me, my dear friend, you cannot render a greater service to your country than to resist this project. Far better will it be to endeavor to obtain from Jefferson assurances on some cardinal points:

1st. The preservation of the actual fiscal system.

2d. Adherence to the neutral plan.

3d. The preservation and gradual increase of the navy.

4th. The continuance of our friends in the offices they fill, except in the great departments, in which he ought to be left free.

—To Oliver Wolcott. *Hamilton*, VI, 487-489.

December 24, 1800

Another subject. *Jefferson or Burr?* the former without all doubt. The latter, in my judgment, has no principle, public or private; could be bound by no agreement; will listen to no monitor but his ambition, and for this purpose will use the worst part of the community as a ladder to climb to permanent power, and an instrument to crush the better part. He is bankrupt beyond redemption, except by the resources that grow out of war and disorder, or by a sale to a foreign power, or by great peculation. War with Great Britain would be the immediate instrument. He is sanguine enough to hope every thing, daring enough to attempt every thing, wicked enough to scruple nothing. From the elevation of such a man may heaven preserve the country!

Let our situation be improved to obtain from Jefferson assurances on certain points: the maintenance of the present system, especially on the cardinal articles of public credit—a navy, neutrality. Make any discreet use you may think fit of this letter.

—To Gouverneur Morris. *Hamilton*, VI, 496-497.

December 26, 1800

[If th]ere be [a man][1] in the world I ought to hate, it is Jefferson. With Burr I have always been personally well. But the public good must be paramount to every private consideration.

—To Gouverneur Morris. Draft in Hamilton's hand. Hamilton Papers, 1st ser.

December 27, 1800

Several letters to myself and others from the city of Washington, excite in my mind extreme alarm on the subject of the future President. It seems nearly ascertained that Jefferson and Burr will come

[1] Bracketed material mutilated in original.

into the House of Representatives with equal votes, and those letters express the probability that the federal party may prefer the latter. In my opinion, a circumstance more ruinous to them, or more disastrous to the country, could not happen.

This opinion is dictated by a long and close attention to the character of B., with the best opportunities of knowing it—an advantage of judging which, few of our friends possess, and which ought to give some weight to my opinion.

Be assured, my dear sir, that this man has no principle, public nor private. As a politician, his sole spring of action is an inordinate ambition; as an individual, he is believed by friends as well as foes to be without *probity*; and a voluptuary by system—with habits of expense that can be satisfied by no fair expedients. As to his talents, great management and cunning are the predominant features; he is yet to give proofs of those solid abilities which characterize the statesman. Daring and energy must be allowed him; but these qualities, under the direction of the worst passions, are certainly strong objections, not recommendations. He is of a temper to undertake the most hazardous enterprises, because he is sanguine enough to think nothing impracticable; and of an ambition that will be content with nothing less than *permanent* power in his own hands. The maintenance of the existing institutions will not suit him; because under them his power will be too narrow and too precarious. Yet the innovations he may attempt will not offer the substitute of a system *durable* and *safe*, calculated to give lasting prosperity, and to unite liberty with strength. It will be the system of the day, sufficient to serve his own turn, and not looking beyond himself. To execute this plan, as the good men of the country cannot be relied upon, the worst will be used. Let it not be imagined that the difficulties of execution will deter, or a calculation of interest restrain. The truth is, that under forms of government like ours, too much is practicable to men who will, without scruple, avail themselves of the bad passions of human nature. To a man of this description, possessing the requisite talents, the acquisition of permanent power is not a chimera. I *know* that Mr. Burr does not view it as such, and I am sure there are no means too atrocious to be employed by him. In debt, vastly beyond his means of payment, with all the habits of excessive expense, he cannot be satisfied with the regular emoluments of any office of our government. Corrupt expedients will be to him a necessary resource. Will any prudent man offer such a President to the temptations of foreign gold? No engagement that can be made with him can be depended upon; while making it, he will laugh in his sleeve at the credulity of those with whom he makes it;—and the first moment it suits his views to break it, he will do so.[1] Let me add, that

[1] A recent incident will give you an idea of his views as to foreign politics. I dined with him lately. His toasts were: "The French Republic," "The Commissioners

I could scarcely name a discreet man of either party in our State, who does not think Mr. Burr the most unfit man in the United States for the office of President. Disgrace abroad, ruin at home, are the probable fruits of his elevation. To contribute to the disappointment and mortification of Mr. J., would be, on my part, only to retaliate for unequivocal proofs of enmity; but in a case like this, it would be base to listen to personal considerations. In alluding to the situation, I mean only to illustrate how strong must be the motives which induce me to promote *his* elevation in exclusion of another.

For Heaven's sake, my dear sir, exert yourself to the utmost to save our country from so great a calamity. Let us not be responsible for the evils, which in all probability will follow the preference. All calculations that may lead to it must prove fallacious.

—To James A. Bayard. Copy. Hamilton Papers, 1st ser.

January, 1801

It is a fact that Mr. Burr is now in frequent and close conference with a Frenchman, who is suspected of being an agent of the French Government, and it is not to be doubted that he will be the firm ally of Buonaparte.

You are at liberty to show this letter to such friends as you think fit, especially Mr. Bayard, of Delaware, in whose principles and sound sense I have much confidence.

Depend upon it, men never played a more foolish game than will do the Federalists if they support Burr.

—To Gouverneur Morris. Draft in Hamilton's hand. Hamilton Papers, 1st ser.

January 10, 1801

So our eastern friends want to join the armed neutrality and make war upon Britain. I infer this from their mad propensity to make Burr President. If Jefferson has prejudices leading to that result, he has defects of character to keep him back. Burr, with the same propensities, will find the thing necessary to his projects, and will dare to hazard all consequences. They may as well think to bind a giant by a cobweb as his ambition by promises.

—To Gouverneur Morris. Draft in Hamilton's hand. Hamilton Papers, 1st ser.

---

who Negotiated the Convention," "Buonaparte," "The Marquis La Fayette." His doctrines, that it would be to the interest of this country to permit the indiscriminate sale of prizes by the belligerent powers; and the building and equipment of vessels—a project amounting to nothing more nor less (with the semblance of equality) than to turn all our naval resources into the channel of France, and compel Great Britain to war. Indeed, Mr. Burr must have war, as the instrument of his ambition and cupidity. The peculiarity of the occasion will excuse my mentioning in confidence the occurrences of a private table.

January 16, 1801

I admit that his politics are tinctured with fanaticism; that he is too much in earnest in his democracy; that he has been a mischievous enemy to the principal measures of our past administration; that he is crafty and persevering in his objects; that he is not scrupulous about the means of success, nor very mindful of truth, and that he is a contemptible hyprocrite. But it is not true, as is alleged, that he is an enemy to the power of the Executive, or that he is for confounding all the powers in the House of Representatives. It is a fact which I have frequently mentioned, that, while we were in the administration together, he was generally for a large construction of the Executive authority and not backward to act upon it in cases which coincided with his views. . . . To my mind a true estimate of Mr. Jefferson's character warrants the expectation of a temporizing rather than a violent system. That Jefferson has manifested a culpable predilection for France is certainly true; but I think it a question whether it did not proceed quite as much from her *popularity* among us as from sentiment, and, in proportion as that popularity is diminished, his zeal will cool. Add to this that there is no fair reason to suppose him capable of being corrupted, which is a security that he will not go beyond certain limits. It is not at all improbable that under the change of circumstances Jefferson's Gallicism has considerably abated. . . .

It is demonstrated by recent facts[1] that Burr is *solicitous to keep* upon *anti-federal* ground, to avoid compromitting himself by any engagements,[2] with the Federalists. . . . He will never choose to lean on good men, because he knows that they will never support his bad projects; but instead of this he will endeavor to disorganize both parties, and to form out of them a third, composed of men fitted by their characters to be conspirators and instruments of such projects. . . . Ambition without principle never was long under the guidance of good sense. Besides that, really, the force of Mr. Burr's understanding is much overrated. He is far more *cunning* than *wise*, far more *dextrous* than *able*.

(*Very, very confidential.*—In my opinion he is inferior in real ability to Jefferson. There are also facts against the supposition. It is past all doubt that he has blamed me for not having improved the situation I once was in to change the government. That when answered that this could not have been done without guilt, he replied, "Les grandes âmes se soucient peu des petits moraux";[3] that when told the things was never practicable from the genius and situation of the country, he answered, "That depends on the estimate we form of the human

[1] My letter to Mr. Morris states some of them.
[2] He trusts to their *prejudices* and *hopes* for support.
[3] Great spirits do not worry much about petty morals.—Ed.

passions, and of the means of influencing them." Does this prove that Mr. Burr would consider a scheme of usurpation as visionary?) . . . Can there be any serious question between the policy of leaving the Anti-federalists to be answerable for the elevation of an exceptionable man, and that of adopting ourselves and becoming answerable for a man who, on all hands, is acknowledged to be a complete Catiline? 'Tis enough to state the question to indicate the answer, if reason, not passion, presides in the decision.

—To James A. Bayard. Copy. Hamilton Papers, 1st ser.

January 21, 1801

. . . I beg of you, as you love your country, your friends, and yourself, to reconsider dispassionately the opinion you have expressed in favor of Burr.

I never was so much mistaken as I shall be if our friends, in the event of their success, do not rue the preference they will give to that *Catiline*. Adieu.

—To Theodore Sedgwick. Hamilton's hand. Hamilton Papers, 1st ser.

[1804]

1. Col. Burr has steadily pursued the track of democratic politics. This he has done either from *principle* or from *calculation*. If the former, he is not likely now to change his plan, when the Federalists are prostrate, and their enemies predominant. If the latter, he will certainly not at this time relinquish the ladder of his ambition, and espouse the cause or views of the weaker party.

2. Though detested by some of the leading Clintonians, he is certainly not personally disagreeable to the great body of them, and it will be no difficult task for a man of talents, intrigue, and address, possessing the chair of government, to rally the great body of them under his standard, and thereby to consolidate for personal purposes, the mass of the Clintonians, his own adherents among the Democrats, and such Federalists as, from personal good-will or interested motives, may give him support.

3. The effect of his elevation will be to reunite under a more adroit, able, and daring chief, the now scattered fragments of the Democratic party, and to reinforce it by a strong detachment from the Federalists. For though virtuous Federalists, who, from miscalculation, may support him, would afterwards relinquish his standard, a large number from various motives would continue attached to it.

4. A farther effect of his elevation by aid of the Federalists will be, to present to the confidence of New England, a man, already the man of the Democratic leaders of that country, and towards whom the mass

of the people have no weak predilection, as their countryman, as the grandson of President Edwards, and the son of President Burr. In vain will certain men resist this predilection, when it can be said, that he was chosen governor of this State, in which he was best known, principally, or in a great degree, by the aid of the Federalists.

5. This will give him fair play to disorganize New England, if so disposed; a thing not very difficult, when the strength of the Democratic party in each of the New England States is considered, and the national tendency of our civil institutions is duly weighed.

6. The ill opinion of Jefferson, and jealousy of the ambition of Virginia, is no inconsiderable prop of good principles in that country. But these causes are leading to an opinion, that a dismemberment of the Union is expedient. It would probably suit Mr. Burr's views to promote this result, to be the chief of the Northern portion; and placed at the head of the State of New York, no man would be more likely to succeed.

7. If he be truly, as the Federalists have believed, a man of irregular and unsatiable ambition, if his plan has been to rise to power on the ladder of Jacobinic principles, it is natural to conclude that he will endeavor to fix himself in power by the same instrument; that he will not lean on a fallen and failing party, generally speaking, of a character not to favor usurpation and the ascendancy of a despotic chief. Every day shows, more and more, the much to be regretted tendency of governments entirely popular, to dissolution and disorder. Is it rational to expect that a man, who had the sagacity to foresee this tendency, and whose temper would permit him to bottom his aggrandizement on popular prejudices and vices, would desert the system at a time when, more than ever, the state of things invites him to adhere to it?

8. If Lansing is governor, his personal character affords some security against pernicious extremes, and at the same time renders it morally certain, that the democratic party, already much divided and weakened, will moulder and break asunder more and more. This is certainly a state of things favorable to the future ascendancy of the wise and good. May it not lead to a recasting of parties, by which the Federalists will gain a great accession of force from former opponents? At any rate is it not wiser in them to promote a course of things, by which schism among the Democrats will be fostered and increased, than on fair calculation to give them a chief, better able than any they have yet had, to unite and direct them; and in a situation to infer rottenness in the only part of our country which still remains sound, the Federal States of New England?

—"Reasons Why it is Desirable that Mr. Lansing Rather Than Col. Burr Should Succeed." *Hamilton*, VII, 851-853.

February 24, 1804

To detach the Federalists from Burr, they must believe *two* things: *one*, that we are in earnest as to our candidate and that it is not a mere diversion; *the other*, that there is some chance of success. All believe, and some leading candidates admit, that if either of the two democratic rival parties should come to expect a defeat, they will range themselves under your banner.

—To Rufus King. *Works*, X, 450.

On George Clinton

In the state of New York a second-rate politician held on to the governorship tenaciously from 1777 to 1795. Hamilton had cooperated with George Clinton during the Revolution and had futilely sought his aid to enlarge the taxing powers of the Congress of the Confederation. Hamilton scored his most brilliant victory over Clinton in the great fight for the ratification of the Constitution, which the governor bitterly opposed. An unreconstructed Antifederalist and particularist, Clinton was a target for some of Hamilton's most devastating literary missiles. Clinton bided his time and took his revenge. As Vice President of the United States he broke the tie in the Senate and cast the deciding vote in 1811 against the renewal of the charter of the Bank of the United States, Hamilton's project.

[1789]

To the Independent and Patriotic Electors of the State of New York.

. . . It is just, for instance, that difference of opinion, on a great political question occasionally arising in a community, does not constitute what is understood by *spirit of party*. Men, in such cases, ought to take their sides according to their convictions, though they should be cautious not to suffer their zeal to hurry them into irrational extremes.

But when the Governor is objected to as the head of a party, we presume it is not on account of the side he took in the question concerning the new Constitution. . . . Discerning men, soon after the peace, perceived that he had formed a close connection with a particular set of characters, in whose public and private views he was continually embarked.

It is asked, What could have been his object in thus devoting himself to a party? The answer is plain: to keep himself in place—to perpetuate himself in the enjoyment of the power and *profit* of the office he holds. . . .

It is asserted, in order to excite prejudice, that the opposition to the Governor arises from the wealthy and the great. We believe it to be true that the principal part of the men of the most considerable property in the State are of opinion that a change is necesssary. But we believe it to be not less true that the same opinion embraces a large proportion of all other classes of the community. Will it follow that it must be wrong because men of property concur in it? Are they less interested than other people in good government? . . .

As to the quantity of property which may have been amassed by the Governor during his administration, this is a subject which we should have left untouched, were it not for some observations in the address which seem to require notice. . . . And though we do not agree in the opinion that the idea of his being possessed of a large fortune is groundless, yet we should not impute blame to him on that account, in any other view than as he may be justly chargeable with *penury* in the manner of acquiring it, and with *disingenuity* in the attempts to conceal it. It is undeniable, that he has received from the state what may be deemed a handsome fortune in a few accumulated payments,[1] and that he has made several profitable speculations in land. Some of these are publicly known, and others of them, we have good grounds to believe, are covered under the names of third persons.

—Pamphlet in New York State Library, Albany, quoted in *Works*, II, 116-127.

February 18, 1789

On this ground it is highly necessary that the Chief Magistrate of the State should be free from all temptation wantonly to perplex or embarrass the National Government,—whether that temptation should arise from a preference of partial confederacies, from a spirit of competition with the national rulers for personal pre-eminence, from an impatience of the restraints of national authority, from the fear of a diminution of power and emoluments, from resentment or mortification proceeding from disappointment, or from any other cause whatsoever. For all attempts to perplex and embarrass, would not only tend to prevent the government from doing the good they may meditate, but would also expose this State to the distrust and ill-will of the others.

—To the Supervisors of the City of Albany. Broadside, N.Y. Pub. Lib.

February 20, 1789

The present Governor was bred to the law under William Smith, Esquire, formerly of this city. Some time before the late revolution he resided in Ulster County, and there followed his profession with reputation, though not with distinction. He was not supposed to possess considerable talents, but, upon the whole, stood fair on the

[1] Hamilton in a footnote gives figures to show amounts paid Clinton on a settlement of his accounts in 1782, plus his salary. Including interest, he estimates the total at around £20,000.

score of probity. It must, however, be confessed, he very early got the character with many of being a very *artful* man, and it is not to be wondered at, if that impression, on the minds in which it prevailed, deducted something from the opinion of his integrity. But it would be refining too much to admit such a consequence to be a just one. There certainly are characters (though they may be rare) which unite a great degree of address, and even a large portion of what is best expressed by the word *cunning*, with a pretty exact adherence in the main to the principles of integrity.

Mr. Clinton, from his youth upward, has been remarkable for a quality which, when accompanied by a sound and enlarged understanding, a liberal mind, and a good heart, is denominated *firmness*, and answers the most valuable purposes; but which, when joined with narrow views, a prejudiced and contracted disposition, a passionate and interested temper, passes under the name of *obstinacy*, and is the source of the greatest mischiefs, especially in exalted public stations. . . .

In the beginning of 1775 the contest with Great Britain had become serious; and we all remember the interesting question then agitated in our Assembly, respecting the co-operation of this State in the general measures of America. Here Mr. Clinton and Mr. Philip Schuyler were the leaders of the minority, who advocated the propriety of that co-operation; and both these gentlemen, for their conduct upon the occasion, will always be entitled to credit from the friends of the revolution. To compare the degree of merit to which they may respectively lay claim would be an invidious task. But as the partisans of Governor Clinton have taken pains to propagate an opinion of superior merit in him, in regard to this transaction, it is but justice to the other gentleman to observe that he was equally *open* and *decided* in the part he took in that question; that as none will pretend to ascribe to Mr. Clinton greater abilities than to Mr. Schuyler, the exertions of the latter must have been at least as useful as those of the former; and that Mr. Schuyler has in his favor the additional circumstance of having risked a large property, which Mr. Clinton had not to risk, upon the event of this revolution.

—*Letters of H. G.*, *I. N. Y. Daily Advertiser*, March 10, 1789.

February 21, 1789

. . . There is, however, no part of his character which has been more misrepresented than the military part of it. His panegyrists describe him to us as the "war-worn veteran"—the complete soldier—consummate general. One would imagine from their stories of him that he had often, in the language of Sergeant Kite, "breakfasted upon ravelins, and picked his teeth with palisadoes,"—that he was the first of American generals—a Marius in courage—a Caesar in skill—inferior in nothing to a Turenne or a Montecuccoli, an Eugene or a Marlborough. But trust me, my dear sir, this is a mere rant and romance. That Mr. Clinton is a man of courage, there is no reason to doubt. That he was upon most occasions active and vigorous, cannot be justly disputed. In his capacity of governor he was ever ready to promote the common cause, prompt in affording the aid of the militia when requisite, and scrupling not, when he thought his presence might be of use, to put himself at the head of them. But here his praise as a soldier ends. Beyond this he has no pretension to the wreath of military renown. No man can tell when or where he gave proofs of generalship, either in council or in the field. After diligent inquiry, I have not been able to learn that he was ever more than once in actual combat. This was at Fort Montgomery, where he commanded in person, and which, after a feeble and unskilful defence, was carried by storm. That post, strongly fortified by nature, almost inaccessible in itself, and sufficiently manned, was capable of being rendered a much more difficult morsel to the assailants than they found it to be. This, I own, was not the common idea at the time; but it is not the less true. To embellish military exploits, and varnish military disgraces, is no unusual policy. Besides, Governor Clinton was at the zenith of his popularity—a circumstance which disposed men's minds to take a great deal for granted. One particular in this affair deserves to be noticed. It is certain that the Governor made a well-timed retreat (I mean personally, for the greatest part of the garrison were captured), a thing which must have occasioned no small conflict in the breast of a commander nice in military punctilio. But squeamishness on this head had been ill-placed. It was undoubtedly the duty of the *Brigadier* to provide in season for the safety of the Governor.

Those who are best acquainted with the particulars of the burning of Esopus, in the fall of the year 1777, assert that his Excellency was culpably deficient in exertion on that occasion. The fact seems to have been that a large body of men remained unemployed in the vicinity, under his direction, while the descent of the enemy was made with little or no opposition. And there is room to suppose that, if a better countenance had been kept up, the evil might have been prevented.

—*Letters of H. G., II.* N. Y. *Daily Advertiser*, March 11, 1789.

February 22, 1789

One of the number *only* I shall name, Egbert Benson, Esq., the present attorney-general; this gentleman, in the capacity of a member of the Assembly, long had a principal agency in giving energy and animation to the measures of the State. In confining myself to the mention of Mr. Benson, it is not because there are not others who have an equal right to it, but because it is his peculiar good fortune *to have virtues and talents, and yet to be unenvied.* And as it is my intention you should be at liberty to make any use of these letters which you may think proper, I am unwilling to attempt an enumeration of all the characters alluded to, lest, if incomplete, it should be the occasion of offence. Though not immediately connected with the subject, there is one circumstance which I cannot forbear mentioning before I conclude. Mr. Benson, during the war, was considered as the confidential friend and adviser of the Governor. Not long after the peace, it was perceived that this relation between the two persons began to be weakened, and it is some time since it has been understood to have entirely ceased. The first appearance of the change was, to discerning men, an ill omen of the future. But Benson was an unfit confidant for the new system of policy. He was honest and independent. Materials better adapted for *tools* were wanted, and they have been selected with admirable judgment.

—*Letters of H. G., III.* N. Y. *Daily Advertiser*, March 12, 1789.

February 24, 1789

. . . *I do not recollect a single measure of public utility, since the peace, for which the State is indebted to its Chief Magistrate.*

—*Letters of H. G., IV.* N. Y. *Daily Advertiser*, March 14, 1789.

February 25, 1789

The inclination of the Governor to hinder tumult or commotion is not to be questioned. In his situation, a man must have been both abandoned and mad not to have had that inclination. Regard to his own authority and consequence, independent of other motives, was sufficient to produce it. But there are circumstances which warrant a conclusion, that he had formed a plan of building up his own popularity in the city upon that of certain individuals who were then advocates for persecution; not, indeed, in the shape of mobs and riots, but of *law;* by banishment, disfranchisement, and the like; and that his conduct was guided by condescensions to them, which, in some measure, involved him in their policy. . . .

It is not undeserving of attention, that the chief agents in promoting the laws passed after the evacuation of the city, of which the inhabitants of the southern district had reason to complain, were men who had been constantly devoted to the Governor; and that the persons who have had the greatest share in mitigating or abrogating those exceptional laws have been in opposite views to him. And it ought not to escape observation, that there has never been any official act of the Governor calculated to effect the alteration or repeal of those laws.

—*Letters of H. G., V.* N. Y. *Daily Advertiser*, March 17, 1789.

February 26, 1789

I shall now proceed to give you a brief history of the Governor's administration since the peace, as it respects the United States, from the whole of which, preferring the evidence of *actions* to that of *professions*, I am persuaded that you will agree with me, that there is satisfactory proof of his being an enemy to the AMERICAN UNION.

The facts from which I shall draw this conclusion are of the following nature:

I. That while he has acknowledged the insufficiency of the old government, he has strenuously opposed the principal measures devised by the joint councils of America for supporting and strengthening it.

II. That he has treated Congress, as a body, in a contemptuous manner.

III. That his behavior towards the individuals composing that body has been of a nature calculated to give them just cause of disgust.

IV. That he disapproved of the very first step taken toward the effectual amendment of the old confederation.

V. That he prejudged and condemned the new Constitution before it was framed.

VI. That he opposed it, after it appeared, with unreasonable obstinacy.

VII. That he has continued his opposition to it even since its adoption by this State. And,

VIII. That he is unfriendly to the residence of Congress in this city.

From the assemblage of these facts, I am mistaken, my dear sir, if you do not think the evidence of his enmity to the Union complete; and I shall not be the less mistaken if you do not consider this as a conclusive objection to his re-election.

Whatever may have been your doubts respecting parts of the new Constitution, I am satisfied that you regard the preservation of the UNION as essential to the peace and prosperity of the country, and will deem it unsafe to trust any man with power, who entertains views inimical to it.

—*Letters of H. G.*, VI. N. Y. *Daily Advertiser*, March 18, 1789.

February 28, 1789

The embarrassments experienced in carrying through the first plan, the increase of the national debt, and other circumstances, induced Congress to devise a new system of impost, which was finally agreed upon on the 18th of April, 1783.

The Governor, undoubtedly, took an active part in opposition to this measure. It is true, he declared in the convention that he had always been a friend to the impost, but *could not agree* to the manner in which Congress proposed to exercise the power. This is plainly a subterfuge. He was a friend to an abstract something, which might be any thing or nothing, as he pleased; but he was an enemy to *the thing proposed.* A general impost, being a measure not within the provision of the confederation, could only be brought about by some general plan devised by the common councils of the UNION, and submitted to the adoption of the several States. There could else be no concert, no common agreement. To oppose, therefore, the specific plan offered, and yet pretend to be a friend to the thing in the abstract, deserves no better name than that of hypocrisy.

I am possessed of unquestionable evidence, to prove that he used personal influence with members of the Legislature to prejudice them against the granting of the impost. You may obtain a confirmation of this from one of the gentlemen who represent your own county in the year 1786. The argument employed with him was, that Congress being a single body, and consequently without checks, would be apt to misapply the money arising from it. This looks like more than an objection to the mode. If the money was to be granted in any shape, that consequence, if to be apprehended at all, might follow.

A question of a very delicate and serious nature arises on the conduct of the Governor. Is it justifiable in the Chief Magistrate of a State to employ his personal influence with individual members of the Legislature in relation to any matter of public concern which is to come under their deliberation? To me an interference of this sort appears highly exceptionable.

—*Letters of H. G., VIII.* N. Y. *Daily Advertiser,* March 23, 1789.

March 2, 1789

The second particular which I have stated, as evidence of Mr. Clinton's enmity to the Union, is, that he has treated Congress, as a body, in a contemptuous manner.

A proof of this exists in his refusal to convene the Legislature of this State in the year 1786, upon pressing and repeated supplications of Congress; sheltering himself under the frivolous pretence that the constitution did not leave him at liberty to do it.

The constitution empowers the governor to convene the Legislature "on extraordinary occasions." This provision is evidently calculated to enable him to call together the Legislature whenever any thing of importance out of the ordinary routine of State business should occur. To put any other meaning upon it is absurd, and would embarrass the operations of government. It cannot be supposed that the constitution intended by "extraordinary occasions" nothing but wars, rebellions, plagues, or earthquakes. The word "extraordinary," as used in this case, can only be construed as equivalent to *special;* and a special occasion is any thing of moment out of the common and expected course. . . .

Now, sir, I will boldly appeal to every candid mind whether this transaction is not evidence, as well of a splenetic and disrespectful disposition toward the government of the United States, as of a temper inflexibly haughty and obstinate. In what humiliating light must he have considered Congress, not to have looked upon their earnest and repeated application on a matter which they and all the other States, thought of the most serious moment to the Union, in a situation notoriously distressing and critical, as an occasion sufficiently special to leave him *at liberty* to call the Legislature together! How much of contempt and disregard toward the representative authority of confederated America was implied in such a construction! The merits of the impost system are of no consequence in the consideration of the subject. The whole is a question of decorum and due deference in the head of a particular member of the confederacy toward the head of the whole confederacy. In this light, it is evident that the conduct of the Governor on the occasion was an insult to the people of the United States, and of course to the people of this State, through their representatives in Congress.

—*Letters of H. G., IX.* N. Y. *Daily Advertiser,* March 25, 1789.

March 3, 1789

I am well informed that his Excellency never made a visit to, or had any intercourse of civilities with, either of the two last Presidents of Congress. This neglect on his part appears the more pointed, as it is well known that he had been upon a footing of intimacy with one of the gentlemen previous to his appointment—I mean General St. Clair. This gentleman had been heard to lament that the Governor's conduct toward him, in an official respect, had put it out of his power to keep up the amicable intercourse which had formerly subsisted between them. It seems as if the character of a President of Congress amounted, in the Governor's estimation, to a forfeiture even of the rights of private friendship.

This behavior to the official head of Congress is to be regarded in a stronger light than mere disrespect to the individual. It may justly be esteemed disrespect to the body themselves, and to have been dictated by a disposition to humiliate the government which they administered.

—*Letters of H. G.,* X. N. Y. *Daily Advertiser,* March 27, 1789.

March 4, 1789

Some time in the latter part of the year 1785, or beginning of 1786, the State of Virginia proposed the holding of a convention for the purpose of devising some system of commercial regulations for the United States. This State, among others, acceded to the proposition, and the deputies from the different States appointed pursuant, met at Annapolis in the fall of 1786. But the number actually assembled formed so incomplete a representation of the Union, that, if there had been no other reason, it would have been inexpedient for them to proceed in the execution of their mission. In addition to this, they were unanimously of opinion that some more radical reform was necessary; and that even to accomplish the immediate end for which they had been deputed, certain collateral changes in the federal system would be requisite, to which their powers in general could not be deemed competent. Under these impressions, they, with one voice, earnestly recommended it to the several States to appoint deputies to meet in convention, in the ensuing month of May, with power to revise the confederation at large, and to propose such alterations and amendments as should appear to them necessary to render it adequate to the exigencies of the Union.

The report of this convention was in course handed to the Governor, on the return of the deputies of this State from Annapolis.

I have ascertained it beyond a doubt that, in a conversation on the subject of this report, he expressed a strong dislike of its object, declaring that, in his opinion, no such reform as the report contemplated was necessary; that the confederation as it stood was equal to the purposes of the Union, or, with little alteration, could be made so; and that he thought the deputies assembled upon that occasion would have done better to have confined themselves to the purposes of their errand. . . .

This, then, seemed to be the true state of the business. On the other hand, Congress, as *constituted*, was not fit to be trusted with power; on the other, it was not expedient to *constitute them differently*. To me it appears impossible to reconcile all this to a sincere attachment to an *efficient Federal Government*. Thus, sir, have I explained to you my meaning in the assertion: that the Governor disapproved of the very first step taken toward the effectual amendment of the old confederation.

—*Letters of H. G., XI*. N. Y. *Daily Advertiser*, March 28, 1789.

March 6, 1789

One of the circumstances stated to you in mine of the 26th of February, to show that the Governor is unfriendly to the *Union*, is, that he prejudged and condemned the new Constitution before it was framed. . . .

The declarations of the Governor on this occasion fix upon him the charge of inconsistency. How can what he said in the instance in question be reconciled with his declaration in the convention, "*that he had always lamented the feebleness of the confederation*"?

—*Letters of H. G., XII*. N. Y. *Daily Advertiser*, March 31, 1789.

March 7, 1789

The next in order of the circumstances alleged in proof of the unfriendly disposition of the Governor to the Union, is that he opposed the new Constitution, after it appeared, with unreasonable *obstinacy*....

I should be the last to blame any man for opposing the adoption of the Constitution while its establishment was yet a question in the United States; but when that was no longer the case; when nine States, the number required by the Constitution to its establishment, had adopted it; when it had thereby become the government of the Union, I think further opposition was not justifiable by any motives of prudence or patriotism. These considerations had their proper weight with a great proportion of the Governor's party.

Out of sixty-four members, of which the Convention of this State consisted, there were at first only nineteen in favor of the Constitution. In the conclusion, there was a majority which did actually adopt it. But the Governor *persisted to the last in his negative.*

—*Letters of H. G., XIII.* N. Y. *Daily Advertiser,* April 2, 1789.

March 8, 1789

The seventh of the circumstances enumerated in proof of his Excellency's enmity to the Union is, that he has continued his opposition to the new Constitution even since its adoption by this State. . . .

I attended the debates of the convention, and I could not forbear remarking that the *Governor,* in the speech alluded to, seemed carefully to confine his assurances to a mere *official compliance.* The impression made upon my mind by the *two* last speeches he delivered was this: that he would, as Governor of the State, in mere official transactions, *conform* to the Constitution; but that he should think it expedient to keep alive the spirit of opposition in the people, until the *amendments proposed,* or another convention (I am not certain which), could be obtained. In this impression I am not singular; there were others who understood him in the same sense.

. . . the Constitution of the United States leaves the mode of appointing ELECTORS to the discretion of State Legislatures. They may therefore, refer them to the choice of the people, if they think proper. This has been done in several of the States, and is, in my opinion, a privilege which it is of great importance should be in the hands of the people. Making the usual allowances for want of punctuality in meeting, disagreement in opinion, difficulties in framing new and untried regulations, it may be safely pronounced that the Legislature was assembled too late to refer the choice of electors to the people; whereby they were deprived of an opportunity of exercising a constitutional discretion, and *the people* of a chance of exercising a privilege of very considerable moment to their interests. May it not be justly said, in this instance, that the Governor UNDERTOOK TO THINK for the Legislature?

—*Letters of H. G., XIV*. N. Y. *Daily Advertiser*, April 8, 1789.

March 9, 1789

The last of the circumstances mentioned by me in my letter of the 20th of February, as evidence of the inimical disposition of the Governor toward the Union, is, that he is unfriendly to the residence of Congress in this city. . . .

To me, my dear sir, the collective view of his conduct will admit of no other supposition than that he has entertained a project for erecting a system of *State Power*, unconnected with, and in subversion of, the Union.

—*Letters of H. G., XV*. N. Y. *Daily Advertiser*, April 11, 1789.

On General Nathanael Greene

After an indifferent start, the fighting Quaker from Rhode Island ended the war in a blaze of glory. Nathanael Greene had a high regard for the military abilities of Hamilton and the latter was one of Greene's most ardent admirers and supporters. When the general died, Hamilton assumed responsibility for straightening out the affairs of his debt-burdened estate. As Secretary of the Treasury, Hamilton was unfairly criticized for the action of one of his Treasury aides, who purchased a pay claim of an officer indebted to Greene and had the entire proceeds turned over to Greene's widow. Complaining that he was "the object of unprincipled persecution," Hamilton wrote Mrs. Greene: "I console myself . . . with this belief, that in spite of calumny the friends I love and esteem will continue to love and esteem me."

July 4, 1789

It is an observation, as just as it is common, that in those great revolutions which occasionally convulse society, human nature never fails to be brought forward in its brightest as well as in its blackest colors; and it has very properly been ranked not among the least of the advantages which compensate for the evils they produce that they serve to bring to light, talents and virtues, which might otherwise have languished in obscurity, or only shot forth a few scattered and wandering rays.

Nathaniel Greene, descended from reputable parents, but not placed by birth in that elevated rank which, under a monarchy, is the only sure road to those employments that give activity and scope to abilities, must, in all probability, have contented himself with the humble lot of a private citizen, or, at most, with the contracted sphere of an elective office, in a colonial and dependent government, scarcely conscious of the resources of his own mind, had not the violated rights of his country called him to act a part on a more splendid and more ample theatre. . .

As long as the measures which conducted us safely through the first most critical stages of the war shall be remembered with approbation; as long as the enterprises of Trenton and Princeton shall be regarded as the dawnings of that bright day which afterwards broke forth with such resplendent lustre; as long as the almost MAGIC OPERATIONS of the remainder of that memorable winter, distinguished not more by these events than by the extraordinary spectacle of a powerful army straitened within narrow limits by the phantom of a military force, and never permitted to transgress those limits with impunity, IN WHICH skill supplied the place of means, and disposition was the substitute for an army—as long, I say, as these operations shall continue to be the objects of curiosity and wonder, so long ought the name of Greene to be revered by a grateful country. To attribute to him a portion of the praise which is due, as well to the formation as to the execution of the plans that effected these important ends, can be no derogation from that wisdom and magnanimity which knew how to select and embrace counsels worthy of being pursued. . . .

Unwilling to do more than merely to glance at a scene in which the meritorious might be involved with the guilty, in promiscuous censure, here let me drop the curtain, and invite you to accompany me to the Heights of Monmouth. There let me recall to your indignant view, the flower of the American infantry flying before an enemy that scarcely dared to pursue—vanquished without a blow—vanquished by their obedience to the commands of a leader who meditated their disgrace. Let me contrast with this the conduct of your Greene; the calm intrepidity and unshaken presence of mind with which he seconded the dispositions of his General, to arrest the progress of the disorder and retrieve the fortune of the day. Let me recall to your recollection that well-timed and happy moment on the left of the enemy, by which he so materially contributed to deciding the dubious event of the conflict, and turning the hesitating scale of victory. . . .

The defeat of Camden, and the misfortune of Gates, opened the career of victory and of glory to Greene. . . .

To estimate properly the value of his services, it is necessary to recur to the situation of the southern extremity of the Union at the time he entered upon the command in that quarter. Georgia and South Carolina subdued and overrun; the spirit of their people dejected and intimidated; the flame of resistance scarcely kept alive by the transient gleams of a few expiring embers; North Carolina distracted by the still recent effects of internal commotion, dreading the hostility of a considerable part of its own citizens, and depending, for its exertions, on the tried valor and patriotism of the rest, more than on the energy of a feeble and ill-organized government; Virginia, debilitated by the excessive efforts of its early zeal, and by the dissipation of its revenues and forces, in Indian hostilities, in domestic projects, encumbered by a numerous body of slaves, bound by all the laws of degraded humanity to hate their masters; deficient in order and vigor in its administration, and relying wholly, for immediate defence against threatened invasion, on the resources of a country, extensive, populous, and fertile, to be put in motion by the same ardent and magnanimous spirit which first lighted up the opposition to Great Britain, and set the glorious example of resistance to America. In such a situation what was to be hoped? What was to be hoped from a general without troops, without magazines, without money? A man of less depth of penetration or force of soul than Greene, would have recoiled at the prospect; but he, far from desponding, undertook the arduous task with firmness—with a firmness which was the result of a well-informed estimate of a situation perilous but not desperate. He knew how much was to be expected from the efforts of men contending for the rights of man. He knew how much was to be performed by capacity, courage, and perseverance. . . .

To retard the progress of the British army was, of course, an indispensable policy on the part of Greene. For this purpose, he practised every expedient which a mind, fertile in resource, could devise. And so efficacious were the expedients he adopted, that, surmounting all the impediments in his way, he completed his retreat across the Dan, without loss of men, baggage, or stores.

Such, nevertheless, was the energy of the pursuit, that in crossing the three principal rivers, the Catawba, the Yadkin, and the Dan, the British troops, in a manner, trod upon the heels of the American. In the passage of the last of the three, the van of the enemy's army reached one shore, almost at the very moment that the rear of ours landed on the opposite.

Cornwallis, upon this occasion, imitating Charles the Twelfth of Sweden, when the celebrated Schulenburgh made good his retreat across the Oder, in spite of the utmost efforts of that vigorous and enterprising monarch, might, with propriety, have exclaimed, "This day, at least, Greene has conquered me!" The art of retreating is perhaps the most difficult in the art of war. To have effected a retreat in the face of so ardent a pursuit, through so great an extent of country; through a country offering every obstacle, affording scarcely any resource; with troops destitute of every thing, who a great part of the way left the vestiges of their march in their own blood;—to have done all this, I say, without loss of any kind may, without exaggeration, be denominated a masterpiece of military skill and exertion. Disappointed at his first aim, Cornwallis now retired from the Dan to Guilford Court-House. Having driven the American army out of North Carolina, he flattered himself that his efforts would at least be productive of the advantage of an accession of force, by encouraging the numerous royalists of that State to repair to his standard. Greene, not without apprehensions that the hopes of his competitor, in this respect, might be realized, lost not a moment, after receiving a small reinforcement from Virginia, in recrossing the Dan, to take post in the vicinity of the British army, and interrupt their communication with the country. Three weeks passed in a constant scene of military manoeuvre: Cornwallis, equally striving to bring his antagonist to an action; and Greene, adroitly endeavoring to elude it, yet without renouncing such a position as would enable him to prevent both supplies and reinforcements. On this occasion he played the part of Turenne; and he played it with complete success. The relative position which he took and maintained, and the tragical fate of a body of royalists, intercepted in their way to the British army, destroyed every prospect of that aid which they, not without reason, had promised themselves from their adherents in North Carolina.

Virginia, in the meantime, awakened by the presence of danger, exerted herself to reinforce the American army. Greene, speedily finding himself in a condition to outnumber his adversary, resolved to offer that battle which he had hitherto declined. He considered that, in the existing circumstances, a defeat must be, to the enemy, absolute ruin; while to him, from his superiority in cavalry, united with other advantages, it could be nothing more than a partial misfortune, and must be compensated at a price which the enemy could not afford to pay for it.

The two armies, now equally willing to try the fortune of a battle, met and engaged near Guilford Court-House. All that could be expected from able disposition towards insuring success, promised a favorable issue to the American arms. But superior discipline carried it against superior numbers and superior skill. Victory decreed the glory of the combat to the Britons; but Heaven, confirming the hopes of Greene, decreed the advantage of it to the Americans. Greene retired; Cornwallis kept the field. But Greene retired only three miles; and Cornwallis, in three days, abandoning the place where the laurels he had gained were a slender compensation for the loss he had suffered, withdrew to Wilmington on the sea-coast.

This victory cost him a large proportion of the flower of his army; and it cost him a Webster.

Here occurred the problem, on the right solution of which depended the fame of Greene and the fate of the Southern States. There was every probability that the next movement of Cornwallis would be towards a junction with Arnold for the invasion of Virginia. Was the American general to keep pace with his adversary in his northern career, in order to resist his future enterprises? Or, was he to return into the field he had lately left, to endeavor to regain what had been there lost? The first, as the most obvious, and, in a personal light, the least perilous course, would have been thought the most eligible by an ordinary mind. But the last, as the wisest, though, to his own reputation, the most hazardous, appeared preferable to the comprehensive eye and adventurous *enterprising* spirit of a Greene.

On the one hand, he concluded, justly, that Virginia might safely be trusted to her own strength and resources, and to the aid which, if necessary, she might derive from the North, against all the force which the enemy were then able to employ in that quarter. On the other hand, he foresaw, that if South Carolina and Georgia should be abandoned to the situation in which they then were, they would quickly have abandoned themselves to despair; would have lost even the spirit of opposition; and might have been rendered, in several respects, subservient to the future progress of their conqueror. Under these impressions, he determined to return into South Carolina, to attempt the recovery of that and its neighboring State.

This was one of those strokes that denote superior genius, and constitute the sublime of war. 'Twas Scipio leaving Hannibal in Italy, to overcome him at Carthage!

The success was answerable to the judicious boldness of the design. The enemy were divested of their acquisitions in South Carolina and Georgia, with a rapidity which, if not ascertained, would scarcely be credible. In the short space of two months, all their posts in the interior of the country were reduced. The perseverance, courage, enterprise, and resource, displayed by the American general in the course of these events, commanded the admiration even of his enemies.

—"Eulogium on Major-General Greene." Hamilton Papers, 1st ser.

On von Steuben

Although Hamilton had reservations about some of the foreign officers in the Continental army, he soon learned to appreciate the contribution that von Steuben's instruction in drill made to the battlefield conduct of the troops, notably at Monmouth. Only a few weeks after Hamilton wrote this letter to Duer, Washington was writing Gouverneur Morris: "Although I think the Baron an excellent officer, I do most devoutly wish that we had not a single foreigner among us, except the Marquis de Lafayette, who acts upon very different principles from those which govern the rest." After the war, Hamilton and other influential friends of the baron, through a friendly mortgage of his New York lands, arranged to settle his debts and stave off bankruptcy.

HEADQUARTERS June 18, 1778

I take the liberty to trouble you with a few hints on a matter of some importance. Baron Steuben, who will be the bearer of this, waits on Congress to have his office arranged upon some decisive and permanent footing. It will not be amiss to be on your guard. The Baron is a gentleman for whom I have a particular esteem, and whose zeal, intelligence, and success, the consequence of both, entitle him to the greatest credit. But I am apprehensive, with all his good qualities, [that] a fondness for power and importance, natural to every man, may lead him to wish for more extensive prerogatives in his department than it will be for the good of the service to grant. I should be sorry to excite any prejudice against him on this account; perhaps I may be mistaken in my conjecture. The caution I give will do no harm if I am; if I am not, it may be useful. In either case, the Baron deserves to be considered as a valuable man and treated with all the deference which good policy will warrant.

—To William Duer, M.C. Hamilton Papers, 1st ser.

November 23, 1785

The poor *Baron* is still soliciting Congress, and has every prospect of indigence before him. He has his imprudences, but, upon the whole, he has rendered valuable services, and his merits and the reputation of the country alike demand that he should not be left to suffer want.

—To Washington. Hamilton's hand. Hamilton Papers, 1st ser.

On "Light Horse Harry" Lee

The high-spirited and mettlesome subject of this letter staged a daring capture of the British fort at Paulus Hook (now Jersey City), and managed to elude his pursuers and get back to the American lines with a bag of prisoners. Lee was then court-martialed on some petty charges and acquitted with honor.

WEST POINT September 11, 1779

. . . The Philadelphia papers will tell you of a handsome stroke by Lee on Powle's Hook. Some folks in the Virginia line, jealous of his glory, had the folly to get him arrested. He has been tried and acquitted with the highest honor. Lee unfolds himself more and more to be an officer of great capacity, and if he had not a little spice of the Julius Caesar or Cromwell in him, he would be a very clever fellow. Adieu.

—To John Laurens. *Works*, IX, 174.

On Lafayette

Lafayette came to America a callow youth and a stanch monarchist. By the end of the Revolution his political thinking had matured and he had come abreast of liberal and Revolutionary ideas. To this change, the close association with his bosom companion, Alexander Hamilton, contributed enormously, for the latter had a precocity and political profundity which the dashing Frenchman lacked. Hamilton and Lafayette fought together on some of the darkest days of the war, and on some of the brightest—at Monmouth and at Yorktown, where Hamilton served under Lafayette's command. Hamilton backed up Lafayette in urging that Washington rebuke Sullivan for his general order criticizing the conduct of Admiral d'Estaing during the Rhode Island campaign. Lafayette tried in every way to get Hamilton a command in the field and to patch up the short-lived quarrel between Hamilton and Washington.

In personality, temperament, and a sense of foreignness, Lafayette and Hamilton had much in common. To Hamilton, Lafayette spoke of "our adopted compatriots," *language he could not have used to a native-born American. Hamilton, Lafayette wrote his wife Adrienne, is* "a man whom I love very much." *Francophobes like John Adams predicted that* "this mongrel character of French patriot and American patriot cannot exist long," *but Hamilton, who knew Lafayette ever so much better, had complete faith in his friend's dedication to American liberty, a faith justified by Lafayette's later career.*

May, 1795

P. S.—I had almost forgotten a principal object of this letter. It concerns the Marquis Lafayette. In conversation, I think, but certainly by letter (this *entre nous*), I suggested to Mr. Jay that, in case the treaty with Great Britain turned favorably, it will be well to hint to the British minister that the United States took a very particular interest in the welfare of Lafayette, and that the good offices of that country, to procure his liberation, would be regarded as a valuable mark of friendship. I believe I also had some conversation, in the same spirit, either with the President or the Secretary of State; but I do not remember if any thing was done.

—To William Bradford. Works, X, 100.

October 16, 1795

I even venture to think it possible that the time is not very remote when the marquis will again recover the confidence and esteem of his country, when perhaps the men in power may be glad to glorify themselves and their cause with his alliance.

—To Washington. Hamilton Papers, 1st ser.

On Robert Morris

[1782]

There has been no material change in our internal situation since you left us. The capital successes we have had have served rather to increase the hopes than the exertions of the particular States. But in one respect we are in a mending way. Our financier has hitherto conducted himself with great ability, has acquired an entire personal confidence, revived in some measure the public credit, and is conciliating fast the support of the moneyed men. His operations have hitherto hinged chiefly on the seasonable aids from your country; but he is urging the establishment of permanent funds among ourselves; and though, from the nature and temper of our governments, his applications will meet with a dilatory compliance, it is to be hoped they will by degrees succeed. . . .

Upon the whole, however, if the war continues another year, it will be necessary that Congress should again recur to the generosity of France for pecuniary assistance. The plans of the financier cannot be so matured as to enable us by any possibility to dispense with this; and if he should fail for want of support, we must replunge into that confusion and distress which had liked to have proved fatal to us, and out of which we are slowly emerging. The cure, on a relapse, would be infinitely more difficult than ever.

—To De Noailles. *Hamilton,* I, 314-317.

April, 1783

As to Mr. Morris, I will give your Excellency a true explanation of his conduct. He had been for some time pressing Congress to endeavor to obtain funds, and had found a great backwardness in the business. He found the taxes unproductive in the different States; he found the loans in Europe making a very slow progress; he found himself pressed on all hands for supplies; he found himself, in short, reduced to this alternative: either of making engagements which he could not fulfil, or declaring his resignation in case funds were not established by a given time. Had he followed the first course, the bubble must soon have burst; he must have sacrificed his credit and his character, and public credit, already in a ruinous condition, would have lost its last support.

He wisely judged it better to resign. This might increase the embarrassments of the moment; but the necessity of the case, it was to be hoped, would produce the proper measures; and he might then resume the direction of the machine with advantage and success.

He also had some hope that his resignation would prove a stimulus to Congress.

He was, however, ill advised in the publication of his letters of resignation. This was an imprudent step, and has given a handle to his personal enemies, who, by playing upon the passions of others, have drawn some well-meaning men into the cry against him. But Mr. Morris certainly deserves a great deal from his country. I believe no man in this country but himself could have kept the money machine a-going during the period he has been in office. From every thing that appears, his administration has been upright as well as able.

The truth is, the old leaven of Deane and Lee[1] is, at this day, working against Mr. Morris. He happened, in that dispute, to have been on the side of Deane; and certain men can never forgive him. A man whom I once esteemed, and whom I will rather suppose *duped* than wicked, is the second actor in this business.

—To Washington. Hamilton's hand. Dated in endorsement by Washington. Hamilton Papers, 1st ser.

On John Jay

PHILADELPHIA July 25, 1783

. . . I have been witness with pleasure to every event which has had a tendency to advance you in the esteem of your country, and I may assure you with sincerity that it is as high as you could possibly wish. All have united in the warmest approbation of your conduct. I cannot forbear telling you this, because my situation has given me access to the truth, and I gratify my friendship for you in communicating what cannot fail to gratify your sensibility.

The peace, which exceeds in the goodness of its terms the expectations of the most sanguine, does the highest honor to those who made it. It is the more agreeable, as the time was come when thinking men began to be seriously alarmed at the internal embarrassments and exhausted state of this country.

—To John Jay. *Works*, IX, 381.

On James Madison

November 23, 1788

I could console myself for what you mention respecting yourself, from a desire to see you in one of the executive departments, did I

[1] A reference to the feud between Silas Deane and Arthur Lee, both American agents in France. Lee accused Deane of extravagance and dishonesty. Congress was sharply divided on this issue.—Ed.

not perceive the representation will be defective in characters of a certain description. Wilson is evidently out of the question. King tells me he does not believe he will be elected into either House. Mr. Gouverneur Morris set out to-day for France, by way of Philadelphia. If you are not in one of the branches, the government may sincerely feel the want of men who unite to zeal all the requisite qualifications for parrying the machinations of its enemies. Might I advise, it would be, that you bent your course to Virginia.

—To James Madison. *Hamilton*, I, 488-490.

October 12, 1789

. . . As I lost the opportunity of a personal communication, may I ask of your friendship, to put to paper and send me your thoughts on such objects as may have occurred to you, for an addition to our revenue, and also as to any modifications of the public debt, which could be made consistent with good faith—the interest of the public and of the creditors.

—To James Madison, Jr. *Works*, IX, 462.

May 26, 1792

In almost all the questions, great and small, which have arisen since the first session of Congress, Mr. Jefferson and Mr. Madison have been found among those who are disposed to narrow the federal authority. The question of a national bank is one example. The question of bounties to the fisheries is another. Mr. Madison resisted it on the ground of constitutionality, till it was evident, by the intermediate questions taken, that the bill would pass; and he then, under the wretched subterfuge of a change of a single word, "bounty" for "allowance," went over to the majority, and voted for the bill. . . .

This kind of conduct has appeared to me the more extraordinary on the part of Mr. Madison, as I know for a certainty, it was a primary article in his creed, that the real danger in our system was the subversion of the national authority by the preponderancy of the State governments.

—To Colonel Edward Carrington. *Works*, IX, 526-527.

On Edmund Randolph

In August, 1795, Washington forced Edmund Randolph to resign as Secretary of State on the ground that he had intrigued with the French minister, Joseph Fauchet, to block the ratification of Jay's Treaty. He was accused of being in the pay of the French, but that was never proven. At the least, however, he was guilty of serious indiscretion in office.

October 16, 1795

There is another subject upon which I will hazard a few words. It is that of Mr. Randolph. I have seen the intercepted letter,[1] which, I presume, led to his resignation. I read it with regret, but without much surprise, for I never had any confidence in Mr. Randolph, and I thought there were very suspicious appearances about him on the occasion to which the letter particularly refers.

I perceive that, rendered desperate, he meditates as much mischief as he can. The letter he calls for, I presume, is that above alluded to. His object is, if he obtains it, to prejudice others; if any part is kept back, to derive advantage to his cause from the idea that there may be some thing reserved which would tend to his exculpation, and to produce the suspicion that there is some thing which you are interested to keep from the light.

Though, from the state of public prejudices, I shall probably for one be a sufferer by the publication; yet, upon the whole, I incline to the opinion that it is most advisable the whole should come before the public. I acknowledge that I do not express this opinion without hesitation, and therefore it will deserve, as it will no doubt engage, your mature reflection; but such is the present bias of my judgment. I am the more inclined to the opinion, as I presume that the subject being in part before the public, the whole letter will finally come out through the quarter by which it was written, and then it would have additional weight to produce ill impressions.

—To Washington. Hamilton Papers, 1st ser.

December 24, 1795

I have read with care Mr. Randolph's pamphlet. It does not surprise me. I consider it as amounting to a confession of guilt; and I am persuaded this will be the universal opinion. His attempts against you are viewed by all whom I have seen, as base. They will certainly fail of their aim, and will do good, rather than harm, to the public cause and to yourself. It appears to me that, by you, no notice can be, or ought to be, taken of the publication. It contains its own antidote.

—To Washington. Hamilton's hand. Hamilton Papers, 1st ser.

On General James Wilkinson

Hamilton had doubts about Wilkinson's character, but that arch double-dealer who became a secret pensioner of Spain, made himself indispensable to the military arm of the government. Despite his later

[1] From Joseph Fauchet, French minister to the United States, intercepted by the British and turned over to Oliver Wolcott, Hamilton's successor.—Ed.

complicity in Aaron Burr's intrigues, he was entrusted with an important command during the War of 1812, where his mismanagement proved disastrous.

June 15, 1799

I have just received a letter from General Wilkinson, dated the 13th April, in which he assures me he will set out in the ensuing month for the seat of government. The interview with him will be useful.

It strikes me forcibly, that it will be both right and expedient to advance this gentleman to the grade of major-general. He has been long steadily in service, and long a brigadier. This, in so considerable an extension of the military establishment, gives him a pretension to promotion.

I am aware that some doubts have been entertained of him, and that his character on certain sides, gives room for doubt. Yet he is at present in the service, is a man of more than ordinary talent, of courage and enterprise; has discovered upon various occasions a good zeal, has embraced military pursuits as a profession, and will naturally find his interest, as an ambitious man, in deserving the favor of the government; while he will be apt to become disgusted, if neglected; and through disgust may be rendered really what he is now only suspected to be. Under such circumstances, it seems to me good policy to avoid all just grounds of discontent, and to make it the interest of the individual to pursue his duty.

—To Washington (Private). Hamilton Papers, 1st ser.

On Gouverneur Morris

In the celebrated oration delivered at the funeral of Hamilton, Gouverneur Morris charged his listeners to protect Hamilton's fame. "It is all he has left—all that these poor orphan children will inherit from their father. But, my countrymen, that fame may be a rich treasure to you also. Let it be the test by which to examine those who solicit your favor. Disregarding professions, view their conduct, and on a doubtful occasion, ask, Would Hamilton have done this thing?"

October 2, 1798

Why does not Gouverneur Morris come home? His talents are wanted. Men like him do not super-abound.

—To Rufus King. *Hamilton*, VI, 362-363.

On Rufus King

Hamilton persuaded Rufus King, the Massachusetts lawyer, to come to New York, and then, in backing King for the Senate, committed a major political blunder. In ignoring the claims to that post of Robert R. Livingston, he permanently antagonized the powerful Livingston family, who shared control of New York politics with Hamilton's father-in-law, Philip Schuyler, and had been on Hamilton's side at the New York ratifying convention. Hamilton successfully urged King's appointment as minister to Great Britain.

May 10, 1796

While I have my pen in my hand, give me leave to mention a particular subject to you. Mr. Pinckney, it is said, desires to return to the United States. In this case a successor will be wanted. If we had power to make a man for the purpose, we could not imagine a fitter than Mr. King. He is tired of the Senate, and I fear will resign at all events. I presume he would accept the mission to England. Can there be a doubt that it will be wise to offer it to him?

—To Timothy Pickering. *Works*, X, 164-165.

May 20, 1796

. . . Mr. King is a remarkably well-informed man, a very judicious one, a man of address, a man of fortune and economy, whose situation affords just ground of confidence;—a man of unimpeached probity where he is best known, a firm friend to the government, a supporter of the measures of the President—a man who cannot but feel that he has strong pretensions to confidence and trust.

—To Washington. Hamilton Papers, 1st ser.

12

On Life and Death

Am I, then, more of an American than those who drew their first breath on American ground?

Birth, Youth, and Family Ties

Few letters are extant about Alexander Hamilton's early life. Hamilton said little about his boyhood and wrote less. The reason is obvious. It is best to forget the past when the past holds humiliation, poverty, and tragedy. If you are driven by ambition it is perhaps easy to do so.

Hamilton was illegitimate. He was the offspring of a liaison between Rachel Faucitt and James Hamilton. Rachel was the beautiful daughter of British parents, whose own marriage had gone on the rocks. Her ambitious mother arranged her marriage on the island of Nevis in the British West Indies to John Michael Lavien (or Levine). Tradition in the Hamilton family made Lavien Jewish, but this is highly improbable. Lavien was a flashy, middle-aged Danish planter, who moved his young bride to the Danish island of St. Croix, but could not hold her. Rachel quickly came to detest him. She ran away and was jailed on her husband's orders under the curious laws of the island. When she was discharged she refused a reconciliation. Abandoning her four-year old son, Peter, she returned to Nevis. There she met the thirty-three year old Scottish merchant, James Hamilton, a younger son of the Laird of Cambuskeith, but something of a drifter and ne'er-do-well, albeit a charming one. Since no divorce was obtainable in the British West Indies Rachel and James set up a home together without benefit of clergy or courts. They had two sons, James, Jr., who was born in 1753, and, a few years later, another son, Alexander.

Hamilton celebrated January 11th as his birthday, but was vague on the year. On the basis of a letter he wrote to a relative in Scotland in

1797, it was generally believed that he was born in the year 1757. However, the records of the Danish probate court in St. Croix which ruled on the distribution of his mother's estate refer to her two "obscene children," and give Hamilton's age in the year 1768 as thirteen, not eleven, indicating their belief that he was born in 1755. This is certainly not conclusive, but it is the best evidence we have.[1]

Lavien was not a patient man, and his situation was humiliating. His wife was living in flagrant adultery. He sued for divorce, and in his petition cited Alexander Hamilton as one of the illegitimate children of Rachel's union with the correspondent James Hamilton. His petition was granted.

Meantime, James Hamilton had gone bankrupt, and young Alexander was brought up in genteel poverty. His mother saw to his early education, sent him to a Jewish school, where his teacher stood him on a table and made him recite the Ten Commandments in Hebrew, and, in addition, gave him a solid grounding in the three r's. Alexander was a precocious student and an avid reader.

In 1765, the year the colonies were seething with protest over the Stamp Act, James Hamilton moved his family from British Nevis to Danish St. Croix, where he had employment awaiting him, but he soon left his wife and two sons for work on another island. Rachel never saw him again. Abandoned by husband and lover, she opened a shop, using the name Rachel Lewine, and sent Alexander to St. John's School, where he made a new and lasting friend, Edward (Ned) Stevens. Alexander took a job as an apprentice clerk in the office of the New York merchants, Cruger and Beekman, where he demonstrated his flair for business and administration. On the death of young Hamilton's mother from a fever in 1768, the probate court awarded all her property to Peter Lavien, son of John and Rachel, leaving Alexander penniless. Hence, his understandable lack of affection for his half-brother and his pardonable desire to get what was his due on the latter's death. Alexander now moved in with Nicholas Cruger and shunned further contact with most of his relatives. He began to handle business transactions on his own account. But he was lonesome. His friend, Ned Stevens, had gone to King's College in New York. Young Hamilton's frustration and ambition are explicit in his early letter to Ned.

In 1771 Hamilton met Hugh Knox, a Presbyterian clergyman who had just come to St. Croix. Knox was greatly impressed by the boy, an impression which was heightened by a remarkable letter Hamilton wrote describing the great storm which gutted the town on August 30,

[1] Recently a wedding ring, reputedly given by Hamilton to Eliza Schuyler, has come to light. In addition to the names of the couple and the date of the wedding, the engraving on the ring records the dates of birth of the parties. Hamilton's appears as "Jan. 11, 1757." If the ring is authentic, it represents the earliest known statement by Hamilton of his exact age.

1772. Knox saw to it that the letter was published in the Royal Danish-American Gazette, *where it appeared on October 3d of that year. Now, Knox felt, Hamilton was truly wasted on the island. He should go to Princeton. Knox arranged for Hamilton to go first to a grammar school at Elizabethtown, New Jersey, in preparation for college. Actually, Hamilton entered King's College (now Columbia) because Princeton refused to take him as a student with advanced standing. Hamilton sailed in midsummer of 1773 as supercargo in Cruger's ship,* Thunderbolt. *His life as an American was about to start.*

These are a few letters dealing with those early days:

St. Croix, November 11, 1769

As to what you say respecting your having soon the happiness of seeing us all, I wish for an accomplishment of your hopes, provided they are concomitant with your welfare; otherwise not; though I doubt whether I shall be present or not, for, to confess my weakness, Ned, my ambition is so prevalent, so that I contemn the grovelling condition of a clerk or the like, to which my fortune, etc., condemns me, and would willingly risk my life, though not my character, to exalt my station. I am confident, Ned, that my youth excludes me from any hopes of immediate preferment; nor do I desire it; but I mean to prepare the way for futurity. I'm no philosopher, you see, and may be justly said to build castles in the air; my folly makes me ashamed, and I beg you'll conceal it; yet, Neddy, we have seen such schemes successful when the projector is constant. I shall conclude saying, I wish there was a war.

—To Edward Stevens. (Copy). Hamilton Papers, 1st ser.

THE HURRICANE LETTER

October 3, 1772

CHRISTIANSTAED

The following letter was written the week after the late Hurricane, by a Youth of this Island, to his Father; the copy of it fell by accident into the hands of a gentleman, who, being pleased with it himself, shewed it to others to whom it gave equal satisfaction, and who all agreed that it might not prove unentertaining to the Publick. The Author's modesty in long refusing to submit it to Public view, is the reason of its making its appearance so late as it now does.

St. Croix, Sept. 6, 1772

Honoured Sir,

I TAKE up my pen just to give you an imperfect account of one of the most dreadful Hurricanes that memory or any records whatever can trace, which happened here on the 31st ultimo at night.

It began about dusk, at North, and raged very violently till ten o'clock. Then ensued a sudden and unexpected interval, which lasted about an hour. Meanwhile the wind was shifting round to the South West point, from whence it returned with redoubled fury and continued so 'till near three o'clock in the morning. Good God! what horror and destruction—it's impossible for me to describe—or you to form any idea of it. It seemed as if a total dissolution of nature was taking place. The roaring of the sea and wind—fiery meteors flying about it in the air—the prodigious glare of almost perpetual lightning—the crash of the falling houses—and the ear-piercing shrieks of the distressed, were sufficient to strike astonishment into Angels. A great part of the buildings throughout the Island are levelled to the ground—almost all the rest very much shattered—several persons killed and numbers utterly ruined—whole families running about the streets, unknowing where to find a place of shelter—the sick exposed to the keeness of water and air—without a bed to lie upon—or a dry covering to their bodies—and our harbours entirely bare. In a word, misery, in all its most hideous shapes, spread over the whole face of the country.—A strong smell of gunpowder added somewhat to the terrors of the night; and it was observed that the rain was surprizingly salt. Indeed the water is so brackish and full of sulphur that there is hardly any drinking it.

My reflections and feelings on this frightful and melancholy occasion, are set forth in the following self-discourse.

Where now, oh! vile worm, is all thy boasted fortitude and resolution? what is become of thy arrogance and self-sufficiency?—why dost thou tremble and stand aghast? how humble—how helpless—how contemptible you now appear. And for why? the jarring elements—the discords of clouds? Oh! impotent presumptuous fool! how durst thou offend that Omnipotence, whose nod alone were sufficient to quell the destruction that hovers over thee, or crush thee into atoms? see thy wretched helpless state, and learn to know thyself. Learn to know the best support. Despise thyself, and adore thy God. How sweet—how unutterably sweet were now, the voice of an approving conscience. Then couldst thou say—hence ye idle alarms, why do I shrink? what have I to fear? a pleasing calm suspense! a short repose from calamity to end in eternal bliss? Let the Earth rend—let the planets forsake their course—let the Sun be extinguished and the Heavens burst asunder—yet what have I to dread? my staff can never be broken—in Omnipotence I trusted. . . .

Thus did I reflect, and thus at every gust of the wind, did I conclude, —'till it pleased the Almighty to allay it.—Nor did my emotions proceed either from the suggestions of too much natural fear, or a conscience overburthened with crimes of an uncommon cast.—I thank God, this was not the case. The scenes of horror exhibited around us, naturally awakened such ideas in every thinking breast, and aggravated the deformity of every failing of our lives. It were a lamentable insensibility indeed, not to have had such feelings—and I think inconsistent with human nature.

Our distressed, helpless condition taught us humility and contempt of ourselves—The horrors of the night—the prospect of an immediate, cruel death—or, as one may say, of being crushed by the Almighty in his anger—filled us with terror. And every thing that had tended to weaken our interest with him, upbraided us in the strongest colours, with our baseness and folly.—That which, in a calm unruffled temper, we call a natural cause, seemed then like the correction of the Deity.—Our imagination represented him as an incensed master, executing vengeance on the crimes of his servants.—The father and benefactor were forgot, and in that view, a consciousness of our guilt filled us with despair.

But see, the Lord relents—he hears our prayer—the Lightning ceases—the winds are appeased—the warring elements are reconciled and all things promise peace.—The darkness is dispell'd—and drooping nature revives at the approaching dawn. Look back Oh! my soul—look back and tremble.—Rejoice at thy deliverance, and humble thyself in the presence of thy deliverer.

Yet hold, Oh vain mortal!—check thy ill timed joy. Art thou so selfish to exult because thy lot is happy in a season of universal woe? Hast thou no feelings for the miseries of thy fellow-creatures? and art thou incapable of the soft pangs of sympathetic sorrow?—Look around thee and shudder at the view. See desolation and ruin where'er thou turnest thine eye? . . . Hark the bitter groans of distress. . . . Oh distress unspeakable! my heart bleeds—but I have no power to solace!—O ye, who revel in affluence, see the afflictions of humanity and bestow your superfluity to ease them.—Say not, we have suffered also, and thence withhold your compassion. What are your sufferings compared to those?—ye have still more than enough left. Act wisely—succour the miserable and lay up a treasure in Heaven.

I am afraid, Sir, you will think this description more the effort of imagination than a true picture of realities. But I can affirm with the greatest truth, that there is not a single circumstance touched upon, which I have not absolutely been an eye witness to.

Our General[1] has issued several very salutary and humane regulations, and both in his publick and private measures, has shewn himself *the Man.*

—*Royal Danish-American Gazette* (St. Croix),
Oct. 3, 1772.

[1] This is a reference to the Danish governor, Ulrich Vilhelm v. Roepstorff.—Ed.

[c. 1782]

Engrossed by our own immediate concerns, I omitted telling you of a disagreeable piece of intelligence I have received from a gentleman of Georgia. He tells me of the death of my brother Levine. You know the circumstances that abate my distress, yet my heart acknowledges the rights of a brother. He dies rich, but has disposed of the bulk of his fortune to strangers. I am told he has left me a legacy. I did not inquire how much. . . .

—To Elizabeth Hamilton. Hamilton Papers

June 23, 1785

. . . The situation you describe yourself to be in gives me much pain, and nothing will make me happier than, as far as may be in my power, to contribute to your relief. I will cheerfully pay your draft upon me for fifty pounds sterling whenever it shall appear. I wish it was in my power to desire you to enlarge this sum; but, though my future prospects are of the most flattering kind, my present engagements would render it inconvenient to me to advance a larger sum. My affection for you, however, will not permit me to be inattentive to your welfare, and I hope time will prove to you that I feel all the sentiments of a brother. Let me only to request of you to exert your industry for a year or two more where you are, and at the end of that time I promise myself to be able to invite you to a more comfortable settlement in this country. But what has become of our dear father? It is an age since I have heard from him, or of him, though I have written him several letters. Perhaps, alas, he is no more, and I shall not have the pleasing opportunity of contributing to render the close of his life more happy than the progress of it. My heart bleeds at the recollection of his misfortunes and embarrassments. Sometimes I flatter myself his brothers have extended their support to him, and that he now enjoys tranquillity and ease. At other times I fear he is suffering in indigence. Should he be alive, inform him of my inquiries; beg him to write to me, and tell him how ready I shall be to devote myself and all I have to his accommodation and happiness. I do not advise your coming to this country at present, for the war has also put things out of order here, and people in your business find a subsistence difficult enough. My object will be, by and by, to get you settled on a farm.

—To James Hamilton, Jr.,—St. Thomas. *Works,* IX, 405-406.

July 25, 1795

I hesitated whether I would not also secure a preference to the drafts of my father, but these, as far as I am concerned, being a voluntary engagement, I doubted the justice of the measure, and I have done nothing. I repeat it lest they should return upon him and increase his distress. Though as I am informed, a man of respectable connections in Scotland, he became, as a merchant, bankrupt at an early day in the West Indies and is now in indigence. I have pressed him to come to us, but his age and infirmity have deterred him from the change of climate.

—To Robert Troup. Hamilton Papers, 1st ser.

May 2, 1797

. . . You, no doubt, have understood that my father's affairs at a very early day went to wreck, so as to have rendered his situation during the greatest part of his life far from eligible. This state of things occasioned a separation between him and me, when I was very young, and threw me upon the bounty of my mother's relatives, some of whom were then wealthy, though by vicissitudes to which human affairs are so liable, they have been since much reduced and broken up. Myself, at about sixteen, came to this country. Having always had a strong propensity to literary pursuits, by a course of study and laborious exertion, I was able, by the age of nineteen, to qualify myself for the degree of Bachelor of Arts in the College of New York, and to lay the foundation by preparatory study for the future profession of the law. . . .

Public office in this country has few attractions. The pecuniary emolument is so inconsiderable as to amount to a sacrifice to any man who can employ his time with advantage in any liberal profession. The opportunity of doing good, from the jealousy of power and the spirit of faction, is too small in any station to warrant a long continuance of private sacrifices. The enterprises of party had so far succeeded as materially to weaken the necessary influence and energy of the executive authority, and so far diminish the power of doing good in that department, as greatly to take away the motives which a virtuous man might have for making sacrifices. The prospect was even bad for gratifying in future the love of fame, if that passion was to be the spring of action. . . .

In the year 1780, I married the second daughter of General Schuyler, a gentleman of one of the best families of this country, of large fortune, and no less personal and political consequence. It is impossible to be happier than I am in a wife; and I have five children, four sons and a daughter, the eldest a son somewhat past fifteen, who all promise well as far as their years permit, and yield me much satisfaction. Though I have been too much in public life to be wealthy, my situation is extremely comfortable, and leaves me nothing to wish for but a continuance of health. With this blessing, the profits of my profession and other prospects authorize an expectation of such addition to my resources, as will render the eve of life easy and agreeable; so far as may depend on this consideration.

It is now several months since I have heard from my father, who continued at the island of St. Vincents. My anxiety at this silence would be greater than it is, were it not for the considerable interruption and precariousness of intercourse which is produced by the war.

I have strongly pressed the old gentleman to come and reside with me, which would afford him every enjoyment of which his advanced age is capable; but he has declined it on the ground that the advice of his physicians leads him to fear that the change of climate would be fatal to him. The next thing for me is, in proportion to my means, to endeavor to increase his comforts where he is.

—To Alexander Hamilton, Laird of Cambuskeith. Hamilton's hand. Hamilton Papers, 1st ser.

Friendship

At the end of the war, long after Yorktown, John Laurens, Hamilton's bosom friend, was killed in a skirmish in the South.

December, 1779

Cold in my professions, warm in my friendships, I wish, my dear Laurens, it [may] be in my power, by actions rather than words, [to] convince you that I love you. I shall only tell you that, till you bade us adieu, I hardly knew the value you had taught my heart to set upon you. Indeed, my friend, it was not well done. You know the opinion I entertain of mankind, and how much it is my desire to preserve myself free from particular attachments, and to keep my happiness independent of the caprices of others. You should not have taken advantage of my sensibility to steal into my affections without my consent.

But as you have done it and as we are generally indulgent to those we love, I shall not scruple to pardon the fraud you have committed, on one condition: that for my sake, if not for your own, you will always continue to merit the partiality, which you have so artfully instilled into [me.]

—To John Laurens. Draft in Hamilton's hand; date in later hand. Hamilton Papers, 1st ser.

ALBANY October 12, 1782

I feel the deepest affliction at the news we have just received of the loss of our dear and estimable friend Laurens. His career of virtue is at an end. How strangely are human affairs conducted, that so many excellent qualities could not insure a more happy fate! The world will feel the loss of a man who has left few like him behind, and America of a citizen whose heart realized that patriotism of which others only talk. I shall feel the loss of a friend I truly and most tenderly loved, and one of a very small number.

—To General Nathanael Greene. Hamilton Papers, 1st ser.

Husband and Father

. . . I love you too much.

Underneath the joshing note in Hamilton's letter to John Laurens lay a serious intention. If he had to marry he would prefer a wife who was pretty, well-bred, wealthy—and chaste. Elizabeth Schuyler filled all these specifications. She was the daughter of General Philip Schuyler, a great landowner and political figure in New York. Her marriage to Alexander on December 14, 1780 was an important step in his career. Elizabeth was completely devoted to her husband. Until the end he was to her an untarnished hero. Hamilton loved her deeply despite his occasional flirtations and deviations from his marital vows. "I have told you and I told you truly that I love you too much," he wrote her on the eve of marriage. "You engross my thoughts too entirely to allow me to think of anything else." There were eight children of the marriage, and as marriages go it was a very good one. The letters between Hamilton and Elizabeth are extremely tender and affectionate.

December, 1779

I anticipate by sympathy the pleasure you must feel from the sweet converse of your dearer self in the enclosed letters. I hope they may be recent. They were brought out of New York by General Thompson, delivered to him there by a Mrs. Moore, not long from England, *soi disante parente de madame votre épouse.* She speaks of a daughter of yours,—well, when she left England, [ ][1] and now, my dear, as we are upon the subject of wife, I empower and command you to get me one in Carolina. Such a wife as I want will, I know, be difficult to be found, but if you succeed, it will be the stronger proof of your zeal and dexterity. Take her description—she must be young, handsome (I lay most stress upon a good shape), sensible (a little learning will do), well bred (but she must have an aversion to the word *ton*), chaste, and tender (I am an enthusiast in my notions of fidelity and fondness), of some good nature, a great deal of generosity (she must neither love money nor scolding, for I dislike equally a termagant and an economist). In politics I am indifferent what side she may be of. I think I have arguments that will easily convert her to mine. As to religion a

[1] Several words obliterated here.

moderate stock will satisfy me. She must believe in God and hate a saint.

But as to fortune, the larger stock of that the better. You know my temper and circumstances and will therefore pay special attention in this article of the treaty. Though I run no risk of going to Purgatory for my avarice, yet as money is an essential ingredient to happiness in this world, as I have not much of my own, and as I am very little calculated to get more either by my address or industry, it must needs be that my wife, if I get one, bring at least a sufficiency to administer to her own extravagancies. *N. B.*—You will be pleased to recollect in your negotiations that I have no invincible antipathy to the *maidenly beauties*, and that I am willing to take the *trouble* of them upon myself.

If you should not readily meet with a lady that you think answers my description, you can only advertise in the public papers, and doubtless you will hear of many competitors for most of the quaifications required, who will be glad to become candidates for such a prize as I am. To excite their emulations it will be necessary for you to give an account of the lover—his *size*, make, qualities of mind and *body*, achievements, expectations, fortune, etc. In drawing my picture you will no doubt be civil to your friend, mind you do justice to the length of my nose, and don't forget that I— [ ][1]

After reviewing what I have written, I am ready to ask myself what could have put it into my head to hazard this jeu *de folie*. Do I want a wife? No. I have plagues enough without desiring to add to the number that greatest of all; and if I were silly enough to do it I should take care how I employed a proxy. Did I mean to show my wit? If I did, I am sure I have missed my aim. Did I only intend to [frisk?] In this I have succeeded, but I have done [more.] I have gratified my feelings, by lengthening [out] the only kind of intercourse now in my pow[er,] with my friend.

—To John Laurens. Hamilton Papers, 1st ser.

August, 1781

In my last letter I informed you that there was a greater prospect of activity now, than there had been heretofore. I did this to prepare your mind for an event which, I am sure, will give you pain. I begged your father, at the same time, to intimate to you, by degrees, the probability of its taking place. I used this method to prevent a surprise, which might be too severe to you. A part of the army, my dear girl, is going to Virginia, and I must, of necessity, be separated at a much greater distance from my beloved wife. I cannot announce the fatal necessity, without feeling every thing that a fond husband can feel. I am unhappy; I am unhappy beyond expression. I am unhappy, because I am to be so remote from you; because I am to hear from you less fre-

[1] Words crossed out.

quently than I am accustomed to do. I am miserable, because I know you will be so; I am wretched at the idea of flying so far from you, without a single hour's interview, to tell you all my pains and all my love. But I cannot ask permission to visit you. It might be thought improper to leave my corps at such a time and upon such an occasion. I must go without seeing you—I must go without embracing you;—alas! I must go. But let no idea, other than of the distance we shall be asunder, disquiet you. Though I said the prospects of activity will be greater, I said it to give your expectations a different turn, and prepare you for something disagreeable. It is ten to one that our views will be disappointed, by Cornwallis retiring to South Carolina by land. At all events, our operations will be over by the latter end of October, and I will fly to my home. Don't mention I am going to Virginia.

—To Elizabeth Hamilton. *Hamilton*, I, 268-269.

HEAD OF ELK September 6, 1781

Yesterday, my lovely wife, I wrote to you, inclosing you a letter in one to your father, to the care of Mr. Morris. To-morrow the post sets out, and to-morrow we embark for Yorktown. I cannot refuse myself the pleasure of writing you a few lines. Constantly uppermost in my thoughts and affections, I am happy only when my moments are devoted to some office that respects you. I would give the world to be able to tell you all I feel and all I wish, but consult your own heart and you will know mine. What a world will soon be between us! To support the idea, all my fortitude is insufficient. What must be the case with you, who have the most female of female hearts? I sink at the perspective of your distress, and I look to heaven to be your guardian and supporter. Circumstances that have just come to my knowledge assure me that our operations will be expeditious, as well as our success certain. Early in November, as I promised you, we shall certainly meet. Cheer yourself with this idea, and with the assurance of never more being separated. Every day confirms me in the intention of renouncing public life and devoting myself wholly to you. Let others waste their time and their tranquillity in a vain pursuit of power and glory; be it my object to be happy in a quiet retreat with my better angel.

—To Elizabeth Hamilton. *Hamilton*, I, 267.

September, 1781

How chequered is human life! How precarious is happiness! How easily do we often part with it for a shadow! These are the reflections that frequently intrude themselves upon me with a painful application. I am going to do my duty. Our operations will be so conducted as to economize the lives of men. Exert your fortitude and rely upon heaven.

—To Elizabeth Hamilton. *Works*, IX, 246-247.

YORKTOWN October 16, 1781

Two nights ago, my Eliza, my duty and my honor obliged me to take a step in which your happiness was too much risked. I commanded an attack upon one of the enemy's redoubts; we carried it in an instant, and with little loss. You will see the particulars in the Philadelphia papers. There will be, certainly, nothing more of this kind; all the rest will be by approach; and if there should be another occasion, it will not fall to my turn to execute it.

—To Elizabeth Hamilton. *Works*, IX, 250.

ALBANY November 3, 1782

I have been employed for the last ten months in rocking the cradle and studying the art of *fleecing* my neighbors. I am now a grave counsellor-at-law, and shall soon be a grave member of Congress. The Legislature, at their last session, took it into their heads to name me, pretty unanimously, one of their delegates.

I am going to throw away a few months more in public life, and then retire a simple citizen and good pater familias. I set out for Philadelphia in a few days. You see the disposition I am in. You are condemned to run the race of ambition all your life. I am already tired of the career, and dare to leave it.

—To Lafayette. Hamilton's hand. Hamilton Papers, 1st ser.

PHILADELPHIA November, 1798

I am always very happy, my dear Eliza, when I can steal a few moments to sit down and write to you. You are my good genius; of that kind which the ancient philosophers called a *familiar;* and you know very well that I am glad to be in every way as familiar as possible with you. I have formed a sweet project, of which I will make you my confidant when I come to New York, and in which I rely that you will cooperate with me cheerfully.

You may guess and guess and guess again
Your guessing will be still in vain.

But you will not be the less pleased when you come to understand and realize the scheme.

Adieu best of wives and best of mothers
Heaven ever bless you and me in you.

A. H.

—To Elizabeth Hamilton. Hamilton Papers.

Friday, October 28 [1802]

This morning, my beloved Eliza, I leave Albany for Claverack, my health greatly mended, and I hope to make but a short stay there. My plan is to go to Poughkeepsie and there embark.

I shall be glad to find that my dear little Philip[1] is weaned, if circumstances have rendered it prudent. It is of importance to me to rest quietly in your bosom.

Adieu, my beloved,

A. H.

Kiss all the children for me.
Love to Cornelia.

—To Elizabeth Hamilton. Special Collections, Columbia Univ. Lib.

SOME FATHERLY ADVICE:

December 5, 1791

I received with great pleasure, my dear Philip, the letter which you wrote me last week. Your mamma and myself were very happy to learn that you are pleased with your situation, and content to stay as long as shall be thought best for you. We hope and believe that nothing will happen to alter this disposition. Your master also informs me that you recited a lesson the first day you began, very much to his satisfaction. I expect every letter from him will give me a fresh proof of your progress, for I know you can do a great deal if you please, and I am sure you have too much spirit not to exert yourself that you may make us every day more and more proud of you. You remember that I engaged to send for you next Saturday, and I will do it, unless you request me to put it off, for a promise must never be broken, and I never will make you one which I will not fill as far as I am able; but it has occurred to me that the Christmas holidays are near at hand, and I suppose your school will then break up for a few days and give you an opportunity of coming to stay with us for a longer time than if you should come on Saturday. Will it not be best, therefore, to put off your journey till the holidays? But determine as you like best, and let me know what will be most pleasing to you. A good night to my darling son.

—To Philip Hamilton. *Works*, IX, 499-500.

September 21, 1793

I was very glad to learn, my dear daughter, that you were going to begin the study of the French language. We hope you will in every respect behave in such a manner as will secure to you the good-will and regard of all those with whom you are. If you happen to displease any of them, be always ready to make a frank apology. But the best way is to act with so much politeness, good manners, and circumspection as never to have occasion to make any apology. Your mother joins in best love to you. Adieu, my very dear daughter.

—To Angelica Hamilton. *Works*, X, 57-58.

[1] This is the second Philip, born June 2, 1802, and named after his eldest brother killed in a duel the year before.

[c. 1800]

From the first of April to the first of October he is to rise not later than six o'clock; the rest of the year not later than seven. If earlier, he will deserve commendation. Ten will be his hour of going to bed throughout the year.

From the time he is dressed in the morning till nine o'clock (the time for breakfast excepted), he is to read law. At nine he goes to the office, and continues there till dinner time. He will be occupied partly in writing and partly in reading law.

After dinner he reads law at home till five o'clock. From this time till seven he disposes of his time as he pleases. From seven to ten he reads and studies whatever he pleases.

From twelve on Saturday he is at liberty to amuse himself.

On Sunday he will attend the morning church. The rest of the day may be applied to innocent recreations.

He must not depart from any of these rules without my permission.

—Rules for Philip Hamilton. Hamilton Papers, 1st ser.

[1804]

My Dear James:

I have prepared for you a Thesis on Discretion. You may need it. God bless you.

Your affectionate father.

—To James A. Hamilton. Works, X, 457.

Women: The Reynolds Affair

My real crime is an amorous connection with his wife. . . .

Hamilton's sister-in-law, Angelica Schuyler Church, worldly, witty, frivolous, and flirtatious, had a girlhood crush on the handsome Alexander which she never lost. It was to Angelica, whom he had not yet met, that Hamilton wrote shortly before his marriage, praising his sweetheart's beauty and perfection. She was a veritable heart-breaker, he confessed, concluding: "It is essential to the safety of the state and to the tranquillity of the army—that one of two things take place, either that she be immediately removed from our neighborhood, or that some other nymph qualified to maintain an equal sway come into it. By dividing her empire it will be weakened and she will be much less dangerous when she has a rival equal in charms to dispute the prize with her. I solicit your aid."

Hamilton was spoofing, but to Angelica, the supreme coquette, this was a challenge. Thereafter she never withheld her affection and ad-

miration from her "petit fripon" (cute rascal). Typical of her correspondence with the Hamiltons was a note she penned from London, April 25, 1788, in which she mentioned reports that "our dear Hamilton writes too much and takes no exercise, and grows too fat." This was deplorable, she pointed out. "He will be unable to flirt as Robert Morris." After advising Elizabeth to get him to exercise, she added: "Embrace poor dear Hamilton for me, it is impossible to know him, and not to wish him health and pleasure, and then I am really so proud of his merit and abilities, that even you, Eliza, might envy my feelings."

When the Churches moved from England to America their relationship to the Hamiltons was a source of discomfiture to the latters' friends. John Barker Church was a promoter and a gambler. Harrison Gray Otis described to his wife a dinner party he attended in Philadelphia. "After dinner," he related, "Mrs. C[hurch] dropped her shoe bow." Her younger sister Peggy picked it up and put it in Hamilton's buttonhole, saying " 'There brother I have made you a Knight.' 'But of what order,' asked Mrs. Church. " 'He can't be a Knight of the Garter in this country.' 'True sister,' replied Peggy, 'but he would be if you would let him.' "

But gallantry might pass the bounds of flirtation or discretion. In one case where it did Hamilton was to pay dearly for his indiscretions.

In 1792 John Beckley, a Republican and professional Hamilton-hater, rushed to James Monroe with a story of the Secretary of the Treasury's alleged criminal operations. Beckley's story was third hand. It came to him from a man named Jacob Clingman. It seems that a clerk in the Treasury named Andrew G. Fraunces had boasted to Clingman that "he could, if he pleased, hang Hamilton." He asserted that Hamilton had given him the power of attorney to purchase a Revolutionary War veteran's certificate for back pay at a substantial discount and just before passage of the bill for payment at par. For his services, Fraunces alleged that he was paid fifty dollars, and also was given other sums. But in addition, another friend of Clingman's named James Reynolds claimed to have received $1,100 from Hamilton for services rendered.

The credibility of Clingman and Reynolds should have been dubious even to one so blind as a Hamilton-hater. Both were under arrest and faced with prosecution for suborning a witness to commit perjury in an attempt to embezzle Treasury funds. Three Congressmen, Monroe, Muhlenberg, and Venable, visited Reynolds, and with the data in their pockets, confronted Hamilton in his office. Hamilton asked them to meet him at his home that evening and took the precaution of requesting Oliver Wolcott, the Comptroller, to be there as a witness.

The congressmen and the Comptroller heard a wierd story that night. It seems that in the summer of 1791, while his wife was away from Philadelphia, Hamilton had had an affair with Reynolds' wife,

Maria, who had come to him for financial aid. Hamilton had fallen into a trap. He was blackmailed by a scoundrel, aided and abetted by the scoundrel's wife. He paid Reynolds a thousand dollars, and some further small sums. The visitors were dumstruck and agreed to treat the affair in the strictest confidence.

But one of Hamilton's enemies did not keep his word. In 1797, some years after Hamilton had left office, James T. Callender, a Republican hatchetman, published his so-called History of the United States for the Year 1796. *The hidden tale of 1792 was now exposed to the public eye. Hamilton accused Monroe, undoubtedly with justice, of breach of faith. A challenge to a duel almost resulted, but Aaron Burr, ironically enough, brought about a peaceful settlement of this personal issue between the parties. Hamilton was now forced to publish the whole story. His integrity as a public man was at stake. His private life must be sacrificed. It was an amazing performance. Never in American history has a public man shown greater candor. However shocked Elizabeth may have been by these sordid disclosures, there is no evidence whatsoever that the ugly episode affected their marriage.*

ALBANY October 1, 1793

Contemptible as you are, what answer could I give to your last letter? The enclosed is a copy of what shortly will appear in one of the gazettes of the City of New York:

"One Andrew G. Francis, late clerk in the Treasury Department, has been endeavoring to have it believed that he is possessed of some facts of a nature to criminate the official conduct of the Secretary of the Treasury, an idea to which, for obvious reasons, an extensive circulation has been given by a certain description of persons.

"The public may be assured that the said Francis has been regularly and repeatedly called upon to declare the grounds of his suggestion, that he has repeatedly evaded the inquiry, that he possesses no facts of the nature pretended, and that he is a despicable calumniator."

—To ——————, *Works*, X, 58.

1797

The spirit of Jacobinism, if not entirely a new spirit, has at least been clothed with a more gigantic body and armed with more powerful weapons than it ever before possessed. . . .

A principal engine, by which this spirit endeavors to accomplish its purposes, is that of calumny. It is essential to its success that the influence of men of upright principles, disposed and able to resist its enterprises, shall be at all events destroyed. . . .

Ought I to regret, if there be any thing about me so formidable to the FACTION as to have made me worthy to be distinguished by the plenitude of its rancor and venom? . . .

I dare appeal to my immediate fellow-citizens, of whatever political party, for the truth of the assertion, that no man ever carried into public life a more unblemished pecuniary reputation, than that with which I undertook the office of Secretary of the Treasury, a character marked by indifference to the acquisition of property rather than by avidity for it. . . .

Without the slightest foundation, I have been repeatedly held up to the suspicions of the world as a man directed in his administration by the most sordid views; who did not scruple to sacrifice the public to his private interest, his duty and honor to the sinister accumulation of wealth.

Merely because I *retained* an opinion once common to me and the most influential of those who opposed me, *that the public debt ought to be provided for on the basis of the contract upon which it was created*, I have been wickedly accused with wantonly increasing the public burthen many millions in order in promote a stock-jobbing interest of myself and friends.

Merely because a member of the House of Representatives entertained a different idea from me, as to the legal effect of appropriation law, and did not understand accounts, I was exposed to the imputation of having committed a deliberate and criminal violation of the laws, and to the suspicion of being a defaulter for millions; so as to have been driven to the painful necessity of calling for a formal and solemn inquiry.

The inquiry took place. It was conducted by a committee of fifteen members of the House of Representatives—a majority of them either my decided political enemies or inclined against me, some of them the most active and intelligent of my opponents, without a single man, who, being known to be friendly to me, possessed also such knowledge and experience of public affairs as would enable him to counteract injurious intrigues. Mr. Giles, of Virginia, who had commenced the attack, was of the committee.

The officers and books of the treasury were examined. The transactions between the several banks and the treasury were scrutinized. Even my *private accounts* with those institutions were laid open to the committee; and every possible facility given to the inquiry. The result was a complete demonstration that the suspicions that had been entertained were groundless.

Those which had taken the fastest hold were, that the public monies had been made subservient to loans, discounts, and accommodations to myself and friends. The committee in reference to this point reported thus: "It appears, from the affidavits of the cashier and several officers of the Bank of the United States and several of the directors, the cashier, and other officers of the Bank of New York, that the Secretary of the Treasury never has either *directly* or *indirectly*, for himself or any other person, procured any discount or credit from either of the said banks upon the basis of any public monies which at any time have been deposited therein under his direction: And the committee are *satisfied* that *no monies* of the United States, whether *before* or *after* they have passed to the credit of the Treasurer, have ever been *directly* or *indirectly* used for or applied to *any purposes* but those of the government, except so far as all monies deposited in a bank are concerned in the *general operations* thereof."

The report, which I have always understood was unanimous, contains in other respects, with considerable detail, the materials of a complete exculpation. My enemies, finding no handle for their malice, abandoned the pursuit. . . .

Of all the vile attempts which have been made to injure my character, that which has been lately revived in No. V and VI of the *History of the United States for 1796*, is the most vile. This it will be impossible for any *intelligent*, I will not say *candid*, man to doubt, when he shall have accompanied me through the examination. . . .

The charge against me is a connection with one James Reynolds for purposes of improper pecuniary speculation. My real crime is an amorous connection with his wife for a considerable time, with his privity and connivance, if not originally brought on by a combination between the husband and wife with the design to extort money from me.

This confession is not made without a blush. I cannot be the apologist of any vice because the ardor of passion may have made it mine. I can never cease to condemn myself for the pang which it may inflict in a bosom eminently entitled to all my gratitude, fidelity, and love. But that bosom will approve, that, even at so great an expense, I should effectually wipe away a more serious stain from a name which it cherishes with no less elevation than tenderness. The public, too, will, I trust, excuse the confession. The necessity of it to my defence against a more heinous charge could alone have extorted from me so painful an indecorum. . . .

The first reflection which occurs on a perusal of the documents is that it is morally impossible I should have been foolish as well as depraved enough to employ so vile an instrument as *Reynolds* for such *insignificant ends*, as are indicated by different parts of the story itself. . . . All the documents show, and it is otherwise matter of notoriety, that Reynolds was an obscure, unimportant, and profligate man. Nothing could be more weak, because nothing could be more unsafe than to make use of such an instrument; to use him, too, without any intermediate agent more worthy of confidence who might keep me out of sight; to write him numerous letters recording the objects of the improper connection (for this is pretended and that the letters were afterwards burnt at my request); to unbosom myself to him with a prodigality of confidence, by very unnecessarily telling him, as he alleges, of a connection in speculation between myself and Mr. Duer. It is very extraordinary, if the head of the money department of a country, being unprincipled enough to sacrifice his trust and his integrity, could not have contrived objects of profit sufficiently large to have engaged the co-operation of men of far greater importance than Reynolds, and with whom there could have been due safety, and should have been driven to the necessity of unkennelling such a reptile to be the instrument of his cupidity.

But, moreover, the scale of the concern with Reynolds, such as it is presented, is contemptibly narrow for a rapacious speculating Secretary of the Treasury. *Clingman, Reynolds,* and his wife were manifestly in very close confidence with each other. It seems there was a free communication of secrets. Yet in clubbing their different items of information as to the supplies of money which Reynolds received from me, what do they amount to? *Clingman* states that Mrs. Reynolds told him, that at a certain time her husband had received from me upwards of eleven hundred dollars. A note is produced which shows that at one time fifty dollars were sent to him, and another note is produced, by which and the information of Reynolds himself through Clingman, it appears that at another time $300 were asked and refused. Another sum of $200 is spoken of by *Clingman* as having been furnished to Reynolds at some other time. What a scale of speculation is this for the head of a public treasury, for one who, in the very publication that brings forward the charge, is represented as having procured to be funded at forty millions a debt which ought to have been discharged at ten or fifteen millions for the criminal purpose of enriching himself and his friends? He must have been a clumsy knave, if he did not secure enough of this excess of twenty-five or thirty millions, to have taken away all inducement to risk his character in such bad hands and in so huckstering a way—or to have enabled him, if he did employ such an agent, to do it with more means and to better purpose. It is curious that this rapacious Secretary should at one time have furnished his speculating agent with the paltry sum of fifty dollars; at another, have refused him the inconsiderable sum of $300, declaring upon his honor that it was not in his power to furnish it. This declaration was true or not: if the last, the refusal ill comports with the idea of a speculating connection; if the first, it is very singular that the head of the Treasury, engaged without scruple in schemes of profit, should be destitute of so small a sum. But if we suppose this officer to be living upon an inadequate salary, without any collateral pursuits of gain, the appearances then are simple and intelligible enough, applying to them the true key. . . .

For frail indeed will be the tenure by which the most blameless man will hold his reputation, if the assertions of three of the most abandoned characters in the community, two of them stigmatized by the discrediting crime which has been mentioned, are sufficient to blast it. The business of accusation would soon become, in such a case, a regular trade, and men's reputations would be bought and sold like any marketable commodity.

Some time in the summer of the year 1791, a woman called at my house in the city of Philadelphia, and asked to speak with me in private. I attended her into a room apart from my family. With a seeming air of affliction she informed me that she was a daughter of a Mr. Lewis, sister to a Mr. G. Livingston of the State of New York, and wife to a Mr. Reynolds, whose father was in the Commissary Department during the war with Great Britain; that her husband, who for a long time had treated her very cruelly, had lately left her to live with another woman, and in so destitute a condition that, though desirous of returning to her friends, she had not the means; that knowing I was a citizen of New York, she had taken the liberty to apply to my humanity for assistance.

I replied, that her situation was a very interesting one—that I was disposed to afford her assistance to convey her to her friends, but this at the moment not being convenient to me (which was the fact), I must request the place of her residence, to which I should bring or send a small supply of money. She told me the street and the number of the house where she lodged. In the evening I put a bank-bill in my pocket and went to the house. I enquired for Mrs. Reynolds and was shown up stairs, at the head of which she met me and conducted me into a bedroom. I took the bill out of my pocket and gave it to her. Some conversation ensued, from which it was quickly apparent that other than pecuniary consolation would be acceptable.

After this I had frequent meetings with her, most of them at my own house; Mrs. Hamilton with her children being absent on a visit to her father. In the course of a short time, she mentioned to me that her husband had solicited a reconciliation, and affected to consult me about it. I advised to it, and was soon after informed by her that it had taken place. She told me besides that her husband had been engaged in speculation, and she believed could give information respecting the conduct of some persons in the department which would be useful. I sent for Reynolds who came to me accordingly.

In the course of our interview, he confessed that he had obtained a list of claims from a person in my department which he had made use of in his speculations. I invited him, by the expectation of my friendship and good offices, to disclose the person. After some affectation of scruple, he pretended to yield, and ascribed the infidelity to Mr. Duer, from whom he said he had obtained the list in New York, while he (Duer) was in the department.

As Mr. Duer had resigned his office some time before the seat of government was removed to Philadelphia, this discovery, if it had been true, was not very important—yet it was the interest of my passions to appear to set value upon it, and to continue the expectation of friendship and good offices. Mr. Reynolds told me he was going to Virginia, and on his return would point out something in which I could serve him. I do not know but he said something about employment in a public office.

On his return he asked employment as a clerk in the Treasury Department. The knowledge I had acquired of him was decisive against such a request. I parried it by telling him, what was true, that there was no vacancy in my immediate office, and that the appointment of clerks in the other branches of the department was left to the chiefs of the respective branches. Reynolds alleged, as *Clingman* relates, No. IV (a), as a topic of complaint against me, that I had promised him *employment* and had *disappointed* him. The situation of the wife would naturally incline me to conciliate this man. It is possible I may have used vague expressions which raised expectation; but the more I learned of the person, the more inadmissible his employment in a public office became. . . .

The intercourse with Mrs. Reynolds, in the meantime continued; and though various reflections (in which a further knowledge of Reynolds' character and the suspicion of some concert between the husband and wife bore a part) induced me to wish a cessation of it; yet, her conduct made it extremely difficult to disentangle myself. All the appearances of violent attachment, and of agonizing distress at the idea of a relinquishment, were played with a most imposing art. This, though it did not make me entirely the dupe of the plot, yet kept me in a state of irresolution. My sensibility, perhaps my vanity, admitted the possibility of a real fondness; and led me to adopt the plan of a gradual discontinuance rather than of a sudden interruption, as least calculated to give pain, if a real partiality existed.

Mrs. Reynolds, on the other hand, employed every effort to keep up my attention and visits. Her pen was freely employed, and her letters were filled with those tender and pathetic effusions which would have been natural to a woman truly fond and neglected. . . .

Mrs. Reynolds more than once communicated to me that Reynolds would occasionally relapse into discontent at his situation, would treat her very ill, hint at the assassination of me, and more openly threaten by way of revenge, to inform Mrs. Hamilton. All this naturally gave some uneasiness. I could not be absolutely certain whether it was artifice or reality. In the workings of human inconsistency it was very possible that the same man might be corrupt enough to compound for his wife's chastity, and yet have sensibility enough to be restless in the situation and to hate the cause of it.

Reflections like these induced me for some time to use palliatives with the ill-humors which were announced to me. . . .

Thus has my desire to destroy this slander completely led me to a more copious and particular examination of it, than I am sure was necessary. The bare perusal of the letters from Reynolds and his wife is sufficient to convince my greatest enemy that there is nothing worse in the affair than an irregular and indelicate amour. For this, I bow to the just censure which it merits. I have paid pretty severely for the folly, and can never recollect it without disgust and self-condemnation. It might seem affectation to say more.

—*Observations on Certain Documents contained in Nos. V and VI of "The History of the United States for the Year 1796," in which the Charge of Speculation against Alexander Hamilton, late Secretary of the Treasury, is fully refuted.* (Philadelphia: printed for John Fenno by John Bioren, 1797), pp. 3, 4-7, 9-12, 17-19, 20, 25, 36-37.

Integrity and Ambition

If you can conveniently let me have twenty dollars. . . .

. . . the malicious intrigues to stab me in the dark. . . .

Hamilton was without question the least affluent man to hold the office of Secretary of the Treasury in American history. He did not enter the public service to make money and he never made any out of it. This was explicit in letters written from the days of the Revolution. While he was handling the multi-million dollar funding operations of the government he had to resort to borrowing small sums, ranging from twenty to one hundred dollars, from friends. Yet he had to earn money to support his family, and after each spell of public service he devoted himself assiduously to the practice of the law. Talleyrand happened to pass Hamilton's law office one night on the way to a party. Hamilton was bent over his desk drafting a legal paper by the light of a candle. The Frenchman was amazed. "I have just come from viewing a man who had made the fortune of his country, but now is working all night in order to support his family," he reflected.

Hamilton's integrity was incessantly attacked by his enemies during his term as Secretary of the Treasury. The climax came in February, 1793, when Congressman Giles of Virginia, a supporter of Jefferson, moved a series of resolutions that Jefferson had drafted denouncing Hamilton's integrity and charging him with exceeding his powers by appropriating funds not authorized by law, specifically with transferring to the United States money raised by loan in Europe. Giles called upon

Hamilton for a full accounting. Congress was about to adjourn and it was thought that this demand would becloud Hamilton's future operations, but the Secretary of the Treasury confounded his enemies by a round-the-clock operation to complete his full report by the middle of February. The resolutions failed of passage by an overwhelming vote. Hamilton felt that Washington did not stand behind him as squarely as he might have on the question whether the Secretary of the Treasury had in his fiscal operations exceeded the authority delegated to him by the President. Washington said that he had approved of Hamilton's actions on the assumption that they were "agreeable to the laws." The incessant attacks and investigations had their cumulative effect on Hamilton's willingness to remain a public target for his foes and contributed to his decision to resign from office.

March 1, 1782

Your Excellency will, I am persuaded, readily admit the force of this sentiment, that though it is the duty of a good citizen to devote his services to the public when it has occasion for them, he cannot with propriety or delicacy to himself obtrude them when it either has, or appears to have none. The difficulties I experienced last campaign in obtaining a command will not suffer me to make any further application on that head.

As I have many reasons to consider my being employed hereafter in a precarious light, the bare possibility of rendering an equivalent will not justify to my scruples the receiving any future emoluments from my commission. I therefore renounce, from this time, all claim to the compensations attached to my military station during the war or afterwards. But I have motives which will not permit me to resolve on a total resignation. I sincerely hope a prosperous train of affairs may continue to make it no inconvenience to decline the services of persons whose zeal, in worse times, was found not altogether useless; but as the most promising appearances are often reversed by unforeseen disasters, and as unfortunate events may again make the same zeal of some value, I am unwilling to put it out of my power to renew my exertions in the common cause in the line in which I have hitherto acted.

I shall accordingly retain my rank while I am permitted to do it, and take this opportunity to declare that I shall be at all times ready to obey the call of the public in any capacity, civil or military (consistent with what I owe to myself), in which there may be a prospect of my contributing to the final attainment of the object for which I embarked in the service.

—To Washington. Hamilton's hand. Hamilton Papers, 1st ser.

ALBANY May 18, 1782

My military situation has indeed become so negative, that I have no motive to continue in it; and if my services could be of importance to the public in a civil line, I should cheerfully obey its command. But the plan which I have marked out to myself is the profession of the law, and I am now engaged in a course of studies for that purpose. Time is so precious to me that I could not put myself in the way of any interruptions, unless for an object of consequence to the public or to myself. The present is not of this nature. Such are the circumstances of this State, the benefit arising from the office you propose would not, during the war, exceed yearly one hundred pounds; for, unfortunately, I am persuaded it will not pay annually into the Continental treasury above forty thousand pounds; and, on a peace establishment, this will not be for some time to come much more than doubled. You will perceive, sir, that an engagement of this kind does not correspond with my views, and does not afford a sufficient inducement to relinquish them.

—To Robert Morris. Draft in Hamilton's hand.
Hamilton Papers, 1st ser.

ALBANY June 17, 1782

The letter which you did me the honor to write me, of the 4th instant, came to my hands too late to permit me to answer it by the return of the same post. The explanation you give of your intention in your late offer makes it an object that will fully compensate for the time it will deduct from my other occupations. In accepting it, I have only one scruple, arising from a doubt whether the service I can render in the present state of things will be an equivalent for the compensation. The whole system (if it may be so called) of taxation in this State is radically vicious, burthensome to the people, and unproductive to government. As the matter now stands, there seems to be little for a continental receiver to do. The whole business appears to be thrown into the hands of the county treasurers, nor do I find that there is any appropriation made of any part of the taxes collected to continental purposes, or any provision to authorize payment to the officer you appoint; this, however, must be made. There is only one way in which I can imagine a prospect of being materially useful—that is, in seconding your application to the State. In popular assemblies much may sometimes be brought about by personal discussions, by entering into details and combating objections as they rise. If it should at any time be thought advisable by you to empower me to act in this capacity, I shall be happy to do every thing that depends on me to effectuate your views. I flatter myself to you, sir, I need not profess that I suggest this, not from a desire to augment the importance of office, but to advance the public interest.

It is of primary moment to me as soon as possible to take my station in the law, and on this consideration I am pressing to qualify myself for admission the next term, which will be the latter end of July. After this, if you should think an interview with me necessary I will wait upon you in Philadelphia.

—To Robert Morris. Hamilton's hand. Hamilton Papers, 1st ser.

ALBANY September 30, 1783

Your Excellency knows that in March, '82, I relinquished all claim to any future compensation for my services, either during the residue of the war, or after its conclusion—simply retaining my rank. On this foundation I build a hope that I may be permitted to preserve my rank, on the peace establishment, without emoluments and unattached to any corps—as an honorary reward for the time I have devoted to the public. As I may hereafter travel, I may find it an agreeable circumstance to appear in the character I have supported in the Revolution.

I rest my claim solely on the sacrifice I have made, because I have no reason to believe that my services have appeared of any value to Congress, as they declined giving them any marks of their notice, on an occasion which appeared to my friends to entitle me to it, as well by the common practice of sovereigns as by the particular practice of this country in repeated instances.

Your Excellency will recollect that it was my lot at York Town to command, as senior officer, a successful attack upon one of the enemy's redoubts; that the officer who acted in a similar capacity in another attack, made at the same time, by the French troops, has been handsomely distinguished in consequence of it by the government to which he belongs; and that there are several examples among us where Congress have bestowed honors upon actions, perhaps not more useful, nor apparently more hazardous.

—To Washington. Hamilton Papers, 1st ser.

December 1, 1789

I have received your letter of the 16th inst. I am sure you are sincere when you say that you would not subject me to an impropriety; nor do I know that there would be any in my answering your queries. But you remember the saying with regard to Caesar's wife. I think the spirit of it applicable to every man concerned in the administration of the finance of a country. With respect to the conduct of such men, SUSPICION is ever eagle-eyed. And the most innocent things are apt to be misinterpreted.

Be assured of the affection and friendship of, etc.

—To Henry Lee. Hamilton's hand. Hamilton Papers, 1st ser.

April 17, 1791

. . . The expectation of promotion in civil as in military life is a great stimulus to virtuous exertion, while examples of unrewarded exertion, supported by talent and qualification, are proportionable discouragements. Where they do not produce resignations they leave men dissatisfied, and a dissatisfied man seldom does his duty well.

In a government like ours, where pecuniary compensations are moderate, the principle of gradual advancement as a reward for good conduct is perhaps more necessary to be attended to than in others where offices are more lucrative.

—To Washington. *Hamilton*, V, 467-469.

September 30, 1791

If you can conveniently let me have twenty dollars for a few days, be so good as to send it by bearer. I have just put myself out of cash by payment of Major L'Enfant's bill.

—To ————————. *Works*, IX, 497.

August 18, 1792

. . . I have not fortitude enough always to hear with calmness the calumnies which necessarily include me, as a principal agent in the measures censured, of the falsehood of which I have the most unqualified consciousness. I trust I shall always be able to bear, as I ought, imputations of errors and judgment; but I acknowledge that I cannot be entirely patient under charges, which impeach the integrity of my public motives or conduct. I feel that I merit them *in no degree*; and expressions of indignation sometimes escape me, in spite of every effort to suppress them. I rely on your goodness for the proper allowances.

—To Washington. *Hamilton*, IV, 247-248.

December 18, 1792

. . . 'Tis not the load of proper official business that alone engrosses me, though this would be enough to occupy any man. 'Tis not the extra attention I am obliged to pay to the course of legislative manoeuvres that alone adds to my burden and perplexity. 'Tis the malicious intrigues to stab me in the dark, against which I am too often obliged to guard myself, that distract and harass me to a point which, rendering my situation scarcely tolerable, interferes with objects to which friendship and inclination would prompt me.

—To John Jay. *Works*, X, 29-30.

June 21, 1793

Considerations relative to both the public interest and to my own delicacy have brought me, after mature reflection, to a resolution to resign the office I hold towards the close of the ensuing session of Congress.

I postpone the final act to that period, because some propositions remain to be submitted by me to Congress which are necessary to the full development of my original plan, and, as I suppose, of some consequence to my reputation, and because, in the second place, I am desirous of giving an opportunity, while I shall still be in office, to the revival and more deliberate prosecution of the inquiry into my conduct which was instituted during the last session.

I think it proper to communicate my determination thus early, among other reasons, because it will afford full time to investigate and weigh all the considerations which ought to guide the appointment of my successor.

—To Washington. Draft in Hamilton's hand. Hamilton Papers, 1st ser.

April 8, 1794

I cannot charge my memory with all the particulars which have passed between us relative to the disposition of the money borrowed. Your letters, however, and my answer, which you refer to in the foregoing statement, and lately reminded me of, speak for themselves, and stand in need of no explanation.

As to verbal communications, I am satisfied that many were made by you to me on this subject; and, from my general recollection of the course of proceedings, I do not doubt that it was substantially as you have stated it in the annexed paper, and that I have approved of the measures which you from time to time proposed to me for disposing of the loans, upon the condition that what was to be done by you should be agreeable to the laws.

—Washington to Hamilton. *Works*, III, 190.

April 9, 1794

I have analyzed the declaration which you have been pleased to make upon the copy of the paper of the first instant delivered by me to the Committee of Inquiry into the State of the Treasury Department, and find, with regret, that the terms used are such as will enable those who are disposed to construe every thing to my disadvantage to affirm, That the declaration of the President has entirely waved [*sic*] the main point, and does not even manifest an *opinion* that the representation of the Secretary of the Treasury is well founded.

To this it would be added, that the reserve of the President is a proof that he does not think that representation true, else his justice would have led him to rescue the officer concerned even from suspicion on the point.

That this will be the interpretation put upon your declaration I have no doubt; and, in justice to myself, I cannot forbear to make this impression known to you, and to bring the declaration under your revision.

I am the more certain that this construction will be put upon the matter, from what has heretofore taken place. In the course of the discussion of the last session, an argument of this kind was, in private, urged against me: "If Mr. Hamilton had really acted by the authority of the President, or in due communication with him, would not the President take some method, either directly to Mr. Madison, or through Mr. Jefferson or Mr. Randolph, to make known to him that this ground of accusation did not exist? His not doing it, which may be inferred from Mr. Madison's urging the point, is a proof that there was no co-operation on his part." . . .

The situation is indeed an unpleasant one. Having conducted an important piece of public business in a spirit of confidence—dictated by an unqualified reliance, on the one hand, upon the rectitude, candor, and delicacy of the person under whom I was acting; on the other, by a persuasion that the experience of years had secured to me a reciprocal sentiment (whatever imperfections it may have otherwise discovered); and by the belief, likewise, that, however particular instances might be forgotten, the general course of proceeding in so important an affair could not but be remembered—I did not look for a difficulty like that which now seems to press me. Knowing, too, that there existed in my written communications with the President (not only those which have been specified, but others), so many direct and indirect indications of what was truly the course pursued, I still less apprehended a difficulty of that nature when the occasion for explanation should occur.

Not seeking to escape responsibility for any improper execution of the laws—if any has happened—I do not imagine that want of intermediate authority from the President to do what they would justify, would be suffered to remain (the appeal being made to him) a topic of objection to my conduct.

In the freedom of these remarks I flatter myself, sir, that you will perceive nothing but that just sensibility which a man of honor, who thinks his veracity exposed to question, ought to feel and that you will be persuaded I continue yet to retain undiminished that respect which a long-established conviction of the existence of an upright and virtuous character ought to inspire.

—To Washington. Hamilton Papers, 1st ser.

May 27, 1794

I some time since communicated my intention to withdraw from the office I hold, towards the close of the present session.

This I should now put in execution, but for the events which have lately accumulated, of a nature to render the prospects of the continuance of our peace in a considerable degree precarious. I do not perceive that I could voluntarily quit my post at such a juncture consistently with considerations either of duty or character; and therefore I find myself reluctantly obliged to defer the offer of my resignation.

—To Washington. Draft in Hamilton's hand. Hamilton Papers, 1st ser.

December 1, 1794

I have the honor to inform you that I have fixed upon the last of January next as the day for the resignation of my office of Secretary of the Treasury. I make the communication now that there may be time to mature such an arrangement as shall appear to you proper to meet the vacancy when it occurs.

—To Washington. Draft in Hamilton's hand. Hamilton Papers, 1st ser.

December 2, 1794

The procuring of military supplies generally is, with great propriety, vested by law in the Department of the Treasury. That department, from situation, may be expected to feel a more habitual solicitude for economy than any other, and to possess more means of information respecting the best modes of obtaining supplies. . . .

Whenever an object of public business is likely to be permanent, it is more fit that it should be transacted by an officer of the government, regularly constituted, than by the agent of a department, specially intrusted.

The officer can be placed, by law, under more effectual checks. In the present case, that idea is particularly important. The person intrusted ought to be prohibited, under penalties, from all dealing, on his own account, in the objects of supply.

The duration and emoluments of mere agency being precarious, a well-qualified man, disposed to make the necessary sacrifices of other pursuits, and to devote himself exclusively to the business, could with much greater difficulty, if at all, be found.

—To Washington. *Works*, X, 80-81.

KINGSTON February 21, 1795

The unnecessary and capricious and abominable assassination of the national honor by the rejection of the propositions respecting the unsubscribed debt in the House of Representatives haunts me every step I take, and afflicts me more than I can express. To see the character of the government and the country so sported with—exposed to so indelible a blot—puts my heart to the torture. Am I, then, more of an American than those who drew their first breath on American ground? Or what is it that thus torments me at a circumstance so calmly viewed by almost everybody else? Am I a fool—a romantic Quixote—or is there a constitutional defect in the American mind?

—To Rufus King. *Hamilton*, V, 624-625.

July 25, 1795

Confiding in your integrity and friendship to me, I have made you executor of my will. My concerns are not very extensive and of course will not give you much trouble. Indeed, I might have dispensed with the ceremony of making a will as to what I may myself leave, had I not wished that my little property may be applied as readily and as fairly as may be to the benefit of my few creditors. For after a life of labor I leave my family to the benevolence of others, if my course shall happen to be terminated here. . . .

I hope what I leave may prove equal to my debts. If it does not, I have the consolation of hoping that the loss will be permitted by himself to fall upon my brother-in-law, Mr. Church, whose friendship and generosity I do not doubt.

I regret that his affairs as well as my own have suffered by my devotion to the public service. But I trust, upon the whole, that the few operations I have made for him will more than recompense him for my omissions, though they will not have been as profitable to him as they ought to have been, and as they would have been if I could have paid more attention. . . .

I have received some large fees for which the parties could not have had equivalents: from Williamson, one hundred pounds; from Constable, one hundred pounds; from Macombe, one hundred pounds; from Mr. Bayard, on behalf of Wilhim and Jan Willink, one hundred pounds. It would be just, if there were means, that they should be repaid. But what can I direct who am, I fear, insolvent?

God bless you, my friend. Be assured always of the attachment of, etc.

—To Robert Troup. Hamilton's hand. Hamilton Papers, 1st ser.

July 17, 1798

I am not, however, ready to say that I shall be satisfied with the appointment of Inspector-General, with the rank and command of Major-General, on the principle that every officer of high rank in the late army, who may be appointed, is to be above me.

I am frank to own that this will not accord with my opinion of my own pretensions, and I have every reason to believe that it will fall far short of public opinion.

Few have made so many sacrifices as myself. To few would a change of situation for a military appointment be so injurious as to myself.

If, with this sacrifice, I am to be degraded below my just claim in public opinion, ought I to acquiesce?

—To Timothy Pickering. *Hamilton*, VI, 326-327.

July 29, 1798

With regard to the delicate subject of the relative rank of the major-generals, it is very natural for me to be a partial judge, and it is not very easy for me to speak upon it. If I know myself, however, this, at least, I may say, that, were I convinced of injustice being done to others[1] in my favor, I should not hesitate even to volunteer a correction of it, as far as my consent could avail. But in a case like this, am I not to take the opinion of others as my guide? If I am, the conclusion is that the gentlemen concerned ought to acquiesce. It is a fact of which there is a flood of evidence that a great majority of leading Federal men were of opinion that in the event of your declining the command of the army, it ought to devolve upon me, and that in case of your acceptance, which everybody ardently desired, the place of second in command ought to be mine. . . .

After saying this much, I [will] add that regard to the public interest is ever predominant with me; that if the gentlemen concerned are dissatisfied, and the service likely to suffer by the preference given to me, I stand ready to submit our relative pretensions to an impartial decision, and to waive the preference. It shall *never* be said, with any color of truth, that my ambition or interest has stood in the way of the public good.

—To Washington. Hamilton's hand. Hamilton Papers, 1st ser.

December 16, 1798

You recollect that, shortly after my first appointment, I was desired to turn my attention to a system of regulations for the tactics and discipline of the army. From that moment I have devoted much of my time to the preliminary investigations, and I shall devote a much larger proportion, if I am to consider myself as now in service, and entitled to the emoluments of the station; for, to be frank with you, it is utterly out of my power to apply my time to the public service without the compensations, scanty enough, which the law annexes to the office. If I were to receive them from the day of the appointment, I should be at least a thousand pounds the worse for my acceptance. From the time that it was fully known that I had re-engaged in military life, the uncertainty of my being able to render services for which I might be retained drove away more than one half of my professional practice, which I may moderately estimate at four thousand pounds a

[1] Charles C. Pinckney and Henry Knox, both picked by Washington for his general staff.—Ed.

year. My pecuniary sacrifices already to the public ought to produce the reverse of a disposition everywhere to compel me to greater than the law imposes. This remark, I am well aware, is not necessary for you personally.

Again, If I am to discharge with effect the duties of my present office, I must make frequent journeys from one part of the army to another. Everybody knows that the expenses of such journeys would quickly eat out the narrow allowances of a major-general.

It will be disagreeable to be exposed to the dilemma of compromitting my reputation and that of the government by not producing the results to be expected from the department, or of ruining myself once more in performing services for which there is no adequate compensation.

The precedent of the last war is a full comment on the propriety of an extra allowance to the inspector-general. It is indeed indispensable, if he is to be useful.

It is always disagreeable to speak of compensations for one's self, but a man past forty, with a wife and six children, and a very small property beforehand, is compelled to wave [*sic*] the scruples which his nicety would otherwise dictate.

—To McHenry. Hamilton Papers, 1st ser.

January 7, 1799

. . . I have discontinued my practice as attorney and solicitor, from which I had derived a considerable part of my professional profits; and I have applied no small portion of my time to preliminary investigations, in order to the collection of the best lights for forming a system of tactics and discipline as perfect as exists anywhere else.

The very circumstance of my having accepted a military appointment, from the moment it was known, withdrew from me a large portion of my professional business. This, it will be perceived, was a natural effect of the uncertainty of my being able in the progress of suits to render the services for which I might be engaged, at the customary previous expense to the parties.

The result has been, that the emoluments of my profession have been diminished more than one half, and are still diminishing, and I remain in perfect uncertainty whether or when I am to derive from the scanty compensations of the office even a partial retribution for so serious a loss.

Were I rich, I should be proud to be silent on such a subject. I should acquiesce without an observation as long as any one might think the minutest public interest required an accumulation of sacrifices on my part. But after having to so advanced a period of my life devoted all my prospects of fortune to the service of the country, and dependent, as I am, for the maintenance of a wife and six children on my professional exertions, now so seriously abridged, it is essential for me to forego the scruples of delicacy, and to ask of you to define my situation, that I may determine whether to continue or to change my present plan.

—To McHenry. Hamilton Papers, 1st ser.

[after 1800]

. . . In the event which would bring this paper to the public eye, one thing at least would be put beyond doubt. This is that my public labors have amounted to an absolute sacrifice of the interests of my family, and that in all pecuniary concerns the delicacy no less than the probity of conduct in public stations has been such as to defy even the shadow of a question.

Indeed, I have not enjoyed the ordinary advantages incident to my military services. Being a member of Congress while the question of the commutation of the half pay of the army for a sum in gross was in debate, delicacy and a desire to be useful to the army by removing the idea of my having an interest in the question, induced me to write to the Secretary of War and relinquish my claim to half pay, which or the equivalent I have never received. Neither have I even applied for the lands allowed by the United States to officers of my rank.

—Unaddressed letter. *Works*, X, 479.

Loyalty to friends is a commendable trait, but it can prove an embarrassment to a person in public life. The fact that some of Hamilton's close friends were speculators who sought to capitalize on their connection with him provided a source of much gossip. Hamilton was disturbed at the speculative rise in bank stock and public securities and thought it necessary to warn his friend William Duer both for his purse and his reputation. The warning was ignored. Duer overreached himself. A shady operator who had in fact embezzled government funds when he was Assistant Secretary of the Treasury, Duer was caught in the speculative downdrift of 1792 and spent the greater part of his last six years in jail where he belonged.

August 17, 1791

The conversation here was: "Bank scrip is getting so high as to become a bubble," in one breath; in another: " 'Tis a South-Sea dream"; in a third: "There is a combination of knowing ones at New York to raise it as high as possible by fictitious purchases, in order to take in the credulous and ignorant"; in another: "Duer, Constable, and some others are mounting the balloon as fast as possible. If it don't soon burst, thousands will rue it," etc., etc.

As to myself, my friend, I think I know you too well to suppose you capable of such views as were implied in those innuendoes, or to harbor the most distant thought that you could wander from the path either of public good or private integrity. But I will honestly own I had serious fears for you—for your *purse* and for your *reputation;* and with an anxiety for both, I wrote to you in earnest terms. You are sanguine, my friend. You ought to be aware of it yourself and to be on your guard against the propensity. I feared lest it might carry you further than was consistent either with your own safety or the public good.

—To William Duer. *Hamilton,* V, 478-479.

March 14, 1792

Be this as it may, act with *fortitude* and *honor.* If you cannot reasonably hope for a favorable extrication, do not plunge deeper. Have the courage to make a full stop. Take all the care you can in the first place of institutions of public utility, and in the next of all fair creditors.

—To William Duer. *Hamilton,* V, 498.

May 23, 1792

. . . I am of opinion that those friends who have lent you their money or security from personal confidence in your honor, and without being interested in the operations in which you may have been engaged, ought to be taken care of absolutely, and preferably to all creditors. In the next place, public institutions ought to be secured. . . .

As to the usurious tribe: these present themselves under different aspects. Are these women, or ignorant people, or trustees of infants? The real principal advanced and legal interest would, in such cases, stand, in my mind, on high ground. The mere veteran usurers may be taken greater liberties with. Their real principal and interest, however, abstracted from usurious accumulation, would stand better than claims constituted wholly by profits from speculative bargains. But the following course deserves consideration: Take care of debts to friends who have aided you by their money or credit disinterestedly, and the public institutions. Assign the rest of your property for the benefit of creditors generally. The law will do the rest. Whenever usury can be proved, the contract, I take it, will be null.

—To William Duer. Works, IX, 510-511.

To Hamilton the speculative excesses could be turned to the advantage of the Treasury and the taxpayers.

TREASURY DEPARTMENT April 16, 1792

. . . The moderate size of the domestic debt of the United States appears to have created the most intemperate ideas of speculation in the minds of a very few persons, whose natural ardor had been measured by great success in some of the early stages of the melioration of the market value of the stock. . . . The extreme indiscretion of the first mentioned speculations and the distress which, it was manifest, they must produce, excited perhaps and animated the movements of the other party and brought on a scene of private distress for money both artificial and real which probably has not been equalled in this country. It happened in the winter season, when the influx of cash articles of trade, as returns from abroad, is nearly suspended, and when quantities of specie were sent from the seaports to the interior country for the purchase of produce, to supply the demand for the spring exportation. . . . The United States, you would presume, would not be insensible to so fit a moment to make purchases of the public stock, and the Treasurer was accordingly authorized to buy. . . .

—To Gouverneur Morris. Gouverneur Morris Papers, Special Collections, Columbia Univ. Lib.

Education and Politics

Hamilton was keenly interested in the problems of higher education, favored a national university supported by federal funds, drafted the legislation setting up the University of the State of New York, and was active in the affairs of his own alma mater, Columbia, which he served as a trustee.

September 4, 1796

I return the draft, corrected agreeably to your intimations. You will observe a short paragraph added respecting education. As to the establishment of a university, it is a point which, in connection with the military schools, and some other things, I meant, agreeably to your desire, to suggest to you as parts of your speech at the opening of the session. There will several things come there much better than in a general address to the people, which likewise would swell the address too much. Had I health enough, it was my intention to have written it over, in which case I would both have improved and abridged. But this is not the case. I seem now to have regularly a period of ill health every summer.

—To Washington. *Works*, X, 190.

August 6, 1800

The president of Columbia College, in this city, has resigned, and we are looking out for a successor. Dr. Wharton has occurred to me as a character worthy of inquiry; and the great confidence I feel in your judgment and candor, induces me to have recourse to you.

We are extremely anxious to have a well-qualified man, as this is the only thing wanting to render our institution very flourishing. We have two very good professors—one of the languages, the other of the mathematics and natural philosophy; and we have a professor of chemistry—this branch having been lately made a part of the academic course,—together with better funds, as I believe, than any similar institution in the United States. I mention these particulars to impress you with the importance of our college to the cause of literature, and with the duty which thence results of peculiar circumspection and care in the choice of a president. It is essential that he be a gentleman in his manners, as well as a sound and polite scholar; that his moral character be irreproachable; that he possess energy of body and mind, and be of a disposition to maintain discipline without *undue austerity*; and, in the last place, that his politics be of the right sort. I beg you to inform me particularly how far Dr. Wharton meets this description, in what, if any thing, he fails. You will, of course, see the propriety of mentioning nothing about this inquiry.

—To James Ashton Bayard. Copy. Hamilton Papers, 1st ser.

Tragedy and Frustration

The curtain rose on the Hamilton tragedy in November, 1801, when his eldest son, Philip, challenged a Republican lawyer named George I. Eacker for publicly attacking his father's reputation. Philip was killed in the duel. Neither parent ever completely recovered from the blow. The shock permanently unsettled the mind of the beautiful Angelica, Philip's eldest sister. This family tragedy of political origin, combined with the ebb in the fortunes of his own party, explains Hamilton's despairing letter to Gouverneur Morris.

February 12, 1802

My loss is indeed great. The brightest as well as the eldest hope of my family has been taken from me. You estimated him rightly. He was a fine youth. But why should I repine? It was the will of heaven, and he is now out of the reach of the seductions and calamities of a world full of folly, full of vice, full of danger—of least value in proportion as it is best known. I firmly [trust][1] also, that he has safely reached the haven [of eternal repose] and felicity.

You will easily conceive that every [memorial of] the goodness of his heart must be precious [to me.] You allude to one recorded in a letter [to your son.] If no special reasons forbid it, I should [be very glad to] have a copy of that letter.

[1] Bracketed material mutilated in original.

Mrs. Hamilton joins me in [affectionate] thanks to Mrs. Rush and yourself; [our wishes for] your happiness will be unceasing.

—To Dr. Benjamin Rush. Hamilton's hand. Hamilton Papers, 1st ser.

February 27, 1802

Mine is an odd destiny. Perhaps no man in the United States has sacrificed or done more for the present Constitution than myself; and contrary to all my anticipations of its fate, as you know from the very beginning, I am still laboring to prop the frail and worthless fabric. Yet I have the murmurs of its friends no less than the curses of its foes for my reward. What can I do better than withdraw from the scene? Every day proves to me more and more, that this American world was not made for me.

—To Gouverneur Morris. Draft in Hamilton's hand. Hamilton Papers, 1st ser.

Grange (New York) December 29, 1802

A garden, you know, is a very useful refuge of a disappointed politician. Accordingly, I have purchased a few acres about nine miles from town, have built a house, and am cultivating a garden. The *melons* in your country are very fine. Will you have the goodness to send me some seed, both of the water and musk melons? My daughter adds another request, which is for three of four of your paroquets. She is very fond of birds. If there be any thing in this quarter the sending of which can give you pleasure, you have only to name them. As *farmers*, a new source of sympathy has arisen between us, and I am pleased with every thing in which our likings and tastes can be approximated.

—To General Charles Cotesworth Pinckney. *Hamilton*, VI, 551-552.

The Duel

"Apology from principle, I hope, rather than from pride, is out of the question."

Failing to win his own party's nomination for the governorship of New York, Burr turned to the Federalists. Hamilton denounced his old enemy as "a man of irregular and unsatiable ambition," a dangerous and despicable person, "who ought not to be trusted with the reins of government." Burr bided his time. After being trounced in the election, he wrote Hamilton demanding satisfaction. When Hamilton refused to repudiate his remarks, the challenge followed. Hamilton believed that his honor was at stake and that, as a public figure, he had no alternative. But in his last years he had shown an aversion to the practice of duelling, doubtless heightened by his son Philip's tragedy.

On the fourth of July, a week before the duel, Hamilton and Burr attended a dinner of the Society of the Cincinnati. Hamilton was gay and sang an old military song, believed by some to be "How stands the glass around?" This was the song General Wolfe was supposed to have written the night before his death on the Plains of Abraham.

Hamilton was prepared to die. He made out his will, put his affairs in order, and wrote two farewell notes to his wife. The night before he died he told his second, Nathaniel Pendleton, that "he had made up his mind not to fire at Colonel Burr the first time, but to receive his fire, and fire in the air." When Pendleton expostulated, he explained: "It is the effect of a religious scruple, and does not admit of reasoning. It is useless to say more on the subject, as my purpose is definitely fixed." It is significant that, while the original account of the duel in the pro-Burr Morning Chronicle *stated that "both parties took aim and fired in succession," this account by mutual agreement of the seconds on both sides was modified to read: "both parties presented," which implied merely an "elevation of the arm." Hamilton did fire a shot into the air, but it was purely involuntary. When he received his pistol, after having taken his position, he was asked if he would have the hairspring set. He answered: "Not this time."*

September 18, 1799

I have received your letter of the 17th instant, and regret extremely the event of which it informs me. Although it is not my intention to contravene military prejudices on the subject, yet I doubt not you will agree with me that it is proper to discourage a spirit which would lead to frequent events of this nature. I have been the more naturally led to this reflection, as I am informed by General Wilkinson that the practice of duelling in the Western army has been carried to an extreme in every view reprehensible and injurious. I must request from you a particular statement of the circumstances of this unhappy affair.

—To Colonel Moore. Draft partly in Hamilton's hand. Hamilton Papers, 1st ser.

June 18, 1804

SIR:

I send you for your perusal a letter signed Charles D. Cooper, which, though apparently published some time ago, has but very recently come to my knowledge. Mr. Van Ness, who does me the honor to deliver this, will point out to you that clause of the letter to which I particularly request your attention. You must preceive, sir, the necessity of a prompt, unqualified acknowledgment or denial of the use of any expressions which would warrant the assertions of Dr. Cooper.

—Burr to Hamilton. *The Balance and Columbian Repository* (Hudson, N. Y.), July 24, 1804; [William Coleman], *A Collection of the Facts and Documents relative to the Death of Major-General Alexander Hamilton* (New York, 1804; repr. Boston, 1904) (hereinafter cited *Coleman Coll.*), pp. 1, 2.

June 20, 1804

SIR:

I have maturely reflected on the subject of your letter of the eighteenth instant, and the more I have reflected, the more I have become convinced that I could not, without manifest impropriety, make the avowal or disavowal which you seem to think necessary. The clause pointed out by Mr. Van Ness is in these terms: "I could detail to you a *still more despicable* opinion which General Hamilton *has expressed* of Mr. Burr." To endeavor to discover the meaning of this declaration, I was obliged to seek in the antecedent part of this letter for the opinion to which it referred, as having been already disclosed. I found it in these words: "General Hamilton and Judge Kent have declared in *substance* that they looked upon Mr. Burr to be a *dangerous man,* and one who *ought not to be trusted with the reins of government.*"

The language of Dr. Cooper plainly implies that *he* considered this opinion of you, which he attributes to me, as a *despicable* one; but he affirms that I have expressed some other, *still more despicable,* without, however, mentioning to whom, when, or where. 'Tis evident that the phrase "still more despicable" admits of infinite shades, from very light to very dark. How am I to judge of the degree intended, or how shall I annex any precise idea to language so indefinite?

Between gentlemen, *despicable* and *more despicable* are not worth the pains of distinction; when, therefore, you do not interrogate me as to the opinion which is specifically ascribed to me, I must conclude that you view it as within the limits to which the animadversions of political opponents upon each other may justifiably extend, and consequently as not warranting the idea of it which Dr. Cooper appears to entertain. If so, what precise inference could you draw as a guide for your conduct, were I to acknowledge that I had expressed an opinion of you *still more despicable* than the one which is particularized? How could you be sure that even this opinion had exceeded the bounds which you yourself deem admissible between political opponents?

But I forbear further comment on the embarrassment to which the requisition you have made naturally leads. The occasion forbids a more ample illustration, though nothing could be more easy than to pursue it. Repeating, that I cannot reconcile it with propriety to make the acknowledgment you desire, I will add that I deem it inadmissable, on principle, to consent to be interrogated as to the justness of the *inferences* which may be drawn by others from what I may have said of a political opponent in the course of fifteen years' competition. If there were no other objection to it, this is sufficient, that it would tend to expose my sincerity and delicacy to injurious imputation from every person who may at any time have conceived the *import* of my expressions differently from what I may then have intended or may afterwards recollect. I stand ready to avow or disavow, promptly and explicitly, any precise or definite opinion which I may be charged with having declared of any gentleman. More than this cannot fitly be expected from me, and especially it cannot be reasonably expected that I shall enter into an explanation upon a basis so vague as that which you have adopted. I trust, on mature reflection, you will see the matter in the same light with me. If not, I can only regret the circumstance, and must abide the consequences.

The publication of Dr. Cooper was never seen by me until after the receipt of your letter.

—Hamilton to Burr. *The Balance*. July 24, 1804; *Coleman Coll.*, pp. 3, 4.

June 21, 1804

SIR:

Your letter of the 20th inst. has been this day received. Having considered it attentively, I regret to find in it nothing of that sincerity and delicacy which you profess to value.

Political opposition can never absolve gentlemen from the necessity of a rigid adherence to the laws of honor and the rules of decorum. I neither claim such privilege nor indulge it in others.

The common-sense of mankind affixes to the epithet adopted by Dr. Cooper, the idea of dishonor. It has been publicly applied to me under the sanction of your name. The question is not whether he has understood the meaning of the word, or has used it according to syntax and with grammatical accuracy, but whether you have authorized this application, either directly or by uttering expressions or opinions derogatory to my honor. The time "when" is in your own knowledge, but no way material to me, as the calumny has now first been disclosed, so as to become the subject of my notice, and as the effect is present and palpable. Your letter has furnished me with new reasons for requiring a definite reply.

—Burr to Hamilton. *The Balance*, July 24, 1804; *Coleman Coll.*, pp. 4, 5.

June 23, 1804

SIR:

Your first letter, in a style too peremptory, made a demand, in my opinion, unprecedented and unwarrantable. My answer, pointing out the embarrassment, gave you an opportunity to take a less exceptionable course. You have not chosen to do it; but by your last letter, received this day, containing expressions *indecorous* and improper, you have increased the difficulties to explanation intrinsically incident to the nature of your application. If by a "definite reply," you mean the direct avowal or disavowal required in your first letter, I have no other answer to give, than that which has already been given. If you mean any thing different, admitting of greater latidude, it is requisite you should explain.

—Hamilton to Burr. *The Balance*, July 24, 1804; *Coleman Coll.*, p. 7.

Major Van Ness and Nathaniel Pendleton, intermediaries for Burr and Hamilton respectively, now took over the correspondence. On June 26th Pendleton wrote Van Ness that Hamilton could not "consent to be questioned generally as to any rumors which may be afloat derogatory to the character of Col. Burr," and considered Burr's attitude as evidence of "premeditated hostility." On June 27th Van Ness replied that "secret whispers" were "equally injurious with slanders publicly uttered," and that Burr regarded Hamilton's reply as "evasive." Hamilton's remarks on the Van Ness letter:

Whether the observations on this letter are designed merely to justify the result which is indicated in the close of the letter, or may be intended to give an opening for rendering any thing explicit which may have been deemed vague heretofore, can only be judged of by the sequel. At any rate, it appears to me necessary not to be misunderstood. Mr. Pendleton is therefore authorized to say, that in the course of the present discussion, written or verbal, there has been no intention to evade, defy, or insult, but a sincere disposition to avoid extremities, if it could be done with propriety. With this view, Gen. Hamilton has been ready to enter into a frank and free explanation on any and every object of a specific nature, but not to answer a general and abstract inquiry embracing a period too long for any accurate recollection, and exposing him to unpleasant criticisms from, or unpleasant discussions with, any and every person who may have understood him in an unfavorable sense. This (admitting that he could answer in a manner the most satisfactory to Col. Burr) he should deem inadmissible in principle and precedent, and humiliating in practice. To this therefore he can never submit. Frequent allusion has been made to slanders said to be in circulation. Whether they are openly or in whispers, they have a form and shape and might be specified. If the alternative alluded to in the close of the letter is definitely tendered, it must be accepted; the time, place, and manner to be afterwards regulated. I should not think it right in the midst of a Circuit Court to withdraw my services from those who may have confided important interests to me and expose them to the embarrassment of seeking other counsel, who may not have time to be sufficiently instructed in their case. I shall also want a little time to make some arrangements respecting my own affairs.

—*Coleman Coll.*, pp. 15, 16.

On my expected interview with Col. Burr, I think it proper to make some remarks explanatory of my conduct, motives, and views. I was certainly desirous of avoiding this interview for the most cogent reasons:

(1) My religious and moral principles are strongly opposed to the practice of duelling, and it would ever give me pain to be obliged to shed the blood of a fellow-creature in a private combat forbidden by the laws.

(2) My wife and children are extremely dear to me, and my life is of the utmost importance to them in various views.

(3) I feel a sense of obligation towards my creditors; who, in case of accident to me by the forced sale of my property, may be in some degree sufferers. I did not think myself at liberty as a man of probity lightly to expose them to this hazard.

(4) I am conscious of no *ill will* to Col. Burr, distinct from political opposition, which, as I trust, has proceeded from pure and upright motives.

Lastly, I shall hazard much and can possibly gain nothing by the issue of the interview.

But it was, as I conceive, impossible for me to avoid it. There were *intrinsic* difficulties in the thing and *artificial* embarrassments, from the manner of proceeding on the part of Col. Burr.

Intrinsic, because it is not to be denied that my animadversions on the political principles, character, and views of Col. Burr have been extremely severe; and on different occasions I, in common with many others, have made very unfavorable criticisms on particular instances of the private conduct of this gentleman. In proportion as these impressions were entertained with sincerity and uttered with motives and for purposes which might appear to me commendable, would be the difficulty (until they could be removed by evidence of their being erroneous) of explanation or apology. The disavowal required of me by Col. Burr in a general and indefinite form was out of my power, if it had really been proper for me to submit to be questioned, but I was sincerely of opinion that this could not be, and in this opinion I was confirmed by that of a very moderate and judicious friend whom I consulted. Besides that, Col. Burr appeared to me to assume, in the first instance, a tone unnecessarily peremptory and menacing, and, in the second, positively offensive. Yet I wished, as far as might be practicable, to leave a door open to accommodation. This, I think, will be inferred from the written communication made by me and by my directions, and would be confirmed by the conversations between Mr. Van Ness and myself which arose out of the subject. I am not sure whether, under all the circumstances, I did not go further in the attempt to accommodate than a punctilious delicacy will justify. If so, I hope the motives I have stated will excuse me. It is not my design, by what I have said, to affix any odium on the conduct of Col. Burr in this case. He doubtless has heard of animadversions of mine which bore very hard upon him, and it is probable that as usual they were accompanied with some falsehoods. He may have supposed himself under a necessity of acting as he has done. I hope the grounds of his proceeding have been such as ought to satisfy his own concience. I trust, at the same time, that the world will do me the justice to believe that I have not censured him on light grounds nor from unworthy inducements. I certainly have had strong reasons for what I have said, though it is possible that in some particulars I may have been influenced by misconstruction or misinformation. It is also my ardent wish that I may have been more mistaken than I think I have been; and that he, by his future conduct, may show himself worthy of all confidence and esteem and prove an ornament and a blessing to the country. As well, because it is possible that I may have injured Col. Burr, however convinced myself that my opinions and declarations have been well-founded, as from my general principles and temper in relation to similar affairs, I have resolved, if our interview is conducted in the usual manner, and it pleases God to give me the opportunity, to *reserve and throw away* my first fire, and I *have thoughts* even of *reserving* my second fire, and thus giving a double opportunity to Col. Burr to pause and reflect. It is not, however, my intention to enter into any explanations on the ground. Apology from principle, I hope, rather than pride, is out of the question. To those who, with me, abhorring the practice of duelling, may think that I ought on no account to have added to the number of bad examples, I answer that my *relative* situation, as well in public as private, enforcing all the considerations which constitute what men of the world denominate honor, imposed on me (as I thought) a peculiar necessity not to decline the call. The ability to be in future useful, whether in resisting mischief or in effecting good, in those crises of our public affairs which seem likely to happen, would probably be inseparable from a conformity with public prejudice in this particular.

A. H.

—*Coleman Coll.*, pp. 24-27.

July 9, 1804

LAST WILL AND TESTAMENT OF ALEXANDER HAMILTON

In the name of God, Amen.

I, Alexander Hamilton, of the City of New York, counsellor at law, do make this my last will and testament, as follows:

First, I appoint John B. Church, Nicholas Fish, and Nathaniel Pendleton, of the city aforesaid, esquires, to be executors and trustees of this my will; and I devise to them, their heirs and assigns, as joint tenants, and not as tenants in common, all my estate, real and personal, whatsoever, and wheresoever, upon trust, at their discretion to sell and dispose of the same at such time and times, in such manner, and upon such terms as they the survivors and survivor shall think fit; and out of the proceeds to pay all the debts which I shall owe at the time of my decease; in whole, if the fund shall be sufficient; proportionably, if it shall be insufficient; and the residue, if any there shall be, to pay and deliver to my excellent and dear wife, Elizabeth Hamilton.

Though, if it should please God to spare my life, I may look for a considerable surplus out of my present property; yet if he should speedily call me to the eternal world, a forced sale, as is usual, may possibly render it insufficient to satisfy my debts. I pray God that something may remain for the maintenance and education of my dear wife and children. But should it on the contrary happen that there is not enough for the payment of my debts, I entreat my dear children, if they or any of them shall ever be able, to make up the deficiency. I without hesitation commit to their delicacy a wish which is dictated by my own.—Though conscious that I have too far sacrificed the interests of my family to public avocations, and on this account have the less claim to burthen my children, yet I trust in their magnanimity to appreciate, as they ought, this my request. In so unfavorable an event of things, the support of their dear mother, with the most respectful and tender attention, is a duty all the sacredness of which they will feel. Probably her own patrimonial resources will preserve her from indigence. But in all situations they are charged to bear in mind that she has been to them the most devoted and best of mothers.

In testimony whereof, I have hereunto subscribed my hand, the ninth day of July, in the year of our Lord one thousand eight hundred and four.

ALEXANDER HAMILTON.

Signed, sealed, published, and declared, as and for his last will and testament in our presence, who have subscribed our names in his presence, the words *John B. Church* being above interlined.

DOMINICK F. BLAKE

GRAHAM NEWELL.

THEO. B. VALLEAU.

—*Coleman Coll.*, pp. 27-29.

July 10, 1804

This letter, my dear Eliza, will not be delivered to you, unless I shall first have terminated my earthly career, to begin, as I humbly hope, from redeeming grace and divine mercy, a happy immortality. If it had been possible for me to have avoided the interview, my love for you and my precious children would have been alone a decisive motive. But it was not possible, without sacrifices which would have rendered me unworthy of your esteem. I need not tell you of the pangs I feel from the idea of quitting you, and exposing you to the anguish I know you would feel. Nor could I dwell on the topic, lest it should unman me. The consolations of religion, my beloved, can alone support you; and these you have a right to enjoy. Fly to the bosom of your God, and be comforted. With my last idea I shall cherish the sweet hope of meeting you in a better world. Adieu, best of wives—best of women. Embrace all my darling children for me.

—To Elizabeth Hamilton. *Works*, X, 475.

Tuesday evening, 10 o'clock 1804

. . . The scruples of a Christian have determined me to expose my own life to any extent, rather than subject myself to the guilt of taking the life of another. This much increases my hazards, and redoubles my pangs for you. But you had rather I should die innocent than live guilty. Heaven can preserve me, and I humbly hope will; but, in the contrary event, I charge you to remember that you are a Christian. God's will be done! The will of a merciful God must be good. Once more,

Adieu, my darling, darling wife.

—To Elizabeth Hamilton. *Works*, X, 476.

Index

"A. B." Letter, 52.
Adams, John, vii, xii-xiii, 1, 400, 421, 433-434, 437, 479, 521, 525, 527-534, 559; letter to, 530-531
Adet, Pierre, 421-422
Agriculture, 368, 374, 376
Albany, supervisors of, letter to, 544
Alexander, William, 44; letter to, 44-45
Alien and Sedition Acts, x, xviii, 492-494
Allen, Ethan, 112
Allen, Ira, 112
Allison, William, 28; letters to, 457-458, 496
Alsop, John, 21
Ambition, 588, 590-591, 595-598
"American, an," 523
"Americanus," 24-25, 416-418; mentioned, xvii
"Americus," 75-76, 425-427
Ames, Fisher, 396
"Amicus," 127-128
Ancestry, 566-567
André, John, 50-60, 449
Annapolis Convention xvii, 87-89, 358
"Answer," xvii, 423
"Aristides," 128
Army, plan for reorganization, 39-41; and government, 255-262; administration of, 437-447
Arnold, Benedict, xvi, 50-61, 556
Arnold, Peggy Shippen, 51-52, 56
Assumption-Residence bargain, 287
Aurora, 478

Bank of New York, xii, 306-307, 336, 582
Bank of North America, 336
Bank of the United States, 263-269, 543, 582
Bayard, James Ashton, xviii, 535, 539; letters to, 536-541, 600-601
Beaumarchais, Pierre Caron de, 428
Beckley, John, 503, 580
Benson, Egbert, 160, 477, 546
Bill of Rights, U.S., 271-275; British, 452
Blackstone, Sir William, 9-10, 14, 156
Bonaparte, Napoleon, viii, 117-118, 120, 536
Boston, Supervisors of, letter to, 252
Boston Tea Party, 1
Boudinot, Elias, letters to 42-43, 401
Bradford, William, 336; letter to, 559
Brown, John, 114
Brown, Moses, 375
Brunswick, Duke of, 431
Burgoyne, John, 31-34, 419, 423
Burke, Edmund, x
Burlamaqui, Jean Jacques, 8
Burr, Aaron, xiii, 118, 284, 453, 534-543, 602-608; letters to, 604-606; letters from Burr to Hamilton, 603-605

Caesar, Julius, 103, 558
"Caesar," 134-135
Callender, James T., vii, 479, 581
"Camillus," 138, 202-208, 385-393, 456, 469-471; mentioned, x, xvii, 384, 396
Cardozo, Benjamin N., 269
Carleton, Sir Guy, 449
Carrington, Edward, letters to, 124-125, 312-313, 522, 562
Carroll, Charles, letter to, 530
"Catullus to Aristides," 128-129, 523-524, 528-529
Chaplain, qualifications, 50
Chase Samuel, 47
Checks and balances 238-239
Church, Angelica Schuyler, 579
Church, John Barker, 580, 595, 609
Cicero, 218
Cincinnati, report for Society of, 132

"Circular," 444
Civil liberties, viii, 271-275, 449-494
Clark, George Rogers, 115-116
Classes 139-143
Clay, Henry, 285
Clingman, Jacob, 580, 584, 586
Clinton, George, 38, 460, 535, 543-553; letters to, 72-73, 76-78, 95, 129-130, 327-328, 378-380, 496
Clinton, Sir Henry, 34, 38, 42, 50, 53-54, 57, 59-60; letter to, 52
Clymer, George, 148
Coercive Acts 6, 19-20
Coke, Sir Edward, 450
Columbia College, 600-601; *also see* King's College
Confederation, weaknesses, 90-112. *also see* Continental Congress, Nationalism.
Congress, viii, 211-213. *also see* Treaties.
Constable, William, 287, 595, 598
Constitution, *see* Contitutional Convention; Government, constitutional
Constitutional Convention, resolution for, xvi, 96-97; member of, xvii; chronology, 145-148; debates, 149-158, 240; Hamilton Plan, 153-159. *also see* Annapolis Convention.
Continental Congress, member, xvi; resolution in, 114; debates in, 288-289, 402-403
"Continentalist," 73, 83-86, 93-94; mentioned, xvi
Conway, Thomas, 495-496
Conway Cabal, 495-497
Cooper, Charles D., 603-605
Cooper, Thomas, 397
Cornwallis, Charles, 30, 38, 83, 448, 555-556, 576
Courts, viii, xii, 215-235. *Also see* Due Process, Judicial Review.
Credit, public, viii-x, 285-325, 343; report on, xvii, 289-303; second report, 320-325
Cromwell, Oliver, 103, 558
Croswell, Harry, 479-480
Croswell, People v., xviii, 479-485
Cruger, Nicholas, xv, 567
Cruges and Beekman, 567
Currency, ix, xvii-xviii, 285, 337-339, 341-342, 349-350, 353-357
"Curtius," 396

Dallas, Alexander James, 410, 414-415
Dana, Francis, 496
Dayton, Jonathan, letter to, 282-284
Deane, Silas, 561
Debt, national, *see* Credit, public
"Defence of the Funding System," 116-117, 142-143, 251-252, 313-316, 329
Delacroix, Jacques, 420
Democracy, xiii, 130-139
Demosthenes, xi
DeNoailles, Masquis de, letter to, 560
"Detector," 427-428
Dickinson, John, letter to, 71
"Discourses on Davila," 527
Duane, James, xvi, 76; letters to, 38-39, 78-83, 91-93
Due process, 449-454
Duels, 43, 603;
Hamilton-Eacker, xviii, 601-602
Lee-Laurens, 45-47;
Hamilton-Burr, xviii, 602-610
Duer, William, 287, 557, 584-585, 598; letters to, 401, 558, 598-599

Eacker, George, xviii, 601
Economic program, viii-ix, 285-376; public credit, viii-x, 285-325, 343; taxation, viii-ix, xii, xvii-xviii, 171-172, 239-255, 326-335; currency, ix, xvii-xviii, 285, 337-339, 341-342, 349-350, 353-357; trade, ix, xii, 326-327, 358-360; national bank, 81-83, 285, 335-354; manufactures, 285, 335, 360-374; labor, 361-364, 375-376; agriculture, 368, 374, 376
Education, of Hamilton, 567-568, 572; of children, 578-579; views of, 600-601
Edwards, E., co-author with Hamilton, 46-47
Edwards, Jonathan, 542
Elizabeth I, 23, 359
Estaing, Jean d', 401, 559
"Eulogium on Major-General Greene," 553-557
Evening Post, xviii

"Fact," 319-320
Factions, 139-143
Family, *see* Marriage
"Farmer Refuted," xv, 8-19
Fauchet, Joseph, 416, 418, 420-421, 562
Federalism, viii, x, 275-280. *Also see* Nullification, Secession.
"Federalist," 25-26, 74-75, 97-111, 140-142, 161-175, 181-195, 211-212, 220-235, 240-251, 257-262, 269, 271-279, 377-378; authorship discussed, 160-161; mentioned, viii, x, 139, 237, 256, 275
Fenno, John, 478; letter to, 522-523
Fish, Nicholas, 609
FitzSimmons, Thomas, 326
Florida, 118, 121
Foreign relations, ix, 377-437; maxims for conduct of, 377-379; Great Britain, 379-400; France, 400-434; Spain and Latin-America, 434-437. *Also see* Jay's Treaty, Treaty of 1778.

Fox, Charles James, viii, x
"Fragment on French Revolution," 422-423
France, 400-434; and Britain, 398-400; French Revolution, x, 403-404, 407-418, 322-423, 431; Treaty of 1778, 404-406, 419, 423; and Britain, 398-400; XYZ affair, 420-432
"France," 419-420
Franklin, Benjamin, 375, 412, 428, 530
Fraunces (Francis), Andrew G., 580-581
French Revolution, x, 403-404, 407-418, 422-423, 431
Freneau, Philip, 477-478
Friendship, 573-574, 598-599
Frothingham, David, 478
"Full Vindication," xv, 1-8

Gallatin, Albert, 325
Gates, Horatio, xvi, 34-35, 38-39, 554; letter to, 35-36
Genêt, Edmond, 115, 406, 410, 412, 414-416, 419-420, 429,
George III, 1
Gerry, Elbridge, 145, 147-148, 421
Giles, William Branch, xvii, 582, 587
Glover, John, 33, 36-37
Gordon, William, 496
Gorham, Nathaniel, 146-147
Government, constitutional, viii, 181-284; Presidency, viii, 181-211; Congress, viii, 211-215; courts and judicial review, 215-237; separation of powers, checks and balances, 237-238; taxation, viii-ix, xii, xvii-xviii, 171-172, 239-255, 326-335; defence, 255-262; implied powers, 263-269; welfare clause, 269-271; Bill of Rights, 271-275; Federalism and states' rights, 275-280; nullification, secession, 280-284
Government, principles of, xiii, 122-144; monarchy v. republic, 122-130; democracy and role of people, xiii, 130-139; classes, parties, factions, 139-143; political tenets, 143-144; public service, 144
Great Britain, ix, 379-400; Nootka Sound incident, 380-381; Jay's Treaty, ix, 199-207, 381-397, 421, 466-471, 562; and France, 398-400; and Latin-America, 434-435
Greene, Nathanael, 51, 59; "Eulogium on," 553-557; letters to, 51, 499, 573-574
Greene, Mrs. Nathanael, 557
Greenleaf's New Daily Advertiser, 477
Grenville, George, 383
Grotius, Hugo, 8

"Guide in Making Tactical Experiments Relative to the Step," 439-440
Gunn, James, letter to, 439

"H. G." letters, 22, 544-553
Haldimand, Sir Frederick, 112
Hamilton, Alexander (Laird of Cambuskeith), 566, 573
Hamilton, Alexander, appraisal of, vii-xiv; chronology, xv-xviii; publications, xv-xviii, *also see* specific titles; and pseudonyms; ancestry, birth, youth, xv, 566-567; education, xv, 567-568, 572; public service, xv-xvii, 587-589, 602; duel with Burr, xviii, 602-610; religion, 422, 569-570, 607, 610; marriage and family, 572, 574-578, 601-602; friendships, 573-574, 598-599; relations with women, 579-587; integrity, 581-588, 591-595, 602-608; ambition, 588, 590-591, 595-598; last will and testament, 609
Hamilton, Alexander, Jr., xvi
Hamilton, Andrew, 479
Hamilton, Angelica, xvi, 601-602; letter to, 578
Hamilton, Eliza, xvi
Hamilton, Elizabeth Schuyler, xvi, 572, 574-575, 580-581, 585-586, 602, 607, 609; letters to, 51-53, 63, 449, 571, 575-578, 610
Hamilton, James, xv, xviii, 566-567, 571
Hamilton, James, Jr., 566; letter to, 571
Hamilton, James Alexander, xvi, letter to, 579
Hamilton, John Church, xvi
Hamilton, Philip (eldest son), xvi, xviii, 578, 601-602; rules for, 579; letter to 578
Hamilton, Philip (younger son), xvi, 578
Hamilton, William Stephen, xvi
Hammond, George, 383
Hancock, John, 528; letter to, 34
Harrison, Benjamin, 498
Helvering v. *Davis*, 269
"Helvidius" letters, 412
"History of the U.S. for 1796," 581, 583
Hoffman, Josiah O., letter to, 478-479
"Horatius," 418-419; mentioned, xvii, 416
House of Representatives, and treaties, 195, 199-202; letters, etc., to, 115, 138, 269-270, 289-303, 329-330, 332-333, 361-376. *Also see* Congress.
Howe, Sir William, 28, 31-33, 38
Huddy, Joshua, 448-450
Hume, David, 146

Humphreys, David, 498
"Hurricane Letter," 568-570; mentioned, xv
Hylton v. *U.S.*, 253-255

Immigration, ix, 285, 363, 366-367. *Also see* Alien and Sedition Acts.
Implied powers, viii, 263-269
"Impost Duty, Report on," 132
Indians, 115-116, 447
Insurrection, 485-492
Integrity, 587-588, 591-595, 602-608
"Intolerable Acts" 6, 19-20

Jackson, Andrew, xii
Jackson, William, 145; instructions to, 70
Jay, John, 21, 91, 160-161, 199, 382, 383, 402, 416, 418, 421, 424, 484, 561; letters to, 21-22, 281, 404, 454-455, 475-477, 561, 591; cabinet papers to, 383
Jay's Treaty, ix, 199-207, 381-397, 421, 466-471, 562; Camillus letters, 385-395
Jefferson, Thomas, cited, vii, ix-xii, xiv, xviii, 1, 115, 119, 124-125, 127-128, 139, 209, 219, 263, 280, 284, 287, 313, 325, 333-334, 375, 377, 383, 396, 399-400, 403, 412, 414-415, 421, 477, 479, 492-494, 502, 521-527, 529, 535-537, 539-540, 542, 562, 587, 593; letters to, 196, 403-404
Johnson, William Samuel, 148
Johnstone, George, 48
Judicial review, viii, 215-225, 253-255
"Junius," 185

Kane, James, 129
Kent, James, 161, 176, 479-480, 604
Kentucky, 114
King, Rufus, 148, 528, 562, 565; letters to, 25, 76, 284, 307, 396-400, 414-415, 427, 435, 527, 529, 543, 564, 594-595
King's College, xv, 1, 27, 450, 567-568, 572
Knox, Henry, 45, 68, 91, 485, 528; letters to, 448-449; co-author of cabinet paper, 410-411
Knox, Hugh, 567-568; letter to, 31-32

Labor, 361-364, 375-376
Lafayette, Adrienne, 559
Lafayette, Marie, Marquis de, 43-44, 65, 78, 411, 497, 557, 559-560; letters to, 63, 65, 143-144, 433, 577
Lamb, John, 27, 477
Lansing, John Jr., 157, 542
Latin-America, policy toward, 434-437
Laurens, John, 43, 45-47, 50, 64, 454-455, 573-574; letters to, 53-60, 86, 496-497, 558, 573-575
Lavien (Levine, Lewine), John Michael, 566-567
Lavien (Levine), Peter, 566-567, 571
Lavien (Levine, Lewine), Rachel Faucitt, xv, 566-567
Lear, Tobias, 505; letter to, 521
Learned, Ebenezer, 37
Ledyard, Isaac, 460
Lee, Arthur, 561
Lee, Charles, xvi, 42-47
Lee, Henry ("Light-Horse Harry"), 33, 485, 558; letter to, 489-491, 590
Lee, Richard Henry, 528
Le Guen v. *Gouverneur and Kemble*, 453
L'Enfant, Pierre, 591
"Letter from Phocion," *see* "Phocion"
Lewis, Francis, 21
Lewis, Morgan, 216, 479
Lincoln, Abraham, xii
Lincoln, Benjamin, 528
Livingston, Brockholst, 216
Livingston, Gilbert, 213
Livingston, Robert R., 21, 28, 336; letters to 30-32, 131-132, 459-460, 477, 495-496
Livingston, William, letter to, 456-458
"Loans," 211-312
Locke, John, 8
Louis XIV, 404, 411-412
Louisiana Purchase, xi, 117-121
L'Ouverture, Toussaint, 433
Loyalists, attitude toward, 450-452, 456-471, 475-477
"Lucius Crassus," 209, 235-237, 239, 333-335, 493-494, 526-527

Maclay, William, vii, 336
Macombe, Alexander, 595
Madison, James, cited, x, xii, 91, 124-125, 147-148, 154, 156, 159-161, 175, 179, 237, 263, 269, 275, 280, 286-287, 312-313, 318, 326, 396, 400, 412, 506, 561-562, 593; letters to, 70-71, 175, 179, 561-562
Mansfield, Earl, *see* Murray, William
Manufactures, 285, 335, 360-374; report on, 269-270, 329, 361-376
Marat, Jean Paul, 417
Marbury v. *Madison*, 220
Marriage and family, 572, 574-578, 601-602
Marshall, John, 220, 263, 421
Matthews, George, 159; letter to, 155-156
McCulloch v. *Maryland*, 263

M'Dougall, Alexander, 80
McHenry, James, 158, 492; letters to, 208-209, 399, 436-437, 439, 442-447, 492, 596-598
Meade, Richard K., letter to, 65
"Measures of Defence," 440-441
Meigs, Return Jonathan, 51
Mendy, Rev. W., 50
"Mentor," mentioned, 460
Mercer, John Francis, 402
"Metellus," 524-525
Mifflin, Thomas, 414-415, 485; letter to, 460-461
Minority rights, 456-471
Miranda, Francisco, 434-435; letter to, 435
Monarchism, 122-130
Monmouth, battle of, xvi, 42-45
Monroe, James, 533, 580-581
Montesqieu, Baron de, 8, 143, 237
Morris, Gouverneur, 28, 148, 336, 460, 557, 562, 564; letters to, 29, 32-33, 130-131, 138-139, 433-434, 457-459, 495-496, 537, 539, 602
Morris, Robert, 80, 286-287, 336, 560-561, 580; letters to, 22, 94-95, 459, 589-590, 599-600
Muhlenberg, Frederick A., 580
Murray, William, 485
Murray, William Vans, 433, 533
Mutiny, 66-71

National Gazette, 477, 502, 522, 524
Nationalism, viii, 72-121, 161-180; national character, 72-76; continental outlook, viii, 76-90; weaknesses of Confederation, 90-112; West and statehood, xi, 111-121, 434-437
Necker, Jacques, 152
Negroes, xvi. *Also see* Slavery.
New Hampshire, ratification in, 175-176, 179
New York, Legislature, member, xvi; speeches in, 74, 90; Assembly, members, xvii; speeches in 112-114, 122-123, 133-134, 218-219, 275-276, 328-329, 452-453, 472-474; Provincial Congress, letter to, 27-28; Convention, letter to committee of, 29; speeches in, 111-112, 123-124, 136-140, 143, 176-179, 212-215, 237-239, 279-280; and import duty, 89-90; address to electors of, 129, 525-526, 543-544; ratification of Constitution, 176-180, 203
New York Society for Promoting the Manumission of Slaves, xii, 454
Nichols, Moses, 458
Nixon, John, 36
"No Jacobin," 413-416; mentioned, xvii
Nootka Sound incident, 380-381
"Notes on Virginia," 493
"Novanglus Letters," 1
Nullification, 280-284

Oaths, 472-474
"Objections and Answers," 125-127, 142, 281, 317-319
"Observation on Certain Documents," 581-587
Ogden, Isaac, 458
Osgood, Samuel, 402
Otis, Harrison Gray, 580; letter to, 436

"Pacificus," 196-198, 378, 409, 411-412; mentioned, x, 407
Paine, Thomas, 502, 524
Parties, 139-143
Paterson (Patterson), John, 35-36
Paterson, William, 146, 151
Peace Establishment, Committee on, draft report, 255-256
Pendleton, Nathaniel, 603, 606, 609
People, role of, xiii, 130-139
"Pericles," 118-119
"Phocion," first letter, 23, 461-464; second letter, 23-24, 450-452, 464-466, 472; mentioned, x, xvii, 460
Pickering, Timothy, 398, 421; letters to, 118, 158-159, 399, 426, 430, 433, 493, 565, 595-596
Pinckney, Charles Cotesworth, 146, 400, 421, 521, 525, 527, 529, 531-534, 565; letters to, 118, 520-521, 524, 602
Pinckney's Treaty, 434
Pitt, William, x
Pontigibaud, Chevalier de, 28
Poor, Enoch, 37
Postlethwayt, Malachy, 285
Powers, separation of, 238-239
Presidency, 181-211; powers, 181-193; and treaties, 193-207; war power, 208-209; code of etiquette, 209-211
Press, freedom of, 475-484
"Public Conduct and Character of John Adams, Esq.," 400, 531-534
Public creditors, address to, 306-397
Public land, 114-115
Public servants, 144
"Publius," xvi, 47-50; *also see* "Federalist"
Pufendorf, Samuel von, 8
Purdy, Samuel, 129
Putnam, Israel, 34-36; letter to, 37-38

Quebec Act, xv, 6-7, 19-21

Randolph, Edmund, 145-146, 153, 159, 263, 375, 416, 418, 485, 562-563, 593; letters to, 378, 487-488
"Reasons Why It Is Desirable," 541-542
Religion, 422-423, 569-570, 607, 610

"Remarks on the Quebec Act," 19-21; mentioned, xv, 6-7
"Report on Impost Duties" 288, 326-327
"Report on Public Credit," 289-303, 330-331, 454; Second report, 320-325; mentioned, xvii, 286, 329
Report on the National Bank," xvii, 138, 343-353
"Remarks on the Quebec Bill," xv, 20-21
"Report on the Subject of Manufactures," 269-270, 329, 361-374; mentioned, xvii, 360, 375
"Report on the U.S. Mint," xvii
Republicanism, 122-130
Revolution, 1-71; right of, x, 1-26; spirit of '76, 22; moderation in, 22-25; as last resort, 25-26; military events, 27-47, 61-65, 553-557; army reorganization, 39-41; profiteering, 47-50; chaplain, 50; Arnold's treason, 50-61; Hamilton at Yorktown, 61-65; mutiny, 66-71. *Also see* French Revolution
Reynolds, James, 580-586
Reynolds, Maria, xviii, 580-586
"Reynolds Pamphlet," 581-587
Rhode Island, and import duty, 86-87; letter to governor of, 86-87
"Rights of Man," 524
Rivington, James, 475-477
Rivington's Gazette, 499
Robespierre, Maximilien, 417, 428
Rodney, Caesar, 47
Roman Catholicism, 6-7, 19-21, 472
Rush, Benjamin, letter to, 601-602
Rush, Richard, xii
Rutgers, Elizabeth, 216
Rutgers v. *Waddington*, 216-219, 460, 469
Rutledge, John, 148; letter to, 536

St. Domingo, 120, 433
Schuyler, Philip, xvi, 33, 80, 545, 572, 574, letters to, 497-499
Scott v. *Sandford*, 220
Seabury, Samuel, 1
Sears, Isaac, 475-477
Secession, 280-284
Sedition, 485-492
Sedgwick, Theodore, letters to, 76, 282, 284, 424, 426, 433, 528-529, 541
Senate, 213-215; and treaty power, 193-206; letters, etc., to, 252-253, 466-467
Seton, William, 336; letter to, 307-308
Short, William, cabinet papers to, 144, 289
Simcoe, Lt. Col. J. G., 50
Slavery, xii, 454-456, 468-469
Smallwood, William, 28
Smith, Adam, 285
Smith, William, 437, 545; letter to, 199-200
Society for Establishing Useful Manufactures, xvii, 361
Sources, xiii-xiv
Spaight, Richard D., 145
Spain, relations with 434-437
'Spirits, Foreign and Domestic," 473-474
"Stand," 22, 429-432; mentioned, xviii, 421
States' rights, viii, 275-284
Steuben, Charles von, 557-558
Stevens, Edward ("Ned"), 27, 567 letter to, 568
Stirling, Lord. *See* Alexander, William
Story, Joseph, 269
Sullivan, John, 401, 559; letter to, 175-176

"T. L.," 522-523
Talleyrand, Charles Maurice De, viii, 383, 432, 587
Taxation, taxes, viii-ix, xii, xvii-xviii, 171-172, 239-255, 326-335
Tilghman, Tench, 63, 497-498
"Titus Manlius," 429, 432
Tories, *see* Loyalists
Trade, ix, xii, 326-327, 358-360
Treaties, powers of President, Congress, 193-207, 396-397; as law of land, 207-208; to be observed, 379-380; abrogation of, 404-406. *Also see* Jay's Treaty, Pinckney's Treaty, Treaty of 1778.
Treaty of 1778 (France), 404-406, 419, 460, 466-467
Tripolitan War, 209
Troup, Robert, 216, 450; letter to, 571-572, 595
"Tully," 488-489; mentioned, xvii, 485

United States Gazette, 477

Van Ness, William W., 603-604, 606
Venable, Abraham, 580
Vermont, 112-114
"Vindication of Congress," 87-88
"Vindication of the Funding System," 308-311
Virginia, ratification in, 175

Wadsworth, Jeremiah, 49, 336
War power, 208-209
"Warning," 424-427; mentioned, xiii, 421
Washington, George, cited, vii, ix, xv-xvii, 8, 28, 33, 36, 38-39, 42-43, 46-47, 50, 54-58, 61, 65-66, 91, 116, 139, 149, 161, 209, 217, 263, 280, 285-286, 332, 335-336, 358, 375, 382, 384, 396-398, 400, 404, 406, 412, 414-415, 421, 437, 448, 478-479, 485,

495-506, 520-521, 527-528, 532-533, 559, 562, 588; letters to, 35-37, 51, 61-63, 67-69, 148-149, 280-281, 374, 385, 402, 407-408, 421-424, 437-439, 485-487, 489, 491, 500-503, 506, 558-565, 588, 590-594, 596; cabinet papers to, 199, 219, 378, 380-385, 403-406, 408-409, 434-435, 467-469; reports, etc., to: "Objections and Answers," 125-127, 142, 281, 317-319; code of etiquette, 209-211; on constitutionality of bank, 263-268; on arrears of pay, 303-306; letter from Washington to Hamilton, 592; drafts of messages, etc.: plan for reorganizing army, 39-42; speeches to Congress, 144, 270-271, 374, 376, 378-379, 438, 447; message to House, 200-202; speech, 376; letter to McHenry, 432-439; Farewell Address, 506-520; mentioned, ix, xviii, 397, 420-421
Wasp, 479
Wayne, Anthony, letter to, 50
Webster, Daniel, ix
Webster, Pelatiah, 336
Welfare clause, xii, 269-271
West, 112-121, 434-437
West Point, 49-60; letter to commandant, 442
"Westchester Farmer," 1
Wharton, 600-601
Whisky Rebellion, xvii, 280-281, 485-492
Wilkinson, James, 437, 563-564, 603
letter to, 117
Willet, Marinus, 477
Williamson, Hugh, 146
Willink, Jan, 595
Willink, Wilhim, 595
Wilson, James, 1, 145, 148, 155, 562
Wilson, Woodrow, xi
Wolcott, Oliver, 354, 580; letters to, 175, 325, 397, 422, 427, 493, 536-537
Wolfe, James, 603
Women, relations with, Angelica Schuyler Church, 579-580; Reynolds affair, 580-587. *Also see* Hamilton, Elizabeth Schuyler
Writs of Assistance, 453-454

XYZ Affair, 420-432

Yates, Robert, 154
Yorktown campaign, xvi, 61-65
Youth, 566-567

Zenger, John Peter, trial of, 479, 483-484